EDITION 2

Essential Skills and Strategies in the Helping Process

Robert E. Doyle

St. John's University

 Brooks/Cole Publishing Company

I⊤P® An International Thomson Publishing Company

Pacific Grove • Albany • Belmont • Bonn • Boston • Cincinnati • Detroit • Johannesburg • London • Madrid • Melbourne • Mexico City • New York • Paris • Singapore • Tokyo • Toronto • Washington

Sponsoring Editor: *Eileen Murphy*
Editorial Assistant: *Lisa Blanton/Susan Carlson*
Production Editor: *Tessa A. McGlasson*
Marketing Team: *Jean Thompson/Christine Davis/*
  Deanne Brown
Marketing Representative: *Gerry Levine*
Manuscript Editor: *Jennifer McClain*
Interior Design: *Vernon Boes*

Cover Design: *Christine Garrigan*
Art Editor: *Jennifer Mackres*
Permissions Editor: *May Clark*
Typesetting: *The Cowans*
Cover Printing: *Phoenix Color Corp.*
Printing and Binding: *Maple-Vail*
  Book Mfg. Group

For more information, contact:

BROOKS/COLE PUBLISHING COMPANY
511 Forest Lodge Road
Pacific Grove, CA 93950
USA

International Thomson Editores
Seneca 53
Col. Polanco
México, D. F., México
C. P. 11560

International Thomson Publishing Europe
Berkshire House 168-173
High Holborn
London WC1V 7AA
England

International Thomson Publishing GmbH
Königswinterer Strasse 418
53227 Bonn
Germany

Thomas Nelson Australia
102 Dodds Street
South Melbourne, 3205
Victoria, Australia

International Thomson Publishing Asia
221 Henderson Road
#05-10 Henderson Building
Singapore 0315

Nelson Canada
1120 Birchmount Road
Scarborough, Ontario
Canada M1K 5G4

International Thomson Publishing Japan
Hirakawacho Kyowa Building, 3F
2-2-1 Hirakawacho
Chiyoda-ku, Tokyo 102
Japan

Printed in the United States of America

10   9   8   7   6   5   4   3   2   1

Library of Congress Cataloging-in-Publication Data

Doyle, Robert E., [date]
    Essential skills and strategies in the helping process / Robert E.
Doyle. — 2nd ed.
        p.   cm.
    Includes bibliographical references (p.   ) and index.
    ISBN 0-534-34879-3 (alk. paper)
    1. Counseling.   I. Title.
    BF637.C6D63   1998
    158'.3—dc21   97-18814
                                                          CIP

THIS BOOK IS PRINTED ON ACID-FREE RECYCLED PAPER

To my wife, Madeleine,
and my daughters, Jeanne and Kristina,
for their infinite patience,
encouragement, and love.

Contents

Preface

This book is intended for students who are enrolled in an introductory counseling course at the graduate or the undergraduate level. It was designed to provide students with a comprehensive understanding of the skills and strategies that are of critical importance in the counseling process and assumes the reader has had little or no background in counseling theory or methodology. Although the book is addressed to students who intend to become professional counselors, it may be used by students in other departments such as human services, nursing, psychology, and social work who are enrolled in a beginning counseling course.

A certain point of view is clearly implicit in any counseling textbook. This book evolved over several years from rny interest in presenting my students with a practical understanding of the counseling process from a skill-based point of view. My own students have found the book to be very helpful, and many of my former students have ccntinued to use the text as a resource book and foundation for further development of their knowledge of and skills in the helping process. I have strived to present the subject matter in a relatively informal writing style and to make the material as readable and concise as possible.

The book is divided into three major parts: the first section provides an overview of the essential components of the counseling process; the second part outlines some of the basic and widely used counseling intervention strategies; and the third section presents a comprehensive model for students to understand and master the communication skills that are essential to any counseling process.

Part 1, which contains three chapters, presents an overview of the primary components of the counseling process—the counselor, the client, and the dynamics of this process. Chapter 1 discusses the counselor's personal qualities, the educational requirements, and the major professional associations as well as the ethical standards and legal issues that counselors should be familiur with. Chapter 2 briefly reviews some of the major reasons why individuals function with varying degrees of effectiveness. The information covered in this chapter is not usually found in introductory counseling textbooks, but I included this material because I have found that many of my oun students need a review of these basic principles and a solid foundation for examining client concerns. Chapter 3 presents a model for conceptualizing and understanding the counseling process as it unfolds or develops over time. In this chapter I also point out the difficulties encountered in working with clients who are reluctant or resistant, and I suggest some ways to facilitate and overcome this complication.

Part 2, which has three chapters, presents an overview and some practical suggestions on how to use some of the fundamental intervention strategies employed in the counseling process. In the introduction section, the movement to integrate various counseling approaches is briefly discussed; then a skills-oriented model is presented, which conceptualizes various counseling approaches as *intervention strategies* rather than theories. Chapter 4 discusses four major cognitively oriented counseling strategies from this skills-oriented point of view. These strategies are: helping clients acquire and retain important factual information; assisting clients with the decision-making process; helping clients restructure their logical thinking; and assisting clients with analogous, inductive, and creative thinking. This chapter includes some intervention strategies that are employed by professional counselors in a variety of settings but rarely found in counseling theory textbooks. Chapter 5 outlines a number of affectively oriented approaches and then describes how these approaches can be used to help clients ventilate, obtain catharsis, gain insight, and improve their self-concepts. Chapter 6 presents the important behaviorally oriented or performance-based counseling strategies that are very useful in helping clients.

Part 3, which contains four chapters, provides a process to enable students to develop the critical communication skills required for effective helping. The introduction section outlines ten communication roles employed by counselors and describes a four-point Likert-type scale for the qualitative evaluation of the counselor's competency and timing in using a particular role. Each chapter describes certain role communication skills; outlines the important subsidiary verbal responses that are associated with each of these roles; furnishes illustrations of these communication skills; and provides numerous examples and practice exercises for developing these skills. Chapter 7 presents the primary communication skills: attending, clarifying, and supporting. Chapter discusses the intermediate communication skills: providing information, probing, responding to client questions, and the use of silence. Chapter 9 describes the advanced communication skills: advising, motivating or prescribing, and analyzing or evaluating. And Chapter 10 provides the opportunity for students to practice communicating various intervention strategies.

New to the Second Edition

This edition of Essential Skills and Strategies in the Helping Process has several significant changes, which are based on the feedback I received from colleagues and students who have read and used the textbook in their classes. Several revisions were made in Part 1. These include major changes in the names of professional associations, significant modifications in the terminology used to describe psychological disorders, and further discussions on topics such as accreditation and licensure, ethical and legal issues, occupational stress, resistant and reluctant clients, and the transitional stages of the counseling process. Two new role communication skills—responding to client questions and advising—were developed and added to Part 3 to provide students with a broader range of skills. Two other roles—motivating and interpreting—were modified to reflect the increased emphasis given to the two new role communication skills and to more clearly specify the skills used in the evaluating or interpreting role. Chapter 10 was rewritten to include a discussion of important factors that counselors-in-training need to take into account as they learn to apply counseling strategies, and to enrich the case study materials. Finally, a discussion of the importance of multicultural issues has been included.

Acknowledgments

I want to thank those with whom I have been associated at St. John's University—students, secretaries and clerical assistants, administrators, and my professional colleagues. My students, by their open, genuine. and sincere interest in learning how to help others, have been a constant source of inspiration to me. Many come from a bilingual and bicultural background, and I am indebted to them for feedback on the cultural aspects of the materials in the book. The departmental secretaries and clerical assistants were always willing to give a helping hand. The administrators provided me with the environment that has allowed me to pursue my interest in counseling. And my colleagues—Shirley Griggs, Donald Sampson, James O'Toole. and Jennie Venezia—provided encouragement, helpful suggestions, and appropriate criticism at the right time.

Second, I would like to express my appreciation to the reviewers who shared their reactions and suggested improvements to the text. Their thoughtful comments are reflected throughout the text. My sincere thanks go to: Nancy DePalma, West Hartford Public Schools; Kim C. Francis, Brooklyn College; Eugene Goldin, Long Island University; Robert Guiry, New York Police Department; Patricia Hudson, George Washington IJniversity; Margaret Olson, University of Wisconsin at Oshkosh; Dovie Jane Gamble, University of Florida; Don Harvey, Trevecca Nazarene University; Patricia Hudson, George Washington University; Mary Kay Kreider, St. Louis Community College; and Bernard Nisenholz, California State University, Northridge. I also extend my thanks to those who reviewed and used the first edition of this book and took the time to offer their insightful and constructive comments.

Finally, I want to express my gratitude to my publisher, Claire Verduin, and to the staff at Brooks/Cole who helped me develop the first edition of this book. And I am indebted to my new editor, Eileen Murphy, my production editor Tessa McGlasson, and to all the others in the Brooks/Cole association who assisted me to prepare this edition. It has always been a delight to work with the members of the Brooks/Cole team. Their continual support has benefited me and helped me work more productively.

Robert E. Doyle

PART 1

The Counselor, the Client, and the Counseling Process

Counseling may be defined as a dynamic interpersonal process where a trained professional assists another individual—who is functioning at an unsatisfactory level in some aspect of life—to become a more effectively functioning person. This definition of counseling (and any others you may encounter) involves three unique factors: the counselor, the client, and the counseling process. This part of the text discusses important aspects of each of these factors.

Chapter 1 briefly describes the personal characteristics important for every counselor, the central components of the counselor's education and training, and the essential ethical standards and significant legal considerations that guide a counselor's behavior in professional practice. Chapter 2 presents a brief review of important psychological concepts and discusses several areas where clients frequently need assistance. Knowledge of the topics covered in this chapter is necessary for you to understand how individuals who are functioning effectively differ from persons who are not. Chapter 3 briefly outlines the counseling process from initiation to completion. It delineates the characteristics of this process through its various developmental phases or stages, and it specifies the distinctive activities that occur in each stage. This chapter also presents some ways to work successfully with clients who are either reluctant about or resistant to receiving counseling.

The Counselor

and

the Counseling Process

INTRODUCTION

This chapter presents several important topics about the counselor and the counseling process. It begins with an outline of the personal and professional characteristics that counselors need to manifest; then it discusses the major professional counseling associations and the educational requirements for counselors; and, finally, it describes essential ethical and legal issues important in the counseling process. After studying this chapter you should be able to:

- indicate the important characteristics of professional counselors;
- describe the professional education and training of counselors;
- name the major counseling associations;
- identify the major ethical standards or codes of conduct that guide practitioners in the counseling field;
- discuss important ethical issues, including the client's welfare, competency of the counselor, the client's right to privacy, and value issues inherent in the counseling relationship; and
- specify some of the major legal issues that affect the counselor.

CHARACTERISTICS OF THE PROFESSIONAL COUNSELOR

Counseling is a unique interpersonal process whose success depends on the attitudes, skills, and knowledge the counselor brings to the relationship. As a counselor you should manifest the following six personal and professional characteristics in order to help another person:

1. the belief that clients are unique individuals of significant value,
2. the belief that clients are capable of change,
3. the knowledge of how effective individuals function,

4. the knowledge and skills necessary to help individuals overcome functional limitations,
5. the willingness to become involved in this interpersonal process, and
6. the knowledge of yourself and your own skills and limitations.

Belief That Clients Are Unique Individuals of Significant Value

The belief that all human beings are worthwhile, valuable, and unique is an essential conviction for every counselor to have. This conviction must be present for you to relate to each client in a positive and constructive manner. The acceptance of and sincere belief in the client must be a felt experience and not an abstract philosophical concept. It does not mean that you must approve or disapprove of a particular act or like or dislike a particular trait manifested by a client; rather, in spite of an act or regardless of a trait, you should have a genuine interest in the client and respect the client as an important, valuable, and worthwhile human being.

You need to be open to clients from diverse cultural backgrounds and comfortable with differences between yourself and others who may be unlike you in terms of race, ethnic background, religious beliefs, and values. Try to understand your clients with their traditions in mind. Remember, however, that the diversity within cultures can be quite considerable and that each of your clients is a unique individual.

Furthermore, as a counselor you must understand that a client's self-perception and perception of the world constitute reality for that person. The beliefs, attitudes, feelings, and cognitive impressions that clients have about themselves and their environment strongly influence the way they behave. As a counselor you need to focus on understanding these perceptions, for they provide valuable vehicles for viewing the client's internal frame of reference, grasping the uniqueness of the client's world, and comprehending the meaning of the client's behavior.

Counselors who manifest this belief in their clients' sense of worth and uniqueness encourage their clients to develop a feeling of trust during the counseling process. This belief is communicated in a number of ways. Nonverbally, it is communicated by promptness, posture, and facial expressions; paraverbally, it is communicated by tonal quality; and verbally, it is communicated by responses that are sensitive to the feelings and attitudes of the client.

Belief That Clients Are Capable of Change

Your theoretical orientation and your basic assumptions about the nature of human beings largely determine your belief regarding the kind of change and the amount or degree of change possible for any individual client. Counselors may hold distinct and varied opinions on the kinds of changes that they believe are possible, but all counselors must believe that individuals are capable of changing.

Counselors tend to be optimists, and they believe that all clients can—at least to some extent—modify their feelings, attitudes, cognitive structures, or overt behaviors.

They recognize, moreover, that helping people to change is hard work and that sometimes they cannot help a particular person. When this occurs, the inability to help the person is not ascribed to the impossibility of change but rather to extenuating causes such as the client's unreadiness for change, the need to modify the client's environmental situation, or the counselor's inexperience or lack of knowledge in dealing with this client's particular type of problem.

As a counselor you must communicate your belief that your client is capable of changing. This communication should be accomplished by your actions and attitudes and should not depend on verbal communication. The use of phrases like "I believe you can solve your problem" will not, by and of itself, persuade your client of your belief. Other communication channels such as body gestures, facial expressions, and voice tone are more subtle, but also more powerful, ways of communicating your real attitudes and beliefs.

Knowledge of How Individuals Function

Counselors need to understand the psychological principles that guide human behavior and to be aware of the environmental factors that influence this behavior. This knowledge is ordinarily acquired through advanced study in graduate psychology courses, which focus on understanding both the *nomothetic* or *general laws*—the psychological characteristics and behaviors common to all people; and the *idiographic phenomena*—the unique characteristics and behaviors of specific individuals under these laws.

It is important for you to take the cultural experiences and social backgrounds of your clients into consideration to fully understand their behavior. Any sort of oppression such as discrimination, stereotyping, or racism can have a negative impact on their lives. Be aware of any institutional barriers that might prevent your clients from using some services or programs. Learn about the cultures of the clients you serve and how their cultural heritage influences their values, beliefs, and behaviors. However, do not expect clients from the same cultural group to be identical—there is considerable diversity among members of all groups. Depend on your clients to tell you how their own culture has influenced them.

Knowledge of how individuals function is essential to the entire counseling process, whether you are trying to build trust necessary to establish a working relationship, attempting to explore and understand factors that are delimiting the client's behaviors, deciding upon a particular treatment strategy, employing an intervention strategy, or deciding when to terminate a case.

Knowledge of How to Assist Individuals

Counseling requires more of you than a willingness to enter into a relationship, a belief in the value of individuals, a belief in change, and the knowledge of how people function. You must also possess important clinical skills that help you to assist individuals in finding the impediments that block their ability to undergo some changes and function at a more effective or higher level.

Clients are helped in many ways. What seems to work in one place or time may not work in another. A wide variety of approaches, methods, and theories of counseling are available. As a beginning counselor, however, you should avoid the meaningless smorgasbord approach that haphazardly takes a bit of this theory and a bit of that theory. As a counselor-in-training you should experiment, under supervision, with a variety of approaches that you can gradually integrate into a personal style through ongoing training and practice.

As you develop your counseling skills you should seek out opportunities that will enhance your ability to work with clients from diverse populations. By learning to attend to your clients' heritage and background you will discover how to modify your intervention strategies and techniques to be relevant to these situations. You will also learn to be flexible, for what works with one client with a particular cultural background may not work with another client from that same background.

Learning how to assist individuals in overcoming their functional limitations is a time-consuming process of personal growth. Counselors-in-training normally obtain entry-level skills through didactic and experimental learning. They read and hear about counseling approaches. They try to emulate the behavior of expert counselors by shaping their responses to fit the pattern of the particular expert whom they are studying at that time. Through sequential clinical experiences such as simulations, role playing, supervised practice, and internships, you will learn to deal with conceptual and actual problems and thereby develop your own personal skills. Skill development is an ongoing process, and you should expect to continue to learn skills and add them to your repertoire throughout your entire professional career.

Willingness to Become Involved

Counselors must demonstrate their willingness to become involved in this interpersonal process called counseling. The commitment to share oneself goes beyond merely giving the time and energy required to assist another person. It includes the effort to bring as much of yourself as necessary into the helping relationship and the ability to communicate to the client that nothing is more important at that moment than the client and what he or she has to say. As you learn to bring yourself into a counseling relationship you will need to become aware of how your own historical and cultural background has influenced your thoughts, actions, and behaviors. Furthermore, this commitment to become involved requires you to be willing to concentrate fully on the client's internal frame of reference, to reach out to help clients understand themselves, to assist clients in understanding the change process and any impediments that may be present, and to take some risks in using yourself as an instrument to facilitate this change.

Counselors who have good feelings of their own self-worth, adequacy, and self-discipline transcend their own limitations and are free to give the necessary attention to their clients and to focus on ways to assist them. You can communicate this willingness to become involved by being warm, understanding, and sincere; by concentrating on the messages your clients are trying to communicate; and by giving genuine, unhurried, and sincere responses.

Knowledge of Oneself

Counselors must have positive self-concepts and feel secure about themselves. By manifesting good psychological health, counselors can have a positive modeling effect on their clients. As a counselor you should be aware of your own feelings, attitudes, and values and how these relate to helping another person. Counselors typically have a high social interest and a strong motivation for working with others; however, being a counselor also requires a high tolerance for dealing with client ambiguity, client defensiveness, and your own frustrations. It is important that you know how you solve your own problems and cope with the conflicts and stresses in your own life. In addition, you need to know your own skills and to willingly acknowledge your limitations. You should be open to self-improvement and growth through additional learning and experience and to the acknowledgment that all persons, including yourself, have a range of talents and limits.

Counselors realize that they cannot help everyone with every functional limitation, and they must be able to recognize when a particular client's concerns require some specialized knowledge or area of expertise they may not possess. You must become sensitive to those areas and exercise appropriate discretion and judgment in referring the client to other specialists.

This process of knowing yourself and facing up to your own limitations has two important influences on counseling. First, the better you can understand and appreciate your own feelings, thoughts, and behaviors, the better you can understand and appreciate the feelings, thoughts, and behaviors of others. Second, counselors who are comfortable with themselves communicate an attitude of genuineness to the client. The client, sensing that genuineness, develops or confirms a sense of trust in the counseling relationship and unfolds more deeply his or her internal frame of reference, thus moving the counseling process along.

THE COUNSELOR'S PROFESSIONAL EDUCATION AND TRAINING

Standards for the education and training of counselors have been published by four major professional associations: the American Counseling Association (ACA), the American Association of Marriage and Family Therapists (AAMFT), the American Psychological Association (APA), and the Council on Rehabilitation Education (CORE). ACA, AAMFT, and CORE have established standards for the preparation of professional counselors in different areas of specialization at the master's degree level; and ACA and APA have specified criteria for doctoral-level programs. Although there is some variability among master's degree standards, they typically specify that counselors-in-training complete a two-year or 48 to 60 semester-hour program to meet minimum entry-level professional requirements. Master's degree programs traditionally offer coursework in one of eight specialized areas: career counseling, community agency counseling, gerontological counseling, marriage and family counseling, mental health counseling, rehabilitation counseling, school counseling, and student affairs practice in higher education. Doctoral programs, which typically require the completion of the entry-level or master's degree program as a prerequisite, customarily offer majors in: counselor education and supervision, rehabilitation counseling, and counseling psychology.

The American Counseling Association is the largest national association for professional counselors. Founded in 1951 as the American Personnel and Guidance Association (APGA), it served as an umbrella organization to unify the work of four national associations. In 1983 APGA changed its name to the American Association for Counseling and Development (AACD) and in 1992 to the American Counseling Association (ACA). It now has 16 member associations or divisions devoted to different aspects of the counseling profession (see Table 1). ACA and several of its member associations conduct annual meetings, and each division publishes a newsletter and a journal of particular interest to the members of that group. Professional counselors keep up their education and training by reading these professional journals, by attending workshops and various training programs, and by actively participating in one of the associations devoted to counseling.

ACA has had a strong influence on the professional practice of counseling in several important ways. First, it has promulgated standards for the training of counselors since 1958—standards that continue to be revised and updated over the years. Second, it has been working for the accreditation of counselor preparation programs since 1978. Third, it has fostered the process of identifying professional counselors through a national certification process since 1982 when it first sponsored the National Board for Certified Counselors (NBCC). And fourth, it has encouraged state branches to seek licensure for professional counselors since 1977 when it developed a model licensing bill.

In 1981 ACA established the Council for the Accreditation of Counseling and Related Educational Programs (CACREP) as its accreditation affiliate. CACREP takes responsibility for the revision of standards for the education and training of counselors and for the accreditation of counselor preparation programs at both the master's and doctoral degree levels. The current training standards outline a common core of knowledge as well as competencies unique to the specialization areas. These standards require students to develop core competencies in each of eight curricular areas:

T A B L E   1-1
Member Associations of ACA

American College Counseling Association (ACCA)
American Mental Health Counselors Association (AMHCA)
American Rehabilitation Counseling Association (ARCA)
American School Counseling Association (ASCA)
Association for Adult Development and Aging (AADA)
Association for Assessment in Counseling (AAC)
Association for Counselor Education and Supervision (ACES)
Association for Counselors and Educators in Government (ACEG)
Association for Humanistic Education and Development (AHEAD)
Association for Multicultural Counseling and Development (AMCD)
Association for Specialists in Group Work (ASGW)
Association for Spiritual, Ethical, and Religious Values in Counseling (ASERVIC)
International Association of Addictions and Offender Counselors (IAAOC)
International Association of Marriage and Family Counselors (IAMFC)
National Career Development Association (NCDA)
National Employment Counseling Association (NECA)

- human growth and development
- social and cultural foundations
- helping relationships
- group methods
- career development
- appraisal
- research and evaluation
- professional orientation

Additional competencies are specified for each area of specialization. Furthermore, supervised practica and internships related to the specialization area are required. CACREP conducts a review of these standards every seven years and obtains input from members of related professional associations before any revisions to these standards are made.

The CACREP accreditation process is a voluntary one. Many counselor preparation programs have sought and obtained this accreditation status, including 111 by early 1997. Other counselor education programs follow the standards for their program offerings but for various reasons have elected not to apply for accreditation.

Many counselors have become National Certified Counselors (NCC) by meeting the standards set by the National Board for Certified Counselors (NBCC), the certification affiliate of the American Counseling Association. This certification process provides professional identity and visibility to professional counselors by publishing a registry of nationally certified counselors. To become nationally certified you have to meet certain specified educational standards, obtain appropriate professional counseling experience, and successfully complete a written national examination designed to test your knowledge of the eight content areas specified in the CACREP standards, listed above. Certified counselors must show evidence of continued professional growth and development to maintain this credential. NBCC also offers counselors the opportunity to obtain additional specialty certification, through additional testing, in five areas: addiction counseling, career counseling, gerontological counseling, mental health counseling, and school counseling.

Counselors can also be nationally certified by three other groups. The American Association of Marriage and Family Therapists (AAMFT) has established requirements for marriage and family therapists, the International Association of Marriage and Family Counselors (IAMFC) has developed standards to become a certified family therapist, and the Commission on Rehabilitation Counselor Certification (CRCC) has specific criteria for becoming a certified rehabilitation counselor (CRC).

Professional counselors may also obtain a license or professional certification in the majority of states in the United States (41 in 1994). A license or professional certificate is granted under state regulations that control the use of a particular title, the scope of practice, or both. State licensure laws normally govern the use of a title rather than the scope of practice because of the considerable overlap of professional activities among counselors, psychologists, social workers, and other mental health practitioners. Several states specify graduation from a CACREP-approved program or its equivalent as the minimum educational requirement, and many call for the National Counselor Examination offered by NBCC as the written examination requirement. Because each state controls its own professional licensure and credentialing legislation, wide variations exist in the terminology and functions defined in each of these statutes.

In some settings professional counselors work closely with other helping professionals such as psychologists and social workers. Standards for the education and training of members of these allied professions have been determined by their respective professional associations, the American Psychological Association (APA) and the National Association for Social Workers (NASW).

ETHICAL CONSIDERATIONS FOR THE COUNSELOR

The overall goal of the counseling process is to help the client become a more effectively functioning person. In this process the counselor's role is to assist clients in modifying their behavior or in choosing between alternative courses of action, or perhaps to support clients while they are experiencing some trauma in the course of life. Ultimately, of course, clients are responsible for choosing whatever behavior they want to adopt, what direction they wish to go, and how they wish to resolve the traumatic episodes in their lives. The counselor's primary job is assisting the client; nevertheless, the counseling relationship has a strong bearing on the counseling outcome. In the relationship, the counselor is the helper, the nurturer, the more effective person, or the mentor and, hence, exerts considerable influence on the client. The counselor can alter counseling outcomes in significant ways.

Ethical principles provide rules for conducting yourself in appropriate ways with your clients. This section briefly outlines important information about codes of ethics that you need to be aware of in working with clients. It also covers four major ethical issues: the client's welfare, the competency of the counselor, the client's right to privacy, and the value issues inherent in the counseling process.

Codes of Ethics

Clearly, counselors have an obligation to work for their clients' best interests. Toward this end, experienced counselors as well as counselors-in-training should be knowledgeable about the standards and principles of conduct that have emerged over the years through the consensus of experienced counselors. These ethical standards or principles are codified and promulgated by national professional associations such as the American Psychological Association (APA), the American Counseling Association (ACA), and the American Association of Marriage and Family Therapists (AAMFT). They provide guidelines for appropriate ethical behavior in dealing with issues relating to professional practice. These written codes of ethics fulfill several functions: first, they help clarify the counselor's responsibility to clients, to employers, to professional groups, and to society in general; second, they provide some guidelines for handling issues and resolving conflicts that may arise in a particular situation; and third, the codes provide a standard by which members of the profession may be judged.

Ethical standards provide broad guidelines and offer a discrete number of statements about general professional behavior. Because of the discreteness and the generality of these statements, they leave gray areas and offer limited direction for some issues that may arise in professional practice. You may find a conflict in interpreting various sections of ethical codes—particularly if you belong to several professional organizations and try to follow each group's codes. At other times you may encounter issues that cannot be handled by relying solely on these guidelines, and you will have to use your own judgment in applying standards to specific situations.

Seven divisions of ACA (ACES, AMHCA, ARCA, ASCA, ASGW, IAMFC, and NCDA) have published their own codes for dealing with issues of primary concern to members of these divisions, and the National Board for Certified Counselors (NBCC) has published its own code of ethics to guide nationally certified counselors. Professional organizations periodically revise their ethical codes as conflicts within the code or new issues come to light. In 1995 ACA published a revised *Code of Ethics and Standards of Practice*, which provides a new code of ethics and offers specific standards to guide the behavior of professional counselors. The ethics committee believes this revision provides a unified approach to ethical decision making, minimizes the conflicts among different codes, and circumvents the need for professional counselors to consult and follow several different codes (Herlihy & Remley, 1995). As a counselor-in-training you should familiarize yourself with the current ethical standards published by the professional associations you identify with, such as ACA, AAMFT, and APA and any of the divisions of ACA that you are interested in joining. Furthermore, the following publications concerning ethical issues can provide you with considerable assistance in understanding the ethical dimensions of practice:

> *Ethical Standards Casebook* (Herlihy & Corey, 1996)
> *Issues and Ethics in the Helping Professions* (Corey, Corey, & Callanan, 1998)
> *Ethical, Legal, and Professional Issues in the Practice of Marriage and Family Therapy* (Huber, 1994)
> *Ethics and Values in Psychotherapy* (Rosenbaum, 1982)
> *Ethical and Legal Issues in Counseling and Psychotherapy* (Van Hoose & Kottler, 1985)

The Client's Welfare

The primary responsibility of every counselor in the counseling relationship is the welfare of the client. Clearly, counselors do not work in a vacuum; they also have responsibilities to themselves, to the agencies and institutions for whom they work, to their profession, and to society in general. Putting the welfare of the client first means that your top priority is helping the client and ensuring that the client obtains appropriate assistance from either yourself or another helping professional. You should be aware of the subtle ways that you can affect the welfare of your client. You may, for example, find yourself in a dual relationship with the client that results in competing role expectations. If you are involved with the client in another role such as teacher or administrative superior, or in a close social relationship, the counseling relationship will be confounded and your ability to be objective will be hindered. Consequently, it is generally better to avoid counseling individuals with whom you have another relationship. Refer these cases to another counselor. Focusing on what is best for the client's welfare should be your paramount ethical concern.

The Competency of the Counselor

Counselors must present themselves and their qualifications in honest, truthful ways and work within their own areas of professional expertise. As a counselor trainee who has had little counseling experience in which to develop proficiency, you should present yourself as a counselor-in-training and work within the parameters of those areas for which you are obtaining adequate supervision. When you finish your formal training, you should apply for the positions that match your qualifications, and you should obtain the credentials and licenses those positions require. When working with clients, you should employ intervention strategies that you are competent in using and that are appropriate for the situation. If a client has concerns that you cannot handle, you should seek consultation, obtain appropriate supervision, or make a referral to an appropriate professional or agency that can deal with the issue. To ensure that you maintain your competency as a counselor, you should keep up with developments in the field by reading and attending workshops and professional meetings and through continued supervision. It is imperative that you be aware of your own professional competence and recognize your limitations at any given stage in your career development.

The Client's Right to Privacy

Individuals have a right to the privacy of their own lives. When clients discuss their concerns with counselors in the counseling process, they reveal considerable information about themselves. In this sharing process, the client places a certain amount of trust and faith in you, and you assume an obligation to protect the client's right to privacy. This protection involves two major concepts that beginning counselors need to be aware of: (1) confidentiality and informed consent and (2) recording the interview.

Confidentiality and informed consent. To the beginning counselor trainee, confidentiality often implies that the counselor should never share any information about the client with any other person. This rigid interpretation is too all-encompassing. There are limits to confidentiality; clearly, confidentiality must be breached when issues are discussed that are potentially harmful to the client or others. The following paragraphs outline further guidelines you should be aware of on the extent of confidentiality.

Information about the client should be used for the welfare of the client. When you honestly and professionally believe that information about the client should be shared with others, you should be prepared to do so. However, you will need to obtain the client's consent and make the client aware of the material to be shared and under what circumstances and with whom it will be shared. If you are working with children (or others who need supervision), you should obtain a parent's—or a legal guardian's—approval and make the guardian aware of the extent and limitations of confidentiality.

Counselors obtain information about clients from the clients themselves during the counseling process and from other sources. In other words, this information can be internally (interview) or externally (noninterview) based. Furthermore, counselors interact with professional supervisors and colleagues, professional workers in other disciplines, and other significant persons in the life of the client, all of whom are interested in the client's welfare. Generally speaking, when interacting with significant other persons, counselors discuss information about their clients in the following hierarchical order:

1. Interview and noninterview data are frequently shared with professional supervisors and colleagues.
2. Noninterview data are often shared with professionals in other disciplines and sometimes with significant other persons.
3. Interview data are not shared with others unless there is a compelling reason for doing so.

Counselors and counselors-in-training share interview data with their supervisors and colleagues to benefit from the experiences of others and thus develop their skills and be better prepared to help their clients. In fact, most counselors-in-training are required to share their notes and audio- or videotapes of their counseling sessions with their supervisors and colleagues for critical reviews. Counselors share noninterview data and inferences from interview data with professionals in other disciplines and with significant others to gain their cooperation and expertise in assisting the client or to keep them informed of the progress of the case. Normally, the counselor does not share interview data with professionals in other disciplines and significant others unless there is an important health or safety issue, a clear danger to human life, or unless the client specifically consents to divulging the information.

If clients are properly prepared—and you present sound reasons why you want to share information with professional supervisors and colleagues—they normally have no objection. In fact, they may be pleased to know that you are in contact with other skilled professionals and that there are many resources available. Likewise, when they are properly prepared, they are usually not apprehensive when you share noninterview data and inferences from interviews with professionals in other disciplines and significant other persons. They may question you if you want to share interview data with individuals from these two groups. If they are made fully aware of the reasons why you want to share this information, their objections normally vanish.

Two general principles that must be kept in mind when sharing both interview and noninterview data with others are: (1) obtain the client's informed consent, and (2) reveal everything that is essential and absolutely nothing that is not essential.

Recording the interview.   Recording the interview in one way or another is essential for several reasons—to remind yourself what happened with a particular client in a particular session, to review your work with your supervisor or professional colleagues, and to show your own growth and development as a counselor.

There are several ways to record a session: audiotaping, videotaping, and note taking. Audiotaping and videotaping are easy and fruitful ways for a beginning counselor trainee to record counseling sessions because of the simplicity of audiocassette tape machines and the portability of video equipment.

These methods provide an excellent means for your supervisor to monitor your growth over time and to see how you handle a given situation. The supervisor can review your moment-to-moment interaction with the client and give feedback, pointing out what was well done, what was not so well done, and what was left undone. It is imperative, of course, that the equipment not get in the way of the counseling relationship.

Beginning counselor trainees often need several experiences with recorders so that they can feel comfortable working with the machinery and hearing their own voices and seeing themselves; gain some expertise in obtaining the informed consent of their clients in truthful but nonanxiety-provoking ways; and learn how to place recorders, microphones, and cameras in inconspicuous places so the client and counselor do not have their attention drawn to these devices and, hence, will focus on the counseling process and not on the recording process.

More experienced counselors and counselors who work in settings where sessions cannot be taped may rely on written notes taken either during or immediately after the counseling session. There is not one specific or correct way to take these notes. As a counselor trainee, you should follow the recommendations of your immediate supervisor until you develop your own style and preferred method. Generally, notes taken during the interview record factual information stated, ideas and feelings mentioned, and plans or goals discussed with the client. Notes written immediately after the session contain a résumé of the points discussed, a summary of the dynamics of the session, and a statement about tentative goals for the next meeting.

Neophyte counselors who are trying to develop many skills simultaneously must be cautioned against two extreme positions: compulsion and scantiness. At the one extreme, trainees may be so intent on taking notes that either they do not concentrate on the relationship and use the note taking as an excuse or a refuge from developing their communication skills, or they become interrogators rather than counselors. At the other extreme, trainees may be so intent on the session or concerned with their skills that they fail to record important and significant events.

When written notes are used to record interviews, clients should be aware that these notes are being kept. When taken during the session, notes should be made in such a way as to be as inconspicuous as possible. They should be brief enough so that the counselor-client relationship is not affected and sufficiently long to record the significant elements.

When recording a session, be honest with your client. Explain the purpose of the note taking or the audio- or videotaping and explain with whom you expect to share the case materials. Do not write anything you do not want your interviewee to see, and allow your client to read your notes or listen to or see the recording if he or she wishes to do so. Remember, counseling is a collaborative effort, and any notes or records of the sessions are taken for the client's welfare.

Notes and recordings of the interview need to be kept in a secure place to which only the counselor has immediate access. Normally they should be shared only with those who are helping the counselor—namely, supervisors or professional colleagues.

Value Issues Inherent in the Counseling Process

Counseling is not a value-free human endeavor. All counseling is intimately involved with cultural, moral, and ethical values related to the three major spheres of life: the educational/vocational dimension, the marital and family dimension, and the social/ cultural dimension. Both counselors and clients bring to the counseling relationship deeply cherished values concerning education, work, marriage and family issues, and people's obligations and responsibilities to those in their immediate environment as well as those incumbent upon them as citizens.

Neither clients nor counselors leave their values at the door of the counseling office. The only value that may appear overtly in a counseling session is the dignity and respect that both participants reveal in their treatment of one another; however, other values are usually implicit in the relationship and are not obvious, principally because both the client and the counselor are working under the same value system and do not need to discuss them. Some examples include:

- the school counselor advising the college preparatory student about various colleges—both have implicitly accepted the value that "a good education is most desirable";
- the vocational counselor educating an unemployed head of household about job placement strategies—both have implicitly accepted the "Protestant work ethic"; and
- the behavioral counselor treating the obese client—both have accepted the value that being overweight is unhealthy.

Generally speaking, value issues become critical in the counseling process when one of the following situations occurs:

- The values of the client and the counselor are different.
- The values of the client are causing some difficulty in his or her environment.
- The counselor would like to employ a treatment that he or she believes, in the long run, will help the client, but knows that the treatment has some side effects, involves some pain or other harm to the client, or could lead to results that may leave the client worse off than if there were no treatment.

When the first situation occurs, and the client and the counselor have different values regarding an issue that is relevant to the counseling relationship, the counselor needs to remain aware of these differences and respect the client's right to his or her own values about a particular issue. The United States is a pluralistic society, and counselors must work within that system. Because the goal of any counseling relationship is to help clients resolve their own problems, you should, if at all possible, try to work within the client's frame of reference and value system to find a solution. However, sometimes you may find that it is impossible to do this. When this occurs, the conflict should be discussed openly with the client, and if further counseling proves unworkable, a referral to another counselor is mandated.

When the second value issue emerges whereby the client's value system is causing the client difficulty, the counseling is clearly value dominated. Again, the counselor must remember that the overall goal of the process is to help clients help themselves. Therefore, you need to help the client discuss his or her values in the context of the client's own environment and assist the client in resolving the difficulty or at least coping with the situation in a more effective way.

The third critical value situation arises when a proposed treatment strategy involves some risk to the client and may cause the client some physical or psychological harm or otherwise leave the client in a worse state than he or she was before treatment. Clearly, risk taking is a normal human behavior. We take chances in virtually all things we do. Usually we do things that involve odds that are overwhelmingly in our favor, but as counselors we should encourage a client to undertake a risky treatment when the following guidelines have been met:

- the client's present situation is very bad or is deteriorating, and some treatment involving risk is necessary, such as an aversion technique (outlined in Chapter 6);
- the client fully understands the risk and consents to the treatment; and
- the proposed treatment has been reviewed by an objective panel of professional supervisors or experts, and the panel agrees that the treatment is warranted.

LEGAL CONSIDERATIONS FOR THE COUNSELOR

Counselors-in-training should be aware of the major legal issues related to the professional practice of counseling. This section of the text briefly discusses the issues related to confidentiality and privileged communication, specific federal and state legislation, and malpractice. More detailed information about these legal aspects of counseling and the helping professions can be found in Anderson (1996), Fischer and Sorenson (1996), Huey and Remley (1989), and Woody and Associates (1984).

First, the distinction between the terms confidentiality and privileged communication must be understood. *Confidentiality* is an ethical term that refers to the client's right to privacy, guiding counselors to disclose information only with the informed consent of the client. Under certain unusual conditions counselors are legally bound to breach confidentiality. These situations involve clear and immediate danger to the client or to a third party—for example, child abuse, potential suicide, or serious harm to another person. *Privileged communication* is a legal term that refers to the right of the client to discuss matters with an appropriate person and not have this communication reported in a court of law. Privileged communication may be absolute or limited. Absolute privileged communication, which protects the helper from disclosing confidential information to any court, is normally extended to certain parishioner-clergy and client-lawyer relationships. However, privileged communication statutes for counselors are usually limited or restricted, which means that in any given case a judge has the authority to decide whether or not the helper should divulge the confidential information. It is also important to note that privileged communication, which is the right of the client, may be waived by a client. Furthermore, legal mandates to report child abuse in all 50 states and regulations to disclose criminal activity in some states take precedence over privileged communication statutes for counselors (Anderson, 1996).

Second, counselors should become familiar with both national and local laws that guide their practice. At the national level the Family Educational Rights and Privacy Act (Public Law 93-380), often referred to as the Buckley Amendment, became public policy in 1974. This act stipulates that clients or their parents have the right to examine all appropriate official records and to challenge any information they feel is inadequate or misleading, and that access to student information is severely restricted. The Education of All Handicapped Children Act (Public Law 94-142) became public policy in 1977. This law mandates the rights of students with disabilities to receive an appropriate education and the rights of parents to participate in the design of the education of their children. School counselors typically become involved with the implementation of this law by helping to develop an individualized educational program (IEP) for a student who has a disability, monitoring the way this program is carried out, and consulting with parents on a regular basis. Because state laws govern what transpires within each of the 50 states, counselors should become familiar with the laws of the state in which they work.

Third, counselors may be sued for malpractice when they fail to render the proper service according to acceptable professional standards, whether through ignorance or neglect, and when some injury or harm to the client or someone else results from actions taken following the counselor's advice or recommendation. Malpractice liability has resulted from such issues as abandoning a client, not being aware of a suicidal tendency, sexual intimacy with a client, failure to obtain consent for a research project, failure to complete a contract, misrepresenting one's professional training, improper diagnosis, and inadequate supervision (Anderson, 1996; Corey & Corey, 1998). Acceptable standards of professional practice clearly require counselors to practice only in areas where they are well trained and to consult with professional colleagues and supervisors when there is any concern about the appropriateness of a treatment or strategy. Counselors who use ethical codes as a standard of practice have some protection from malpractice litigation. As a further precaution, counselors-in-training should consider obtaining malpractice liability insurance, which can be acquired at a reasonable price through ACA and several other professional organizations.

Summary

This chapter has presented information about the counselor and the counseling process. After reading it you should be familiar with several important aspects of counseling. First, you should be able to discuss some of the important personal and professional characteristics that are important for counselors. Second, you should be able to describe the professional education and training requirements for counselors. Third, you should be able to name the major professional counseling associations. Fourth, you should be able to identify the major ethical standards or codes of conduct that guide counselors. Fifth, you should be able to discuss the major ethical issues involved in the counseling profession. And finally, you should be able to identify some of the major legal issues that affect the counselor.

References

American Association for Marriage and Family Therapists. (1991). *AAMFT code of ethics.* Washington, DC: Author.

American Counseling Association. (1995). *Code of ethics and standards of practice.* Alexandria, VA: Author.

American Psychological Association. (1987). *Casebook on ethical principles of psychologists.* Washington, DC: Author.

American Psychological Association. (1992). *Ethical principles of psychologists and code of conduct.* Washington, DC: Author.

Anderson, B. S. (1996). *The counselor and the* law (4th ed.). Alexandria, VA: American Counseling Association.

Corey, G., & Corey, M. S. (1998). *Becoming a helper* (3rd ed.). Pacific Grove, CA: Brooks/Cole.

Corey, G., Corey, M., & Callanan, P. (1998). *Issues and ethics in the helping professions* (5th ed.). Pacific Grove, CA: Brooks/Cole.

Fischer, L., & Sorenson, G. P. (1996). *School law for counselors, psychologists, and social workers* (3rd ed.). New York: Longman.

Herlihy, B., & Corey, G. (Eds.). (1996). *Ethical standards casebook* (5th ed.). Alexandria, VA: American Counseling Association.

Herlihy, B., & Remley, T. P. (1995). Unified ethical standards: A challenge for professionalism. *Journal of Counseling and Development, 74,* 130–133.

Huber, C. H. (1994). *Ethical, legal, and professional issues in the practice of marriage and family therapy* (2nd ed.). Columbus, OH: Merrill.

Huey, W. C., & Remley, T. P. (Eds.). (1989). *Ethical and legal issues in school counseling.* Alexandria, VA: American Counseling Association.

National Association of Social Workers. (1990). *Code of ethics.* Washington, DC: Author.

Rosenbaum, M. (Ed.). (1982). *Ethics and values in psychotherapy.* New York: Free Press.

Van Hoose, W. H., & Kottler, J. A. (1985). *Ethical and legal issues in counseling and psychotherapy* (2nd ed.). San Francisco: Jossey-Bass.

Woody, R. H., & Associates. (1984). *The law and the practice of human services.* San Francisco: Jossey-Bass.

The Effectively Funcioning Person

The Effectively Funcioning Person

INTRODUCTION

This chapter presents a brief overview of several areas where clients frequently manifest some difficulties in their lives. Helping clients become more effective, more fully functioning, and more independent is the ultimate goal of any counseling relationship and is implicit in all counseling approaches. The sections of this chapter should help you understand many of the ways in which individuals who function quite effectively differ from those who function less effectively. After careful review of the material in this chapter you should be able to:

- describe how a person functions effectively or ineffectively in one or more of the following dimensions of life: need satisfaction, stress and the coping processes, developmental task attainment, social contact and interpersonal relationship skills, and other personal or characteristic attributes; and
- discuss some of the major problems that can impede the effective functioning of individuals, such as handicapping conditions, serious vocational problems, substance abuse problems, and psychological disorders.

IMPORTANT PSYCHOLOGICAL DIMENSIONS OF FUNCTIONING

Individuals who are functioning effectively usually

1. satisfy their needs in appropriate ways,
2. deal with the stresses of life and their emotional reactions by using effective coping processes,
3. learn tasks that are appropriate to their developmental stage,
4. have worthwhile social interactions and interpersonal relationships, and
5. demonstrate other positive attributes in their lives.

Individuals who are functioning less than optimally often manifest problems in one or more of these areas.

Need Satisfaction

Needs, drives, and motives are the energizing forces that propel us toward or away from some action or thing that we require for our survival or well-being (Coon, 1995; Weiten, 1995).

Many theorists postulate that all human beings have a primary motivation that provides the general direction or outlines the major thrust of human life (Maddi, 1996). Freud (1967) maintained that we all have two primary tendencies: first, to gratify our instinctual drives, and second, to minimize our feelings of guilt and punishment. Because these two basic tendencies have different aims, they impel us in different directions. Therefore, according to Freudian theory, we need to make compromises between these tendencies in order to function effectively.

The humanistic theoreticians such as Adler (1964), Maslow (1970), and Rogers (1959) have a different view of the primary thrust in our lives. According to these theorists, this primary force is a general striving or growth motivation to fulfill our inherent potential. Adler, Maslow, and Rogers held slightly divergent positions about the source and nature of this primary motivation but not about the essential belief that life has an overriding goal-directed purpose. The behavioral psychologists, such as Skinner (1953), maintain that we are not born with an overriding central purpose or thrust in life but rather that all our behaviors are a result of the learning process.

Regardless of these differing views about the existence or the source of a primary tendency in our lives, most authorities agree that certain needs are common to all of us. Needs are usually discussed in terms of two separate domains. Needs related to our physiological nature and required for our bodies to function effectively are referred to as *drives*. Needs associated with social functioning and important for our psychological well-being are referred to as *motives*.

In the physiological domain we have certain needs that must be met if we are to remain alive, comfortable, and in good health. These biological imperatives, drives, or survival needs include the need for food, liquids, clothing, shelter, activity, rest, and appropriate body temperature. An important part of this physiological need structure is the tendency for our bodies to seek *homeostasis*, or a balanced state of equilibrium or stability. When we are in a state of deprivation (in need of food or liquids) or in a state of discomfort (too hot or too tired), this drive for homeostasis causes us to change our activity to improve our body's well-being. Because these needs are activated by a lack of something that the body requires, they are considered to be deficiency motives by Maslow (1970) and primary drives by the behavioral psychologists (Coon, 1995; Weiten, 1995). It is important to note that when our physiological needs are not adequately met, they limit our entire well-being: for example, when one is starving, one's entire physical and psychological makeup is affected.

In the psychological domain we also have certain needs that we must satisfy to function in an adequate and appropriate manner. As these needs primarily concern our relationship to society, they are considered by behavioral psychologists to be *socially derived needs* learned in the process of socialization (Coon, 1995; Weiten, 1995) and are referred to as acquired needs or secondary drives. However, other experts, such as the Adlerians (Dreikurs & Soltz, 1987), the humanistic psychologists (Maslow, 1970), and the transactional analysts (Elson, 1979) imply that certain of these needs are so imperative for our well-being that they are neither acquired nor secondary in nature. Regardless of the theoretical differences concerning the origin of these psychological needs, they do motivate much of human behavior and must be satisfied for us to function effectively.

Because our psychological needs greatly influence how we function, counselors must have a knowledge of these needs and how they control our behavior. The psychological needs that counseling and psychotherapy authorities consider extremely important are summarized in the following paragraphs.

The need for safety, security, and self-preservation.   According to Maslow (1970) all human beings need to feel safe and secure and to live in a nonthreatening environment. We are motivated to shun painful and dangerous situations, avoid chaos in our lives, minimize anxiety, and protect our sense of self. This self-protection need can cause any one of us to become quite assertive or aggressive. According to Dinkmeyer, Dinkmeyer, and Sperry (1987) and Sweeny (1989) this need impels discouraged children, who mistakenly feel attacked and deeply hurt, to seek revenge in order to protect themselves from further challenges to their safety and security.

The need for structure and order.   In addition to feeling safe and secure, we all need to have structure and order in our lives (Maslow, 1970). Elson (1979) and Wollams and Brown (1979) describe how we structure our time in different ways. This can range from becoming involved in very meaningful activities or relationships to engaging in quite meaningless ones. Individuals who are functioning effectively typically have better structure in their lives than those who are functioning less effectively.

The need for attention, contact, and positive regard.   We are all social entities, and we have a basic need to obtain attention and establish contact with other human beings that impels us to make physical and emotional contact with others. The need for recognition or strokes is extremely important and powerful. Those of us who do not have these needs satisfied in a positive manner by receiving smiles, hugs, or words of approval will seek to have them satisfied in negative ways by seeking frowns, slaps, or words of admonition. According to Rogers (1972) satisfying this need for positive regard is crucial to the healthy personality. Dinkmeyer, Dinkmeyer, and Sperry (1987) maintain that children who misbehave are very often seeking attention but are doing so in ill-advised and inappropriate ways.

The need for affection, belonging, and love.   Closely aligned to the need for attention is the need to engage in reciprocal relationships with significant others. Every individual strives to find and maintain a relationship with other individuals and to be a member of some group. This need to belong, to love and be loved, and to relate to other human beings in significant ways influences much of human behavior. When this need is not met it is one of the more prominent causes of behavioral problems among individuals (Maslow, 1970). This need is quite evident in adolescence, when the need to identify with a peer group becomes a strong motivator of behavior.

The need to feel unique and for positive self-regard.

Each one of us needs to feel unique and worthwhile and to have a positive feeling of self-worth. Having a positive self-regard is crucial for being well adjusted or fully functioning (Rogers, 1972). Furthermore, out of this need to feel unique, we all need to take time occasionally to reflect, meditate, and be by ourselves. Extremely discouraged children express this need by withdrawing from situations and giving up on some or all aspects of their behavior (Dreikurs & Soltz, 1987). This withdrawal can be manifest in a variety of ways such as being sick, failing coursework, or being in a sad or depressed state.

The need to influence and control one's environment.

We all have the need to influence and control our environment for our own benefit. This need impels us to learn things and engage in activities that are important to us. People sometimes seek to fulfill this need to achieve and gain control in ways that are ill-advised. Children, in particular, can assert this need for power and control of their environment in ways and at times that are most inappropriate (Sweeny, 1989). They may be disruptive, seek attention in unsuitable ways, or scapegoat other children. Parents, teachers, and significant other adults ought to be aware of this and take suitable steps so that power struggles can be avoided.

Needs are complex energizing processes that influence the direction and the intensity of our behavior. The strength of any particular need at any particular time differs among us and also within us. Whether a particular need or motive will activate any of us toward a particular behavior is the product of several factors:

- The opportunity for the need to be satisfied must be available; circumstances beyond our control can prevent a need from being actively pursued.
- The appropriate target, object, or person to whom our need is directed must be present.
- The notion of having at least a reasonable chance for success must be perceived.
- Our anxiety level should not be too intense; being overly anxious frequently leads to self-defeating behaviors.
- The incentive value of other needs must be less intense.

In the process of helping clients, it is important for counselors to understand how these needs and motives influence behavior. Clients who experience frustrations or manifest ill-advised and maladaptive behaviors often have unsatisfied needs, or they may be attempting to meet their needs in inappropriate ways. As counselors, we need to help our clients explore and understand these factors and aid them in developing more effective strategies for meeting their important needs.

Stress and the Coping Process

Stress.

At every stage of life it is normal for any one of us to encounter challenging situations or taxing and potentially stressful conditions. The major sources of psychological stress are frustrations, conflicts, changes, and pressures (Weiten, 1995). These challenging conditions often occur at transitional points in our lives, and they always produce anxiety or some other emotive reactions.

When we are *frustrated* either an external or an internal obstacle prevents us from acting or obtaining some desired goal. External blockages can be caused by social, economic, legal, or other environmental conditions. Internal blockages are often related to some personal limitation such as a handicap, insufficient knowledge, or lack of a specific ability, skill, or talent. Some frustrations are quite brief and relatively insignificant, and although stressful, the blockage can be removed in a short time. For example, a flat tire may prevent you from keeping an important appointment, but the tire can be changed and the appointment rescheduled. Other frustrations are much more serious—for example, the parents of an addict who are unable to involve their child in a suitable treatment program are probably quite frustrated and may be experiencing chronic stress.

When we are faced with a *conflict* we have to choose between two or more incompatible alternative courses of action. There are three classic types of conflicts. In the *approach/approach* conflict you must choose between two or more incompatible goals or situations, all of which are equally desirable; for example, people in a restaurant who are presented with a list of desirable entrées or desserts. Normally this type of conflict is the least stressful since no matter what one chooses the outcome is pleasant. In the *avoidance/avoidance* conflict you must select from two or more undesired objects or events that you want to avoid. This conflict might be experienced by the student who does not want to study a foreign language but must take one to graduate. Typically, this type of conflict is very stressful and frequently leads to delaying the decision in the hope that a better alternative might develop. In the *approach/avoidance* conflict you want to obtain an objective that has both positive and negative aspects—such as when you want to buy something very much but don't want to spend that amount of money. Conflicts are often a result of more complex situations and can involve a matrix of goals that you desire and situations that you wish to avoid (Coon, 1995; Weiten, 1995).

Any *change* in your life, whether perceived as positive or negative, may also cause stress. In a mobile society such as ours, come people have experienced considerable shifting in their lives. These changes, which may have been in educational or occupational endeavors, financial conditions, or geographical locations, have exposed individuals to a wide variety of new or different demands and increased the potential for stress. Other changes, such as personal illness, sickness in the family, marital separation or divorce, and loss of a loved one can also cause considerable stress on an individual and in a family.

A fourth cause of stress is *pressure*. According to Weiten (1995) this pressure is caused by the expectations and demands for us to act in ways deemed appropriate by society, our reference groups, or ourselves. This pressure may be the expectation for us to *perform* or achieve at a certain level in some area—for example, a student may be expected to earn honors in schoolwork. In other cases, the pressure may be to *conform*—a young person may be expected to like a certain type of food, music, or recreational activity simply because of peer pressure.

Emotional reactions.
Anger, anxiety, and sadness are three major emotional reactions we experience when faced with a frustration, a conflict, or another stressful condition. Each of these feelings can vary in intensity from a mild reaction to an extremely strong one. Anger, our typical reaction to a frustration, can range from being slightly annoyed to being in a rage. Anxiety, which we normally experience when we face a situation that has an uncertain outcome, can vary from a minor apprehension to an

immobilizing fear. And sadness, which may be our reaction to a bad experience, can range from feeling glum or slightly dejected to sorrow or grief or deep depression (Weiten, 1995).

Coping strategies.   The active efforts that we employ to solve our concerns, ameliorate the stressful conditions we experience, and lower our anxiety are our coping strategies (Kagan & Segal, 1994). Some of the ways that we cope are proactive, whereas others are more reactive. When we are functioning effectively, we handle stressful concerns and any thwarting conditions we encounter in productive ways by using a wide variety of adaptive, healthy, and constructive coping skills or positive adjustment mechanisms. When we are functioning less effectively, we typically use maladaptive, unhealthy, and counterproductive coping skills or defense mechanisms (Calhoun & Acocella, 1990; Rathus & Nevid, 1995).

Proactive or constructive coping strategies involve taking direct and effective steps to handle a given issue, problem, or demand of life. Employing positive coping strategies, however, does not automatically ensure a successful outcome in any particular situation. Nonetheless, since the coping process is an ongoing one that is repeated over and over again, the use of these constructive actions generally leads to positive outcomes. These proactive skills have been classified into various types by Moos and Schaefer (1993) and Weiten (1995) according to their focus or goal. Constructive coping strategies involve efforts to:

> *Appraise the situation in realistic ways.* This means making an accurate and realistic evaluation of the situations and circumstances that cause the stressful events in our lives. This process should provide a clear understanding of these problems and their ramifications. Having a lucid perception of a problem and the circumstances that caused it is an important coping process of and by itself.
>
> *Use appropriate problem-solving skills.* Learning how to solve, modify, or circumvent the problems we face in life is a major coping process. This includes mastering the steps necessary to choose wisely among alternative courses of action, learning how to accept the compromises that have to be made in our lives, accepting and living constructively with a blockage that cannot be removed, acting assertively to remove conditions that are preventing us from taking appropriate actions, and when necessary, learning new skills to enhance our competence.
>
> *Deal effectively with emotional reactions to stress.* It is often important to reduce the emotional reactions caused by stress. This can be accomplished indirectly by either of the methods mentioned above or directly by learning how to release pent-up emotions in mature and socially acceptable ways, learning how to put problems aside for a while, and learning effective relaxation techniques.
>
> *Maintain good physical condition.* Keeping our bodies in reasonably good physical condition enables us to deal more effectively with the demands placed on us by any stressful condition. Learning to eat nutritional foods, developing and maintaining good hygienic habits, and engaging in a reasonable amount of exercise are activities that can not only help prevent but also serve to ameliorate the problems of stress.

Nonconstructive coping skills tend to be reactive rather than proactive. Although these tactics can relieve stress or any other emotional reaction temporarily, they ultimately have serious negative physical and psychological repercussions. These maladaptive tactics can be grouped into the following general patterns or styles: aggressive, defensive or transformed, self-blaming, and withdrawn.

Aggressive coping reactions occur when we attack another person verbally or physically. This type of reaction is often associated with anger. Anger can take various forms—directing our feelings at the person or thing that caused the stress or problem, venting our hostility at an innocent party and thus finding a scapegoat, or having a generalized raging anger and acting in an aggressive manner with everyone.

Defensive or transformed coping reactions are present when we change or disguise the cause of our frustration or thwarting condition. These reactions typically take the form of one of the classic defense mechanisms: compensation, projection, rationalization, reaction formation, or sublimation.

Self-blaming coping reactions are manifest when we engage in highly critical negative self-talk that assumes we are responsible for the problems in our lives and blaming ourselves for all our misfortunes.

Withdrawn coping reactions are evident when we either passively accept or inappropriately remove ourselves from dealing with the frustrations, conflicts, and other concerns of life. This type of reaction is frequently associated with an emotional state of sorrow and depression. This retreat from the challenges of life may be exhibited by fantasizing, regressing, mental wandering, or apathy. An apathetic reaction is probably the most maladaptive form of the reactive or poor coping mechanisms.

Clients who manifest poor skills in coping often have weak convictions about their abilities to overcome the stressful conditions they encounter. Consequently, any proactive attempts they make are rather limited in methodology, duration, and energy expended. Counselors who have clients with ineffective coping skills frequently need to develop treatment strategies that assist clients in improving their feelings of self-worth, appraising their situations more realistically, and marshaling their resources more efficiently. Normally, such treatment strategies employ a graduated or step-by-step approach and incorporate one or more of the interventions outlined in Part 2.

Developmental Task Attainment

As we progress through life from infancy to old age, certain physiological and psychological changes occur within us. These changes and the theories or models that attempt to find the broad underlying principles that describe these changes are investigated in the field of developmental psychology. Numerous theories try to explain how we change over our life span. Some theories focus on one aspect of behavior such as cognitive development (Piaget, 1966) or moral behavior (Kohlberg & Kramer, 1969), whereas other theories analyze one period of life such as childhood, adolescence, middle age, or maturity and old age (Berk, 1997; Birren & Schaie, 1996; Rice, 1996). This section of the text outlines some of the well-known theories of development, cites some references that you may wish to review, and makes suggestions about working with clients who have not mastered the appropriate developmental tasks.

Developmental psychologists frequently divide our life span into a series of *stages,* or dynamic transitional periods, in which all aspects of our physical and psychological development occur. Psychologists often differ on the exact meaning of the term *developmental stage* and the concepts and formulations they have about these stages (Shaffer, 1996). Many theoreticians believe that life stages are structural entities that are universal (applicable to all of us), invariant (we must progress through these steps in a particular sequential order), and qualitatively rather than quantitatively different (distinctive laws govern us or unique phenomena apply to us at each stage). Furthermore, some theoreticians maintain that these life stages are transitional, overlapping, and continuous periods of time because elements of any stage may be present at another stage. The way we ascertain a person's developmental stage is by observing the modal or most common behaviors he or she manifests. Examples of stage theories include Freud's psychoanalytic theory of development, Piaget's theory of cognitive development, Kohlberg's theory of moral development, and Erikson's theory of psychosocial development.

Other psychologists either do not use the word *stage* to discuss developmental concerns or use this word to refer to a particular *phase* or period of life without implying all the characteristics of stages as outlined above. For example, Havighurst (1972) outlined certain developmental tasks or skills that we are expected to master at particular ages in our society, and Neff (1985) discussed how important it is for us to master certain work-related developmental tasks in order to become contributing members of society. Clearly, the age at which these developmental tasks are expected to be mastered can and does vary among and within different societies. Therefore, the age at which developmental tasks are appropriate is related to the expectations of a particular society or a unique reference group within that society, rather than universally related to a particular age group.

The major concepts of the developmental theories of Piaget, Erikson, and Havighurst, which are of interest to counselors, are briefly discussed in the following paragraphs.

Piaget's theory (1966) concerns the cognitive development of children and adolescents. According to this theory, our abilities to conceptualize objects in the world differentially occur at specific age-related stages. Our ability to accomplish the tasks of each stage depends on our biological readiness and how well we accomplished the tasks of the previous stage. Counselors who work with children and adolescents should be familiar with this theory and its possible relationship to a client's learning process. The four major stages of cognitive development, their approximate ages, and the major cognitive activities of each stage are outlined briefly in Table 2-1.

Erikson's theory (1993, 1994) postulates that crucial aspects of our psychological development occur during eight stages that each of us is expected to progress through in our lifetime. During each age-related period, we must learn how to deal effectively with specific issues or *psychosocial* crises. Each crisis is a crucial event leading to an outcome that lies somewhere between two bipolar opposites. The most successful and healthy outcome is at one end of the continuum; the least successful and most unhealthy outcome lies at the other end. Accomplishing this task successfully helps us gain the strength

TABLE 2-1
Piaget's Stages of Cognitive Development

Sensorimotor period (birth to 2 years)	Knowledge of the world obtained through senses and motor activities. Development of cognitive patterns begins with immediate here-and-now experiences and then progresses to tendency to repeat interesting events, to an awareness that objects have a permanence, and to a curiosity about novel objects and events.
Preoperational period (2 to 7 years)	Gradually develop the ability to use symbols to represent objects; tend to focus on only one characteristic of an event or object at a time and ignore other features of the object; not able to think about a process or idea in an opposite or reverse way.
Concrete operational period (7 to 11 years)	Develop the ability to think logically, to classify objects, and to understand how various items are interrelated; develop ability to reverse our thinking, which allows us to learn the fundamental arithmetic operations of addition, subtraction, multiplication, and division.
Formal operations period (11 to 16 years)	Develop the ability to think abstractly, to formulate hypotheses, to generate alternative solutions to problems, and to think about the future.

to cope with the crisis that occurs at the next stage. Individuals who go through the developmental stage with a negative or unsuccessful outcome will be limited in their future development.

Erikson's model suggests that counselors should be able to assess whether a client has successfully accomplished certain of these developmental challenges. However, Erikson's theory must be used with some caution. Hershenson, Power, and Waldo (1996) have pointed out that Erikson's theory is culturally bound to some extent and that each bipolar trait construction has built-in limitations. For example, the theory implies that failure to achieve autonomy by the age of 3 years leads to shame and doubt. Clearly, autonomy is never fully accomplished by age 3, nor is shame and doubt caused only by failure to achieve autonomy. Erikson's eight life stages and their approximate ages, and the psychological crisis associated with each stage, are listed in Table 2-2.

Havighurst (1972) has a more detailed model of the developmental process than Erikson. Havighurst divides our life span into several major age-related periods and identifies certain developmental tasks that we should master during each of these specific periods. When we successfully accomplish these tasks, we obtain positive feedback from others and a deep sense of personal satisfaction and are well prepared to meet the challenge of our next developmental period. If we do not learn the task at the appropriate time it is more difficult to learn the task later in life, and we are poorly prepared to meet the tasks associated with the next developmental period.

Havighurst's list of developmental tasks can be used by counselors to assess a client's developmental progress. The specific age at which these tasks ought to be accomplished varies among cultures and among social classes within cultures, so these tasks must be

TABLE 2-2
Erikson's Life Stages

Life period	Psychosocial crisis	Desired outcome
First year	Basic trust vs. mistrust	Acceptance, trust, and hope
Second year	Autonomy vs. shame and doubt	Control
Third through fifth years	Initiative vs. guilt	Purpose or goal
Sixth year to puberty	Industry vs. inferiority	Competence
Adolescence	Identity vs. confusion	Self-identity
Young adulthood	Intimacy vs. isolation	Mutuality and sharing
Middle adulthood	Generativity vs. self-absorption	Helping others
Mature age	Integrity vs. despair	Satisfaction with life

seen as normative concepts rather than as absolute standards. The approximate age-related periods and the major developmental tasks associated with each of these periods are briefly outlined in Table 2-3.

Although the term *stage development* has different meanings and not all experts agree on a particular developmental theory, there is a general consensus that we all pass through certain age-related periods in which specific challenges should be met. Individuals who are functioning effectively accomplish the developmental tasks that are appropriate for their age and cultural group. They encounter a minimal amount of difficulty in progressing from one stage or phase of life to another. On the other hand, individuals

TABLE 2-3
Havighurst's Developmental Stages and Their Related Developmental Tasks

Infancy and early childhood (up to age 6)	Learning to walk
	Learning to take solid foods
	Learning to talk
	Learning to control elimination of body wastes
	Learning sex differences and sexual modesty
	Forming concepts and learning language to describe social and physical reality
	Getting ready to read
	Learning to distinguish right and wrong and beginning to develop a conscience
Middle childhood years (6 to 12 years)	Learning physical skills necessary for ordinary games
	Building wholesome attitudes toward oneself as a growing organism
	Learning to get along with age-mates
	Learning the appropriate masculine or feminine social role
	Developing fundamental skills in reading, writing, and calculating
	Developing concepts necessary for everyday living
	Developing conscience, morality, and a scale of values
	Achieving personal independence
	Developing attitudes toward social groups and institutions

TABLE 2-3   (continued)

Adolescent years *(12 to 18 years)*	Achieving new and more mature relations with age-mates of both sexes
	Achieving a masculine or feminine social role
	Accepting one's physique and using the body effectively
	Achieving emotional independence from parents and other adults
	Preparing for marriage and family life
	Preparing for an economic career
	Acquiring a set of values and an ethical system as a guide to behavior—developing an ideology
	Desiring and achieving socially responsible behavior
Early adulthood years *(18 to 30 years)*	Selecting a mate
	Learning to live with a marriage partner
	Starting a family
	Rearing children
	Managing a home
	Getting started in an occupation
	Taking on civic responsibilities
	Finding a congenial social group
Middle years *(30 to 60 years)*	Assisting teenage children to become responsible and happy adults
	Achieving adult civic and social responsibility
	Reaching and maintaining satisfactory performance in one's occupation
	Developing adult leisure-time activities
	Relating to one's spouse as a person
	Accepting and adjusting to the physiological changes of middle age
	Adjusting to aging parents
Later maturity years *(60 years and older)*	Adjusting to decreasing physical strength and health
	Adjusting to retirement and reduced income
	Adjusting to death of one's spouse
	Establishing an explicit affiliation with one's age group
	Adopting and adapting social roles in a flexible way
	Establishing satisfactory physical living arrangements

who manifest developmental difficulties have not mastered the educational, vocational, and social tasks that their society expects persons of that age group to have achieved.

During the early phases of the counseling process, you should assess the client's developmental progress. If the problem is related to a deficiency in developmental task attainment, a treatment strategy that focuses on developing self-understanding and awareness of one's potential and a methodology to overcome this deficiency need to be implemented. Even though a wide variety of intervention strategies may be used clients often benefit from an approach that incorporates the goal of developing these tasks. In the school counseling field, programmatic approaches to dealing with developmental needs of students have been put forth under the *Comprehensive Developmental Guidance* program model (Gysbers & Henderson, 1994; Paisley & Hubbard, 1994; Trotter, 1995). This school counseling approach is designed to assist children and adolescents in educational settings become more effectively functioning people. It is a proactive and preventive model that includes a variety of activities in curriculum, individual and group planning, and support service areas.

Social Contact and Interpersonal Relationship Skills

Interaction with other human beings is one of the most basic needs that we have. Our lives revolve around one another. We enjoy the company of other people, and our friends are important in our lives. We think, write, and talk about one another. We have developed both written and unwritten rules that govern the way we eat, dress, travel, and get married. We have organized ourselves into political entities for our own well-being. This process of social interaction strongly influences the standards that we are expected to live by, the attitudes that we have toward others, and the actions that we take in particular circumstances.

Some of the difficulties individuals face in the social sphere of their lives include role conflicts and ineffective relationships with others.

Role expectations and role conflict.   We grow up and live in a social/cultural milieu composed of four interrelated groups that strongly influence our attitudes, customs, values, and social mores. These four groups are composed of (1) the members of our immediate home and family environment; (2) our peers and the members of our immediate community (including school, church, and club contacts); (3) the members of our subculture; and (4) the members of the general society that surrounds us (see Figure 2-1). The influence that members of any one group have on us may vary; in general, however, the members of the groups closest to us exert the most direct influence, while the members of the groups furthest away exert the least direct influence.

As members of various groups in this social/cultural milieu, we learn to behave in ways that these groups expect. Thus, we behave in a particular *role* in a way that we are expected to behave. Roles represent the ways we carry out the duties and obligations incumbent in our membership in different groups. Role theory and role expectations are important in understanding the social dynamics of human behavior and the transactions that occur between and among individuals. The major constructs of role theory are that:

- we all occupy one or more positions in our society (for example, mother, aunt, student);
- all of us who occupy a particular position (counselors in a particular setting) behave in distinctive ways that are common to all occupants of that position (all counselors);
- this characteristic way of behaving is expected by other members of society as well as the occupants of that position; and
- the other members of society fall into other distinctive groups that form a network of interrelated groups.

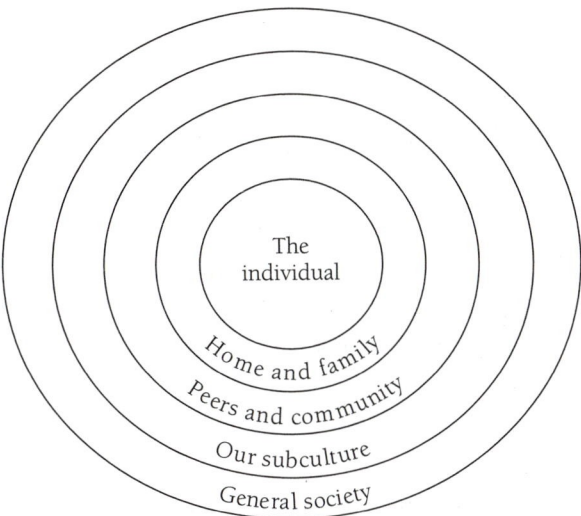

FIGURE 2-1
Our social/cultural milieu

Role expectations are normally quite clear when there is agreement among the members of the occupant group and among the members of other interrelated groups. Role conflicts may occur when there is a lack of agreement among group members or among the members of the group and the members of the interrelated groups, or when an individual behaves in a manner that is contrary to the standards expected by the group members.

Effectively functioning individuals may not experience role conflicts, or they may consider these conflicts an inevitable part of life and resolve them in a proactive way by using any of the constructive coping skills discussed previously. Individuals who are functioning less effectively encounter difficulty handling these role conflicts, and they often experience tension, anxiety, and dissatisfaction in the role in which the conflict exists. Furthermore, the less effective person typically uses nonconstructive or reactive adjustment mechanisms in resolving these role conflicts.

Counselors who are sensitive to multicultural factors can minimize conflicts and problems related to cultural differences (Lee, 1996). Being sensitive to multicultural issues involves the following dimensions. First, you need to be aware of the values, beliefs, and role expectations that are related to your own cultural background as well as the values, beliefs, and role expectations of your client, based on his or her cultural history. Second, you need to be aware of individual differences and the breadth and depth of diversity within and among cultures. Third, you need to be sensitive enough to use counseling techniques and strategies that are compatible with the cultural traditions of the client. For example, using self-disclosure with certain individuals might cause difficulty because this process is considered incompatible with the traditions of many Asian Americans, Latinos, and Native Americans (Sue & Sue, 1990).

Loneliness, shyness, and ineffective communication skills.

In addition to role conflicts, three major difficulties that people may experience in the social sphere of their lives are loneliness, shyness, and an ineffective communication process.

Loneliness has been classified into three distinctive forms by Young (1979). First, there is the brief and momentary feeling of isolation, or a *transient* type of loneliness, that anyone may have. This form of isolation is not a serious problem for most people. Second, there is the *transitional* type of loneliness, which lasts longer; it may be caused by a geographical move, a divorce, or the death of a spouse. This kind of loneliness can cause considerable pain and lasts until some coping process is employed. Finally, there is the *chronic* type of loneliness, which is experienced by those who are socially isolated and not meeting their needs for a satisfactory social life. This form of loneliness can be quite serious and is often related to other problems.

Lonely people usually have poor self-regard, a lack of self-confidence, and low self-esteem. Socially isolated students of all ages do poorly academically and experience little satisfaction in school settings (Rice, 1996). Loneliness is also related to a lack of effective social skills, a fear of intimacy, and an irrational thinking process (Murphy & Kupshik, 1992). Socially isolated people want to be liked by others, but they either engage in self-defeating behaviors or withdraw from interacting with others.

Shyness is another major social problem for many people. It can be the cause of social isolation. Children who do not learn how to interact effectively with other children can become lonely and withdrawn (Marshall, 1994). Although shyness and loneliness are interrelated, they are not the same. Shy people have difficulty making friends—they are not necessarily lonely. Shy people exercise an extreme amount of caution in social situations, whereas lonely people have a chronic feeling or sense of being alone. According to Zimbardo (1977) shyness tends to be experienced in specific social encounters such as large groups or new situations and with specific groups of people such as strangers and authority figures. Shyness is not considered to be an enduring personality trait. Helping a client deal with shyness is often less difficult than helping someone overcome loneliness.

An important aspect of our interaction with others is effective communication. Good communication occurs when two or more people focus their attention on the same issue at the same time and understand the meaning of the expressed comments. Effective communication is essential for good relationships. Poor communication is a common problem with those who have inadequate and dysfunctional relationships with others. The primary cause of a communication difficulty may be with the speaker, the listener, or both. A major cause of poor communication is lack of careful attention to what is being said. The speaker may communicate self-centered, irrelevant, or tangential information; send different verbal and nonverbal messages; create an interrogative atmosphere; employ distracting nonverbal or paraverbal mannerisms; or not think about the effect the words will have on the listener. The listener may not attend to the speaker or be preoccupied or may selectively listen and hear only parts of the speaker's message. Effective communication requires effective speaking and effective listening. Clients who exhibit poor skills in this area can benefit from an intervention strategy that incorporates communication-skill training.

The effectively functioning person has developed ways to interact with others that are useful, helpful, and supportive. Role conflicts are dealt with in proactive ways, and the effective person manifests positive attitudes, thoughtfulness, and empathic understanding of others. He or she has developed satisfying relationships and effective two-way communication systems with significant other persons in all spheres of life. These communication systems are based on mutual respect, warmth, and understanding. The person who is functioning less effectively often demonstrates role conflicts, loneliness, shyness, and ineffective communication skills.

During the initial phases of counseling, you should gain some insight into how your client is functioning in human relationships. A client who manifests one or more of the characteristics of the less effective type of person may need an intervention that incorporates three different objectives: obtaining insight into the problem area, improving self-esteem, and/or improving social skills. Treatment programs for clients who have these socially oriented problems frequently include role-playing exercises, assertiveness training, and cognitive-restructuring procedures.

Other Characteristic Attributes

Our ability to function effectively is manifest by other personal attributes and by the characteristic ways that we interact with our environment. The self-actualizing, emotionally healthy, and effectively functioning person manifests positive personal attributes and has a pattern of interaction with the environment that is rich and dynamic. The effective or more fully functioning person exhibits positive attributes and characteristic ways of behaving such as a sense of personal identity and self-worth, a commitment to some meaningful goals, a sense of responsibility for self-control and tolerance, and initiative and spontaneity (Maslow, 1970). Furthermore, the effectively functioning person typically manifests good cognitive skills. These hallmarks of psychological independence and interdependence are amplified in the following sections.

Sense of personal identity and self-worth.   Effectively functioning individuals have a good sense of their own personal identity and positive feelings about themselves. Having this positive self-evaluation enhances their self-concept and enables them to function at high levels. Individuals who function less effectively do not feel good about themselves. Low self-esteem is highly correlated with emotional problems, poor school achievement, and poor interpersonal relationship skills.

Commitment to meaningful goals.   Self-actualizing persons are aware of societal demands and the necessity to make choices throughout life. Healthy individuals accept this challenge and commit themselves to some meaningful goals or objectives that both enhance the self and contribute to the overall well-being of others. Effective individuals have a good sense of immediate, intermediate, and long-term goals, and they direct their efforts in a meaningful way toward appropriate goals. Less effective individuals are unable to develop plans, or they may be unable to implement the plans they have made.

Responsible self-control and tolerance.   Healthy individuals experience the full range of human desires and emotions and have learned to respond to these feelings in a responsible, self-controlled manner. Individuals who are functioning effectively accept responsibility for their actions and recognize that conflicts often exist between one's personal needs or desires and the needs and desires of others. The effective individual

accepts these conflicts as normal and healthy. Individuals who are functioning less effectively often have difficulty with self-control and are frequently intolerant of others.

Initiative and spontaneity.

Self-actualizing individuals tend to be proactive rather than reactive. They anticipate the many problems and concerns that individuals must deal with in the course of life. This anticipatory preparation facilitates problem solving during developmental periods and crisis situations and fosters positive growth. Effective individuals do not see themselves from static points of view such as being perfect or having all the things they need in life. Rather, they recognize their own imperfections and the transience of acquiring physical things and that all humans are in a dynamic state of growing and becoming. Their actions tend to be reasonably spontaneous and in concert with highly prized values (Fromm, 1996; Rogers, 1972). Individuals who are functioning less effectively tend to be reactive rather than proactive. This reactive process is a defensive and protective way of behaving. Ineffective individuals frequently lack spontaneity and initiative.

Effective cognitive skills.

Functioning effectively in the cognitive domain is usually manifest in good learning patterns, accurate perceptions of reality, sound logical and inferential thinking processes, good decision-making skills, and intellectual openness.

> *Good learning patterns.* Learning is a complex process that strongly influences the behavior of individuals. Learning theorists state that we learn through observational learning, classical and operant conditioning, and through a cognitive-information-process model that includes sensory stimulation, examining available information, selecting and weighting the importance of the data, and forming meaningful associations (Hilgard & Bower, 1981; Kintsch, 1982). Effective individuals have mastered good learning habits; they realize the importance of multisensory input, repetition, and selectivity when exposed to information and are able to categorize this information in an organized way.
>
> *Accurate perceptions of reality.* An important element in our cognitive functioning is how we select, organize, and interpret the information we have obtained. Effective people can select appropriate information from an array of data, organize the various pieces of this information into a meaningful hierarchical order, and interpret the information in ways that facilitate their awareness of reality (Hochberg, 1978).
>
> *Sound logical and inferential thinking processes.* An important cognitive skill is our ability to think logically and reach sound conclusions on the basis of given information. Effective individuals can think both deductively and inductively. They can reach meaningful conclusions or make reasonable inferences about new and previously unknown objects and events on the basis of previous observations of similar phenomena (Kintsch, 1982; Wickelgren, 1974).
>
> *Good decision-making skills.* The ability to make a decision has several cognitive components. The process involves
>
> 1. becoming aware of the decision-making process,
> 2. identifying the problem,

3. determining appropriate goals,
4. describing all the important factors related to the problem,
5. identifying alternatives and the consequences of these alternatives,
6. judging the desirability of the alternatives, and
7. selecting, implementing, and evaluating the chosen alternative.

Effective individuals have manifested a history of decision making that has enhanced their quality of life in one or more of the major spheres of life (Krumboltz & Thoresen, 1976).

Intellectual openness. Intellectual openness is the ability to think about things in a fresh or new way, to conceptualize new behaviors, and to try them out intellectually. The effective individual recognizes that many aspects of life must be thought of in terms of probabilities and chance factors, rather than absolutes, and is willing to take some intellectual risks (Fromm, 1996; Rogers, 1972).

Counselors with clients who manifest poor images, who lack meaningful goals, who have limited self-control, or whose cognitive functioning is ineffective must develop treatment programs that focus on improving these aspects of their clients' personality. A variety of techniques for accomplishing these goals is available. Chapters 4, 5, and 6 outline several important cognitive, affective, and behavioral strategies that can be used in working with clients who have these concerns.

SPECIAL PROBLEMS THAT IMPEDE EFFECTIVE FUNCTIONING

Several distinctive problems may impede the effective functioning of individuals. Four of these problems are handicapping conditions, serious vocational problems, substance abuse problems, and psychological disorders.

Handicapping Conditions

The adjustment and behavioral patterns of individuals are influenced by personal characteristics such as physical limitations caused by birth defects, sickness, or accidents; intellectual impairments brought about by neurological damage or learning disorders; and other concerns related to health problems. Effectively functioning individuals will react to these blockages in proactive ways, whereas persons functioning at less effective levels will be more reactive in their responses.

Disabilities.
A person who is disabled has a permanent condition caused by an accident, disease, or congenital problem that interferes with that person's ability to function. Counseling clients with disabilities frequently involves helping them make realistic assessments of their strengths and limitations and assisting them in learning how to adjust and compensate for any known limitation. Because disabling conditions are blockages or frustrations that cause emotional feelings of anger, the counseling process should

include helping clients assess their coping skills. When necessary, the client should be given the appropriate assistance to overcome nonconstructive adjustment mechanisms and to develop more constructive coping strategies.

Learning difficulties. Individuals of average or above average intelligence who encounter serious difficulties in learning are considered learning disabled. They often see themselves as slow or incompetent. Although the origin of any learning disability is assumed to be neurological, it is often impossible to determine the specific cause of a learning problem for a particular client. Consequently, when working with individuals who have learning disorders, it is appropriate to focus not on the cause of the problem but rather to pinpoint specific behavioral learning deficits and formulate appropriate remedial programs. Typically, clients with learning disabilities have perceptual learning deficits that have concomitant effects on their educational progress, socialization, and self-esteem.

Counselors who work with individuals who have some physical or neurological damage and either a physical or learning disability must work cooperatively with a team of other knowledgeable persons. This team may include diagnostic experts, classroom teachers, special education teachers, specialists in reading or speech and hearing, rehabilitation counselors, and the parents of the client. The counseling process typically focuses on helping clients improve their self-images, change their illogical thinking processes, improve their study skills and habits, and enhance their social skills.

Serious Vocational Concerns

The occupations people choose have a profound influence on all aspects of their lives. This choice may determine who they marry, how much money they earn, where they live, and how they spend their leisure time. The notion that an occupational choice is made at a particular point in life is misleading. Occupational selection is not really a onetime event; it is a lifelong process that involves developing abilities, interests, and values and making numerous and varied educational and vocational decisions.

Vocational counseling experts such as Brown and Brooks (1991) and Zunker (1994) maintain that decisions about occupational and career choice require individuals to have a sound understanding of themselves, a comprehensive knowledge about the occupational opportunities available, and a thoughtful career planning process. There is clear evidence that not all individuals function effectively in the vocational aspects of their lives—their behavior may be considered vocationally maladaptive. Although no universal taxonomy of vocationally maladaptive behavior has been developed, those who are having vocational problems may belong to one or more of the following groups.

Those who are unable to make a career decision. This group consists of individuals who are at the appropriate age to make a vocational decision but who cannot make one. There are several different categories of undecided groups (Osipow, 1980): (1) those who have low self-confidence or high anxiety, (2) those who believe that there are serious barriers to their appropriate vocational choice, (3) those who have difficulty deciding among alternatives, and (4) those who lack sufficient information about themselves or the occupational world to make a sound decision.

Those who have defective work personalities.   The individuals in this group tend to have problems with independence, acceptance of the work ethic, interpersonal relationships, authority figures, and emotional stability. Neff (1985) has suggested that there are five distinctive patterns among defective work personalities. The five types are:

1. The *dependent*—an individual whose major response to the work demand is dependency and childlike reliance on others for support.
2. The *impulsive*—one whose major response to the work demand is indifference, who lacks a concept of responsibility, and whose impulse gratification is strong.
3. The *socially naive*—a person whose response to the work demand is marked by naiveté and who needs experience to gain skills in the social mores and customs of work.
4. The *hostile*—an individual whose response to the work demand is hostility and aggression and who can work well alone but whose anger is easily aroused.
5. The *fearful*—one whose major response to the demand to work is fear and anxiety and who has a history of learned helplessness.

According to Neff, potential workers who manifest one of these five patterns need a carefully developed rehabilitation program to ensure their employability.

Those who are structurally unemployed.   The structurally unemployed are individuals who are not employed because their skills do not match the requirements for the available jobs. They include individuals who are inadequately prepared or inappropriately educated for the demands of the available jobs and those who are geographically immobile, inexperienced, or handicapped (Herr & Cramer, 1992). Structurally unemployed people are often very discouraged and may not be considered part of the labor force because they do not actively seek work.

Those who are underemployed.   The underemployed are individuals who are either working part-time but seeking full-time employment or working in positions that require much less education and training than they have (Herr & Cramer, 1992). Underemployed workers are probably also dissatisfied because of their unmet needs.

Those who are vocationally dissatisfied.   This group represents a wide spectrum of workers whose present jobs fail to provide important economic, psychological, or sociological satisfactions. Nevertheless, many dissatisfied workers remain in their positions for one reason or another.

Those who are burned out.   For many individuals occupational stress is a serious health problem. This stress can lead to physical and psychological exhaustion or *burnout* (Herr & Cramer, 1992). Some of the factors that are related to this vocational difficulty are: long working hours, poor interpersonal relationships on the job, policies of the workplace, financial issues, poor working conditions, boredom, and lack of control over the outcomes of one's labor (Forney, Wallace-Schultzman, & Wiggers, 1982). Individuals who are burned out have little energy or enthusiasm for their work and frequently manifest negative and cynical attitudes and behaviors. Such stress may be associated with other emotional problems and with the increased use of alcohol (Maslack, 1982). Burnout can be alleviated by removing or reducing the factors causing the stress, by incorporating significant recreational activities into one's lifestyle, and by obtaining social support from colleagues, family members, and mutual self-help groups.

Clients who are vocationally maladaptive can benefit from vocational counseling. The vocational counseling process will typically help clients develop more insight, acquire some necessary vocational skills, receive emotional support during any retraining process, learn the techniques necessary to explore various occupational opportunities, learn how to search out potential jobs, and embark on appropriate job-seeking endeavors. The specific treatment strategies used will vary depending on the unique needs of a particular client.

Substance Abuse Problems

Substance abuse involves the use of alcohol, or another drug to such an extent that one's personal and social functioning are impaired. All drugs have a physiological and a psychological effect. They induce a chemical reaction in the cells of the brain that affects the nervous system and causes changes in perceptions, emotions, and behavioral patterns. The major difficulties in using any drug are the potential for physical and psychological dependence, the potential for causing serious harm to oneself and others, and the enormous costs to society.

Although alcohol is similar to other drugs in many respects, the issues associated with each of the following substances are different enough to be considered as separate concerns.

Alcohol abuse.   Alcohol is widely used throughout the world. It is not considered an illegal substance, nor does it require a prescription as do many other drugs. Although there are a variety of methods for classifying people who drink, a very useful way is to group them by their degree of alcoholic dependency (Forrest, 1994; Peer, Lindsey, & Newman, 1982). *Social drinkers* are not dependent upon alcohol. They consume a moderate amount of alcohol, but they do not feel a compulsion to drink, and they can accept or refuse a drink. *Problem drinkers* have a psychological dependence on alcohol and consume a considerable amount, often daily, to relieve tension. They usually reserve their drinking, however, for times that do not interfere with their work or their other major responsibilities. *Alcoholics* have both a psychological and a physiological dependence on alcohol. They usually consume a large amount daily, and they need a drink to reduce the stress they feel and to cope with the situations they encounter. Other authorities have classified alcoholics into further subdivisions (Jellinek, 1960).

Addiction to alcohol is one of the most serious health and social problems of our era (Gitlow & Peyser, 1988; Muisener, 1994; Velleman, 1992). This maladaptive behavior is believed to be significantly related to one-eighth of our national health costs, 50% of all automobile fatalities, 60% of all homicides, and high accident and absentee rates and low productivity in industry. Furthermore, a large number of diseases (cirrhosis of the liver, pancreas disorders, and various nutritional problems) are specifically related to alcohol addiction. It is considered the third leading cause of death in the United States, after heart disease and cancer.

Alcoholics often deny that they have a drinking problem, and they frequently resist suggestions that they go for treatment. However, this maladaptive behavior pattern can be altered. Most treatment programs involve individual counseling, family counseling, and involvement in a support group such as Alcoholics Anonymous, Al-Anon, or Alateen. In cases where the alcoholism is severe, a client may be hospitalized to overcome withdrawal symptoms.

Individual counseling sessions focus on helping clients abstain from drinking, improve their feelings of self-worth, and learn to cope successfully with the stressful conditions in their lives. Family counseling sessions are designed to help families understand and deal with their feelings of denial and shame, improve their dysfunctional communication patterns, and modify behaviors that have unwittingly reinforced the drinking process. Many treatment programs strongly encourage clients to join Alcoholics Anonymous, their spouses to meet with an Al-Anon group, and their teenage children to become associated with an Alateen group. These groups not only provide emotional support to the members but also help the individual and the family deal with the temptations of alcohol and the problems of remaining sober.

Drug abuse.   The use and abuse of psychoactive substances has increased significantly in the last several years and has become a problem in all parts of the nation (Ray & Ksir, 1992). Addicts may be found in all age groups and in all classes of society; however, drug abuse appears to be more serious among adolescents and young adults. Furthermore, a considerable amount of illegal behavior is involved in the abuse of drugs. Elaborate smuggling and illicit distribution are required to get the drugs to their users, and serious addicts frequently turn to crime in order to obtain the money to support their habits. Drugs are classified by their effect on the user, by chemical composition, or by the source of the drug and can be categorized in the following ways:

Narcotics (analgesics). A narcotic is a drug that has both a pain-relieving (analgesic) and a sleep-inducing (sedative) effect. Because these drugs are made from the opium or poppy plant, which is grown in hot, dry climates, they are also referred to as *opiates.* Well-known narcotics include codeine, heroin, and morphine. Narcotics can also be manufactured—examples of synthesized narcotics are methadone, meperidine (Demerol), and oxycodone (Percodan). Narcotics act on the nervous system, producing drowsiness, a feeling of euphoria, and a sense of detachment from pain. Using this type of drug often causes physical and psychological dependence, a lowering of social motivation, and the possibility of infections from nonsterile injections.

Hallucinogens (psychedelics). Hallucinogens are drugs that do not have any known medical value. However, they do have an extremely powerful effect on emotional, intellectual, and motor functioning. Representative examples are mescaline (obtained from the peyote cactus), psilocybin (derived from a rare mushroom plant), dimethyltriptamine (DMT), and lysergic acid diethylamide (LSD). This type of drug acts on the central nervous system to alter auditory, visual, and tactile perceptions. It tends to induce a highly euphoric or extremely depressed emotional state and seriously impairs memory and problem-solving skills. Potential hazards from the use of this sort of drug are changes in mood, feelings of intense anxiety, panic, or depression, and the inability to distinguish between reality and fantasy.

Stimulants. A stimulant is a drug that elevates the mood, emotions, alertness, and physical activity of the user. Sometimes referred to as "speed" or "uppers," the primary stimulants are amphetamines (Dexedrine and Benzedrine), cocaine, and caffeine. These drugs stimulate the central nervous system, thereby increasing alertness, suppressing appetite temporarily, and increasing optimism. The major dangers in using stimulants are psychological dependence and a deterioration of physical health. Heavy use can cause aggressiveness, confusion, and psychotic-like behavior.

Sedatives. A sedative is a drug that has both a sleep-inducing and a depressant effect. The opposite of the stimulants, sedatives tend to relax and soothe and combat anxiety and restlessness. Sometimes referred to as "downers," examples of sedatives include the barbiturates (Amytal, Luminal, Nembutal, Seconal), the chlorpromazines (Thorazine and Serpasil), the meprobamates (Miltown and Equanil), chlordiazepoxide (Librium), and diazepam (Valium). Large doses have similar effects to those of consuming large amounts of alcohol (euphoria, slurred speech, and poor motor coordination). The major risks in using sedatives are physical and psychological dependence and the strong possibility of physical injury due to poor motor coordination.

Cannabis sativa (marijuana). Marijuana, hashish, and tetrahydrocannabinols (THC) are obtained from the *Cannabis sativa* or hemp plant, which can be grown easily in many parts of the world. Marijuana is a mixture of the flowers, leaves, and stems of the plant, hashish is extracted from the resins, and THC is the active chemical in the plant. The major physiological effects of the drug are an increase in heart rate and a reddening of the eyes. Psychologically, the drug tends to produce a mild state of intoxication, induce a sense of relaxation and euphoria, distort the sense of taste and touch, and impair memory and reaction time.

Substance abuse counseling is a distinct specialization. Treatment for drug abusers typically involves placement in a highly structured residential facility, which is often staffed by former addicts. These programs typically involve medical treatment for the withdrawal process and both individual and group counseling sessions based on the principles of behavioral counseling. Although many counselors have little direct experience with the rehabilitation of substance abusers, this problem is so widespread in our society that all counselors need to be knowledgeable about substance abuse for at least three reasons. First, counselors have an important role in primary prevention (Baker & Shaw, 1988); second, counselors must know how to make referrals to appropriate substance abuse specialists; and third, counselors working in schools and other institutional settings often need to provide supportive counseling for clients receiving specialized counseling outside the institutional setting.

Psychological Disorders

Individuals who exhibit extreme forms of personal distress, unrealistic or irrational behavior, social deviance, or other manifestations of maladaptive behavior are considered to be mentally ill, abnormal, psychologically deviant, or pathological. The most widely used method for diagnosing individuals who suffer from these psychological difficulties is outlined in the fourth edition of the *Diagnostic and Statistical Manual of Mental Disorders* (DSM IV). The DSM IV employs separate dimensions, called *axes*, to describe five different aspects of a client's functioning. The first two axes are used to diagnose clinical syndromes (Axis I) and long-term personality concerns (Axis II). The other three axes are employed to describe general medical conditions (Axis III), psychosocial and environmental problems (Axis IV), and global assessment of functioning (Axis V). For complete diagnosis and treatment planning, clients need to be assessed on all five axis measures.

The major psychological and personality disorders described in the first two axes are indicated in the following paragraphs.

Disorders usually first diagnosed in infancy, childhood, or adolescence.
This category includes several major disorders that appear in infancy, childhood, or adolescence. Individuals with a *mental retardation* disorder show below average intellectual functioning and concomitant deficits in adaptive functioning. Those who have a *learning* disorder function significantly below what is expected for their age, measured IQ, and educational experience. Persons who have a *communication* disorder have difficulties in speech and language. Individuals with a *pervasive developmental* disorder have severe deficits in multiple areas. Those who exhibit an *attention deficit and disruptive behavior* disorder manifest prominent symptoms of inattention or hyperactivity. And those who have a *feeding and eating* disorder demonstrate gross disturbances in feeding and eating. Other afflictions in this diagnostic category include disorders characterized by tics and elimination dysfunctions.

Delirium, dementia, amnesic, and other cognitive disorders.
Individuals with these disorders manifest either a temporary or a permanent impairment of the brain. The most prevalent syndromes are delirium, dementia, and amnesia. Individuals who have a *delirium* disorder experience difficulty sustaining or shifting attention and maintaining a coherent thought pattern. Persons with a *dementia* disorder exhibit multiple cognitive deficits that include the impairment of memory, of abstract thinking, and of the ability to make sound judgments. Those with an *amnesia* disorder have a memory impairment in the absence of other significant deficits.

Substance-related disorders.
Substance-related disorders are characterized by the maladaptive use of alcohol and drugs. Individuals with this disorder use a mood-changing or behavior-altering substance frequently, suffer some noticeable impairment because of its use, become dependent upon the substance, and manifest an impaired ability to control their patterns of use.

Schizophrenia and other psychotic disorders.
Schizophrenia disorders are evidenced by individuals who have psychotic symptoms that have been present longer than six months. They have delusions and severe thought disturbances and appear to be out of contact with reality. There are several major schizophrenia disorders. Persons with a *paranoid-type* disorder experience delusions of persecution and grandeur. Those who manifest a *catatonic-type* disorder have rather extreme motor disturbances, and some experience catatonic stupor. Individuals with a *disorganized-type* disorder have severe deterioration of adaptive behavior and often act in rather silly and disorganized ways.

Persons who have an *undifferentiated-type* disorder display schizophrenic symptoms but cannot be classified into one of the previously mentioned categories. Finally, those with a *residual-type* disorder have had at least one schizophrenic episode but presently do not have any obvious psychotic symptoms.

A number of other psychotic disorders are recognized as well. Individuals with a *schizophreniform* disorder display schizophrenic symptoms for less than six months. Those who suffer from a *schizoaffective* disorder exhibit symptoms of schizophrenia or mood disorders but do not meet the criteria for either classification. Persons who exhibit *delusional disorder* have delusions of persecution or grandeur but do not have the severe deterioration seen in paranoid schizophrenia. Individuals who manifest a *brief psychotic* disorder have short episodes of psychotic symptoms that last anywhere from a few hours to less than a month. Those with a *shared psychotic* disorder experience delusions that materialize from being in a close association with a person who has a psychotic disorder. Persons fall into the category of *psychotic disorders due to other conditions* when their impairment does not fit into one of the categories outlined here.

Mood disorders.
Mood disorders are marked by persistent disturbances in mood, affect, or emotional tone. There are two major categories of mood disorders. Persons who have a *depressive* disorder exhibit emotional extremes only at one end of the mood continuum and experience feelings of sadness, dejection, and despair that become paramount in their lives. In severe cases of depression, delusions and hallucinations may occur. Individuals who suffer from a *bipolar* disorder experience extreme swings in moods, going through depression and its bipolar opposite, a euphoric or manic state.

Anxiety disorders.
Anxiety disorders are psychological disturbances in which an individual's behavior is dominated by feelings of excessive tension, fear, apprehension, and avoidance. There are several major anxiety disorders. Persons who manifest a *panic* disorder have recurrent attacks of overbearing anxiety that occur without warning. Individuals who have a *phobic* disorder experience chronic and irrational fears of objects or situations that pose no real danger. Those who suffer from an *obsessive-compulsive* disorder have unwanted thoughts, ideas, or impulses to engage in certain repetitive actions that appear absurd and useless. Persons who exhibit a *post-traumatic stress* disorder have had a very stressful experience and maintain a strong reaction to this event for relatively long periods. Those with an *acute stress* disorder show an elevated degree of anxiety immediately after a distressing incident. Finally, individuals who manifest a *generalized anxiety* disorder have a chronic and high level of apprehension not related to any known threat.

Somatoform disorders.
Somatoform disorders are characterized by physical symptoms for which no authentic organic basis can be discovered. There are several major somatoform disorders. Those who have *hypochondriasis* are preoccupied with health concerns and are perpetually worried about the possibility of contacting a serious illness. People who manifest a *somatization* disorder have a long and recurring history of chronic but diverse medical complaints that appear to have no physical origin. Individuals who exhibit a *conversion* disorder experience a significant loss of some physiological function that seems to be an expression of a psychological need. Individuals who suffer from a *somatization pain* disorder are preoccupied with a pain of unknown origin. Persons with

a *body-dysmorphic* disorder are preoccupied with some imagined defect in their physical appearance. Finally, those who manifest an *undifferentiated somatoform* disorder have unexplained physical complaints lasting six months or longer—but their condition does not meet the full requirements of the other somatoform categories.

Factitious disorders.

Individuals who demonstrate disorders in this classification have physical and/or psychological symptoms of illness that are deliberately produced or feigned in order to satisfy a need to be sick. They may exaggerate their current medical conditions, fabricate, or self-inflict an illness. This motivation to be ill is accompanied by the absence of any known incentive for the behavior.

Dissociative disorders.

Dissociative disorders are those disturbances manifested by individuals who lose contact with portions of their consciousness or memory and suffer disturbances in their sense of identity. There are several major dissociative disorders. Those who exhibit a *dissociative amnesia* disorder have a sudden and extensive memory loss and are unable to recall their own names or home addresses. Individuals with a *dissociative fugue* disorder suddenly leave home, cannot recall all or part of their past, and are either confused about their own identity or assume a new one. Persons who have a *dissociative identity* disorder appear to have multiple personalities or two or more very distinct personalities. Finally, individuals who experience a *depersonalization* disorder seem to live in a dream world, temporarily lose their own sense of personal identity, and behave in a robotic fashion.

Sexual and gender identity disorders.

There are three major classifications of these disorders. Persons who manifest a *paraphilia* disorder have recurring sexual urges, fantasies, and/or behaviors that are not part of normal sexual expression—such as exhibitionism, fetishism, and voyeurism. Individuals who have a *sexual-dysfunctional* disorder experience difficulties with appropriate desire, arousal, and responses during sexual relations. Those who suffer from *gender identity* disorders are bothered because their sexual identity does not coincide with their physical gender.

Eating disorders.

There are two major eating disorders. Individuals who display an *anorexia nervosa* disorder have a disturbed perception of their body and refuse to maintain a normal body weight. Those who suffer from a *bulimia nervosa* disorder have repeated binges of eating followed by inappropriate compensatory behaviors such as self-induced vomiting, misuse of laxatives, extreme fasting, or overexercising.

Sleep disorders.

There are two major subgroups of sleep disorders: dyssomnia and parasomnia. Those who suffer from *dyssomnia* experience difficulty in the amount of time that they sleep or the appropriateness of the time when they fall asleep or in not feeling rested after an appropriate period of sleep. Individuals who experience *parasomnia* have abnormal occurrences during their sleep such as frightening dreams or sleepwalking.

Impulse control disorders.

These disorders are exhibited by those who are unable to control an impulse, drive, or temptation to act in some way harmful to themselves or to another person. There are five major types of disorders in this category. First, individuals who have *intermittent explosive* disorder may either aggressively assault other individuals or destroy property. Second, persons with a *kleptomania* disorder cannot resist the tendency to steal property that they do not need. Third, those with a *pathological gambling* disorder cannot resist the temptation to gamble. Fourth, individuals who have a *pyromania* disorder cannot resist the impulse to set fires. Finally, those who have a *trichotillomania* disorder cannot overcome their temptation to pull out their own hair.

Adjustment disorders.

Individuals who have an *adjustment* disorder experience maladaptive reactions to some stressful condition in their lives. The adjustment difficulty may be characterized by extreme irritability, loss of appetite, poor sleep, or other physical complaints. Problems may also become evident in one or more areas of life such as in school, at work, or in social situations.

Personality disorders.

When the personality traits of individuals become inflexible and cause functional impairment or subjective distress for relatively long periods of time, the result is considered to be a personality disorder. These disorders often become evident during the teenage years and may continue throughout adult life. The DSM IV uses Axis II to list ten personality disorders grouped into three clusters that have shared features. Individuals who fit into the first group, considered the *odd* or *eccentric* disorders, typically reveal a lack of interpersonal relationships, restricted affect, and peculiar ideas. Three specific disorders are in this cluster: the paranoid, the schizoid, and the schizotypal personality disorders. Clients who fall into the second group, called the *dramatic, emotional,* or *erratic* disorders, usually manifest considerable affect and lack of stability. This cluster includes the antisocial, the borderline, the histrionic, and the narcissistic personality disorders. Individuals who fit into the third group, labeled the *anxious* or *fearful* disorders, attempt to meet the demands of life by rigid behaviors, anxiety, passive compliance, or withdrawal. The specific afflictions in this cluster are the avoidant, the dependent, and the obsessive-compulsive personality disorders.

SUMMARY

This chapter has briefly outlined several ways that effective individuals differ from ineffective ones. After studying this chapter you should be able to describe the major needs individuals have, discuss the role of stress and the emotions in the coping process, outline the major developmental concerns, indicate some important social interaction and relationship skills, and name some other major characteristics of effectively functioning individuals. In addition, you should have gained some understanding of individuals with special concerns, such as those with handicapping conditions, serious vocational concerns, substance abuse problems, and psychological disorders. To attain a high level of understanding of these concerns, in-depth study of these topics is required.

REFERENCES

Adler, A. (1964). *Social interest: A challenge to mankind.* New York: Capricorn.
American Psychiatric Association. (1994). *Diagnostic and statistical manual of mental disorders* (4th ed.). Washington, DC: Author.

Baker, S. B., & Shaw, M. C. (1988). *Improving counseling through primary prevention.* Columbus, OH: Merrill.

Berk, L. E. (1997). *Child development* (4th ed.). Boston: Allyn & Bacon.

Birren, J. E., & Schaie, K. W. (Eds.). (1996). *Handbook of the psychology of aging* (4th ed.). San Diego, CA: Academic Press.

Brown, D., & Brooks, L. (1991). *Career counseling techniques.* Boston: Allyn & Bacon.

Calhoun, J. F., & Acocella, J. R. (1990). *Psychology of adjustment and human relations* (3rd ed.). New York: McGraw-Hill.

Coon, D. (1995). *Introduction to psychology: Exploration and application* (7th ed.). St. Paul, MN: West Publishing.

Dinkmeyer, D. C., Sr., Dinkmeyer, D. C., Jr., & Sperry, L. (1987). *Adlerian counseling and psychotherapy* (2nd ed.). Columbus, OH: Merrill.

Dreikurs, R. R., & Soltz, V. (1987). *Children: The challenge* (rev. ed.). New York: E. P. Dutton.

Elson, S. E. (1979). Recent approaches to counseling: Gestalt, transactional analysis, and personality theories. In H. M. Burks & B. Stefflre (Eds.), *Theories of counseling* (3rd ed.) (pp. 254–316). New York: McGraw-Hill.

Erikson, E. H. (1993). *Childhood and society* (3rd ed.). New York: Norton.

Erikson, E. H. (1994). *Identity: Youth in crisis.* New York: Norton.

Forney, D., Wallace-Schultzman, F., & Wiggers, T. T. (1982). Burnout among career development professionals: Preliminary findings and implications. *Personnel and Guidance Journal, 60,* 435–439.

Forrest, G. G. (1994). *Intensive psychotherapy of alcoholism.* Northvale, NJ: Jason Aronson.

Freud, A. (1967). *The ego and the mechanisms of defense* (rev. ed.). New York: International Universities Press.

Fromm, E. (1996). *To have or to be.* New York: Continuum.

Gitlow, S. E., & Peyser, H. S. (Eds.). (1988). *Alcoholism: A practical treatment guide* (2nd ed.). New York: Grune & Stratton.

Gysbers, N. C., & Henderson, P. (1994). *Developing and managing your school guidance program* (2nd ed.). Alexandria, VA: American Counseling Association.

Havighurst, R. J. (1972). *Developmental tasks and education* (3rd ed.). New York: David McKay.

Herr, E. L., & Cramer, S. H. (1992). *Career guidance and counseling through the life span: Systematic approaches* (4th ed.). New York: HarperCollins.

Hershenson, D. B., Power, P. W., & Waldo, M. (1996). *Community counseling: Contemporary theory and practice.* Boston: Allyn & Bacon.

Hilgard, E. J., & Bower, G. H. (1981). *Theories of learning* (5th ed.). Englewood Cliffs, NJ: Prentice Hall.

Hochberg, J. (1978). *Perception* (2nd ed.). Englewood Cliffs, NJ: Prentice Hall.

Jellinek, E. M. (1960). *The disease concept of alcoholism.* New Haven, CT: Hillhouse Press.

Kagan, J., & Segal, J. (1994). *Psychology: An introduction* (8th ed.). New York: Harcourt Brace.

Kintsch, W. (1982). *Memory and cognition.* New York: Krieger.

Kohlberg, L., & Kramer, R. (1969). Continuities and discontinuities in child and adult moral development. *Human Development, 12,* 93–120.

Krumboltz, J. D., & Thoresen, C. E. (Eds.). (1976). *Counseling methods.* New York: Holt, Rinehart and Winston.

Lee, C. C. (Ed.). (1996). *Multicultural issues in counseling: New approaches to diversity* (2nd ed.). Alexandria, VA: American Counseling Association.

Maddi, S. R. (1996). *Personality theories: A comparative analysis* (6th ed.). Pacific Grove, CA: Brooks/Cole.

Marshall, J. R. (1994). *Social phobia: Shyness to stage fright.* New York: Basic Books.

Maslack, C. (1982). *Burnout: The cost of caring.* Englewood Cliffs, NJ: Prentice Hall.

Maslow, A. H. (1970). *Motivation and personality* (2nd ed.). New York: Harper & Row.

Moos, R. H., & Schaefer, J. A. (1993). Coping resources and processes: Current concepts and measures. In L. Goldberger & S. Breznitz (Eds.), *Handbook of stress: Theoretical and clinical aspects* (2nd ed.). New York: Free Press.

Muisener, P. P. (1994). *Understanding and treating the adolescent substance abuser.* Thousand Oaks, CA: Sage.

Murphy, P. M., & Kupshik, G. A. (1992). *Loneliness, stress, and well being: A helper's guide.* London: Tavistock/Routledge.

Neff, W. (1985). *Work and human behavior* (3rd ed.). New York: Aldine-Atherton.

Osipow, S. (1980). *Manual for the career decision scale.* Columbus, OH: Marathon Consulting Press.

Paisley, P. O., & Hubbard, G. T. (1994). *Developmental school counseling programs: From theory to practice.* Alexandria, VA: American Counseling Association.

Peer, G. G., Lindsey, A. K., & Newman, P. A. (1982). Alcoholism as a stage phenomena: A frame of reference for counselors. *Personnel and Guidance Journal, 60,* 465–469.

Piaget, J. (1966). The origins of intelligence in children. New York: International Universities Press.

Rathus, S. A., & Nevid, J. S. (1995). Adjustment & growth: The challenges of life (6th ed.). Fort Worth, TX: Harcourt Brace.

Ray, O. S., & Ksir, C. (1992). *Drugs, society, and human behavior* (6th ed.). St. Louis, MO: Times, Mirror/Mosby.

Rice, P. F. (1996). *The adolescent: Development, relationships, and culture* (8th ed.). Boston: Allyn & Bacon.

Rogers, C. R. (1959). A theory of therapy, personality, and interpersonal relationships as developed in the client-centered framework. In S. Koch (Ed.), *Psychology: A study of science* (Vol. 3, pp. 184–256). New York: McGraw-Hill.

Rogers, C. R. (1972). *On becoming a person.* Boston: Houghton Mifflin.

Shaffer, D. R. (1996). *Developmental psychology: Childhood and adolescence* (4th ed.). Pacific Grove, CA: Brooks/Cole.

Skinner, B. F. (1953). *Science and human behavior.* New York: Macmillan.

Sue, D. W., & Sue, D. (1990). *Counseling the culturally different: Theory and practice* (2nd ed.). New York: Wiley.

Sweeny, T. J. (1989). *Adlerian counseling: A practical approach for a new decade* (3rd ed.). Muncie, IN: Accelerated Development.

Trotter, T. V. (1995). *Walking the talk: Developing a local comprehensive school counseling program.* Alexandria, VA: American School Counseling Association.

Velleman, R. (1992). *Counseling for alcohol problems.* Thousand Oaks, CA: Sage.

Weiten, W. (1995). *Psychology: Themes and variations* (3rd ed.). Pacific Grove, CA: Brooks/Cole.

Wickelgren, W. A. (1974). *How to solve problems.* San Francisco: W. H. Freeman.

Wollams, S., & Brown, M. (1979). *The total handbook of transactional analysis.* Englewood Cliffs, NJ: Prentice Hall.

Young, J. (1979, September). *Cognitive therapy and loneliness.* Paper presented at the meeting of the American Psychological Association, New York.

Zimbardo, P. G. (1977). *Shyness: What it is, what to do about it.* Reading, MA: Addison-Wesley.

Zunker, V. G. (1994). *Career counseling: Applied concepts of life planning* (4th ed.). Pacific Grove, CA: Brooks/Cole.

Transitional Stages in the Counseling Process

INTRODUCTION

This chapter outlines five important counseling stages and describes the distinctive activities that occur in each of these stages. This is followed by a discussion of the characteristics of reluctant and resistant clients, outlining some of the ways to deal with these clients. Finally, important sources of information about clients are reviewed. After studying this chapter, you should be able to:

- identify the five transitional counseling stages;
- discuss the reasons for calling counseling stages transitional, overlapping, and continuous;
- describe the major characteristics or themes found in each counseling stage;
- outline some of the ways you should deal with reluctant and resistant clients; and
- name six different sources that counselors may use to obtain information about clients and describe the advantages and limitations of each.

THE TRANSITIONAL STAGES

Counseling is a developmental process; it has a beginning, progresses through an orderly, transitional sequence, and has an ending. This developmental process can be described in terms of the following five stages:

1. relationship-building stage—developing the foundation for a sound collaborative working association;
2. exploratory stage—examining and understanding the client and his or her frame of reference;
3. decision-making stage—formulating a counseling goal and an intervention strategy;
4. working or implementation stage—expending effort to ameliorate the situation or solve the problem; and
5. termination stage—concluding the counseling process.

The characteristics of the counseling process have been discussed by a number of authors (Brammer & MacDonald, 1996; Burke, 1989; Cormier & Hackney, 1996; Egan, 1994; Hansen, Rossberg, & Cramer, 1994; Ivey, Ivey, & Simek-Morgan, 1997; Okun, 1997; Patterson & Welfel, 1994). An analysis of their writings indicates that, even though there is no agreement on the number of phases or stages, the names of these stages, or the characteristics of each stage, there is a consensus that the counseling process moves through a sequential, orderly progression of stages. There is also considerable agreement that the relationship aspects of counseling permeate the entire process (Waehler & Lenox, 1994).

It is my viewpoint that the five stages of counseling are not distinct units but developmental in nature. Therefore, they need to be seen as transitional, overlapping, and continuous stage processes rather than as rigid, discrete, and discontinuous divisions (see Figure 3-1). This transitional concept implies that, while each of these stages has its own theme and developmental tasks, elements of any stage—or of all stages— may be evident at any other stage. For example, after you say hello to a new client, you may have many of the following questions in the back of your head: "Who is this person? Can we work together? I wonder what the problem is? I wonder if I can help the client deal with this concern? I wonder how long it will take?" The particular counseling stage can be discerned by the dominant activities or the major focus of that time span. Thus, the issue that you are paying most attention to—perhaps getting to know your client—is the transitional stage that you are in. There is considerable variability in the time and efforts spent on each stage. In some cases you may spend a large amount of time in developing the foundation for a good relationship before moving the counseling process along, while in other cases you may need to spend little time on this basic stage.

Furthermore, because these stages are developmental, the emphasis or major theme of each stage must be accomplished at least to a minimal degree before counseling can *fully progress* to the next stage. If some of the developmental tasks of the prior stages have not been accomplished, or if they were only minimally met, then the counseling process will be somewhat constrained and the outcomes severely limited. The more completely these tasks are performed, the more thorough the counseling outcomes.

The counseling process may be refocused at any given point in counseling—that is, at any point the counselor may choose to concentrate on the developmental tasks of an earlier stage to enrich the process or overcome difficulties or blockages. A shift in emphasis may be necessary and appropriate to enhance the relationship, to explore additional dimensions of the problem, to reformulate the targeted issue, to employ a different strategy, or to attend to some other task that may further enhance the counseling effort. This refocus to another task should not be seen as a regression but, rather, as part of the normal transitional stage development process. This concept of stages is similar to the structured-stage concepts outlined by developmental stage theories (Lerner, 1986; Turiel, 1969). When a particular concern of a client has been resolved, the process may be repeated to focus on another unresolved issue faced by the client.

Counseling, by its very nature, often does not progress on a steady, even, time-predictable course. The character, duration, and intensity of the counselor-client interaction in different counseling cases vary considerably. Consequently, the character, duration, and intensity of each of these stages also vary. Occasionally, all five stages may occur in one counseling session; however, they normally take a minimum of several sessions and

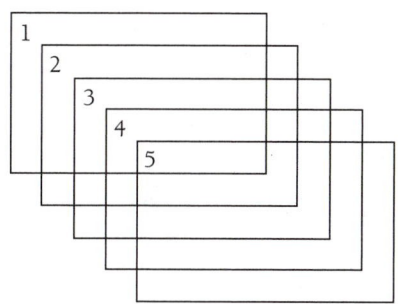

Stage 1–Relationship building

Stage 2–Exploration and understanding

Stage 3–Decision making

Stage 4–Working or implementation

Stage 5–Termination and follow-up

FIGURE 3-1
The five transitional counseling stages

often take many, many sessions. Some counseling cases require considerable time on one or two stages and little time on other stages. Other counseling cases will require considerable time on all stages.

The tasks outlined in each of these five stages appear to be pantheoretical or orientation free; therefore, all types of counseling—regardless of the approach, the problem area, or the intervention used—should progress through these stages. The specific counseling tasks associated with each stage are outlined in the following sections. As counselors-in-training you should become aware of these tasks; realize that the burden of accomplishing these tasks is on you, the counselor—the trained professional—and not on the client, the person in need; and try to develop your skills in accomplishing these tasks in a logical sequence.

The Relationship-Building Stage

When the counseling process begins, the counselor and the client ordinarily do not know one another, so the foundation for a collaborative working relationship must be developed. Building this relationship is the focus of the initial counseling stage, and it is achieved through four interrelated tasks: (1) establishing the facilitative conditions, (2) determining the initial counseling goals, (3) structuring the relationship, and (4) exemplifying ethical standards. This initial stage is normally relatively short, ranging from a few minutes to several sessions.

Establishing facilitative conditions.

At the beginning of this process clients are frequently unsure of themselves, unsure about you, and most of all, unsure about the counseling process. Furthermore, clients may even be unaware of their major concerns. This cautiousness means that clients may be quite guarded in what they say. Clients need to feel a sense of trust, genuineness, and respect. As the counselor you must take the responsibility for providing the conditions that will facilitate open, honest, and complete communication. Clients need to feel a sense of being at ease in the relationship and of being accepted by you and to feel that they are understood in appropriate ways. You need to communicate an interest in and a positive regard for clients and an understanding and respect for their feelings, attitudes, and concerns.

These attributes are behaviorally communicated by:

- being fully present to the client and focusing on the client as a person of real value and worth,
- listening intensively and attempting to identify the client's underlying feelings and thoughts, and
- responding to the client with high-level attending responses.

These high-level responses communicate to the client that he or she has been understood—they help the client feel more comfortable in the relationship, and they encourage the client to fully express concerns.

Determining initial counseling goals.

Clients come to counselors for a variety of reasons: to resolve a conflict, solve a problem, or to obtain some help in becoming a more effectively functioning person. They may be extremely aware of their problems or rather vague and uncertain about why they feel the way they do or even why they came to the counselor. Clients may present an initial problem that is not their major concern. Motivation to work on the solution to the problem may be weak, moderate, or strong. In any case, some mutually agreed-upon purpose for meeting must be identified. This first goal may be an agreement to work on the presenting problem, to listen to the client in order to help the client gain some insight and a better understanding of himself or herself, or to explore the client's rather diffuse concerns in order to develop an understanding of the client and thereby identify a more precise counseling goal.

Structuring the relationship.

All counseling relationships need to be structured in order to provide the client with a sense of clarification, direction, and understanding of the process. Initially, clients may not have a clear picture of what to expect or how changes are likely to occur, and they may be uncertain of the logistic and procedural aspects of this process. As the counselor you should develop a mutual understanding and agreement between yourself and the client regarding three important issues: the dynamics and methodology of the process; the logistical, pragmatic, and procedural issues involved; and the client's personal or consumer-oriented concerns (Day & Sparacio, 1980).

First, to develop an understanding of the dynamics of the counseling process you may need to discuss how counseling works, the nature of the interaction, the responsibilities of both yourself and the client, and information about how positive results can be achieved. For example, as a college counselor you may provide structure to a student who is undecided about his major by stating, "My job is to help you think about the issues that are involved in making this decision. You are responsible for obtaining any additional information that you need, judging its relative importance, and weighing it in light of your own personal background and values."

Second, as the counselor you should be sure that the arrangements are clear for all the important logistical and practical details such as time (including time of meeting, session length, frequency of contact, and how long the process may last), location (including address, building, and room number), arrangements for absences, cancellation, and emergency situations, costs, and other details. For example, as a rehabilitation counselor you may say to your client, "John, we will meet every Thursday afternoon from three until three forty-five in room 415 in the rehab center. If for some reason you cannot make it, please call the office and leave a message for me. We can reschedule our session for another time that week."

The third aspect of structuring is to make sure that there is an agreement about those items that deal with the personal concerns of the client such as the confidential nature of the relationship, the arrangements for recording the sessions, the qualifications of the counselor, and what the client's responsibilities are in the process. For example, as a counselor working in a community agency you may say, "Anything you say in these sessions will be kept confidential. Our sessions will be taped so that I can review the highlights of your case with my supervisor."

The amount of structure that is provided differs from case to case and will depend on the needs of the client, the environmental setting, the type of problem presented, and the counselor's theoretical orientation. Frequently, counselors structure the relationship in general terms initially and provide additional structure as the need develops. Too much structuring can increase a client's anxiety rather than lower it, and too little can create an erroneous perception of what the counseling process is all about.

Maintaining ethical standards.

As the counselor you need to exemplify appropriate ethical behavior throughout the counseling process. At the initial stage of counseling the major ethical concerns involve confidentiality, informed consent, and the appropriate representation of your skills and credentials. These issues should be addressed when you structure the relationship, but you will need to continue to be concerned about ethical standards throughout the entire counseling process.

The Exploratory Stage

During the second transitional stage you should focus on assisting clients in exploring, perceiving, analyzing, and understanding the parameters of self and their problems. To gain an understanding of clients and their internal frames of reference, it is most helpful to address the following four major tasks:

1. explore the scope or depth and breadth of the client's presenting problem;
2. analyze the client's degree of functioning in several major dimensions of the client's life;
3. understand the historical and idiosyncratic ways that this particular client has changed and the amount of resistance that presently exists toward change; and
4. identify the client's internal strengths and the external resources available to the client.

At this stage you may help your client move from a surface awareness of his or her concern to a recognition of any underlying issues that need to be addressed.

The scope of the problem.

The major task at this stage is to explore and understand the reasons the client came for help. To facilitate this exploratory process, both you and the client need to: clarify whether the presenting problem is the major or real problem; identify the context of the environmental situation where the problem occurs; evaluate the nature, severity, and duration of the problem; assess the consequences that this particular problem has caused the client and significant others; and estimate the effects that any change would have on both the client and significant others in the client's life. This exploratory process is often best done by actively listening to the client, clarifying issues, and supporting and encouraging the client as a person of value. Open-ended inquiries may be used, but care must be taken to avoid creating a dependency relationship or an interrogative atmosphere.

The client's degree of functioning.

To understand the client's internal frame of reference, it is usually helpful to examine the client's degree of functioning in several major aspects of life. As the exploratory process unfolds, you may form a professional judgment about whether the client is

- progressing through the developmental life stages with a minimum of problems;
- meeting his or her physiological, psychological, and social needs in effective ways;
- functioning at an appropriate cognitive level;
- relating in positive ways to significant others;
- coping and adjusting well to the conflicts, frustrations, and other thwarting conditions encountered in life; and
- manifesting appropriate behavioral patterns.

An examination of these dimensions will provide further insight into the client and will increase both the client's and the counselor's awareness of the client's ability to function in a variety of dimensions of life.

Historical patterns.

As the counselor you may want to help clients explore and understand how they have historically dealt with problems similar to the presenting one. For example, it may help a particular client for you to know if the client has discussed important problems with significant others, sought new factual information to clarify issues, tried out new experiences or roles, changed his or her environment, or taken chances when the future was uncertain. This exploratory process can reveal the client's resistance to handling life issues or the client's ability to deal with the uncertainty of the problem-solving process. During the exploration process, you will begin to formulate some tentative plans about the intervention strategy you may want to employ with the client.

Strengths and resources.

The client's internal strengths and the source and kinds of resources available to the client may also be explored during this stage. To understand the scope of the client's strengths, it is helpful to ascertain the client's sense of ownership for the problem, sense of responsibility for resolving the issue, awareness of strengths and limitations, and knowledge of available external resources. Helping clients obtain this awareness and sense of responsibility is essential in counseling. The way you treat and respond to your clients will affect their willingness to take responsibility and ownership for their own thoughts, feelings, and actions. If clients experience you as a caring, trusting, and concerned helper, they will slowly become less defensive and more open to self-exploration and self-understanding. Helping clients uncover issues they may not be aware of brings about clarification of the problem and often suggests an intervention strategy.

The Decision-Making Stage

The third transitional stage is intermediate between the exploration of a client's concerns and the application of a particular intervention plan. Two interrelated tasks need to be accomplished at this stage: The goals of the counseling process must be mutually agreed upon by you and the client, and a decision should be made by you regarding the particular intervention strategy that will be used. The initial goals may be redefined or revised on the basis of the understanding reached in the first two stages of counseling. It is critical that the goals be mutually agreed upon because progress will be most unlikely if you are working on one concern while the client has a need to work on something quite different. The extent to which this agreement should be explicit varies from one approach to another. If you plan to use strategies based on a person-centered approach, you could accept an implicit agreement; whereas if you plan to employ a behavioral approach, you would want to have a very explicit agreement.

Deciding on a goal is not always a clear-cut process. Some clients present a multitude of issues that may impede their ability to function effectively. In these cases it is strongly recommended that as a beginning counselor you give serious consideration to working on one concern that is causing major discomfort and yet is a goal that can be reached within a reasonable length of time. Reaching a decision on a counseling goal and the type of intervention is a task that cannot be accomplished effectively unless the tasks of the prior stages have been met. There are a number of client, counselor, and environmental variables that influence the specificity of these counseling goals and the intervention strategy used.

Client variables.   The client characteristics that strongly influence the counseling goal and the intervention approach include:

- the kind of problem—for example, does the client have poor interpersonal skills or does he or she have poor decision-making skills?
- the historical and idiosyncratic pattern employed to solve problems and resolve issues—for example, does the client typically let others make the decisions or does he or she have the habit of investigating all possibilities so thoroughly as to become paralyzed in the process?
- demographic characteristics—for example, does the client's age, gender, or income level have a bearing on the college and the financial aid that he or she is eligible for?
- personality characteristics—for example, the dependent client will have to be handled somewhat differently from the independent client.
- cultural background—for example, using certain techniques with clients from some cultures may cause resistance because the process may be considered incompatible with the culture (for instance, self-disclosure).

Counselor variables.   The counselor variables that strongly influence the counselor's choice of the appropriate intervention method include:

- knowledge of the cognate area—for example, theories and research in motivation, cognition, relationship, adjustment, and personality of behavior;
- knowledge and experiences in using various counseling approaches—for example, person-centered, cognitive-restructuring, or behavioral; and
- level and skill in communicating appropriate high-level responses—for example, helping skills, verbal responses, and role-communication skills.

Environmental variables.   The setting (school, college, vocational rehabilitation agency, or private practice) where the counseling takes place may have a moderate to strong influence on the appropriateness of a particular goal or intervention strategy. Counselors who work in institutional settings often delimit their goals in order to help the client function more effectively within that setting. For example, a school counselor working with a child who has an alcoholic parent must have an immediate goal of helping the student function more effectively at school despite the family problem.

The Working or Implementation Stage

The fourth counseling stage is the application of an appropriate intervention strategy. The major task at this stage is helping clients resolve their concerns and learn to function more effectively. This may require you to provide emotional support, encouragement, and reinforcement of newly gained insights. You may want to use one particular strategy or a multivariate treatment approach. The strategies employed in counseling can be classified as interventions that emphasize improvement in the client's level of mental functioning, sense of well-being or emotional state, or ability to behave more appropriately. Thus, treatment strategies may be cognitively focused, affectively focused, or performance focused. *Cognitively focused* interventions should be considered when you believe that the client needs assistance to obtain or retain factual information, when the client needs help making decisions, or when the client reveals faulty deductive or inductive thinking processes. *Affectively focused* interventions should be considered when you conclude that the client reveals inadequate feelings of self-worth, poor acceptance of others, and minimal skills in dealing with his or her own attitudes, beliefs, emotions, or values. *Performance-focused* interventions may be appropriate when the client's behavioral repertoire is limiting his or her functioning. More often than not, counselors will employ a multimodal approach using strategies from all three domains. Intervention strategies based on these three modalities are explained more fully in Chapters 4, 5, and 6.

In the working or intervention stage of counseling, counselors often use several resources to assist clients in resolving their concerns. These resources may be significant others in a client's life, community resources, or published materials.

Significant others.   Frequently, an appropriate intervention strategy involves significant other persons in a client's life. The client may be required to interact in a different way with a parent, spouse, child, teacher, or employer. When this is probable, your treatment approach must give careful attention to this aspect of the client's life. At times you may want to involve these significant other persons in the intervention strategy. When this is desirable, appropriate consultation with the concerned parties should be conducted.

Community resources.   Community resources are used in the counseling process for three distinct purposes. First, clients may be referred to another person or agency for complete treatment if it becomes apparent that the client has a problem that can best be resolved through the assistance of another professional, group, or association. Examples of such referrals include optometrists, physicians, psychologists, and speech and hearing specialists. Referrals may also be made to a specialized agency such as the Association for the Help of Retarded Children or the United Cerebral Palsy Association. Second, clients may be referred for concurrent treatment if the counselor recognizes that other professional help is needed by the client as part of or perhaps parallel to the counselor's intervention. For example, as a school counselor you may refer a student who has an alcoholic parent to Alateen, a support group for children of alcoholics. Finally, community resources are also used to enable clients to obtain the information necessary to advance the counseling process. Examples of this type of referral include the following:

- You are a vocational counselor and your client is concerned with career choice, so you want that client to interview a person who is working in a particular occupation.
- You are a school counselor and your client is in the process of selecting a college, so you want your client to visit the colleges that he or she is considering.
- You are a vocational rehabilitation counselor and your client may have recently suffered some disabling event and needs to be directed to a particular agency to learn a new trade.

Published materials.   Published materials and references are valuable in the treatment phase of counseling to help the client obtain information that will enhance the treatment. For example, a student who is interested in becoming a dental hygienist may be directed to the *Occupational Outlook Handbook* to learn more about the occupation.

The Termination Stage

During the fifth and final transitional counseling stage, the termination process occurs. This is an extremely important period in which you need to focus on accomplishing three interrelated tasks. First, progress made should be summarized and evaluated. Second, other issues that require attention at this time should be brought forward. And third, methods to foster client growth after the counseling process terminates need to be established. When these tasks are handled effectively, the counseling process is successfully completed. When these tasks are not dealt with, the process is truncated and the important growth that has occurred is curtailed.

To evaluate the counseling process you and the client should determine whether the desired goals were met. The major responsibility for accomplishing this first task should be placed on the client (Ward, 1984). The client may be asked to prepare a progress report indicating how the counseling goals were reached. This may entail having the client state how he or she has changed, what new learning has occurred, or how he or she is better able to deal with specific situations or significant other persons. To consolidate the process you ought to review the client's progress report carefully and then verbally summarize and review what happened and why it happened. This consolidation will serve to reinforce attainment of the goals.

Determining the client's preparedness to terminate requires an assessment of the client's overall level of functioning and whether or not other client concerns or unresolved issues need to be addressed at this time. One issue that frequently needs attention is dependency. There is often a natural tendency to maintain the bond that was established in the counseling process, and the dependent client will manifest this tendency to a high degree. These dependency feelings must be dealt with before the termination process can occur. Clearly, not all client issues can be resolved—clients will never function fully in all aspects of their lives. But once the agreed-upon goals have been met, unless another goal that is mutually agreed to is selected and the counseling stages are recycled, the counseling process should move toward closure.

The final task in the termination process is helping the client develop a systematic method to ensure that the growth and change process will continue. This ordinarily includes arrangements for periodic follow-up sessions, as well as developing a self-monitoring plan and rehearsing ways this plan will be implemented. Self-monitoring plans and follow-up efforts serve to improve clients' self-confidence and provide a necessary support system.

Termination is often a hard step, but when the tasks of this stage have been accomplished the client should be ready to leave. During the final session the client should be informed that the relationship is not being ended but the meetings are being adjourned; the client should be encouraged to return whenever he or she needs further assistance.

RELUCTANT AND RESISTANT CLIENTS IN THE COUNSELING PROCESS

Many clients come to see a counselor on a voluntary basis. These clients recognize that they have an unresolved problem—they have the motivation to obtain professional assistance, and they have made a commitment to involve themselves in the change process. Other clients, however, are referred to a counselor involuntarily. They are compelled to enter the process by some pressure outside themselves. Dyer and Vriend (1988) maintain that most of the clients seen in institutional settings are involuntary. This section discusses some of the basic issues counselors face in dealing with both voluntary and involuntary clients.

The Reluctant and Uncommitted Client

The reluctant client is one who is unmotivated to seek help; if it were left up to this person, he or she would never go talk to a counselor. The counseling process is not seen by such a person as a reasonable or realistic approach. When a reluctant client does appear and starts this course, the likelihood that the counseling process will be incomplete is strong unless you take some preventive effort. In school and other institutional settings involuntary clients include students referred for poor classroom achievement, disciplinary concerns, and other maladaptive or ill-advised behaviors. In rehabilitation and other community agencies uncommitted clients may be referred by a concerned or overwhelmed parent, another agency, the probation system, or the courts.

These uncommitted clients may be unwilling to become committed for a variety of reasons. Many see the counseling process as an affront to their own self-concepts. They believe that the way they are functioning is okay; any action showing a willingness to change or to seek help is an admittance of their own weakness, a sign of failure. Others see the counselor as part of the system that they are already at odds with—the very authorities who have caused the client difficulty are now using one of their colleagues to set the client straight! Still others are reluctant to change because their ill-advised behavior may have given them some status with their peer group. Thus, any change in behavior will necessarily result in a change of status, and that may be quite undesirable. Others see the counselor as a person who is trying to control their lives; therefore, the clients' attempts to be independent are threatened. In certain cases reluctance can be related to cultural factors. You may have a client who comes from an environment that does not encourage discussion of problems outside the family—not with strangers and certainly not with a counselor.

Client reluctance is manifested in many ways. A principal one is the silent treatment. Reluctant clients may refuse to discuss anything, and when they do, they nod, shrug their shoulders, or give short answers to any and all questions. Beginning counselors who are not careful and are not prepared to deal with reluctant clients may intensify their questioning, creating an interrogative atmosphere; they get nowhere, and their reluctant clients remain apathetic, indifferent, and minimally communicative.

Another reluctant group consists of the avoiders—individuals who are seemingly quite agreeable and compliant, but who are forgetful, come late, or miss their appointments. Some avoiders are willing to talk about anything and everything but the real issues. Their avoidance of work on the important topics is signaled by their loquaciousness, silly actions, efforts to focus on small talk, or willingness to work only on small, inconsequential concerns. Other avoiders appear forgetful or will keep you waiting for them to show up or complete an assigned task. Reluctance is shown in a third way by clients who have excuses for everything they do. They take little responsibility for their actions, complain about everything, or appear quite dependent, and their defense mechanisms are powerful and serve as a protective shield. A final way that this unwillingness is displayed is by hostile behavior—a defiant disposition, a supercritical attitude, and a tendency to verbally attack everything. The angry client appears to have no tolerance for any institution or system and vents this hostility at the least provocation.

Handling the uncommitted and involuntary client is difficult for any counselor and extremely frustrating for the beginning counselor. Trying to deal with this type of client can cause counselors to blame themselves, feel a sense of personal failure, and develop a lower professional self-regard. Furthermore, when little progress is made in counseling, there is a very strong possibility that a counselor will reinforce the client's reluctance. This behavior is reinforced by being impatient; ignoring the client's signals; getting upset and directing irritation at the client, to whom one should be sending signals of positive regard; and, ultimately, giving up and refusing to do any further work with the unwilling client.

To deal with an uncommitted client, you should first be aware of the need to establish realistic expectations for the client and the counseling session. Asking yourself the following questions can be helpful:

- Is the client coming voluntarily or was the client referred by a third party?
- Did you expect to accomplish a great deal or did you expect to move rather slowly?
- Did you expect a compliant, easygoing individual or a person who was defending his or her own concept of self?
- Is this reluctance related to the client's cultural background?

Formulating realistic expectations will help you prevent feelings of frustration and will positively influence the counseling process. It is also important to continue communicating a warm, deep respect for the client. Unless the client feels that you are on his or her side, the reluctance will be maintained. In addition, the client's feeling of self and self-expression must be dealt with in the counseling process. The reluctant client's major interest is the self. Therefore, almost any technique that enhances the client's self-understanding will serve to reduce or lower the reluctance.

Reluctance should be dealt with as it comes up in counseling. As in dealing with any other deeply felt issue, you will need to help the client gain an understanding of the reluctance, become aware of this reluctance, and take steps to deal with it in an effective manner. You must be in touch with the client, acknowledge his or her feelings, and possibly interpret the client's behaviors. This interpretation could be done in ways similar to the following: "Silence helps you feel more comfortable, and discussing issues that are of concern to you appears to be too painful"; "Your reluctance to discuss this important topic may be saying to both of us that you are quite comfortable in staying where you are"; or "Your not wanting to discuss the important issues appears to be counterproductive." Ritchie (1994) suggests using a variety of techniques, including puppets, media or stories, paradox and reframing, and modeling and role playing, to help overcome reluctance among schoolchildren. Counselors can anticipate how they will work with reluctant clients by simulating these cases before they occur with role-playing and role-reversal techniques.

Strategies that go beyond those used within the typical dyadic counseling process are frequently very helpful when working with reluctant clients. Many effective strategies have been developed to work with clients who manifest ill-advised behaviors (Brown, Pryzwansky, & Schulte, 1995; Kottler, 1992). In order to help clients overcome some self-defeating behaviors, you may need to work with significant other persons in the client's world. Modification of the client's environment may be helpful, and other resource persons also may be useful.

The Resistant but Committed Client

The resistant client is typically one who volunteered to come for help, entered into the relationship, and became at least superficially involved in the counseling process but is unwilling to change his or her feelings, thoughts, or overt behaviors. This resistance to reach a decision, to recognize symptoms, or to give up self-defeating activities is counterproductive for the client and quite frustrating for the counselor. Some believe that resistance is pervasive throughout all counseling and therefore present to some extent with every client (Peterson & Nisenholz, 1995). As a counselor-in-training you should become aware of the reasons for client resistance, discover how to anticipate it, and learn how to handle it.

Committed clients may be resistant for many reasons. Many clients are afraid to examine themselves and issues related to their concerns. Learning about oneself and taking the steps to change self-defeating thoughts, feelings, or behaviors can be threatening. Some clients are unsure of themselves and do not feel a sense of complete trust and confidence in the relationship. Others may fear change—they are aware of where they are at the present time and are scared to modify their lifestyle. Still others may not know what is expected of them in the counseling process and may passively expect some spontaneous resolution to occur.

Resistance often is not a conscious attempt to thwart the counseling process, but it is a real barrier to progress. The resistance to avoid dealing with the issues and doing any hard work takes many forms: some clients are silent, some appear very tired and listless, some act quite forgetful or evasive, some hide behind a barrage of words, and some become defensive or argumentative.

As a counselor you can learn to deal with this resistance when clients manifest it. First, you must anticipate that it may occur, and you must not become anxious or defensive or try to placate your client. You should perceive the resistance as a sign of what your client is ready to work on and not ready to work on. Second, you need to continue showing a warm, caring, and concerned interest in your client. Take time to deepen your relationship and enhance the trusting climate. Third, remain patient and calm and do not get distracted. Don't become discouraged or give up trying to work through the problem. Fourth, try to understand what is causing the resistance: Is there an overt or covert payoff for the client if he or she does not change, or are there significant disadvantages that may occur if he or she does? And finally, deal with the resistance in a constructive and helpful way.

There are several alternative ways to handle resistance positively. If the resistance is relatively mild, it may be best to ignore it and move ahead. If the resistance is more serious, you may wish to downplay it and direct the client to move ahead with the next step in the counseling process. If the client is highly anxious and fearful of moving forward, however, humor, reframing, and diversionary tactics may be useful. Gladding (1996) and Roloff and Miller (1980) suggest that it is helpful to have clients take steps to do something quite minor and then something quite major, or to ask them to do something impossible and then something quite reasonable. Either way, some action is accomplished and a resistance block may be broken. Another way to handle this situation is by confrontation. Help the client understand the resistance, point out the conflicts and contradictions that are present, and use this to help your client become aware of this resistance as part of the counseling process.

SOURCES OF INFORMATION ABOUT THE CLIENT

The purpose of this section is to describe several important ways that counselors typically obtain information about clients. Although the primary means of obtaining information about the client is through the verbal interchange between the client and the counselor, information is often obtained before and during the counseling process in a variety of other ways. The most common methods are (1) prior personal knowledge of the client, (2) reports from significant others, (3) life-history questionnaires, (4) environmental or situational observations, (5) observations of nonverbal behaviors, and (6) psychometric data. Each of these data collection techniques and resources is discussed briefly in the following sections.

Personal knowledge of the client.

Counselors sometimes know their clients before beginning the counseling process. Many counselors work in institutional settings such as schools, colleges, or residential treatment programs and have previously met clients and observed them in a variety of situations within the institutional setting. This prior knowledge can minimize the amount of time spent on the relationship-building stage and often facilitates the exploratory stage. As a counselor, you should acknowledge this previous information early in the counseling process in order to ensure that the interpretations of these previous observations are valid and known to both the client and the counselor.

Reports from significant others.

Reports about the client may be written or verbal, brief or extensive, and may come from people who have known the client either in a professional or in a personal relationship. One of the more common forms is a report written by another professional person. These reports vary in the type and extent of information supplied. One example is a minimally informative school anecdotal record, such as "John was quiet in the sixth grade." Another is an informative referral from a teacher, such as "John is failing in sixth grade. He can respond well to verbal questions; however, on written tasks he responds poorly. I suspect his auditory learning style is good but his visual one is poor. Can you pursue this matter with John and/or his parents?" Another example is a rather extensive psychological report concerning the client's past behavior and the prognosis for his or her future.

Life-history questionnaires.

Many counseling agencies require new clients to complete a life-history questionnaire prior to the initial or intake interview. The purpose of this questionnaire is to obtain a comprehensive picture of the client's background and to facilitate the exploratory process. These questionnaires probe into the client's background and often inquire about the following areas:

- general information: name, age, sex, height, weight
- residential data: address, phone number, living environment
- familial data: marital status, children, parents, siblings
- educational data: schools attended, years of attendance, major
- occupational history: jobs held and companies worked for
- avocational interests: hobbies, sports, civic activities
- history of physical health: previous illnesses and accidents, present health status, medication currently taken
- the presenting problem: its history and any previous counseling experience

A life-history questionnaire may be relatively short or quite long and extensive depending on the philosophy of the agency.

Environmental or situational observations.

To gain a better understanding of their clients, counselors often see their clients in the environment that is related to the clients' concerns. This is particularly true for counselors who work in institutional settings as well as for those who work in marital counseling. For example, counselors visit the classroom to see how a child or student is functioning with his or her peers in that room; rehabilitation counselors visit the sheltered workshop to see how a rehabilitation plan is working; and marriage counselors frequently see a couple together and also schedule sessions when the entire family can be present.

Observations of nonverbal behaviors.

As part of the observation process counselors need to pay close attention to nonverbal behaviors to gain a better understanding of their clients. As you know from your own personal experience, body language often says as much as or more than an individual's verbal expressions. One's body language can confirm, emphasize, minimize, or contradict what is said verbally. It can reveal attempts to control what one says or does not say. And facial expressions or physiological responses can reveal emotional reactions to the topics under discussion and can give clues about the client's self-concept. Some nonverbal behaviors you should pay attention to include:

- automatic body reactions such as change of facial color (blushing or turning pale) and pace of breathing
- facial expressions and body movements such as smiles, frowns, eye movements, and gestures
- general appearance such as dress, grooming, and posture
- physical characteristics such as height, weight, general fitness, and complexion

You need to be sensitive to the meaning of these nonverbal behaviors and interpret them in the context of the conversation and the environment where they occur.

Psychometric data.

Standardized tests provide an objective and standardized methodology that counselors in various settings often use. These instruments are employed for four different reasons.

First, they are used to identify individuals who can benefit from the counseling process. Counselors who work in institutional settings are responsible for counseling large numbers of individuals, so they use various screening inventories or checklists for identifying clients who can most benefit from counseling.

Second, counselors use psychological instruments to help clients see an objective picture of their strengths and limitations. For example, school and rehabilitation counselors administer and interpret scholastic aptitude tests, achievement tests, and interest inventories so that their clients can compare themselves to others objectively and gain further insight into their educational and vocational development.

Third, counselors use tests to measure the growth of individuals or groups of individuals over time or to see if a particular counseling intervention facilitated a particular growth. For example, a school counselor may give an interest inventory to a student before vocational counseling and again after the counseling to see if the individual's interests have changed as a result of the counseling process.

Fourth, counselors sometimes use tests to gain knowledge about the counseling process by comparing the relative efficacy of two or more counseling approaches or interventions. For example, a vocational counselor may wish to research whether biblio-therapy (reading about occupations) is a more effective treatment than seeing role models or hearing lectures by experts. To investigate this question, the counselor would set up an appropriate experimental study to find the answer.

SUMMARY

This chapter has outlined the characteristics of the counseling process as it progresses through the five transitional development stages. The chapter also provided some important concepts for working with resistant and reluctant clients. In addition, six different sources that counselors often use to obtain information about their clients were briefly presented. After reading and studying this chapter you should be able to identify the five transitional counseling stages and discuss the major characteristics of each stage. You should be able to discuss the differences between reluctant and resistant clients. And you should be able to describe the advantages and limitations of the six different sources of information about clients.

REFERENCES

Brammer, L. M., & MacDonald, G. (1996). *The helping relationship: Process and skills* (6th ed.). Boston: Allyn & Bacon.

Brown, D., Pryzwansky, W. B., & Schulte, A. C. (1995). *Psychological consultation: Introduction to theory and practice* (3rd ed.). Boston: Allyn & Bacon.

Burke, J. F. (1989). *Contemporary approaches to psychotherapy and counseling: The self-regulation and maturity model.* Pacific Grove, CA: Brooks/Cole.

Cormier, L. S., & Hackney, H. (1996). *The professional counselor: A process guide to helping* (3rd ed.). Boston: Allyn & Bacon.

Day, R. W., & Sparacio, R. T. (1980). Structuring the counseling process. *Personnel and Guidance Journal, 59,* 246–249.

Dyer, W. W., & Vriend, J. (1988). *Counseling techniques that work.* Alexandria, VA: American Counseling Association.

Egan, G. (1994). *The skilled helper: A problem-management approach to helping* (5th ed.). Pacific Grove, CA: Brooks/Cole.

Gladding, S. T. (1996). *Counseling: A comprehensive profession* (3rd ed.). Columbus, OH: Merrill.

Hansen, J. C., Rossberg, R. H., & Cramer, S. H. (1994). *Counseling: Theory and process* (5th ed.). Boston: Allyn & Bacon.

Ivey, A. E., Ivey, M. B., & Simek-Morgan, L. (1997). *Counseling and psychotherapy: A multicultural perspective* (4th ed.). Boston: Allyn & Bacon.

Kottler, J. A. (1992). *Compassionate therapy.* San Francisco: Jossey-Bass.

Lerner, R. M. (1986). *Concepts and theories of human development* (2nd ed.). New York: McGraw-Hill.

Okun, B. F. (1997). *Effective helping* (5th ed.). Pacific Grove, CA: Brooks/Cole.

Patterson, L. E., & Welfel, E. R. (1994). *The counseling process* (4th ed.). Pacific Grove, CA: Brooks/Cole.

Peterson, J. V., & Nisenholz, B. (1995). *Orientation to counseling* (3rd ed.). Boston: Allyn & Bacon.

Ritchie, M. H. (1994). Counselling difficult children. *Canadian Journal of Counseling, 28,* 58–68.

Roloff, M. E., & Miller, G. R. (Eds.). (1980). *Persuasion: New directions in theory and research.* Beverly Hills, CA: Sage Publications.

Turiel, E. (1969). Developmental processes in the child's moral thinking. In P. H. Mussen, J. Langer, & M. Covington (Eds.), *Trends and issues in developmental psychology* (pp. 92–133). New York: Holt, Rinehart and Winston.

Waehler, C. A., & Lenox, R. A. (1994). A concurrent (versus stage) model for conceptualizing and representing the counseling process. *Journal of Counseling and Development, 73,* 17–22.

Ward, D. E. (1984). Termination of individual counseling: Concepts and strategies. *Journal of Counseling and Development, 63,* 21–25.

PART 2

How Counselors Help Individuals Change: Counseling Intervention Strategies

The beginning student in the field of counseling is often bewildered by the sheer number and the conceptual diversity of approaches to counseling. This confusion can be resolved in one of three ways. One way is to focus on one and only one theoretical approach and practice it until you become an expert in using that approach. The counselor-in-training who follows this method will become identified with a particular theory such as a person-centered counselor, a trait-factor counselor, or a behavioral counselor. A second way is to focus on one theory or approach, practice it until some basic competencies are achieved, and then go on to develop some skills using another theory. Thus, you can learn to counsel by mimicking Rogers, then perhaps Perls or Ellis or Lazarus, until you become familiar with a variety of approaches. In this training modality, the counselor trainee is faced with the responsibility of mastering a variety of schools and learning to employ a particular model for a particular client need. This is the menu approach to the counseling process. A third way is to formulate a unified conceptual model that slowly but systematically integrates ideas and techniques from all the major approaches as you develop you own counseling style and modality.

This section of the book discusses contemporary approaches to integrating various counseling approaches; provides a rationale for working with clients from the cognitive, the affective, and the behavioral modalities; and outlines important counseling intervention strategies based on these modalities. Chapter 4 delineates several important cognitively focused interventions. Chapter 5 is devoted to a discussion of the major affectively focused interventions. And Chapter 6 describes the counseling interventions based upon behaviorally focused modalities.

CONTEMPORARY THEORETICAL DEVELOPMENTS

There is ample evidence in the literature that various counseling approaches have merit and that one theory or approach is not superior to all others (Cormier & Cormier, 1991; Frank & Frank, 1991; Strupp, 1982). Most helpers use a variety of approaches

(Corey, 1996; Norcross & Prochaska, 1988). Several indications in the counseling field point to a trend toward developing a pantheoretical, or more universal or united, approach to the helping process. First, increased emphasis has been placed on teaching beginning counselors a repertoire of communication skills that are useful in different stages of counseling and in a variety of approaches to the counseling process (Doyle, 1982; Egan, 1994; Evans, Hearn, Uhlemann, & Ivey, 1993; Hill, 1978; Ivey, Ivey, & Simek-Morgan, 1997; Kagan, 1972). Second, there is a greater focus on learning theory and more awareness of the role and importance of the client's motivation, self-expectations, and self-attributions as essential ingredients to the process of change (Frank & Frank, 1991; Kanfer & Gaelick-Buys, 1991; Linehan & O'Toole, 1982). Third, there is a general consensus that counseling is based on developing a sound interpersonal relationship and employing sound technical strategic interventions (Frank & Frank, 1991; Strupp, 1982; Waehler & Lenox, 1994). Fourth, efforts have been made to organize the many theoretical approaches into meaningful taxonomies of intervention strategies (Frey & Raming, 1979; Hutchins, 1979; L'Abate, 1981). Finally, there is considerable discussion in the literature about the feasibility of developing an integrated approach to the helping process (Erskine & Moursund, 1988; Goldfried, 1982; Goldfried, Castonguary, & Safran, 1992; Patterson, 1985; Prochaska & Norcross, 1994).

CHANGE IS A NATURAL OCCURRENCE

Clients do not change in mysterious ways. In fact, change is a dynamic and normal part of our everyday existence—we grow, develop, and modify our behavior. The following examples illustrate twelve distinct ways in which change can and does occur.

1. *Receiving direct instructions.* People respond to direct instructions and factual information. For example, the Postal Service reminds us to mail our letters early at Christmastime with the admonition "Mail Early!"; and on the ski slope, the ski instructor is heard saying, "Keep your weight on the downhill ski."

2. *Learning how to make choices.* Choosing between and among alternative courses of action is important in our everyday lives. Individuals must learn to weigh the alternatives, consider the advantages and disadvantages, and recognize and accept some degree of risk in every choice. Examples of some major choices that affect our behavior include the college sophomore asking "What shall I major in?" and the newlywed couple pondering "What neighborhood should we live in?"

3. *Learning how to think deductively.* Thoughts and beliefs can and do influence our emotions and our daily activities. Consequently, thoughts that are based on a faulty reasoning process lead to faulty conclusions and perceptions; thus, we can change by learning to think more logically. For example, the statement "I am no good" may be based on the two premises "I have difficulty doing something" and "People who have difficulty doing something are no good"; thus, "I am no good." In this case, the error in the second premise needs to be pointed out and emphasized so that the individual can reason more logically.

4. *Discussing an issue with someone you respect.* A discussion of one's thoughts, feelings, or frustrations can often help a person change. For example, when you are very angry or feeling a deep loss, a close friend can provide the atmosphere for you to air your concern and thus talk out the anger or the depression.

5. *Gaining more insight.* Helping individuals look at themselves in a way that promotes self-knowledge can influence how they think, feel, or act. For example, the student who becomes aware of the fact that certain actions have a negative effect on others should gain some feeling that his or her behavior ought to change.

6. *Enhancing one's self-esteem.* People who have more self-confidence and positive feelings about themselves are more likely to behave assertively than those who have a poor self-image. For example, the young man who has a good self-image is more likely to have positive interpersonal relationships than the individual who has a poorer self-image.

7. *Watching another person.* When an individual observes another person perform, that individual is likely to replicate that behavior. For example, tennis students carefully watch their tennis coach, and counselors-in-training want to see an expert, such as their instructor, perform.

8. *Drilling and practicing.* Performing a new activity over and over again until it is part of our repertoire is one way to ensure that a particular action is likely to be repeated. For example, an individual who is unsure of his or her performance in a potential job interview will practice or role-play an imaginary interview until more confidence is gained.

9. *Changing the environment.* Individuals can increase the probability that they will act in a certain way by changing the conditions under which the activity takes place. For example, when an individual is studying for a final examination, he or she probably wants to remove distracting cues by studying in a quiet place. Another example is the person who wants to stop smoking—he or she does not buy cigarettes and does not associate with people who smoke.

10. *Learning how to reduce anxiety.* Some individuals are unable to do certain things because a great deal of anxiety is associated with that particular situation. By learning how to reduce the anxiety, they can be freer to act. For example, students can be taught to relax before taking an examination, or employees can be taught to think of pleasant scenes when they have to do something anxiety provoking at work.

11. *Receiving positive feedback.* When an individual acts in a positive way and receives praise for that endeavor, that behavior is likely to be repeated in the future. For example, the counselor-in-training who is told by a group of peers or a supervisor that a particular skill was performed well will be apt to use that skill again under similar circumstances.

12. *Receiving negative feedback.* When people do things that cause others to frown or look down on them, then they are likely to avoid acting that way in the future. For example, the young boy who picks up an ashtray may be admonished by his parents with the sharp words "No, No!" or the student who doesn't hand in his or her homework on time may receive a demerit. The vocal rebuff and the demerit are forms of punishment that are used to decrease the likelihood

of those behaviors. Although negative feedback can be effective, too much negative feedback can enhance feelings of inadequacy, so it should be used very sparingly.

THE THREE DOMAINS OF FUNCTIONING

Human beings are in a dynamic interactive relationship between themselves and their environment. Individuals strive to maintain their equilibrium throughout experiences that bring about constant changes and adaptations. Everyone learns new things and begins to think, feel, believe, and behave differently as a result of interactions with societal or environmental influences. Because individuals are unique, the influence that societal forces have varies with their patterns of interactions and their striving for equilibrium. Individuals change in a variety of ways and for unique reasons.

Historically, counseling strategies or interventions were classified using two-dimensional and linear formats. In the fifties and early sixties the directive versus nondirective dichotomous scale was in vogue. This was replaced by the rational-affective framework discussed by Barkley (1968), Patterson and Watkins (1995), and Shertzer and Stone (1980) and employed by Frey (1972) in the analytical goal and process taxonomy.

Hutchins (1979) and L'Abate (1981) have maintained that counseling theories need to be viewed from a three-dimensional construct. Hutchins used the terms *thinking, feeling,* and *acting* for his T-F-A model, which classifies theories into various combinations of these modalities depending on the primary counseling intervention. Thus, Rogers is seen as an F-A-T (feeling-acting-thinking) or F-T-A (feeling-thinking-acting) counselor, whereas Ellis is considered to be a T-A-F (thinking-acting-feeling) or T-F-A (thinking-feeling-acting) interventionist. L'Abate presented a very similar eclectic model. It uses the terms *emotionality, rationality,* and *activity,* and hence is labeled the E-R-A model. This model classifies theorists using a process and goal format and comes to slightly different conclusions on the placement of various theoreticians.

Strupp (1982) pointed out that the therapeutic process is essentially a tutorial, collaborative, educational one and that success in therapy should be demonstrable in one or more of three functioning domains—that is, in the client's mental functioning, sense of emotional well-being, and social functioning or behavioral activities.

The three major interactive functioning domains should not be used only to classify theorists and to measure the success of the counseling process. They can and should be used in understanding a client's functioning status and in suggesting a meaningful taxonomy for classification of counseling interventions. Thus, the specific strategies or technical interventions that counselors employ may be described as cognitively focused, affectively focused, or performance focused. These three domains are illustrated in the diagram that follows.

It is important to note and realize that changes in one of these domains can have an effect on one or both of the other domains. Therefore, when we alter the way we think about something, we normally change the way we feel about it and the way we behave toward it. Similarly, when we change the way we feel about somebody, we usually alter

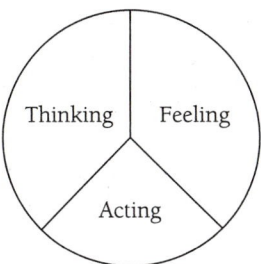

The major domains of functioning

the way we think about and act toward that person. The same is true for the third domain; that is, when we change the way we behave, modifications occur in our thinking and feeling domains as well.

THE COUNSELOR'S ROLE

The counselor's role in helping individuals change is to facilitate these natural avenues. Counselors, by definition of this role, interject themselves into their clients' interactive relationship with their environment and attempt to facilitate natural growth and the dynamic process. The major goals of the counseling process are to assist clients in overcoming impediments to change and in becoming more self-directed and to facilitate both psychological independence and interdependence, so that clients are free to act for their own good as well as the good of society.

In the process of understanding these technical interventions or counseling strategies, it is essential for counselors-in-training to be aware that three important concepts underlie all interventions: the professional working relationship between the counselor and the client; the counselor's linguistic and communication skills; and the client's motivation, expectations, and self-attributions. Furthermore, it must be noted that interventions are rarely used alone; more often counselors use multimodal approaches that employ strategies from the cognitive and affective as well as the performance domains.

Specific intervention techniques based on cognitive, affective, and performance concepts are outlined in the following three chapters.

MULTICULTURAL CONSIDERATIONS

While learning these intervention techniques you should be sensitive to the cultural issues that can affect the counseling process. Locke and Parker (1994) discuss seven dimensions that counselors should be mindful of in order to provide effective services to culturally diverse clients. Being attentive to these seven aspects is really the first step of a

lifelong learning process. Culturally sensitive counselors will continually strive to become more competent in each of these areas. The seven dimensions are:

1. self-awareness;
2. awareness of one's own cultural background;
3. awareness of the presence of racism, sexism, and poverty in our society;
4. awareness of individual differences;
5. awareness of other cultures;
6. awareness of the diversity within and among cultures; and
7. awareness of professionally solid skills and techniques.

In learning to apply the interventions and techniques outlined in the following
three chapters, you will need to take your client's cultural background into consideration and to respect your client's beliefs and values—which may be different from your
own. Avoid premature judgments and stereotyping of any client according to cultural
characteristics, and remember also that there is wide diversity within and among all
cultural groups. When applying these strategies and interventions keep in mind that an
individual's cultural background can influence the counseling process and the type of
independence that individual manifests. For example, clients from some cultures may:

• expect the counseling process to be highly structured and solution oriented
  rather than unstructured and emotionally oriented;
• encourage indirect rather than direct forms of communication;
• interpret the expression of feelings as a sign of personal weakness;
• foster a very high degree of respect for parents, teachers, and all authority
  figures—including all counselors;
• promote a high degree of respect for—and want conformity to—family
  traditions and expectations;
• perceive individuals to be selfish if they concentrate on self-determination
  rather than emphasizing what is best for the family or the group;
• be averse to the exploration and open discussion of personal problems and
  family issues outside the family constellation; and
• inhibit the display of assertive behaviors.

As you learn to develop your counseling skills, seek out opportunities to work
under supervision with clients from diverse populations. Learn to be comfortable with
the differences between yourself and others who have another cultural heritage. You will
need to discover how to be flexible, to become aware of the cultural influences that affect
your clients, and to learn how to modify and adapt your techniques to meet their needs.

REFERENCES

Barkley, J. (1968). Counseling and philosophy: A theoretical exposition. In B. Shertzer &
    S. C. Stone (Eds.), *Guidance Monograph Series, Series II: Counseling*. Boston: Houghton
    Mifflin.
Corey, G. (1996). *Theory and practice of counseling and psychotherapy* (5th ed.). Pacific Grove, CA:
    Brooks/Cole.

Cormier. W., & Cormier, L. S. (1991). *Interviewing strategies for helpers: Fundamental skills and cognitive behavioral interventions* (3rd ed.). Pacific Grove, CA: Brooks/Cole.

Doyle, R. E. (1982). The counselor's role in communication skills: The roles counselors play. *Counselor Education and Supervision, 22,* 123–131.

Egan, G. (1994). *The skilled helper: A problem-management approach to helping* (5th ed.). Pacific Grove, CA: Brooks/Cole.

Erskine, R., & Moursund, J. (1988). *Integrative psychotherapy in action.* Newbury Park, CA: Sage Publications.

Evans, D. R., Hearn, M. T., Uhlemann, M. R., & Ivey, A. E. (1993). *Essential interviewing: A programmed approach to effective communication* (3rd ed.). Pacific Grove, CA: Brooks/Cole.

Frank, J. D., & Frank, J. (1991). *Persuasion and healing* (3rd ed.). Baltimore: Johns Hopkins Press.

Frey, D. H. (1972). Conceptualizing counseling theories: A content analysis of process and goal statements. *Counselor Education and Supervision, 11,* 243–250.

Frey, D. H., & Raming, H. E. (1979). A taxonomy of counseling goals and methods. *Personnel and Guidance Journal, 58,* 26–33.

Goldfried, M. R. (Ed.). (1982). *Converging themes in psychotherapy: Trends in psychodynamic, humanistic, and behavioral practice.* New York: Springer.

Goldfried, M. R., Castonguary, L. G., & Safran. J. D. (1992). Core issues and future directions in psychotherapy integration. In J. C. Norcross & M. R. Goldfried (Eds.), *Handbook of psychotherapy integration.* New York: Basic Books.

Hill, C. E. (1978). Development of a counselor verbal response category system. *Journal of Counseling Psychology, 25,* 461–468.

Hutchins, D. E. (1979). Systematic counseling: The T-F-A model for counselor intervention. *Personnel and Guidance Journal, 57,* 529–531.

Ivey, A. E., Ivey, M. B., & Simek-Morgan, L. (1997). *Counseling and psychotherapy: A multicultural perspective* (4th ed.). Boston: Allyn & Bacon.

Kagan, N. (1972). *Influencing human interaction.* Unpublished manuscript. Michigan State University.

Kanfer, F. H., & Gaelick-Buys, L. (1991). Self-management methods. In F. H. Kanfer & A. P. Goldstein (Eds.), *Helping people change* (4th ed.) (pp. 305–360). New York: Pergamon.

L'Abate, L. (1981). Classification of counseling and therapy: Theorists, methods, processes, and goals: The E-R-A model. *Personnel and Guidance Journal, 59,* 263–265.

Linehan, E., & O'Toole, J. (1982). Effect of subliminal stimulation of symbolic fantasies on college student self-disclosure in group counseling. *Journal of Counseling Psychology, 29,* 151–157.

Locke, D. C., & Parker, L. D. (1994). Improving the multicultural competence of educators. In P. Pedersen & J. C. Carey (Eds.), *Multicultural counseling in schools* (pp. 39–58). Boston: Allyn & Bacon.

Norcross, J. C., & Prochaska, J. O. (1988). A study of eclectic (and integrative) views revisited. *Professional Psychology: Research and Practice, 19,* 170–174.

Patterson, C. H. (1985). *The therapeutic relationship: Foundations for an eclectic psychotherapy.* Pacific Grove, CA: Brooks/Cole.

Patterson, C. H., & Watkins, C. E. (1995). *Theories of counseling and psychotherapy* (5th ed.). Reading, MA: Addison-Wesley.

Prochaska, J. O., & Norcross, J. C. (1994). *Systems of psychotherapy: A transtheoretical analysis* (3rd ed.). Pacific Grove, CA: Brooks/Cole.

Shertzer, B., & Stone, S. C. (1980). *Fundamentals of counseling* (3rd ed.). Boston: Houghton Mifflin.

Strupp, H. H. (1982). The outcome problem in psychotherapy: Contemporary perspectives. In
    J. H. Harvey & M. M. Parks (Eds.), *Psychotherapy research and behavior change* (Vol. 1, pp.
    39–71). Washington, DC: American Psychological Association.
Waehler, C. A., & Lenox, R. A. (1994). A concurrent (versus stage) model for conceptualizing
    and representing the counseling process. *Journal of Counseling and Development, 73,*
    17–22.

Cognitively Focused Counseling Strategies

INTRODUCTION

Four distinctive cognitively focused intervention strategies are presented in this chapter. These approaches can be seen as educative in nature since they help clients learn to do things in new or different ways. They have rather clearly outlined techniques that, when used in appropriate situations, should bring about desired client goals. After studying this chapter you should be able to:

- discuss three ways that you can help clients acquire and retain factual information,
- describe how you might help a client learn the decision-making process,
- identify the characteristics that might indicate poor logical thinking on the part of a client,
- outline the steps that you might take to help clients restructure their thought processes, and
- name several ways that you could help a client think more analogously, inductively, or creatively.

Cognitively focused counseling strategies are based on the notion that individuals are rational beings whose cognitive and mediational processes influence all aspects of their ability to function. Consequently, counselors who want to help their clients change in significant ways need to use strategies that focus on the cognitive domain. This chapter discusses four major ways to work with clients from a cognitive point of view. These four approaches help clients (1) acquire and retain accurate and relevant factual information; (2) learn how to choose among various courses of action to make satisfactory decisions and solve problems; (3) learn how to think logically about themselves and the world around them; and (4) learn how to use their resources in creative, imaginative, and inventive ways. Each of these approaches contains different intervention strategies. This chapter outlines those strategies, suggests when these interventions ought to be used, and makes specific recommendations on how to employ these techniques.

ACQUIRING AND RETAINING FACTUAL KNOWLEDGE
Basic Concept

One major cognitive approach that is often employed, particularly by counselors who work in schools, colleges, and community agency settings, is helping clients acquire and retain factual information. Three specific strategies are used in this approach. These strategies help clients

- learn more about educational and vocational opportunities,
- increase their knowledge about themselves by understanding the results of psychometric instruments, and
- develop the skills necessary to manage the learning process more effectively.

Each of these strategies is discussed in this section. They may be used alone or combined with other interventions to help individuals resolve issues and solve problems.

Educational and Vocational Information

One of the critical developmental issues that students face is the need for vocational selection and career development (Zunker, 1994). Similarly, many adults need assistance in seeking employment opportunities and career information (Lea & Leibowitz, 1992). In fact, career development is considered to be a lifelong process (Herr & Cramer, 1992). Career counseling can be defined as the process of helping an individual, or a group of individuals, with appropriate vocational development tasks at any point throughout life— in other words, vocational counseling may be concerned with helping people prepare for, make choices about, enter into, adjust to, succeed in, or retire from active involvement in the world of work. Three divisions of the American Counseling Association are directly concerned with assisting individuals who face career developmental issues: the National Career Development Association (NCDA), the National Employment Counseling Association (NECA), and the American Rehabilitation Counseling Association.

The choice of an occupation is one of the major decisions an individual makes in life. It affects the economic, psychological, and sociological activities of the individual. Economically, it determines certain financial rewards and, as Hoppock (1976) has pointed out, whether one will experience employment or unemployment, satisfaction or dissatisfaction, and success or failure. In the psychological and sociological domains, one's occupation provides a sense of identity and offers status and prestige; it strongly influences the selection of friends, leisure-time activities, who one marries, where one lives, and how one's children are educated.

One of the many interventions that all counselors should be aware of, and many will be called upon to provide, is to assist clients in obtaining relevant educational and occupational information. Practical information should be provided to students and clients to help them discover the variety of occupations available in our society; the similarities and differences among various occupations; what economic and psychological rewards are provided by different occupations; whether an occupation is increasing or decreasing in the number of people it employs; what individuals actually do in various occupations; the qualifications necessary for entry-level positions in specific occupations; how one advances; and how particular occupations affect other dimensions of life.

Hoppock (1976), Isaacson and Brown (1993), and Zunker (1994) have all stressed the importance of counselors having an adequate and appropriate file of educational and occupational information. In general, they suggest that the counselor's file contain the following items:

Government publications such as the *Occupational Outlook Handbook, Occupational Outlook Quarterly, Dictionary of Occupational Titles,* and the *Standard Occupational Classification Manual.*

Up-to-date files of pamphlets on occupations, careers, and educational information. This material is probably best obtained by purchasing a complete set from one of the principal publishers of occupational information such as Careers, Chronicle Guidance Publications, and Science Research Associations. These publishers also provide a subscription service for keeping the file current.

Bulletins and directories that are related to the educational and vocational interests of students and clients. These directories may include such items as bulletins for various colleges and educational programs, directories of trade unions and employers, and the local telephone book.

Computer software now contains considerable educational and occupational information. For example, the *Guidance Information System* (GIS) (1996) provides a procedure for obtaining national and local educational and occupational information through a time-sharing process. Another program, *ExPan* (1996), presents information on careers, colleges, financial aid, and scholarships. Other examples are the *DISCOVER* (1996) program and *SIGI PLUS* (1996), which provide systematic approaches for the career exploration process. These programs are available in software packages for use with most of the popular desktop computers. Counselors who have computers and microcomputers should become familiar with the resources available in this medium. For a further discussion of this area, readers are referred to Isaacson and Brown (1993), Maze and Cummings (1982), Sampson and Reardon (1990), and Zunker (1994).

Publications and resource materials from the National Occupational Information Coordinating Committee (NOICC) and the local State Occupational Information Coordinating Committee (SOICC). NOICC, established by Congress in 1976, has the responsibility to develop and share occupational information at the national, state, and local levels, and to foster the development and growth of parallel committees at the state level. Furthermore, NOICC has promulgated guidelines for the development of career guidance standards at the state and local levels. School counselors need to keep up with the activities of NOICC as well their local SOICC.

The vast amount of educational and occupational information available will preclude you from having detailed knowledge about many occupations or educational programs. Consequently, you will rarely provide clients with the required information during an actual counseling interview. As a counselor who is concerned with the career development of your clients, you will need to become familiar with the available career guidance resource materials and computer software packages. Furthermore, you should be able to instruct your clients in how to get this information so that it can be discussed in further sessions. The instructional process should include a discussion of appropriate resource materials, how the information can be obtained, how the material can be used by the client, and a timetable for accomplishing the search. Whenever possible, you should show the client how to use the resource library or the computer program or both.

The career development of individuals is facilitated by helping clients ascertain the implications of educational choices, the realities of the world of work, and the environmental factors that influence educational and vocational trends. Assisting clients in obtaining educational and vocational information includes accomplishing the activities specified in the following steps:

1. Orient clients to the availability of educational and vocational information. This should involve a discussion of:
   a. Educational and vocational opportunities that are available
   b. Sources of meaningful and reliable information
   c. Specific factors one should look for in seeking appropriate information

2. Help clients focus on several specific educational or vocational possibilities that they would like to investigate. This can be done in a variety of ways, including having clients:
   a. Provide a self-generated list
   b. Brainstorm with the counselor
   c. Take an interest inventory

3. Explain to clients that specific details are important and necessary to learn about each opportunity. For example, if clients are seeking information about a specific occupation, they should obtain information on the occupation's:
   a. Outlook
   b. Qualifications
   c. Rewards
   d. Work environment
   e. On-the-job activities
   f. Entrance requirements
   g. Advantages and disadvantages

4. Advise clients about the availability of resource materials on occupations and the world of work. This includes:
   a. Educational and occupational files
   b. Brochures, pamphlets, and books
   c. Computer programs
   d. Audio and visual resources
   e. Interviews with original sources

5. Help clients activate their search by providing:
   a. Instruction on how to use the resource materials
   b. Help in understanding the content of the information available
   c. Continued encouragement and positive feedback

6. Assist clients in examining this material in light of other needs. Clients need to assess this information in light of their:
   a. Background
   b. Aspirations
   c. Needs
   d. Decision-making skills
7. After a client has had the opportunity to evaluate this factual material, one of three outcomes is possible:
   a. The information is sufficient and the client needs no other help at this time
   b. Further information is necessary and the client needs continued help in obtaining it
   c. The information appears sufficient at this time, but the client needs help in decision-making skills or with some other problem

Counselors who work in school settings are called upon to be the experts in the school's developmental career guidance program. Thus, in addition to helping students on an individual or group basis, you may be expected to design and implement a career guidance program that incorporates into the curriculum appropriate career information and decision-making skills. Counselors who work with clients on career decisions need to be thoroughly familiar with the contemporary theories of vocational development. An excellent summary of these theories is presented in Osipow and Fitzgerald (1996). And on a more pragmatic level, counselors should keep abreast of the latest career guidance materials available from NOICC and their local SOICC.

Interpretation of Psychometric Data

In addition to helping clients obtain good educational and vocational information, counselors often must assist clients who want to learn more about themselves and their characteristic traits. This process can be facilitated by employing appropriate psychometric instruments and interpreting these results in ways that are useful to clients. As a counselor you may or may not be involved in the administration of these instruments. That will depend on your theoretical orientation and your place of employment. Nevertheless, because of the importance of these psychological tools, you need to have a good understanding of testing theory and how to use tests in the counseling process. Before you discuss any psychological test result with a client, you should be thoroughly familiar with the instrument. You must know the validity and reliability of specific instruments; the types of scores that are available; and how to select, administer, and interpret appropriate tests. Important aspects of these concepts are presented in this section; however, a further discussion of these may be found in Anastasi and Urbina (1997), Cronbach (1990), Lyman (1991), Mehrens and Lehmann (1991), and Walsh and Betz (1994).

Validity. The most important characteristic of a psychological test is its *validity*—that is, the degree to which it measures what it is intended to measure. A test may be valid for one situation (when it is used for the purpose it was designed for) and not valid in another situation (when it is used for a purpose it was not designed for). Validity can be and is expressed in several different ways: face validity, content validity, construct validity, and concurrent or predictive validity.

Face validity is a term that is used when a test looks like it assesses what it claims to measure. Technically speaking, the term has nothing to do with whether or not the instrument does what it is purported to do. It is a useful notion, however, because people are more apt to take a test seriously if it appears to do what it is supposed to do. This type of validity is based on the opinion of the user and is purely subjective.

Content validity is a phrase that is employed when the instrument assesses a representative sample of the subject matter that it intends to measure. This type of validity is established by examining whether the items on the test truly represent an appropriate sample of the content areas. It is most often used when the domain or the universe of the subject matter is clearly defined. For example, standardized tests of academic achievement should have good content validity because academic subject areas are fairly well established. Test batteries that use this construct include the Stanford Achievement Test Battery and the Iowa Tests of Basic Skills.

Construct validity is the type of validity that is used when the instrument measures a theoretical psychological construct. This sort of validity is determined by examining the test to see if the items are logically consistent with the theory underlying the construct. The concepts of intelligence and personality traits are examples of psychological constructs. Examples of instruments that use construct validity include the Otis Lennon Mental Ability Test, which is based on a particular definition of intelligence, and the Edwards Personal Preference Schedule, which is designed to measure particular personality characteristics.

Concurrent validity and predictive validity are terms used when the instrument is compared to another independent criterion measure. The major distinction between the two terms is the time at which the criterion measures are taken. When the criterion measure is obtained at approximately the same time as the test data taken, concurrent validity is computed; when the criterion measure is obtained at a future time, predictive validity is acquired. Both concurrent and predictive validity are established by statistical means and expressed as a correlation coefficient. Values of this coefficient range from .00, or no relationship, to +1.00, or a perfect relationship. Acceptable instruments usually report correlation coefficients with validity of .60 or higher.

Concurrent validity is most important when the instrument is used as a more efficient alternative to obtaining desired information. For example, if a paper-and-pencil test of scholastic aptitude has a high correlation with an individual intelligence test, the first instrument can be used to obtain nearly the same information as the longer, second test. Thus, the Otis Lennon Mental Ability Test will yield scores that should be comparable to IQ scores obtained on the Wechsler Intelligence Scale for Children.

Predictive validity is most important when the instrument is used to help someone choose a future program or when employed to select the most promising candidates for a program. Examples of tests that report predictive validity are the Law School Admission Test (LSAT) and the School and College Ability Tests (SCAT).

Reliability.   A test is considered to be *reliable* when it measures the same phenomena in a consistent or stable manner. Because educational and psychological constructs are more dynamic than stable, and since any measurement of these constructs is a sample measure, reliability is usually thought of in probability terms. In other words, the reliability of a test can be thought of as the probability that the same person at *different times* or on a *different sample of equivalent items* will obtain the same score. Similar to concurrent and predictive validity, the reliability of a test is usually expressed statistically as a correlation coefficient. This statistic shows the degree of relationship between two sets of measures and varies from +1.00, a perfect relationship, to .00, no relationship. In general, a test should have a reliability coefficient of .80 or higher.

Test scores and standard references.
An individual who takes an educational or psychological test obtains a raw score on that instrument. This score, of and by itself, has no meaning unless the results of the test are associated with some standard. The standard may be a criterion reference or a population reference. A *criterion* reference is used when the score is based on a clearly defined content domain. Criterion-referenced tests are very useful for educational purposes in which mastery of certain knowledge and skills is deemed important. Note how important the criterion reference is in the following two examples: "Peter scored 85 out of 1OO on an eighth-grade vocabulary test"; "Susan typed 60 words per minute on a sixth-grade vocabulary typing test." A *population* reference is employed when the score is compared to the scores of a representative sample of individuals, called the *standardization sample* or the *norm group*. When the standard is a population reference, the raw score is converted to some relative score such as derived IQ, grade equivalent, percentile, stanine, *t* score, or *z* score. Each of these derived scores allows us to compare the individual tested to some reference group. For example, the statement "He scored in the 55th percentile on a fifth-grade arithmetic test" really says, "He scored better than 54 percent of all fifth-grade students in the United States, and 44 percent scored better than he did."

Purposes of tests.
Psychological tests provide a standardized and objective methodology for assessing certain educational and psychological characteristics of people. They can be used for classification, selection, evaluation, verification, and further understanding.

Tests are used for *classification* purposes when the user wishes to classify individuals into some characteristic group that the test measures. For example, if a group of students is administered the Strong Vocational Interest Inventory, we could classify them by their highest scores according to the six personality types identified by Holland (1985)—namely, realistic, investigative, artistic, social, enterprising, and conventional. Tests are employed for *selection* purposes when the scores are used to select individuals for some purpose. For example, a company may wish to hire only individuals who have typing proficiency; thus, a minimum score on a standardized typing test for employment is set. Tests are used for *evaluation* when the user wishes to measure the results of an intervention, treatment, or teaching program. For example, a teacher wishing to evaluate the usefulness of a particular teaching modality may give a pretest and posttest to an experimental and a control group of students. Tests are employed for *verification* when the user wants to verify a scientific hypothesis. For example, a counselor wants to know if the self-concept of individuals can be improved by training subjects in experiential focusing. To verify this hypothesis the counselor would have to set up an appropriate experimental design. Finally, tests are used for *self-understanding* when individuals can learn more about themselves by taking a test. For example, a student may learn that her scores on the Strong Vocational Interest Inventory reveal interests very similar to accountants, an occupation she hadn't considered previously, and quite dissimilar to elementary school teachers, an occupation she had seriously thought of entering.

Although tests can be given for any of these five purposes, it should be noted that the purposes are not mutually exclusive—a particular test may be given for a number of different reasons.

Test administration.
Several major points need to be made about administering educational and psychological tests in a counseling situation. First, careful thought must be given to selecting tests that measure characteristics that are important to the client. The instruments that are available can assess aptitudes, achievement, interests, or personality characteristics in different ways, and they all have distinctive purposes. Therefore, in selecting a test it is helpful to answer the question "How will the results of this test help the client?" Second, be sure the client is interested in taking the test and obtaining the results. Insofar as possible, involve the client in selecting the appropriate instrument. This requires careful explanation by the counselor of the strengths and attributes of any testing instrument under consideration. Third, explain who will have access to the results. Individuals have a right to privacy, and if any significant others, such as parents, have a right to see the results, that fact should be discussed with the client. Fourth, the directions for administering the test should be adhered to so that the test is always given with the same set of instructions. Counselors must be thoroughly familiar with the test manual and follow the directions specified. Respondents should know what is expected of them, how they should take the test, and how they should gauge their time. Finally, while the client is taking the test, any individual or environmental conditions that might affect the outcome of the test should be observed and recorded.

Test interpretation.
Relevant psychometric data must be carefully interpreted by counselors so that the information is useful to their clients. There are four basic types of test interpretation: descriptive, genetic, predictive, and evaluative. A *descriptive* interpretation helps the client learn what kind of person he or she is. For example, "Your scores on the Kuder Interest Inventory indicate that you prefer outdoor activities to computational ones." A *genetic* interpretation informs the client why he or she acts in a certain way. For example, "The discrepancy between your son's quantitative and verbal scores indicates a strong possibility that he has a learning disability, and that may be the reason for his poor schoolwork." A *predictive* interpretation helps clients ascertain whether or not they are likely to succeed in a given endeavor. For example, "Students with scores like yours are usually accepted at a state college." Finally, an *evaluative* description helps clients compare themselves to some performance standard or criteria. For example, "Your score placed you in the 75th percentile. That means you did better than three-fourths of the students your age, and about one-fourth of the students did better than you."

Involve your client.
A good testing procedure involves the client as much as possible. He or she should feel involved in the test selection and its evaluation and interpretation. The client can be involved in the interpretation process by following these four steps:

1. Encourage the client to share any relevant personal information with you. Try to ascertain: (a) the client's motivation for taking the test; (b) the conditions under which the test was taken; (c) how serious the client was when he or she responded to specific test items; and (d) how the client felt about the process.

2. Tell the client about the nature of any of the test instruments that may be used. Describe what these tests purport to do, how the scores can vary from one administration to another, and how the results can be used. Whenever possible, involve the client in the selection of the testing instruments.

3. Interpret the results to the client using all the empirical evidence available. This may involve comparing the client's score to available statistical and normative information and assisting the client in understanding his or her probability of success in pursuing a particular course of action.

4. Discuss the meaning of the test results with the client in light of other known factors. Use both test and nontest data to help the client learn more about himself or herself. Involve the client in the interpretation of the test. Have the client state what he or she believes the test score means in light of these other known factors. Allow the client to evaluate the test score as it applies to himself or herself.

The Management of Learning

In addition to helping clients learn about themselves from test data and obtaining educational and vocational information from good source materials, counselors often must assist clients in managing the learning process more effectively. Counseling programs at the primary and secondary education levels need to work with students from a developmental and preventive approach. Such an approach calls for helping students accomplish appropriate developmental tasks such as those specified by Havighurst (1972). In addition, counselors need to be attuned to the fact that several conditions influence the learning process (Griggs, 1994). These include:

- environmental conditions such as light, sound, and temperature;
- sociological characteristics such as peer and group pressure;
- perceptual strengths and weaknesses; and
- internal factors such as drive, persistence, motivation, and other psychological characteristics.

Helping students learn how to learn more effectively is an important component of a developmental counseling approach.

Furthermore, counselors who work in schools and colleges often must work in a remedial situation and deal with clients who manifest difficulties living up to their potential. This problem may be the result of a number of factors such as lack of interest, poor motivation, or overwhelming personal problems; or it may be the result of poor learning habits and skills. When the lack of academic achievement is related to the former concerns, the use of group or individual counseling procedures based on a combination of different intervention strategies is often called for (Baker, 1996). When the lack of achievement is related to learning deficiencies, counselors have to help clients manage the learning process more effectively.

In learning how to manage the learning process more effectively, students need to develop a variety of skills. Among these are learning how to:

- be prepared for their lessons with the necessary tools;
- allocate, schedule, and use their time effectively;
- concentrate and minimize external distractions;
- read contextual materials;
- take notes from both oral and written presentations;
- organize their notes in systematic ways; and
- outline materials for oral and written presentations.

Green (1993) discusses a number of useful techniques for helping students improve their study skills.

Learning is notably affected by both external conditions and by a student's physiological and psychological status. External conditions such as the physical setting (light, sound, temperature, physical plant, and time of day) and the sociological and cultural expectations of the groups the student belongs to (peer, family, and role models) create an environment that can enhance or detract from learning. An individual's physical health and perceptual strengths and weaknesses (auditory, visual, tactual, and kinesthetic) often influence how that individual progresses with certain educational tasks. And, clearly, a person's psychological characteristics (aptitudes, interests, motivation, and other personality traits) strongly shape how that person learns.

As a counselor you can help clients manage the learning process more effectively by using the following procedures:

1. Learn as much as you can about any conditions related to the client's physical, environmental, sociological, or psychological characteristics that may enhance or delimit the learning process. Investigate the possibility of modifying the environmental factors that hamper this process. Note the client's strengths.
2. Encourage the client to develop habits conducive to learning. These minimally include:
   a. having the proper tools,
   b. working in an appropriate physical environment,
   c. learning how to use time wisely,
   d. discovering how to read and outline textual materials,
   e. seeking help and feedback as warranted, and
   f. using all available resources (for example, teachers and books).
3. Prepare the client for learning by facilitating the conditions that foster learning. These include:
   a. motivating the client by stressing how and why certain material is meaningful and important;
   b. providing feedback to help the client see logical relationships between new materials and previously obtained information; and
   c. helping the client develop a useful system that can reinforce the learning process.
4. Help the client learn how to organize materials for learning more effectively. The client may have to be taught how to:

    a. group or categorize the information to be learned into associated clusters;

    b. arrange this material in a logical sequence that builds on previous knowledge;

    c. establish relationships between old and new materials; and

    d. use various mnemonic devices such as stories, sentences, words, jingles, and mental images to facilitate recall.

5. Assist the client in developing a plan for distributed practice. Help the client understand that three one-hour sessions are normally better than one three-hour session because the difficulty of learning increases disproportionally with time due to limits of attention span, fatigue, and environmental factors, and individuals tend to remember and recall the primary and most recent information.

6. Encourage the client to use a multisensory approach to learning. Have the client incorporate as many of the five senses as feasible. Teach the client to use a good study method such as the SQ3R method (Survey, Question, Read, Recite, Review).

In the process of learning, an individual establishes a pattern or set that facilitates recall and fosters learning similar concepts and facts. If the client has had a bad experience in learning or has learned to do things incorrectly, the set must be modified through a reeducational process. This process is often harder to accomplish than the initial learning process because connections that have been made previously need to be changed so that a new pattern can be established. For example, a student who has learned to add a column of numbers incorrectly needs to unlearn this procedure as well as learn the correct way. As a result of continued or unwarranted failure or possible misuse of reinforcement procedures, an individual learns to become less competent, and a state of learned helplessness can develop. This set is a difficult but not impossible pattern to alter.

SYSTEMATIC PROBLEM-SOLVING AND DECISION-MAKING SKILLS

Basic Concept

Another major cognitive approach is one that teaches clients a decision-making process. The need for effective decision making is an ongoing process throughout the life span of an individual; it is also something everyone must do several times a day. Concerns may vary from simple daily tasks such as "What shall I eat for breakfast?" to more complex and difficult ones such as choosing a college, selecting an occupation, or picking a community in which to live. Choosing one thing over another can be confusing, stressful, and sometimes immobilizing. Counselors are often required to help their clients learn how to make decisions and solve problems. Clients need assistance in learning how to weigh facts, resolve conflicts, deal with frustrations, choose between alternative courses of action, cope with various life problems, and overcome indecisiveness.

Decision making is a procedure that can be learned and applied when one needs to solve a problem or make a decision. Typically, the decision-making process involves systematically working through a logically ordered series of steps (Blocker, 1987; Krumboltz and Thoresen, 1976; Yates, 1990). Although experts articulate slight differences in the number and content of each of these steps, there is considerable similarity in the overall development process. The following eight steps are fairly typical of the chronology for a decision-making procedure:

1. becoming oriented to the decision-making framework,
2. identifying the decision that needs to be made,
3. generating a list of alternative courses of action,
4. gathering information relative to each alternative,
5. weighing the relative merits of each option,
6. making a choice among the alternatives,
7. implementing and evaluating the decision, and
8. generalizing the decision-making process to other situations.

The decision-making process is typically not a completely rational process; it involves a considerable amount of uncertainty and subjective self-evaluation on the part of clients (Kaye, 1992; Russo & Schoemaker, 1990). They should analyze their own needs and characteristics and relate these to the information they have collected or learned about each option. In assessing themselves clients often need to evaluate one or more of the following characteristics:

- the immediacy of their need to make a decision;
- their personal, economic, social, and psychological needs;
- their personal beliefs and values;
- their previously learned patterns of making decisions;
- the degree of risk they are willing to take;
- their personal feelings about the seriousness and the importance of this decision;
- how this decision will affect other aspects of their lives; and
- how this decision will affect significant other persons in their lives.

This subjective evaluation of their previous adequacy in making decisions, how they have typically dealt with barriers and obstacles, and how their decisions have affected them and others provides clients with an awareness of the dimensions of their choice process and the critical information necessary for making sound decisions.

Making appropriate decisions requires clients to use constructive coping strategies to handle life situations (see p. 24), but many clients have developed poor decision-making habits (Gelatt, 1989). Gelatt, Varenhorst, and Carey (1972) discuss seven poor patterns or styles of dealing with the need to make a decision.

In the four patterns indicated below, clients make decisions but use inadequate procedures to reach a solution. This process can lead to unsatisfactory or inadequate results.

1. An *impulsive* decision occurs when clients use little thought or examination, often choosing the first available choice—"Leap before you look."
2. A *fatalistic* pattern is exhibited when the individual leaves the decision to chance—"It's beyond my control."
3. A *compliant* procedure is at work when the person follows someone else's plans—"I'll do whatever you say."
4. An *intuitive* decision is made when the client follows an inner feeling about the choice—"It feels right."

In the following three patterns, clients often undergo considerable stress and still can be unable to reach an appropriate resolution to their situation.

1. A *delaying* procedure occurs when the client postpones action until a later time—"I'll solve that one later."
2. An *agonizing* feeling happens when the person receives too much information or too many alternatives and is overwhelmed—"There are so many possibilities, I don't know what to do."
3. *Paralysis* occurs when the individual has the necessary information and accepts the need to make a decision but cannot deal with it emotionally because of tension or anxiety—"I can't face it."

The counseling process is a good vehicle for helping clients learn how to make appropriate decisions and learn the problem-solving process. Because of the similarity in the steps involved in reaching a decision and in finding a resolution to a problem, the terms are often used interchangeably, or the decision-making process is considered a form of the problem-solving process (D'Zurilla, 1988). The counselor's role in this process is fourfold. First, a warm, accepting atmosphere that is conducive to exploration and self-evaluation should be created. Second, the systematic steps necessary for making sound decisions must be taught or reviewed. Third, the client should be helped in learning more about the kind of information that he or she needs and the sources of that information. And fourth, the client must be assisted in considering each option in light of the information available and with due consideration to his or her own personal characteristics and subjective factors. It is, of course, the client's responsibility to reach a decision or solve a problem—this often needs to be made clear and reinforced with clients, particularly with those who like to procrastinate or those who want to foster a dependency relationship.

Individuals with low self-esteem often have difficulty with the decision-making process for several reasons. They may be unwilling or unable to take any sort of a risk, or they may feel that they have no control over their future and are unable to change things. They may be too sensitive to the feelings and ideas of others as well as to various social pressures and, thus, do what others believe is right. Such individuals are often poorly motivated and will question—either consciously or unconsciously—the need to study and learn the decision-making process (Brown & Lent, 1992; Janis & Mann, 1979; Wheeler & Janis, 1980). In such cases you will need to use other intervention strategies as well as to teach the client decision-making procedures.

Clients can and do differ in their personalities and in their decision-making styles. For example, some rely more on the objective data that they gather during the process; others rely more on their own subjective feelings and perceptions about the information. Some need considerable time to move through the process; others can move through it more rapidly. Some like to weigh their decision verbally, whereas others rely more on their own internal thought process. Clearly, you should be aware of these different styles and work with clients in their own modalities for the benefit of the client.

Teaching the decision-making procedure in the counseling process should lead to two outcomes. First, the client should be able to come to a resolution of the immediate problem that he or she is concerned about. Second, the client should learn the process so that he or she can generalize and apply the process to other situations that require decision-making skills. The process of using the decision-making procedure in counseling should be approached in a well-planned developmental manner. The following eight-step model illustrates such an approach.

1. *Orientation.* Orient the client to the decision-making or problem-solving process. Help the client:

   a. recognize that decision-making and problem-solving skills are used daily and throughout life;
   b. understand that learning the process of decision making is necessary to solve immediate as well as distant problems;
   c. make a commitment for the necessary time and effort to learn these skills; and
   d. agree to act only after facts are weighed.

2. *Identify problem.* Help the client define the problem and his or her concerns in specific, concrete terms. This step can be facilitated by:

   a. articulating the goals, values, and objectives as concretely as possible, and
   b. subdividing the overall objective into several subproblems or more manageable issues.

3. *Generate alternatives.* Encoumge the client to generate a comprehensive list of possible alternative solutions. This process can be facilitated by:

   a. brainstorming,
   b. free-associating, and
   c. obtaining opinions of others.

   Initially the client should list as many alternatives as possible, no matter how foolish some may first appear. This tends to ensure that no reasonable alternative will be overlooked. This list should then be arranged in order of preference.

4. *Collect information.* Instruct the client in ways of collecting information about each of the possible alternative solutions. The client may need help in developing appropriate questions and seeking the proper resources. Suggested resources include:

   a. interviewing knowledgeable persons,
   b. visiting appropriate sites,
   c. reading various resource materials, and
   d. engaging in exploratory activities.

5. *Evaluate alternatives.* Assist the client in examining the consequences of each possible or probable solution. The positive and negative consequences of each alternative should be examined in terms of:

   a. rewards,
   b. obligations,
   c. probability of accomplishment,
   d. implications for self, and
   e. implications for significant others in the client's life.

6. *Plan action.* Help the client select and decide on a course of action. This often involves:

   a. eliminating the least desirable solution and selecting the most promising in terms of the consequences;

    b. reevaluating one's objectives in light of the implications of each solution;

    c. specifying the tactics or ways the alternative or strategy will be carried out (note what is to be done, when, by whom, how); and

    d. note the possibility of revising the decision if new information becomes available or if an unexpected event occurs (new information and/or unexpected events are often cues to reconsider the entire decision-making process).

7. *Implement decision.* Encourage the client to act on his or her decision in order to evaluate and test the chosen alternative. If the solution proves to be satisfactory, then the decision process is complete; if not, then the process must be continued and the client must be assisted in going back to an earlier step.

8. *Generalize.* Assist the client in generalizing the problem-solving and decision-making model to other aspects of his or her life. For example, the model can be used:

    a. in everyday situations when one decides what to wear and how to spend leisure time;

    b. at critical developmental points in life when one decides what college to select or what occupation to pursue; and

    c. at stressful moments when one needs to decide on a course of action under painful or unpleasant circumstances.

Learning the decision-making model helps individuals anticipate problems, minimizes the probability of acting impulsively, and lessens the anxiety and tension often associated with crises and indecisiveness.

The Trait-Factor Approach

A unique form of the decision-making process is the trait-factor theory of counseling, which was developed to help clients make better educational and vocational choices (Williamson, 1965). This approach to counseling applies the decision-making process to help clients assess their *traits,* consider them in light of *the factors* in the environment, and reach some conclusion regarding their future behaviors. In this approach the counselor takes an active role in helping the client come to a better understanding of his or her abilities, interests, and values; the opportunities, requirements, and consequences of possible courses of action; and the steps necessary to accomplish an objective. The counselor assumes the responsibility for guiding the client through the following five stages of the counseling process: analysis, synthesis, diagnosis, treatment, and follow-up.

In the *analysis* stage, you should try to understand the client's concern or problem and learn as much about the client's traits and factors as possible. This information is obtained by means of psychological tests, interviews, and any other feasible means of collecting data. Next you need to *synthesize* this information into a meaningful pattern and make some *diagnosis* or prognosis regarding the meaning of these data for the client. In the *treatment* stage you should guide the client in his or her understanding and interpretation of these traits and factors, and suggest possible courses of action based on the available data. Furthermore, during the treatment stage the client is expected to come to some decision and plan to implement this decision in the foreseeable future.

The *follow-up* stage takes place some time later when you check with the client to ascertain whether he or she is encountering any difficulty implementing the planned action.

The trait-factor approach to counseling seems to be used mostly in helping clients make educational and vocational decisions (Patterson & Watkins, 1995). Its use, however, is not restricted to these areas because it provides a systematic methodology for guiding counselors in dealing with a variety of issues (Ivey, Ivey, & Simek-Morgan, 1997).

SYSTEMATIC IMPROVEMENT OF THE DEDUCTIVE THINKING PROCESS
Basic Concept

A third major cognitive approach deals with clients' deductive reasoning powers, their perceptions of themselves, and their perceptions of the situations they are confronted with in life. This approach is based on the concept that the sources of clients' problems are the mistaken beliefs and perceptions they have about themselves and the negative constructs and connotations they have about their life experiences. The emphasis is placed on making clients aware of their mental processes; helping them eliminate unproductive and debilitating thought patterns, beliefs, and opinions; and enabling them to learn more adaptive, constructive, and useful patterns of thinking.

There are three important reasons why helping clients to think systematically and logically is important. First, expectations and assumptions have significant implications for emotional reactions and overt behavior in the real world. What you believe and what you expect to happen can influence how you feel and act. Second, a person's thought processes about an event or situation—rather than the event itself—are frequently the cause of erroneous feelings, distorted perceptions, or ill-advised behaviors. What you think about an event is often more important than the event itself. Third, because the process of thinking uses language as a reasoning tool, language itself plays an important role in a person's cognitive feelings and actions. Identifying certain things as "good" or "bad" or "so-so" will shape one's reactions to those items. Therefore, clients can be helped to modify their beliefs, attitudes, and behavior by changing the way they label things.

Clients' expectations or other assumptions about events, their logical thought processes, and how they label things are three important issues to address in helping clients overcome dysfunctional cognitions. Beck and Weishaar (1995), Ellis (1995), Mahoney (1991), and Meichenbaum (1977) offer distinctive approaches for helping clients who reach conclusions based on faulty reasoning processes. Often this reasoning contains one or more of the following distorted ways of speaking or thinking that reveal negative feelings about oneself.

> *Self-deprecating statements.* These expressions, when made repeatedly, reveal poor self-worth. For example, "I'm not a good student" or "No one really likes me."
>
> *Absolute or perfectionistic terms.* When individuals set up overly stringent guidelines for their behavior, they set themselves up for self-criticism and negative self-images. Conclusions that are absolute or perfectionistic often include the words "must," "ought," "should," "unless," or "until." For example, "I should have been the one promoted" or "Unless I get an A, I can't go home."

Overgeneralization of negative experiences. These are deductions based on too few examples or situations. Frequently, they are based on negative experiences that make clients think there are many obstacles making the future hopeless and bleak. For example, "Since I failed the first exam, I will fail the course" or "All the children in school hate me."

Negative exaggerations. These statements greatly magnify the true meaning of an event or reality. For example, "All professional athletes are greedy" or "You insulted my mother—you hate my family!"

Factually inaccurate statements. These remarks are based on inadequate or incorrect information. These erroneous data distort the client's perceptions of reality. For example, "You need an A average to get into college" or "Autistic children are lazy."

Ignorance of the effects of time. These assertions ignore growth, maturation, and the effect that the passage of time can have on an experience or event. For example, "He was a very poor student last year—he will surely fail this year" or "I have to go back to the lake and relive my vacation there."

These examples reveal a faulty deductive thinking process. This type of thinking can be analyzed by careful examination of the premises, facts, or assumptions involved and the conclusion reached from those facts or assumptions. The deductive reasoning process involves at least two premises, factual statements, or assumptions to reach a conclusion that logically flows from the two premises. In analyzing a client's faulty reasoning, it can be very helpful to write out the premises, facts, or assumptions and the conclusions based on these premises. Sometimes one or more of the premises, facts, or assumptions are false. At other times the conclusion cannot be logically deduced from the premises. For example, using six of the statements from the previous section, the premises and conclusions could be reconstructed and written in the following way:

1. My mother bawled me out.
   My father bawled me out.
   No one really likes me.
2. My parents expect me to do well
   For me, to do well means to get an A.
   I can't go home unless I get an A.
3. Mary doesn't talk to me.
   John calls me the teacher's pet.
   All the children hate me.
4. Professional athletes make a lot of money.
   Those who make a lot of money are greedy.
   All professional athletes are greedy.
5. Autistic children have difficulty in learning how to read.
   Lazy children have difficulty reading.
   Autistic children are lazy.
6. He was a very poor student last year.
   Once a poor student, always a poor student.
   He will surely fail this year.

The first three examples are illustrations of faulty reasoning using premises or assumptions that may be true. The last three examples are prototypes of logical or syllogistic reasoning that is faulty due to erroneous assumptions. Generally, of course, the client's faulty logic is not stated in the syllogistic format but only as an abbreviated conclusion. Therefore, to help clients see the errors in their faulty thinking processes, it is helpful to write down the premises and conclusions on a piece of paper or constantly point out the faulty premises leading to the distorted conclusions. Furthermore, clients sometimes need to investigate the evidence that supports their assumptions. This may require homework assignments. Two intervention strategies, thought stopping and cognitive restructuring, are very useful techniques when counselors want to help clients improve their deductive reasoning processes.

Thought Interference or Thought Stopping

Thought stopping is a technique used to help clients recognize inappropriate thinking patterns and then terminate the unwanted thought (Cautela & Wisock, 1977; Mahoney & Arnkoff, 1978; Wolpe, 1958). It is often employed with clients who consistently present self-deprecating, negative self-concepts and poor images of themselves; exhibit unwarranted fear or anxiety in anticipating a future action; or display a strong emotional reaction to ordinary, everyday life situations. Clients may ruminate on the past, present, or future; engage in illogical or worry-oriented thinking; present self-distortions; or engage in self-destructive descriptions. This procedure is designed to restrain and inhibit the clients' negative self-talk and force them to speak in more realistic, accurate ways. Typical thought-stopping methodology involves the following steps:

1. Identify with the client one of the thoughts that the client would like to control, and explore the details surrounding the situations that seem to arouse the self-limiting thoughts.
2. Instruct the client to imagine himself or herself in a situation that raises irrational, poor, or self-defeating thoughts or thought sequences. If necessary, help the client verbalize the scene.
3. As soon as the irrational or poor thought is emitted by the client, interrupt with strong intervention—for example, "Stop! Your statement makes no sense."
4. Help the client change his or her inappropriate thought pattern and appreciate the reality of the situation by labeling the incident more accurately. The client needs to learn that any statement has four possible truth values: always, necessarily true; possibly true or true under certain circumstances; probably not true, true under rare circumstances; and never true, impossible.
5. To realistically effect changes in the client's cognitions, this process must be repeated with other visualizations until the client verbally changes labels and the direction of the thought patterns.
6. As with any other cognitive strategy, continuing guided practice should be combined with simulations until proper perspective is obtained. Homework

should be assigned to obtain the experience and skills necessary for improving the thought process on one's own.

The thought-stopping procedure normally involves several sessions. In applying this strategy you should slowly shift the burden for interrupting the thought pattern from yourself to the client. This may be accomplished by gradually lowering your voice when you command the client to stop the thought; eventually, ask the client to take the responsibility for saying "Stop!" whenever a disturbing thought occurs. Repeated practice is often necessary.

Systematic Cognitive Structuring and Restructuring

Cognitive restructuring is a technique based on the underlying assumption that the way clients structure or think about their experiences determines how they feel and behave (Beck & Weishaar, 1995; Burns, 1992). This technique is designed to help clients modify maladaptive thought patterns and improve and extend their logical thinking process. It is often used when unwarranted conclusions are drawn because of erroneous premises or assumptions, or poor syllogistic or deductive reasoning, and when clients need help in extending their logical thinking process. Counselors who use the cognitive-restructuring process should employ the following procedures:

1. Take an extensive client history to find out how the client handles current problems and how he or she has handled them in the past.
2. Help clients become aware of their thought processes. For each conclusion, ask the client to discuss the evidence for the particular conclusion, alternative ways of viewing the evidence, and what would happen if one or more of the alternatives were true.
3. Review the rational thinking process, showing the client the four possible truth values of any statement or assumption. Discuss and review how the thinking process works, using syllogisms when necessary. Show the client how the underlying assumptions, premises, and poor reasoning affect his or her thinking, feeling, and performance. It is helpful to present illustrations of irrational thinking in an exaggerated way so that clients can see them more easily.
4. Help the client analyze self-statements, assumptions about others, and logical thought patterns in light of the major dimensions of his or her life. A three-column procedure can help do this. In the first column the client should describe any and all anxiety-provoking situations. In the second column, the client can record his or her thoughts and conclusions about this situation. And in the third column the client should list the types of errors found in these thought patterns and conclusions.
5. Teach the client to modify internal self-statements, erroneous labels, and any poor assumptions about others.
6. Drill and review the logical reasoning process with concrete cases from the client's frame of reference. When appropriate, help clients determine

reasonably attainable goals. Having clients understand the importance of realistic goals decreases illogical thought processes.

7. Combine thought stopping with simulations, homework, and relaxation techniques until logical patterns become set.

Occasionally, clients face difficulties extending their thinking processes. When this occurs, they need help understanding the interrelationships between and among complex constructs and data; the relationship of past, present, and future events; or how environmental factors are related to current behavior or events. This often requires factual instruction techniques rather than cognitive restructuring.

The thought-stopping and rational-restructuring techniques may be useful with individuals who tend to be extremists (that is, perfectionist, overly dependent, isolationist, or irresponsible types); who exhibit fears and anxiety in regard to performance in social situations, public speaking, or test taking; and who display extreme emotional reactions to normal life situations (that is, depression or anger).

ANALOGOUS, INDUCTIVE, AND CREATIVE THINKING
Basic Concept

A fourth major cognitive approach is one that encourages clients to be open to new thoughts and ideas and to think in creative ways (Cole & Sarnoff, 1980). Individuals are frequently called upon to act or make a decision when it is not possible to use the deductive reasoning process to reach positive, certain conclusions. They must learn to think analogously, inductively, and creatively as well as deductively. They connect one case to another and learn from this comparison. They generalize from individual cases and learn to act in creative ways. This type of thinking provides clients with conclusions that go beyond observations or known facts. It is helpful to foster analogous, inductive, and creative thinking when we want to motivate clients to

- try to do something new,
- raise their aspirational levels,
- gain new perspectives on common, everyday problems, and
- obtain some awareness about or insight into themselves.

Individuals reason analogously when they compare two or more things, find a resemblance in some respects between and among them, and therefore conclude that the items are probably alike in other respects as well. *Analogous thinking*, in other words, is a process of reasoning by comparison. Individuals find a similarity among objects and experiences and reach a conclusion regarding the relationships between or among other objects and experiences. For example, a counselor-in-training has helped an undecided college freshman make a choice of college major by using some occupational information, having the client interview several individuals, and helping the client sort out the meaningfulness of these data. The next time the novice counselor has a client with a similar problem, the counselor will compare his or her previous experience to this new experience to see if there is enough in common to use the same intervention strategy.

Individuals think *inductively* when they generalize from a limited set of observations. A person starts with a number of observations, attempts to integrate or find a conceptual way to connect these observations, and then comes to some generalized conclusions based on both the observations and some thoughts about the relationships among these observations. For example, a new counselor encouraged ten of his clients to discuss their personal interests with him. Subsequently, he administered an interest inventory to each of them. From these ten cases he concluded that, although discussion of the students' expressed interests provided useful insights into their backgrounds, the measured interests provided additional information relevant to a discussion of potential occupations. Thus, the counselor decided that he should use both expressed and measured interests when he does career counseling.

Creative thinking is very often employed when a solution is sought for a problem that cannot be resolved by the deductive reasoning process alone. Various methods have been suggested to free the creative potential that is inherent within each person. These include the use of metaphors (Gordon, 1978), lateral thinking (DeBono & DeSaint-Arnaud, 1983), and imagery (Wolpin, Shorr, & Krueger, 1986). Typically, the creative process involves recalling one's previous experience with similar problems; using both analogous and inductive thinking to brainstorm and obtain new visual images of situations, problems, or issues; and breaking out of the usual or traditional ways of doing things in order to reach a new and perhaps unconventional solution to the problem. Creative thinking requires a fairly thorough knowledge of the subject in question. For example, a counselor who has studied cognitive, affective, and behavioral approaches to counseling and who has gained experience using a variety of techniques during the training process soon discovers that each client is different and that, although one can employ a particular intervention, the application of that intervention often requires novel approaches and creative thought.

Although using analogous, inductive, or creative reasoning with clients in certain types of counseling situations may be beneficial, these approaches have not received much attention in the counseling literature (May, 1994). This kind of reasoning is characterized as progressing through a definite four-stage process that provides the client with a useful understanding of analogous, inductive, and creative thinking. The four stages are: preparation/observation, incubation/analysis, illumination/tentative conclusion, and verification.

During the *preparation/observation* stage, the problem or concern is identified, the facts and observations are gathered, the material is studied in detail, and questions are posed regarding the observations made. In the *incubation/analysis* stage, time is allowed for pondering all the observations and facts previously gathered, the data are compared and contrasted, and ideas and concepts are considered and reviewed until the components of a problem are reformulated into a solvable issue. During the *illumination/tentative conclusion* stage, provisional solutions are reached. This stage often requires considerable time to reach an answer, which frequently comes when one is not consciously forcing it. The *verification* stage occurs when one tries out a tentative solution, revises it if need be, and/or generalizes to other examples (Bernard & Huckins, 1975; Moore, 1985).

Suggested Methods

Counselors who want to foster analogous, inductive, and creative thinking in their clients can use a variety of methods. You should help the client move through the observation, analysis, conclusion, and verification process. The following four questions may be used by clients as guides to facilitate this process:

- What do I want to observe in this process?
- What meaning does this information have for me, my family, and my friends?
- What inferences, suggestions, or conclusions can I tentatively draw from this process?
- How can I try out these notions to see how realistic they are?

The seven methods suggested below can be used by counselors to encourage clients to be open to new ideas, to gain new perspectives, and to think in different ways.

1. Encourage creative problem solving. Have clients use the brainstorming technique to generate as many ideas as possible. Explain this concept and then ask some open-ended questions to foster imagination and new lines of thought. Allow the ideas to be a little wild, fragmented, unconnected, and unconventional. Instruct clients to defer judgment on all of the notions. The emphasis is to break out of the typical ways of thinking and open new thought patterns.

2. Try having clients dream, think, or write about ways to solve a problem or about the future. Try to have them look at questions addressing the future, such as: "In two years what would you like to be doing?"; "In three years how would you look back on this problem?"; "In four years what issues will you face?"; or "In five years where would you like to live?"

3. Use the open-ended question technique to help clients think more openly. Provide the client with a printed list of unfinished sentences regarding his or her life. Examples might include the following: "I wish that . . .."; "If I could I would . . ."; or "In what ways could I . . . ."

4. Help clients understand that many activities and the conclusions we are called upon to make are not based on deductive thinking. Individuals often resolve problems by using analysis or by viewing the problem from another perspective. Ask your client how he or she might solve a problem that is somewhat different, or ask what suggestions the client would make if the problem belonged to a friend.

5 Encourage clients' use of imagery, relaxation, and meditational processes. Have clients learn the relaxation procedures and then the meditational and imagery techniques to become more aware of themselves (Cole & Sarnoff, 1980).

6 Encourage clients to interview possible role models. Help them identify possible interviewees who might provide them with some future direction or help them resolve an issue. Assist clients in formulating appropriate questions and, if possible, role-play the interviews. After the interviews are concluded, help clients integrate this experience and reach new conclusions.

7. Instruct clients to use various references to investigate alternative solutions to a problem. Suggest books and reading materials, audiovisual materials, or various computer software packages. Help them understand that there are often alternative

ways to resolve an issue. Assist them in the process of integrating this material into a meaningful conclusion for themselves.

SUMMARY

This chapter has outlined four cognitively focused intervention strategies. These strategies are based on the concept that human beings are rational and their cognitive and mediational processes exert a strong influence on all their endeavors. Cognitively focused strategies are designed to help clients: acquire and retain accurate and relevant factual information; learn how to choose among alternative courses of action to make satisfactory decisions and solve problems; learn how to think more logically about themselves and the world about them; and learn how to use their resources in more analogous, inductive, or creative ways. In these strategies the counseling process is primarily an educative one, and as the counselor your major function is to help the client learn new material and different ways of handling various situations. These intervention strategies typically involve a series of structured steps and frequently require clients to do a considerable amount of work outside the counseling session.

After reading this chapter on cognitively focused strategies you should be able to describe the major cognitive interventions. You should have an understanding of when these strategies can be used, and you should recognize the steps involved in employing these methods. To attain proficiency in applying these methods in counseling sessions requires in-depth study of these techniques as well as considerable clinical practice with actual clients under the supervision of a qualified professional.

REFERENCES

Anastasi, A., & Urbina, S. (1997). *Psychological testing* (7th ed.). Upper Saddle River, NJ: Prentice Hall.

Baker, S. (1996). *School counseling for the twenty-first century* (2nd ed.). Columbus, OH: Merrill.

Beck, A. T., & Weishaar, M. E. (1995). Cognitive therapy. In R. J. Corsini & D. Wedding (Eds.). *Current psychotherapies* (5th ed.) (pp. 229–261). Itasca, IL: F. E. Peacock.

Bernard, H. W., & Huckins, W. C. (1975). *Dynamics of personal adjustment* (2nd ed.). Boston: Holbrook.

Blocker, D. H. (1987). *The professional counselor.* New York: Macmillan.

Brown, S. D., & Lent, R. W. (1992). *Handbook of counseling psychology* (2nd ed.). New York: Wiley.

Burns, D. (1992). *Feeling good: The new mood therapy* (2nd ed.). New York: Morrow.

Cautela, J. R., & Wisock, P. A. (1977). The thought-stopping procedure: Description, application and learning theory interpretations. *The Psychological Record, 2,* 255–264.

Cole, H., & Sarnoff, D. (1980). Creativity and counseling. *Personnel and Guidance Journal, 59,* 140–146.

Cronbach, L. J. (1990). *Essentials of psychological testing* (5th ed.). New York: Harper & Row.

DeBono, E., & DeSaint-Arnaud, M. (1983). *The learning-to-think coursebook.* Larchmont, NY: DeBono Resource Center.

DISCOVER: A computer based career development and counselor support system. [Computer program]. (1996). Iowa City, IA: American College Testing Program.

D'Zurilla, T. J. (1988). Problem solving therapies. In K. S. Dobson (Ed.), *Handbook of cognitive-behavioral therapies* (pp. 85–135). New York: Guilford.

Ellis, A. (1995). Rational and emotive therapy. In R. J. Corsini & D. Wedding (Eds.), *Current psychotherapies* (5th ed.) (pp. 162–196). Itasca, IL: F. E. Peacock.

ExPan. [Computer program]. (1996). New York: The College Board.

Gelatt, H. B. (1989). Positive uncertainty: A new decision-making framework for counseling. *Journal of Counseling Psychology, 36,* 252–256.

Gelatt, H. B., Varenhorst, B., & Carey, R. (1972). *Deciding: A leader's guide.* Princeton, NJ: College Entrance Examination Board.

Gordon, D. (1978). *Therapeutic metaphors.* Cupertino, CA: Meta Publishers.

Green, G. W. (1993). *Getting straight A's* (rev. ed.). Secaucus, NJ: Lyle Stuart.

Griggs, S. A. (1994). *Learning styles counseling.* Greensboro, NC: Eric/Cass.

Guidance information system 3.0. [Computer program]. (1996). Chicago: Riverside.

Havighurst, R. J. (1972). *Developmental tasks and education* (3rd ed.). New York: David McKay

Herr, E. L., & Cramer, S. H. (1992). *Career guidance through the life span* (4th ed.). New York: HarperCollins.

Holland, J. L. (1985). *Making vocational choices: A theory of careers* (2nd ed.). Englewood Cliffs, NJ: Prentice Hall.

Hoppock, R. (1976). *Occupational information* (4th ed.). New York: McGraw-Hill.

Isaacson, L. E., & Brown, D. (1993). *Career information, career counseling, and career development* (5th ed.). Boston: Allyn & Bacon.

Ivey, A. E., Ivey, M. B., & Simek-Morgan, L. (1997). *Counseling and psychotherapy: A multicultural perspective* (4th ed.). Boston: Allyn & Bacon.

Janis, I. L., & Mann, L. (1979). *Decision-making: A psychological analysis of conflict, choice, and commitment.* New York: Free Press.

Kaye, H. (1992). *Decision power: How to make decisions with confidence.* Englewood Cliffs, NJ: Prentice Hall.

Krumboltz, J. D., & Thoresen, C. E. (1976). *Counseling methods.* New York: Holt, Rinehart and Winston.

Lea, H. D., & Leibowitz, Z. B. (Eds.). (1992). *Adult career development: Concepts, issues and practices* (2nd ed.). Alexandria, VA: American Counseling Association.

Lyman, H. B. (1991). *Test scores and what they mean* (5th ed.). Boston: Allyn & Bacon.

Mahoney, M. J. (1991). *Human change process: The scientific foundations of psychology.* New York: Basic Books.

Mahoney, M. J., & Arnkoff, D. (1978). Cognitive and self-control therapies. In S. L. Garfield & A. E. Bergin (Eds.), *Handbook of psychotherapy and behavioral change* (2nd ed.) (Part IV, pp. 689–722). New York: Wiley.

May, R. (1994). *The courage to create.* New York: Norton.

Maze, M., & Cummings, R. (1982). *How to select a computer assisted guidance program.* Madison, WI: University of Wisconsin, Vocational Studies Center.

Mehrens, W. A., & Lehmann, I. J. (1991). *Measurement and evaluation in education and psychology* (4th ed.). Fort Worth, TX: Harcourt *Brace.*

Meichenbaum, D. H. (1997). *Cognitive behavior modification: An integrative approach.* New York: Plenum.

Moore, L. P. (1985). *You're smarter than you think.* New York: Holt, Rinehart and Winston.

Osipow, S. H., & Fitzgerald, L. F. (1996). *Theories of career development* (4th ed.). Boston: Allyn & Bacon.

Patterson, C. H., & Watkins, C. E. (1995). *Theories of counseling and psychotherapy* (5th ed.). Reading, MA: Addison-Wesley.

Russo, E. J., & Schoemaker, P. J. (1990). *Decision traps: The ten barriers to decision making and how to overcome them.* New York: Simon & Schuster.

Sampson, J. P., & Reardon, R. C. (Eds.). (1990). *Enhancing the design and use of computer-assisted career guidance systems.* Alexandria, VA: American Counseling Association.

SIGI PLUS (System of interactive guidance and information): A computerized guidance program. [Computer program]. (1996). Princeton, NJ: Educational Testing Service.

United States Department of Commerce, Office of Federal Statistical Policy and Standards. (1987). *Standard occupational classification manual.* Washington, DC: United States Government Printing Office.

United States Department of Labor. (1991). *Dictionary of occupational titles* (4th ed. rev.). Washington, DC: United States Government Printing Office.

United States Department of Labor. (1996). *Occupational outlook handbook: 1996–1997.* Washington, DC: United States Government Printing Office.

Walsh, W. B., & Betz, N. E. (1994). *Tests and assessments* (3rd ed.). Englewood Cliffs, NJ: Prentice Hall.

Wheeler, D. D., & Janis, I. L. (1980). *A practical guide for making decisions.* New York: Free Press.

Williamson, E. G. (1965). *Vocational counseling.* New York: McGraw-Hill.

Wolpe, J. (1958). *Psychotherapy by reciprocal inhibition.* Stanford, CA: Stanford University Press.

Wolpin, M., Shorr, J., & Krueger, L. (Eds.). (1986). *Imagery: Recent practice and theory.* New York: Plenum.

Yates, J. F. (1990). *Judgement and decision making.* Englewood Cliffs, NJ: Prentice Hall.

Zunker, V. G. (1994). *Career counseling: Applied concepts of life planning* (4th ed.). Pacific Grove, CA: Brooks/Cole.

5 Affectively Focused Counseling Strategies

INTRODUCTION

This chapter is devoted to a discussion of affectively oriented counseling approaches. The person-centered, the Gestalt, and the existential approaches are briefly outlined. Suggestions are offered for using the affective approaches to help clients ventilate, obtain catharsis, and gain insight and improve self-awareness. After careful review of the material in this chapter you should be able to:

- discuss the key concepts in the three affective approaches: person-centered, Gestalt, and existential;
- identify the differences among the ventilation, the cathartic, and the self-awareness and self-insight processes; and
- describe how you could use an affective approach to assist clients in gaining insight into themselves.

Individuals sometimes want or need to explore feelings about themselves, their self-perceptions and self-responsibilities, their relationships with significant others, and the meaningfulness of their experiences. The concerns they present may reveal a positive desire to learn more about themselves, or they may present issues that reveal limited awareness of self, negative feelings of self-worth, feelings of helplessness or of having few options, or an inability to deal with their emotions in an effective manner. When any of these are present, clients may be helped by using an affectively focused counseling strategy.

Affectively oriented approaches are based on a view of human nature that emphasizes the following major points. First, human beings have the capacity to understand themselves, to regulate their own behavior, to choose among alternative courses of action, and to develop their inherent potential. Second, individuals view the world from their own subjective frame of reference. Third, healthy individuals live in the present and deal with phenomena at the conscious level. Fourth, the ultimate aim of any counseling process is to help clients move in a positive direction to find self-satisfaction through living a meaningful and authentic life. And fifth, any and all attempts to facilitate client growth must be based on a deep respect for the client as a human being, an understanding of the importance of the client's unique perception of the world, and a focus on or concern with conscious phenomena or the here-and-now events of life.

Three Affectively Focused Approaches

This chapter presents three major affectively oriented counseling theories. Each of these approaches helps clients gain a better understanding of themselves and thus become better able to deal with their problems, issues, and concerns. The *person-centered* theory developed by Carl Rogers (1951) emphasizes helping clients focus inwardly to help them move toward the process of self-development and self-actualization. The *Gestalt* theory founded by Fritz Perls (1992) focuses on assisting clients in improving their self-awareness by becoming more cognizant of the totality and the meaningfulness of their experiences. Individuals who become more aware of their experiences learn to function more effectively. The *existential* approach has been promulgated by several different theorists including Frankl (1985), May (1986), and Van Kaam (1966). This school emphasizes helping clients focus on the meaningfulness of their experiences to obtain a better understanding of their existence. Through this process clients gain more positive feelings of self, and more self-actualization or insight about self is likely to occur. After the presentation of the theories, the text outlines specific suggestions that can be employed to help clients ventilate, obtain catharsis, and develop greater insight and self-awareness.

Because each of these three major theories is reviewed only briefly in this chapter, readers are encouraged to read about them in detail either in the books written by the original theorists (Perls, 1992; Rogers, 1972; May, 1986) or in texts that present another description of the essential concepts of these theories (Burks & Stefflre, 1979; Corey, 1996; Corsini & Wedding, 1995; Gilliland, James, & Bowman, 1994; Gladding, 1996; Ivey, Ivey, & Simek-Morgan, 1997; Patterson & Watkins, 1995).

The Person-Centered Approach

An important affectively oriented counseling approach is the person- or client-centered one. This humanistic approach emphasizes that all human beings have within themselves the potential to be creative and behave in a responsible and wholesome manner. The client is the central focus of his or her own therapy, and it is the client who ultimately reaches his or her own conclusions about what is causing any disturbance or problem, the steps that need to be taken to resolve the issue, and the consequences for living with any therapeutic outcome.

The person-centered approach to counseling was developed by Carl Rogers. It is based on the underlying premise that human beings, by their very nature, are inherently good; that they have a tendency to act positively; and that they can and do strive to become self-actualized. The emphasis in person-centered counseling is placed on developing an atmosphere that is conducive to client growth rather than on diagnosis or prescriptive interventions. In his writings (1942, 1951, 1957, 1972), Rogers stresses the following major concepts, which outline the frame of reference he used to understand how people function and how to assist them. These concepts are: the dignity and worth of each person; the inherent potential of each person to become self-actualized; the importance of each individual's private world of experience; the natural characteristic of people to be good and trustworthy; the notion of self-concept and the feelings of positive regard that must be present for individuals to function effectively and fully; and the role and function of the counselor.

The dignity and worth of individuals.

Rogers maintains that every person is a valuable member of the human race and deserves to be treated in a dignified and humanistic way. Each person, regardless of looks, economic status, or behavior, should be respected and treated warmly and genuinely. Having this nonjudgmental, positive, and genuine attitude toward others is essential for dealing with others in all relationships.

Self-actualization potential.

Rogers stresses that every person by nature has the inherent potential to become self-actualized. This self-actualization process is the prime reason clients change and grow in positive directions. It implies that individuals have the innate capacity to function in ways that satisfy their physical and psychological needs in an autonomous but self-controlled and self-disciplined manner. This process serves to enable the person to develop those capacities that enhance the individual as well as significant others in his or her life. Self-actualization is a dynamic process of becoming (Rogers, 1972), and it is a growth and developmental phenomenon rather than a static terminal state or fixed stage of existence. Self-actualized individuals are dynamic, function fully, and live effectively in socially responsible ways.

Internal frame of reference.

A third major concept articulated by Rogers is the importance of understanding the individual's internal frame of reference. Each person lives in an ever-changing private world or field of experience that they alone know and encounter. This subjective or phenomenological world provides a frame of reference for the individual that in turn acts as a guide for the behavior of the individual in satisfying perceived needs. Thus, an understanding of this perceptual world is basic to understanding a client's behavior.

Trustworthiness.

Rogers believes that individuals are intrinsically good and trustworthy. By this concept he means that all human beings have an innate tendency to manage their own affairs and behave in ways that are personally satisfying and socially responsible. Individuals who behave in irresponsible, socially undesirable, or destructive ways have become alienated from their own inherent nature. Their behavior is a defensive process that projects a poor self-image or poor self-concept. This underlying discrepancy within the individual causes anxiety, and the individual is in a state of incongruence.

Self-concept and positive regard.

Rogers postulates that two interrelated factors influence the self-actualization process. The first is the person's self-concept. This self-concept is the awareness of one's being. This view of self is composed of the constellation of attitudes, feelings, and thoughts about one's self. It includes concepts of one's abilities, skills, personality, goals, desires, values, relationships with others, and experiences. The self-concept is subjective and personal.

The second factor is the degree of positive regard that one has had and continues to experience. All human beings have the need to be accepted, respected, and loved, but it is of critical importance during the childhood developmental years. Positive regard is a valuating concept; the degree to which one experiences this positive regard influences one's self-concept and thus the way one functions and tends toward self-actualization. If during the developmental period a child receives affection based only on his or her behavior, then the child experiences *conditional positive regard,* which can and does cause problems within the person. For positive mental health it is essential for the child to experience *unconditional positive regard,* a basic ingredient in Rogerian counseling.

Maladaption comes about as a result of experiencing conditional positive regard and a blockage of the natural tendency toward self-actualization. Rogers labels this as an incongruity that has developed within the person. This *incongruity is* often reflected in one of the following ways: a discrepancy between the individual's awareness and his or her functioning; a discrepancy between the individual's potential and his or her attainment; negative feelings about one's self or one's characteristics; strong feelings of guilt, tension, or anxiety; or poor interpersonal relationships.

The role and function of the counselor.

Rogers stresses that, because clients have this inherent potential to self-actualize, the counselor's role is to facilitate this process by providing the appropriate climate so that self-exploration, self-understanding, and personal growth can occur. In this process the clients' self-actualizing tendencies will help them overcome any blockages or obstacles that have interfered with their ability to function. Rogers (1957) states that certain necessary and sufficient conditions must be present for positive client growth to occur. Five of these conditions focus on the counselor and one focuses on the client. They are as follows:

1. *The individuals must be in psychological contact.* This first condition places the responsibility on the counselor for creating a nonjudgmental, nondiagnostic, and nonauthoritarian atmosphere in which a relationship based on mutual respect and trust can develop. In this warm, genuine, and authentic climate the counselor should encourage the client to explore his or her own feelings, attitudes, and prescriptions; help the client focus on the present rather than past occurrences; and accept whatever the client says without a value judgment.

2. *The client must be in a state of incongruence, being vulnerable or anxious.* The second condition indicates that the client is truly a person in need and is quite anxious, disturbed, or upset about some events, persons, or things in his or her life. This incongruence can manifest itself in a variety of ways. In some cases clients may distort or deny their feelings, perceptions, or factual events; in other cases they may not be able to deal with experiences in their lives as they believe they should. This anxiety may appear as a relatively minor concern or an extremely serious one.

3. *The counselor must be congruent or integrated in the relationship.* The third condition requires that the counselor be receptive to the client and focus intensely on what the client is saying. The counselor must leave any personal concerns out of the

relationship and not allow any barriers to interfere with listening to the client's words and being attuned to the client's underlying messages. This congruence allows the counselor to pay close attention to the client and to be genuine in his or her contact. Congruence further allows the counselor to be aware of self in the relationship and to communicate in an open, sincere, and meaningful way. This in turn facilitates the client's willingness to open up to the counselor.

4. *The counselor must experience unconditional positive regard for the client.* The counselor needs to feel a deep and genuine caring for the client as a person of value no matter what condition the client is in, how the client behaves, or what the client says. The counselor does not have to like the condition, the behavior, or the expressions but must accept the client as a fellow human being who is entitled to respect without any conditions. This unconditional positive regard is a nonpassive caring for the client, and it encourages a mutual respect that is essential for the collaborative nature of person-centered counseling.

5. *The counselor must experience an empathic understanding of the client's internal frame of reference and endeavor to communicate this experience to the client.* Through the process of listening to the client's words and underlying messages, the counselor senses what the client is feeling and what meanings these feelings have for the client. The counselor conveys his or her own perceptions of these feelings to the client in an open, respectful, and sharing manner. This sensing of the client's inner world may be limited at times, but the communication of this intention has considerable value. It can foster further discussion of the client's hidden self and encourage more awareness of self.

6. *Communication to the client of the counselor's empathic understanding and unconditional positive regard must be achieved to a minimal degree.* The client hears that the counselor really cares, understands his or her problems and concerns, and is aware of the client's underlying feelings and perceptions. This results in the client's feeling a sense of genuine interest and concern and of being a mutual partner in the counseling process; the client gains a level of security, which allows a gradual discussion of inner feelings, attitudes, and perceptions.

The focus of the person-centered approach is not to help a client solve a particular problem but rather to help the person grow and develop a better understanding of self. Through the process of providing acceptance, respect, and understanding, the client slowly allows his or her inherent self-actualization process to be activated. Clients also gain increasing insight, become more aware of the meaning of their own thoughts, feelings, and behavior, and begin to see for themselves how they can deal more effectively with the problems and issues of their own lives.

The person-centered counseling process goes through the following phases:

1. the experience of being cared for and the sense of freedom to discuss anything that is on one's mind;
2. a slow unfolding and airing of one's attitudes and perceptions and a release of one's pent-up feelings;
3. a gradual movement toward becoming less defensive or anxious;
4. an awareness of one's incongruities and the factors related to these issues;
5. a more accurate perception of one's self, one's problems, and one's relationships to others;

6. an increase in the strength to deal with problems and an enhanced ability to make decisions; and

7. a gradual but definite sense of being more integrated—an increased facility for self-direction, more self-confidence, and a greater positive insight into self.

The process of uncovering feelings that have been distorted or denied in one's awareness is not always a smooth path but rather a route that has numerous ups and downs. In gaining insight and gradual self-awareness, the client may have to recognize some internalized patterns about his or her concept of self. Thus, the process for some clients is painful and anxiety provoking. Genuineness, unconditional positive regard, and an empathetic understanding of the client are essential conditions for guiding the client through this process.

The Gestalt Approach

A second major affectively oriented counseling method is the Gestalt approach, developed by Frederick S. Perls (1992; Perls, Hefferline, & Goodman, 1994). This counseling approach is process oriented and focuses on what is happening to the client during the counseling rather than on the content of the client's discussion. Client feelings are emphasized, and the therapeutic goal is to help clients become more aware of what they are doing and how they are doing it—and, at the same time, to learn to accept and respect themselves and their own behavior. Perls was influenced by a number of psychological movements, including psychoanalysis, psychodrama, existentialism, and Gestalt psychology. They all contributed to his understanding of the spectrum of human emotions, feelings, and body sensations. Gestalt counseling emphasizes the following major concepts: the wholeness of individuals; the ability of individuals to focus on their perceptual fields, to select one need at a time in a spectrum of needs, and to shift focus from one need to another as needs are met; the inherent tendency of individuals to self-actualize and to direct their lives in an effective manner; the importance of the present; the homeostatic or self-regulating process; the concept of awareness; and the intervention techniques used in the counseling process.

Wholeness. The essential ideas of Gestalt psychology are based on the notion that human behavior is more than a mere collection of unrelated stimuli or events and that the parts of life have meaning in relation to the whole. Thus, individuals do not see phenomena as isolated bits and pieces; rather, we have a tendency to organize these factors into meaningful configurations. The human experience cannot be compartmentalized—it needs to be understood as a *gestalt,* integrated, or unified whole (Van de Reit, Korb, & Gorrell, 1980). The original Gestalt theory was formulated in Germany by Wertheimer, Kohler, and Koffka, who were studying the field of perception (Hartmann, 1974). The Gestalt psychologists found that human beings have a strong need to impose a meaning on, and achieve closure with, relevant portions of their perceptual fields. Three major principles guide this need: (1) the principle of closure, which says that people have a need to complete the incomplete; (2) the principle of proximity, which says that the distance between objects has a bearing on how they are seen (thus, people tend to relate items that are close to one another and not those that are farther apart); and (3) the principle of similarity, which says that people have a tendency to group similar items together. These three principles can be visually represented by the following examples:

- What shape is suggested by this diagram?
- How do you organize the following sets of dots?
- Which figures would you group together?

Each one of these principles shows that individuals constantly seek to put things together in order to make sense or to develop an organized pattern out of a variety of factors, and that individuals need to find a connection or to have closure in dealing with life's issues.

The concept of wholeness also refers to the agreement between the physical and the psychological dimensions of a person. When clients reveal discrepancies between verbal statements and nonverbal behavior, a lack of wholeness is present. Gestalt counselors look for evidence of this lack of wholeness and make their clients aware of these discrepancies, thus challenging their clients to assume responsibility for this incongruence.

Concepts of perceptual field.

Another important notion is that individuals organize their perceptions to meet their needs. The perceptual field of an individual is described by Gestalt psychologists in terms of the *figure* and the *ground*. Within the individual's environment or perceptual field, the item that the person is focusing on or is most aware of is called the figure, and the rest of the perceptual field is called the ground. Only one item or event can be the figure at one time. The object that the client focuses on can be the figure, and the ground is anything within the client's knowledge and awareness levels. A good gestalt, or meaningful perception pattern, is created when a person's greatest need becomes the figure and other needs fade into the background or the ground. When this need is met, the gestalt is completed and that figure fades into the ground, allowing the individual to go on to another need. If needs are not met, gestalts are incomplete, new gestalts cannot be made, and the client has some *unfinished business*. Furthermore, when gestalts are not complete, or closure has not occurred in previous experience, the individual's self-regulatory process has malfunctioned. Thus, a hidden agenda for many individuals is their unfinished business. This unfinished business, which is often an unexpressed feeling or unresolved situation, interferes with the effective functioning of the individual.

Self-actualization.

Perls (1992) stressed that human beings are inherently neither good nor bad, but they can use their nature effectively or ineffectively. All have the potential to self-actualize. This self-actualization process is manifested by the ability of individuals to find their own way in life and to accept responsibility for directing their own lives in an effective manner, coping with the problems and frustrations of life, and choosing between and among alternative courses of action. Therefore, self-actualized people take responsibility for their actions, live productive and proactive lives rather than reactive or defensive ones, and thoughtfully select from among options to meet their unique needs in a systematic manner. Ineffective or maladaptive individuals have not taken responsibility for their decisions and have not acted on appropriate figures in their perceptual fields.

The importance of the present.
An important tenet of the Gestalt approach is concentration on the here and now. People must live in the present because it is the only time one has control over. The focal point of life is the here and now; the past is gone and the future has not yet come (Polster & Polster, 1973). Consequently, individuals need to appreciate and fully experience themselves as they live life rather than dwelling on the past or the future. The past and future are of importance only if they are related in a meaningful way to the present. In the counseling process this concept is stressed by encouraging clients to relate their feelings to the present and by keeping clients from ruminating or focusing on past or future events. Concentrating on the present facilitates the client's awareness of self and enhances introspection, exploration, and resolution. This here-and-now orientation is fostered by the counselor, who uses questions such as "What are you feeling right now?" and "What are your feet doing while you are talking?"

Self-regulation.
All human beings are constantly striving to meet their needs and are in an interactive relationship with their own unique environments (Latner, 1984). This relationship is a homeostatic process—a tendency toward balancing—wherein the individual strives for equilibrium within himself or herself or between the self and the environment. This balance can be threatened by demands of the environment (outside of self) or by demands of various needs of the individual (internal conflicts).

When an imbalance occurs, often a strong emotional experience, such as anxiety or exuberance, arises and indicates that the individual is out of balance. This emotional state usually signals the need for self-regulation and self-control and normally supplies the energy for the organism to meet this need and return to a balanced state. When this fails to happen, the regulatory process has malfunctioned. This imbalance may be related to different spheres of life or to different intrapsychological phenomena. Examples of the former type of imbalance include how a student's poor interpersonal peer relationships influence her academic performance and how a person's home life affects his job performance. Examples of the latter type of imbalance include how the need for recognition becomes a self-defeating behavior in one's attempt to relate to significant others.

Gestalt counselors endeavor to make their clients aware of the characteristic ways of maintaining an unhealthy state. Gestalt theory outlines five patterns whereby individuals become imbalanced: introjection, projection, retroflection, deflection, and confluence (Polster & Polster, 1973). *Introjection* refers to ways clients take on their feelings and behaviors or embrace the rules and regulations of life. Individuals who introject adopt the views or the behaviors of others without analyzing those views to see if they agree with their own self-structures. This can cause them to function poorly because they may accede without any careful thought to the demands of others and act and behave as others expect them to; they are not their own persons. *Projection* is the process of dismissing or disowning parts of one's self that are inconsistent with one's self-image and placing these outside one's self, or assigning them to others. In this situation individuals make others (or the environment) responsible for what occurs in their lives; thus, they are not accountable for their own behavior. Another person is assigned guilt or blame for the individual's own shortcomings (for example, when a student blames an instructor for his failure). *Retroflection* occurs when something that is originally directed away from a person is reversed and returns to that person. For example, retroflection occurs when clients do for themselves what they want others to do for them or when they want to direct a feeling or a behavior towards another and end up directing the feeling or behavior inward. Thus, clients may do projects that they really want others to do for them or, when their aggression toward another is turned inward, they wind up hating themselves. *Deflection* consists of avoiding any serious or long contact with an issue. This process serves to help clients circumvent the topic and diminishes their emotional experiences. They may diffuse the issue by using humor, overgeneralizing, or talking incessantly. For example, you may have a client who avoids his real concern by talking around the problem. *Confluence* occurs when clients cannot make a clear distinction or boundary between themselves and others or their environment. For example, a parent who has invested so much of self in a child may lose a sense of where his or her emotions stop and where the child's begin—in fact, the parent may see or feel the child as an extension of self.

Awareness.

The objective of the Gestalt counselor is to help the client become fully aware of self and his or her present experience. Self-awareness is of major importance in an individual's self-regulation process. It is perhaps the single most important feature of the self-actualized person. This is the central concept of the Gestalt approach. Awareness touches virtually every aspect of life: one's internal ideas, feelings, and physiological actions, as well as one's appreciation for and relationship to one's environment. When one is aware of self, one is in touch with one's own existence and reality; one has a sense of responsibility for one's own attitudes, behaviors, and feelings; and one can exercise greater self-control. Helping the person become aware of self at every instant assists the client in seeing his or her difficulties, what may be producing them, and what actions may be necessary to solve them.

The aware person understands things as unified wholes or gestalts. When awareness is blocked, needs can be unmet, feelings unexpressed, self-actualization frustrated, and gestalts incomplete. These incomplete gestalts cause considerable imbalance within the individual and serve as a continual distraction for the person. People become maladjusted because they are fragmented and unable to determine which objects or phenomena in their environments will satisfy their needs. The major sign of a maladjusted person is being unaware of self or environmental factors or both. Energy is spent suppressing unfinished business. Hence, the key to self-actualization is self-awareness, and the major way to help individuals overcome their maladaptive behaviors is to increase their self-awareness.

The role and function of the counselor.

The aim of the Gestalt counselor is to assist clients in becoming more aware of themselves, their environments, and their personal needs in the here-and-now situation. Thus, the counselor helps clients come to grips with their emotions, feelings, and attitudes and to discover what is causing an imbalance in their lives. This increased self-awareness in turn makes the client more self-reliant and hence more self-actualized. In other words, the aim is to foster self-dependency by helping individuals learn about their own strengths and self-regulation activities. Gestalt therapy is not interested in why a person behaves the way he or she does but in what a person is doing and how he or she is doing it.

The Gestalt approach attempts to go beyond clients' verbal statements by helping them experience themselves in the present and work through their unfinished business. Client self-awareness is enhanced by encouraging clients to: listen to what they themselves are saying; recognize the processes of what they are feeling and thinking; observe how they act in certain situations; and note any discrepancies between their thoughts, feelings, expressions, and behaviors. Rather than providing answers to the client's concerns, the Gestalt counselor encourages the client to deal with the unfinished business by structuring the situation so the impasse comes into the open. The counselor's goal is to help the client recognize the unfinished business or the impasse, realize that he or she has the ability to resolve the issue, and assume the responsibility of taking the necessary steps to act on the unfinished business. The counselor encourages clients to make their own interpretations and find their own meanings as they struggle to experience the process of completing their gestalts. By experiencing these problems and solutions, clients are able to increase their awareness and improve their self-regulation processes.

The role and function of the counselor in this process is to provide an atmosphere that is conducive to developing self-awareness in the here-and-now situation (Passons, 1975). Any techniques can be used to facilitate this process. Typically, Gestalt counselors are rather active, directive, and forceful in trying to help clients focus their awareness on the present. The task of the counselor is to bring out this awareness by attending to clients and their perceptual fields, heightening or highlighting the essential elements of these experiences, and when necessary, expressing feelings that are too abstract or personal for clients to verbalize. It is not the role of the counselor to pass judgment on the client but rather to point out discrepancies, to challenge incomplete gestalts, and to give feedback.

Although Gestalt counseling does not mandate a step-by-step procedure, this approach does stress having clients experience themselves in problem situations. Gestalt counselors emphasize having clients take ownership of their own statements, act out conflicts, and see different sides of the issues. Although specific techniques are not mandated, Gestalt counselors frequently use the following strategies.

1. *Help clients modify their verbal statements.* In order to stress to clients that they must live in the present, take ownership over their lives, and take responsibility for their feelings, behaviors, or attitudes, counselors direct their clients to modify their verbal messages using one of the following techniques:

   a. Use the personal pronoun. The client is encouraged to use "I" and to avoid the impersonal "it." Speaking in the first-person singular forces the client to take ownership of his or her statements and enhances the client's awareness of what is being communicated. For example, a client is instructed to change, "It will not happen again" to "I will not let that happen again."

   b. State that they are responsible for themselves. One way to do this is to have clients end all their statements or beliefs with the phrase "and I take responsibility for my feelings, actions, or thoughts." For example, a client is told to change

"I was mad" to "I was mad, and I take responsibility for my feelings." Another technique is changing the words "can't" to "won't" or switching "but" to "and." For example, "I want to stop smoking but I can't" is a statement that avoids responsibility. "I want to stop smoking and I won't" puts the responsibility for the action in the client's lap.

c. Talk in the present tense. This encourages the client to focus on the here-and-now situation. For example, clients are asked to change "I hated him" to "I hated him yesterday, and today I am still very angry with him."

d. Convert questions into statements. Forcing clients to make statements encourages them to focus on themselves and their own perceptions and beliefs and avoids deflecting the focal point away from the client. For example, "Do you believe me?" should be changed to "I do not think you believe me."

2. *Use simulations.* Simulated techniques are used to help clients gain insight into their own behaviors, emotions, perceptions, and thoughts. By using these techniques they can learn to bring past experiences into the present, understand both sides of a question or situation, feel the opposite sides of an internal conflict, or get in touch with a part of themselves they may have been unaware of. These simulations are also used when the client has some unfinished business that is limiting the client. Such techniques as role playing, role reversal, rehearsing, dialoguing, playing the projection, and the empty chair can be employed. After acting out these simulations the counselor helps the client see the unfinished business that emerges.

a. Role playing occurs when the counselor has the client play himself or herself in a given situation or relationship. It provides the client with the opportunity to engage in a behavior without any risks. Gestalt counselors often ask clients to say out loud or enact what they are thinking about.

b. Role reversal happens when the client plays someone else in a given situation or relationship. It gives clients the chance to see themselves and the situation from another perspective. One technique used is asking clients to play part of themselves that they rarely or never express.

c. Rehearsal is the act of practicing a specific behavior or situation. It affords the client the opportunity to strengthen the behavior and belief so that the target behavior can be carried out.

d. Dialoguing is the process of speaking on both sides of an issue or a conflict. This brings the issue out into the open and provides the client with new insight.

e. Playing the projection occurs when the client has projected something on another person and the counselor has the client play the role of the person on whom the projection was made. Thus, clients may see that they have the same questions as the other person.

f. The empty-chair technique is similar to the dialogue, but it is more dramatic because the process involves having the client talk to an empty chair that stands for a significant other person or the opposite side of an issue. This technique is sometimes carried out by having the client change seats each time he or she speaks on a different side of the issue.

3. *Direct clients to discuss unpleasant feelings and emotions.* Gestalt counselors do not preach or use "why" questions, but they do direct clients to focus on unpleasant

experiences. This is done to help the client experience the emotion during the counseling process. The threatening fantasies are brought out into the open, and the client is encouraged to see how he or she can handle the obstacles. Strong resistance to this is often encountered, and the counselor needs to point out how the client is stuck at a prohibitive point. This awareness of being "stuck" helps clients overcome their resistance to the process. One of the following methods is often used:

a. Asking clients to finish open-ended sentences such as "Right now I feel . . ." or "I would like to. . . ."

b. Encouraging clients to stay with a feeling and even exaggerate their emotional experiences during the counseling session—for example, "Stay angry, get real mad at him, show me how angry you can be" or "Cry, go ahead and cry if you feel that sad." One variation of this is to ask the client to become the emotion: "Be your anger, stay with it."

c. Confronting clients with discrepancies between their statements and nonverbal gestures or body language—for example, "You say you are relaxed, but you are biting your nails."

d. Encouraging clients to share how they might feel if they had just revealed a well-guarded secret to a group or to a particular person—for example, "Suppose you just told your innermost feelings to the people you work with. How would you feel?"

e. Sharing your hunches about how you think a client might feel about a given situation—for example, "It seems to me that you would feel very hesitant to tell your boss off."

The Existential Viewpoint

The third major affectively oriented counseling approach is based on the existential notion that human existence, by its very nature, causes individuals to search for the meaning of their lives. Thus, many of the problems that clients bring to the counseling process are related to their search for identity and purpose in life, their examination of their relationships with others, and their questioning of their own abilities and developmental processes. The existential approach does not offer specific techniques for working with clients; rather it recommends issues that counselors ought to be aware of and endorses the creation of an atmosphere conducive to examining the meaningfulness of life and its ramifications.

The existential approach to counseling does not represent the work of a single person nor is there one major proponent of this school. It has its roots in existential philosophy, which was originally discussed and written about by such men as Kierkegaard, Nietzsche, Sartre, and Heidegger. A number of individuals such as Frankl (1985), Fromm (1996), May (1990), Van Kaam (1966), and Yalom (1981) have been influential in advancing the existential approach in counseling. These experts have articulated a number of characteristics that distinguish those who are living a meaningful existence from those who are functioning inadequately. Among the major characteristics of those who live an

authentic existence are awareness of self; a sense of freedom to make responsible decisions; the ability to relate to significant others in their lives; the willingness to accept the
negatives of life and death; and the acceptance of anxiety as a constructive force in one's
life.

Self-awareness and uniqueness.

Individuals have the innate tendency to be
self-aware—a unique capacity that allows them to think and feel about themselves. This
awareness is primarily a self-centered subjective perception or the "I am" experience
(May & Yalom, 1995). This awareness facilitates an understanding of the fact that one is
unique in the world, and the process of learning underscores the experience that each
person travels the road of life in a way that no one else does. This quality of aloneness can
lead to loneliness and isolation. When clients feel this strong sense of isolation, a prime
therapeutic goal is to help them become more aware of themselves and their uniqueness.
Increased awareness of self leads to greater courage to face life's loneliness, greater responsibility, greater openness to options, and richer existential living. Failure to be aware
of self leads to passivity and reactive behavior rather than a productive and proactive
lifestyle.

Freedom and responsible decision making.

Individuals have the capacity
to make choices in their lives, and they are responsible for their actions. Human beings
are essentially free to make decisions and to take alternative courses of action in many
dimensions of their lives. These choices are often made with a degree of risk and uncertainty. Existentialists hold that individuals grow, learn, and develop in a process that does
not simply follow a behavioral conditioning process. People are responsible for the choices
they make and the ones they refuse to make; thus, they are responsible for their behavior
and the direction of their lives. Individuals who do not use their capacity to make decisions, or who are fearful of the consequences and thus become immobilized, act as if
their lives were controlled completely by external forces. When clients are immobilized
by conflicts, the major existential goal is to help them understand that freedom is a basic
human quality.

Relationship.

Individuals have a basic need to relate to significant others in a meaningful way. The need to be a part of a group, the need for recognition from others, and
the need to share oneself with others are all manifestations of this need for relatedness.
Individuals who are open to others show a caring and respectful attitude toward them
and feel responsible for their well-being. Individuals who do not have a good relationship with others become estranged and alienated from society. This lack of relationship
can also lead to isolation and self-centeredness. The therapeutic process aims at helping
the client become more aware of the need to relate and the interdependence of all members of the human society.

Meaningfulness.

Human beings have an innate desire to search for a personal
meaning for their existence. This desire to understand the meaningfulness of existence is
the major characteristic of existentially oriented approaches. Individuals who are functioning effectively accept the mysteries of existence and the dualities of that existence—
birth and death, joy and sadness, elation and pain, and happiness and suffering. This

acceptance does not imply a passivity nor any avoidance of the desire to ameliorate or improve the negative aspects of that existence but, rather, that life, by its very nature, has these components to it. Having a sense of the meaning of life gives a purpose to one's existence and enables one to form a set of moral and spiritual values. Searching for this meaning in the face of the sufferings and dilemmas of life is an ongoing existential quest. The existential counseling process helps clients deal with these issues and learn to resolve these ultimate questions about life.

The role of anxiety. Anxiety is natural to the human condition. Rather than viewing anxiety as a negative state of imbalance, individuals must learn to use anxiety as a constructive awareness to act. Living life fully can and does cause anxiety. Choices must be made with elements of risk. Taking responsible actions can cause unpleasant reactions from others, and intensive and worthwhile task accomplishment can have concurrent pressures. Anxiety is not something to avoid; rather, it should motivate the individual to take proactive, positive, and responsible steps to deal with the causes of the anxiety. Individuals who avoid anxiety have relinquished control of themselves and lead a reactive and passive existence.

The role of the counselor. Existentially oriented counselors focus on helping clients recognize that seeking meaningful life satisfaction from material objects and physical things is a nonauthentic lifestyle and that true satisfaction comes from living life in an existential manner (Fromm, 1990). Thus, existentialists tend to help their clients become more

- aware of their actions and their ability to choose alternatives and to be responsible for these actions;
- aware of themselves, their uniqueness, their loneliness, their independence;
- sensitive to the factors that influence their relationships to others;
- open to their quest for searching out a meaningful purpose or value in life; and
- accepting of anxiety as a healthy human experience that naturally occurs in living one's life.

Ultimately, the goal of the existential counselor is to help the client experience a more authentic life.

The existential counselor must see the client as a unique person who needs to map out a role for self in this world. Thus, the concern is with helping the person become free to follow his or her authentic self and face the challenges of life. Existentialists do not employ a step-by-step procedure to accomplish these objectives nor do they offer a set of practical techniques. Emphasis is placed on developing a sound working relationship and creating an honest, open, and nonauthoritarian atmosphere. The counselor is actively engaged in giving caring messages: expressing authentic responses, helping clients gain insight into their own thoughts and feelings, and aiding clients in dealing with the values and meaning of life.

Existentialists can and do use a wide variety of methods to accomplish these objectives. Any methodology that helps the client focus on understanding a personal meaning of life, that has a distinct emphasis on personal responsibility, and that helps the client explore his or her own notions of self and the process of living may be used. The crucial concept is developing a warm, trusting relationship with the client. This relationship process is the key to enabling the client to become more authentic in his or her own life.

AFFECTIVELY ORIENTED COUNSELING PROCEDURES

Affectively oriented counseling strategies direct the counseling process inward—that is, toward the client—to help the client deal with his or her own perceptions and feelings about self. This inward attention is based on the notion that clients have the inherent ability to function more effectively and that the counselor's role is to act as a catalyst to allow and encourage this process. Although various experts use different processes to assist their clients, a number of major counseling strategies employ affective approaches. These intervention strategies foster ventilation, catharsis, and insight and self-awareness, and thus help clients gain improved feelings and perceptions of themselves. In general, the affectively focused intervention strategies include the following concepts or guidelines.

- Deal with the client in an open, respectful, and genuine way.
- Focus on understanding the client from his or her subjective, internalized frame of reference.
- Work with the client on a conscious, focused, here-and-now orientation.
- Accept the client as having tremendous dignity and worth, regardless of his or her present condition.
- Focus on developing client self-awareness by using techniques that encourage the client to see himself or herself more clearly; use reflective and self-awareness procedures to enhance this process.
- Help the client understand self, his or her underlying motivation, and the environmental and personal factors that influence his or her behavior.
- Assist the client in seeing alternative ways of thinking, feeling, or behaving. This will tend to enhance the client's sense of freedom and responsibility.
- Help the client understand how he or she can influence the direction and activities of life and enhance self-responsibility.
- Help the client explore personal values and the meaningfulness of life experiences, search for greater self-fulfillment, and become more self-actualized.

Ventilation

One important affectively oriented counseling strategy is ventilation. *Ventilation* can be defined as the process of allowing clients to talk about things that are of concern to them. This process of providing clients with an outlet to examine, discuss, and investigate their feelings, thoughts, opinions, and experiences is an important counseling strategy that often makes clients psychologically healthier (May, 1990). Creating a warm, accepting climate gives clients the freedom to discuss whatever is of concern to them in a nonthreatening way, allows them to release inhibitions, makes possible a flow of internal feelings, and helps them see things more objectively. Although fostering this atmosphere is an essential ingredient for all counseling processes, it is often appropriate to concentrate on this skill or climate on its own.

Focusing on the ventilation process is often very useful when clients are under some stress due to the following conditions: indecisiveness, a recent trauma or negative experience, or a recent profound positive experience. Ventilation can be useful to clients who know how to make decisions but who need help to reflect on various components of themselves, their relationships with family, friends, and significant others, and the decisions they need to make in the foreseeable future. This process can also be of considerable value to clients whose functioning level is normally quite satisfactory but who need to talk about a recent profound or negative experience. The ventilation allows clients to express themselves openly and air their feelings, and thereby find release from the tension they are experiencing. Thus, they become more free to make decisions and to regain their normal level of functioning.

The ventilation process is facilitated by providing the fundamental counseling conditions articulated by Rogers (1957): (1) create an empathic, warm, and respectful climate conducive to client openness and self-disclosure; (2) allow the client the opportunity to experience and explore the full range of whatever is bothering him or her; (3) try to feel and understand the client from his or her internal frame of reference by intensively listening with the "third ear" and reflecting on the meaning of the client's statements rather than the surface content; (4) respect the client as a human being of significant worth and value; and (5) encourage the client to talk about things that are difficult for him or her.

Some important issues that the counselor should be mindful of in the ventilation process include the following.

> *Attend to the client.* Actively listen to what the client has to say. Manifest your active listening by using a variety of attending skills such as accents, simple minimal verbal responses, paraphrases, reflections of content and feelings, and summarizations. Be attentive to the client's internal frame of reference rather than to surface statements. Concentrate on listening to what the client is saying and the meaning of these messages, and communicate back to the client that you know and understand what he or she is trying to say.
>
> *Clarify when necessary.* When some confusion or doubt exists about what the client means or is trying to communicate, or when the client presents double messages, ask an appropriate question that is designed to clear up the confusion, resolve the doubt, or identify the duality of an issue more clearly. Clarifying is often needed to define what the real issue is. Perception checks such as "It seems to me that you are trying to say this . . ." and questions clarifying alternatives such as "Do you mean this or do you mean that?" are helpful communication tools that can facilitate the clarifying process.
>
> *Support the client as a person of significant value.* Provide the client with positive feedback about himself or herself. Inform the client that he or she seems like a fine person to you. Communicate feelings of reassurance and

encouragement and thus reaffirm the client's sense of personal value. This support or reassurance is frequently communicated by expressing approval of a present, past, or future action or feeling or by providing consolation for some unhappy event. Helping clients relax by using a warm, friendly tone or by employing specific relaxation techniques is another supportive measure that can facilitate the ventilation process.

Use open-ended questions or statements when appropriate. Active listening is also facilitated by the use of open-ended statements and questions such as "Tell me more about that" or "What happened then?". The judicious use of these open-ended statements and questions, posed with a warm, understanding tone, encourages further self-exploration and discussion.

Catharsis

A second affectively oriented counseling strategy is catharsis. Considered a more complex and focused intervention than ventilation, catharsis is a purging or cleansing action that results from a release in tension or the elimination of an emotional blockage by bringing it out into the open. This process is based on the concept that one's emotions can control the way one thinks and the way one acts, so that feelings that haven't been expressed build up inside until the pressure or tension causes maladaptive behavior (Bohart, 1980). These pent-up feelings keep one from functioning adequately, use up a considerable amount of internal energy, and often result in avoidance of situations, withdrawal from life, and keeping oneself at a considerable emotional distance from significant persons in one's life. These unexpressed feelings may be relatively recent but often are based on traumatic experiences that occurred long ago. The buried feelings associated with that experience need to be expressed so that the built-up tension can be discharged and the pressure within the person restored to normal.

In cases in which emotions are related to deep feelings of bitterness, anger, and frustration, discharges can be dramatic and possibly explosive. Catharsis can be used to help relieve grief, fear, embarrassment, rage, anger, boredom, and tension (Scheff, 1979). The cathartic process can be facilitated by encouraging the ventilation process. Catharsis may be further enhanced by helping clients remember and express the circumstances under which their emotions became blocked and by observing and understanding the discrepancies in their lives that may have caused the emotional difficulty.

The cathartic process unfolds over two phases. First is the recall of the past experience, and second is the release of the blocked emotion in one form or another (Nichols & Efran, 1985). The first stage is facilitated by encouraging the ventilation process and allowing clients to recollect their experiences. The second phase not only allows the pent-up emotional release but also focuses on helping clients deal with these emotions. During this release-and-recovery phase clients should be assisted in the following ways:

- encourage them to relive their suppressed traumatic emotional experiences;
- foster the examination of these experiences so that they understand why the blockage occurred and what ramifications this suppression has caused for self and for others;

- help them understand how this experience can be seen as a valuable part of their lives; and
- encourage them to explore how they can overcome any problems or interpersonal relationship difficulties that may be related to this blockage.

No attempt should be made to foster other counseling strategies at this time. Allow the client to discuss whatever he or she thinks is of importance. Do not respond with solutions to the content of the client's problem, but recognize the issues as real concerns. Do not expect to hear complete stories or logical sequences—the ventilation and cathartic processes are often erratic, emotionally charged, and disjointed. During the ventilation process do not feel that you, as the counselor, need to know the whole story or foster a resolution to the issues presented. During the cathartic process, the release of tension and pent-up feelings should be the primary emphasis. The object of these strategies is to allow the client to ventilate and to experience the release of the tension or stress blocking his or her ability to function. Sometimes the ventilation process alone can improve the client's functioning levels. At other times the cathartic process seems necessary. These strategies can take place over one session or unfold gradually over several interviews.

Insight, Self-Awareness, and Improved Self-Esteem

A third important affectively oriented counseling strategy focuses on helping the client gain insight and improved self-awareness. Insight is the process of looking inside oneself to gain a deep understanding of one's own existence. People can gain insight into one of three major dimensions of their lives. First, they can gain a more complete knowledge and awareness of themselves. Second, they can obtain a better understanding of the relationship between themselves and significant other persons in their lives. And third, people can explore and come to a better understanding or acceptance of the meaningfulness of their experiences in the world. Helping clients acquire insight in any or all three of these dimensions facilitates self-awareness.

In the process of understanding themselves, clients need to gain a more accurate analysis of their own personality characteristics and psychological attributes. They may have a confused, distorted knowledge of themselves and need help to overcome this confusion and distortion. They may need assistance in learning to become more aware of themselves and need help to:

- discern which thoughts and beliefs are held superficially and which ones are held deeply;
- distinguish between or among various feelings and attitudes;
- detect their needs, interests, and motives through deeper understanding;
- obtain a view of their strengths and weaknesses from another perspective.

Obtaining insight also has a dimension of becoming more aware of one's relationship to significant others and how one's own thoughts, feelings, and activities affect these relationships. Individuals can be aware of the images they present to others and the reasons why people relate to them the way they do; or individuals may present themselves in a distorted manner in the belief that the distortion is necessary to maintain the relationship. The counseling process can foster insight and self-awareness by helping individuals:

- understand how their self-perceptions affect their relationships with others;
- learn how they feel about others and how they believe they treat them;
- discover the importance of their relationships with others; and
- perceive how these behaviors affect their social existence, personal growth, and satisfaction.

Fostering insights has existential connotations as well as personal and interpersonal ones. The individual who is insightful and has self-awareness should be aware of the realities of life and feel responsible for self, others, and the well-being of society. Being aware of the meaningfulness of one's experience implies an openness to the existential world and an acceptance of the vicissitudes and temporalness of life. Counselors often help clients gain insights into the meaningfulness of their experiences by assisting them in:

- understanding their own values and beliefs about the world;
- becoming more accepting of unpleasant, painful experiences;
- realizing the limitations of the human condition; and
- striving to become open in their experiences and the realities of their existence.

Clients who can benefit from an insightful-oriented approach typically manifest a lack of self-knowledge, a subjective view of themselves that is incongruent and confused, or a self-image that is not in agreement with the views of other significant persons. They may present themselves as shy, docile, or confused people whose behavior or conversation reveals confused, unproductive, counterproductive, or self-defeating ways. The picture clients portray of themselves may be accurately described by them, or they may be only vaguely aware or unaware of this lack of self-knowledge. Other clients may present themselves as individuals who function at a fairly high level but need help sorting out the meaning of their existence, or they may be suffering from a traumatic experience and may benefit from the insightful counseling process.

Insight and self-awareness typically make up the second phase of an intervention strategy that employs the ventilation process as the first stage. In other words, providing the facilitative conditions, or a warm, open, and respectful climate, is necessary to enhance insight. Often, the skills that are used to foster the ventilation process are sufficient of and by themselves to allow insight to occur. Rogers (1972) has presented both theoretical and research findings to support his claim that his facilitative conditions are necessary and sufficient for positive changes to occur. However, although the Rogerian conditions may be all that are necessary for some clients under certain circumstances, additional techniques are available and can be used to foster insight.

The insightful process can be developed by a variety of methods that enable clients to see reality more accurately, trust self-decisions more certainly, and understand others more completely. One or more of the following communication skills may facilitate this process.

Provide the client with appropriate factual information or explanations of how various structures work or how they may be organized. Frequently, clients lack knowledge about themselves, environmental factors, and available resource materials. If some important knowledge is lacking, insight may be facilitated by providing this essential material. The information may be presented by the counselor, or the counselor may help the client find it by directing the client to it and guiding the client through it.

Inquire about specific relevant data. Ask the client questions that are designed to elicit appropriate data, and learn more about the client and his or her concern. The skillful use of questioning can facilitate insight when the probe helps the client recall important data, promotes more comprehensive discussion during the counseling process, and enhances awareness on the part of the client.

Use direct, forceful statements that are designed to encourage the client to think or feel in a new or different manner. This communication process is used when the counselor believes it is necessary to produce some movement on the part of the client. These deliberate statements are designed to upset the client by showing disapproval or rejection of a client's statement, to confront the client by sharply pointing out discrepancies, to direct the client by strongly advising the client to do something, to center the client by not digressing, or to self-disclose and thereby help the client see things from a different perspective.

Interpret and evaluate various data and information with the client. This process is used when counselors share their knowledge and insight to help clients understand the relationship between various factors. It assists clients in learning more about their strengths and weaknesses, thus providing a deeper understanding of themselves.

SUMMARY

This chapter briefly outlined the person-centered, the Gestalt, and the existential approaches to counseling. The affectively oriented approaches to the counseling process are based on the notion that individuals have the ability to understand themselves, regulate their own behaviors, choose wisely among alternative courses of action, and fulfill their inherent potential. These strategies stress developing a strong relationship with clients understanding clients from the clients' own subjective views of life, and dealing with clients in the here-and-now situation. In these strategies the counselor's objective is to have clients improve their ability to deal with their emotions, beliefs, and values; develop more awareness of themselves; and gain more positive feelings of self-worth. Suggestions were made on methods to use to help clients ventilate, obtain catharsis, and gain insight, self-awareness, and self-esteem.

After your comprehensive review of this chapter, you should be able to discuss the major concepts in the three affectively oriented approaches. You should have a clear perception of how and when to employ these strategies. And you should be aware of the processes employed in using these interventions in practice. To develop a high level of competency in applying affectively focused intervention strategies, you will need further study of these approaches and some experience using them under the guidance of an expert.

REFERENCES

Bohart, A. C. (1980). Towards a cognitive theory of catharsis. *Psychotherapy: Theory, research and practice, 17,* 192–201.

Burks, H. M., & Stefflre, B. (1979). *Theories of counseling* (3rd ed.). New York: McGraw-Hill.

Corey, G. (1996). *Theory and practice of counseling and psychotherapy* (5th ed.). Pacific Grove, CA: Brooks/Cole.

Corsini, R. J., & Wedding, D. (Eds.). (1995). *Current psychotherapies* (5th ed.). Itasca, IL: F. E. Peacock.

Frankl, V. E. (1985). *Psychotherapy and existentialism.* New York: Washington Square Press.

Fromm, E. (1990). *The sane society.* New York: Henry Holt.

Fromm, E. (1996). *The art of loving* (rev. ed.). New York: HarperCollins.

Gilliland, B. E., James, R. K., & Bowman, J. T. (1994). *Theories and strategies in counseling and psychotherapy* (3rd ed.). Boston: Allyn & Bacon.

Gladding, S. T. (1996). *Counseling: A comprehensive profession* (3rd ed.). Columbus, OH: Merrill.

Hartmann, G. (1974). *Gestalt psychology: A survey of facts and principles.* Westport, CT: Greenwood.

Ivey, A. E., Ivey, M. B., & Simek-Morgan, L. (1997). *Counseling and psychotherapy: A multicultural perspective* (4th ed.). Boston: Allyn & Bacon.

Latner, J. (1984). *The Gestalt therapy book.* Highland, NY: Gestalt Journal.

May, R. (1986). *The discovery of being: Writings in existential psychology.* New York: Norton.

May, R. (1990). *The art of counseling* (rev. ed.). Nashville: Gardner Press.

May, R., & Yalom, I. (1995). Existential psychotherapy. In R. J. Corsini & D. Wedding (Eds.), *Current psychotherapies* (5th ed.) (pp. 262–292). Itasca, IL: F. E. Peacock.

Nichols, M. P., & Efran, J. S. (1985). Catharsis in psychotherapy: A new perspective. *Psychotherapy, 22,* 46–58.

Passons, W. R. (1975). *Gestalt approaches in counseling.* New York: Holt, Rinehart and Winston.

Patterson, C. H., & Watkins, C. E. (1995). *Theories of counseling and psychotherapy* (5th ed.). Reading, MA: Addison-Wesley.

Perls, F. S. (1992). *Gestalt therapy verbatim* (rev. ed.). Highland, NY: Gestalt Journal.

Perls, F. S., Hefferline, R. F., & Goodman, P. (1994). *Gestalt therapy: Excitement and growth in human personality* (rev. ed.). Highland, NY: Gestalt Journal.

Polster, E., & Polster, M. (1973). *Gestalt therapy integrated: Contours of theory and practice.* New York: Bruner/Mazel.

Rogers, C. R. (1942). *Counseling and psychotherapy.* Boston: Houghton Mifflin.

Rogers, C. R. (1951). *Client-centered therapy.* Boston: Houghton Mifflin.

Rogers, C. R. (1957). The necessary and sufficient conditions of therapeutic personality change. *Journal of Consulting Psychology, 21,* 95–103.

Rogers, C. R. (1972). *On becoming a person.* Boston: Houghton Mifflin.

Scheff, T. J. (1979). *Catharsis in healing, ritual, and drama.* Berkeley: University of California.

Van de Reit, V., Korb, M. P., & Gorrell, J. J. (1980). *Gestalt therapy: An introduction.* New York: Pergamon Press.

Van Kaam, A. (1966). *The art of existential counseling.* Wilkes Barre, PA: Dimension Books.

Yalom, I. D. (1981). *Existential psychotherapy.* New York: Basic Books.

Performance-Focused Counseling Strategies

Introduction

This chapter presents the information necessary to understand the behavioral or performance approach to helping clients. The techniques outlined in this chapter are seen as ways of helping clients learn to modify their activities and thus are considered educational in nature. You should be able to respond to the following discussion questions after studying this chapter:

- Indicate the differences among the three major behavioral approaches to counseling.
- Identify the important steps in the behavioral counseling process.
- Specify the elements of a contingency contract.
- Name the major techniques used in the social learning approach and indicate when they might be useful in a counseling situation.
- Describe how positive and negative reinforcements and punishments can be used to change behavior.
- Discuss some key behavioral techniques such as assertiveness training, aversion techniques, flooding, paradoxical intention, and systematic desensitization.

This chapter discusses ways to work with clients from a performance or behavioral point of view. The basic premise in this approach is that individuals develop their personalities or characteristic ways of behaving as a result of their life experiences, and they have *learned* to behave or act the way they do. Some of this behavior is appropriate and desirable, whereas other behavior can be inappropriate and undesirable. Individuals who manifest maladaptive behavior have failed to learn correctly, and the way to help these people is to teach them appropriate ways to behave. Furthermore, because all aspects of a person's life are influenced by how that person acts, helping an individual change a behavior often helps that person modify other dimensions of his or her life in significant ways. Performance-focused interventions are those that help clients increase or decrease the likelihood of performance of an existing activity, initiate a new activity, or eliminate a present activity.

This chapter contains five sections. First, an overview of the essential steps used in the behavioral counseling approach are outlined. Second, the meaning and use of contingency contracts are explained. Third, the basic principles of observational and simulated learning are delineated. Fourth, the major concepts of contingency management and operant conditioning are presented. And finally, the essential ideas of stimulus response and classical conditioning are specified. In each section, suggestions are offered for using these intervention strategies in the counseling process.

Behavioral Counseling

The term *behavioral counseling* can be defined as a learning process by which the counselor helps the client learn something new or learn how to change a specific behavior in a particular situation. Behavioral counseling emphasizes identifying the client's problem, clearly labeling the problem in behavioral terms, defining the desired behavioral goals or changes, specifying a plan to bring about the desired changes, and observing and recording the client's behaviors. The counselor takes an active role in teaching the client new ways of behaving and involves the client as much as possible. Typically, after a counseling relationship has been established and the problem has been identified, the behavioral counselor should follow these nine sequential steps.

1. Describe the problem behavior and the context in which it occurs. Identify the items in the behavioral formula ($S^D \rightarrow R \rightarrow S^R$) where S^D is the discriminative stimulus, or antecedent or situation that occurs prior to the behavior; R is the problem behavior, or response to the discriminative stimulus; and S^R is the consequence or behavior that occurs after the problem behavior, reinforcing the problem behavior. It is helpful to find answers to the following questions:
   a. What stimuli or events occurred before the target behavior?
   b. What was the biological and psychological state of the individual when the behavior occurred?
   c. What is the problem behavior or the response to the prior events?
   d. What is the nature of the relationship between the problem and the reinforcers (S^R)?
   e. What types of reinforcers are present?
2. Identify the observable and measurable components of the problem behavior.
   a. Note the *frequency* of occurrence or number of times the response occurred in a period of time; the *intensity* or forcefulness of the response; the *duration*; and the *topology* or form or shape of the behavior.
   b. Collect these data by means of the continuous, time-interval, or situation sampling method and record it in a way that is relatively simple, portable, and economical. Suggested methods include using notebooks, logs, diaries, mechanical devices, tape recorders, charts, and graphs. Martin and Pear (1996) provide more details on appropriate recording procedures.

3. Specify the desired goal. Indicate whether the behavioral goal is:
   a. *response acquisition,* or learning new skills or behaviors;
   b. *response facilitation,* or learning to use presently existing skills more frequently or in a variety of situations; or
   c. *response inhibition,* or learning to decrease the likelihood of undesirable responses.

4. Agree on the set of standards or performance criteria to be achieved.
   a. Identify what needs to be modified in the behavioral formula ($S^D \rightarrow R \rightarrow S^R$).
   b. State the environment where the behavior should be performed or the most favorable discriminative stimuli (S^D).
   c. Indicate the level of performance or criterion level in terms of frequency, intensity, or duration.
   d. State what reinforcements will be used to bring about the new behavior.

5. Develop a plan for the behavior changes.
   a. State the stimulus-response conditioning, simulation, or operant conditioning techniques that will be employed.
   b. Indicate who will be responsible for what activities.
   c. Identify the consequences for meeting or not meeting targeted goals and the procedures for applying the consequences.

6. Describe to the client the methodology planned, the reason for each activity, and the responsibilities of the client and the counselor.

7. Implement the plan. During this treatment phase, continued observations should be made on the frequency, duration, and intensity of the target behavior in order to evaluate the client's progress and the factors that facilitate or impede the client's development.

8. As the client manifests the appropriate behavioral changes, make every effort to develop variable schedules of reinforcement and to practice the new behaviors in realistic settings.

9. When the new behaviors become established, make plans to terminate counseling, and establish methods for client follow-up.

CONTINGENCY CONTRACTS

Counselors using a behavioral approach to counseling often employ a technique known as the *contingency contract.* This is also referred to as a behavioral or psychological contract. Contracts indicate a mutual agreement to work toward a specific goal or to exchange services or goods. The contract normally specifies who is responsible for what and under what conditions and what contingencies apply if the contract is broken. Contracts form the basis of much of our society. We often have explicit written contracts for legal activities such as buying property, opening bank and brokerage accounts, and marketing our personal services. On the other hand, much of our social interaction is made by implicit verbal agreements in which the contingencies of breaking the contract are not determined. For example, when someone is late for a dinner engagement, the consequences of that behavior are not often spelled out in advance. Behavioral or contingency contracts are similar to our other social contracts. However, for the sake of clarity and complete understanding, they should be explicit and should specify the following points:

1. Outline a realistic, clear, and detailed description of the client's goals. These goals can be stated in terms of a range of behaviors, such as "I will compliment my neighbor at least once a day," and "I will try to compliment him three times a day."

2. State the time and frequency by which the goal or behavior is to be measured—for example, "Within three weeks I will visit my mother-in-law three times."

3. Indicate the contingencies or the consequences of meeting or not meeting the goal. Specify the positive or negative consequences that will be given, when and where they will be given, and who will give them. Articulate how these are contingent upon fulfilling or not fulfilling the time and frequency goals. These rewards and punishments should be minimal, immediate, and frequent—for example, "You will earn one dollar each time you do this," and "You will forfeit two dollars when you do that more than twice a day." Be careful not to agree to consequences that are too intense and thus unrealistic; for example, a consequence of $100 is too large for most clients.

4. Specify the means by which contract terms are recorded, measured, or observed and how these terms and observations will be reviewed; for example, the person who is trying to stop smoking may be instructed to keep a daily log of the time, place, and events that preceded his or her smoking a cigarette or having a desire for one.

5. Attach a bonus clause to the contingency contract to indicate additional rewards that can be earned if and when the minimal goals are exceeded; for example, the client who is trying to learn to get his or her homework done on time may be given the target goal of finishing the work by 9 P.M. every day and given the reward of watching television from 9 P.M. to 10 P.M. If the client finishes by 8:30 P.M., he or she may be awarded the pleasure of watching an extra half hour of television.

OBSERVATIONAL AND SIMULATED LEARNING
Basic Concept

The first important behavioral counseling approach discussed is based on the concepts of observational and simulated learning. Observational and simulated learning stresses that individuals learn new ways of behaving by observing others behave in certain ways and by practicing behaviors in simulated ways. The principles underlying this approach to learning have been articulated by Bandura and Walters (1963). Individuals can learn through this social learning process in two distinctive ways: by observation and by simulated experiences. In the observational learning approach, some individual or group acts as a model or a stimulus for changing the thoughts, feelings, or behaviors of the client. The client observes the model's performance and, without actually engaging in the behavior, may obtain new knowledge, modify attitudes, and acquire new behavior. In the simulation learning approach, clients play a role, or simulate themselves in a situation or relationship. This behavioral practice enables clients to overcome inhibitions, deal with their anxieties, and learn appropriate skills. It is common to use both observational and simulated approaches in a sequential process.

Observational Learning

Observational learning is a common occurrence in life—people learn by observing the behavior of others. Informally, this learning process is used throughout our daily lives, as evidenced by the influence others have on our dress codes and our moral and ethical behavior. In a more formal setting, this learning process is used by mentors, teachers, and instructors who model certain skills and expect their students to spend hours learning to copy their actions. The observational learning process is also referred to as modeling, imitation, copying, and mimicry. This learning process has two phases: the *acquisition* phase, which occurs when the observer attends, watches, and listens to the model; and the *performance* phase, which occurs when the observer performs the desired activity.

Modeling procedures can be overt, symbolic, or covert. *Overt* behaviors are activities that are performed in the here-and-now situation. Overt or participant modeling occurs when a live model performs the behavior in the presence of the observer—for example, when the counseling instructor demonstrates how to open a counseling session. This method has the advantage of allowing the observer to identify with the model and see actions that the observer wants to emulate. The disadvantage is that the model's actions or behaviors cannot be controlled; thus, clients may see undesirable behaviors as well as desirable ones.

Symbolic behaviors take place in an abstract or symbolic way. The symbolic modeling procedure is being used when the target behavior is presented through the media—for example, when students who are studying Rogerian counseling view a film of Rogers counseling a client. This technique has the advantage of allowing the counselor to have control over the modeled behaviors; the counselor can select relevant portions of the target behavior, and replications are easy to do. But the observer cannot identify personally with the model, and relevant symbolic models who demonstrate the desired performance may not be available or may be difficult to find.

Covert behaviors take place in our thoughts. Covert modeling procedures are employed when the model is presented through the imagination—for example, when the instructor asks you to imagine yourself in a particular situation or in a role-playing exercise. This approach has the advantage of having complete control of the target behavior because one's imagination can supply relevant materials. It has the disadvantage of the possible loss of reality.

The modeling process can have one of three major effects on the learner: the observer learning effect, the response facilitative effect, or the disinhibiting effect. The *observer learning effect* occurs when a person learns something by observation alone. Because human beings learn simply by seeing things, clients can learn new behaviors solely by observing a model's behavior; for example, by seeing someone bake a cake or solve a problem, an individual can learn how to bake a cake or solve problems. The *response facilitative effect* occurs when an individual sees a model do something that he or she knows how to do and the observer then does it, providing there are no constraints. In other words, the model prompts the behavior; for example, one person may light a cigarette after another person has lit one. In the *disinhibiting* or *inhibiting effect,* an individual sees something done that he or she knows how to do but that person is either disinhibited from repeating the behavior (for example, the player who carries out a particular play after seeing the coach demonstrate the play) or inhibited from repeating the behavior (for example, the person who does not buy an airplane ticket after seeing or reading about a serious airplane accident).

Observational or imitative learning is fostered by using the following eight-step process:

1. Assist the client in identifying the behavior or skill that he or she wants to learn.
2. Eliminate or minimize distracting stimuli and intensify relevant stimuli. This may be done by helping the observer relax.
3. Help the observer focus on what to look for in the model by giving a set of instructions or relevant questions.
4. Select a warm, nurturing model whom the client can respect and identify with. Identification can be enhanced by matching the observer with the model in terms of competence, age, gender, and cultural characteristics. However, the model should be sufficiently distant from the observer in age or competency so that the observer will respect the model and be motivated to learn.
5. Break down any complicated behavior into small, incremental steps that can be modeled and observed.
6. Observe the model and discuss the observed behavior with the client. Review the behavior in order from the least difficult responses to the most difficult. The client should carefully observe the antecedents and the consequences of the behavior.
7. Have the client practice the new behavior or skill as soon after the observation stage as is practical. Provide support and verbal encouragement. This practice should occur both under the direction of the counselor, who can guide the practice, and as homework, so the practice is rehearsed.
8. Evaluate the procedure with the client. If the desired skill was obtained, the intervention was successful. If the desired skill was not obtained, further modeling or assistance with other interventions may be called for.

Simulated Learning

Simulated learning has proved to be an effective learning process. It is a common occurrence in our everyday experiences. Skiers who practice in their basements and job applicants who mentally prepare for an interview are using this learning process. Simulations can deal with realistic or exaggerated situations, overt events or covert thoughts, or past, present, or future occurrences. Simulations are sometimes referred to as replications, practice, or drills.

Three major forms of simulations exist: role playing, role reversal, and dialoguing. *Role playing* is used when clients play themselves in a particular situation or relationship.

It has the advantage of allowing the client to practice being in a certain situation. For example, a placement counselor may have a client play himself in a mock job interview so the client can experience what a job interview is like. *Role reversal* is employed when the client plays someone else in the situation. This has the advantage of having the client experience how another person may react in a given scenario. For example, the placement counselor may have the client play the personnel manager in a mock job interview so the client can gain an understanding of what the employer may be looking for in a job applicant. *Dialoguing* is the process used when the client plays himself or herself and someone else at the same time and conducts a dialogue between the two. For example, the placement counselor can have the client play himself and the personnel manager during the mock job interview. This has the advantage of having the client experience both sides of an issue.

Learning through the simulation process is facilitated by the following five-step procedure:

1. Help the client specify the target behavior, attitude, or performance to be learned. Be as specific and concrete as you can.
2. Encourage the client to determine the environment or situation where the skill needs to be used, the fear reduced, or the attitude changed.
3. Arrange the simulations in a hierarchical order; start with small scenes, minimal interchanges, least difficult or least anxiety-provoking situations, and plan a gradual expansion to more difficult, more complex scenes. Involve the client in planning the hierarchy.
4. Apply the hierarchy. Begin with the first simulation, using covert methods and practice. Have the client discuss the experience, and provide feedback and verbal reinforcement. Move on to more complex situations and progress from minimal-risk to minor-risk situations. Provide ample practice, vary simulations, and give the client plenty of feedback and reinforcement.
5. Have the client apply the new behavior or skill in a real situation. It is important to review the experience with the client to give the client a chance to reflect on this experience and gain some insight into his or her behaviors. If the trial was successful, encourage the client to repeat the experience several times, while providing support and feedback. If the experience was of limited success, repeat the simulated experience until more mastery and comfort are assured. If the experience was not successful, repeat the simulation and investigate the possibility of incorporating other techniques into the intervention program.

Applications and Advantages of Observational and Simulated Approaches

Modeling and simulated learning approaches are extremely useful in a variety of counseling situations, including educational and vocational exploration; decision-making interventions; catharsis, insight, and self-awareness concerns; and modification of social behaviors. The counseling process, which relies on verbal interchanges, lends itself well to observational learning and simulations. The counselor has considerable control in this approach through the selection of appropriate situations, the amount of repetition, and the intensity of the experience. This technique can be used in a systematic manner, and the process is fun and engaging for clients.

CONTINGENCY MANAGEMENT
Basic Concept

The second major behavioral counseling approach is contingency management. *Contingency management* is the name given to those behavioral counseling strategies based on the concept that the responses that follow the behavior are the behavioral modifiers. This can be represented by the second part of the behavioral formula (R→S^R) and is often referred to as instrumental, operant, or type-R conditioning. This learning method can be stated as the *principle of reinforcement*. This principle, sometimes called the *law of effect,* can be stated in three ways:

- behavior is controlled by its consequences;
- behavior that is followed by a satisfying state of affairs is strengthened or stamped in, whereas behavior that is followed by an annoying state of affairs is weakened or eliminated; or
- acts that are rewarded are enhanced, and acts that are punished are curtailed.

This conditioning can be exemplified by the student who studies for an exam. If he gets a good grade, his study behavior is reinforced and likely to be repeated. If he fails his exam, he is apt to feel his studying did not pay off and hence may be less likely to study for an exam in the future. Another example is the child who puts her hand in the cookie jar. If she gets a cookie, her behavior is reinforced. If she doesn't find a cookie, her behavior is not reinforced and is not likely to be repeated in the near future. Skinner (1938, 1953, 1989) made significant contributions to our understanding of these behavioral principles, and Kanfer and Goldstein (1991), Kazdin (1994), and Krumboltz and Thoresen (1976) provide excellent examples of how these principles can be used in a variety of settings.

Before discussing how contingency management techniques can be used to increase or decrease the likelihood of a behavior, it is important to understand the following terms: operants, behavioral consequences, primary and secondary consequences, reinforcement schedules, aversive stimuli, the effectiveness of operant contingencies, and the meaning of other operant terms.

Operants.   Operants are the behaviors or the responses (R) that precede and are related to the reinforcing stimulus (S^R). In the previous examples the behavior (R) "studying" was reinforced by the stimulus (S^R) "the good mark on the test"; and the behavior "putting the hand in the cookie jar" was reinforced by the cookie. Activities that operate on or have an effect on our environment are considered to be operant behaviors. Thus, most human behaviors, such as walking and speaking, are considered to be operants.

Operant behaviors have three major characteristics. First, operants are voluntary or freely emitted behaviors that operate in and on the environment; thus, they are controlled only by their environmental consequences. Theoretically, there is no pairing of the prior stimulus and the response. The contingent reinforcer is in control, and the instrumental response is influenced by its outcome. For example, the behavior of studying is controlled by the result of studying or the mark on the exam, and putting the hand in the cookie jar is controlled by the reward of getting or not getting a cookie. Second, operants are learned behaviors. These behaviors are distinct from respondent behaviors, which are usually innate or maturational. For example, a knee jerk is an innate, respondent behavior; studying and putting one's hand in a cookie jar are learned behaviors. Third, operants have a contingent relationship to the environmental events that follow. To be in a *contingent relationship,* event B may follow event A, but need not do so—for example, if you go to the beach, you may get wet. In contrast, to be in a *dependent relationship,* event B must necessarily follow event A—for example, if you swim, you will get wet. Both studying and putting one's hand in the cookie jar are operant behaviors that may be followed by different consequences. Although the term *free operant* is often used to describe the absence of constraints, human behavior almost always occurs in a context that sets some boundaries; hence, there is usually an interdependence between the behavior (R) and the prior events (S^D) or the environment.

Behavioral consequences.   Operant behavior can result in behavioral consequences or operant contingencies that may be pleasant or unpleasant; they may occur or be given, or they may not occur or be removed. It is important to understand how these four contingencies can be employed to help increase or decrease the likelihood of a behavior.

When the consequence or contingent response tends to *maintain* or *increase* the probability of that operant behavior, then *reinforcement* has occurred. Reinforcement can be positive or negative. It is positive when a pleasant consequence follows or is added or given—for example, when a pleasant feeling follows doing a favor for a neighbor or when a gold star is given. It is negative when an unpleasant consequence disappears or is removed or taken away—for example, when a pain goes away after medication or when a detention is removed. In all these cases, reinforcement of the desired behavior has occurred.

When the consequence or contingent response tends to *extinguish* or *decrease* the probability of that operant behavior, *punishment* has occurred. As with reinforcement, punishment can be positive or negative. Punishment is positive when an unpleasant consequence follows or is added—for example, when a student fails a test for not studying or when detention is assigned. The punishment is negative when a pleasant consequence goes away or is removed—for example, when the gold star is taken away or when the cookie jar is deliberately left empty. In either case the target behavior is less likely to occur in the future. Four possible consequences or operant contingencies are illustrated in Table 6-1.

Another way to portray these four contingencies is by the following outline:

1. Reinforcement is used to increase or start a behavior.

    a. It is positive when something pleasant occurs or is given.
    b. It is negative when something aversive is removed or disappears.
2. Punishment is used to decrease or stop a behavior.

    a. It is positive when an aversive result occurs or is given.
    b. It is negative when something pleasant is taken away or lost.

T A B L E   6-1
The Four Possible Operant Contingencies

	Added = Positive	*Removed = Negative*
Pleasant consequence	Positive reinforcement	Negative punishment
Unpleasant consequence or aversive stimulus	Positive punishment	Negative reinforcement

Rewards.   Rewards are not always reinforcers. A reward is considered to be something given to a person for completing a particular activity—for example, giving a student a candy bar for getting 100 percent on a test. However, a reward may not be valued by the person and hence not really serve as a consequence for increasing the target behavior. The student may not like candy, or he or she may feel it is a bribe and not at all related to the activity of studying. Rather than using a reward, it is more desirable to have the person see the consequence as a logical and natural one. For example, instead of using a candy bar as a reward for going into a pool on a hot day, the natural consequence of the cooling of the body should be allowed to serve as the reinforcer. Rewards, however, can and are used as reinforcers; to be useful, they must be valued by the persons concerned and applied in a consistent fashion.

Primary and conditioned consequences.   Consequences can be primary or conditioned. A *primary* or *universal reinforcer* is a consequence that is related to maintaining and perpetualizing life or the satisfaction of physiological needs. Examples of primary reinforcers include food, water, a balanced body temperature, rest and sleep, procreation, and breathing. A punishment is considered primary and universal when the consequences have a universally aversive reaction. Examples of aversive stimuli include loud noise, bright lights, temperature extremes, loss of sleep, and other painful situations.

A *conditioned consequence* is a stimulus or an object that initially has no value but that, by continued pairing with a primary consequence, assumes reinforcing or punishing qualities. Conditioned positive reinforcers include verbal praise such as "That was a nice thing to do," nonverbal gestures like smiles and winks, and symbolic or token objects such as money or gold stars. Conditioned positive punishments include verbal rebukes such as "Don't do that!", nonverbal gestures like frowns and stares, and symbolic objects such as demerits. Conditioned consequences are used when the goal is to reinforce desired behaviors and punish undesired ones.

Attention is a powerful reinforcer because it meets a basic human need. It can serve to reinforce both appropriate and inappropriate behaviors. Thus, a child whose ill-advised behavior gains attention is likely to repeat that behavior because it was reinforced. Similarly, withdrawing attention is an excellent form of negative punishment because it removes something desirable. Thus, the child who engages in an ill-advised behavior such as a temper tantrum should not be given the attention he or she wants.

Reinforcement schedules.   For new behaviors to become established, they do not have to be reinforced every time they occur. Reinforcement can be scheduled at different times and rates. The major kinds of reinforcement schedules are continuous, or uninterrupted, and intermittent, or periodic. When trying to establish a new behavior, it may appear that constant reinforcement is desirable to encourage the behavior to become habitual; however, the fact is that the exact opposite is true. This principle is known as *Humphrey's paradox*. Thus, in order for a behavior to become "stamped in," it is desirable to start with a continuous reinforcement schedule and move to an intermittent schedule with longer gaps between reinforcers.

Continuous reinforcement (CR) occurs when a behavior is reinforced every time it occurs. When one wants to develop or establish a new behavior, this is a very effective schedule. However, when the behavior reaches a plateau (called the *asymptotic level*), continuous reinforcement is no longer effective; thus, one must learn to reinforce on an intermittent basis. For example, when one wants to establish a behavior such as doing homework, cleaning a room, or practicing the piano, the behavior initially should be reinforced each time it is done by praise or some token reinforcer like a gold star. However, as soon as feasible, the reinforcement schedule should be switched to an intermittent one, which lessens the density or frequency of the reinforcement gradually and progressively.

Intermittent reinforcement (IR) occurs when the behavior is reinforced on a periodic basis. Reinforcing a behavior periodically increases the likelihood that the behavior will be repeated. The reinforcement can be scheduled to occur on a time (interval) basis or an event (ratio) basis and can occur at fixed or variable points or places. There are four possible ways to reinforce on an intermittent basis: the fixed-ratio schedule, the variable-ratio schedule, the fixed-interval schedule, and the variable-interval schedule.

The two *ratio schedules* require that a certain number of responses be given before the reinforcement can be administered. Ratio schedules are similar to piecework, in which one is paid for accomplishing a certain task. This form of reinforcement tends to increase the pace of the target behaviors, because the more rapidly one accomplishes a task, the sooner a reinforcement occurs. The *fixed-ratio* schedule (FR) is a pattern of reinforcement that is presented on a regular-event basis; for example, one might give written compliments to a student for every fifth problem or every tenth page of work. This schedule is associated with a tendency for the person to slow down after the reinforcement is given. The *variable-ratio* schedule (VR) is a reinforcement pattern that is constructed to present the reinforcement on a variable-event basis; for example, one may develop a reinforcement system to give five gold stars for a term paper but vary the events that will be reinforced. The schedule may grant the star after the 1st, 8th, 12th, 20th, and 22nd pages. Playing slot machines follows a variable-ratio reinforcement schedule. Variable-ratio schedules are not effective when reinforcement is too spread out.

The two *interval schedules* require that a certain amount of time lapse or pass before reinforcement is given. Interval schedules are preferred by many behaviorists because this type of schedule avoids having people rush to accomplish a task. *The fixed-interval* schedule (FI) is a pattern of reinforcement that occurs at specific, or fixed, time intervals; for example, one might use verbal praise as a reinforcer and compliment the individual every 10 minutes. The *variable-interval* schedule (VI) is a reinforcement pattern that is based on a variable time interval. For example, one might develop a token reinforcement system that gives a gold star five times during the day and decide to vary the time that the reinforcer is given, such as after 1 hour, 3 hours, 4 hours, 5 hours, and 8 hours. The variable-interval schedule explains why it is sometimes hard to extinguish an undesired behavior. If an acting-out behavior occasionally gains a child attention, that behavior is being reinforced, and thus it is likely to be maintained.

Aversive stimuli or unpleasant consequences.

In helping clients modify their behaviors, it is often desirable to assign an unpleasant consequence (positive punishment) or to remove an aversive stimulus (negative reinforcement). The use of severe primary aversive stimuli such as loud noises, extreme temperatures, and intense pain raises serious ethical issues and is justified only when less aversive means have not or cannot work and when the maladaptive behavior is serious enough to warrant the use of these extreme means. Conditioned aversive stimuli such as verbal rebukes and minor primary aversive stimuli such as slight shocks are employed when aversive methods are appropriate.

It should be noted that a contingent stimulus can be pleasant or aversive, depending on its effect on a particular behavior, and a particular behavior may have aversive and pleasant consequences simultaneously. For example, when a student misbehaves in class, other students may cheer (the pleasant consequence) while the teacher scolds (the aversive consequence); and when the team commits an error, the home fans boo (an aversive consequence) while visiting fans cheer (a pleasant consequence). Careful thought must be given to select consequences that are truly reinforcing when one wants to increase the likelihood of a behavior and truly punishing when one wants to decrease or eliminate a behavior.

Aversive consequences can also have undesirable side effects. These side effects occur when an individual learns to deal with the unpleasant consequences in one or more of the following three ways: operant escape, operant avoidance, and aggression. *Operant escape* occurs when individuals remove themselves from the aversive or painful experience; for example, when a father is yelling at his son, the son can try to escape the unpleasant event by leaving the room (physical escape) or by daydreaming (mental escape). *Operant avoidance* occurs when the individual acts to avoid a painful result or experience; for example, when a student believes that taking a particular class will result in failure or boredom, the student will try to avoid the class. *Aggression* occurs when the individual reacts hostilely to an aversive stimulus; for example, when a teacher scolds a student, the student sasses or physically rebuffs the teacher.

Effectiveness of reinforcement and punishment.

Reinforcement and punishment are most effective when the consequences are (1) contingent upon the behavior, (2) consistently used for the same behavior, (3) immediately used with minimal time delays, (4) intense enough to be seen as a consequence of the behavior and yet weak enough to allow for an increase in the intensity of the consequences in the future, and (5) appropriate to the behavior. Furthermore, punishment is most effective when combined with positive reinforcement of alternating behaviors and when chances for escape, avoidance, and aggression are minimized.

Other operant terms.

Several other terms are used when behavioral and contingency management methods are employed. These terms are response differentiation, shaping, chaining, prompting and fading, satiation, deprivation, restraint, and the Premack principle.

Response differentiation is the process of reinforcing one level or variant of an existing behavior while punishing or withdrawing reinforcement from other levels or variants of the behavior. For example, a parent who is trying to help a child lose weight may compliment the child every time he or she eats a desirable food and frown or show no reaction to the child when he or she eats an inappropriate food.

Shaping is the process of reinforcing successive approximations to a target behavior until the new behavior has been learned. The terminal goal is broken down into a series of steps, and each slight change is reinforced. The size of each step and its intensity must be determined on an individual basis. For example, in learning how to reflect the content and feelings of a client statement, the behavior might be broken down into the following sequences: a response that mirrors the content of a client's statement, a response that mirrors the feeling of a client's statement, and a response that goes beyond the surface of the client's statement and reflects the underlying content and feeling. In training someone to learn this behavior, it is possible to shape the responses by systematically teaching the sequence and reinforcing appropriate student responses at each level.

Chaining is the process of combining previously learned behaviors into a more complex behavior. Each event or activity has a triple function: it is a behavior, it is the discriminative stimulus for the behavior that follows, and it is the reinforcement stimulus for the prior behavior. The behaviors "walk to the office," "sit down," "talk to the counselor," "relax," and "leave the office" can be labeled as the discriminative stimulus S^D, the behavior R, or the reinforcing stimulus S^R, depending on which link of the chain of human behavior is being analyzed. Three links of a chain of human behavior are represented in Table 6-2. In learning a new complex behavior, a chain of simple behaviors is reinforced until the complex behavior is learned.

Prompting is the act of providing a stimulus or a cue for a person to act in a certain way (for example, when mother says, "Set the table"). In starting a new behavior, a conspicuous prompt is often necessary. The prompt should be gradually removed so that the new behavior is eventually done without a hint or a cue. The process of gradually removing the prompts is called *fading*—for example, to teach a child to set the table, a prompt such as "John, set the table" can be used. Because it is most desirable for the child to set the table without the prompt, the parent would gradually remove and not offer the cue.

T A B L E 6-2
Links in a Chain of Human Behavior

Discrimination stimuli	Behaviors	Contingent stimuli
1. walk to office (S_1^D) →	sit down (R_1) →	talk to counselor (S_1)
2. sit down (S_2^D) →	talk to counselor (R_2) →	relax (S_2)
3. talk to counselor (S_3^D) →	relax (R_3) →	leave office (S_3^R)

Satiation occurs when too much reinforcement of one type has been given. If an individual has too much of a good thing, the reinforcer loses its power to reinforce the behavior; for example, a student who has recently had a lot of candy at a birthday party is probably satiated and will not see a piece of candy as an incentive to act in a particular way. Sometimes satiation causes other actions; for example, when a person praises others continuously, his or her sincerity may be questioned.

Deprivation is the term used when no reinforcement has been provided. The deprivation of reinforcement normally increases the reinforcing power of a stimulus. Thus, if a child likes candy but has not had any in a long time, the child has been deprived of candy as a reinforcer and the candy can probably serve as a strong incentive to act in a particular way. Deprivation of important reinforcers can cause severe problems; for example, students who receive no praise for their work can be damaged or turned off from a subject.

Restraint is the word employed when physical force is used to prevent a behavior from occurring. This method of behavioral change implies an authoritarian approach and is best used when the client's well-being or some other person's well-being suffers as a result of the behavior; for example, a mentally retarded child may be prevented from hitting his or her own head by restraining the movement of the child's arms.

The Premack principle is the premise used when we attempt to increase low-probability behaviors by making them contingent upon high-probability behaviors; for example, "You can watch TV (the high-probability behavior) after you do your homework" (the low-probability behavior). The term was named after the psychologist Dave Premack (1965), who wrote about its applications in behavioral techniques. This principle is also referred to as grandma's rule.

Increasing the Likelihood of a Behavior

Contingency management methods can be used to increase the likelihood of a behavior. Because the operant definition of reinforcement is the procedure by which the operant behaviors are increased or maintained, the way to help clients increase the probability of a particular behavior is by positive and negative reinforcement methods. Positive reinforcement methods provide a pleasant consequence as the result of the behavior. Positive reinforcement is a normal and consistent process throughout our entire lives. Some typical examples are good grades and a sense of accomplishment from studying, verbal praise for doing something helpful for others, and the salary check or the token reinforcer for performing a work-related task.

Negative reinforcement methods remove aversive consequences as the result of the behavior. Removing aversive stimuli is usually less desirable than positive reinforcement—not because it does not work but because the aversive stimuli may not be present (student is not in detention, pain is not present) or because the use of aversive stimuli has some undesirable side effects. Some common examples of how negative reinforcement is used in our lives include removing anxiety by studying, removing pain by going to a physician, and removing teasing when we do what others want us to do.

The following steps outline a systematic way to help clients increase and maintain the likelihood of a particular behavior using operant conditioning methods:

1. Help the client identify the target behavior or performance to be changed. Be as specific and concrete as possible. If necessary, break down compli-cated behaviors into the links of a chain.

2. Analyze the behavioral chain and determine what current reinforcers, if any, exist for the target behavior, and notice what reinforcement schedule is in effect.

3. Identify reinforcers for the target behavior. Determine what pleasant consequences can be added and what unpleasant ones can be removed. Many behavioral patterns of individuals are the result of poorly arranged or poorly thought-out reinforcers. It is therefore important to analyze the consequences of the client's present behaviors in terms of the type of reinforcer as well as the frequency, intensity, and duration of these reinforcers. What changes might be made to this pattern?

4. Look into the possibility that the client has experienced saturation or deprivation of some reinforcers. If either situation exists, can these reinforcers be avoided or used to increase behavior?

5. Is a high level of behavior present? If so, can the Premack principle be used to increase the likelihood of the lower-level behavior by making the high-level behavior contingent on the lower-level behavior?

6. Identify a schedule of reinforcement. Note the frequency and the duration of the reinforcement pattern and specify by whom, how, and when the reinforcement will be administered.

7. If the targeted behavior is complex, break it down into incremental sequences and plan to shape the desired behavior.

8. Encourage the client to implement the program. If necessary, combine with observational and simulated learning experiences to help the client.

9. Provide positive feedback and evaluate the client's progress step-by-step through the behavioral change program.

10. Continue the conditioning until the behavior is increased and maintained for a reasonable period.

11. Plan client follow-up to see if the targeted behavior has been maintained.

Decreasing the Likelihood of a Behavior

Operant conditioning methods may be used to decrease or eliminate the likelihood of a behavior. Because punishment is defined as a contingent stimulus that decreases a be-havior, the contingent methods used to decrease or eliminate a behavior are positive and negative punishment.

Positive punishment methods present an unpleasant consequence as a result of engaging in a particular behavior. The use of unpleasant consequences or aversive stimuli is a common phenomenon in our society. When an individual engages in an undesirable behavior, that individual is subject to some type of undesirable consequence. Children who misbehave get scolded, and the team member who plays poorly gets booed. Punishment used effectively can stop an unwanted behavior quickly, facilitate discriminatory learning, and serve as an instructional example to observers.

Punishment can have three bad side effects. First, it can lead to the use of escape, avoidance, and aggression. Second, it can provide a poor social learning model (for example, when the teacher scolded a student, Jim, he and his peers learned to scold, and they in turn scolded Jim's younger sister). And third, the use of primary aversive stimuli can have severe physiological side effects; thus, it can do more harm than good.

Negative punishment methods remove pleasant consequences as a result of engaging in a particular behavior. Removing pleasant consequences is an effective tool in the learning process. In order to use it, of course, the pleasant consequences must be present. Negative punishment can be given in one of three ways: time-out, response cost, and extinction. *Time-out* occurs when the possibility for all reinforcement is removed or all pleasant consequences are cut off for a time—for example, when a player is removed from a game. *Response cost* occurs when part or all of a pleasant consequence previously earned is removed. For example, when one receives a fine for passing a red light or for some other infraction, the previously earned money is the pleasant consequence that is removed. *Extinction* occurs when consequences are discontinued or withdrawn completely, and neutral consequences or events are presented where positive outcomes used to exist—for example, deliberately keeping the cookie jar empty or ignoring a loud child when loudness had previously obtained attention. The use of this form of negative punishment often increases the behavior rather dramatically before the new consequences become evident.

Natural and logical consequences.

Whenever possible, it is desirable to allow the natural or logical consequences of an ill-advised behavior to serve as the punishment. *Natural consequences* are those that result from a behavior without the intervention of another person. These are the universal, inevitable consequences that are true for all human beings regardless of ethnic background or social class. Examples include "If I forget my lunch money, I can't buy lunch"; "If I oversleep, I will be late"; and "If I don't take care of my laundry, I will not have clean clothes to wear."

Logical consequences are the results that follow logically from an ill-advised behavior. These consequences require the intervention of another person or the application of a rule or law. Social conventions, mores, and group expectations usually require certain behaviors and built-in reinforcement procedures. These consequences might be avoided, but another person or group is normally present to impose the sanctions. Examples include "If I go to school late, I will get detention"; "He who breaks the window fixes it"; and "If I don't show up Thursday, the gang will ignore me."

The following steps indicate a procedure that can be used to help clients decrease or eliminate the likelihood of a particular behavior using type-R conditioning:

1. Help the client identify the behavior to be decreased. If the behavior is complicated, break it down into links of a chain. Help the client be as specific as possible.

2. Analyze the behavioral chain to determine what contingencies presently exist for the target behavior. Note all the positive and negative reinforcers for the current behavior. How strong are these reinforcers?

3. Identify ways to punish the target behavior. What natural and logical consequences are available to help decrease the ill-advised behavior? Determine what aversive stimuli can be given or positive consequences removed. Specify who will administer the punishment and how and where the punishment will be carried out.

4. Look into the possibility of initiating or strengthening a desired behavior. It is frequently wise to increase one behavior while decreasing another one.

5. Is it possible to eliminate the current reinforcers by satiation? If so, what are the consequences?

6. Encourage the client to implement the program. If necessary, combine with other techniques, such as observational and simulated experiences, to lessen the likelihood of the behavior.

7. Provide positive feedback and evaluate the client's progress step-by-step through the program.

8. Continue the conditioning until the targeted behavior is decreased or eliminated for a reasonable period.

9. Plan to follow up with the client periodically to see if the desired behavioral change has occurred.

Classical Conditioning
Basic Concept

A third major behavioral counseling approach is based on the concepts of classical conditioning. *Classical conditioning* is the name given to those behavioral intervention methods based on the idea that the events that *precede* the targeted behavior are the things that control the behavior. These events can be represented symbolically by the first part of the behavioral formula ($S^D \rightarrow R \rightarrow S^R$). These techniques are frequently labeled stimulus-response, respondent, or type-S conditioning methods. The basic law that summarizes stimulus-response methods says that "behavior is controlled by its antecedent stimuli." Because certain stimuli cause certain responses, new stimuli can be associated with the old stimuli that give the desired response, and soon the associated stimuli bring about the given response.

Classical conditioning methods are based on the work of a Russian physiologist, Ivan Pavlov (1927), who, while studying the salivation process of dogs, noticed that food brought about the salivation response in the animals. When he made a certain noise at the same time he introduced the food, he discovered that, after repeated pairing, the noise became capable of producing the saliva.

Four elements must be present for classical conditioning to occur: first, an unconditioned event or stimulus (UCS) such as the food in Pavlov's experiments; second, the unconditioned response (UCR), which follows the unconditioned stimulus, or the saliva in Pavlov's studies; third, a conditioned stimulus (CS), which is a natural event (such as

Pavlov's noise) that is introduced at the same time as the unconditioned stimulus (UCS); and fourth, a conditioned response (CR), which has been matched or associated in some way with the unconditioned response (UCR).

This law can be illustrated as follows:

$$UCS \rightarrow UCR$$
$$(CS)\ (UCS) \rightarrow (UCR)$$
$$(CS) \rightarrow (UCR)\ (CR)$$
$$CS \rightarrow CR$$

The repeated pairing of the conditioned stimulus (CS) with the unconditioned stimulus (UCS) ultimately causes the conditioned stimulus (CS) to bring about the unconditioned response (UCR). It is also possible to match the unconditioned response (UCR) with a conditioned response (CR) so that ultimately the conditioned stimulus (CS) can bring about a conditioned response.

Stimulus-response conditioning is a very important learning tool and has affected us in a myriad of ways. For example, if every time you were awakened by an alarm someone in your house was simultaneously cooking bacon, you would soon wake up with the desire for bacon even when it was not being prepared. Another example is that of a young child who was bitten by her cousin's dog. At the sight of that dog or one similar to it, she would probably cry or show another type of anxious or tense behavior.

Stimulus Conditioning Phenomena

Several major learning processes can occur as a result of stimulus control methods. They are stimulus generalization, stimulus discrimination, reinforcement, extinction, and spontaneous recovery.

Stimulus generalization takes place when a response that has been associated with a particular stimulus occurs after other similar stimuli cues are presented. In other words, an association of similar discriminative stimuli has occurred, and both the original stimuli and similar stimuli elicit the same response; for example, a student who has done poorly in a particular math class may generalize and want to avoid all math classes in the future.

Stimulus discrimination occurs when similar discriminative stimuli do not bring about the same response. In other words, a discrimination has occurred between and among the various stimuli; for example, a student who has done poorly in a particular math class may want to avoid the teacher who taught that math class but does not want to avoid other math classes or teachers.

Reinforcement occurs when the matching of the conditioned and unconditioned stimulus is repeated. In other words, the association between the unconditioned stimulus and the conditioned stimulus is strengthened; for example, the periodic matching of the alarm and the cooking of bacon is a reinforcement of this respondent conditioning. (Note how this term has different meanings in operant and in classical conditioning.)

Extinction occurs when the response is no longer elicited as a result of the conditioned stimulus. In other words, the conditioned stimulus is no longer

effective in bringing about the desired response; for example, when after a
while the alarm does not bring about a desire for bacon. (Again, note how
this term has distinctive meanings in operant and classical conditioning.)

Spontaneous recovery occurs when the conditioned response returns unexpect-
edly after it has become extinct. In other words, after the set or relationship
between the conditioned stimulus and conditioned response appears to have
been broken, it reappears; for example, after extinction has occurred one
wakes up to the alarm without the desire for bacon, but spontaneous recovery is evident when suddenly one morning the alarm again brings a desire for
bacon.

Conditioning based on the first part of the behavioral formula ($S^D \rightarrow R$) is useful
under two different sets of circumstances. First, it is used to modify or change the stimulus that causes a certain behavior. Second, it is used when a relatively neutral stimulus
causes an unwarranted response and modification of the response is necessary.

Stimulus Change

There are two stimulus change methods: discrimination training and stimulus control
techniques. Discrimination training is used when it is desirous to have only a very specific behavior cause a specific response. It is accomplished by reinforcing a particular
behavior regularly in the presence of a specific stimulus and not reinforcing, or extin-
guishing, that behavior in the presence of another specific stimulus. For example, discrimination training is used to teach individuals the fact that red lights signal danger and
green lights signal safety.

Stimulus control techniques are used when it is desirous for the response to be
eliminated. This is done by removing the discriminative stimulus or by developing a
new pairing pattern so that the unwanted behavior occurs only in the presence of an
undesired stimulus; for example, stimulus control methods are used when individuals
avoid smoking by not buying cigarettes or by not associating with friends who smoke.

Changing Responses

When relatively neutral stimuli bring about an inappropriate or undesired response, the
response pattern must be changed. This type of respondent conditioning is often used
with clients who have a high degree of anxiety, fear, phobia, or avoidance. The object is
to replace the conditioned response (tension or anxiety) rather than the stimulus. This
conditioning relies on the fact that the organism cannot respond in incompatible ways at
the same time (tension and relaxation). Therefore, it is possible to desensitize or inhibit
the learned response (tension) by substituting an incompatible newly learned response
(relaxation). There are four major procedures used in changing response patterns: systematic desensitization, assertiveness training, flooding and implosive therapy, and aversion methods. Another method that appears to be based on similar principles but is
usually not included in respondent conditioning is paradoxical intention.

Systematic desensitization.

Systematic desensitization can be described as a counterconditioning or deconditioning process that is used to eliminate negative feelings, anxiety, or other aversive reactions to various stimuli that elicit these unpleasant emotions. Systematic desensitization has been used extensively by Joseph Wolpe (1958, 1990), who employed this technique with phobic clients. It is based on two concepts. The first is that two opposite emotive states—anxiety and relaxation—cannot exist at the same time. Second, if anxiety can be eliminated or inhibited in the presence of situations that produce it, those situations will eventually lose their power to evoke anxiety in the future. This latter notion is referred to as the *reciprocal inhibition principle*. It is used with individuals whose anxiety is so intense that they are incapable of doing the things they want to do or need to do; for example, the woman whose fear of dogs prevents her from visiting friends who own a dog, or the man with a disability whose fear of trains prohibits him from attending a rehabilitation program. The systematic desensitization procedure can be employed to help the woman visit her friends or to help the man with a disability attend the rehabilitation program.

Systematic desensitization has been found to be effective with a wide variety of anxiety-related problems in human beings. Among these are fear of heights, open spaces, public speaking, flying, and test taking; school phobia; stuttering; interpersonal anxiety arising from poor interpersonal relationships such as jealousy and fear of criticism, disapproval, or rejection; and psychophysiological illness such as asthma, headaches, insomnia, speech disorders, and various kinds of sexual dysfunctioning (Kalish, 1981; Schwartz, 1982). The procedure has been effective with both individual and group counseling.

There are three major aspects to this strategy: training clients in deep muscle relaxation, constructing an appropriate hierarchy of anxiety-provoking situations, and counterpoising relaxation and the anxiety-provoking stimuli. It often takes six months or longer to guide a client through this intervention strategy. The typical steps in this procedure are as follows:

1. Identify the target behavior. A comprehensive history of the client should be obtained to analyze the problem and the events related to it. This is done by extensive questioning and through the use of the Life History Questionnaire, which was developed for this purpose (Wolpe & Lazarus, 1966).

2. Determine the factors related to the client's phobic condition. Obtain a detailed description of all the situations related to the fear and discomfort that the client experiences. This is frequently done through verbal discussion; however, the Fear Survey Schedule, the Willoughby Questionnaire, or the Bernsenter Self-Sufficiency Inventory (Wolpe, 1990) may be used.

3. Help the client construct an anxiety hierarchy. Assist the client in identifying and then ranking a list of anxiety-provoking situations. This is done by determining which stimuli cause the least discomfort, then identifying those that cause increasing feelings of discomfort to isolate the situations that cause the most anxiety. These hierarchies should be as real and as concrete as possible and deal with relevant situations, people, times, and places.

4. Teach the client progressive relaxation techniques. This consists of teaching the client how to relax different muscles of the body. In a soothing voice, guide the client through an orderly sequence of relaxing different muscles until a state of complete relaxation is achieved. Clients often need considerable

practice before they can relax completely. Plan to give relaxation exercises for homework.

5. Develop a plan for presenting scenes from the anxiety hierarchy to the client. The plan should present different scenarios for each item on the anxiety hierarchy and should have a logical progression from covert scenes having little intensity to overt and more realistic situations. Expect to progress slowly and deliberately, and include homework assignments.

6. Desensitize systematically by presenting the anxiety hierarchy while maintaining relaxation. Progress slowly through scenes from the anxiety hierarchy until the client signals that discomfort is being experienced. At this point, reinforce the relaxation until the client again experiences complete relaxation. The procedure is repeated over and over until the connection between these stimuli and the response of anxiety is eliminated and fear is neutralized. The process is continued until the situation that originally provoked the anxiety no longer does so.

7. Plan to follow up treatment periodically. Expect to reinforce the treatment when necessary.

There are several variations to Wolpe's technique, including in vivo desensitization, which uses real-life situations; covert desensitization, which employs the imagination; contact desensitization, or participant modeling desensitization, which uses observation and simulated experiences; automated desensitization, which employs tape-recorded sessions; and emotive imagery, which uses the imagination to desensitize fears caused by thoughts, images, and wish fulfillments in children.

Assertiveness training.

Assertive individuals are those who act in their own best interest without too much anxiety and without infringing on the rights of others. Assertive people are aware of their rights, communicate their opinions, needs, and feelings in appropriate ways, and make reasonable demands on others. This behavior has been learned by the assertive person over the course of his or her lifetime. Unassertive individuals allow themselves to be treated as persons of little or no consequence. Typically, unassertive people are taken advantage of by others; lack spontaneity; have difficulty expressing their thoughts, opinions, and emotions; fail to rise to meet unjust treatment; allow others to make decisions in social and work situations; and lack self-esteem (Alberti & Emmons, 1995; Shaw, Wallace, & LaBella, 1980).

Assertiveness training is a process designed to help clients explore new alternatives that can be open to them. It encourages them to respect their own feelings while at the same time respecting the feelings of others. The technique is designed to reduce the fear or anxiety response that has been caused by, or is related to, a particular situation or event and therefore frees the person to express his or her feelings and ideas. Thus, the individual should be able to make more appropriate choices and act more responsibly in his or her daily life. The basic concept involves a counterconditioning process that replaces the fear and anxiety response (the conditioned response) that occurs as a reaction to a particular stimulus or set of stimuli with a new conditioned response (assertive behavior). The principal method used in assertiveness training is counterconditioning; however, other effective intervention strategies such as modeling, role playing, role reversal, direct instruction, coaching, and contingency reinforcement are often used along with this deconditioning process.

Learning to become assertive is hard work for some clients and extremely difficult for others. Those who encounter the most difficulty are often enmeshed in an environment that reinforces unassertive behavior and punishes assertive behavior. In these cases, clients have to work on modifying the environment as well as their own behavior. Sometimes clients confuse assertiveness with aggression. They need to learn that aggression is quite the opposite of assertiveness and that aggression is really violating the rights of others by strongly acting out one's desires or frustrations in a hostile manner.

The usual steps employed in this process are as follows:

1. Help the client recognize that his or her inhibitions are causing a great deal of tension and unpleasantness. The client must learn to overcome these inhibitions while respecting the rights of others.

2. Obtain detailed descriptions of all the situations that are related to unassertive behavior, and identify specific instances of unassertiveness and the stimuli that cause and reinforce the behavior.

3. Help the client arrange a hierarchy, from the situations where the client has a higher probability of being assertive to those where the client is nonassertive.

4. Teach the client the distinction between assertiveness and aggression and between unassertiveness and politeness. Help the client identify and accept his or her own personal rights as well as the rights of others by helping to clarify the client's understanding of what is appropriate behavior in different situations.

5. Develop a plan to teach the client more assertive behavior. Use covert and symbolic means with weak stimuli or mundane events initially, and then have the client practice assertive behavior. Plan to move on to more intense stimuli and more overt situations. In these graduated situations, incorporate modeling, role playing, role reversal, direct instruction, and contingent reinforcement.

6. Implement the plan. Be systematic and provide positive feedback and reinforcement. Do additional role playing, modeling, homework, and practice sessions as needed. Do not rush the client. Instruct the client to do homework and take notes on his or her behavior and report back on how he or she felt and how the assignment went. Provide assertiveness training for a variety of situations; otherwise, generalization is less likely to occur.

7. Encourage the client to evaluate his or her own behavior and any changes that have taken place. Plan to follow up with the client periodically. Reinforce the treatment when necessary.

Flooding.   The term *flooding* of and by itself indicates that too much of something is present. In counseling it involves exposing a client to a stimulus, then repeatedly or gradually increasing the time or the intensity of the experience without allowing the client to escape or avoid the exposure. It can be used to extinguish or lessen certain behaviors, or it can be used to help clients overcome behavioral deficits. When it is used to overcome a behavioral deficit, the assumption is made that the client has had a prior real or imagined experience that paired the target behavior with an aversive consequence. Hence, the client wants to avoid or escape from these situations or things that evoke the anxiety or fear. The process involves repeated exposure to the feared stimulus until the client learns that no aversive consequences will follow (Groden & Cautela, 1981). For example, a person who cannot ice-skate because of fear of having an accident can be taught to overcome this fear through the covert method of imagining himself or herself skating and watching himself or herself fall on the ice over and over and over again.

When the method is used to help with a behavioral excess, the assumption is made that certain conditions foster or cause inappropriate responses. The process is designed to present the inappropriate behavior for long periods or in massive doses so that the individual becomes exhausted or tired of the behavior (Rachman, Hodgson, & Marks, 1972). This exhaustion teaches the client to act differently when presented with the same or similar conditions. For example, a student who constantly taps a pencil or chews gum can be taught to avoid this behavior by being kept after school and instructed to tap the pencil or chew gum continuously for prolonged periods. The technique, sometimes referred to as the *massing of trials*, employs the following steps:

1. Identify the target behavior by obtaining an extensive client history.
2. Obtain detailed descriptions of all the situations that are related to the maladaptive behavior.
3. Ask the client to arrange in hierarchical order scenes that facilitate the maladaptive behavior, from most likely to least likely.
4. Plan a flooding program. From the client's history and situational hierarchy, plan an intervention at a scene that is most likely to cause the maladaptive behavior. Plan how to use covert, symbolic, and overt means to present the stimuli in massive doses until avoidance is eliminated or anxiety reduced. Plan homework assignments.
5. Activate the plan. If appropriate, combine with fading to remove other prompting cues. Provide positive feedback as a systematic contingent reinforcement. Do not allow the client to escape from the stimuli.
6. Plan to follow up with the client periodically. Reinforce when necessary.

Another form of flooding, known as *implosive therapy*, relies on cues and covert procedures that are frightening to the client (Shipley, 1979).

Flooding as a technique has some side effects; for example, using this strategy with the behavior of excessive cigarette smoking does produce the exhaustion phenomenon but it also causes more tar and nicotine to be inhaled, which is poor for the health of the client. Consequently, this technique has to be carefully thought out prior to its use to minimize or avoid the side effects.

Aversion techniques.

Aversion techniques can be employed when the counselor wants to assist the client in eliminating or stopping an undesired behavior. The undesirable behaviors may be behavioral excesses, such as overindulgence in food, sweets, or alcohol, or they may be unwanted behaviors, such as compulsive gambling, self-injurious body behavior, cigarette smoking, or enuresis. The basic concept in aversion methods is repeatedly pairing an aversive or noxious stimulus with the undesired behavior. This association of the painful or noxious stimulus with the unwanted behavior should ultimately lead to the cessation of the target behavior. For example, a person who smokes excessively is taught to snap a rubber band against his or her wrist when the urge to smoke occurs. This repeated pairing of the pain and the urge to smoke is designed so that, ultimately, the urge to smoke will elicit pain and thus curtail the smoking habit. Aversive techniques have been used throughout human history to bring about desired changes (Kazdin, 1978). The ancient Greeks and Romans used such techniques to cure tics and excessive alcoholism. These methods have proved to be successful with many behavioral excesses, including drinking, eating, and smoking, by pairing them with aversive stimuli such as electric shock or a nauseating incident.

Aversive methods should be well thought out before their use, for several reasons. First, care should be given to minimize the possibility that the client will use avoidance, escape, or aggression in reaction to the stimulus. Second, every effort should be made to keep the strength or the intensity of the stimulus as low as possible, because the actual presence of the aversive or noxious stimulus can bring about the desired change, rather than the strength of the stimulus. Third, the counselor should try to ensure that the stimulus is truly aversive to the client and not neutral or positive. And fourth, repetition and follow-up need to be incorporated into the treatment so that the aversive stimulus does not have transient or limited-time effects. As a general rule, aversive techniques should be considered only when an individual's biological or psychological well-being is severely affected by the inappropriate behavior and other treatment alternatives are not appropriate.

Typically, an aversion intervention program should include the following steps:

1. Identify the target behavior by obtaining a detailed client history.

2. Have the client describe the maladaptive behavior and the situation that is normally related to the behavior.

3. Plan what aversive stimulus should match with the undesired behavior. What have other investigators used in similar circumstances? Does the aversive stimulus have any negative side effects? Plan how the pairing will occur, how much homework to assign, and how records will be kept. Plan to use covert, symbolic, and overt techniques, and start with less intensive stimuli.

4. Implement the program. Associate the unpleasant stimulus as closely with the inappropriate behavior as possible. Make sure that the induced stimulus is presented when, and only when, the unwanted behavior occurs to ensure a strong association.

5. Monitor the program continually. Individuals differ in their responses to aversive stimuli, so careful supervision is required.

6. Continue the conditioning until the inappropriate response no longer occurs in an overt or natural setting or in circumstances where the behavior previously occurred most frequently.

7. Plan to follow up with the client periodically, and reinforce the pairing when necessary.

The aversion technique is often best combined with other contingency management techniques that are designed to initiate or increase the likelihood of another behavior. Thus, although one behavior is being curtailed, another is taking its place; for example, by this process clients can be taught to eliminate fattening foods and eat more nutritious ones.

Paradoxical intention.   In this technique the counselor instructs the client to engage in a behavior that appears to be incompatible with or the direct opposite of the desired goal. This strategy is called *paradoxical* because it is designed to eliminate a problem behavior by the unusual means of encouraging it. The technique has been used extensively by Frankl (1960, 1991), who employed it with clients who manifested phobias, obsessions, and anticipatory anxiety. Individuals who have a fearful expectation of an aversive reaction become enmeshed in a vicious cycle—the anxiety causes the aversive reaction to occur, and thus the thing that the client fears does in fact happen. In dealing with clients who became immobilized, Frankl required them to intend to act toward the item or event that would raise the unwarranted fear. This would be done in a humorous way. He discovered that this experience, which he reinforced in a variety of ways, brought about a change in attitude toward the item that caused the anxiety, and the symptom or the response would be diminished.

Paradoxical intention is designed to change the client's attitude toward his or her behavior; thus, this method can and has been used for a variety of problems. Some have used it to reduce stress (Shoham-Salomon & Jancourt, 1985), treat insomnia (Espie & Lindsay, 1985), or work with alcoholic families (Held & Heller, 1982). Others (Dreikurs, 1967; Grunwald & McAbee, 1985; Sweeney, 1989) have used this approach in working from an Adlerian frame of reference and have illustrated its use with clients whose maladaptive behavior is an attention-getting device. For example, a client who screams with a loud voice at inappropriate times is told by the counselor to scream as loud as he or she can. As the client responds, the counselor teases the client by saying something like, "Oh, that only earned you a C. I know you have an A scream inside of you." This is periodically repeated until the inappropriate behavior stops. This technique is often used in family counseling in which the counselor instructs parents on how to use the technique. The usual procedures involved are:

1. Identify the inappropriate behavior.
2. Persuade the client to produce the behavior in the most intense way possible.
3. Inject humor into the situation as the client engages in the behavior. This allows the client to become somewhat detached from the problem by laughing at it.
4. Repeat steps 2 and 3 until the inappropriate behavior is minimized.

As with other techniques, paradoxical intention is not a panacea. It does not always work, nor can or should it always be used. Its effectiveness can be enhanced by using it with other procedures to teach clients more appropriate ways of behaving.

SUMMARY

The essential concepts of behaviorally focused interventions were briefly outlined in this chapter. Behavioral techniques are based on the premise that all behavior is learned and that individuals develop habits and reinforce their behavioral activities. These strategies are designed to help clients learn a new behavior, increase the likelihood of a present behavior, or eliminate an unwanted or undesirable behavior. Behavioral counselors focus on concrete behaviors and activities; they employ very specific, highly structured, goal-directed, and sequentially ordered steps to assist clients. Homework assignments are often given. Contingency contracts, which outline the goals, responsibilities, and contingencies involved in the counseling process, are frequently employed. Behavioral approaches include the concepts of observational and simulated learning, which promote the acquisition of new skills by using modeling and role-playing strategies; the operant conditioning principles, which explain the modification of behavior by the appropriate use of reinforcement and punishment contingencies; and the classical conditioning theory, which gives the basis for strategies such as stimulus control, systematic desensitization, assertiveness training, flooding, aversion techniques, and paradoxical intention.

After reading this chapter on the behaviorally focused strategies, you should be able to identify the major aspects of the social learning, operant conditioning, and classical conditioning interventions. You should be able to understand how and when to use these strategies, to discuss the sequential steps involved in applying a behavioral technique, and to describe the contents of a contingency contract. In order to accomplish a high level of facility in using these methods, you will have to study these techniques further and obtain supervised practice in applying these strategies with actual clients.

REFERENCES

Alberti, R. E., & Emmons, M. L. (1995). *Your perfect right: A guide to assertive* behavior (7th ed.). San Luis Obispo, CA: Impact.

Bandura, A., & Walters, R. H. (1963). *Social learning and personality development.* New York: Holt, Rinehart and Winston.

Dreikurs, R. (1967). *Psychology in the classroom.* New York: Harper & Row.

Espie, C., & Lindsay, W. (1985). Paradoxical intention in the treatment of insomnia. *Behavior Research Therapy, 23,* 703–709.

Frankl, V. E. (1960). Paradoxical intentions: A logotherapeutic technique. *American Journal of Psychotherapy, 14,* 520–525.

Frankl, V. E. (1991). Paradoxical intention. In G. R. Weeks (Ed.), *Promoting change through paradoxical therapy* (pp. 99–110) (rev. ed.). New York: Brunner/Mazel.

Groden, G., & Cautela, J. R. (1981). Behavior therapy: A survey of procedures for counselors. *The Personnel and Guidance Journal, 60,* 175–180.

Grunwald, B. B., & McAbee, H. V. (1985). *Guiding the family.* Muncie, IN: Accelerated Development.

Held, B., & Heller, L. (1982). Symptom prescription as a metaphor: A systematic approach to the psychosomatic-alcoholic family. *Family Therapy, 9,* 133–145.

Kalish, H. I. (1981). *From behavioral science to behavioral modification.* New York: McGraw-Hill.

Kanfer, F. H., & Goldstein, A. P. (1991). *Helping people change: A textbook of* methods (4th ed.). Elmsford, NY: Pergamon Press.

Kazdin, A. E. (1978). *History of behavior modification.* Baltimore, MD: University Park Press.

Kazdin, A. E. (1994). *Behavior modification in applied settings* (5th ed.). Pacific Grove, CA: Brooks/Cole.

Krumboltz, J. D., & Thoresen, C. E. (1976). *Counseling methods.* New York: Holt, Rinehart and Winston.

Martin, G., & Pear, J. (1996). *Behavior modification: What it is and how to do it* (5th ed.). Englewood Cliffs, NJ: Prentice Hall.

Pavlov, I. P. (1927). *Conditioned reflexes: An investigation of the physiological activity of the cerebral cortex.* (G. V. Anrep, Trans.). London: Oxford University Press.

Premack, D. (1965). Reinforcement theory. In D. Levine (Ed.), *Nebraska symposium on motivation* (pp. 123–180). Lincoln, NE: Nebraska Press.

Rachman, S., Hodgson, R., & Marks, I. M. (1972). The treatment of chronic obsessive-compulsive neurosis: Follow-up and findings. *Behavior Research and Therapy, 10,* 181–189.

Schwartz, A. (1982). *The behavior therapies.* New York: Free Press.

Shaw, M. E., Wallace, E., & LaBella, F. (1980). *Making it assertively.* Englewood Cliffs, NJ: Prentice Hall.

Shipley, R. H. (1979). Implosive therapy: The technique. *Psychotherapy: Theory, Research, and Practice, 16,* 140–147.

Shoham-Salomon, V., & Jancourt, A. (1985). Differential effectiveness of paradoxical intention for more versus less stress-prone individuals. *Journal of Counseling Psychology, 32,* 449–543.

Skinner, B. F. (1938). *The behavior of organisms: An experimental analysis.* New York: Appleton-Century-Crofts.

Skinner, B. F. (1953). *Science and human behavior.* New York: Free Press.

Skinner, B. F. (1989). *Recent issues in analysis of behavior.* Columbus, OH: Merrill.

Sweeney, T. J. (1989). *Adlerian counseling: A practical approach for a new decade* (3rd ed.). Muncie, IN: Accelerated Development.

Wolpe, J. (1958). *Psychotherapy by reciprocal inhibition.* Stanford, CA: Stanford University Press.

Wolpe, J. (1990). *The practice of behavior therapy* (4th ed.). Boston: Allyn & Bacon.

Wolpe, J., & Lazarus, A. (1966). *A behavior therapy technique: A guide to the treatment of neuroses.* Elmsford, NY: Pergamon Press.

The Counselor's Role Communication Skills

Counselors-in-training develop their counseling skills through a process that involves both didactic and experiential learning. The didactic process focuses on cognitive learning in which students read the technical literature, hear about various theoretical counseling approaches, see demonstrations of these approaches, and study typescript, audiotaped, and videotaped vignettes of actual counseling case material. The experiential process focuses on learning obtained from direct experience in which counselors-in-training develop their skills through modeling the behavior of admired experts; practicing appropriate counselor response patterns; obtaining peer feedback on their counseling practices; and receiving professional supervision of their counseling practices in the typical sequential learning steps of role playing, practicum, and internship.

Typically, students entering their first experientially based course in counseling are confused about how to begin a counseling relationship. They may be familiar with the theoretical literature and may be able to discuss intellectually the Adlerian, behavioral, Rogerian, and some other major approaches to the counseling process. Nevertheless, to be effective counselors, they need to develop important communication skills.

Counseling involves a dynamic communication process between two people who are interacting with one another. This interactive process is a collaborative effort in which the counselor and the client undertake certain roles, responsibilities, and behaviors. In this collaboration, you as the counselor must take the responsibility for providing a facilitative climate and enhancing the client's motivation to change. Thus, the burden is on you to employ appropriate verbal, paraverbal, and nonverbal communication skills to influence the direction, the duration, and the eventual effectiveness of the counseling process. The client must feel free enough to reveal his or her real concerns and eventually must learn that he or she is the only one who can assume the ultimate responsibility for bringing about the desired changes.

As the counselor you must be concerned about both perceiving what the client is attempting to communicate and responding to that message in an appropriate manner. Client messages have cognitive, as well as affective, components. On the surface the cognitive content of a message is normally rather easy to identify; on the other hand, clients frequently communicate vague and incomplete pictures of themselves and their concerns. They may exhibit a lack of congruity between their verbal and nonverbal signals or a tendency to verbalize about irrelevant material. Clients also frequently show their lack of personal ownership of a problem by speaking about an unidentified person or group (for example, "*It* is a common fault . . ."; "*Some people* believe that . . ."; or "*Everybody* cannot stand for . . ."); or by speaking for someone who is not present (for example, "*Bill* believes . . ."; *John* says . . ."; *Mary* does . . ."). Speaking for others may or may not represent the other person's position, but it can distract from the major focus of the conversation. While listening to the cognitive component of the client's message, you need to be aware of these tendencies to avoid or deflect the problem.

The affective component of a client's message is the manifestation of the internal reaction that individuals have to their experiences. Clients may identify their feelings by labeling them or describing how they feel, or they may vaguely allude to how they feel. Frequently, these internal reactions are communicated by outward signs, such as crying when one is sad or extremely disappointed, shouting when one is angry, and smiling when one is happy or has experienced a pleasant event. Some clients have difficulty expressing themselves, particularly when they have a fear of being rejected or not being taken seriously. Feelings are more frequently communicated through nonverbal and paraverbal means than they are by verbal channels. You need to pay attention to your client's facial expressions, voice inflections, and other cues. You should also be aware of the vagueness that may be present in some messages and the contradictions that can exist between the verbal and nonverbal channels. You must make every effort to recognize and accept your client's feelings in order to facilitate the client's awareness and expression of these inner reactions, any conflicts that he or she may experience about these feelings, and any barriers that may prevent the expression of these feelings.

Barriers to effective dialogue between counselors and their clients can arise from causes such as making value judgments about clients, having selective or erroneous perceptions of the issues that clients present, and giving inappropriate responses to client messages. You should avoid making value judgments about your clients, labeling them or their actions, or questioning their motives. When issues arise that require evaluations of your client's thoughts, feelings, or behaviors, or an analysis of your client's motives, you should focus on helping clients make these judgments for themselves so that effective growth can occur. Because it is often difficult to really feel the problems and sense the difficulties that another person is experiencing, selective or erroneous perceptions can occur. Your experiences of life are different from your clients'. Hence, as a counselor you must try to understand the perceptual views of your clients who, because of different cultural backgrounds, personal interests, age, and other factors, may have different perceptions of their experiences and quite distinctive meanings for certain words and phrases. Learning to respond to clients in appropriate ways is a skill that can be learned. This section of the text is devoted to helping you as a counselor-in-training understand, develop, and master the important communication skills used in counseling.

COMMUNICATION AS A ROLE FUNCTION

The counseling relationship is based on effective communication between two people. The client is the person who seeks some resolution of a problem. The counselor is the skilled professional who uses his or her skills and knowledge of human behavior to assist the person in need. Because the purpose of this interaction is to improve the client's well-being, the burden is on you as the counselor to employ appropriate communication skills that will influence the shape, the duration, and indeed the eventual effectiveness of the counseling process.

Considerable attention has been focused on improving the communication skills of counselors since Robinson (1950) outlined a verbal response system based on the degree of lead involved. His use of the term *lead* implies that counselors have the responsibility of employing responses that anticipate the client's needs and enable the client to progress further in the interviewing or counseling process. These efforts to develop a skills-oriented approach to the education and training of counselors have led to:

1. the identification of a number of distinctive types of verbal responses that counselors employ within the counseling dyad (Benjamin, 1987; Brammer & MacDonald, 1996; Danish, D'Augelli, Hauer, & Conter, 1980; Hackney & Cormier, 1994; Hill, 1978; Hoffman, 1959; Spooner & Stone, 1977);
2. the development of several scales to evaluate counselors' skills in using responses (Danskin, 1955; Hill, 1978; Hoffman, 1959; Spooner & Stone, 1977); and
3. the formulation of several programs that systematically teach these skills (Carkhuff, 1969; Danish et al., 1980; Doyle, 1982; Evans, Hearn, Uhlemann, & Ivey, 1993; Ivey & Authier, 1978; Kagan, 1972a).

These efforts to develop counselor skills have been found useful for understanding the counseling process and have been effective in a variety of training programs (Baker, Daniels, & Greeley, 1990; Carkhuff, 1969; Francis, McDaniel, & Doyle, 1987; Hill, 1978; Hudson, Doyle, & Venezia, 1991; Ivey & Authier, 1978). Counselor education programs that have used the skills-oriented approach typically have their students learn a repertoire of helping in prepracticum courses. These skills are further developed in later courses until, as Kagan (1972b, p. 44) pointed out, a critical phenomenological change occurs when the trainee "puts it all together" and "becomes truly capable of therapeutic intervention."

This section of the text presents a comprehensive system for describing counseling skills that are used throughout the entire counseling process. The system includes an adequate methodology for evaluating the counselor's verbal as well as paraverbal and nonverbal modalities. Blum and Rosenberg (1968), Hill, Charles, and Reed (1981), and Lambert, DeJulio, and Stein (1978) have all indicated that such models are necessary. This model, entitled the *role communication skill model,* has two dimensions. Because communication presupposes role-taking opportunities (Kohlberg, 1969) and because counseling is a dynamic interactive communication process, the first dimension used to describe the counselor's functional behaviors is the *role* construct. This construct was employed earlier by Danskin (1955), Hoffman (1959), Muthard (1953), and Robinson (1955) in their investigations of the types of verbal responses used by counselors. In this interactive communication process, it is the counselor who must take the responsibility for acting or behaving in ways that provide the facilitative climate and the conditions necessary to enhance the probabilities for client change. Furthermore, because counselors engage in different behaviors and act in several ways in the various stages of counseling, these distinctive ways of behaving are considered to be unique roles. In the present configuration, this model has ten role communication skills, listed below. Eight counselor roles were initially described by the author (Doyle, 1982) and discussed in detail in the first edition of this text (Doyle, 1992). In this edition, two additional roles (with one asterisk) are defined and illustrated and two other roles (with two asterisks) were significantly modified. These counselor roles are:

- attending
- clarifying
- supporting or reassuring
- informing or describing
- probing or inquiring
- responding to client questions*
- advising*
- motivating or prescribing**
- evaluating or interpreting**
- problem solving

In this model, roles are seen as the critical or most important behavioral messages, and verbal responses or counselor leads, such as those mentioned by Buchheimer and Balough (1961), Hill (1978), and Spooner and Stone (1977), are seen as having second-ary importance. Thus, verbal responses are subsidiary skills necessary for each role. The model includes the four response modes (paraphrasing, approval, self-disclosure, and interpretation) that Hill and associates (1988) found to be the most helpful. And it incor-porates the six responses that Elliott and associates (1987) reported as being critical because of the significant differences in the use of the responses among seven diverse therapeutic approaches. These responses are: questioning, providing information, and advising; and using reflections, interpretations, and self-disclosures.

Furthermore, because communication takes place through paraverbal and nonver-bal channels as well as through words, a particular verbal response can convey a different role, depending on the counselor's attitude, expertise, and intention. This variation in the meaning of a particular phrase appears to be in agreement with Greenberg's conten-tion (1986) that speech acts have different meanings depending on the context or the episode in which they occur. Paraverbal elements include tonal quality, such as intensity, pitch, amplitude, velocity, and raspingness; and voice differentiators, such as laughter, sobbing, and a cracking or breaking voice. Nonverbal messages are communicated by various facial and other body movements. Messages are sent by such things as eye con-tact, nodding the head, and manipulating the facial muscles to produce frowns, indiffer-ence, quizzical looks, and smiles. Other nonverbal messages are sent by posture, muscle tone, twitching, and gestures. Changes in the meaning of a particular verbal response and hence the role used by the counselor are thus affected by tonal quality as well as gestures, body movements, and facial expressions. The ten counselor roles and the sub-sidiary verbal responses associated with these eight roles are outlined in further detail in the chapters of this section.

The second dimension employed to describe counselor behaviors is the *level* con-struct. This dimension is employed as a method for the qualitative evaluation of the counselor's competence and timing in using a particular role with appropriate nonverbal and paraverbal characteristics. Qualitative phenomena, such as therapeutic knowledge, insight, accuracy, and appropriateness in terms of pace and timing in using the role, can be accounted for with this construct. Furthermore, the level construct provides a methodology for indicating whether the paraverbal and nonverbal channels of communication are used appropriately.

The counselor's effectiveness in using roles can be ascertained by employing a competency continuum with a Likert-type scale. For convenience, a four-point rating scale is used:

Level 1: Poor use of the role
Level 2: Mediocre use of the role
Level 3: Good use of the role
Level 4: Excellent use of the role

The overall Level-of-Response Scale for rating the counselor's proficiency in using appropriate responses is indicated at the end of this section. The specific competency criteria for rating the counselor trainee's use of each role is incorporated in the chapters that follow. Counselors-in-training sometimes prefer to use the descriptive terminology—poor, mediocre, good, or excellent—rather than the numerical rating.

The level construct was first proposed by Carkhuff (1969), who outlined a five-point scale for rating the counselor's effectiveness in both discriminating and communicating responses. Responses rated below 3 were considered to be distractive and had the potential for doing more harm than good. A response with a rating of 3 was considered to be minimally facilitative, and a response above 3 was thought to be additive—that is, quite helpful to the client and the counseling process. Gazda and associates (1995) revised Carkhuff's scale to a four-point one. The Level-of-Response Scale used in this text is similar to the scales employed by Carkhuff and Gazda in terms of effectiveness, but it is based on the role construct rather than the "facilitative conditions" stressed by these authors.

The role communication skills discussed in the four chapters of this section have been arranged along a continuum having four major domains. The primary role communication skills—attending, clarifying, and supporting—are presented in Chapter 7. These roles focus on accepting and understanding the client and the client's frame of reference and communicating warmth, interest, and respect to the client. The intermediate role communication skills—providing information, inquiring, responding to questions, and the use of silence—are described in Chapter 8. These roles require the counselor to give more direction to the counseling process by describing phenomena, probing for more information, and using silence as an effective tool. Chapter 9 outlines the advanced role communication skills—advising, motivating, and evaluating. These skills require that the counselor use more direct, deliberate, and rather forceful responses. And Chapter 10 discusses the skills that are needed in the problem-solving role, when the counselor uses specific cognitive, affective, or performance intervention strategies. Hansen, Rossberg, and Cramer (1994), Robinson (1950), and Shertzer and Stone (1980) discuss similar concepts of a continuum of counselor responses using counselor lead as the construct.

Each role is discussed in some detail. First, the purpose of the role and what it is designed to accomplish are described. Second, the importance of the role is indicated and some guidelines in using the role are outlined. Third, the typical verbal responses associated with each role are given, and illustrations of these responses are presented. Fourth, a methodology for evaluating the effectiveness of the use of this role is discussed, and examples of effective and ineffective responses are shown. Finally, a variety of exercises designed to help you as a counselor-in-training to develop these skills are provided. Initial practice in using these skills sometimes feels awkward and clumsy, and you may find yourself focusing on your own words and phrases rather than on the needs of the client. Learning these communication skills requires practice, and repeated practice is usually necessary to attain mastery.

In learning these role communication skills, you will need to keep in mind the following general principles:

1. Avoid allowing any of your personal concerns to creep into the counseling process and distract from the client's concerns.
2. Help your clients keep the focus on themselves rather than on a third party who is not present in the session.
3. Carefully observe whether your client's nonverbal and paraverbal signals are in agreement with his or her verbal statements.
4. Pay careful attention to any emerging themes and repeating thoughts, feelings, or behaviors that may reveal overriding patterns for your client.
5. Be consciously aware of how your own inner perceptions, values, and experiences affect your interpretation of your client's statements. This is even more important when your client's cultural background is different from yours.
6. Make every effort to use language that is appropriate to the cultural experience and the educational background of your client.

The exercises in each role have been designed to enable you as a counselor-in-training to learn and practice a variety of verbal responses within that role; to develop the skills necessary to discriminate between low- and high-quality responses; and to practice communicating high-level responses. Each role contains three distinctive types of practice exercises: the discrimination exercises, the communication exercises, and the solo exercises. The discrimination exercises are designed to help you

- practice identifying a client's initial or stated concern;
- understand that there are different methods of responding to perceived needs with empathy, respect, and warmth;
- practice identifying the different types of responses;
- recognize that responses are truly different in the degree of their effectiveness; and
- practice discriminating among different levels of responses.

The communication exercises have been planned to provide the opportunity for you to practice giving appropriate high-level responses to a variety of client statements. For each communication exercise, you will be asked to give several different types of appropriate verbal responses. The solo exercises are intended to give you further opportunities to practice your skills under supervisory conditions.

These exercises have been used in a number of ways under the supervision of experienced counselors. Some supervisors have assigned the exercises as homework, others have assigned counselors-in-training to triads for practice, whereas others have had small groups discuss the exercises intensively. The exercises have been found to be most useful when the reasons for the ratings are discussed in the group. Obviously, an exercise in print form does not adequately convey any nonverbal aspects, nor does it reflect any tonal quality. These communicative channels can be employed in ways that convey very distinct meanings. It is therefore critical that the exercises be used as an *aid* in the training program and not as a substitute for intensive supervision. Indeed, it is imperative that the responses given by the counselors-in-training be discussed fully and completely in a supervised small-group discussion. The nuances and the reasons counselors-in-training give for their responses and the ratings they assign to these responses are the focal point of the exercises.

LEVEL-OF-RESPONSE SCALE

Because there are qualitative as well as modal differences in responding to clients, the counselor's proficiency in using each of the roles can be thought of as lying along a continuum with four integral points: poor (1); mediocre (2); good (3); excellent (4). The following descriptions should be used as a guide in rating the counselor's responses. Note that responses may be rated with a decimal rating (that is, 2.3, 2.5, 2.9) depending on the closeness or distance from the ordinal integers given in the rating scale.

Level 1: poor use of the role.   The counselor does not attend to the client's concerns or uses a role that is inappropriate at this point in the counseling process. The reflective, paraphrasing, or clarifying responses have little or no relationship to the content and feeling expressed by the client; the counselor is informing, describing, or explaining things incorrectly; irrelevant material is sought; the probing or motivating roles are used prematurely; or the counselor is using a particular problem-solving technique incorrectly or inappropriately. The counselor may show lack of interest, may ridicule, or may try to punish the client.

Level 2: mediocre use of the role.   The counselor partially attends to the feelings or content expressed by the client, or a role is used that is not very helpful at this stage of counseling. The reflective, paraphrasing, or clarifying responses are superficial interpretations of the client's cues. The counselor may provide the client with partial or incomplete information, or probe for appropriate data but not at a sufficient depth. When the motivating role is used, it is done in a weak manner. The problem-solving role is used prematurely, incorrectly, or incompletely. The counselor may show minimal interest, give cheap advice, or ask rather meaningless questions.

Level 3: good use of the role.   The response mode attends to the stated content and to the feelings of the client, or the counselor uses a role that is very suitable at this point in the counseling process. The counselor interprets messages correctly and communicates this effectively to the client. The attending and clarifying roles are used appropriately, phenomena are explained correctly, and probes are topical and at sufficient depth.

Motivational statements are adroit, and the problem-solving role is used competently. The counselor shows a high degree of interest, makes appropriate inquiries, and interprets the verbal, paraverbal, and nonverbal messages in meaningful ways.

Level 4: excellent use of the role.

The response mode used goes beyond attending to the stated content and the surface feelings of the client, or the counselor uses a role that is very appropriate and advances the counseling process. The counselor interprets the client's messages fully and responds adroitly. Factual information and descriptions are given completely and in an understanding manner. The probing and motivational roles are used when called for and facilitate the progress of the counseling. The problem-solving role is used in a timely way, and the counselor demonstrates his or her mastery of the technique employed. The counselor reveals an intensive interest, makes wise inquiries, and takes some appropriate risks in the interpretation of the verbal, paraverbal, and nonverbal messages.

REFERENCES

Baker, S., Daniels, T, & Greeley, A. (1990). Systematic training of graduate level counselors: Narrative and meta-analytic reviews of three major programs. *Counseling Psychologist, 18,* 355–421.

Benjamin, A. (1987). *The helping interview* (4th ed.). Boston: Houghton Mifflin.

Blum, A. F., & Rosenberg, L. (1968). Some problems involved in professionalizing social interaction: The case of psychotherapeutic training. *Journal of Health and Social Behavior, 9,* 72–85.

Brammer, L. M., & MacDonald, G. (1996). *The helping relationship: Process and skills* (6th ed.). Boston: Allyn & Bacon.

Buchheimer, A., & Balough, S. C. (1961). *The counseling relationship: A casebook.* Chicago: Science Research Associates.

Carkhuff, R. R. (1969). *Human and helping relationships* (2 vols.). New York: Holt, Rinehart and Winston.

Danish, S. L., D'Augelli, A. R., & Brock, G. W. (1976). An evaluation of helping skills training: Effects on helpers' verbal responses. *Journal of Counseling Psychology, 3,* 259–266.

Danish, S. L., D'Augelli, A. R., Hauer, A. L., & Conter, J. J. (1980). *Helping skills: A basic training program* (2nd ed.). New York: Human Sciences Press.

Danskin, D. G. (1955). Roles played by counselors in their interviews. *Journal of Counseling Psychology, 2,* 22–27.

Doyle, R. E. (1982). The counselor's role communication skills, or the roles counselors play: A conceptual model. *Counselor Education and Supervision, 22,* 123–131.

Elliott, R., Hill, C. E., Stiles, W. B., Friedlander, M. L., Mahrer, A. R, & Marigison, F. R. (1987). Primary therapist response modes: Comparison of six rating systems. *Journal of Consulting and Clinical Psychology, 55,* 218–223.

Evans, D. R., Hearn, M. T., Uhlemann, M. R., & Ivey, A. E. (1993). *Essential interviewing: A programmed approach to effective communication* (4th. ed.). Pacific Grove, CA: Brooks/Cole.

Francis, K., McDaniel, M., & Doyle, R. (1987). Training in role communication skills: Effects on interpersonal and academic skills of high-risk freshmen. *Journal of College Student Personnel, 28,* 151–156.

Gazda, G. M., Asbury, F. R., Balzer, F. J., Childers, W. C., & Phelps, R. E. (1995). *Human relations development: A manual for educators* (5th ed.). Boston: Allyn & Bacon.

Greenberg, L. S. (1986). Change process research. *Journal of Consulting and Clinical Psychology, 54,* 4–9.

Hackney, H., & Cormier, L. S. (1994). *Counseling strategies and interventions* (4th ed.).Boston: Allyn & Bacon.

Hansen, J. C., Rossberg, R. H., & Cramer, S. H. (1994). *Counseling theory and process* (6th ed.). Boston: Allyn & Bacon.

Hill, C. E. (1978). Development of a counselor verbal response category system. *Journal of Counseling Psychology, 25,* 461–468.

Hill, C. E., Charles, D., & Reed, K. G. (1981). A longitudinal analysis of changes in counseling skills during doctoral training in counseling psychology. *Journal of Counseling Psychology, 28,* 428–436.

Hill, C. E., Helms, J. E., Tichenor, V., Spiegel, S. B., O'Grady, K. E., & Perry, E. S. (1988). Effects of therapist response modes in brief psychotherapy. *Journal of Counseling Psychology, 35,* 222–233.

Hoffman, A. E. (1959). An analysis of counselor subroles. *Journal of Counseling Psychology, 6,* 61–67.

Hudson, P., Doyle, R. E., & Venezia, J. (1991). A comparison of two group methods of teaching communications skills to high school students. *Journal for Specialists in Group Work, 16,* 255–263.

Ivey, A. E., & Authier, J. (1978). *Microcounseling: Innovations in interviewing, counseling, psychotherapy, and psychoeducation* (2nd ed.). Springfield, IL: Charles C. Thomas.

Kagan, N. (1972a). *Influencing human interaction.* Unpublished manuscript, Michigan State University.

Kagan, N. (1972b). Observations and suggestions. *The Counseling Psychologist, 3*(1), 42–45.

Kohlberg, L. (1969). Stage and sequence: The cognitive-development approach to socialization. In D. A. Goslin (Ed.), *Handbook of socialization theory and research* (pp. 347–480). Chicago: Rand McNally.

Lambert, M. V., DeJulio, S. S., & Stein, D. M. (1978). Therapist interpersonal skills: Process, outcome, methodological considerations, and recommendations for future research. *Psychological Bulletin, 85,* 467–489.

Muthard, J. E. (1953). The relative effectiveness of larger units used in interview analysis. *Journal of Consulting Psychology, 18,* 184–188.

Robinson, F. P. (1950). *Principles and procedures in student counseling.* New York: Harper & Bros.

Robinson, F. P. (1955). The dynamics of communication in counseling. *Journal of Counseling Psychology, 2,* 163–169.

Shertzer, B., & Stone, S. C. (1980). *Fundamentals of counseling* (3rd ed.). Boston: Houghton Mifflin.

Spooner, S. E., & Stone, S. C. (1977). Maintenance of specific counseling skills over time. *Journal of Counseling Psychology, 24,* 66–71.

7 Primary Role Communication Skills

Introduction

The counselor's primary role communication skills are covered in this chapter. The attending, clarifying, and supporting roles are explained, examples demonstrating the effective use of each of these roles are given, and exercises are provided to allow you to practice and master these skills. After studying this chapter you should be able to:

- Describe the purposes of the attending, clarifying, and supporting roles.
- Discuss the characteristics that distinguish high-level responses from low-level responses in each of these roles.
- Give examples of the types of responses used in each of these roles and illustrate good and poor uses of these responses in helping interviews.
- Apply these skills in appropriate situations.

The Attending Role

Before you can help another person, you must pay attention and listen to what the other person is saying. *Attending* is the process of trying to understand a client without making any evaluative judgments about the person. It is accomplished when you actively listen to the client in order to discern the client's primary or essential message; demonstrate an interest, acceptance, and respect for the client and the client's internal frame of reference; and communicate by an appropriate phrase or gesture that you understand what the client is saying or is attempting to say. You need to listen to the essential or underlying message expressed by the client and not the superficial words or phrases. This active listening requires you to be patient and keep an open mind. It involves focusing on the content of the phrases the client uses, the emotions or affect the client is feeling or expressing, and the body language the client is using, and putting these signals into a composite message in light of the client's background and experience.

Demonstrating interest, acceptance, and respect for the client requires you as the counselor to establish and maintain good eye contact and attentive body posture and to be fully present for the client. Your responses to the client should accurately communicate your understanding and may vary from a nonverbal gesture, such as a nod of the head, to a simple minimal verbal response, such as "mm-hmm" or "I see," to a more verbal response, which reflects the client's feelings and content, to a deeper-level paraphrasing response, which goes beyond what the client has stated in an attempt to catch the internal meaning of the client's statement.

Because the attending role involves the process of being receptive and involved with another person, it is the prerequisite for all other responses to clients. It sets the tone for the relationship, demonstrates to the client that the counselor cares and is sincerely interested, and provides the opportunity for the client to discuss whatever is bothering him or her. The way one attends to the client can have a great deal of influence on the client and the counseling process. Good attending responses tend to reduce a client's fear about revealing himself or herself; thus, they decrease the client's defensiveness and increase his or her sense of trust in the counselor and the counseling process.

Four guiding principles should be followed in communicating an attending response to the client. First, give yourself a chance to reflect before responding—take time to integrate the totality of the client's message and to formulate an appropriate response. Second, try to use responses that are brief and to the point rather than long and all-inclusive. Long responses tend to be counterproductive because clients can be distracted by them or give short responses to them. Third, use terms, phrases, and expressions that are familiar to the client. You should employ a vocabulary appropriate to the client's age, educational level, and cultural background. And fourth, be reasonably spontaneous. Although you can take time to think and reflect on the meaning of a client's statement, the silence caused by a pause that is too long can be distracting.

Types of Attending Responses

The following four types of verbal responses are all normally used in this role and are quite helpful in attending to clients.

1. *Simple minimal verbal.* This is a short response, such as "I see," "Uh-huh," or "Mm-hmm," which is considered the verbal equivalent of a head nod (Okun, 1997). It indicates to a client that the counselor is listening and following his or her statements. A simple verbal response can encourage the client to continue talking (Benjamin, 1987) and can have a significant reinforcing value that increases a client's use of a particular word or topic (Hackney & Cormier, 1994).

2. *Reflection of content and feelings.* This is a response that mirrors or reflects to the client the message that the counselor hears. The counselor responds to what is being said, how it is being said, the underlying feelings that are evident, and the nonverbal body expressions that are communicated. It is important to sense the feelings and attitudes not expressed by the client and to bring these to the surface (Benjamin, 1987). Words identical or similar to the client's are used to convey to the client the essence of the message that the counselor heard.

3. *Accent.* This is a short response that selects a part of the client's previous statement and brings it into focus by repeating it. It is said slowly with a soft voice and in a tonal quality that encourages the client to elaborate further on the part of the message that the counselor thinks is most important (Hackney & Cormier, 1994).

4. *Paraphrasing.* This response is a restatement of the client's essential message using different words or phrases that are carefully chosen (Cormier & Cormier, 1991). Because different words are used, this not only communicates the counselor's understanding of the client's message but also helps clients see their thoughts, feelings, and behaviors from another perspective. In paraphrasing it is helpful to use responses that go beyond the client's verbal message in order to catch the deeper internal meaning. Counselors often use images and analogies to capture this deeper meaning.

Illustrations of Different Types of Attending Responses

The following three examples demonstrate the use of the attending role. Note how the client's statement can be responded to in different ways and still convey warmth and understanding to the client.

■ *Client 1, a 20-year-old woman:* I feel as if my friends have been letting me down lately. Until recently I was very popular in school—I had a lot of friends, and I enjoyed being with them. But all of a sudden I feel like I've been losing them. I've been snubbed by some, and I really don't know why this is happening.

1. *Simple minimal verbal:* I understand.
2. *Reflection of feeling and content:* You're upset because you seem to have lost some of your popularity.
3. *Accent:* You've been snubbed.
4. *Paraphrasing:* You feel your friends have been ignoring you, and you're confused as to why this is happening. You're really hurt.

■ *Client 2, a teenager:* My mother is constantly on my back. Every time I turn around, there's something else she wants me to do or some more advice she wants to hand out. She really burns me up.

1. *Simple minimal verbal:* That hurts.
2. *Reflection of feeling and content:* You're angry at your mother because she wants you to follow her advice and do her errands for her.
3. *Accent:* Your mother burns you up.
4. *Paraphrasing:* You're behind the eight ball, and every time you want to get out from behind, you're shoved back there by your mother.

■ *Client 3, a 23-year-old woman:* I'm working part-time as a dental assistant; it's the only job I could get. It seems that I've spent my whole life wanting and training to be a teacher, but it's impossible to get a job. I hate what I'm doing now, and I'm so afraid I'll be stuck there for the rest of my life and my education will just go down the drain.

1. *Simple minimal verbal:* I see.
2. *Reflection of feeling and content:* You're angry because you have a job you hate and cannot obtain one for which you were trained.
3. *Accent:* You're afraid you will be stuck.
4. *Paraphrasing:* You feel that you are in a rut and the walls are too high for you to get out.

Levels of Attending Responses

The attending role can be used with various degrees of effectiveness. When you use the role effectively, it shows that you understand both the content and feelings expressed by the client, tend to focus on issues and situations that appear most relevant, communicate to the client that you have heard the major message, and often get behind the stated words to capture or sense the client's underlying message. High-level responses communicate to the client that you are a person who is sincerely interested in the client and a person to whom the client can relate in a nonthreatening, trustful manner. The role is used ineffectively when the counselor responds only to the surface level concerns expressed by the client. This is often manifested by the counselor's repeating the content of the client's message. This "parroting" usually causes a circular movement in the dialogue and feelings of discomfort on the part of the client (Evans, Hearn, Uhlemann, & Ivey, 1993). Low-level responses are often ineffective and may be counterproductive. They are often said in a tonal quality that creates a questioning atmosphere rather than a permissive or encouraging one. Low-level responses can also imply disapproval and criticism of the client's thoughts, feelings, or behaviors. On the four-point scale, the use of this role can be rated as follows:

Level 1: Poor use of the role. The counselor is least effective when he or she reveals little or no interest in the client, when messages are glaringly misinterpreted, when responses reveal little or no awareness of the underlying feelings or concerns of the client, when body movements or voice quality is distracting, or when the role is used at an inappropriate place in the relationship.

Level 2: Mediocre use of the role. The counselor's responses are mediocre when he or she attends partially to the feeling or the content expressed by the client; when the response is a superficial interpretation of the client's verbal, paraverbal, and nonverbal messages; when tonal quality or gestures are somewhat misleading; or when the counselor shows only minimal interest in the client.

Level 3: Good use of the role. The counselor is effective when he or she attends to the stated content and feelings, when messages are interpreted correctly and communicated back accurately, and when the counselor manifests a high degree of interest in the client.

Level 4: Excellent use of the role. The counselor is most effective when he or she demonstrates intense interest in the client; interprets messages fully; responds to the underlying feelings and messages expressed by the client; maintains appropriate eye contact, tonal quality, and physical attentiveness; and uses the role at appropriate times.

Illustrations of Different Levels of Attending Responses

There are three client statements below, each of which is followed by four different responses. The responses are rated according to the Level-of-Response Scale, and the reasons for each of these ratings are indicated. Study these examples to see if you agree with the ratings and the reasons stated. You may find that you do not agree with these ratings. Because the nonverbal and paraverbal aspects of the client's statement and the counselor's responses cannot be adequately conveyed by the printed word, it is quite possible that you will read one or more of these statements differently from the person who rated them. Any counselor response may be rated differently depending on how it is heard. When rating responses it is extremely important that you state the reasons for your rating so that you can discuss any differences with your supervisor and classmates.

■ *Client 1, a high school senior:* I'm worried about what I'll do in the future, and I was wondering whether you can tell me if there are any good jobs in accounting.

Responses	*Ratings and Reasons*
1. It sounds like you are looking for some area to direct your energy, and accounting is on the top of your list.	2.8 Attends to the surface content and feelings of the client. Supports the client's questioning as having value, and hence the client has value. Open to further dialogue.
2. Where have you been for the last three years? You are a poor lost soul.	1.0 Counselor ridicules the client, shows lack of caring, and ignores the client's feelings.
3. If you don't know what the opportunities are in the field of accounting, you might like to see someone in the business department or check the *Occupational Outlook Handbook.*	2.0 Gives advice without understanding situation. Attends only to the content of the client's statement and doesn't deal with feelings. Does nothing to involve self in the client's concern.
4. Graduation is a few months away, and you're scared that you will get out of here without any place to go. It sounds like accounting is an occupation that you may be vaguely interested in.	3.5 Goes beyond statement by attempting to attend to the underlying message. Solicits action on the part the client.

■ *Client 2, a 25-year-old man:* I'm exhausted. My work has been building up for weeks. The harder I try to finish, the more there seems to be to do. I'm cranky with my wife and baby. I don't know what to do.

Responses	*Ratings and Reasons*
1. Your job is getting to be too much, and you're worried about the effect it will have on your family.	2.5 Paraphrases statements and hence shows attentiveness to client's concern.

2. This will pass. Once part-time help is employed, things will ease off. Don't worry.

1.0 Responds by giving cheap advice. Behaves in a manner congruent with preconceived role.

3. You feel you've hit the bottom of the pit. You work hard, but there is no end; you love your family but fight with them. And you sure don't want to stay there.

4.0 Goes beyond client statement. Designed to elicit reaction to the underlying message.

4. What do you want me to do? I have enough problems of my own.

1.0 Shows total lack of caring. Ridicules client by ignoring his appeal for help.

■   *Client 3, a college freshman:*   You know, lately everything seems to be going wrong. My grades are slipping, my mother keeps hassling me, and my boyfriend has been threatening to break up with me.

Responses
1. You know, I had the same problem when I was your age. . . . Don't worry, it will go away.

Ratings and Reasons
1.0 Gives advice without really understanding the problem, and an inappropriate selfdisclosure.

2. You're having difficulty dealing with your mother and your boyfriend and keeping up your grades.

2.5 Attends to content by reflecting the main points made by the client.

3. You're very upset. You feel like you're being pulled in three different directions by your school, your mother, and your boyfriend.

3.5 Attends to feelings and content. Encourages the client to go further by naming the three directional pulls.

4. It's very hard for you to decide what's best for you. And the pain only complicates the issue.

4.0 Goes beyond client statement; encourages the client to react to deeper-level feelings.

Practice Attending Exercises: "What Do I Do After I Say 'Hello'?"

The following exercises have been designed to enhance your attending skills. The discrimination exercises are designed to give you the opportunity to identify the client's underlying message, to recognize various types of attending responses, and to gain experience in learning how to distinguish effective from ineffective responses. The communication exercises offer you the chance to practice giving a variety of high-level attending responses. Finally, the solo exercises provide further opportunities to develop your attending skills. When you do these exercises assume that some of the clients may have a cultural background that is different from yours.

Discrimination exercises.   For each of the following excerpts identify the feeling and the content underlying the client's statement, and then indicate the *type* of attending response illustrated. Finally, point out the appropriateness of the response by rating the *level* of the response. Please be prepared to share the reasons for your ratings with your classmates and your supervisor. You may find that one or more of your classmates read the excerpts with another intonation or emphasis than you did and consequently rated the responses quite differently.

■ **Client 1, a high school sophomore:**   I just got my report card, and I flunked geometry. I don't know how I'm going to face my parents. They're planning on a trip to Europe this summer, and now I'll have to go to summer school.

Underlying message: _____

Responses	*Type and Level of Response*
1. It's painful to disappoint your parents, but even more painful when you disappoint yourself.	1. _____
2. How am I going to face my parents . . .	2. _____
3. You seem to be upset for three reasons: first, because you failed school; second, because you upset your parents; and third, because you might miss a trip to Europe.	3. _____
4. Wow!	4. _____

■ **Client 2, a 30-year-old man:**   I'm thinking about getting a divorce. My wife and I do nothing but tear each other to pieces. Whatever love we had for each other has long since been destroyed.

Underlying message: _____

Responses	*Type and Level of Response*
1. What was once a beautiful relationship has deteriorated and become so painful that you feel there is only one way out.	1. _____
2. Uh-huh.	2. _____
3. Being torn or tearing—it's so painful.	3. _____
4. You seem to be living painfully with your wife. Your love for each other has gone, and you are wondering if divorce is the only sensible thing to do.	4. _____

■ **Client 3, a 40-year-old woman:**   Ever since my breast surgery I have no desire to have sex with my husband. He's gentle and patient and doesn't mind looking at my scar. I have sex with him, but there's no feeling.

Underlying message: _____

Responses	*Type and Level of Response*
1. It's difficult to adjust to a painful experience. You feel that your relationship with your husband will never be the same again.	1. _____
2. Even though you appreciate your husband's efforts to be sensitive, you feel as though you've lost your desire for sex.	2. _____
3. You have no feeling . . .	3. _____
4. Your adjustment to your breast surgery has dimensions you never anticipated.	4. _____

■   *Client 4, a high school junior:*   My older brother thinks he's my father. Do you know what he did? He went to the bar where I go once in a while for drinks with my friends, and he told the bartender not to serve me anymore because I'm not twenty-one.

Underlying message: _____

Responses	*Type and Level of Response*
1. You are mad at your brother because he embarrassed you, and because you can no longer be served in that bar.	1. _____
2. You resent someone else running your life. You wonder who is going to be in charge—you or someone else.	2. _____
3. Your big brother playing "father's role" is really upsetting to you.	3. _____
4. He told him not serve you . . .	4. _____

■   *Client 5, a 30-year-old homemaker:*   I don't know what I want to do with my life.

Underlying message: _____

Responses	*Type and Level of Response*
1. You sound frustrated because you want to change, but you are unsure of where to go or what to do.	1. _____
2. You're confused, you feel you want to do *something* with your life.	2. _____

3. Thinking about the future is scary.   3. _____

4. I understand.   4. _____

■ *Client 6, a middle-aged man:*   You know, I work hard all day. . . . I have lots of pressure. . . . People make me feel uptight. . . . Can I help it if I blow off a little steam in my wife's direction once in a while?

Underlying message: _____

Responses	*Type and Level of Response*
1. Something at work gets you so angry that when you get home you take it out on your wife.	1. _____
2. In your wife's direction . . .	2. _____
3. Continue.	3. _____
4. You really are burdened at this moment. Something seems to be making you uptight.	4. _____

■ *Client 7, a 19-year-old man:*   The whole white society is corrupt. They're just out to manipulate and exploit the brothers, and that's just the way it is.

Underlying message: _____

Responses	*Type and Level of Response*
1. It's damning when everything is against you.	1. _____
2. You're angry at the way you feel white society treats you.	2. _____
3. The whole white society is corrupt.	3. _____
4. Damn.	4. _____

■ *Client 8, a young man:*   I don't know why the courts suggested I come and see you. So I got busted—that's no big deal. People get busted every day. The courts are always sending us to see this one or that one; they think I'm sick in the head. But I'm not, I'm not. I'll show them! I'll show them!

Underlying message: _____

Responses	*Type and Level of Response*
1. It's tough to be on the bottom. You'll climb the ladder to the top and tell them off.	1. _____

2. You're angry. The courts sent you here.   2. _____
   You think it's because you're not
   functioning the way they want you to.

3. I see, they sent you to me.   3. _____

4. And I'm not sick in the head.   4. _____

■ *Client 9, a middle-aged woman:*   This past weekend my cat died. She
drank a can of paint thinner I left in the kitchen after I finished painting. I don't know
how she got into the can. . . . She must have knocked the top off. I feel terrible now. . . .
Oh, I just can't seem to do anything right.

Underlying message: _____

Responses   *Type and Level of Response*

1. It's awful to lose your pet, particularly   1. _____
   one that you have been so attached to.
   But it is even more painful to have this
   feeling that you can't do anything right.

2. It's hard when a pet dies, particularly if   2. _____
   you feel you're partly at fault.

3. I can't seem to do anything right . . .   3. _____

4. Your cat's dying is painful, but it's more   4. _____
   bothersome to you because you feel
   you can't do anything right.

■ *Client 10, a newly married woman:*   When I get home from work, I
just can't stand doing the housework anymore, especially washing the dishes. I'm so sick
of them—I'm just letting them pile up in the sink! And I feel so guilty when my husband
yells at me to do them. That's all he seems to be doing now—yelling!

Underlying message: _____

Responses   *Type and Level of Response*

1. It appears that you have ambivalent   1. _____
   feelings about your relationship. Your
   husband constantly yells at you, and
   yet you seem to provoke him by not
   doing the dishes.

2. You have to do the housework when   2. _____
   you come home, a chore you hate, and
   your husband fails to understand you.

3. You are upset at your husband's yelling   3. _____
   at you. He doesn't understand the
   pressure you have on the job.

4. You can't stand doing housework   4. _____
when you come home, so you don't do
it. Your husband yells at you and
makes you feel guilty.

Communication exercises.   For each excerpt given below, give three different types of high-level attending responses.

■   *Client 11, a 30-year-old man:*   I really love my work, but the foreman is really getting to me. He used to be my best friend, but he's changed. I thought he knew a lot, but now I see that he's not very good at his job.

■   *Client 12, a middle-aged woman:*   I have a difficult problem. I went back to work after being home for many years. Now I'm working and making much more money than my husband, and it's tearing him apart. I don't know what to do.

■   *Client 13, a 40-year-old woman:*   I'm beginning to feel very useless . . . no one needs me anymore. My husband and I don't seem to communicate. I don't see my children that much—they have their own friends and interests. Most of the time I'm alone.

■   *Client 14, a 25-year-old man:*   My girlfriend has cancer, and it's driving me crazy. The doctors say it's terminal. I don't have much faith in doctors. If anything happens to her, I don't know what I'll do . . . I love her so much.

■   *Client 15, a 40-year-old man:*   I'm overwhelmed by the amount of work I have. My wife died five years ago, and my son is on drugs. I don't know what to do.

■   *Client 16, a 24-year-old woman:*   I'm really having a bad time at home. I just wish I weren't there. I'm twenty-four years old, and my parents expect me to act like a child. They just don't understand much about the world. I don't know what to do about it.

■   *Client 17, a high school junior:*   My grades are so bad I'm sure I won't be able to make any of the colleges I want to go to.

■   *Client 18, a 30-year-old woman:*   I feel very depressed lately. I have a good job, but it's not enough. My family thinks I should get married, but I don't know anyone I'd like to marry.

■   *Client 19, a 25-year-old woman:*   I'm so hurt. We've been married only six months, and John wants a divorce. He has completely rejected me. I don't know where I failed.

■   *Client 20, a college junior:*   I don't know whether I should go to law school or not. I'd like to be a lawyer, but everyone tells me how tough law school can be. I'm afraid of flunking out.

Solo exercises.   Practice your attending responses in a triad. Each counselor-in-training should take a turn at being a client, a counselor, and a supervisor. Role-play on a tape recorder. After 5 minutes the "supervisor" should lead the critique of the counselor's use of the attending role. Repeat the exercise until all members of the triad have had the opportunity to practice.

THE CLARIFYING ROLE

This role is employed when the counselor actively attempts to make various issues clearer or to dispel any confusion that may exist. As the counselor, you may be unsure of what the client is actually trying to say or what the client means by his or her statement; or you may feel that the client is confused and needs help in clarifying an issue; or you may believe that the client needs to provide more information or elaborate on a problem or concern (Cormier & Cormier, 1991). Egan (1994) points out that it is important to understand what clients are attempting to express rather than feign understanding. The clarifying role is often used in conjunction with the attending role because it can facilitate the understanding of the client's thoughts and feelings.

Your clarifying response should encourage your client to reflect, restate, or redefine a statement he or she has made about a situation, problem, or concern. The request for clarification may be communicated nonverbally by silence or by a quizzical look; paraverbally by an inquisitive tonal quality; or verbally by an open-ended question that cannot be answered with a simple yes or no or by a statement that reflects your perception of the issue.

Types of Clarifying Responses

The clarifying role generally includes the following types of responses:

1. *Perception checking.* In this response the counselor seeks to verify the accuracy of his or her perception of all or part of the client's message, and the counselor asks the client to confirm or modify this perception (Brammer & MacDonald, 1996). A typical perception check is "It seems your major concern is . . ."

2. *Clarification of alternatives.* This response is used when the counselor has some doubt or confusion about which alternative is of major importance to the client or when the counselor believes the client is not sure of what he or she really wants to focus on. Often this response takes the form, "Do you mean this or do you mean that?"

3. *Request for further information or elaboration.* In this response the counselor makes a specific request for further information in order to clear up any confusion that may be present. A response of this sort is, "I'm not sure what you mean; please go on."

Illustrations of Different Types of Clarifying Responses

The following examples illustrate the use of the clarifying role.

■   *Client 1, a 20-year-old woman:*   I feel as if my friends have been letting me down lately. Until recently I was very popular in school—I had a lot of friends, and I enjoyed being with them. But all of a sudden I feel like I've been losing them. I've been snubbed by some, and I really don't know why this is happening.

1. *Perception checking:* I gather your major concern is looking at yourself to see what you've done to cause your friends to pull away.
2. *Clarifying alternatives:* I'm not sure what your real concern is. Are you angry because you may have done something to lose some of your friends, or do you feel you've done nothing and can't understand it?
3. *Request for further information or elaboration:* I'm not sure I completely understand your concern. Tell me more about your situation.

■ **Client 2, a teenager:** My mother is constantly on my back. Every time I turn around, there's something else she wants me to do or some more advice she wants to hand out. She really burns me up.

1. *Perception checking:* Are you saying your mother is controlling your whole life?
2. *Clarifying alternatives:* Is it really your mother who is bothering you, or is it your own lack of skill in speaking up for your rights that bothers you?
3. *Request for further information or elaboration:* I'm uncertain about your relationship with your mother and other family members. Please amplify this.

■ **Client 3, a 23-year-old woman:** I'm working part-time as a dental assistant; it's the only job I could get. It seems that I've spent my whole life wanting and training to be a teacher, but it's impossible to get a job. I hate what I'm doing now, and I'm so afraid I'll be stuck there for the rest of my life and my education will just go down the drain.

1. *Perception checking:* You seem to feel that the most important thing for you is to get another job, either in education or in a closely related field.
2. *Clarifying alternatives:* You seem to be very angry, but I'm not sure whether that anger is directed toward yourself for not adjusting to this situation or toward others who may have encouraged you.
3. *Request for further information or elaboration:* I hear an angry voice, and I'm puzzled about whom this anger is directed toward. Please continue.

Levels of Clarifying Responses

This role is often used in the early phases of the counseling process. High-level responses are communicated by words and by paraverbal and nonverbal means that reveal a sincere and genuine interest in the client and focus on critical issues or situations that need clarification. The effective use of this role greatly enhances both the client's and your understanding of issues stated by the client or within the client's internal frame of reference. It can be ineffective and even counterproductive when you employ incongruous paraverbal or verbal channels, constantly attempt to clarify some trivial points, show approval or disapproval, or use the role excessively. The excessive use of this role is distracting to clients and tends to interrupt their thought processes (Hackney

& Cormier, 1994). The use of this role can be rated on the four-point scale indicated below.

> *Level 1: Poor use of the role.* The counselor is most ineffective when he or she reveals little or no interest in the client's underlying concern, communicates a value judgment in the response, or uses the role at an inappropriate point in the counseling process. Low-level responses reveal little relationship to the feeling or content expressed by the client, and the counselor may reveal a preoccupation with other matters.
>
> *Level 2: Mediocre use of the role.* The counselor is not very effective when he or she tries to clarify only a part of the client's underlying message; when the response is a superficial interpretation of the client's verbal, paraverbal, and nonverbal message; and when only minimal interest in the client is revealed.
>
> *Level 3: Good use of the role.* The counselor is effective when he or she focuses on the stated content and feelings of the client; attempts to clear up garbled, confused, or unclear messages; and manifests a high degree of interest in the client.
>
> *Level 4: Excellent use of the role.* The counselor is most effective when he or she goes beyond the stated content and surface feelings expressed by the client; helps the client articulate issues more clearly; assists the client in focusing on the underlying concerns; avoids value judgments; and shows an intense interest in the client.

Illustrations of Different Levels of Clarifying Responses

To give you some practice in learning to distinguish between effective and ineffective counselor responses, three client statements are presented below. Each statement is followed by four different clarifying responses. The Level-of-Response Scale was used to rate each of the counselor's responses, and the reasoning behind each of these ratings is stated. In studying these examples, you may find that you do not agree with these ratings. Because tonal quality and other paraverbal aspects of the client's statements and the counselor's responses are not conveyed, it is possible that you will read some of these statements in another way than the person who rated them. Any response may obtain a different rating depending on the paraverbal message that the reader hears. Thus, when rating responses, it is crucial to indicate the reasons behind the ratings so that any differences among these ratings can be understood.

■   *Client 1, a high school senior:*   I'm worried about what I'll do in the future, and I was wondering whether you can tell me if there are any good jobs in accounting.

Responses	*Ratings and Reasons*
1. I'm not sure what your real concern is. Are your unsure about your future in general or unsure about accounting as an occupation?	3.0 Goes beyond the stated message and attempts to clarify between two reasonable alternative meanings.

2. Your major concern seems to be whether or not you should go on to college and major in accounting.

2.8 Counselor is checking whether or not his or her perception of the client's underlying message is correct.

3. Is the concern about your future coming only from you, or is there pressure from home?

2.8 Counselor clarifies between alternatives to see if there is another issue in the client's presenting problem.

4. Are your grades good enough to get into a good accounting program?

1.5 Attempts to have the client elaborate, but communicates a value judgment in the response.

■ **Client 2, a 25-year-old man:**   I'm exhausted. My work has been building up for weeks. The harder I try to finish, the more there seems to be to do. I'm cranky with my wife and baby. I don't know what to do.

Responses

1. You seem to be saying that the pressure of the job is causing problems with your health and family life.

Ratings and Reasons

2.5 Counselor checks on his or her perception of the client's statement. Does not go much beyond surface level.

2. I'm unclear about your relationship with your boss and your work; please tell me me about that situation.

2.8 Requests the client to elaborate. Focus is on one area that is reported by the client.

3. I'm not sure what you mean. Is your health affecting your work, or is it vice versa?

3.0 Counselor is clarifying between two important alternatives.

4. You seem frustrated and think that the cause lies in your work, but you are uncertain if that is the true cause.

3.5 Goes beyond the stated message in order to clarify the underlying causes of the client's feelings.

■ **Client 3, a college freshman:**   You know, lately everything seems to be going wrong. My grades are slipping, my mother keeps hassling me, and my boyfriend has been threatening to break up with me.

Responses

1. You feel you'd like to stop the world and start all over again.

Ratings and Reasons

2.5 Counselor checks perception of the seriousness of the problem. May sound too flippant for some clients.

2. You seem to feel that everyone is against you.

3.0 Perception check goes beyond the problems stated by the client.

3. I'm not sure which one irks you more—your poor school work, your relationship with your mother, or your boyfriend.

2.5 Counselor's clarification among the stated alternatives may sound a bit superficial to the client.

4. And you're wondering whether you should quit school, move out of the house, or get another boyfriend.

3.0 By injecting humor into clarification among alternatives, counselor is attempting to go beyond surface meaning of the client's statement.

Practice Clarifying Exercises: "What Do I Say After I Say 'I See'?"

These exercises have been prepared to assist you in developing your clarifying skills. The discrimination exercises give you the chance to further practice: identifying the client's underlying messages, recognizing the different ways that client statements may be clarified, and discriminating between more and less effective responses. The communication exercises enable you to practice giving high-level clarifying responses in a variety of client situations. Finally, the solo exercises give you the chance to sharpen both your attending and clarifying role communication skills. You should consider the possibility that some clients in these exercises come from a cultural background that is not the same as yours.

Discrimination exercises.   For each of the following excerpts identify the feeling and the content of the client's message, and then specify the *type* of clarifying response used; finally, rate the *level* of the response. Be ready to discuss the reasons for your ratings with your classmates and your supervisor. You may find that the excerpts were read differently by one or more of your classmates; thus, they may have given another rating to the response.

■   *Client 1, a high school sophomore:*   I just got my report card, and I flunked geometry. I don't know how I'm going to face my parents. They're planning on a trip to Europe this summer, and now I'll have to go to summer school

Underlying message: _____

Responses	*Type and Level of Response*
1. I'm not sure why you're upset. Is it because of failing, missing the trip to Europe, or disappointing your parents?	1. _____
2. Are you fearful that your parents might punish you because you upset their plans?	2. _____
3. Please tell me more. I'm a bit vague about what you're most fearful about.	3. _____

■   *Client 2, a 30-year-old man:*   I'm thinking about getting a divorce. My wife and I do nothing but tear each other to pieces. Whatever love we had for each other has long since been destroyed.

Underlying message: _____

Responses	*Type and Level of Response*
1. I'm not sure what you're saying. Is it, "It's too late to patch this marriage up" or, "I'd really like to try to bring the relationship back to where it was"?	1. _____
2. What hurts the most—the fighting, the pain, or the loss of the relationship?	2. _____
3. I sense some ambiguity in what you're feeling. Please tell me more.	3. _____

■ *A 40-year-old woman:* Ever since my breast surgery I have no desire to have sex with my husband. He's gentle and patient and doesn't mind looking at my scar. I have sex with him, but there's no feeling.

Underlying message: _____

Responses	*Type and Level of Response*
1. Are you upset because you're having difficulty adjusting to the surgery, or because you can't talk to your husband about it?	1. _____
2. You seem to be saying that your reaction to your breast surgery has affected your relationship with your husband more than anything else.	2. _____
3. I'm somewhat uncertain about your adjustment to your surgery. Go on.	3. _____

■ *Client 4, a high school junior:* My older brother thinks he's my father. Do you know what he did? He went to the bar where I go once in a while for drinks with my friends, and he told the bartender not to serve me anymore because I'm not twenty-one.

Underlying message: _____

Responses	*Type and Level of Response*
1. I'm not sure why you're mad at your brother. Is it because of this one incident, or does it go beyond this?	1. _____
2. You feel that you do not have a good relationship with your brother.	2. _____
3. I'm a bit confused about your relationship with your brother. Please tell me more about that.	3. _____

■   *Client 5, a 30-year-old homemaker:*   I don't know what I want to do with my life.

Underlying message: _____

Responses	*Type and Level of Response*
1. It sounds like you want a change in your daily routine. It seems you might want to go back to work.	1. _____
2. I'm not sure what you mean. Is it that you don't have a road map, or is it that you have the map but don't know what direction to go in?	2. _____
3. You sound a little overwhelmed, and I'm vague about why this is. Tell me more about yourself and your situation.	3. _____

■   *Client 6, a middle-aged man:*   You know, I work hard all day. . . . I have lots of pressure. . . . People make me feel uptight. . . . Can I help it if I blow off a little steam in my wife's direction once in a while?

Underlying message: _____

Responses	*Type and Level of Response*
1. You seem to be saying that things are a mess at home, and it's because of the pressure from your job.	1. _____
2. I'm uncertain about your real source of anger. Is it the boss, the system, or the whole ball of wax?	2. _____
3. I'm not clear on the point you're making. Please help me by describing your life situation in more detail.	3. _____

■   *Client 7, a 19-year-old man:*   The whole white society is corrupt. They're just out to manipulate and exploit the brothers, and that's just the way it is.

Underlying message: _____

Responses	*Type and Level of Response*
1. Is it really the whole white society that you're upset about, or did a recent incident upset you?	1. _____

2. You seem to be blaming society for something. I'm not sure what that something is.

2. _____

3. Go on.

3. _____

■ **Client 8, a young man:** I don't know why the courts suggested I come and see you. So I got busted—that's no big deal. People get busted every day. The courts are always sending us to see this one or that one; they think I'm sick in the head. But I'm not, I'm not. I'll show them! I'll show them!

Underlying message: _____

Responses

Type and Level of Response

1. Are you angry because you had to come to see me, or are you upset because others are in control of your life?

1. _____

2. You are really very upset. It sounds like you're angry at yourself because you got caught.

2. _____

3. You sound very angry. But I'm not sure who you are really mad at. Please continue.

3. _____

■ **Client 9, a middle-aged woman:** This past weekend my cat died. She drank a can of paint thinner I left in the kitchen after I finished painting. I don't know how she got into the can. . . . She must have knocked the top off. I feel terrible now. . . . Oh, I just can't seem to do anything right.

Underlying message: _____

Responses

Type and Level of Response

1. You're so angry at yourself because of your cat dying that you feel you can't do anything but cry now.

1. _____

2. Is it the loss of the cat that has hurt you, or is it really something else?

2. _____

3. I'm a bit puzzled. The cat's death seems to have set you off. Please tell me more about yourself.

3. _____

■ **Client 10, a newly married woman:** When I get home from work, I just can't stand doing the housework anymore, especially washing the dishes. I'm so sick of them—I'm just letting them pile up in the sink! And I feel so guilty when my husband yells at me to do them. That's all he seems to be doing now—yelling!

Underlying message: _____

Responses	*Type and Level of Response*
1. I'm not sure who you're really angry at—your husband or yourself?	1. _____
2. Is it the pressure from work that's getting to you, or is there something at home that's causing this problem?	2. _____
3. Several things appear to be bothering you, perhaps some more than others. Let's talk about them.	3. _____

Communication exercises.   For each excerpt given below, give three different types of high-level clarifying responses.

■ *Client 11, a 30-year-old man:*   I really love my work, but the foreman is really getting to me. He used to be my best friend, but he's changed. I thought he knew a lot, but now I see that he's not very good at his job

■ *Client 12, a middle-aged woman:*   I have a difficult problem. I went back to work after being home for many years. Now I'm working and making much more money than my husband, and it's tearing him apart. I don't know what to do.

■ *Client 13, a 40-year-old woman:*   I'm beginning to feel very useless . . . no one needs me anymore. My husband and I don't seem to communicate. I don't see my children that much—they have their own friends and interests. Most of the time I'm alone.

■ *Client 14, a 25-year-old man:*   My girlfriend has cancer, and it's driving me crazy. The doctors say it's terminal. I don't have much faith in doctors. If anything happens to her, I don't know what I'll do . . . I love her so much.

■ *Client 15, a 40-year-old man:*   I'm overwhelmed by the amount of work I have. My wife died five years ago, and my son is on drugs. I don't know what to do.

■ *Client 16, a 24-year-old woman:*   I'm really having a bad time at home. I just wish I weren't there. I'm twenty-four years old, and my parents expect me to act like a child. They just don't understand much about the world. I don't know what to do about it.

■ *Client 17, a high school junior:*   My grades are so bad I'm sure I won't be able to make any of the colleges I want to go to.

■ **_Client 18, a 30-year-old woman:_**   I feel very depressed lately. I have a good job, but it's not enough. My family thinks I should get married, but I don't know anyone I'd like to marry.

■ **_Client 19, a 25-year-old woman:_**   I'm so hurt. We've been married only six months, and John wants a divorce. He has completely rejected me. I don't know where I failed.

■ **_Client 20, a college junior:_**   I don't know whether I should go to law school or not. I'd like to be a lawyer, but everyone tells me how tough law school can be. I'm afraid of flunking out.

Solo exercises.   Practice your attending and clarifying responses in a triad. Be careful not to use any other type of response. Give all members in the triad a chance to practice their responding skills. Tape-record your sessions so you can review why some responses were better than others.

THE SUPPORTING OR REASSURING ROLE

Communicating support is an important relationship skill (Johnson, 1997). Everything that a counselor does to build the foundation for a solid counseling relationship is a form of support and reassurance. Your attitude and effective use of attending and clarifying responses demonstrate support by showing a real interest in the client. The specific skills discussed in this role are used when you want to convey this support and reassurance in a more concrete way. This role involves actively providing positive feedback; communicating feelings of security, reassurance, and encouragement; and reaffirming the client's sense of self. In effect, you are saying "I like you" or "You are okay" to the client. This role may be explicitly or implicitly communicated by nonverbal and paraverbal, as well as verbal, means. This role is often necessary in a counseling relationship because clients usually need to feel accepted, and they are frequently unable to marshal their own strengths to engage in new behaviors, to bring about desired changes, or to find appropriate solutions to their problems without the counselor's support.

The supporting or reassuring role is used when you want to acknowledge the experience of the client as very real and to make the client feel that he or she is heard, understood, and accepted as a person of value even though his or her behavior or specific actions may not be acceptable or liked by you or significant others. Benjamin (1987) suggests that reassurance responses help clients overcome blockages and deal with difficult problems and situations, and Brammer and MacDonald (1996) point out that supportive responses are used with clients who are grief stricken or in a state of crisis.

Supportive and reassuring responses should stress that you have faith in the client, believe in the client's ability to resolve issues, have an understanding of the frailty of the human condition, and respect the dignity and worth of the client. In using supportive responses, you should avoid comparisons with others and focus on the idea of being and doing rather than on the attainment of a prize or status symbol. This role is employed at various stages in the counseling process.

Types of Supporting or Reassuring Responses

Typical responses that demonstrate this role are:

1. *A person-of-value response.* This type of response is designed to show uncondi-tional respect. It communicates to clients that they are individuals of significant worth and value regardless of their actions. Responses of this sort focus on the uniqueness of the person; the intrinsic aspects of life rather than the extrinsic aspects; the person's existence rather than the person's productivity; the effort rather than the end product; and *what* one is doing rather than *how* one is doing. "You seem like a fine person to me" emphasizes one's uniqueness. And phrases such as "You handled that nicely" and "It sounds like you had fun" separate worth from accomplishment and can provide encouragement and solid humanistic support to clients.

2. *An approval response.* This sort of response is used to help clients feel more positive about themselves. This is accomplished by showing approval, agreement, or reassurance for a particular thought, feeling, or behavior that the client has revealed. The response may applaud some previous event, compliment some present activity, or reassure that a future event will turn out appropriately. Phrases such as "It was nice for you to help Mary," "You look nice today," and "You have the ability to do that" praise the person and tend to make the client feel better.

3. *A consolation response.* Consolation responses communicate a caring concern and show clients that you are supportive of them when they are not feeling good about something. This kind of response can be very useful when a client has gone through a recent unhappy occurrence, is currently dealing with an uncomfortable situation, or is facing an unpleasant future event. The response may be an expression of comfort, sympathy, or condolence. Phrases such as "What an awful experience for you," "You have my sympathy," and "You are really facing a tough situation" can show your understanding of the client's problem and your support for the client.

4. *A relaxation response.* Relaxation responses can be very supportive when clients are tense, excited, and overstimulated. They are designed to get clients to pause, to become calmer, and to become more in touch with all their emotions. Phrases such as "Take a deep breath," "Close your eyes for a few minutes," and "I want you to think about a pleasant scene" can communicate a sincere interest in the client.

Illustrations of Different Types of Supporting or Reassuring Responses

The following three examples illustrate the use of the supporting role.

■   *Client 1, a young woman:*   My father and I fight all the time, especially about the boys I know. He won't even let a boy in the house. He says they're all no good. I think he just doesn't trust me.

1. *A person-of-value response:* You really are quite a young lady. You are willing to stick up for the things you believe in.
2. *An approval response:* It is really hard for you to feel that you're not trusted. It's very good to tell your father how you feel about your rights.
3. *A consolation response:* I can see you're very angry. It's really hard when your father doesn't understand your position and comes down hard on you.
4. *A relaxation response:* Wow, that's a tough spot to be in. You're very excited. Before we begin, I want you to sit down and think about something pleasant for 30 seconds.

■ *Client 2, a middle-aged man:* All my life I've never been able to hold a job for very long. Everything goes okay for a while, but then I get into a fight with the boss or something like that and I'm fired. I can't seem to help it.

1. *A person-of-value response:* Even though you may have had some problems with some jobs you've held, I am confident you can learn to handle this kind of concern.
2. *An approval response:* Yet, every time that you spoke up I'm sure you felt there was a good reason for it.
3. *A consolation response:* It's really tough not being able to hold on to a job for a long time.
4. *A relaxation response:* I want you to tell me some more about yourself; but first, I want you to take a deep breath and systematically relax different parts of your body.

■ *Client 3, a middle-aged woman:* My mother died a few months ago, and I haven't been the same since. I just can't seem to get my life back on track again. I've been very preoccupied with death and dying.

1. *A person-of-value response:* Your reaction tells me that you miss your mother. After her death, it's normal to feel derailed and upset.
2. *An approval response:* Even though being unable to think or act clearly is upsetting, your mourning of your mother's death is a healthy response. Your feelings are appropriate. Allow yourself time to grieve.
3. *A consolation response:* I'm sorry to hear about her death. The death of a parent is painful and a big loss for you.
4. *A relaxation response:* Mourning takes time and, unfortunately, you are not going to be able to turn it off or rush it. When the thoughts of death and dying come, remember that they are letting you know how much you loved your mother and to value the people in your life more fully. You need to take time to reflect on this.

Levels of Supporting or Reassuring Responses

Counselors who use this role skillfully show respect for their clients, reveal an understanding of the strengths and weaknesses of human beings, normally employ a relaxed, warm tone in their voice, and use attentive body gestures. The effective use of the role can help clients reduce the intensity of their feelings, lower their anxiety about some activity, feel more secure in the counseling relationship, and gain a sense of confidence. These responses should help clients mobilize their strengths by allowing them to put the past into perspective and to explore alternatives and face the future positively. Support and reassurance help reinforce these desired behaviors.

This role is ineffective and may be counterproductive when the counselor fails to acknowledge the depth of the client's feelings or the seriousness of the client's concerns, and when it is used in inappropriate ways. This can occur when the counselor sounds insincere, downplays the seriousness of the client's problem, overuses the role, or fosters a dependency relationship, or when there is real danger that the counselor's words could be interpreted as cheap advice rather than support. Such phrases as "Don't worry, things will turn out okay" convey disinterest or lack of understanding rather than support or reassurance. The timeliness and appropriateness of the counselor's explicit use of support is a function of the immediacy of the client's need for reassurance.

Similar to other counselor role responses, the supporting and reassuring role may be used with various degrees of effectiveness. Here is a four-point scale to rate the counselor's use of this role.

> *Level 1: Poor use of the role.* The counselor is ineffective in using this role when reassurance is inopportune, when it is conveyed in a sterile or condescending voice, when gestures are distracting, or when the counselor is insincere or fails to show meaningful support. Ritualistic reassurance, including clichés, may be used.

> *Level 2: Mediocre use of the role.* The counselor is somewhat ineffective when support is given in a lukewarm manner, when it is poorly phrased, or when the role is of limited value at the point it is used in the counseling process.

> *Level 3: Good use of the role.* The counselor is effective when he or she is responding appropriately to the needs of the client, reassuring or supporting properly, and using this role at a suitable time in the counseling process.

> *Level 4: Excellent use of the role.* The counselor is most effective when the counselor's tone and words are very supportive, and when the counselor's use of the role is an appropriate response to the client's needs.

Illustrations of Different Levels of Supporting or Reassuring Responses

The following illustrations are provided so that you can learn to perceive the differences between effective and ineffective use of the supportive or reassurance role. In each of the examples, the responses have been rated using the Level-of-Response Scale, and the reasons for assigning these ratings are reported. Examine each of these examples to see if you agree with the ratings and the reasons stated. If you do not agree with these ratings, you may have read one or more of these statements with another intonation than the person who rated them. Because the paraverbal aspects of the client's statements and the counselor's responses are never adequately indicated by the printed word, any response may be rated quite differently depending on how it is heard. It is very important that you give reasons for your ratings so that you can discuss any differences with your supervisor and classmates.

■ *Client 1, a college senior:* I'm so mad at that dean. He just asked why I took part in that demonstration. He acted as if I did something wrong.

Responses	Ratings and Reasons
1. You sound like you acted according to your principles. It was an important issue for you.	3.0 This person-of-value response shows respect for the client and focuses on the client's values as having worth.
2. Wow! You sound so agitated—he eally got to you. I want you to sit down, take a deep breath, and relax.	3.0 This relaxation response should enable the client to become more relaxed and calmer.
3. You felt justified in participating in the demonstration, and it hurts when someone in authority questions actions that you think are most important.	3.5 Shows approval for the client's feelings and support for acting in concert with one's principles.
4. Next time there is a demonstration, let me know and I'll go with you.	1.0 Misguided approval and inappropriate support.

■ *Client 2, a college senior:* John and I have had a serious relationship for over a year, and he suddenly tells me he's going to live in Chicago to take care of his father's business—he left just like that.

Responses	Ratings and Reasons
1. That's okay. If you need to cry cry. It's okay.	3.0 Shows approval for the client's deep feelings of hurt.
2. It's understandable how you can feel hurt and discarded after such an experience.	3.5 This consolation response reveals the counselor's understanding and concern.
3. I know you are hurting now, and you have a right to feel that way.	3.0 Counselor's approval response shows awareness of the client's emotions and the situation.
4. I know you can overcome this loss. You have great strengths and can make new friends.	1.5 Although the counselor attempts to demonstrate high regard for the client, it doesn't sound genuine and may hold out false hope.

■ *Client 3, a 35-year-old woman who recently lost her husband:* It's only when I'm alone that these feelings and memories keep returning. If I don't do something right away to divert my attention, I just start crying and feeling sorry for myself.

Responses	Ratings and Reasons
1. Your feelings and memories are part of your life. They are telling you how much you miss your husband. There's nothing wrong with feeling sorry for yourself as you miss him.	3.5 Shows appropriate approval for the client's feelings and behaviors.

2. You must have had a fine relationship. This battle going on between your head and your heart shows your respect for your husband and yourself.

3.5 This person-of-value response is combined with an approval response and shows respect for the client's deep feelings.

3. I really feel for the struggle you are experiencing while you're mourning your husband.

3.0 Shows consolation for the client's feelings and loss.

4. I understand your desire to resume a normal life, but your grieving may be more important and take a while to resolve. It's important to allow yourself time to cry.

3.5 Shows awareness of the client's needs and pressures. The approval reveals an understanding of these dynamics.

Practice Supporting Exercises: "How Do I Say 'You're Okay'?"

The following set of exercises is designed to facilitate the development of your supporting and reassuring role skills. Similar to the previous sets of exercises, it contains three types of skill-building practices: discrimination exercises, communication exercises, and solo exercises. As you do the three sets of exercises allow for the possibility that several clients have backgrounds that are significantly different from yours.

Discrimination exercises.   For each client statement given below, indicate the feeling and the content underlying the client's statement. Then identify the *type* of supporting or reassuring response employed, and show the appropriateness of the response by rating the *level* of the response. Anticipate your classmates' questions about the reasons for your answers, and be prepared to discuss your reasons in class. The excerpts may have been read differently by your classmates, and hence their ratings may not agree with yours. It is important to understand the reasons why these differences exist.

■   *Client 1, a middle-aged woman:*   My husband and I are very upset with our daughter. Every time she comes home it ends up in some sort of conflict. She's twenty-three years old and collecting unemployment. She doesn't seem to be going anywhere. I just wish she would get married.

Underlying message: _____

Responses

1. You are a good mother to be concerned for her welfare.

2. It's quite normal to be upset when children disappoint you.

3. You're under a great deal of pressure. Take a deep breath and relax.

Type and Level of Response

1.   _____

2.   _____

3.   _____

4. It's hard to face these daily fights. I understand your desire to see her settle down.

4. _____

■ *Client 2, a young man:*   I think I want to get a divorce. When I married Susan I thought we had a lot in common. But I found out otherwise. Her values are so materialistic that I find them repulsive.

Underlying message: _____

Responses	*Type and Level of Response*
1. You're hurting now. You feel that the marriage is not working out the way you wanted it to.	1. _____
2. Wanting to live by values that you cherish is really wonderful. You are a fine person for wanting to do that.	2. _____
3. Right now you're angry with Susan and see only where you disagree. Before we start discussing this issue, I want you to take a deep breath.	3. _____
4. It really is difficult to live with some-one who doesn't share your values.	4. _____

■ *Client 3, a man in his late fifties:*   I just got laid off from my job. I worked for the place for eighteen years, and just like that I'm out on the street. It's impossible for a man my age to begin again.

Underlying message: _____

Responses	*Type and Level of Response*
1. After eighteen years, it's tough to be laid off. You were not ready for a change.	1. _____
2. You must have been a good employee, having remained with the same company for eighteen years.	2. _____
3. Sometimes we think that the cards in this life haven't been dealt from a fair deck. The injustice gets to you.	3. _____
4. How can a good man be kept down? It might be hard work to find another job, but with your tenacity I'm sure it can be done.	4. _____

■   *Client 4, a young woman, a high school senior:*   I'm not sure where I'm at. I'd like to go to college and get married. I think raising a family can be a full-time commitment. But then again I should think of some career or occupation. Suppose I don't marry or can't have kids. I'm kind of muddling through.

Underlying message: _____

Responses	*Type and Level of Response*
1. The kinds of questions you're asking yourself are good ones, even though there may not be an immediate answer to them.	1. _____
2. Women are spending more and more of their lives in the world of work. So it's good that you're thinking about college and its vocational implications.	2. _____
3. Hey, you're great. Many girls your age don't think about their future with such insight.	3. _____
4. Women today can find fulfillment through a variety of options. I'm happy to see you examining them.	4. _____

■   *Client 5, a 20-year-old woman:*   Everything was great when I first met Tom. We had so much in common, and he seemed like the right guy to marry. But lately we're fighting a lot. I'm starting to see a different side of Tom, and I don't like it. I still really love him though. He's a great guy. Maybe we'll work things out when we're married.

Underlying message: _____

Responses	*Type and Level of Response*
1. You're a very capable girl. I'm sure you'll be able to handle any problems that come up.	1. _____
2. It's very common for people to see the other aspects of a person as they grow closer. It's good that you are seeing this side of Tom now.	2. _____
3. The closer two people get, the more they have to learn to deal with their differences. It's okay to recognize that there are things you don't like in each other. It doesn't mean your relationship is good or bad . . . it just means you're both more aware.	3. _____

4. It's normal to have doubts about your relationship. Before you say anything else, I want you to close your eyes and relax for 30 seconds.

4. _____

■ **Client 6, a 20-year-old man:** Last week I lost my job. My boss told me to do something I didn't think was right. I wouldn't do it, and he fired me. I don't know what I should do. I have a family to support.

Underlying message: _____

Responses	*Type and Level of Response*
1. I admire your willingness to maintain your principles. You were willing to lose your job. That took courage.	1. _____
2. You must be under some pressure. I know we can work things out for you and your family.	2. _____
3. You're a man with integrity and conviction. Many firms are looking for people with those characteristics.	3. _____
4. I know you are very concerned, but I don't see how you had much choice. After all, what the boss wanted you to do was illegal, unethical, or both.	4. _____

■ **Client 7, a young man, 16 years old:** There's this girl that I like, but I can't ask her out because my friends tell me that I'm too short and ugly, and no girl would go out with me. I don't know what to do. I really like this girl.

Underlying message: _____

Responses	*Type and Level of Response*
1. You are being very hard on yourself. You have many good qualities that many people admire.	1. _____
2. Some may say you're short and ugly, but I don't see you that way. To me you're a heck of a nice guy.	2. _____
3. It's natural to want to ask a girl out whom you admire. And unfortunately, it's also typical for friends to tease.	3. _____
4. I'm glad you came to see me. Let's think about various ways you can get to know this young lady better.	4. _____

■   *Client 8, a young woman:*   If I could tell my boss, just once, where to get off, I know I'd feel better, but I know I'd lose my job. I don't think it would be worthwhile.

Underlying message: _____

Responses	*Type and Level of Response*
1. I know you'll find a creative way to deal with the situation. Let's talk about it for a while.	1. _____
2. When you find yourself holding in too much anger, find a way to relax and get the anger out—talk to a friend, jog, listen to relaxing music, or close your eyes and take a deep breath.	2. _____
3. You have a great deal of patience and determination in staying with your job. It's a sign of maturity as you seek a solution to your problem at work.	3. _____
4. Sometimes we have to choose to put up with frustration. It's an awful choice. I really feel for you.	4. _____

■   *Client 9, a college sophomore:*   I just quit my job because I found it too hard to keep up my studies and work after school. By the time I got home I was too tired to study. My father thinks I'm copping out on my responsibilities, and he's really mad.

Underlying message: _____

Responses	*Type and Level of Response*
1. You surely felt that you did the right thing in quitting. You must have felt you had to quit the job or fail out of school.	1. _____
2. You are a fine person. You seem to have a considerable amount of good sense.	2. _____
3. Fathers can be tough.	3. _____
4. It's difficult to try to maintain a good average and a job at the same time. You deserve some credit for trying to support yourself while you're in school.	4. _____

■   *Client 10, a middle-aged man:*   My son and I don't get along very well. I guess one could call it the generation gap, but I'm only trying to do what's best for him.

Underlying message: _____

Responses	Type and Level of Response
1. Being a parent is not easy.	1. _____
2. You are really concerned about your son, and I'm sure you only have his best interests at heart.	2. _____
3. Mark Twain once said that at eighteen he thought his father was awfully stupid; but when he was twenty-one he couldn't get over how much his dad had learned in three years.	3. _____
4. I know the generation gap is a difficult one to bridge, but we can learn to span that gap fairly well. Before we begin I want you to take a deep breath.	4. _____

Communication exercises.   Please respond to each client statement in this set of exercises by furnishing at least two different types of high-level supportive statements. Try to construct your responses as quickly as possible.

■ *Client 11, a college freshman:*   I came because I had a terrible feeling of depression. My boyfriend, who's nineteen, is threatening to break up with me because I won't have sex with him. We've been going together for sixteen months, and everything was great until about two months ago. Now he has this big thing about going to bed. He keeps saying I'd do it if I really loved him. He doesn't understand my viewpoint at all.

■ *Client 12, the wife of an alcoholic husband:*   My problem is that my husband is an alcoholic. I'm the sole supporter of my family, and although I loved him once, and suppose I still do, I don't think that staying with him is helping the children.

■ *Client 13, a woman who has had three miscarriages:*   I've been so terribly depressed lately that I can no longer function effectively. My husband is considerate and understanding, but he says I must resign myself to the fact that I will never have children. I just can't accept that.

■ *Client 14, a 10-year-old girl:*   Nobody likes me. I don't have any friends. My mother says not to feel bad. I can't help it if I want other kids to like me.

■ *Client 15, a teenager:*   When I get home from school my mother is always drunk. The house is a mess. She doesn't do the dishes or clean up, and she hardly cooks any supper. She just lies there and drinks and screams at me, and I scream back. I'm so ashamed I can't ask my friends to come over, and I'm so disgusted sometimes that I think I'll just leave home.

■   *Client 16, a teenager:*   I know someone who is selling drugs, and I don't know what to do about it.

■   *Client 17, a single, middle-aged woman:*   I'm so depressed. I went to the doctor and found out that I'm pregnant. I feel like this is the end of the world.

■   *Client 18, a foreign student:*   This is my first year in the United States. I had a fellowship during this past year, and applied for one for next year but didn't get it. So now I am forced to consider a job. You know I am a foreigner and have only a student visa. I am not supposed to work here, and as I don't have a degree from the U.S. it will be very difficult to get a job. What would I do if I couldn't get a job? What kind of life do I expect to lead? How can I go back home without completing my studies? I don't even have enough money to go back.

■   *Client 19, a teenager:*   Both my parents think I'm still a little kid. I just turned fifteen, and they won't let me go out on a single date with my boyfriend. All of my friends are allowed to date, so I don't see why I can't.

■   *Client 20, a mother of two young children:*   My husband had a stroke. He'll be in the hospital a long time, and I need money to support us while he's there.

Solo exercises.   Practice all five role communication skills in the triad. Try to have your minisessions run for 15 minutes, and after each session, review the counselor's responses. Make sure each counselor-in-training has a chance to practice and can consistently give higher-level responses.

SUMMARY

This chapter has required your active participation to develop an understanding of the attending, the clarifying, and the supporting role communication skills. After learning about these primary skills and practicing them in the simulated exercises, you should be able to describe these skills, discriminate among higher- and lower-level responses, and demonstrate appropriate use of these skills in your counseling sessions.

Attending has been defined as the process of actively listening to another person and reporting back to that person what you believe was communicated to you. Attending responses include simple minimal verbals, reflections of content and feelings, accents, paraphrases, and nonverbal signals. High-level responses are characterized by demonstrating interest in the other person, maintaining appropriate body language, responding to the underlying feeling and content of the other person, and employing appropriate tonal qualities in your voice.

Clarifying has been defined as the process of clearing up any confusion that may be present in the counseling process. Clarification responses include perception checking, clarification among alternatives, and requests for elaboration. High-level responses focus on critical issues or situations that need clarification and demonstrate a sincere and genuine interest in the client.

Supportive responses are designed to communicate your belief and faith in the client, provide emotional security, reduce client anxiety, and provide encouragement. Supportive responses include person-of-value responses, approval responses, consolation responses, and relaxation responses. High-level responses show concern for clients, reveal an understanding of the problems that human beings face, and are presented in a warm and relaxed tone.

In addition to reading the chapter and practicing the primary role communication exercises, these skills should be practiced in your daily conversations with other people. These primary skills are extremely useful in all human conversations, and their effective use can improve your understanding of another person's point of view. Because these skills are necessary in each phase or stage of the counseling process, it is crucial that you master them as soon as possible.

REFERENCES

Benjamin, A. (1987). *The helping interview* (4th ed.). Boston: Houghton Mifflin.

Brammer, L. M., & MacDonald, G. (1996). *The helping relationship: Process and* Skills (6th ed.). Boston: Allyn & Bacon.

Cormier, W. H., & Cormier, L. S. (1991). *Interviewing strategies for helpers: Fundamental skills and cognitive behavioral interventions* (3rd ed.). Pacific Grove, CA: Brooks/Cole.

Egan, G. (1994). *The skilled helper: A problem-management approach to helping* (5th ed.). Pacific Grove, CA: Brooks/Cole.

Evans, D. R., Hearn, M. T., Uhlemann, M. R., & Ivey, A. E. (1993). *Essential interviewing: A programmed approach to effective communication* (4th ed.). Pacific Grove, CA: Brooks/Cole.

Hackney, H., & Cormier, L. S. (1994). *Counseling strategies and interventions* (4th ed.). Englewood Cliffs, NJ: Prentice Hall.

Johnson, D. W. (1997). *Reaching out: Interpersonal effectiveness and self-actualization* (5th ed.). Boston: Allyn & Bacon.

Okun, B. F. (1997). *Effective helping: Interviewing and counseling techniques* (5th ed.). Pacific Grove, CA: Brooks/Cole.

8 Intermediate Role Communication Skills

INTRODUCTION

This chapter is devoted to a discussion of intermediate role communication skills used in informing, probing, and responding to client questions. These skills are described and illustrated, examples of the effective use of these roles are presented, and exercises are furnished to enable you to practice them. A discussion of the counselor's use of silence is incorporated in this section as well. After careful review of the material in this chapter you should be able to:

- Outline the objectives of the roles of informing, probing, and responding to client questions.
- Describe the purposes and meaning of silence in a helping relationship.
- Discuss the characteristics that distinguish high-level responses from low-level responses in informing and probing roles.
- Identify the types of responses used in each of these roles, and cite examples of good and poor uses of these responses in helping interviews.
- Apply these communication skills in appropriate situations.

THE INFORMING OR DESCRIBING ROLE

The informing or describing role is used when the counselor wants to provide the client with specific, relevant, factual information or with descriptions or explanations of how various structures work or how they may be organized. Giving information and describing how entities function or work are essential counselor roles. Providing clients with information is generally done for one of the following reasons. First, counselors need to apprise clients of how the counseling process works, including information about procedural matters, the roles of the client and counselor, what the process is like, what the ground rules are, and what generally can be expected. Second, counselors need to supply clients with specific information necessary for the counseling process and at levels that clients can understand. This factual material is often educational or occupational information, the meaning of test data, and descriptions of appropriate resource materials. Third, counselors frequently need to supply clients with basic information about essential psychological principles such as the importance of human drives and needs, the themes of different developmental periods of life, the role of anxiety in life, the difficulties of choosing between alternative courses of action, or the inappropriate use of certain coping strategies. Finally, there is the need to inform clients about particular intervention strategies.

Presenting information is not the same as giving advice, suggestions, or directives; it is not value-laden material but, rather, objective and accurate factual material about people, places, or things. It should be stated in an impersonal, matter-of-fact, neutral tone (Benjamin, 1987). The kind of information that you provide to your clients should be directly related to their needs and concerns at any given moment in the counseling relationship. This type of response is employed when clients are not likely to have the information or when they have some misinformation and it is important for them to know the correct information for the counseling process to advance.

The amount of time spent providing factual information varies according to the needs of the client and the type of counseling that is being provided. In some cases a considerable part of an interview or even several interviews may be spent presenting and reviewing important constructs or databases, and in other cases only a minimal amount of time is spent using this role. In either case, you must have solid knowledge and a good information base to use this role efficaciously.

Types of Informing or Describing Responses

The informing role is typically employed for one of the following purposes:

1. *To structure the counseling process.* Responses of this sort inform the client about what the counseling process entails. As the counselor, you may need to describe how the counseling process works and the role and responsibilities of the counselor and the client; provide the client with practical detailed information such as time, location, duration, and cost for each session; or inform the client about taping requirements, record keeping, and confidentiality. Providing clients with these descriptions can reduce anxiety and enable clients to verify their expectations (Hackney & Cormier, 1994).

2. *To provide clients with relevant, factual information.* This type of response is designed to present clients with important facts that are germane and necessary to advancing the counseling process. Frequently, this response communicates information that facilitates the client's self-knowledge and the client's knowledge of the educational and vocational process. This may involve furnishing relevant information about the career development process, the meaning of psychological tests and test scores, the availability of educational and vocational resource materials, or specific data about the rules and regulations of a particular educational institution or community agency. The information presented must be clear and applicable to the client's concerns (Egan, 1994).

3. *To inform clients about some basic psychological principles.* Responses of this type present clients with information about important principles of human nature including such phenomena as human drives and needs, the developmental process, the decision-making or problem-solving process, and ways to reframe issues in order to analyze them from another perspective. Helping clients with the problem-solving process may involve providing information about new or different alternatives or the possible outcomes of various alternatives, or stating the fact that decisions and choices usually involve some risk and are rarely made with absolute certitude.

4. *To present information that is relevant to a particular counseling intervention strategy.* When a specific intervention strategy is employed, clients may need to be given an explanation of the rationale for the strategy, the meaning of certain terms used in the process (such as raw score, contingency reinforcement, or covert modeling), their role and what they have to do in this process, and the steps that you plan to use as the process unfolds. Specific information about a counseling intervention technique is often given to clients during the decision-making and working stages of the counseling process.

Illustrations of Different Types of Informing or Describing Responses

The following set of examples illustrates how this role is used.

■ *Client 1, a 23-year-old woman:*   I lost my job about seven months ago. I went on unemployment instead of looking for other work. I thought it would be fun, just staying home. Now, all I do is lie in bed or stay in my nightgown all day. My husband's been complaining that I look like a slob, and the house is a mess. I can't seem to get myself together.

> *Structuring the counseling process: It* sounds like you think coming here for counseling can help you get yourself together. It probably can, but first you must understand that the counselor has no magic. Any change will depend on you and the goals you set for yourself.

■ *Client 2, a 19-year-old college freshman:*   I'm not sure what I'd like to major in at college. My dad said you would have the latest information on the job outlook for economists, lawyers, and accountants.

> *Important factual information:* Yes, we do have a number of resources that can supply you with that information. First, there's the *Occupational Outlook Handbook,* and information about each of the fields you mention is in the occupational library files. Also, the respective departments have very current information posted on their bulletin boards.

■ *Client 3, a high school junior:*   I'm not sure what I want to do with my life. There are lots of things that appeal to me. I think it would be fun to major in English in college and read and analyze great literature, but then again something exotic like zoology or anthropology might be even more interesting. Maybe you have some tests or something that can tell me what I should do.

> *Information about some basic psychological principles:* Being open to a variety of occupational choices is healthy at your age. Decisions about occupational choices involve learning more about yourself, learning more about the world of work, and engaging in some exploratory activities. Even though there isn't any test that can tell you how to spend your life, some tests might be useful in beginning this exploration process by first helping you learn more about yourself.

■ ***Client 4, a college junior:*** I'm afraid I would blow any job interview. I won't know what to say. . . . My mind goes blank. I have good grades, yet I panic when I have to speak to someone I don't know. You helped me once before when I almost dropped out of college. Can you help me now?

> *Information relevant to a particular intervention strategy:* It sounds like you have a great deal of anxiety when you are faced with a new or an unknown situation. If you want me to help you overcome this fear, you will need to tell me quite a bit about your life, particularly about other events or situations that have caused a similar type of response in you. After we obtain your life history, I will teach you a systematic way of relaxing.

Levels of Informing or Describing Responses

The informing or describing role can be used in ways that differentially affect its potency. Individuals who are effective in using this role provide relevant information, describe things or circumstances accurately, respond in ways that are understood by their clients, and ensure that the material is understood. If the information is complex, it should be broken down into units that the client can assimilate (Cormier & Cormier, 1991; Evans, Hearn, Uhlemann, & Ivey, 1993). Counselors who employ this role at appropriate times advance the counseling process and communicate that they are trained professionals knowledgeable about their field. Information responses are ineffective and counterproductive when unnecessary information is imposed on the client, when the responses fail to provide meaningful and complete descriptions, or when they are given with evaluative overtones or are otherwise value laden. On the four-point scale, the effectiveness in using this role can be rated according to factors such as furnishing accurate and relevant information, employing appropriate terms and phrases, providing data and descriptions that can be readily understood, presenting materials when clients need the information and are ready to receive it, and providing information in a value-free manner.

> *Level 1: Poor use of the role.* The counselor uses this role in an ineffective way when he or she describes or explains matters of concern incorrectly, uses distracting gestures, informs the client prematurely, or provides irrelevant material. The role is also counterproductive when it is used excessively or in a tone that conveys a belaboring or demeaning manner.

Level 2: Mediocre use of the role. This role is used somewhat ineffectively when the counselor provides the client with partial or incomplete information, when the information presented is correct but not germane to the client at the point it is given in the counseling process, or when the counselor's messages are too wordy or the terminology too complex.

Level 3: Good use of the role. The counselor is using this role effectively when he or she responds to the needs of the client by explaining phenomena in sufficient detail to be useful to the client at the time it is given in the counseling process.

Level 4: Excellent use of the role. The counselor is most effective when he or she describes things completely and responds to the client's need for information propitiously. The information is provided in a warm tone and with gestures that can help the client relate to the factual material presented.

Illustrations of Different Levels of Informing or Describing Responses

The following illustrations of responses are provided so that you can see the differences between effective and ineffective use of the informing role. Each of the counselor's responses has been rated using the Level-of-Response Scale, and the reasoning behind each of these ratings is indicated. Study these examples to determine if you agree with the ratings. You may find that you do or do not agree; any response may be rated differently depending on the paraverbals that the reader hears. Thus, it is important to discuss these ratings and the reasons behind them with your classmates and your supervisor so that any differences can be understood.

■   *Client 1, a 22-year-old:*   About three years ago I got stuck in an elevator. I was alone, and I was very scared. But after about five minutes the elevator started up and I was fine. Since then, I can't ride in an elevator without feeling boxed in, shaking, and getting sweaty palms. It's okay when there are stairs and I can walk up to where I want to go, but sometimes I avoid visiting friends because they live above the sixth floor.

Responses	*Ratings and Reasons*
1. Fears are sometimes hard to overcome but with a commitment to change and some hard work, fears can be overcome or at least lessened so they can be handled.	2.4 Counselor briefly outlines the counseling process. Although the words are accurate, it sounds like a lecture.
2. I think we can help you ride in an elevator again. First, we will need to discuss any other fears that you may have.	2.5 This initial outline of a counseling strategy is good but quite limited.
3. Your fear of elevators can be overcome. You must learn to get control of your emotions.	1.0 This authoritarian response is not informative or descriptive.

4. I sense a feeling of helplessness on your part, and I will be glad to work with you. It will take us some time to reduce your anxiety, but I believe we can have you visiting your friends again.

3.0 This very brief description of the counseling process shows an understanding and feeling for the client's problem.

■ *Client 2, a college sophomore:*   My parents want to know what I plan to do after college. They think I should major in accounting or economics or something that has a definite orientation toward an occupation. I want to major in history, which they believe is a total waste of time. Do you have any tests that I can take to show them that accounting is not for me?

Responses

1. I know you are feeling a great deal of pressure, but I'm afraid that in your present condition we would not get an accurate picture from any test.

2. Parents always want to live your life for you. Yes, I have a good inventory that will reveal your true interest patterns.

3. You don't want to do something just because your parents want you to. We have some tests that may help; how-ever, they may or may not come out the way you want them to.

4. You feel pulled in two directions, your parents' and your own, and you'd like to resolve this in some way. I feel the pressure you have, but I do not believe a battery of tests will ease this pressure. It may prove that you are right, or it may prove that your parents are right, about your abilities. But I think it will prove neither.

Ratings and Reasons

3.0 This information about tests is appropriate and helpful.

1.0 This attempt to identify with the client is poor, and the information about testing is probably misleading given the client's motivation.

2.7 Shows awareness of client's feelings and situation. The information about testing, although brief, should further the client's awareness.

3.5 Counselor shows perception of the client's struggle and provides infor-mation about tests that should be beneficial to the client.

■ *Client 3, a middle-aged woman:*   I have to do something. My children are all grown. My husband is extremely busy with his work. I would like to get a job, but I don't know how to begin.

Responses

1. Many women return to the labor force when their children are grown. Our office has helped many women return-ing to work. Working together we

Ratings and Reasons

2.8 Counselor presents factual informa-tion and begins to structure the counseling process.

should be able to help you find a job
that will meet your needs.

2. You really have an empty feeling and
   sense you must do something. I think
   we can work with you on this problem, and we can help you begin by
   talking about you as a person—your
   likes, dislikes, and previous
   accomplishments.

3.0 Counselor shows awareness of the
    client's concern and briefly outlines
    the initial steps of the counseling
    process.

3. Yes, well, the first step is to take a
   battery of tests that will outline your
   abilities and competencies. Then we
   will match these up with various
   occupations and job openings, and see
   which one is the best for you.

1.5 Counselor falsely implies that
    vocational selection is primarily a
    psychometric function.

4. There are several steps. These involve
   helping you understand yourself a
   little better, learning about the kinds of
   work available, and exploring the
   occupational choices that appear to
   meet your needs.

2.8 Counselor briefly outlines the
    vocational counseling process.

Practice Informing and Describing Exercises: "How Do I Provide Specific Information or Descriptions of How Things Function?"

The following exercises have been prepared to assist you in developing your informing role skills. The discrimination exercises afford you the chance to further practice identifying clients' underlying messages and the different ways to inform and describe various things to clients, and to learn to discriminate between more and less effective responses. The communication exercises enable you to practice giving high-level informing and describing responses in a variety of client situations. Finally, the solo exercises give you the chance to enhance your attending, clarifying, supporting, and informing role communication skills. It would be helpful for you to assume that some clients represented in these exercises come from a cultural background that is unlike your own.

Discrimination exercises.
For each of the following excerpts, first identify the feeling and the content underlying the client's statement, and then specify the *type* of informing and describing response illustrated; finally, indicate the appropriateness of the response by rating the *level* of the response. Please be prepared to share the reasons for your ratings with your classmates and your supervisor. You may find that one or more of your classmates read the excerpts with another tonal quality than you did and consequently rated the response quite differently.

■   *Client 1, a recent high school graduate:*   I never seem to be a success at anything. Everything I try seems to end in failure. I've never had a job that lasted for more than six months.

Underlying message: _____

Responses	*Type and Level of Response*
1. We should plan to meet at this time for an hour each week to explore your experiences and help you rediscover your strengths.	1. _____
2. Taking one or two of the career inventories can help us understand your occupational interests. They can be done in an hour, and they ask questions about the kinds of things you enjoy doing.	2. _____
3. You are facing up to the difficulties of finding the right job. Your experiences may have helped you become more aware of yourself and your vocational interests.	3. _____
4. You were successful in graduating from high school. Many people are not. It's not uncommon for people to experiment with different jobs before they find one suitable to their own interests.	4. _____

■   *Client 2, a high school freshman:*   I get really worried about my friends— sometimes I can't get to sleep at night I'm so worried. They all recently began to use the real heavy stuff.

Underlying message: _____

Responses	*Type and Level of Response*
1. You have good reason to worry about your friends. The stuff they are using is dangerous and destructive.	1. _____
2. It sounds like you're in a tough spot. You've taken the first step to deal with this concern. We will need to plan some further steps.	2. _____

3. I understand how upset you are. I have   3. _____
   no magic to solve this problem, but if
   you are willing to work with me, we
   can resolve this issue.

4. And you hope I can tell you what to do   4. _____
   about it. I wish I could just tell you the
   answer. That would make it easy, but
   that's not the way counseling works. If
   we work together, you can discover
   how to tell yourself what to do.

■   *Client 3, a college sophomore:*   My father's giving me a hassle because
my grades aren't that great, and he keeps telling me to make up my mind about my
career. I get sick of him telling me that all the financial sacrifices he's making better be
worth it. Oh, maybe I shouldn't be here in the first place . . . maybe I ought to be out
working.

Underlying message: _____

Responses   *Type and Level of Response*

1. It sounds like if you don't improve   1. _____
   your grades, you will have no choice
   but to be out working. We need to
   look seriously at what is bothering you
   so you can free yourself and be able to
   concentrate more on your studies.

2. The pressure coming from your father   2. _____
   is only part of the problem we are
   dealing with. How you handle this
   type of pressure is another part.

3. It sounds like you want to work at   3. _____
   changing things. Counseling can help
   you clarify what's going on and probably help you make a decision. It
   means an investment of time for both
   of us.

4. I'm happy you can ask yourself the   4. _____
   questions "Should I be here? Maybe I
   ought to be out working?" There are
   several interest inventories that are
   easy to take. They can help you make
   a decision about where you're at in this
   whole education scene.

■   *Client 4, a 25-year-old woman:*   I've been constantly tired lately. I just can't seem to keep my mind on anything. I have so much work to do, but I just can't get up the energy to do it.

Underlying message: _____

Responses	*Type and Level of Response*
1. There are several reasons why you may have this feeling. You may have accepted too many responsibilities or set a demanding pace for yourself. You may be fighting something and need some vitamins, a good rest, or both. But in your case, your lack of energy and inability to concentrate appear to have other causes.	1. _____
2. You must stop thinking the way you do. You keep saying everything must be done perfectly.	2. _____
3. Sometimes the counseling process helps us get at the bottom of why you are feeling the way you do. We can explore some of the things that are going on in your life, and I feel confident you will discover some new ways to look at things.	3. _____
4. It sounds like you are confused about what's going on inside you. There are some simple tests you can take that save time and energy and help me to focus more quickly on your difficulty.	4. _____

■   *Client 5, a 30-year-old engineer:*   I really don't know what I should do. My boss is driving me crazy. He knows that I'm scared to death about flying. And now he wants me to go to St. Louis to estimate a job.

Underlying message: _____

Responses	*Type and Level of Response*
1. We need to separate the pressures of your job from your fear of flying. Through desensitization you might be able to overcome your fear; however, your relationship with your boss may be quite a different issue.	1. _____

2. It sounds as though you feel that I can tell you what to do. I can do that, but it will be much more beneficial to look at some different ways to respond to your boss and their consequences.

2. _____

3. By exploring some of the feelings you have about the situation, you probably will discover what you should do. However, if you need an immediate response to your boss, we can talk about it today and help you decide on a way to approach this problem.

3. _____

4. You seem to be torn between your desire to succeed and your fear of flying. There are some things that you can do to reduce your fear of flying to manageable proportions. But it will take practice to learn, and you must be willing to try.

4. _____

■   *Client 6, a 65-year-old widow:*   My children don't understand. They question me about everything—where I go, what I do, who I'm dating. They think I've flipped.

Underlying message: _____

Responses

Type and Level of Response

1. As people grow and change, it is not uncommon for children to assume parental roles concerning their parents, and you are experiencing this now. It is quite a role reversal.

1. _____

2. Your children's perception of you and your own perceptions are quite different. You don't want to live within the mold they have created for you. The counseling process can help you learn how to tell your children about your own needs.

2. _____

3. During the counseling process we will explore some of the feelings you have about your children as well as the feelings you have about yourself. By exploring these feelings, we should have a better understanding of the situation.

3. _____

4. We will be able to meet here every Thursday at 4:00 p.m. The fee will be _____ dollars. If you need to cancel an appointment, please call as early as possible.

4. _____

■ *Client 7, a 21-year-old man:*   I'm so confused. Here I am engaged to a wonderful girl. Everything is going my way, and yet I'm not content with myself. I feel as if there's something missing in my life.

Underlying message: _____

Responses	*Type and Level of Response*

1. The counseling process can help explore the feelings and expectations you have in your life, and that can be helpful in discovering the basis of some of the confusion you feel. How you change things will be up to you.

1. _____

2. Sometimes people can't get at the root of their confusion. Counseling can help. If you are interested in going that route, I can set up an appointment for you next week.

2. _____

3. Your test results seem to indicate that you are very creative, yet the job you are working at gives you no room for creativity. They also indicate that you like to work with people, and right now you are tied to a machine. Part of your difficulty may be that most of the day, five days a week, you are doing a job you hate.

3. _____

4. Yes, and you keep telling yourself that you're no good. This negative self-talk is causing you a lot of pain.

4. _____

■ *Client 8, a 30-year-old mother:*   I can't cope with my children anymore. They come home from school, turn on the radio, tie up the phone, and totally ignore me when I speak to them. We fight all day long, and my nerves feel tied up in knots.

Underlying message: _____

Responses

1. We will need to look at some of your parenting practices. I think you may be reinforcing your children's poor behavior unknowingly.

2. The fact that your children may be healthy adolescents is not consoling. Counseling can help you become more comfortable with yourself and your role as mother, and show you how to communicate more effectively with your children.

3. Sometimes, talking about these things helps clarify exactly what it is you are feeling. Then it becomes easier to deal with the situation. That's what counseling involves: talking, changing some things, and learning to cope better.

4. I understand what you're saying. As we begin to talk about you and your family, I will want to review with you some basic psychological needs that all children have and that many children try to satisfy in inappropriate ways.

Type and Level of Response

1. _____

2. _____

3. _____

4. _____

■ *Client 9, a middle-aged man:*   Mary and I have been married for twenty years. It was really good in the beginning, but these past few years our marriage has been terrible. I'm considering a divorce. I just can't take it anymore; it's not worth it.

Underlying message: _____

Responses

1. It sounds like your dream has re-emerged. Individuals your age often assess where they are and compare it to where they want to be. It's one of the most difficult times in a marriage. Earlier you were busy establishing yourself in your job and your wife was busy with all the homemaking chores—your relationship never grew. Now it's obvious that you've lost contact and you feel you are living with a stranger.

Type and Level of Response

1. _____

2. When there are difficulties in the   2. _____
   marriage, very often both parties are
   struggling with communication. Some
   blaming is taking place on both sides.
   Walls build up and get higher and
   thicker. Before that happens, we can
   look at the whole picture as both of
   you see it. So often it is the system in a
   family that's in trouble, and no one
   person is to blame.

3. Through the counseling process you   3. _____
   will be able to discover more clearly
   what is going on with you and Mary.
   The decision for or against divorce
   might then be made with more
   understanding.

4. Since the problem seems to be be-   4. _____
   tween you and Mary, it would be a
   good idea for both of you to come to
   talk together. The situation works out
   better if both of you are involved in the
   counseling process.

■ *Client 10, a 28-year-old woman:*   I'm depressed all the time. Everything turns out to be a failure. My family criticizes me. My boss yells at me. Nothing is
right for me. Please help me.

Underlying message: _____

Responses   *Type and Level of Response*

1. I'm glad you came. You are certainly   1. _____
   confused about what is going on inside
   you, and you need some help. We will
   talk for a while and see if we can learn
   more about you and how we can work
   together.

2. You are not a failure at everything. You 2. _____
   dress attractively; you take care of your
   physical self and your appearance.
   Your depression has specific causes
   and is not caused by everything in
   your life, although you may feel like it
   is at the moment.

3. Depression has a way of feeding itself,   3. _____
and often we make more mistakes in
activities or in interpreting other responses because of how we feel. This
self-defeating behavior makes us more
depressed and angry with ourselves.

4. In order to help you, we will have to   4. _____
work together. It means a process of
counseling that involves hard work for
us, but if we meet consistently every
week for an hour, I'm sure things will
get better for you.

Communication exercises.   For each of the following client statements, please
formulate at least two high-level informing or describing counselor responses.

■   *Client 11, a young woman, 17 years old:*   It's my father. For years
now, I can't remember the last time he came home sober. He's drunk all the time now. He
thinks that he's fooling everybody, but he isn't. All my friends know what's going on. I
can't take it anymore.

■   *Client 12, a 25-year-old woman:*   I still can't believe I'm divorced. I
don't have anyone to share my life with now. And I have to start the dating scene all over
again. I don't know what I'm going to do!

■   *Client 13, a 40-year-old woman:*   My problem is that I have twin boys,
7 years of age, and I can't find the energy or patience to be with them anymore. I wish I
were back at work—they're driving me crazy. I feel so guilty about this.

■   *Client 14, a high school senior:*   I think I'm going to quit school. I can't
stand the courses. I don't feel I'm learning anything.

■   *Client 15, a 50-year-old man:*   I caught my daughter smoking marijuana, and I've put her on restriction. It really hurt me, and now I'm wondering what else
she might be doing.

■   *Client 16, a 23-year-old man:*   I'm thinking that I've made the biggest
mistake of my life. I got married two months ago, and now it's not working out. We live
upstairs from her parents. My wife and I fight constantly, and her family always takes
her side.

■   *Client 17, a 23-year-old homemaker:*   My drinking is starting to frighten
me. It seems like I'm climbing into the bottle more and more often.

■ *Client 18, a 22-year-old college student:* In two months I graduate from college. I don't have a job to go to or any plans for that matter. I don't really want to move back home, but there's nothing else for me to do. I just don't know.

■ *Client 19, a high school freshman:* I feel very lonely. I don't seem to have any friends. When lunchtime comes I eat by myself. I don't see anyone after school.

■ *Client 20, a 21-year-old man:* I'm twenty-one years old and am basically dissatisfied with my life. I'm not happy with my job—I'd like to go back to school, but I don't know for what. I'm wasting my time, and I see my whole life as meaningless.

Solo exercises. Team up with two of your classmates to form a triad. Take turns being "the counselor," "the client," and "the supervisor." Role-play in order to further develop your skills. Use the four role communication skills you have learned, and try to employ a variety of responses within each role. Spend at least 10 minutes in each minisession.

THE INQUIRING OR PROBING ROLE

The inquiring or probing role is often employed when you as the counselor seek to obtain further information from the client. It may be used when you want to

- begin an interview;
- encourage the client to speak or elaborate on a topic;
- help clients focus or describe their thoughts, feelings, and behavior more completely;
- assist clients in identifying concrete examples of their concerns; or
- discover what resources clients have at their disposal.

The inquiring or probing role can be employed to guide the discussion and help the client obtain certain insights. This role is most often exemplified by interrogative statements or questions, but it also includes incomplete sentences, in which the client is expected to complete the thought; accents, in which the counselor repeats part of a client's statement to elicit further information; and paraverbal or nonverbal messages, in which the counselor uses a tonal quality or a quizzical look to convey the probe in a clear manner.

Inquiries or probes should normally be made in the form of open-ended questions or statements. This type of questioning requires more than a simple yes or no response. Open-ended questions encourage clients to share their feelings and thoughts with the counselor and permit clients to respond in the way they prefer. Open-ended questions often contain the words *how, what, when, where,* or *who.* These words are associated with seeking out different kinds of information: *how* probes into procedures or processes that caused or preceded the stated event, thought, or feeling; *what* inquires about specific facts and details; *when* and *where* look for information concerning circumstance and occasion; and *who* seeks information about individuals (Evans, Hearn, Uhlemann, & Ivey, 1993; Ivey, Ivey, & Simek-Morgan, 1993).

Why questions seek reasons for thoughts, feelings, or behavior and should generally be avoided because they ask clients to justify their actions or speculate about their motives when they may be unaware of the causes of their feelings and behaviors (Brammer & MacDonald, 1996). This type of question often provokes defensive feelings (Evans, Hearn, Uhlemann, & Ivey, 1993). *Why* questions can also indicate approval or criticism or offer advice to a client that is counterproductive to the inquiring role (Johnson, 1997).

Probes or inquiries can be phrased in a statement form rather than a questioning form when the counselor wants to avoid creating an interrogative atmosphere. For example, "What happened before you did that?" can be restated as "Describe the events that led up to that situation." Benjamin (1987) refers to this as the indirect question, and Okun (1997) maintains that it is highly preferable to use the statement form of the probe. Many counselors-in-training have found this approach more effective than the direct question—when they use it, their clients give more elaborate responses. The statement form acts as an encouragement for clients, and it appears to help them elaborate and continue to express themselves.

When you need to find out a specific or concrete detail, a close-ended question is appropriate; otherwise, it is usually better to avoid using this type of probe. Close-ended probes typically can be answered with a very brief retort, or a yes or no response. They tend to elicit factual materials that often have little bearing on the major concerns of the client and frequently do more to satisfy the counselor's curiosity than to advance the counseling process. Close-ended questions often contain a form of the verbs *to be* or *to do* such as "Are you feeling okay?" or "Do you like that?"

You should minimize the use of the probing role in order to avoid creating an interrogative atmosphere. This climate allows your client to play a more passive role in the counseling process and contributes to dependence rather than independence on the client's part. Counselors who probe a great deal communicate that they are willing to take the major responsibility for the content and direction of the counseling sessions. Furthermore, the excessive use of this role can put your client on the defensive or communicate disapproval of the client's activities.

Types of Probing or Inquiring Responses

The following examples illustrate the use of various types of inquiring or probing responses.

1. *Open-ended questions.* Open-ended questions are often used to:
   a. open the interview—for example, "What would you like to talk about today?"
   b. invite the client to speak or to elaborate on a topic—for example, "Could you tell me more about that?"
   c. ask the client to focus or explore a feeling or thought more completely—for example, "How did you feel then?"
   d. request an example or an illustration of a situation—for example, "Would you give me an example of that?"
   e. help a client identify internal or external resources—for example, "Do you think you can handle that situation?" or "Who can give you some information about that?"

The question must always be relevant to the concern of the client and should encourage the client to discuss any thoughts, feelings, or behaviors that would facilitate the counseling process.

2. *Exploratory or elaborative statements.* Instead of asking open-ended questions, many counselors prefer to use statements that ask clients to elaborate or explain a situation, thought, or feeling more completely. Notice how the five following examples inquire into the same areas as the open-ended questions illustrated above:

   a. Open the interview—for example, "Tell me how I can help you today" or "I wonder how I can help you today."
   b. Invite the client to speak or elaborate on a topic—for example, "Describe that situation more completely" or "I'd be interested in hearing more about that situation."
   c. Ask the client to focus or explore a feeling or thought more completely—for example, "Explain how you felt when that happened to you" or "I'm sure you had some strong reactions to that situation."
   d. Request an example or an illustration of a situation—for example, "Describe a typical incident when that happens to you" or "I'd like to hear about a particular time when that occurred."
   e. Help a client identify internal or external resources—for example, "Tell me how you could handle a situation like that" or "I wonder if you know two or three people who could give you some specific information about that."

In each of these examples two different styles of the statement form of the probe have been used: one form is direct, whereas the other is more indirect. The open-ended statement form of the probe normally facilitates a more comfortable climate and often leads to richer and more complete responses than open-ended questions.

3. *Close-ended questions.* It is often necessary to inquire about relevant details and to obtain specific information. These inquiries are designed to help complete the picture that the client is painting about his or her life. This information is usually obtained by close-ended questions such as:

   a. "How old were you then?"
   b. "Do your parents know about this?"
   c. "Did you have to see a doctor?"
   d. "Have you ever thought about entering a program like this?"
   e. "Would you like to enroll in that class?"

Repeated use of this type of questioning should be avoided because it tends to restrict the flow of the conversation.

Illustrations of Different Types of Probing or Inquiring Responses

The following examples illustrate the use of the inquiring response. Compare the purposes and effectiveness of the open-ended questions used in the first example, the interrogative statements used in the second example, and the close-ended questions used in the third illustration. Also note how many of these examples use the attending or supporting role before the probe. This combination is employed to convey to the client that he or she is being listened to but further information is needed to advance the counseling process.

■ *Client 1, an 18-year-old woman:*   My mother is always criticizing me for the way I look and dress. She thinks there's something wrong with me because I don't date. It's not that I'm not interested, but most men I've met so far are dull and boring.

   1. *Interview opening:* It sounds like an awful situation. What is the major issue that you would like to talk about today?
   2. *Elaborative inquiry:* You're very upset. I'm not sure whether it's because of your mom, your social life, or both. Could you tell me more about yourself?
   3. *Exploration of feelings:* It really gets you down when someone picks on you. It's doubly hard when things aren't going the way you would like them to. How do you feel when your mother picks on you?
   4. *Request for an example:* I know how you feel when people don't see things the way you do. Would you give me an example of how your mother criticizes you?
   5. *Inquiry about resources:* It's painful to be picked on, particularly by someone close to you. How do you meet members of the opposite sex?

■ *Client 2, a high school sophomore:*   My parents don't understand. Everything I do seems wrong to them. It's impossible living with them.

   1. *Interview opening:* It sounds like you want to talk about your parents today. Tell me about them.
   2. *Elaborative inquiry:* Your parents seem to you to be supercritical. You can't do anything right, and it's tough when you're home. I'd like to hear more about your situation.
   3. *Exploration of feelings:* It hurts a lot when you're treated like a child. Adults, and your folks in particular, want you to do things their way. Tell me how you feel about that.
   4. *Request for an example:* It's tough to live with people who don't understand you. Give me an example of what they say to you and how you respond.
   5. *Inquiry about resources:* It is painful to be misunderstood. Name someone—a friend, anyone else in your family—that you can talk to who understands you.

■ *Client 3, a 32-year-old man:*   My wife just had a hysterectomy. She'll never be able to have children. She's only been out of the hospital for about two weeks, and now all she'll talk about is adopting a child. Before this, we'd always thought we'd wait a couple of years before starting a family. I don't know what to say to her.

   1. *Interview opening:* It sounds like you need to learn how to improve your communication with your wife. Would you like to learn how to do that today?
   2. *Elaborative inquiry:* You sound like you're a little stunned. You're concerned about your wife and her present health, and she's already planning for the future. How is your relationship with your wife?

3. *Exploration of feelings:* She shifted gears and you didn't. Wow! Did you feel surprised or angry about this?
4. *Request for an example:* You're startled and confused. Your wife is still recuperating, and she changed her mind and expects you to change your mind too—not only about the time to start a family, but about this whole idea of adoption. Did you ask her what this would mean to your relationship?
5. *Inquiry about resources:* She wants a family right now, and you're not sure about that. Do you know how to go about adopting a child?

Levels of Probing or Inquiring Responses

The inquiring role can be quite effective when the client is given the time to respond to the probe and one question is not followed by another (Cormier & Cormier, 1991). The skillful use of the probing role is a function of the relevancy of the inquiry, the appropriateness of the depth of the probe, the pacing and timing of the questions, and the warmth, respect, and genuineness associated with the probe. This role is very ineffective when leading questions are posed or when double or multiple questions are used. The repeated use of questions can produce a "ping-pong" effect (Hackney & Cormier, 1994), which may cause confusion or create an atmosphere of cross-examination (Evans, Hearn, Uhlemann, & Ivey, 1993). Asking too many questions in any given session also tends to reduce the client's personal responsibility for the counseling process, increase client dependency, and encourage socially acceptable responses (Brammer & MacDonald, 1996). Seeking tangential or superficial material, satisfying the counselor's curiosity, obtaining excessive factual data, or using a brusque manner can also create an interrogative atmosphere, which is counterproductive to the counseling relationship.

The inquiring role is used throughout the counseling process; however, it is usually not employed extensively in the initial stage of counseling because it intimates that counseling is a question-and-answer or cross-examination process. The probing or inquiring role can be used at various levels of effectiveness and rated on this four-point scale:

Level 1: Poor use of the role. The counselor is using this role ineffectively when he or she: probes or inquires about irrelevant data; uses antagonistic or accusative questions such as "Why did you do *that?*"; probes to satisfy his or her own curiosity; asks questions that suggest responses; or uses a voice quality or body movement that communicates an abrupt, authoritative, or dull, uninterested attitude.

Level 2: Mediocre use of the role. The counselor is somewhat ineffective when he or she is probing for related but unessential information, when the inquiries are poorly phrased, and when too many questions cause an interrogative atmosphere.

Level 3: Good use of the role. The counselor is effective in using this role when his or her probes are relevant and well phrased, when the role is used at a suitable time in the counseling process, and when the counselor's voice quality shows interest and concern for the client.

Level 4: Excellent use of the role. The counselor is most effective when his or her inquiries are phrased in a way that encourages the client to go beyond the surface or stated message. Normally, this role is most effective when used sparingly in the counseling process.

Illustrations of Different Levels of Probing or Inquiring Responses

The following examples are provided so that you can learn to distinguish among the levels of responses. Similar to the previous exercises, three client statements are presented followed by four different probing responses. The responses are rated according to the Level-of-Response Scale, and the reasons for each of these ratings are indicated. Study these examples to see if you agree with the ratings and the reasons stated. You may find that you do not agree with these ratings. Because the nonverbal and paraverbal aspects of the client's statements and the counselor's responses cannot be adequately conveyed by the printed word, it is quite possible that you will read one or more of these statements differently from the person who rated them. Any counselor response may be rated quite differently depending on how it is heard. It is extremely important that you state the reasons for your rating so that you can discuss any differences in class with your supervisor and classmates.

■   *Client 1, a middle-aged woman:*   My twenty-year-old daughter has been giving me problems. She stays out all night and does God knows what. When I ask her what she did, she tells me that it's none of my business.

Responses	*Ratings and Reasons*
1. What do you believe about your daughter?	2.3 Open-ended question requesting the client to elaborate, but focus is placed on the daughter and not the mother.
2. You're frightened and worried about your daughter. You feel your relationship with her is not what it should be. Tell me more about your relationship with her.	3.0 Shows awareness of client's feelings. Uses the direct statement form of probe.
3. Your daughter is irritating you. She doesn't want to live by your rules. I'm wondering what goes on inside of you when she says it's none of your business.	3.5 Counselor reflects client's content and feeling. The indirect statement form of the probe focuses on the client's feelings.
4. Any relationship you had with your daughter has been shattered, and you feel very badly about it. Tell me when when you first noticed that you were having problems.	2.5 Counselor is aware of the client's concern; however, the close-ended question probes into material that may not be appropriate at this time.

■ *Client 2, a 29-year-old man:* Every time I go into a singles bar, I feel lost. If I try to talk to a woman, I stutter and stammer. If I try to make small talk, I get embarrassed. I wish I were more self-confident.

Responses	*Ratings and Reasons*
1. You feel pretty awful when you go into a bar. Tell me about other situations or other times when you have this same feeling.	3.5 Shows concern and requests appropriate information using the declarative form of the probe.
2. You'd like to feel more selfconfident not only in bars but in dealing with women in general. Is this lack of self-confidence evident in other aspects of aspects of your life?	2.5 This response demonstrates the counselor's awareness, but the close-ended probe is likely to result in a yes or no response.
3. You probably feel quite confident in other dimensions of your life. Tell me about them.	2.0 Assumes too much about the client. Open-ended probe would be good if first statement were appropriate.
4. You wish you were more selfconfident when you're in a singles bar. What do you do when you get embarrassed?	2.3 Shows awareness of client's problem, but the close-ended probe is inappropriate.

■ *Client 3, a 22-year-old man:* My mother always bossed me around when I was growing up. Now every time my wife tells me what to do, I see red. I start yelling and screaming and telling her to mind her own business. Last night she said she would leave me if I didn't change.

Responses	*Ratings and Reasons*
1. You can't stand being bossed around. Describe a typical situation when you lose your temper.	3.0 Shows awareness of the client's concern. Request for example appears germane.
2. When someone tells you what to do, you come out fighting. That reaction sure doesn't help your marriage. How is your communication with your wife at other times?	2.5 Good initial response to client's concern. However, the close-ended question will probably lead to a limited response.
3. You're upset and angry. You want to be in charge of yourself, but you can't. Tell me about other situations in your life where you do feel in control.	3.0 Counselor's response shows understanding of the problem. The open-ended probe seeks to discover if the problem is only in this relationship.
4. I understand. Tell me how you feel when your wife tells you what to do and how you react when she or others boss you around.	2.5 Counselor's request for the client's feelings and the request for the example are too much to ask at one time.

Practice Probing and Inquiring Exercises: "How Do I Say 'Tell Me More About That'?"

These exercises have been provided to help you enhance your probing and inquiring role skills. The discrimination exercises afford you the chance to obtain additional practice in identifying the client's underlying messages, in recognizing the different ways to probe or inquire for different purposes, and in discriminating between more and less effective responses. The communication exercises enable you to practice giving high-level probing or inquiring responses in a variety of client situations. Finally, the solo exercises give you the chance to polish your attending, clarifying, informing, and probing role communication skills. As you do all three sets of these exercises take the position that several clients have backgrounds that are significantly different from yours.

Discrimination exercises.   For each of the following exercises: first, indicate the feeling and the content of the client's message; second, point out whether the probing and inquiring response is an open-ended question, an open-ended statement, or a close-ended question; and finally, rate the *level* of the response. Be ready to discuss the reasons for your ratings with your classmates and your supervisor. You may find that the excerpts were read in another way by one or more of your classmates; thus, they may have rated the response differently. It is important to understand the reasons for the different ratings.

■   *Client 1, recent high school graduate:*   I never seem to be a success at anything. Everything I try seems to end in failure. I've never had a job that lasted for more than six months.

Underlying message: _____

Responses	*Type and Level of Response*
1. I'm not sure I understand when you say everything ends in failure. Tell me more about yourself and your job history.	1. _____
2. You are telling me you have no sucess keeping jobs, and I understand why that upsets you. Tell me about your last job and why you left it.	2. _____
3. It's as if you just can't win at anything you try to do. Did you have a specific career plan in mind when you graduated?	3. _____
4. Tell me about the last job that you had, how you got it, and what caused you to be unable to keep it.	4. _____

■ **Client 2, a high school senior:** I get really worried about my friends— sometimes I can't get to sleep at night I'm so worried. They all recently began to use the real heavy stuff.

Underlying message: _____

Responses	*Type and Level of Response*
1. When did you first begin to feel this way?	1. _____
2. Drugs are scary things. What did you do when they acted this way?	2. _____
3. How are you affected or influenced by their actions in other ways?	3. _____
4. Your concern is causing you to lose sleep. Tell me more about your relationship with your friends.	4. _____

■ **Client 3, a college sophomore:** My father's giving me a hassle because my grades aren't that great, and he keeps telling me to make up my mind about my career. I get sick of him telling me that all the financial sacrifices he's making better be worth it. Oh, maybe I shouldn't be here in the first place . . . maybe I should be out working.

Underlying message: _____

Responses	*Type and Level of Response*
1. You and your father seem to disagree about grades and your indecision about a career. Tell me about your grades and your feelings about school.	1. _____
2. Tell me about any thoughts, ideas, or dreams you've had about choosing a major or occupational field.	2. _____
3. Who else can you or do you talk to about your schoolwork and your future plans?	3. _____
4. I understand. I'd be interested in hearing more about this.	4. _____

■ **Client 4, a 25-year-old woman:** I've been tired constantly lately. I just can't seem to keep my mind on anything. I have so much work to do, but I just can't get up the energy to do it.

Underlying message: _____

Responses   *Type and Level of Response*

1. Has your physician made any sugges-   1. _____
   tions to you?

2. You have no energy for doing what   2. _____
   you have to do. Tell me more about
   yourself and what you expect of
   yourself.

3. I wonder what a typical day in your   3. _____
   life is like. I want to know what you do
   from the time you get up in the morning until the time you go to bed at
   night.

4. Describe any unusual changes or   4. _____
   events that have happened in your life
   recently.

■   *Client 5, a 30-year-old engineer:*   I really don't know what I should do.
My boss is driving me crazy. He knows that I'm scared to death about flying. And now he
wants me to go to St. Louis to estimate a job.

Underlying message: _____

Responses   *Type and Level of Response*

1. Your boss asked you to fly. Tell me   1. _____
   about any other things that he has
   asked you to do that you feel you cannot do.

2. I'm wondering what it is that is causing   2. _____
   this fear. When did you first become
   aware of this fear of flying?

3. Have you looked at another means of   3. _____
   getting to St. Louis so you won't have
   to fly?

4. That sounds painful. I'd like to hear   4. _____
   about your job situation and your
   relationship with your boss.

■   *Client 6, a 65-year-old widow:*   My children don't understand. They
question me about everything—where I go, what I do, who I'm dating. They think I've
flipped.

Underlying message: _____

Responses   *Type and Level of Response*

1. Tell me more about your relationship   1. _____
   with your children.

2. Have they always been this concerned   2. _____
   about your welfare?

3. Describe one or two things that seem   3. _____
   to irk them.

4. I'd be interested in knowing why they   4. _____
   appear to be so concerned with your
   actions lately.

■ *Client 7, a 21-year-old man:* I'm so confused. Here I am engaged to a wonderful girl. Everything is going my way, and yet I'm not content with myself. I feel as if there's something missing in my life.

Underlying message: _____

Responses   *Type and Level of Response*

1. You can't allow yourself to feel good   1. _____
   about yourself, and you're wondering
   why. Tell me more about yourself.

2. Elaborate on this a little more so I can   2. _____
   try to understand what it is that is mak-
   ing you so discontented with yourself.

3. When did this feeling first come to you?   3. _____

4. Your job, your family, your recreational   4. _____
   activities, your relationship with your
   girlfriend are all going well and yet . . .

■ *Client 8, a 30-year-old mother:* I can't cope with my children anymore. They come home from school, turn on the radio, tie up the phone, and totally ignore me when I speak to them. We fight all day long, and my nerves feel tied up in knots.

Underlying message: _____

Responses   *Type and Level of Response*

1. How long have you felt that your   1. _____
   situation is out of control?

2. The only way they pay attention to you   2. _____
   is when you fight . . . and you feel anxious about this and unable to change
   things. How does your husband manage
   with this?

3. You feel you have lost control. I would
like to hear about the times when you
have enjoyed your family.

3. _____

4. Please tell me more about your home
life—your daily routine, the makeup
of your immediate family.

4. _____

■ *Client 9, a middle-aged man:*　Mary and I have been married for twenty years. It was really good in the beginning, but these past few years our marriage has been terrible. I'm considering a divorce. I just can't take it anymore; it's not worth it.

Underlying message:　_____

Responses	*Type and Level of Response*

1. It must be very painful for you to live
as you do right now. What have you
done to modify or change the
situation?

1. _____

2. You can't take it, but something tells
you that you value or cherish something in the relationship. Tell me about
those things that you value in this
relationship.

2. _____

3. You seem to keep asking yourself
"How can something that was so sweet
become so bitter?"

3. _____

4. Is this feeling only yours? Do you
think Mary feels the same way?

4. _____

■ *Client 10, a 28-year-old woman:*　I'm depressed all the time. Every-thing I do turns out to be a failure. My family criticizes me. My boss yells at me. Nothing is right for me. Please help me.

Underlying message:　_____

Responses	*Type and Level of Response*

1. It's lonely having to get through your
day with no support. Is there anyone
you can talk to?

1. _____

2. As I listened to your feelings of failure
and loneliness, I was wondering about
the circumstances that surround your
family's and boss's criticisms. Tell me
about them.

2. _____

3. You feel like quitting your job and moving away from your family, but you're wondering if that would really help.

3. _____

4. I'd like to know how you respond when you are criticized by your family or yelled at by your boss.

4. _____

Communication exercises. Make two different high-level probing or inquiring responses for each of the following ten excerpts. Try to use open-ended or probing statements, and be spontaneous in composing your replies.

■ *Client 11, a young woman, 17 years old:* It's my father. For years now, I can't remember the last time he came home sober. He's drunk all the time now. He thinks that he's fooling everybody, but he isn't. All my friends know what's going on. I can't take it anymore.

■ *Client 12, a 25-year-old woman:* I still can't believe I'm divorced. I don't have anyone to share my life with now. And I have to start the dating scene all over again. I don't know what I'm going to do!

■ *Client 13, a 40-year-old woman:* My problem is that I have twin boys, 7 years of age, and I can't find the energy or patience to be with them anymore. I wish I were back at work—they're driving me crazy. I feel so guilty about this.

■ *Client 14, a high school senior:* I think I'm going to quit school. I can't stand the courses. I don't feel I'm learning anything.

■ *Client 15, a 50-year-old man:* I caught my daughter smoking marijuana, and I've put her on restriction. It really hurt me, and now I'm wondering what else she might be doing.

■ *Client 16, a 23-year-old man:* I'm thinking that I've made the biggest mistake of my life. I got married two months ago, and now it's not working out. We live upstairs from her parents. My wife and I fight constantly, and her family always takes her side.

■ *Client 17, a 23-year-old homemaker:* My drinking is starting to frighten me. It seems like I'm climbing into the bottle more and more often.

■ *Client 18, a 22-year-old college student:* In two months I graduate from college. I don't have a job to go to or any plans for that matter. I don't really want to move back home, but there's nothing else for me to do. I just don't know.

■ *Client 19, a high school freshman:* I feel very lonely. I don't seem to have any friends. When lunchtime comes I eat by myself. I don't see anyone after school.

■　*Client 20, a 21-year-old man:*　I'm twenty-one years old and am basically dissatisfied with my life. I'm not happy with my job—I'd like to go back to school, but I don't know for what. I'm wasting my time, and I see my whole life as meaningless.

Solo exercises.　Develop your probing skills by trying them out in a triad. Each counselor-in-training should practice for at least 10 minutes using all five counseling roles. Each "supervisor" should take the responsibility for criticizing the mini counseling sessions. Repeat the exercise until all members of the triad have had the opportunity to practice.

The Role of Responding to Client Questions

In addition to learning how to pose questions, you need to learn how to handle questions directed at you. You might have had experiences where you were questioned during an interview and became a bit anxious because you were not sure how to respond. You need not become alarmed—client questions are quite normal, and you will learn how to deal with them in this section of the text. As you do the practice exercises you will discover that one of the previous responses you learned may be the most appropriate response to a client's question; hence, these exercises also provide you with additional experience using other role communication skills.

Every client question, like every client statement, has meaning and needs to be actively listened to and responded to appropriately. However, not every question should be answered directly. When your client asks a question that implies another meaning or one that has a deeper implication or one that raises an issue that your client needs to think some more about, it is usually better to use another role communication skill as a response. You may wish to: attend to your client's message; clarify an issue implicit in the question; support or reassure your client that the question is an important one that needs to be explored; or probe to uncover some relevant information related to your client's concern. Whatever the question, your response needs to be sensitive, openly genuine, and focused on the underlying client message.

Types of Responses to Client Questions

The following guidelines may be helpful to you in learning how to respond to your clients' questions.

First, when you are asked a question seeking factual information it is often best to accept the question at face value and answer the question directly. However, you should be aware that there may be an implicit message in the question, or a particular aspect of the question, that is an important issue to focus on. Thus, your informational response may be followed by another response that encourages your client to discuss the topic in more detail. For example, a freshman in high school who asks "Can you tell me if there are any special high school requirements to be able to major in psychology at college?" may be answered in this way: "There are no special requirements above having a good academic high school program. I'm wondering why you asked—is this one of several possibilities or is there a particular reason why you'd really like to be a psychology major?"

Second, your client will probably ask you questions that tend to focus on self-concerns, or on issues related to others who are not present, or on factors about you, the counselor (Benjamin, 1987). Questions of this sort often imply another meaning, and your response need not be a direct reply to the question but may address the issues raised by using another communication skill. For example, a college student who asks "Should I major in English or mathematics?" may be responded to by saying "I'm not sure I fully understand your dilemma. Are you concerned about which one you'll like better or which major has the best job prospects?"

Third, a different role response may be called for when your client's question is rhetorical, irrelevant, trivial, or out of context. In these cases you need to listen and understand the meaning behind the question and be as helpful as you can in your response. For example, a seventh-grade student asks "Is it going to rain today?" can be told "I don't know, but I suspect you have a good reason for wanting to know that. I'd like to know what it is."

Finally, some questions should never be answered directly for ethical reasons. In situations where you are asked to take sides in a dispute or requested to reveal something you heard in confidence, it is best to indicate why you cannot respond and follow this with another response that attends to the implicit meaning behind the client's question. For example, a husband who asks "What did my wife say to you?" might be answered "It wouldn't be right for me to tell you what she said to me. I can tell you that she is interested in trying to work with you to resolve this issue."

Practice Exercises Responding to Client Questions: "How Do I Answer That One?"

The following exercises have been prepared to give you practice in responding to client questions. The discrimination exercises give you the opportunity to analyze the type of client question, identify the underlying message, review different ways to respond to these inquiries, and practice identifying and rating responses. The communication exercises provide you with practice in giving your own high-level responses.

Discrimination exercises. To rate the following exercises use the information that you have learned from the previous role communication exercises. High-level responses address the client's concerns, while mediocre-level responses only partially address them and low-level responses do not address them at all. When you do these exercises remember that many of your clients may have cultural backgrounds that are dissimilar to your own. Please be prepared to discuss the reasons for your ratings with your classmates and your supervisor. As in the previous exercises the responses may be read with different tonal qualities and thus be rated differently by your classmates. Again, it is important to understand the reasons for your ratings.

■ *Client 1, a 24-year-old female:* I've been going out with John about a year now. He keeps hinting that we should get married. I don't know—I'm very fond of him, but I'm not sure that I want to settle down. How can I handle this without hurting his feelings?

Underlying message: _____

Responses	Type and Level of Response
1. You feel somewhat ambivalent about your relationship. It sounds like you're very concerned about his feelings.	1. _____
2. You seem very upset. I'm not sure if you want to work on keeping this relationship or if you'd like to end it.	2. _____
3. You're not sure you want to settle down. What have you thought about doing?	3. _____
4. You're under a great deal of stress. It's good that you want to handle this situation now.	4. _____

■ **Client 2, a 17-year-old high school student:** I'm on the basketball team, and the coach says I have a great deal of talent and a good chance for an athletic scholarship. Given my grades, can you help me identify the schools I should apply to?

Underlying message: _____

Responses	Type and Level of Response
1. Yes, I think I can do that, but before we take that step, I'd like to know more about your interests.	1. _____
2. You're unsure of what to do. Although you've been encouraged to apply for a scholarship, you don't know what schools to consider.	2. _____
3. That sounds great. I'm wondering if you or the coach have some schools in mind, or do we need to develop a list with you?	3. _____
4. You sound excited about the coach's comments. That's a great feeling to have.	4. _____

■ **Client 3, a 20-year-old college student:** I'm a junior in college, but my mother still treats me the way she did in grammar school. She tells me what to wear, who I should hang out with, and even where I should go when I go out at night. Why can't she understand that I can control my own life?

Underlying message: _____

Responses	Type and Level of Response
1. You are very upset. You're really having a problem discussing your activities with your mother.	1. _____
2. Her actions really bother you. I'd like to know how you typically respond when your mother tells you what to do.	2. _____
3. You sound quite frustrated. I wonder what you have said to her or thought about saying to her.	3. _____
4. And you really want to change things. Is it her control or your inability to communicate to her that causes this problem?	4. _____

■ *Client 4, a 50-year-old male:*   My mother lives alone. She is very forgetful and cannot manage things by herself. We try to help her as much as we can. We do her shopping and help her clean her apartment. I pay all of her bills and take care of her financial concerns. Our kids need us too; we feel pulled in two directions. Do you have any idea how I feel?

Underlying message: _____

Responses	Type and Level of Response
1. While I don't have parents in that situation, I can sense the tension that you are experiencing.	1. _____
2. You feel responsible for taking care of three generations. The burden is very heavy at times.	2. _____
3. Are you stressed because of the time you spend on activities for your mother or are there other factors that contribute to this tension?	3. _____
4. You sound overwhelmed. Tell me about your family situation. I'd like to know who else is available to help take care of your mother.	4. _____

■ *Client 5, a female college student:*   I have a very good friend who tends to embroider her stories. She exaggerates so much that she is dishonest. I want to tell her what a phony she is; but I don't think it would do much good. What would you do in my situation?

Underlying message: _____

Responses	Type and Level of Response
1. You're very concerned for your friend. You really want to help her but you don't know how to do it.	1. _____
2. She really gets to you. Tell me some reasons why she might have a tendency to exaggerate her stories.	2. _____
3. Helping anyone change a behavior can be a difficult process. I'm not sure you want to help her change or if you want to move away from her . . .	3. _____
4. You're bothered by your friend's behavior. She has some fine qualities but her dishonesty overshadows them.	4. _____

■ **Client 6, a college freshman:** I'm a physics major. I really like the subject, and I understand the text and the class lectures very well. But I never do well on the exams. I know the subject better than most of my classmates, yet they do better on their exams. Did you ever have this experience?

Underlying message: _____

Responses	Type and Level of Response
1. I have had the experience of not doing as well as I would have liked to have done, but I'd like to hear more about your situation.	1. _____
2. This sure is an irritating situation for you. And you're wondering if there is any wayto overcome this problem.	2. _____
3. You sound quite frustrated. Is your tendency to do poorly on tests limited to physics or does it occur in other subjects also?	3. _____
4. I'm wondering when you first noticed this problem. Did you have this difficulty in high school or is this a recent development?	4. _____

■ **Client 7, mother of two young children:** My husband had a stroke, and he will be out of work for a long time . . . maybe forever. I don't know what to do— I need money; the kids need me. How can I handle this? What should I do?

Underlying message: _____

Responses	*Type and Level of Response*

1. You sound very upset. Your husband's illness is really putting a lot of pressure on you.

    1. _____

2. You have a big burden on your shoulders and you'd like some help. I'll be glad to assist you, but first I need to understand more about your family situation.

    2. _____

3. At the moment you're overwhelmed. Let's take one step at a time. Tell me what help you will need immediately and in the foreseeable future.

    3. _____

4. Do you know about his financial resources? You should find out about any medical and disability insurance he may be eligible for and his eligibility for social security benefits.

    4. _____

■ *Client 8, a 21-year-old:* All my friends think I'm strange. I don't like many of the things they do. I hate the club scene. The music is so loud; I can't hear anyone. And the smoke—why do they allow it? I don't like any part of those situations; I don't fit in. Why do I have to be so different ?

Underlying message: _____

Responses	*Type and Level of Response*

1. You're quite concerned about this. It's really tough to have different interests.

    1. _____

2. You seem to be saying there are a few things that your friends do that you like but most of their activities you dislike.

    2. _____

3. You feel somewhat frustrated when you're with friends. Tell me some things you have in common with them.

    3. _____

4. You're very confused and upset. You like your friends and do some things you like together, but several things they do you dislike. And they give you a hard time about those.

    4. _____

■   *Client 9, a 55-year-old male:*   We have been married for 28 years. She has always been a wonderful wife and a good mother to our children. But all of a sudden she wants to change things; last night she told me she wanted a divorce. I know you saw her last night. Can you tell me what is going on in her head?

Underlying message: _____

Responses	*Type and Level of Response*
1. I'm sorry I can't tell you what she said. I think it would be best if the three of us met to discuss these issues.	1. _____
2. You feel that you have had a good marriage and all of a sudden some-thing happened. You're really hurting and want to know why this is happen-ing to you.	2. _____
3. You felt you had a good relationship for many years; tell me about any aspects of this relationship that were less than ideal for you.	3. _____
4. Although I can't tell you what she said, I think the fact that both of you have come to see me is an important first step in understanding your difficulties.	4. _____

■   *Client 10, a 79-year-old woman:*   Since my husband died three months ago I've been a lonely lost soul. At first, a lot of people would call or visit and my time was taken up; but now I am alone in my thoughts. I miss my husband more than ever. My doctor gave me some medication to take but . . . I hate to take it . . . I don't know which way to turn or what to do. Have you ever seen anybody like me?

Underlying message: _____

Responses	*Type and Level of Response*
1. I talk to a lot of people who have lost a loved one and many people who are lonely. But none of them have had the same experiences that you've had.	1. _____
2. It's tough to lose a loved one. And now you feel you have very little that's worthwhile to spend your time on.	2. _____
3. You feel very lonely. Tell me about any activities you enjoyed doing before your husband died.	3. _____

4. You must miss him a lot. I'd like to   4. _____
   know more about your family. Please
   tell me as much as you care to say.

Communication exercises.   Ten client statements are provided below. For each excerpt please respond to the client's question with at least three distinctive responses.

■ *Client 11, a 24-year-old female:* When someone asks me for a date I back away and change the subject to talk about something else. I grew up with the impression that I wasn't very capable and I wouldn't marry. I felt I was completely undesirable to the opposite sex. What do I have to do to change?

■ *Client 12, a high school sophomore:* I am interested in taking everything I have this year again next year . . . math, science, English, French, social studies, art, music, and phys ed. Do you think you can add another science course to my schedule?

■ *Client 13, a 48-year-old homemaker:* I've got to talk to someone. I think my husband is having an affair. I don't think I'm imagining it. He leaves home early in the morning and returns late at night and smells of beer. We hardly have an intimate relationship anymore. I don't know what I'm doing to chase him away. What would you do in my situation?

■ *Client 14, a 40-year-old male:* I am having a terrible time at my present job. My boss always picks on me and gives me a hard time. I hate the place—I wish I could quit. But I have a family to support and they say that the job market is lousy. I don't know where to turn. Can you help me?

■ *Client 15, a 24-year-old mother:* My husband and I have different ideas on how to handle the kids. They make me nervous and I'm always screaming at them. I don't know what to do. Did you ever have any difficulty in raising your kids?

■ *Client 16, a 35-year-old female:* My husband's first wife died of breast cancer, and we married two years ago. He has three children: a boy 15, a girl 12, and a son 8. I'm really having trouble taking on this parent role. I don't know how to handle them. Please give me some tricks or techniques or something I can use with them.

■ *Client 17, a middle-aged woman:* I feel that I've been a failure as a mother. My daughter went off to California a year ago and I have not heard from her since she left. Then a few months ago I found out that my son was experimenting with drugs. Can you imagine how I feel?

■ *Client 18, a junior high school student:* I don't know where I will be next year. I want to go to a special high school. The school has some special programs that interest me, but it is very large and quite far away. My folks want me to go to the local high school; it's more convenient. What makes my parents so rigid?

■ *Client 19, a 16-year-old male:*   I know what you are going to say: "You can't get along without a decent education." But I hate this place. The teachers are boring. There is nothing to hold me here. Don't you think the teachers are bad? Don't they get on your nerves?

■ *Client 20, a 26-year-old male:*   I lost my job three months ago and I can't seem to find a job I really would like. My funds are running low. My parents have invited me to live with them, but I don't know—I've been on my own since I went to college. What would you do in my situation?

Solo exercises.   Form a triad with two of your classmates. Take turns being the counselor, the client, and the supervisor. Use all the role communication skills you have previously learned in role-playing situations that you create. In these role-playing scenarios employ a variety of responses within each role to further develop your skills. Spend at least 10 minutes in each minisession.

The Meaning and Use of Silence

Beginning counselors often do not know how to deal with silence in the counseling process. For counselors-in-training it can be a frightening experience (Hackney & Cormier, 1994). In the ordinary social communication process, silence is often interpreted as a negative response. If a person says something, he or she normally expects a response. However, silence is a very effective tool in a counselor's repertoire. Used correctly, it is an active and positive response mode that fits into any number of the counselor's role functions. The use of silence requires a detailed discussion and explanation.

First, silence actively demonstrates your capacity to attend and to listen to a client. Used as an attending response, silence can show that you are sincerely interested in your client and what he or she has to say. This receptive role provides the client with the opportunity and, indeed, in some cases, the pressure to speak about and focus on or develop his or her problem. Used in this way, silence conveys the message "I care about you and I am interested in what you have to say." According to Okun (1997), there are times when silence is the only effective way to attend to a reluctant client.

Second, silence can also show support for the client and provide motivation for the client to speak. Silently waiting for another person to speak indicates that you believe that the client is a significant person and worthy to be heard. For clients who are shy or less articulate, silence can actively show openness and respect and provide space for a client to speak. Silence also communicates to clients that they have the responsibility for major inputs in the counseling process. As a counselor-in-training you need to learn to use silence in this motivating way and to avoid the temptation to talk or fill in to remove pressure from the client.

Third, your silence provides an opportunity for your client to clarify his or her thoughts and feelings. This reflective use of silence allows your client to sort out, think about, and reflect on what has occurred so far in the interview. Your client may periodically need to stop, observe what is going on, and gain some insights into his or her progress in the counseling session. This use of silence allows your client the space for his or her own growth-producing thoughts (Evans, Hearn, Uhlemann, & Ivey, 1993).

Fourth, silence can be used in the probing or inquiring mode. This inquisitive use of silence can be employed when you actively encourage the client to: elaborate on a topic; focus on or delve deeper into a particular thought, feeling, or action; or perhaps weigh alternative courses of action. Silence used in this way communicates that more client information, thought processes, or insights are to be developed and expressed. Using silence as a quest for information reinforces to clients that they have responsibility for progress in the counseling session.

Finally, silence is used in the restive sense. This use of silence occurs when either you, the client, or both of you are intellectually or emotionally fatigued or when the session has moved too quickly and a pause to rest is needed. You can employ this response mode to slow down the pace of the interview.

Silence is not an indiscriminate tool that you can use in an unsystematic, passive way. It must be used at appropriate times—that is, when it will enhance the role functions mentioned previously. The indiscriminate use of silence often reveals a counselor who is passive and reactive rather than dynamic and active. This passive silence is the hallmark of a counselor who takes minimal responsibility for the therapeutic process. Excessive use of silence runs the same risk.

Beginning counselors often use silence unintentionally rather than indiscriminately. Its use is rarely purely unintentional, for it does provide the beginning counselor with a reflective time to ingest the client's internal frame of reference and to try to determine what to do next. However, this unintentional use of silence frequently serves concurrently as another role function for the client and hence can be a productive response for the client as well as for the counselor.

As a beginning counselor, you should also be aware of the reasons why clients use silence. "Nonverbal client statements" are used when clients are in one of four different conditions or states: resistive, reflective, inquisitive, or exhaustive.

The client's resistive state may be caused by pain and discomfort or anger and hostility. In the former case, the client may find it hard to discuss something because it causes uneasiness or embarrassment. The client may not feel comfortable enough in the counseling relationship to reveal more about himself or herself (Brammer & MacDonald, 1996). In the latter case, the client may not want to discuss some aspect of the problem—the pain or discomfort may be too difficult to come to grips with in the session. When resistance is encountered, the relationship has not been well established, and as the counselor you should focus on improving the relationship to enhance the trust between you and the client.

The client is in a reflective state when he or she is silently pondering something during the process of counseling. During this time of reflection, the client may be reviewing what has just occurred in counseling, thinking about what he or she wants to say, searching for some information that is not immediately at the conscious level, or solving some internal problem that may lead to some insight or step in the problem-solving process. This reflective use of silence is labeled *integration silence* by Hackney and Cormier (1994) because clients use this time to absorb what is going on in the counseling session. This reflective state is normally quite productive, and you should allow the client ample time to deal with these inner thoughts before trying to proceed with any verbal responses.

The client is in an inquisitive state when he or she is confused and awaiting some action on the counselor's part (Benjamin, 1987). Normally, the client is waiting for some information, support, evaluation, or assistance from the counselor in the problem-solving process. You need to respond to this request for help in a way that minimizes a dependency relationship with the client. Frequently, it is in the best interest of the client and the counseling process to provide the information and assistance that is requested. However, to foster the client's sense of responsibility and to help the client learn how to do certain things, it is sometimes best to help the client learn how to obtain the information and assistance from others.

The client is in a restive, or exhaustive, state when he or she is intellectually or emotionally worn out and needs a moment to catch a breath before responding verbally. When this occurs, you should allow the client sufficient time and wait patiently until the client is ready to proceed.

Because most counselors-in-training have not learned how to use silence effectively in the counseling process, it often leads to rather awkward experiences for beginning counselors. Learning how to use silence requires you to understand what clients are communicating by their pauses and to employ silence as an effective response. To practice being more comfortable with silence, try the following exercises:

1. Form a triad. After the "client" and the "counselor" have started a practice session, the client should try to use silence in one of the four ways outlined in this section. The "supervisor" should monitor this carefully and discuss the client's meaning when appropriate.
2. Form a triad. After the "counselor" and the "client" have started a practice session, the counselor should try to use silence in one of the four ways outlined in this section. The "supervisor" should monitor this session and stop the session when necessary to discuss how silence was used.

SUMMARY

The intermediate role communication skills were presented in this chapter in a manner that required your active involvement in the learning process. After reading and practicing the skills outlined in the chapter, you should have a good understanding of the informing role, the probing role, the role of responding to client questions, and the effective use of silence. Furthermore, you should be able to identify these skills, explain the differences between higher- and lower-level responses, and employ these skills appropriately in your counseling interviews.

The informing or describing role is used when you need to provide the client with relevant facts or descriptions of how various entities function. Informing responses are frequently employed for one of the following reasons: to structure the counseling process, to provide the client with appropriate factual information, to inform the client about some psychological principles, or to present information about a particular intervention strategy. In high-level responses the material presented is necessary and appropriate to advancing the counseling process and the descriptions are factually accurate; these responses are presented in a manner that is understood by the client.

The inquiring or probing role is employed when you seek to obtain information from the client. Probing responses are typically used to open an interview or to encourage clients to elaborate on a topic; to discuss a thought, feeling, or behavior more completely; to provide concrete examples of their concerns; and to identify their internal or external resources. Inquiring responses include open-ended questions, open-ended statements, and close-ended questions. High-level responses focus on critical issues or situations that need further elaboration and discussion, and they demonstrate a sincere and genuine interest in the client. To avoid excessive questions in an interview and to enhance the client's sense of responsibility for the counseling process, it is recommended that the statement form of the probe be used whenever possible.

Learning how to handle client questions is an important skill for the counselor-in-training to learn. Every client question has meaning and needs to be actively listened to. When your client asks a question that implies another meaning, has a deeper implication, or raises an issue that needs further exploration, it is often better not to answer the question directly but to respond with another role communication skill. Your response should be genuine, sensitive and focused on the underlying message.

Silence can be an effective communication skill and can serve a variety of functions in the counseling process. It can be used to show interest and active listening, to show support and concern, to provide clients with the opportunity to clarify their thoughts and feelings, to probe, or to provide time for reflection.

The skills presented in this chapter require extended practice to be mastered. Many counselors-in-training have practiced the statement form of the probe in a variety of situations and have found it to be quite helpful in enhancing their conversations. Because informing, probing, responding to client questions, and silence are important communication skills in the counseling process, it is important for you to practice them until you feel comfortable using them.

REFERENCES

Benjamin, A. (1987). *The helping interview* (4th ed.).Boston: Houghton Mifflin.

Brammer, L. M., & MacDonald, G. (1996) *The helping relationship: Process & skills* (6th ed.). Boston: Allyn & Bacon.

Cormier, W. H., & Cormier, L. S. (1991). *Interviewing strategies for helpers: Fundamental skills and cognitive behavioral interventions* (3rd ed.). Pacific Grove, CA: Brooks/Cole.

Egan, G. (1994). *The skilled helper: A problem-management approach to helping* (5th ed.). Pacific Grove, CA: Brooks/Cole.

Evans, D. R., Hearn, M. T., Uhlemann, M. R., & Ivey, A. E. (1993). *Essential interviewing: A programmed approach to effective communication* (4th ed.). Pacific Grove, CA: Brooks/Cole

Hackney, H., & Cormier, L. S. (1994). *Counseling strategies and interventions* (4th ed.). Boston: Allyn & Bacon.

Ivey, A. E., Ivey, M. B., & Simek-Morgan, L. S. (1993). *Counseling and psychotherapy* (3rd ed.). Boston: Allyn & Bacon.

Johnson, D. W. (1997). *Reaching out: Interpersonal effectiveness and self-actualization* (6th ed.). Boston: Allyn & Bacon.

Okun, B. F. (1997). *Effective helping: Interviewing and counseling techniques* (5th ed.). Pacific Grove, CA: Brooks/Cole.

9 Advanced Role Communication Skills

Introduction

This chapter delineates advanced communication skills: the advising role, the motivating or prescribing role, and the evaluating or interpreting role. The purposes that these skills are used for are given, the types of responses that are used in each of these roles are outlined and illustrated, and practice exercises are provided. You should be able to respond to the following discussion questions after studying this chapter:

- Summarize the purposes of the advising, motivating, and evaluating roles.
- Discuss the characteristics that distinguish high-level responses from low-level responses in each of these roles.
- Identify the types of responses used in the advising, motivating, and evaluating roles and give examples of good and poor uses of these responses.
- Apply these advanced communication skills in appropriate situations.

The Advising Role

Many clients come to counseling with the expectation of receiving some advice. They are accustomed to obtaining suggestions and recommendations from family members, close friends, and significant others in their lives. They often look for—and assume they will get—advice from the experts they know. Parents, teachers, physicians, and other important figures have conditioned them to this role expectation. Thus, you can anticipate that your own clients will seek advice from you at some point in the counseling process.

The advising role is used when you want to help your client think about a solution to a problem, reflect on an idea offered for possible adoption, plan a course of action or develop a list of options. The role can also be employed as a means of bringing some recommendations into the discussion: asking your client to mention any advice he or she has heard about that deals with the problem under consideration is a desirable method to introduce and examine that advice in an objective manner. This role is also applicable when you feel that a referral to another professional is in order.

Any suggestions you offer as the counselor ought to be carefully thought out, meaningful to your client's frame of reference, and practical for your client to follow. Furthermore, recommendations should be made only when you think it necessary to advance the counseling process and only in areas where you have some clear and expert knowledge (Benjamin, 1987; Cormier & Cormier, 1991; Epstein, 1985).

Advising responses should be given with clear directions. However, the phrasing of these responses can vary from a strongly worded recommendation, stated in a directive tone, to a milder, more permissive suggestion, conveyed in a very warm manner. Notice the differences in wording and tonal qualities that can be used in the following advice offered by a college counselor: "You really have to make an appointment with your program advisor"; "I wonder if you have considered seeing your program advisor"; "I think you might want to talk to your program advisor." As a counselor you may prefer to use a more permissive, conditional wording and a warm tone to ensure that your client does not forgo the responsibility for resolving the problem.

Normally, advising responses are employed in the third and fourth phases of the counseling process—after you have developed a solid working relationship and explored issues related to your client's concerns. Advising responses are more directive than the information responses discussed earlier in the text; advice has an evaluative or a corrective connotation whereas information is factual (Johnson 1997; Moursund, 1990).

When you want your client to learn some new skills, advice can be offered as a collaborative effort by proposing that you work on a project together. For example, if your client has manifested difficulties in speaking to authority figures you may want to say, "We need to help you learn how to become more assertive." Another good time to phrase your recommendation in a collaborative way is when you want your client to consider some options or examine alternative courses of action. For example, if your client asks you what college major to select, you might respond, "Let's work together to list the advantages and disadvantages of each possibility."

The use of direct advice in counseling is controversial, and it can be counterproductive for several reasons. First, it can thwart effective communication with your clients when it is used prematurely or when it cuts off important dialogue or interferes with building a solid relationship. Second, it may foster dependency and encourage your clients to avoid responsibility when the advice interferes with their struggle to learn how to deal with important issues and concerns. Third, it can enhance defensiveness when your clients resist or reject the advice. Fourth, it can be inappropriate or trivial when you offer it in an area in which you are not an expert or when you put forth an easy or simplistic solution to a complex problem. Fifth, your advice can be misinterpreted by your clients. Sixth, your clients may not follow your advice or recommendation because it may be something they cannot or will not do. And finally, your clients may not see the sense of your advice, or your recommendation may not agree with their beliefs or opinions about the topic (Benjamin, 1987; Brammer & MacDonald, 1996; Evans, Hearn, Uhlemann, & Ivey, 1993).

Clearly, there are times when direct advice should not be given. One important situation where this occurs is when you do not know what your client should do. You may not know because you are not an expert or you do not have enough information about the situation. When you feel you are being pressured for advice it is best to be open and genuine in your response—state that you do not know what recommendation to make and mention the reasons why. In these situations you can say you will think about the issue or look it up; or you may prefer to refer your client to an expert or, with the client's permission, consult the expert yourself. For example, you can say, "I don't know what advice to give you. You might like to consult Dr. Chen; or would you prefer that I talk to him about this?" The other times when it is usually unwise to give direct advice is when your client asks about crucial individual decisions (Epstein, 1985). Issues such as who to marry, what occupation to select, and whether or not one should leave a job are quite personal; and, while friends and significant others may offer opinions on what to do, advice from a counselor in these areas is always counterproductive and unwise (Brammer & MacDonald, 1996; Epstein, 1985; Johnson, 1997; Moursund, 1990). Rather than offering specific and direct advice on these topics, you need to help your clients weigh the alternatives and the consequences of their possible choices.

Types of Advising Responses

The following types of advising responses are typically used in this role.

1. *Direct advice.* One way to give advice is to be rather direct in proposing a suitable course of action for your client to follow (Benjamin, 1987). In this response you offer a definite opinion about a decision your client must make, recommend a specific solution to your client's problem, or advise your client to take some concrete action. There are several typical situations when this method of offering advice is warranted:

   a. When your client wants to take some action but is unaware of the generally accepted (or a more desirable) way to do it. For example, as a school counselor you may say to a senior, "It would be good to type that college application."
   b. When your client wants to take some step but is unaware of the implications or the nuances related to that particular action. For example, as a career counselor you might state to your client, "If I were you, I'd wear a suit to that job interview."
   c. When your client needs help and you can offer some recommendations based on your expert knowledge. For example, as a family counselor you might advise a parent, "You need to give your child attention when he is not making a bid for it."

   In some cases it is helpful to offer the client several possibilities. When you place different options on the table for consideration you afford your client the opportunity to weigh the value of the various choices and to think about alternatives. Direct advice can vary from a strong admonition to do something to a more permissive suggestion to consider some possible action. These responses are often phrased in collaborative terms to underscore the mutual nature of the counseling relationship.

2. *Probes about familiar advice.* Rather than offering direct advice to your clients it is often worthwhile to get advice into the discussion by inquiring about the sugges-

tions and recommendations they are already aware of and know about (Benjamin, 1987). This is normally done by using one of the following three inquiring responses:

a. You can have them identify any recommendations and alternatives they have considered. For example, you may say to a client, "I'd like to know what solutions to this problem you considered before you came to see me."

b. You can ask what suggestions they have heard from significant others in their lives. For example, you might ask a client, "I'm wondering what advice you have heard from your friends about this matter."

c. You may ask them to report on any recommendations that they know about from any source. For example, you can say, "What suggestions would you give to another student who had this concern?"

You might also ask your clients to talk about the circumstances under which these recommendations could be followed. This technique for getting advice into the discussion enables your clients to discuss their feelings and their reactions to this advice. It has the distinct advantage of allowing you to remain impartial while your clients evaluate and weigh the usefulness of the various suggestions. This method of bringing advice into the discussion may be all the direction your clients need to resolve the issue (Benjamin, 1987).

3. *The referral.* Chapter 3 explained how referrals are designed to help the client in two distinctive ways:

a. when the client needs to obtain specific facts or information to incorporate into the ongoing sessions and facilitate the counseling process; and

b. when you feel the client can benefit from another helping professional who has some expertise needed by the client.

Brammer & MacDonald (1996) indicate that the referral is an important skill for the novice as well as the experienced counselor. Making an effective referral requires you to know what resources are available, to determine your client's needs and readiness for the referral, to select an appropriate and suitable professional and to explain to your client in concrete and realistic terms why the referral is being made. It is most important for you to maintain your relationship with your client to ensure that the referral is worthwhile and useful. Similar to other advising responses a referral can be offered in a directive manner or in a more permissive way.

Illustrations of Different Types of Advising Responses

The following three examples demonstrate the use of the advising role.

■ *Client 1, a 30-year-old woman:* I hate to go shopping in a supermarket. Every time I get on a checkout line someone is always trying to get ahead of me. I can't say no and I feel so used. What do I have to do to change?

1. *Direct advice:* You feel you can't stand up for your own rights. You would feel better if you were more assertive. Learning these skills will take us some time, but you can learn more effective ways to deal with situations like this.

2. *Probes about familiar advice:* That sounds painful for you. I think we can help you resolve your concern. I really would like to know some of the things you've thought about doing to overcome this behavior.

3. *A referral:* You feel awful when people take advantage of you. We have a fine assertiveness training program here at our center. I'd like to tell you about it; you might like to enroll in it.

■ *Client 2, a 16-year-old male student:*   My father keeps telling me that I should become a physician; they make a lot of money. But I don't like science or math courses. I'm doing okay in those subjects, but I really like my art and English classes. Can you tell me what to say to him?

1. *Direct advice:* You sound quite frustrated. Your father wants what he thinks is best for you and you disagree. We need to help you find another way to talk to him.

2. *Probes about familiar advice:* It seems that you and your father have different opinions about your future. I'd like to know what other members of your family have said to you about this.

3. *A referral:* It's tough when you can't communicate with your parents. Mrs. Walsh, one of the other school counselors, runs a counseling group once a week for students who want to improve their communication skills with their parents. I think you might be interested in going to it.

■ *Client 3, a 40-year-old male:*   I was always a social drinker—a scotch or a beer once or twice a week. Then, I guess, I started this new job and had a martini for lunch every day. Now, I don't know; last night I drank myself to sleep. And my wife is now talking about a separation. I really want to change. Please tell me what I should do.

1. *Direct advice:* What was once a casual habit has turned into a bad one that has all kinds of consequences. We need to develop a plan to help you change. Let's decide on some of the details we want to put into that plan.

2. *Probes about familiar advice:* You appear to be in a difficult situation and you want me to tell you what to do. I suspect you might be able to think of several suggestions that you'd give to a friend who had a similar problem.

3. *A referral:* You really want to change but you can't do it on your own. We can talk for a while about this, but I also want you to eventually see Dr. Tseng, who is an expert in dealing with concerns like yours.

Levels of Advising Responses

Advising responses, if not carefully used, can be counterproductive and interfere with building a good relationship. Communication can be thwarted, and clients can become dependent or resistant. Care must be taken to make them feel involved and responsible for the outcomes of the counseling process. High-level advising responses are based on the clients' needs and their readiness for this type of response. The advice should be specifically related to their concerns and stated in a warm, friendly manner. The advice should offer suggestions for them to examine their behavior, feelings, or situations in new ways and encourage them to become more aware of possible courses of action. Normally, this role is used sparingly and only after a good counselor-client relationship has been established. The role may be used at all counseling stages; however, it is seldom used in the earlier stages and more frequently found in the later stages. The effectiveness and appropriateness of a particular advising response is a function of the counselor's timing and the connotation conveyed. The use of this role can be ranked on the following four-point scale:

Level 1: Poor use of the role. The counselor is ineffective in using this role when it is used prematurely; when it cuts off dialogue; when the counselor gives advice without being aware of the needs of the client; when it is offered with an intonation that communicates another role; or when the advice interferes with the client's attempt to learn how to deal with an important issue or concern.

Level 2: Mediocre use of the role. The counselor is somewhat ineffective in using this role when the recommendations are unclear, when suggestions are too vague, when referrals are incomplete, when voice intonation is not in tune with the message that is intended, or when the role is used under circumstances when the counselor is unsure of what advice to give to the client.

Level 3: Good use of the role. The counselor is effective in employing this role when recommendations, suggestions, or referrals are sound, focused, and timely; when the counselor solicits recommendations from the client; and when the role is used at a fitting time in the relationship.

Level 4: Excellent use of the role. The counselor is most effective in using this role when he or she is aware of the need to give useful advice; when appropriate referrals, good recommendations, or alternative suggestions are offered; or when the client is tactfully encouraged to articulate his or her own options while the counselor demonstrates sensitivity to the client's concerns.

Illustrations of Different Levels of Advising Responses

Advising responses are illustrated and rated in the following three examples. The Level-of-Response Scale is used to rate each of the counselor's responses, and the reasoning behind each of these ratings is stated. In studying these examples, you may find that you do not agree with these ratings. Because tonal quality and other paraverbal aspects of the client's statement and the counselor's responses are not conveyed, it is possible that you will read some of these statements in another way than the person who rated them. Any response may obtain a different rating depending on the paraverbal quality that the reader hears. Thus, it is crucial to indicate the reasons behind the ratings so that any differences among these ratings can be understood.

■ *Client 1, a college student:* My roommate is a pain. She makes my life miserable. She wants to know where I go and everything I do. She listens to my phone conversations. She tells everybody in the dorm everything. I have no privacy in my life. What can I do about her?

Responses

1. It must be very unpleasant not to have privacy in your own room. You ought to be fairly assertive with her and develop some mutually agreed-upon rules for living together.

2. It sounds like she is trying to be your alter ego. I'd like to know what you would say to a friend of yours if she were in the same situation.

3. That must be awful for you. You need to see the residential dorm assistant to see what can be done about this situation.

Ratings and Reasons

2.8 When offered at an appropriate time this can be a worthwhile response.

3.0 This response can be an effective way to get good suggestions into the discussion.

2.1 Reply may appear warranted; however, it may be unsuitable or may be heard as a rejection.

■   *Client 2, a 55-year-old male:*   I'm really fed up. I'll never get promoted. I've worked at my job for 20 years and every time there is an opening for a supervisory position, I get passed over. Do you think I should quit my job?

Responses

1. Wow; you must be very angry and upset. Getting passed over is very difficult; but before you quit we need to discuss other possible solutions to your problem.

2. Well, let's talk about that. When faced with an unpleasant situation it's helpful to think about options. I'm wondering what possibilities ou've considered.

3. You seem extremely frustrated. Before we do anything, I want you to see Dr. Kapoor for some tests The results will help us shed light on your problems.

Ratings and Reasons

2.8 Response seems to be a good way to encourage the client to evaluate options.

3.0 This is a very good way to have the client start to think about other choices.

2.3 Referral may be worthwhile, but it appears to be offered without preparing the client.

■   *Client 3, a high school student:*   I'm in a tough situation. I want to go to college but we can't afford it. My parents can't send me, I have no money, and I don't think I can get a scholarship. Can you help me figure out a way to go to a good college?

Responses

1. It's nice to hear your determination. I'm sure we can figure out a way for you to go to college. There are many programs available to help students further their education.

Ratings and Reasons

3.0 This can be a very effective reply to the client's request.

2. It's great that you want to go on with your college education. I'm curious to hear about what options you think may be open to you.

3.0 Response is an effective way to bring alternatives into the discussion.

3. You want to go to college, but you think you can't afford it. You will need to talk to Mrs. Alverez who is the college advisor. She has helped many students in your situation.

2.4 Referral sounds useful and encouraging; however, it may seem like a rejection to some students.

Practice Advising Exercises: "How Do I Offer Advice?"

Similar to the previous sets of exercises, this set also provides the same three types of practice: discrimination exercises, communication exercises, and solo exercises. The first two sets of exercises should be completed in the same way as those in prior chapters. When you do the solo exercises, try to practice all previous roles. Assume that some of the clients have cultural backgrounds that are different from yours.

Discrimination exercises. For each client statement given below identify the feeling and the content underlying the client's statement, and then specify the *type* of response employed. Finally, indicate the appropriateness of the response by rating the *level* of the response. Anticipate your classmates' questions about the reasons for your answers, and be prepared to discuss your reasons in class. The excerpts may have been read differently by your classmates, and hence their ratings may not agree with yours. It is important to understand the reasons why these differences exist.

■ *Client 1, a high school sophomore:* All my parents do is fight. I can't concentrate on my schoolwork, and sophomore year is hard. My grades are falling fast. If things don't settle down at home, I don't know what I'll do. Can you give me some advice?

Underlying message: _____

Responses

1. It's hard to concentrate when things are not comfortable at home. While we talk about your concerns, I can also arrange some extra help for you at school.

2. That's hard on you. Mrs. Lehner, one of the other counselors, runs a group that helps students deal with problems at home. I think you could feel comfortable joining it.

Type and Level of Response

1. _____

2. _____

3. Wow, you sure feel a lot of pressure.
Let's put our heads together and list
three or four things you might try to
do to help you at school and at home.

3. _____

■   *Client 2, a high school freshman:*   My mother is constantly comparing
me to my older brother and sister. I am sick and tired of hearing about them; how well they
did in school and how easy they were to raise. What do you think I should say to her?

Underlying message: _____

Responses

Type and Level of Response

1. You've about had it. You're not your
brother nor your sister and you need
to let your mother know that. Tell me
what you *want* to say to her and what
you think you *could* say to her.

1. _____

2. I'm glad you spoke up about your
concern. Before you say anything to
your mother you might consider talking to your brother and sister about
your feelings on this matter.

2. _____

3. It's tough when you're always compared
to others. I'd like us to think about several things we can do to help you. Let's
brainstorm and list any possibilities.

3. _____

■   *Client 3, a college junior:*   I need a break from college. If I took off for a
while, I'd be in a better frame of mind and would do better in my studies. If I take a leave, my
parents will be really upset. I'm really quite frustrated. What do you think I should do?

Underlying message: _____

Responses

Type and Level of Response

1. You feel that there is something pre-
venting you from doing as well as
you'd like to do. Let's try to think of
three reasons why you might not be
doing as well as you want to do.

1. _____

2. Things are not going right for you. If
you had a chance to discuss your concerns with someone close to you, what
advice would they give you?

2. _____

3. It's hard when you don't do as well as
you'd like. Let's think about the consequences of staying in school and also
dropping out.

3. _____

■ *Client 4, a 16-year-old female:* I hang out with five girls in my class; we do just about everything together. There is another girl in our class who is not part of any group. I feel sorry for her; a lot of kids tease her or ignore her. I think she is a nice person, a bit shy—and she does some really stupid things. I'd like to get to know her and help her fit in, but the group would be on my case. Do you have any ideas?

Underlying message: _____

Responses   *Type and Level of Response*

1. You're really concerned for her. Tell me   1. _____
   if there are times you could see her
   without the group. For example, what
   would happen if you invited her to
   your house to do some homework
   together?

2. It's hard on you when you see some-   2. _____
   one lonely. Let's try to list five or ten
   things we might do to try to help her.

3. You're very sensitive to the feelings of   3. _____
   others, maybe more than others in the
   group. Tell me what you'd say to someone else in a similar situation who
   asked *you* what to do.

■ *Client 5, a 26-year-old female:* I just found out that I am pregnant. My husband will probably hit the roof! I don't know what to do. We thought we would wait and save some money. I don't know what to do. What would you do in my place?

Underlying message: _____

Responses   *Type and Level of Response*

1. It sounds like life is full of unforeseen   1. _____
   surprises. I'd like us to think about
   what you might do. First, tell me what
   you might say to your husband.

2. If he hits the roof, what's the worst   2. _____
   thing he will do or say after he hits it?

3. You're really concerned about this. Tell   3. _____
   me what advice you have gotten or
   might expect to get from your friends.

■ *Client 6, a 19-year-old college sophomore:* I can't decide what to major in. None of my subjects has any great appeal to me. My grades are okay—I'm passing everything—but I'm a long way from being on the dean's list. What do you think I should do?

Underlying message: _____

Responses	*Type and Level of Response*
1. Selecting a major is a hard decision for lots of students. You might talk to Dr. DePalma in the career development center. She may help you find some areas interesting to you.	1. _____
2. You're being pressed to make a choice you feel you can't make. I'd like us to forget school for a while and talk about any other interests you have.	2. _____
3. It's not at all unusual for students to be unsure of a major. Selecting a major requires you to know a lot about yourself as well as a lot about what each major involves. We might start by helping you learn as much about yourself as we can.	3. _____

■   *Client 7, a 55-year-old male:*   I saw a doctor recently and he told me that I have a serious heart problem. I don't know what to do. I don't have any insurance. I can't tell anybody at home yet because I don't want them to worry. How do you think I can handle this?

Underlying message: _____

Responses	*Type and Level of Response*
1. You feel a lot of pressure right now. Without insurance you feel you might not get the best care. However, I believe you really need the emotional support of your family to help you at this time.	1. _____
2. The doctor gave you some bad news and you know you must take some action. I'd like the two of us to plan some things we could do to deal with these concerns. First, tell me about the options that you believe you have.	2. _____
3. That's a real burden on you. You have raised three important issues—your health, your lack of insurance, and your reluctance to discuss your problems with your family. If you did tell your family, what is the worst reaction you could possibly get?	3. _____

■ *Client 8, a 46-year-old male:* My wife resents the time I spend with my sister-in-law helping her out. My brother died a year ago and she doesn't know how to handle things. I spend two hours at her house every night after work. Hard feelings have developed and that complicates matters. What do you think I should do to get out of this mess?

Underlying message: _____

Responses	*Type and Level of Response*
1. You feel you're under a great deal of pressure and you'd like some help. Let's brainstorm and list some things you could do. Say anything that comes to your mind.	1. _____
2. It seems like you ought to do something fairly soon. To ease the pressure, you might consider stopping the visits to your sister-in-law or bringing your wife along with you when you visit her.	2. _____
3. Sounds like you're caught in a bind. Before we look at what you *could* do, let's consider how you see your relationships and how you think your wife and sister-in-law see them.	3. _____

■ *Client 9, a 17-year-old high school student:* I guess I'm going to be out of here soon. I stopped going to most of my classes so I'll probably fail everything. What jobs do you think I can get?

Underlying message: _____

Responses	*Type and Level of Response*
1. You're not wild about this place; but if you do drop out, you'll find very few jobs available for school dropouts. It's important to get a high school education—if not here, then in an alternative school. That may be a more appropriate place for you now.	1. _____
2. You sound determined to get out of here. Before we talk about any immediate plans, I'd like to know where you see yourself in five years. Where do you think you will be living and what kind of job will you have?	2. _____

3. You feel you're going to drop out of   3. _____
   school soon. I'd like you to list the
   jobs you think you can get now and
   the ones you might get with a high
   school diploma.

■   *Client 10, a young adult male:*   We're not really married. We've been
living together for two years now and we have a good relationship. It doesn't make sense
to be married. . . what do I need that piece of paper for? Carla thinks otherwise. She
wants a family! What should I do?

Underlying message: _____

Responses   *Type and Level of Response*

1. Being in a relationship requires both   1. _____
   good communication and compro-
   mises. What would you advise a friend
   to do if he had the same problem?

2. You'd like to keep the relationship the   2. _____
   way it is, but Carla has other ideas. Tell
   me about the options you think you
   have and the consequences of each one.

3. From my experience, any relationship   3. _____
   between a man and a woman involves
   other people as well. I suspect both
   your families and many of your friends
   have given advice to you. Tell me what
   they have said to you.

Communication exercises.   Please respond with three different high-level advising responses for each of the ten client statements provided below.

■   *Client 11, a 12-year-old:*   I don't have any real friends. The kids are nice
during school, but whenever I suggest doing something after school they always have a
good excuse not to see me. Everybody sticks to their own group and I'm left out. Can
you tell me what I should do?

■   *Client 12, a high school student:*   My parents are getting a divorce. My
mother wants me to live with her, but my father wants me to live with him. I don't know
what to do. Why do they have to split anyway? Can you give me any suggestions?

■   *Client 13, a 28-year-old female:*   My sister is a psychological case study.
She doesn't know how to raise kids. She constantly criticizes her two boys—and she

doesn't care who hears her. She belittles them for the least imperfection. I feel sorry for the kids, but I am even sorrier for my sister who is missing the fun of being a parent. What suggestions can you give me?

■ *Client 14, a college freshman:* Several people on my floor are using some drugs. They keep after me to try it. I don't want to, but . . . what do you think I should do?

■ *Client 15, a 25-year-old female:* I'm really confused. I've been going out with Peter for six months now and I feel we have a great relationship. But lately things seem to be different. He doesn't call when he says he will, and he cancelled three dates in the last two weeks. I don't know what to think. What would you do in my situation?

■ *Client 16, a 46-year-old female:* I lost my husband six months ago and it hurts a lot. And yes, it makes me angry, but I never show the hurt or the anger. My nerves feel like they are really stretched. Can you give me some help?

■ *Client 17, a 46-year-old male:* I've had a bad week as far as my ego goes. My boss yelled at me several times this week and I didn't feel good about that. I'm not concentrating on my job—my mind is elsewhere. What do you suggest I do?

■ *Client 18, a 28-year-old female:* My husband and I are having a terrible conflict. He wants to start a family and I don't. I like my job, it's very interesting, and I get paid very well. I'm not ready to have kids, but he says the biological clock is running fast. Can you offer me some way to resolve this conflict?

■ *Client 19, a 36-year-old female:* I'm very mixed up. I always thought that I would marry someone with the same religious background. That's what my parents always encouraged me to do and that's what I wanted for myself. Now I find myself in love with a man who comes from a different tradition—very different. I'm really very concerned because our religious traditions are so dissimilar. Can you give me any suggestions?

■ *Client 20, a high school senior:* I need two extra courses this semester to get into the college I want to go to. I know I can do the work; I have a decent index and I know I'm willing to work hard. My parents told me to take the courses in summer school and not during the school year. What do you think?

Solo exercises. Form a triad with two of your classmates. Take turns being the counselor, the client, and the supervisor. Use all the role communication skills you have learned in the situations that you create. In these role-playing scenarios employ a variety of responses within each role to further develop your skills. Spend at least 10 minutes in each mini-session.

THE MOTIVATING OR PRESCRIBING ROLE

Motivating the client to act is a function of the entire counseling process; hence, this role is implicit in every response or statement you make. Nevertheless, there may be times when you need to employ a role that is more explicitly motivational. This role is manifested when you use direct, deliberate, focused, and forceful statements that are specifically employed to initiate some growth, movement, or productive action on the part of the client. The use of this role requires you to take a different tack in the counseling relationship from the previous roles, and it involves some degree of risk. This type of response is ordinarily used only after a good working relationship has been established. This allows you time to obtain sufficient information about the client, to determine whether a motivational response is appropriate, and to use this response to strengthen rather than weaken the relationship. The role is normally undertaken to overcome some impasse or to encourage the client to think, feel, or behave in some new or different way. You need to be sensitive to your client when using these responses so you can monitor their effects on your client.

Responses that are used in the motivating role can vary in their potency and strength from relatively mild to extremely strong. If you think that the relationship is not sufficiently well established or that the client is unable to respond in an appropriate way, you should give some thought to employing milder forms of the motivating and prescribing statements. If the relationship is solid, you may wish to use stronger forms of these responses.

Types of Motivating or Prescribing Responses

Although a variety of verbal responses can be used in this role, the following ones are the most common:

1. *Focusing.* This directive response is designed to concentrate the client's attention on the issues that you as the counselor perceive to be most important at that moment of the interview. This response can be used very effectively when the client presents a confusing or vague situation, rambles on with too many details or too much tangential information, wanders away from an important topic, or provides an incomplete or confusing picture (Brammer & MacDonald, 1996). The response is ineffective when the counselor focuses on irrelevant data or fosters further digressions. Attending, clarifying, or probing responses can be used as focusing techniques when the counselor's purpose is to have the client look at or center on a core critical notion. The responses can vary from a relatively mild reminder to keep the conversation on track, to a strong request to discuss one's feelings in further detail, to a command to elaborate on the meaning of one's nonverbal behaviors.

2. *Setting Goals.* For the counseling process to be productive, it is important to identify the purpose of the relationship and to establish meaningful goals for the client. Chapter 3 outlines when and how this process should occur. Briefly stated, these goals should be attainable (Evans et al., 1993), mutually agreed upon (Okun, 1997), subject to modification (Hackney & Cormier, 1994), and specifically tailored for each client (Brammer & MacDonald, 1996).

In many cases your client will clearly indicate what he or she wants to accomplish in the counseling process. However, in other cases, the client may appear unable to articulate a reasonable goal. When this is the situation you can take a rather directive stance and suggest a goal. This step is often taken when the client is unable to identify the problem, when you need to translate a vague or diffuse issue into a concrete objective, or when you need to establish one goal when the client has several major concerns.

3. *Confronting.* The purpose of a confrontation is to have a client face up to something that he or she may not be fully aware of or may wish to avoid. It is an extremely useful response that can challenge your client to examine his or her own statements and behaviors more thoroughly (Hackney & Cormier, 1994). Confrontation can be used very effectively when a client reveals discrepancies and contradictions in thoughts, feelings, or behaviors; manifests rationalizations and other poor coping strategies; employs mixed messages; or demonstrates differences between personal and social values (Evans, Hearn, Uhlemann, & Ivey, 1993). A confronting response may also offer a point of view different from the client's that may help the client understand other positions or objective reality (Brammer & MacDonald, 1996; Okun, 1997).

Because a confrontation may deal with matters that are anxiety provoking to the client, it should be stated in a matter-of-fact tone and employed only after a good relationship has been established. Confrontations can be counterproductive when they sound accusatory or judgmental; when they are stated in a blunt, harsh, or critical manner; and when too many are given in one session (Cormier & Cormier, 1991).

A typical confrontation is an honest and direct statement such as "You said this; however, the evidence suggests something else" or "Your words and your actions do not agree with one another." When the available evidence appears to be contrary to what the client has said, the confrontation may be quite sharp. This "shock treatment" may, as Okun (1997) has indicated, get the client off dead center. However, it may be interpreted as criticism and upset the client. This sharp confrontation has a high degree of risk, and you need to exercise caution to ensure that it leads to the desired outcome.

4. *Self-disclosing.* The purpose of self-disclosure is to help the client focus and expand on an issue by offering a germane personal illustration of a similar situation or concern. If you have a personal experience that can help a client, Egan (1994) believes that sharing this information should be a matter of common sense. There are advantages and disadvantages in using self-disclosures in counseling. On the positive side, they have the possibility of improving the relationship, enhancing the client's feeling of trust, helping the client understand that other human beings have similar kinds of problems, motivating the client to share feelings and personal concerns, and helping the client gain another perspective on an issue or learn how to handle a specific situation (Cormier & Cormier, 1991). On the other hand, self-disclosures have the negative possibilities of: shifting the focus of the discussion from the client to you, the counselor; being irrelevant to the topic or to the client's perceptual world; or trivializing the client's experience (Evans, Hearn, Uhlemann, & Ivey, 1993).

Self-disclosures are often quite helpful when a client has recently had a rather traumatic experience that you have also experienced. Used in this type of situation, your self-disclosure can be a manifestation of your empathic understanding of the depth and seriousness of the client's problem.

When used appropriately, your response should share relevant personal feelings and experiences, relate these experiences implicitly or explicitly to the client's concerns (or point out their differences), and maintain the focus of the interview on the client. Egan (1994) points out that self-disclosures can be a form of modeling and can be used effectively with a client who is reticent and reluctant to talk about self. Your self-sharing will show the client how to talk about self and will encourage the client to reveal more about himself or herself.

In order not to distract from the client's concerns and to keep the focus on the client and not on you, the counselor, self-disclosures should be selective, focused on the issue, and used relatively infrequently and only after a good relationship has been established (Egan, 1994; Evans, Hearn, Uhlemann, & Ivey, 1993).

Illustrations of Different Types of Motivating or Prescribing Responses

The following three examples illustrate the different types of motivating or prescribing responses.

■ *Client 1, a 14-year-old girl:* My father and I fight all the time, especially about the boys I know. He won't even let a boy in the house. He says they're all no good. I think he just doesn't trust me.

1. *Focusing:* You feel that he doesn't trust you. But it sounds to me that the issue is not just one of trust—you also cannot talk to your father.
2. *Setting goals:* I sense that you have difficulty communicating with your father. I think we need to work on helping you improve this communication process.
3. *Confronting:* You have some rights, but at your age your father also has something to say about your friends.
4. *Self-disclosing:* I remember when I was fourteen—I thought my parents' attitude was positively medieval. I know times are different now.

■ *Client 2, a middle-aged man:* All my life I've never been able to hold a job for very long. Everything goes okay for a while, but then I get into a fight with the boss or something like that and I'm fired. I can't seem to help it.

1. *Focusing:* Tell me, what were the circumstances like when you lost your last job?
2. *Setting goals:* You are very wise to look into this problem. I'm glad you came to see me. We'll look into your behavior and find out what causes you to have a fight with your boss.
3. *Confronting:* You know that fights with bosses are unwise, yet you continue to do it.
4. *Self-disclosing:* I've had trouble with bosses also. I don't like to be pushed around either.

■ *Client 3, a middle-aged woman:* My mother died a few months ago, and I haven't been the same since. I just can't seem to get my life back on track again. I've been very preoccupied with death and dying.

1. *Focusing:* Tell me what your day was like yesterday and then how you would have liked to have changed it.
2. *Setting goals:* First we need to help you mourn, to find some time during the day for you to cry. Then we can plan on getting your life reorganized again.
3. *Confronting:* You appear to be using your mother's death as an excuse for ignoring the needs of others in your life.
4. *Self-disclosing:* When my mother died it took me six months to regain my daily routine. It might take about the same length of time for you.

Levels of Motivating or Prescribing Responses

Motivating responses, if not carefully used, can put your clients on the defensive. This is counterproductive because clients may become indecisive and resistant. Care must be taken not to make your clients feel inferior but, rather, to make them feel involved and responsible for the outcomes of the counseling process. High-level motivation responses are based on the client's need and readiness for a motivational or prescription statement. They focus on specific major issues raised directly or indirectly by the client and are usually stated in a warm, friendly manner. Effective responses offer suggestions for your clients to examine their behavior, feelings, or situations in new ways and encourage them to become more aware of themselves. Normally, this role is used after a good relationship has been established and is used sparingly during any interview. The effectiveness and appropriateness of a particular motivational response is a function of its timing and the connotation it conveys. The role is used at all counseling stages; however, it is normally used moderately in the earlier stages and more extensively in the later stages. The use of this role can be ranked on the following four-point scale:

Level 1: Poor use of the role. The counselor is ineffective in using this role when it is used prematurely; when it is blurted out without reference to the needs of the client; when it is presented with an intonation that communicates another role; or when it is conveyed in an accusatory, judgmental, or hostile manner.

Level 2: Mediocre use of the role. The counselor is somewhat ineffective in using this role when suggested goals are unclear, confrontations are vague, voice intonation is not in tune with the message, and the counselor seems unsure of what direction to move the client or the process.

Level 3: Good use of the role. The counselor is effective in employing this role when the suggested goal is sound, confrontations are focused or timely, self-disclosures are appropriate, the role is used at a fitting time in the relationship, and the counselor responds properly to the needs of the client.

Level 4: Excellent use of the role. The counselor is most effective in using this role when he or she: is aware of the need to use forceful statements to obtain some progress within the relationship; demonstrates sensitivity to the client; and gives an impetus to move the counseling process along.

Illustrations of Different Levels of Motivating or Prescribing Responses

The motivating or prescribing roles are illustrated in the following three examples. The Level-of-Response Scale is used to rate each of the counselor's responses, and the reasoning behind each of these ratings is stated. In studying these examples, you may find that you do not agree with these ratings. Because tonal quality and other paraverbal aspects of the client's statements and the counselor's responses are not conveyed, it is possible that you will read some of these statements in another way than the person who rated them. Any response may obtain a different rating depending on the paraverbal aspect that the reader hears. Thus, it is crucial to indicate the reasons behind the ratings so that any differences among these ratings can be understood.

■   *Client 1, a college senior:*   I'm so mad at the dean. He just asked why I took part in that demonstration. He acted as if I did something wrong.

Responses	*Ratings and Reasons*
1. You seem to be responding to the dean very strongly. We may need to explore your feelings about authority figures.	3.0 This appears to be an appropriate goal.
2. You are *really sure you* were right in acting the way you did.	2.8 Counselor is trying to confront the client in an attempt to have the client focus on her inner feelings.
3. When I was an undergraduate, I led several student boycotts.	1.0 Poor self-disclosure—not shown to be related to the client's problem; leaves focus on counselor.
4. Let's look at what happened during your meeting with the dean more carefully.	3.0 Counselor directs the client to focus and describe the situation.

■   *Client 2, a college senior:*   John and I have had a serious relationship for over a year, and he suddenly tells me he's going to live in Chicago to take care of his father's business—he left just like that.

Responses	*Ratings and Reasons*
1. I gather from the little bit that you said that you are hurt, but you want to forget him. It sounds like you want help in learning how to deal with this.	3.0 Counselor attends to the client and identifies some goals to help her deal with her emotions.
2. I was engaged to be married once. She gave me the ring back the week before graduation. Although I realize my experience is different from yours, I sense the frustration and anger that you feel.	2.5 Self-disclosure has some danger of not being germane, but counselor relates it back to the feelings of the client.

3. What happened the last few times you were together? Were there any signs of his lack of seriousness?

3.0 Counselor focuses on relationship and requests the client to reflect on the meaning of the relationship.

4. It may have been very serious on your side, but not serious at all for him.

3.5 Confrontation response may be upsetting. Counselor is forcing the client to face up to a possible explanation.

■ *Client 3, a middle-aged woman:* My husband and I are very upset with our daughter. Every time she comes home it ends up in some sort of conflict. She's twenty-three years old and collecting unemployment, and she doesn't seem to be going anywhere. I just wish she would get married.

Responses

1. You appear to be having a great deal of difficulty in talking to your daughter. We need to help you improve your skills in communicating with her.

Ratings and Reasons

2.7 Counselor restates the client's concern and suggests a reasonable goal for the counseling process.

2. Give me some specific information about these conflicts. Describe how they get started.

3.0 Counselor is requesting the client to focus on the conflicts in order to gain important information.

3. Yes, and I know you would be happy if she moved out of the house, far away—wouldn't it be peaceful.

2.8 Response is designed to confront the client and have her come to grips with how she feels about her daughter.

4. So, it's all your fault. You've been a rotten parent, and it sounds like you're on a guilt trip.

2.8 Counselor confronts the parent about her possible guilt feeling. This is somewhat risky but can be productive.

Practice Motivating and Prescribing Exercises: "How Do I Say 'Get On with It'?"

Similar to the previous sets of exercises, this set also provides the same three types of practice: discrimination exercises, communication exercises, and solo exercises. The first two sets of exercises should be completed in the same way as those in Chapters 7 and 8. When you do the solo exercises, try to practice all previous roles. It would be helpful for you to assume that some clients represented in these exercises come from a cultural background that is unlike your own.

Discrimination exercises: For each client statement given below identify the feeling and the content underlying the client's statement, and then specify the *type* of motivating and prescribing response employed. Finally, indicate the appropriateness of the response by rating the *level* of the response. Anticipate your classmates' questions about the reasons for your answers, and be prepared to discuss your reasons in class. The excerpts may have been read differently by your classmates, and hence their ratings may not agree with yours. It is important to understand the reasons why these differences exist.

■   *Client 1, a young man:*   I think I want to get a divorce. When I married Susan, I thought we had a lot in common, but I found out otherwise. Her values are so materialistic that I find them repulsive.

Underlying message: _____

Responses	Type and Level of Response
1. I'm glad you came to see me. We can discuss your feelings about Susan and you can gain some insight into your own feelings about yourself and your relationship with her.	1. _____
2. My wife is also quite materialistic, and it's a problem in our relationship. But I see her really appealing traits too, and our relationship continues to grow in spite of the rocky moments.	2. _____
3. Let's explore your feelings about Susan. When did you first begin to feel your outlook on life might be different from hers?	3. _____
4. And you're perfect. Susan thinks you're her knight in shining armor.	4. _____

■   *Client 2, a 35-year-old woman who recently lost her husband:*   It's only when I'm alone that these feelings and memories keep returning. If I don't do something right away to divert my attention, I just start crying and feeling sorry for myself.

Underlying message: _____

Responses	Type and Level of Response
1. I haven't experienced the depth of your loss, but I know when my father died, I cried every night for a month.	1. _____
2. And the eleventh commandment is "Thou shall not cry!"	2. _____
3. When you're alone you feel very sad. Tell me if these feelings interfere with other aspects of your life.	3. _____

4. From what you say it is important for
you to learn how to mourn and at the
same time you want some help to plan
some future goals for yourself.

4. _____

■ *Client 3, a male in his late fifties:*   I just got laid off from my job. I
worked for the place for 18 years, and just like that I'm out on the street. It's impossible
for a man my age to begin again.

Underlying message: _____

Responses	*Type and Level of Response*
1. Should I call the undertaker or the old folks' home? You must be out of commission.	1. _____
2. You are very wise to come in for help. It's important for us to understand your talents and then see how they can be employed in today's job market.	2. _____
3. Tell me what you mean by the phrase "just like that"?	3. _____
4. My father was laid off after twenty-five years with the same firm. I can sense what you're going through.	4. _____

■ *Client 4, a high school senior:*   I'm not sure where I'm at. I'd like to go to
college and get married. I think raising a family can be a full-time commitment. But then
again I should think of some career or occupation. Suppose I don't marry or can't have
kids. I'm kind of muddling through.

Underlying message: _____

Responses	*Type and Level of Response*
1. From what you said, I think it's important for us to help you think about a tentative career choice.	1. _____
2. So, who cares. If you want to go to college, you'll get your application in on time. If you don't, you'll diddle daddle.	2. _____
3. I was in the same boat. I was very confused, but I wasn't able to explore my options with a counselor. I think we can help you do the kind of planning that will help you.	3. _____

4. Well, let's try to get a handle on this.   4. _____
   Let's talk about one aspect at a time.
   First, let's talk about your parents' per-
   ceptions about your future.

■   *Client 5, a 30-year-old man:*   Last week I lost my job. My boss told me to
do something I didn't think was right. I wouldn't do it, and he fired me. I don't know
what I should do—I have a family to support.

Underlying message: _____

Responses	*Type and Level of Response*

1. I had a boss who was awful, very un-   1. _____
   ethical and unprofessional; we never
   got along. I know my experience is not
   the same as yours, but I can imagine
   what you're going through.

2. You're paralyzed. You think you're the   2. _____
   only father and husband who ever lost
   a job.

3. It seems that you paid a high price to   3. _____
   live up to your values. Let's look at what
   kind of a job you would like to find.

4. We need to help you resolve some per-   4. _____
   sonal conflicts you have about this
   experience.

■   *Client 6, a 20-year-old woman:*   Everything was great when I first met
Tom. We had so much in common, and he seemed like the right kind of guy to marry.
But lately we're fighting a lot. I'm starting to see a different side of Tom, and I don't like
it. I still really love him though. He's a great guy. Maybe we'll work things out when we're
married.

Underlying message: _____

Responses	*Type and Level of Response*

1. Tell me more about the two sides of   1. _____
   Tom that you see.

2. Are you desperate? Do you want to be   2. _____
   in the boxing ring for twenty years?

3. I've had the experience of beginning a   3. _____
   relationship and thinking I knew the
   person. I realize that my experience is
   somewhat different from yours. Tell
   me more about yours.

4. From the problems you have described, we need to examine your relationship with Tom more closely.

4. _____

■ *Client 7, a middle-aged man:* My teenage son and I don't get along very well. I guess one could refer to it as the generation gap, but I'm only trying to do what's best for him.

Underlying message: _____

Responses	*Type and Level of Response*
1. So, you tell him what to do all the time.	1. _____
2. I had a similar problem with my own children. It took me a long time to learn how to work with teenagers effectively. Let's focus on your concerns.	2. _____
3. You're only trying to do what's best for him. Tell me what you do for him; be as specific as you can.	3. _____
4. If you're on his back all the time that might be the reason for your difficulties in communicating with him.	4. _____

■ *Client 8, a young man, 16 years old:* There's this girl that I like, but I can't ask her out because my friends tell me I'm too short and ugly, and no girl would go out with me . . . I don't know what to do. I really like this girl.

Underlying message: _____

Responses	*Type and Level of Response*
1. When I was your age I was afraid to ask a girl out; I was afraid I would be turned down. My experience was not the same as yours, but I believe we can help you work this out.	1. _____
2. Let's forget about the girl for the moment. I would like you to tell me about your friends and your relationships with them.	2. _____
3. Your friends like to give you a hard time. I think we should work on helping you become more assertive.	3. _____
4. Yes, I know, you're short and ugly. She's tall and just won the Miss Universe contest.	4. _____

■ *Client 9, a young woman:* If I could tell him, just once, where to get off, I know I'd lose my job. I don't think it would be worthwhile.

Underlying message: _____

Responses	*Type and Level of Response*
1. What would you say to him? Tell me.	1. _____
2. He really gets you angry, yet you don't want to lose your job. We need to help you find a way to ventilate your frustrations and deal with this situation more effectively.	2. _____
3. The solution to your problem is in your hands, not your boss's. He can handle himself. You are having problems dealing with him.	3. _____
4. Why don't you antagonize him or quit and get another job? You need to learn to stand up for what you believe are your rights.	4. _____

■ *Client 10, a college sophomore:* I just quit my job because I found it too hard to keep up with my studies and work after school. By the time I got home I was too tired to study. My father thinks I'm copping out on my responsibilities, and he's really mad.

Underlying message: _____

Responses	*Type and Level of Response*
1. It's not easy working your way through school. I know how hard it is—I had to do it myself, and it was a struggle. I know we can help you work this out.	1. _____
2. Do you think he may have any other reasons for being mad?	2. _____
3. I think you need to learn another way to talk to your father. He seems to want to make sure that your time is being well spent. Let's work on improving your communication skills.	3. _____
4. The majority of students who attend here also work, yet there's something different about your experiences. I wonder what that is.	4. _____

Communication exercises.   Ten client statements are provided in this exercise. For each excerpt please try to make three different high-level motivational responses.

■   *Client 11, a college freshman:*   I came because I had a terrible feeling of depression. My boyfriend, who is nineteen, is threatening to break up with me because I won't have sex with him. We've been going together for sixteen months, and everything was great until about two months ago. Now he has this big thing about going to bed. He keeps saying I'd do it if I really loved him. He doesn't understand my viewpoint at all.

■   *Client 12, the wife of an alcoholic husband:*   My problem is that my husband is an alcoholic. I'm the sole support of my family, and although I loved him once, and suppose I still do, I don't think that staying with him is helping the children.

■   *Client 13, a woman who has had three miscarriages:*   I've been so terribly depressed lately that I can no longer function effectively. My husband is considerate and understanding, but he says I must resign myself to the fact that I will never have children. I just can't accept that.

■   *Client 14, a 10-year-old girl:*   Nobody likes me. I don't have any friends. My mother says not to feel bad. I can't help it if I want other kids to like me.

■   *Client 15, a teenager:*   When I get home from school my mother is always drunk. The house is a mess. She doesn't do the dishes or clean up, and she hardly cooks any supper. She just lies there and drinks and screams at me, and I scream back. I'm so ashamed that I can't ask my friends to come over, and I'm so disgusted sometimes that I think I'll just leave home.

■   *Client 16, a teenager:*   I know someone who's selling drugs, and I don't know what to do about it.

■   *Client 17, a middle-aged woman:*   I'm so depressed. I went to the doctor and found out that I'm pregnant. I feel like this is the end of the world.

■   *Client 18, a foreign student:*   This is my first year in the United States. I had a scholarship this year, and applied for one for next year but didn't get it. So now I am forced to consider a job. You know I only have a student visa. I am not supposed to work here, and since I don't have a degree from the U.S. it will be very difficult to get a job. What would I do if I couldn't get a job? What kind of life do I expect to lead? How can I go back home without completing my studies? I don't even have enough money to go back.

■   *Client 19, a teenager:*   Both my parents think that I'm still a little kid. I just turned fifteen, and they won't let me go out on a single date with my boyfriend. All of my friends are allowed to date, so I don't see why I can't.

■   *Client 20, a mother of two young children:*   My husband had a stroke. He'll be in the hospital a long time, and I need money to support us while he is there.

Solo exercises. Your minisession should now be expanded to a minimum of 20 minutes; continue to practice each previous role communication skill and try to incorporate the new role into your counseling repertoire. Give each person in the triad a chance to practice being the counselor, the client, and the supervisor. Rate your peers on their responses, and review the previous roles when necessary.

THE EVALUATING OR INTERPRETING ROLE

The purpose of the evaluating or interpreting role is to help clients expand or modify their frame of reference. The role is used when you want your clients to become more aware of themselves and their thoughts, feelings, and behaviors; to crystallize, rearrange, and gain a new perspective about these experiences; and to enhance their understanding of these personal events.

This role requires you to use your professional knowledge of human behavior, clinical judgment, and personal sensitivity to assess, interpret, or integrate various pieces of information that you have obtained about your clients. This information may come from signals and messages communicated by clients, psychometric data or other resource material, reports from other significant individuals, or your own professional insights. Your evaluation is then shared with your clients in order to provide them with the opportunity to integrate and make connections between and among seemingly unrelated factors, to identify their personal resources and strengths, and to view themselves and their concerns in different ways. Responses in this role may focus on helping clients understand how their typical patterns of behavior cause problems in their lives, how excessive stress or anxiety has developed, how they meet their needs in inappropriate ways, or how they use nonconstructive coping strategies.

In using this role you, as the counselor, assume a more authoritarian, judgmental, and active stance in the relationship. Care must be exercised in using the role because an evaluation process can put your client in a defensive mood. Interpretive responses should be used only after establishing a solid relationship—when you have a good understanding of your client's experiences. These responses should be reasonably close to the client's previous knowledge or perceptions. To ensure that your client is not overwhelmed, use relatively mild forms of interpretations and evaluative responses—and use them sparingly. However, if your response varies considerably from your client's frame of reference it will need to be repeated periodically in order to be assimilated.

Cormier and Cormier (1991) believe that interpretations are generally more effective when they are stated with positive implications ("These events indicate you can . . .") rather than negative ones ("These events indicate you cannot . . ."); and in conditional terms ("Your strengths appear to be . . .") rather than in absolute ones ("Your strengths are . . ."). Effective use of this role can facilitate the counseling relationship and help your client understand possible explanations for his or her behaviors and gain insight or a deeper and better understanding of self. Counselors who believe that interpretations should only emanate from the client—and not the counselor—will not employ this type of response.

Types of Evaluating or Interpreting Responses

The evaluating or interpreting role is typically employed in one of the following ways.

1. *Associating, integrating, or summarizing a variety of factors.* During the counseling process a considerable amount of personal information about clients and their concerns is normally obtained. This information may have been presented by clients, derived from psychometric testing, given by significant others, or acquired from individuals who made the referral. This response should help clients become more aware of their personal experiences, and the possible meanings of, or the relationships among, these experiences. Effective responses may require you to identify related material, analyze, synthesize, and integrate this information into a coherent picture, then highlight themes, convey impressions, and provide appropriate feedback to your clients.

An effective integration or summarization response should pay careful attention to the major affective and cognitive themes presented by the client (Okun, 1997) and may associate similar material, identify connections among seemingly unrelated information, or point out discrepancies among this matter (Brammer, Shostrum, & Abrego, 1989). Associating or integrating material can serve as a summarization process to regulate the pace of the interview, give the session a clearer focus, or review the progress of the counseling (Cormier & Cormier, 1991).

2. *Reframing or redefining the client's perspective.* Interpretations of behavior frequently involve reframing or redefining your clients' experiences from a different perspective. This response, which may relabel or rename these experiences, offers a way for clients to change how they view various phenomena (Ivey, 1994). By offering another frame of reference your clients can obtain alternative meanings about their experiences, view themselves and their concerns in other ways, gain a better understanding of their problems or situations, and become more aware of their strengths and resources as important ingredients in resolving these concerns.

This reframing of your client's experience is based on your own personal and theoretical orientation. Your responses can vary in direction and intensity by stating specific experiences in different ways or offering much more complex meanings for these same experiences. For example, you may relabel your client's self-reported "forgetful" behaviors as "pre-occupied," or you may decide on a more profound response and relabel these same "forgetful" behaviors as an indication of your client's use of avoidance as a poor coping strategy.

3. *Interpreting reasons for the client's experiences.* In addition to giving responses that integrate and summarize various experiences, or redefine and relabel them, you may want to explain or give some reasons why your client has had certain experiences or behaves in a certain manner (Patterson & Welfel, 1994). You may want to provide explanations that establish causal relationships among factors not previously connected by the client. This response often links your client's experiences to some psychological quality or attribute sometimes explained in terms of a particular personality or counseling theory (Brammer & MacDonald, 1996; Clark, 1995; Johnson, 1997). For example, a client's poor interpersonal skills may be linked to

poor developmental tasks attainment, an overprotective family atmosphere, or the desire to be well-liked and admired by everyone.

Illustrations of Different Types of Evaluating or Interpreting Responses

The examples below portray the use of evaluating or interpreting responses. Each example assumes that counseling has progressed for some time.

■   *Client 1, a 25-year-old woman:*   I still can't believe I'm divorced. I don't have anyone to share my life with now. And I have to start the dating scene all over again. I don't know what I'm going to do!

   1. *Associating, integrating, or summarizing a variety of factors:* As we've discussed your recent divorce these last few sessions, I think I've been hearing some different messages. You've talked about how relieved you are about the divorce and how anxious you are to begin life all over. What I also hear is that the future is becoming scary for you now that you are alone. I have a hunch that the idea of meeting new people, especially men, is not as exciting as you say it is—your voice even becomes less forceful when you talk about it.

   2. *Reframing or redefining the client's perspective:* I can understand your feelings of being lost without having a husband, but I suspect that you're selling yourself short. During the times we've met, you've reflected on how you were the one who really had to make the decisions in your marriage. Also, your job seems to allow you to support yourself comfortably. In terms of meeting men, you appear to be active in many ways—and those probably offer you opportunities that you may not be aware of.

   3. *Interpreting reasons for the client's experiences:* With the points you've just made and other insights you've shared before, I have the feeling you are engaging in a lot of negative self-talk. I sense you are still blaming yourself for the divorce. All the other problems of adjusting, such as living alone and meeting men, are probably also scary because you believe you will fail there as well.

■   *Client 2, a middle-aged woman:*   I have a difficult problem. I went back to work after being home for many years. Now I'm working and making much more money than my husband, and it's tearing him apart. I don't know what to do.

   1. *Associating, integrating, or summarizing a variety of factors:* From the tone of your voice, I have a feeling that you are enjoying some of your husband's discomfort. At the same time, you apparently want to alleviate the tension your job is causing in this relationship and restore harmony to your marriage. To do that, you will probably need to resolve your feelings about your work as well as your relationship with your husband.

   2. *Reframing or redefining the client's perspective:* Your concern for your husband seems to be interfering with your ability to deal with this problem. Yet, you appear gentle in many ways; you might be more compassionate towards your husband, so he feels he's still important to you. You've said your husband has always supported you before this. I suspect that if you explain to him why you enjoy this job, he might

support you on this issue as well. I also suspect if you listen to him, this issue could be used in a way to deepen your marriage.

3. *Interpreting reasons for the client's experiences:* It sounds like your husband's role as provider has been taken away from him. Your career has apparently progressed very rapidly, while his has seemingly reached a plateau. I have a hunch that your responses to his behavior may be reinforcing his feelings of inadequacy.

Levels of Evaluating or Interpreting Responses

This role may also be used with different degrees of effectiveness. These responses are most effectively used after you have obtained considerable data about your client, had a chance to integrate this information, and the client has indicated some readiness for an evaluative or an interpretive response. When using this role it is usually desirable to use relatively simple language, to employ ideas and concepts close to the understanding expressed by your client, and to keep your interpretations very general or tentative. Use positive terms to describe the issue, highlight those factors that your client can control, and employ the role when your client has ample time left in the interview to integrate and respond to these evaluative responses.

If you employ this role in the early stages of counseling you may be basing your interpretation on unclear connections, and if you use the role too frequently you can foster a dependency relationship. The role is used inappropriately—by any counselor—when it comes into play too early, when it is based on unclear connections, when the interpretation of the data is not theoretically sound, or when the counselor's body language or tone conveys uncertainty. When used ineffectively, the evaluating or interpreting role puts the client in a defensive posture and discourages clients from revealing more about themselves. Its use can be ranked on the following four-point scale:

Level 1: Poor use of the role. The counselor is ineffective in using this role when he or she interprets and evaluates data incorrectly, integrates factual materials based on poor logical connections, reframes things inappropriately, or uses poor clinical judgment. The role is also employed ineffectively when the counselor is insensitive to the client's concerns, uses negative terms, or uses the role too early in the counseling process.

Level 2: Mediocre use of the role. The counselor is somewhat ineffective in using this role when connections among various data are offered in a vague way, the relevant data is interpreted or evaluated only partially, or the evaluation is superficial. The role is also used in a mediocre way when the counselor uses semi-negative phrases, offers perspectives divergent from the client's frame of reference, or employs the role at inopportune times.

Level 3: Good use of the role. The counselor is effective in the use of this role when disparate data phenomena are associated or evaluated appropriately and logically, when reframing the issues offers a sound perspective, and when clients can understand the connection between their experiences and the psychological interpretation. The role is also used in an effective way when the counselor uses positive phrases, offers perspectives convergent with the client's frame of reference, and when the role is employed at a suitable and opportune time.

Level 4: Excellent use of the role. The counselor is most effective in using this role when he or she interprets or evaluates data skillfully, makes corrections adroitly, redefines the issue in ways that foster growth, and offers very relevant psychological interpretations. The role is also used in a very effective way when the counselor stresses positive aspects, offers perspectives convergent with the client's frame of reference, and employs the role at a timely point in the counseling relationship.

Illustrations of Different Levels of Evaluating or Interpreting Responses

To give you practice discerning the types and levels of responses, three examples are given below. Each client statement is followed by three responses. Each response has been identified by type and rated using the Level-of-Response Scale, and the reasons for assigning these ratings are reported. Examine each of these examples to see if you agree with the ratings and the reasons stated. If you do not agree with these assessments, you may have read one or more of these statements with another intonation than the person who rated them. Because the paraverbal aspects of the client's statement and the counselor's responses are never adequately indicated by the printed word, any response may be rated differently depending on how it is heard. It is very important that you give reasons for your ratings so that you can discuss any differences in class with your supervisor and classmates.

■   *Client 1, a 30-year-old man:*   I can't seem to get things organized. I don't finish any of my projects at work—at least the way I want to finish them. And things at home aren't any better—my children don't always do what I want them to do. And my friends tell me I'm too bossy.

Responses	*Ratings and Reasons*
1. You seem to have a strong need to have things highly organized and be in control in every situation. Yet, you seem to finish your work, and apparently your children and friends liketo be with you.	3.0–3.5 Counselor summarizes the client's previous statements.
2. Being highly organized is an attribute you seem to cherish. Let's see how this desire can mesh with your desire to work with others who do not have this same attribute.	3.0–3.5 Counselor offers a different frame of reference for the client's concern.
3. Wanting to be in control of things is a normal human need. When that need interferes with the needs of others—	3.0–3.5 Counselor suggests a cause of the client's concern.

perhaps your colleagues, children, or friends—it seems to cause you problems.

■ *Client 2, a college sophomore:* I don't know where I am really headed. I'm always in some sort of trouble with my parents—they have high expectations for me and I don't always live up to them.

Responses	Ratings and Reasons
1. Steve, you say you've always apparently disappointed your parents by being socially focused than academically oriented; and you seem to imply that a lot of your resentment is justified because you feel you are not accepted for being yourself.	3.0–3.5 Counselor connects and summarizes the client's experiences.
2. I have a hunch that you have very high expectations for yourself also. And your primary concern might be living up to your own self-image.	3.0–3.5 Counselor reframes the client's concerns.
3. It seems that you are struggling with your own independence. I wonder if the real conflict is caused by you wanting to go in a direction that's different from your parents.	3.0–3.5 Counselor offers some reasons for the client's problems.

■ *Client 3, a 24-year-old woman:* I never seem to be successful in holding a job. I've never had one that lasted more than six months. Everything I do seems to end up in failure.

Responses	Ratings and Reasons
1. You seem to have had the same problem with each of your former employers. Isn't it fair to say you left each job because you had a dispute with your employer?	3.0–3.5 Counselor integrates and summarizes the client's behaviors.
2. Finding the right occupation is difficult for many people. I have a hunch that your dissatisfaction would be alleviated by some effective career counseling.	2.5–3.0 Counselor tries to define the issue as a vocational counseling concern.
3. I suspect that you have a problem dealing with all authority figures in your life, and right now the problem appears most evident at work.	3.0–3.5 Counselor makes a clinical judgment and interprets the client's experiences.

Practice Evaluating and Interpreting Exercises: "How Do I Tell the Client 'These Data Have the Following Meanings'?"

The following set of exercises is provided to help you develop further your evaluating and interpreting communication skills. In each case assume that the counselor and the client have had considerable interaction. As you do these exercises remember that some of your clients may have a cultural background that is different from yours.

Discrimination exercises.   For each excerpt given below, identify the feeling and the content underlying the client's statement. Then state the *type* of response illustrated, and indicate the appropriateness of the response by rating the *level* of the response. Share the reasons for your ratings with your classmates and your supervisor. You may find that one or more of your classmates read the excerpts differently from you and consequently gave a higher or lower rating to the response.

■   *Client 1, a 19-year-old college student:*   I constantly do things only to gain the approval of others. It seems like I need this praise more than anything else.

Underlying message: _____

Responses	*Ratings and Reasons*
1. You appear to have a lot of strengths. During our meetings you mentioned many things you do that no one appears to know about. Is that because you need to praise yourself?	1. _____
2. Seeking approval from others is normal. We all need approval periodically, particularly from those we love and respect. Your constant quest, however, seems to reveal some unmet needs.	2. _____
3. You mentioned several instances in our last session when you were able to function without this praise. I have a hunch that you only seek it from those who are significant or important to you.	3. _____

■   *Client 2, a 15-year-old student:*   I just don't understand my parents. Sometimes they want to know everything I'm doing and thinking. And other times they don't seem to care about what I do or what I think.

Underlying message: _____

Responses	*Ratings and Reasons*
1. This seems to be a recent problem, and from the little you said, for your	1. _____

brother and sister as well. It seems that
the problem has become a serious one
since your parents started a new business venture.

2. Understanding your parents is sometimes very hard. At times you may feel
fairly independent, and at other times
rather dependent on them. That's not
at all unusual.

2. _____

3. You really want to be your own person.
ou respect your parents, but something has caused a breakdown in your
dialogue with them. I have a hunch
that we can improve this situation if
we work on your communication skills.

3. _____

■ **Client 3, a high school senior:** My grades are terrible. I used to be great
in school, but lately I don't seem to care. When I try to study my mind wanders, and I
can't focus on my work.

Underlying message: _____

Responses

1. You've always seemed to have the
desire to do absolutely great in school.
And I wonder if you are now setting
standards you cannot meet.

Ratings and Reasons

1. _____

2. I suspect something happened recently
to affect your grades. You've been on the
honor roll for three years. I have a
hunch it's related to your social life.

2. _____

3. And you are concerned that if you
keep wandering, you'll be wandering
through these halls again next year.
The problem seems to have started
right after you were turned down by
your father's alma mater. That was
disappointing for both of you.

3. _____

■ **Client 4, a 30-year-old man:** I can't seem to say no to anyone. If someone asks me to do something, I'll do it, even though I don't want to. I like myself, but I
don't like that part of me that is a gofer for everybody else.

Underlying message: _____

Responses

1. It's important for you to be liked. That's a learned behavior. You have learned to service everyone, regardless of the inconvenience that it causes you.

2. From what you've said, you appear to like yourself and seem to a have a lot of friends. You apparently know when you want to do something for someone and when someone is taking advantage of you. You appear very aware of things.

3. Yet last week you told me about an incident when you didn't go for a cup of coffee for someone. I suspect there is a pattern to when you are a gofer and when you are not.

Ratings and Reasons

1. _____

2. _____

3. _____

■ *Client 5, an 18-year-old woman:* I smoke too much and so do all my friends. I've tried to stop. I know it's not good for my health, but I do enjoy smoking and so do my friends.

Underlying message: _____

Responses

1. From the little you have told me about yourself, you seem to be able to accomplish just about anything else you've tried. And you appear to have done many things your peers have not. I wonder if you really want to stop?

2. You also told me that you do not smoke at work or in your parents' home. I have a hunch that you could stop, but you are afraid of what your friends would say.

3. Your smoking is apparently a learned behavior. It's possible that it gets reinforced by the approval you obtain from others and the periodic sense of relaxation you get from inhaling.

Ratings and Reasons

1. _____

2. _____

3. _____

■ *Client 6, a 45-year-old man:* I lost my oldest daughter three years ago. She was hit by a drunk driver and was on the critical list in the hospital for five days before she died. It was hard to accept her loss. I know if I hadn't given her permission to go out that night, she would still be with us.

Underlying message: _____

Responses	Ratings and Reasons
1. Grieving is normally a long process that involves several phases. You've acknowledged the loss of your daughter, but I suspect you still have to get over being angry at yourself. It will probably take a long time for you to move through this process.	1. _____
2. You seem to have some ambivalent feelings about the events that occurred before her death. While you feel guilty, you also said that she was so anxious to go out, you could not have kept her home.	2. _____
3. From what you tell me, you have a lot to be proud of. All your children, including your oldest daughter, were good students and admired by both students and teachers. You've done a fine job as a parent, and you will, I'm sure, continue to do so.	3. _____

■ *Client 7, a 55-year-old man:* My wife and I seem to have little in common. For years we were busy raising a family, but now that the children are all young adults we should have time for one another again.

Underlying message: _____

Responses	Ratings and Reasons
1. The problems in your marriage seem to have occurred after the children no longer required your care. It sounds like your family was extremely child centered. That focus has now disappeared, and your relationship needs to be reestablished on a new plateau.	1. _____
2. From what you told me in our last meeting, the burden of raising your family was mostly on your wife. You said you were busy earning money to support them and had little time left over. It appears that you want to make that time up and adjust to a new role.	2. _____

3. When you were raising your family,
   you apparently did what you thought
   you had to do. Now, looking back, you
   have some regrets, and are starting to
   feel some guilt. I wonder if you really
   want to do that?

3. _____

■ *Client 8, an 18-year-old high school senior:* My boyfriend, John, keeps hinting about getting married. We've been going out, more or less steady, for a couple of years. I don't want to hurt him, but I don't know what I want to do.

Underlying message: _____

Responses

1. From what you have said to me,
   you've been accepted at State College
   and your parents would like you to go
   there. I wonder if you also have some
   anxiety related to leaving home and
   losing contact with your friends.

2. From what you told me I gather that
   you're normally quite determined and
   sure about most things in your life.
   What you want, you usually go for
   and get. It sounds to me like you
   might know what you want to do in
   this case.

3. Choices are sometimes hard to make.
   It sounds like you are fond of John,
   and you don't want to hurt him.
   That's a classical sort of conflict—it
   can cause a lot of anxiety and stress in
   your life.

Ratings and Reasons

1. _____

2. _____

3. _____

■ *Client 9, a 20-year-old college sophomore:* I don't know what I really want to do when I finish school. I enjoy my English, history, and philosophy courses, but they don't lead to a specific occupation. I have several friends who are majoring in accounting. Their future is fairly well set, but mine . . ..

Underlying message: _____

Responses

1. You appear concerned because business majors seem to have a definite
   career orientation while you do not.
   While it's normal to be a bit anxious,

Ratings and Reasons

1. _____

your choice appears to be a good fit for you. And I have a hunch that you would not like accounting.

2. It's not at all unusual for college sophomores to be unsure about an outlet for their talents. Your vocational development has apparently progressed quite nicely so far. You've decided to go to college, major in one of the liberal arts, and master your coursework. You do need to do some fine-tuning about further choices.

2. _____

3. From what you have said, you feel there is pressure from home to identify a vocational goal. That's understandable, and we can start to do that. But there are other things you mentioned that suggest there may be other problems at home as well.

3. _____

■ *Client 10, a 16-year-old high school student:* My father is really upset. He wants me to be on the football team. He thinks it will help me get into a good college. I hate that idea. I never liked that sport.

Underlying message: _____

Responses

Ratings and Reasons

1. Let's focus on your assets for getting into college for the moment and not think about pressure from home. Your grades appear to be quite good, you're a talented violin player, and you've been active in a number of school activities. Your chances of getting into a good school without playing football seem to be excellent.

1. _____

2. Last week when you mentioned colleges your father is interested in, they all appeared to have Division I football teams and outstanding orchestras. I gather that you'd like to go to one of these schools and please your Dad. But you are determined not to give in on the football issue.

2. _____

3. I suspect there is a lot more to your   3. _____
   disagreement with your Dad than foot-
   ball. It's quite normal for individuals to
   have different interests than their
   parents. But your differences seem
   more intense than most students.

Communication exercises.   For each of the following client statements, make two different high-level evaluating or interpreting responses.

■   *Client 11, a high school junior:*   My father spends most of his time on the sofa. He usually isn't really bombed—he's just slightly drunk. He's not mean or nasty, but he is really an embarrassment. I can't bring any friends into the house. I don't know what to do.

■   *Client 12, a 13-year-old student:*   I do just about everything with a group of girls in my class. There's one girl who is not part of the group; she never was. My friends make fun of her because she doesn't belong. She doesn't fit in. They tease her, make fun of her, or ignore her. Sometimes she reacts very strongly. I feel sorry for her. I'd like to get to know her better, but my friends would get on me if I did.

■   *Client 13, a college junior:*   I think I'm going to fail out of college. I've been able to keep up so far, but the work seems to be piling up. I don't know what to do.

■   *Client 14, a 28-year-old man:*   I just found out that my wife is pregnant. My job doesn't pay very much. I'd like to find another job so I can support my family better.

■   *Client 15, a 20-year-old:*   I think a lot about death. My father died last year. He was only forty-six. It seems that a lot of people die young and leave families that need support. Death seems so unfair and even unnatural.

■   *Client 16, a 45-year-old man:*   I'm fed up. I have another new boss. She's the fourth one in six years. None of them was any good. I don't know how they got their jobs, but my sixteen years of experience on the job tells me that many supervisors get promoted beyond their competence.

■   *Client 17, a 35-year-old woman:*   I should never have gotten married. My mother said that wives are live-in maids. The children demand this and demand that, and my husband never takes a stand. Oh, I wish I knew what to do.

■   *Client 18, a 16-year-old student:*   All my friends think I'm strange just because I don't go along and do the same things they do. I really don't enjoy going to ball games or to the movies that much. I go, and it's okay, but I'd rather spend my time doing other things.

■   *Client 19, a 50-year-old woman:*   I don't know what to do with myself now that my kids are grown and gone. Nothing interests me anymore. I don't have the energy or the enthusiasm I used to have. I wish I could find something to do with my time.

■   *Client 20, a 25-year-old college graduate:*   My wife and I disagree about a family. I would like to have her stop work and have a family. She wants to continue with her job and save some more money. The money's nice, but I know I'll get another raise soon, and with her salary there's not too much left after taxes anyway.

Solo exercises: Practice all the role communication skills in a triad. Try to conduct a 20-minute mini counseling session. Each counselor-in-training should take turns being the counselor, the client, and the supervisor. Be constructively critical of your classmates' responses.

SUMMARY

The advanced role communication skills presented in this chapter have required your active participation. After reading about the advising, motivating, and evaluating responses and completing the structured exercises, you should have developed a good understanding of these skills. You should be able to specify the types of responses used in these roles, discuss the differences among higher- and lower-level responses, and use these skills in an effective manner in your counseling practice.

The advising role is employed when the counselor wants to help a client think about a solution to a problem, reflect on an idea offered for possible adoption, plan a course of action, or develop a list of options. The role is also applicable when the counselor wants to make a referral or probe in order to bring any previously known advice into the discussion. High-level responses tactfully encourage the client to evaluate and feel involved in any decision-making process. This role is used sparingly and only after a good relationship has been established.

The motivating or prescribing role is employed when the counselor uses rather directive and forceful comments to initiate movement in the counseling process. The following types of responses are typically used in this role: focusing on critical issues, setting goals, confronting, and using self-disclosures. High-level responses are related to clients' readiness for this type of response; they address the major concerns raised by clients, offer different ways for clients to examine their situations, and encourage clients to become more aware of themselves. This role must be used with caution because it can put clients on the defensive or foster dependency. It is recommended that you use a warm and friendly tone when making responses in this role.

The evaluating or interpreting role is used when the counselor calls upon his or her professional knowledge of human behavior to make clinical judgments and interpret, analyze, and integrate various pieces of information. Responses of this sort typically include integrating or summarizing factors, reframing or redefining the client's perspective, and interpreting complex data. High-level responses require the counselor to have a solid knowledge of human behavior and sufficient information about the client, and call for a degree of readiness on the part of the client. In this role the counselor must take a very active and judgmental stance in the relationship. To avoid a dependency relationship and to minimize defensive reactions, it is recommended that the responses be expressed in conditional language such as "It seems possible that . . ." or "Your strengths appear to be . . .".

In addition to reading the chapter and practicing the exercises, you will require considerable clinical practice and critical feedback from your professional peers and supervisors to master these skills. Because these advanced skills are used in many different intervention strategies and approaches, it is important for you to master them as soon as possible.

REFERENCES

Benjamin, A. (1987). *The helping interview* (4th ed.). Boston: Houghton Mifflin.

Brammer, L. M., & MacDonald, G. (1996). *The helping relationship: Process and skills* (6th ed.). Boston: Allyn & Bacon.

Brammer, L. M., Shostrum, E. L., & Abrego, P. J. (1989). *Therapeutic psychology: Fundamentals of counseling and psychology* (5th ed.). Englewood Cliffs, NJ: Prentice Hall.

Clark, A. J. (1995). An examination of the technique of interpretation in counseling. *Journal of Counseling and Development 73*, 483–489.

Cormier, W. H., & Cormier, L. S. (1991). *Interviewing strategies for helpers: Fundamental skills and cognitive behavioral interventions* (3rd ed.). Pacific Grove, CA: Brooks/Cole.

Egan, G. (1994). *The skilled helper: A problem-management approach to helping* (5th ed.). Pacific Grove, CA: Brooks/Cole.

Epstein, L. (1985). *Talking and listening: A guide to the helping interview.* St. Louis, MO: Times/Mirror.

Evans, D. R., Hearn, M. T., Uhlemann, M. R., & Ivey, A. E. (1993). *Essential interviewing: A programmed approach to effective communication* (4th ed.). Pacific Grove, CA: Brooks/Cole.

Hackney, H., & Cormier, L. S. (1994). *Counseling strategies and interventions* (4th ed.). Boston: Allyn & Bacon.

Ivey, A. E. (1994). *Intentional interviewing and counseling: Facilitating client growth in a multicultural society* (3rd ed.). Pacific Grove, CA: Brooks/Cole.

Johnson, D. W. (1997). *Reaching out: Interpersonal effectiveness and self-actualization* (6th ed.). Boston: Allyn & Bacon.

Moursund, J. (1990). *The process of counseling* (2nd ed.). Englewood Cliffs, NJ: Prentice Hall.

Okun, B. F. (1997). *Effective helping: Interviewing and counseling techniques* (5th ed.). Pacific Grove, CA: Brooks/Cole.

Patterson, L. D., & Welfel, E. R. (1994). *The counseling process* (4th ed.). Pacific Grove, CA: Brooks/Cole.

10 Problem-Solving Skills

INTRODUCTION

The purpose of this chapter is to provide you with the opportunity to gain experience with the major intervention strategies outlined and explained in Part 2 of the text. First, several factors are discussed that are important to observe when you use the problem-solving role. Second, the relationship between an identified counseling goal and the type of problem-solving response that may be employed is reviewed. Third, several examples illustrating the use of the problem-solving role in the counseling process are presented. Finally, a number of simulated cases are provided to enable you to practice using your problem-solving skills. After studying this chapter you should be able to:

- Describe several factors that are important in using any intervention strategy.
- Discuss techniques involved in cognitively, affectively, and behaviorally focused intervention strategies.
- Identify the types of intervention strategies appropriate for different kinds of counseling goals.
- Indicate how high-level or effective problem-solving responses differ from low-level or ineffective responses in these interventions.
- Outline the specific details you would consider before deciding on an intervention strategy.

THE PROBLEM-SOLVING ROLE

The problem-solving role occurs when you employ specific counseling strategies and intervention techniques to help your client learn to function more effectively. The entire counseling process is aimed at resolving your client's concern and improving your client's well-being. However, the major thrust of this process to bring about desired change is when a particular counseling strategy is applied. The activities completed in the three previous phases helped both you and your client prepare for this important phase; and the successful implementation of any strategy depends on how well these stages have

271

progressed. Both of you will be ready to work on a problem solution after you have established a solid working relationship, explored important client concerns, and agreed to the direction the counseling process should take (Epstein, 1985; Parsons & Wicks, 1994).

Problem-Solving Strategies: Factors to Remember

Problem-solving interventions include a variety of cognitively oriented, affectively oriented, and behaviorally oriented strategies. In planning a counseling strategy it is important to consider the environment where the counseling takes place and the time available. In many schools and other institutional settings, counselors emphasize cognitive and behavior interventions; and because of time and size of case loads, they tend to use short-term strategies. Your choice of a counseling strategy also depends on your understanding of the problem and the goals you and your client have agreed upon. The relationship between an identified counseling goal and specific counseling strategies is discussed in the next section of this chapter. Furthermore, your knowledge and skill in using various strategies needs to be experientially learned and practiced thoroughly under professional supervision. The following paragraphs highlight several important factors to keep in mind as you learn to apply these skills and strategies.

Interventions may require specific instruction.   The communication skills you studied and practiced in the previous chapters are all used in the implementation stage of counseling, and your competent use of these skills will continue to facilitate client growth and enhance your client's effectiveness. In addition, many intervention strategies require you to provide specific instruction to your client indicating the concrete actions you want taken (Ivey, Ivey, & Simek-Morgan, 1997). Two situations where you must provide clear instructions are role-playing activities and homework assignments. Other situations occur, for example, when you use Gestalt techniques or any of the behavioral methods. In these directives, you consciously use your communication skills to tell your client what to do, what role to play, or what action to follow (Epstein, 1985). Your effectiveness in giving these assignments can be limited if you give instructions tentatively or give too many directives at the same time. When you give instructions in a provisional or tentative manner you run the risk of indicating that compliance is not required, and your client may choose not to follow them. When you offer too many instructions at the same time your client may feel overwhelmed and not follow any of them. Instructions should be given when they help your client accomplish something that is an important part of an overall counseling strategy and when you are reasonably sure your client has the ability, skills, and available resources to implement the instructions. The instructional task has to be meaningful to your client's frame of reference and stated as plainly and clearly as possible (Cormier & Cormier, 1991; Epstein, 1985).

Involve your client in strategy selection.   Involve your client in the selection of a strategy as much as you possibly can (Cormier & Cormier, 1991; Okun, 1997). This does not mean that the overall strategy should be decided by your client. However, your

client can be provided with the rationale for a counseling plan and informed about the general direction, the types of activities, and the possible outcomes of the program you expect to implement (Epstein, 1985). Helping your client see the benefits of a strategy, and any interventions you plan to use, increases the likelihood that your instructions will be followed. Even when your client is involved in choosing a strategy, he or she will not be aware of all the details and techniques you might be considering, and you will have to provide instruction on these techniques. The possibility of dependency can also be lessened when your client feels some responsibility for the actions taken (Benjamin, 1987). Whenever possible, consider offering your client the option of using different techniques or having input into when to finish a particular assignment in order to enhance this sense of responsibility. Nevertheless, remember you have the professional knowledge and skills to facilitate growth and thus the ultimate responsibility to decide on what strategy to employ and when to use a particular technique.

Expect resistance.

When you apply a counseling strategy you should expect to encounter some resistance (Meier & Davis, 1997). There are several reasons why your client may have difficulty in carrying out your strategy or your instructions. First, anything new your client is asked to do may feel awkward, unfamiliar, and difficult to perform. Second, your client may fear the risk of failure, or looking stupid, and some emotional blockage may be present. Third, any meaningful change will probably require some internal reorganization; your client will have to learn and experience—or relearn and reexperience—and incorporate into his or her lifestyle some new ways to think, feel, or behave. Fourth, your client's typical way of thinking, feeling, or behaving may be stamped in and have built-in reinforcements; any change can reduce or threaten these associated rewards. Finally, you may discover your implementation was premature and your client, who you thought was committed to a particular objective, is not as committed to the goal as you believed (Egan, 1994). Whatever the cause of your client's resistance, it normally takes some time to overcome. Specific suggestions for helping you deal with your client's resistance were outlined in Chapter 3. If you have a client who is overly critical of self, be careful not to reinforce this discouragement. While working with resistance, maintain your patience and support and continue to guide your client through the counseling process (Moursund, 1990).

Obtain supervision.

As a counselor-in-training you may not be comfortable in applying several of the approaches outlined in the textbook or discussed in your classes. You may feel pressure to do something, but you may be unsure of yourself; or you may not know what to do. You may be concerned that you will give instructions vaguely or incorrectly or that you will compound your client's problem because you are not an expert in a particular intervention or technique. If you think the strategy is worthwhile, and you believe the intervention will advance your client's progress, you should apply the strategy under professional supervision. Okun (1997) recommends that you let your client know any time you are trying out a new method or technique.

You may want to combine strategies.

When you want to help your client accomplish something, you may think about using one particular strategy alone or combining that strategy with methods and techniques from another strategy. Cormier and

Cormier (1991) indicate that intervention strategies are very often used in an integrated manner. Nevertheless, as a beginning counselor do not be in a great hurry to combine strategies. Initially, consider using one strategy by itself and stay with that approach until you master that skill. As you practice these strategies, interventions, and techniques—under proper supervision—you will slowly gain experience and learn how to incorporate methods and techniques from several approaches into an overall counseling plan.

Plan to monitor your progress.   Plan to continually monitor the usefulness and the effectiveness of any applied strategy. Even though all strategies take time to work, and they typically progress in an uneven and hesitant fashion, you can obtain some indications of your effectiveness by careful observation of yourself and your client or by obtaining feedback from significant others. Okun (1997) maintains that behavior changes provide the best criteria for evaluation because they are reflective of cognitive and affective changes as well. One measure of your effectiveness is how adequately you implement the techniques you plan to use and how successfully your client is responding to your efforts. Other indications of positive growth may be observed by noting such changes in your client as appearance, spontaneity, frequency of positive self-reports, and the degree or depth of involvement with others. Feedback about your client may also be obtained from other significant persons in your client's life such as a teacher, a parent, a spouse, a peer, or a friend. As a counselor-in-training your supervisor will help you review your progress and discuss any changes in your client that may have occurred. Your continual evaluation during this implementation stage may suggest your strategy or technique is not working. If this is the case, you may need to reexamine the counseling goal and revise it if necessary, or plan to use another strategy or technique.

Anticipate termination.   During the implementation of the problem-solving role, anticipate the termination process as well as the possibility of a premature termination. As indicated in Chapter 3, three interrelated activities occur at the termination stage: summarizing and evaluating the counseling process; exploring other concerns that may need attention; and developing a plan to ensure that any changes accomplished are maintained. Positive actions taken during implementation can help you plan for these closing activities. The careful observations you make while monitoring the implementation phase, and the feedback you receive from your peers and supervisor, can facilitate the summary process and alert you to other issues your client may have. In addition, resolving and dealing with your client's feeling of dependency is a major concern during the termination process (Okun, 1997). The willingness of your client to follow your instructions, the involvement that your client shows in selecting a strategy, and the way your client expresses resistance are indications of how he or she will manage dependency and how amenable he or she might be to formulating a follow-up plan.

Counseling can also be prematurely terminated during the implementation stage—either by your client or by you. For example, you may have a client who makes significant progress between sessions; the client reaches a desired goal after your last session, does not feel the need to see you again, and terminates without telling you. This situation may be prevented by preparing your client ahead of time for the concluding process. If your preparation is inadequate, you can remedy this complication by contacting your client as part of a follow-up procedure and settling for a brief conclusion. On the other hand you may have a client who terminates because he or she felt that adequate progress was not being made. Your continual and careful monitoring of the intervention process and feedback from your supervisor can alert you to the probability of this untimely event and prepare you to take appropriate action. Another one of your clients may terminate because of factors outside of his or her control, such as illness, transfer, or lack of financial resources. In any case, contact your client to discover the reasons for the termination and, whenever possible, assist your client in making other plans for help. Your relationship can also end prematurely because of factors related to you. You may have been transferred, changed jobs, have time constraints, felt you could not handle the problem, or have other reasons. When you initiate the termination prematurely, plan to refer your client to another professional counselor as soon as you become aware of any circumstance that prevents you from completing the closure process.

Types of Problem-Solving Responses

The problem-solving role requires you to implement a counseling strategy that you believe will help your client reach a particular goal. A detailed description of each of the major cognitively focused, affectively focused, and behaviorally focused strategies was presented in Chapters 4, 5, and 6. You may wish to reread these chapters to refresh your memory and recall the methodologies and techniques involved in each approach. This section discusses how the selection of a particular counseling goal can be related to each of these counseling strategies.

Cognitively focused interventions.
Cognitively focused intervention strategies are based on the premise that your clients are rational, logical, thinking individuals whose functioning may be impaired by their lack of appropriate factual information, difficulty in making sound decisions, poor deductive thinking processes, or inadequate inductive reasoning. When your goal is to help your client overcome any one of these concerns, consider using a cognitively focused strategy for your overall counseling plan. The specific interventions and techniques involved in these methods are outlined more fully in Chapter 4, and guidelines for the selection of each of these strategies are presented below.

You may have a client who needs help selecting an appropriate educational and vocational goal or one who wants your assistance in managing the learning process more successfully. Another one of your clients may wish to increase his self-knowledge by understanding the results of psychometric instruments. If one of these issues is the goal with a particular client, you may want to concentrate on helping your client obtain or retain relevant factual information.

At another time, you may have a client who needs your assistance in learning how to weigh different facts, choose among alternative courses of action, resolve internal conflicts, deal with frustrations, cope with various life problems, or overcome indecisiveness. If one of these is the agreed-upon counseling goal, you may focus your efforts on helping your client improve her decision-making skills or problem-solving procedures.

Another time, you may have a client who needs help understanding and overcoming unproductive or debilitating thought patterns. Your client may need encouragement to think more logically and develop more constructive and rational thinking processes. Another client may want your assistance in learning how to think analogously, inductively, or creatively. If one of these areas is your objective, you may wish to emphasize techniques that modify your client's deductive thinking methods or enrich his inductive reasoning processes.

Affectively focused interventions.

The concerns of some of your clients may be related to the affective domain, in which case you may wish to help them obtain a keener awareness of themselves, improve their ability to deal with their emotions, improve their feelings of self-worth, or gain better acceptance and appreciation of others. Affectively oriented counseling approaches ought to be considered when any of these goals is to be met. You may want to review each of these strategies and the more detailed explanation of the techniques in Chapter 5. Suggestions for the selection of each of these strategies are presented below.

Your client may need an outlet to discuss, examine, and investigate his feelings, thoughts, opinions, or experiences in an open, accepting atmosphere. When one of these matters is the focus of your counseling, encouraging your client to ventilate can be very worthwhile. In this process, fostering a warm, accepting climate where he can experience the freedom to discuss whatever is bothering him is essential.

You may occasionally have a client who has been unable to express a deeply felt emotion. A client who desires to be free of this burden requires a more complex intervention than pure ventilation. In this situation you need to focus on your client's inner self in order to encourage the release of any pent-up tensions, bring these emotional blockages into the open, and help your client purge himself of this restrictive feeling.

Another client may need your assistance to become more aware of herself and the factors that influence her behaviors. You may also consider an affectively oriented strategy when your primary emphasis is to help your client understand herself, her relationships to significant others, and the meaningfulness of her life experiences. Furthermore, another one of your clients may need help developing a more positive view of himself or his self-esteem. This requires you to move your client beyond the awareness and insight levels in order to facilitate the reorganization of internal self-structures. Achieving any of these goals ordinarily takes considerable time and can be accomplished by the skillful use of an affectively oriented strategy.

Performance-focused interventions.

Your clients may present concerns that are clearly related to their behaviors. They may want to learn a new behavior, increase the likelihood of an existing behavior, or eliminate or decrease the likelihood of a present behavior. When one of these issues is your client's objective, consider using one or more of the performance-oriented counseling strategies. These strategies are based on the principles of observational and simulated learning, contingency management, and classical conditioning. The major methodologies and techniques used in the performance-focused strategies are outlined in Chapter 6, and guidelines for their selection are presented briefly in the following paragraphs.

When you have a client who wants to learn a new behavior, consider using the principles of observational and simulated learning. The observational learning approach requires you to select a model to portray the desired behavior and then coach your client on how to carefully observe the targeted behavior. The simulated learning approach stipulates that you instruct your client on how to practice the desired behavior in a controlled environment. Specific techniques employed in this strategy include role playing, role reversal, and the dialogue process.

Your client may ask for your help to increase the likelihood of a specific behavior or to decrease the likelihood of an unwanted behavior. When one of these goals is desired, your strategy should be based on the principles of contingency management. You will need to instruct your client in these principles and then help your client develop a carefully thought-out plan to implement the steps involved in this approach. The client will need your assistance in selecting appropriate positive or negative reinforcers and in choosing procedures that may serve as positive or negative punishments.

You may have other clients who need support to overcome blockages that prevent them from performing some behavior. When this situation is present, consider using an intervention strategy based on the principles of classical conditioning. This will challenge you to develop a well-constructed plan to instruct your client on the process and carefully guide your client through the systematic procedures involved in this method. Specific classical conditioning interventions include stimulus control methods, relaxation and systematic desensitization procedures, assertiveness training, aversion techniques, flooding applications, and paradoxical intention approaches.

Levels of Problem-Solving Responses

As with other counselor communication roles, you can use this role with varying degrees of effectiveness. When you use the role effectively it indicates that you know your client, that you have satisfactorily progressed through the three previous stages of counseling, and that you have manifested some mastery of the strategy chosen. High-level responses are communicated using verbal, paraverbal, and nonverbal channels. As in all other roles, your attentive body language, good eye contact, and appropriate tonal quality are essential ingredients to effective communication. On the four-point scale, your use of the role can be rated according to the following criteria:

Level 1: Poor use of the role. You will be least effective when you attempt to assist your client and are unaware of your client's resistance; or when you try to use a strategy or technique that you know little about, or use it incorrectly or at an inopportune time. Low-level responses occur also when your overall strategy, general interventions, or specific techniques bear little relationship to your client's concern.

Level 2: Mediocre use of the role. You will be somewhat ineffective when you are only partially aware of any resistance; choose an appropriate strategy too soon in the relationship; introduce one that has little meaning to the client; pose the intervention very tentatively; present incomplete instructions; or provide too many directives at the same time.

Level 3: Good use of the role. You can be effective in using this role when you employ strategies, techniques, and instructions that are related to the counseling goal, suitable to deal with any resistance, theoretically sound and based on solid empirical knowledge, presented at a suitable time in the counseling process, and communicated in clear and concrete terms.

Level 4: Excellent use of the role. As a counselor you will be most effective when you use a strategy, technique, or instruction that helps your client accomplish his or her goals; that is meaningful to your client; that demonstrates your mastery of the intervention; and that offers clear, timely, and easy-to-follow instructions.

Illustrations of Different Levels of Problem-Solving Responses

The following three cases illustrate the use of the problem-solving role in the fourth stage of the counseling process. In each case, assume that a good working relationship has been established, issues related to the client's problem were explored, a counseling goal was decided on, and a strategy to reach that goal was selected. Each example presents critical information about the client obtained in an earlier stage and provides a rationale for the choice of the counseling strategy.

In each illustration the counselor's responses have been rated, and the reasons for these ratings are explained. Study each of these examples, examine the counselor's responses, and see if you agree with the ratings and the reasons stated. You may disagree with the assigned ratings; you could have read the responses with a different tonal quality than the person who rated them, or you may have another view about the intervention utilized. If you do disagree, indicate the reasons why you disagree, and be prepared to discuss the reasons for your ratings with your supervisor and classmates.

■   *Case 1:*   Sandy is 26 years old and single. For the past four years she has been employed as an office manager in a small firm owned by her family. She has a degree in speech pathology, but she never used her professional training. She came to see a counselor because she wants to change her job and find something she really likes. The counselor has established a relationship with Sandy and has given her the Strong Interest Inventory. Sandy appeared to have good feelings about herself and there were no specific behaviors that she wanted to change. The counselor felt that the presenting problem was her real concern and a career counseling approach stressing vocational information would be helpful. The following material was taken from the transcript of this case.

Excerpts and Responses	*Ratings and Reasons*
COUNSELOR: Sandy, you've had a chance to look over the results of the Strong Interest Inventory. I see that your interests tend to cluster in the social area.	2.7 This appears to be a good response; however, the interpretation of the Strong Interest Inventory is too limited.
CLIENT: Yes, I saw that. When I was studying speech pathology, I really enjoyed my classmates. We had a lot in common.	

COUNSELOR: You must have had a good reason not to pursue that as a career since you put so much time and effort into it.

3.5 Good use of the indirect form of the probe. Identifying the reason why a client did not pursue an occupation compatible with her interest is important.

CLIENT: Yes, I didn't for a couple of reasons. First, even though I did quite well, I found that I really didn't like the work involved. And second, there weren't many jobs available at that time.

COUNSELOR: So then you got a job in your family's business and entered the business management field.

2.8 This appears to be a reflection of previously stated information. It may encourage the client to elaborate on her interests.

CLIENT: Yes, but I don't want to stay in this line of work. Office work is not for me.

COUNSELOR: Do you see any relationship between your interests as measured by the Strong and any of your vocational experiences?

3.2 This probe can help the client see if her measured interests are supported by her personal experiences.

CLIENT: Yes, the Strong suggests that my interests are similar to people in the helping fields and dissimilar to those people in the enterprising areas. I guess that's a reflection of why I liked the people in speech pathology and dislike the work I'm doing now.

COUNSELOR: Your actual or manifest interests were reflected by the scores on the inventory.

3.0 Counselor reflects the content of the previous statement to reinforce this concept.

CLIENT: Yes, but while I enjoyed working with people in speech pathology, I didn't enjoy the actual work that much.

COUNSELOR: In your case, it sounds like we need to help you find an occupation that can meet your interest in the helping process and at the same time has tasks that you find more enjoyable.

3.5 Counselor outlines in very general terms the next steps involved in this career counseling situation.

CLIENT: That sounds great. How do we do this?

COUNSELOR: Are you familiar with the *Occupational OutlookHandbook*?

1.0 Introducing reference at this point is irrelevant.

CLIENT: No.

COUNSELOR: Well, at some point we may want to look at that. It's a government reference book that describes specific occupations and tries to forecast the need for people in these areas.

2.5 Counselor realizes the inappropriateness of the previous response and explains the general contents of the text for clarification.

CLIENT: I see . . .

COUNSELOR: Well, what I think we should do now is generate a list of potential occupations. Then we can cull from that list the occupations that may be more realistic for you.

3.0 Counselor moves the process along and encourages the client to think about possible choices she has in mind.

CLIENT: Well, I've often thought that I might want to become a special education teacher or a counselor or a psychologist.

COUNSELOR: Those are three possible choices. In addition to those we should use the Holland codes on the Strong to help us generate occupations that you might not have thought of.

2.4 Although this is often a good way to generate additional choices, the counselor never fully interpreted the Strong nor explained the meaning of the Holland codes.

CLIENT: I'm beginning to get a little excited about this. It feels good to finally begin to move to do something that I really would like.

■   *Case 2:*   Keith is a 21-year-old senior in college. He came to see the counselor to do some postcollege planning. His grades for the first three years were very good; however, this semester he has not kept up with his studies and his grades have been poor. Presently, Keith's social life seems to be more important than his schoolwork. He knows why he is having difficulties, but he is not really committed to changing his behavior. The counselor thought Keith could benefit from gaining insight into his personal goals and his current experiences. The following dialogue was taken from this phase of the counseling process.

Excerpts and Responses

COUNSELOR: Hi, Keith, how are you today?

Ratings and Reasons

3.0 Good opening.

CLIENT: Not too good. As I told you last time we met, I need to improve my grades.

COUNSELOR: You need to improve your grades.

3.0 Counselor makes good use of accent to attend to the client.

CLIENT: Yes, I was a solid A student and all of a sudden it seems my grades are going downhill.

COUNSELOR: And you're not sure why this happened.

3.0 Counselor uses indirect form of the probe to gain further information.

CLIENT: Well, I met a group that likes to party. They're fun to be with, but I'm not spending much time on the books.

COUNSELOR: It sounds like you want to do both—keep going to the parties, but at the same time keep up with your work.

3.5 Counselor uses a paraphrase to communicate back to the client the message that the counselor heard.

CLIENT: Yes, it's hard to do. I tried to stop the partying, but I just can't. I'm really mad at myself.

COUNSELOR: You tried to stop partying, but you can't. There is something there that's too attractive to give up.

3.5 Another good use of the paraphrase.

CLIENT: I don't know. . . . I guess there is.

COUNSELOR: You feel like you're being pulled in two directions. You want to stop partying, yet something draws you to it. You want to resume studying, but you don't have any energy left.

3.0 Counselor tries to clarify between the two alternatives to see if one has a stronger attraction.

CLIENT: I guess I'm trying to play to two different audiences—one wants one play and the other wants a different one. Which play should I pick?

COUNSELOR: It sounds like you're trying to meet two different needs that you have—one to interact with your peers and the other to master your work. And you want to satisfy both.

3.5 Counselor interprets the client's problem in terms of his needs and implies that both activities have meaning for the client.

CLIENT: Yes, I do. But when I'm trying to study, all it takes is one call from a friend and I run to the party.

COUNSELOR: I'm not sure I understand. Is it the call that makes you go, or is it a that you'll miss out on something?

4.0 Counselor uses the clarification response to see if the client takes some ownership of the problem.

CLIENT:　I guess it's me. I guess I can't blame the phone call or my friends.

COUNSELOR:　Well, there's nothing wrong with spending time with your friends, but it sounds like there's more to this issue.	2.5　This attentive response is fair; it goes over previously mentioned material.

CLIENT:　Oh, why is it that I can't seem to say no? Why do I give in to myself?

COUNSELOR:　And if we could find the answers to those questions, it would really help.	3.5　Very good paraphrase of the client's statement.

■　*Case 3:*　Arlene is a 23-year-old client who lives and works in the suburbs. She has friends who live downtown in a tall building, but she is very reluctant to visit them because she gets quite upset and panics whenever she approaches an elevator. Arlene is quite aware of her feelings and knows what is causing her extreme discomfort. She is determined to overcome her fear because she feels so handicapped. The counselor decided to use a systematic desensitization process, and in the following dialogue introduced this strategy to her.

Excerpts and Responses	*Ratings and Reasons*
CLIENT:　I can't stand it. Every time I go downtown to meet my friends, I have to ride the elevator to the seventeenth floor. I break into a cold sweat, and by the time I get there I feel faint and clammy all over.	
COUNSELOR:　This fear really causes you a lot of discomfort.	3.0　Good paraphrase of the client's statement.
CLIENT:　Yes, it sure does.	
COUNSELOR:　Perhaps I can help. I would like to know when you first experienced this fear.	4.0　Counselor provides support by offering to help and then probes for important information.
CLIENT:　It started about two years ago. I was downtown and alone in an elevator car when it suddenly stopped. It was five minutes before it started up again but it felt like five hours.	
COUNSELOR:　You didn't have this fear before this incident.	3.0　Counselor continues to probe for additional information.
CLIENT:　No, I was fine, except in one of those high-speed cars where they zoom you to the top floor in seconds.	

COUNSELOR: In the last two years you have experienced a lot of pain and anxiety when you ride an elevator.

2.8 Counselor summarizes previous statements. Response may be a bit redundant.

CLIENT: Yes; fortunately, I don't have to take an elevator to work. I walk up two flights of stairs—it's good exercise.

COUNSELOR: You could take an elevator at work, but you would rather avoid it and the pain that goes with it.

3.5 Counselor gives a good paraphrase of the client's message.

CLIENT: Well, I do feel some anxiety when I see my friends getting on, but I try to think of other things right away.

COUNSELOR: So even seeing other people walk into an elevator causes you some discomfort.

4.0 Counselor very wisely checks out the importance of this visual stimulus.

CLIENT: Yes, I guess it does.

COUNSELOR: How do you feel when we talk about elevators?

3.5 Counselor continues to probe to see if the anxiety is present when the stimulus is covert.

CLIENT: Right now I feel a bit uncomfortable, but I know I have to resolve this problem.

COUNSELOR: You are determined to overcome this fear.

4.0 Good paraphrase that also supports the client's resolve.

CLIENT: Yes, I really need to.

COUNSELOR: In addition to your daily encounter with the elevator at work, tell me about how often you may need or want to ride an elevator in a typical week.

3.5 Counselor continues to probe to obtain a more complete understanding of the problem.

CLIENT: I would say about two or three times. It's hard to do a lot of things. Can you tell me how long it will take me to overcome this fear?

COUNSELOR: It will take us some time. There is a systematic way to help you overcome this fear. First, I'll teach you a method to relax. Then we will slowly begin to talk about elevators. And eventually we should be able to have you visit your friends on the seventeenth floor as often as you like.

3.5 Counselor provides important information and briefly outlines the counseling process for the client.

Practice Problem-Solving Exercises:
"How Do I Say 'I Know I Can Help You;
This Is What You Need to Do Next'?"

Discrimination exercises.   The following excerpts from several different counseling cases are designed to help you develop your skills in applying a variety of intervention strategies. In each example information about the client that was obtained earlier
is summarized and the intervention strategy that was selected is stated. The exercises
illustrate the content, direction, and communication skills the counselor used in each
case. For each example, indicate whether or not the chosen intervention strategy, the
direction of the interview, and the specific techniques used are, in your view, appropriate. Then rate the effectiveness of each response. Please be prepared to share your opinions about the interventions used and the ratings of each response with your classmates.

■   *Case 1:*   John is a high school junior who came to see his counselor for assistance in career planning. He is in a college preparatory program and has a B+ average.
His test scores indicate that he has above average ability. His father is an electrician for a
large company and his mother is a homemaker. He is the oldest of three children. John is
active in several clubs and is well liked by his classmates. His teachers report that he is
currently doing very well in his classes. The counselor believed that the presenting problem was the main issue and that John could benefit from vocational exploration. The
following excerpt illustrates part of the intervention used by the counselor.

Excerpts and Responses	*Ratings and Reasons*

CLIENT: I don't know what I want to do
with my life. I mean, I don't know what
field or occupation I should go in for.

COUNSELOR: Picking out an occupation
seems to be a pretty scary thing, but you
don't need to make a decision now.
What you should do is begin the exploration process so you can learn more
about yourself and find out what kinds
occupations might meet your interests.

CLIENT: You mean I don't have to decide
today or even for a while? How can I
start this exploratory process?

COUNSELOR: First, we need to help you
get to know yourself better. Then we
should take a look at various occupations that seem like a possibility for
you. By this process we should be able
to eliminate many occupations that are
of no interest to you and identify
several that you might like to consider.

CLIENT: It sounds like a time-consuming process.

COUNSELOR: Well, it can take some time. But this investment is usually very worthwhile.

CLIENT: Can you describe this process in more detail?

COUNSELOR: Sure, let's break it down into a series of steps.

CLIENT: Yes, I'd like to know the whole process.

COUNSELOR: Well, the first phase is helping you get to know yourself better. To do this, we'll need to take a close look at the things that interest you, your values, and the kind of person you are.

CLIENT: That's fine. How do we do this? Do you want me to take some of those psychological tests?

COUNSELOR: That's one way to do it. We could also use one of the computer programs to help us do some of this.

CLIENT: I'll use the computer.

COUNSELOR: Great. Let's schedule you right now for time to use the program.

■ *Case 2:* Thomas is 55 years old, and his first wife died four years ago. He has a son 30 years old and a daughter 26 years old. He is currently dating Connie, a widow, who is 45 years old and who has three teenaged children. He is thinking about becoming engaged, but he is very anxious about this move. Thomas has a good position in a local firm and has been active in several community organizations. He is trying to stop smoking, but that is not what he came to see the counselor about. He feels he would really like to marry Connie, but he is not sure he wants to become involved in the parenting role again. The counselor decided to stress a decision-making strategy; an example of the approach used is indicated below.

Excerpts and Responses	*Ratings and Reasons*
CLIENT: I don't know what I want to do.	
COUNSELOR: You sound confused, and you become anxious because you feel you ought to do something.	

CLIENT: The situation is complex. I have two adult children, and Connie has three teenagers.

COUNSELOR: In addition to you and Connie there are at least five others who will be influenced by what you do.

CLIENT: Yes, and some others too. My wife's parents and mine are deceased. But Connie's parents have been a tremendous support to her, both financially and emotionally, since she became a widow.

COUNSELOR: She's real close to her folks and has depended a great deal on them.

CLIENT: You have a good picture. The older and the younger generations will influence us in one way or another.

COUNSELOR: I see. Your relationship with Connie will be strongly influenced by both sets of children and by her parents.

CLIENT: I feel like I'm being pulled in two directions. One way I take on a lot more responsibilities, and the other way I can be relatively carefree.

COUNSELOR: Let's try to think this out in a logical manner.

CLIENT: What do you have in mind?

COUNSELOR: Let's write things down— the pros and cons of getting married again. Often when we write things down they become clearer.

CLIENT: I should make a list of the reasons why I should and the reasons why I should not marry Connie.

COUNSELOR: Kind of brainstorm. Do all the cons first; then wait a while and list all the pros. Put the lists away for a while, then take them out and look them over.

CLIENT: I've got to do something. This sounds like a good start.

COUNSELOR: When you've finished, bring in your lists and we'll look them over together.

■ *Case 3:* Karen is a 20-year-old college sophomore who transferred from another college at the end of her freshman year. She had excellent grades in high school and during her first year of college; she hoped to finish college in the top of her class. She came to the counseling center very well dressed. She was having trouble in one of her classes, an experience she never had before. Karen had high aspirations for herself and became distraught if she did not meet her self-imposed standards. The counselor decided to use a cognitive-restructuring approach. Excerpts from the interview are presented below.

Excerpts and Responses　　　　　　　　　　　　*Ratings and Reasons*

CLIENT: Oh, I can't keep up with the work in Professor Smith's class.

COUNSELOR: You sound angry and upset.

CLIENT: Yes, he has a reputation as a demanding teacher. They say he rejects papers that are not up to his standards.

COUNSELOR: I'm not sure whether it is the content of the course, Professor Smith, or your tendency to be perfect that is bothering you the most.

CLIENT: His standards are so high, and he even wants us to present our papers orally in class.

COUNSELOR: So, in addition to writing a perfect paper, you will have to give a perfect speech.

CLIENT: I can't get his paper finished— it's not right. And he'll be so critical.

COUNSELOR: What is the worst thing that can happen to you if you don't meet his standards?

CLIENT: He'll ask me to rewrite it. But I'll feel awful.

COUNSELOR: You'll feel awful because you didn't get an F?

CLIENT: Well, that would be far worse. But he'll still make me give an oral report.

COUNSELOR: What will happen if you
  stand in front of the class and can't
  open your mouth?

CLIENT: I'd be so embarrassed.

COUNSELOR: So get a little embarrassed.
  It's better than a failing grade.

CLIENT: I can't do it—my friends will
  laugh at me.

COUNSELOR: It sounds to me like "I won't
  do it because my friends will see that I
  am a complete idiot."

■   *Case 4:*   Tony is 23 years old and has a degree in art education. He has not
been able to find a permanent job in his field and is concerned about his future. He lives
with his parents, who would like to see him get established in an occupation. Tony
reports that he feels pulled in two directions. He would like to be an art teacher, but he
feels pressure to find a steady job. He has several friends in various professional occupations and has an active social life. The counselor believed Tony would benefit from discussing his situation in a nonjudgmental counseling environment. The following excerpts
are taken from a section of this interview.

Excerpts and Responses

CLIENT: My father is on my case. He
  wants to know when I'm going to use
  my art degree in a useful way.

COUNSELOR: You sound angry because
  your father doesn't understand the
  problems you face in your desire to
  become an art teacher.

CLIENT: Yes, I can get some work sub-
  bing for two or three days a week, but
  that only pays for my transportation
  and basic expenses. I can't live on that
  kind of money.

COUNSELOR: And to your father, that
  seems like a dead end.

CLIENT: Yes, he feels that after five years
  of college, I should be able to settle
  down into a job and begin to earn a
  decent salary.

COUNSELOR: It hurts for several reasons.
  First, you have your heart set on work-

Ratings and Reasons

ing with adolescents and helping them
appreciate art. Second, you can't seem
to find a permanent position in this
field. And then there's your father, who
is forcing you to question your commitment to this field.

CLIENT: I know that a job will eventually
open up for me. It's hard enough without his pressure.

COUNSELOR: In spite of his pressure and
this hurt feeling, you are committed to
staying in this field, even if it takes you
a long time to find the job you want.

CLIENT: Yes. What can I tell him to get
him off my back?

COUNSELOR: It sounds like you're searching for ways to have him ease up on
this pressure.

CLIENT: Yes, I sure am. You know he
would like me to take a job in his firm.
He always wanted me to follow his lead.

COUNSELOR: So part of the problem is related to your choosing an occupation
that is different from his.

CLIENT: He's got the ammunition to
really give it to me on that issue.

COUNSELOR: And you need to be able to
talk to him about what's right for you.

■   *Case 5:*   Lois came to talk to a counselor on the advice of her physician. She is
45 years old and reportedly in good health. She complains that she feels listless and
cannot organize her time the way she used to. Her mother died a year ago, and she lives
with her husband and two children. She has a good job and is active in several community groups. The counselor believed that there were some unresolved issues related to
her mother's death. The counselor thought Lois needed to become more aware of her
own feelings about her relationship with her mother. The following dialogue is part of
the transcript from this case.

Excerpts and Responses   *Ratings and Reasons*

CLIENT: I'm so angry at that doctor. He
could have helped Mom more than he
did.

COUNSELOR: You really miss your mother, and you are angry with the physician.

CLIENT: He said he could help, but he didn't.

COUNSELOR: It's okay to be angry, but I want you to take some responsibility for feeling this way.

CLIENT: What do you mean?

COUNSELOR: Instead of saying, "That doctor made me so mad," I want you to say, "I am really angry at that doctor."

CLIENT: Well, he makes me mad, and I am really angry with him. I'm sure he could have done more.

COUNSELOR: That's good. You really miss your mother and you blame the doctor.

CLIENT: He said he could help, and I didn't have time to take care of her.

COUNSELOR: So you feel guilty.

CLIENT: Yes, she was such a great mother. She was kind. She was super with my kids.

COUNSELOR: So you feel guilty because your mother raised you, took care of you when you were sick, and helped a lot with your kids. And you were not able to take care of her, so you really feel guilty.

CLIENT: Yes, she was really wonderful. And that cancer—it's so vile.

COUNSELOR: Suppose you could talk to your mom now. What would you say?

CLIENT: How can I do that?

COUNSELOR: Let's pretend your mother is sitting in this chair. What would you say to her?

CLIENT: Mom, I miss you. I can't do what you did. You managed to do everything so easily, and I'm always struggling.

COUNSELOR: That's good. Continue talking to her.

■   *Case 6:*   Jim is a high school sophomore who moved into the community six weeks ago. He appears to be doing well academically and has recently gone out for one of the school's teams. However, he seems to be somewhat shy and introverted. He would like to ask a classmate out on a date, but he has not been able to do so. The counselor thought that Jim's problem could be handled in several ways. However, because Jim never asked a girl for a date before, he chose to use a role-playing technique. A section of the interview is reported below.

Excerpts and Responses   *Ratings and Reasons*

CLIENT: I would really like to ask Susan to the prom.

COUNSELOR: Well, perhaps I can help you. Tell me more about your situation.

CLIENT: I never do anything right. Every time I see her I get tongue-tied.

COUNSELOR: You feel as if she will ignore you or turn you down.

CLIENT: She doesn't ignore me. She usually smiles and always has a friendly hello.

COUNSELOR: So, she is friendly and seems to like you, but you can't say more than a few words to her.

CLIENT: I can say hi and talk about school or things like that, but I can't seem to get up the nerve to ask her out. I don't know why.

COUNSELOR: Well, let's role-play that situation. You be yourself, and I'll be Susan. Pretend we're in school and we meet going into a classroom about two minutes early, and I say "Hi."

CLIENT: "Hi, Sue. He sure gave a lot of homework. Could you finish yours?"

COUNSELOR: Yes, but it took me hours, and I had to get my dad to help. Maybe I should have called you."

CLIENT: If she ever made a statement like that, I'd really get embarrassed.

COUNSELOR: Well, then suppose she did; or is it out of character for her to say that?

CLIENT: No—she hasn't said anything like that, but she could.

COUNSELOR: So, Susan is friendly toward you. But you are afraid of rejection.

CLIENT: I guess so.

COUNSELOR: Let's role-play three different situations. In the first, she says no. In the second, she says she would really like to, but she is busy that weekend. And in the third, she says yes.

■   *Case 7:*   Bruce is a 20-year-old college junior who is majoring in mathematics. His cumulative average is 2.95, but he received Ds on the first quizzes in each of his math classes this semester. Bruce is an active member of a major organization on campus. He has never had a D before and is quite upset and wants to improve his performance. The counselor decided to try an operant conditioning approach with Bruce. The following excerpts illustrate the approach taken by the counselor.

Excerpts and Responses

CLIENT: I need to improve my study habits. With this new major, they really have piled on the work.

COUNSELOR: And you can't seem to get organized.

CLIENT: Yes, I've broken all my resolutions. I find myself reading the *Times* or a magazine before I settle down to study.

COUNSELOR: It's good to keep up with current events and do some leisure reading, but you have to set some priorities.

CLIENT: Yes, I know—bad marks, angry parents, and I wind up the loser.

COUNSELOR: We need to develop a plan to help you.

Ratings and Reasons

CLIENT: What do you have in mind?

COUNSELOR: First, we need to make up a schedule of your week so we can identify the possible times you can devote to studying.

CLIENT: Well, I do have two free periods every day, but that's the time I spend in the cafeteria with my friends.

COUNSELOR: Let's try to put you on a self-reward system. What would you give yourself if you earned a reward?

CLIENT: Well, I like to socialize.

COUNSELOR: Would you, or can you, use this as a reward?

CLIENT: Yes, I think so.

COUNSELOR: Let's develop a study schedule for you for this coming week. Then we need to see how we can use your social contacts as a reward for studying when you follow it.

CLIENT: Well, if I study the first free period, I'll socialize the second one.

COUNSELOR: And, if you don't study the first period?

CLIENT: I have to give it a try. I have to improve or it's good-bye for me.

■ *Case 8:* Jane is a widow who has three children who live with her. She referred herself to your agency because of her lack of assertiveness; she appears anxious and rather sad. She feels her lack of assertiveness is causing her to function poorly at work and at home. During an earlier phase of counseling, Jane indicated that she rarely showed any emotions. She claimed she was brought up to keep her feelings inside herself. She has a part-time job and an income from her husband's pension, which she feels is quite adequate for her to live on. She is active in her church and talks to several good friends regularly. The counselor thought she could benefit from an assertiveness training program; first, however, she needed to learn how to express her feelings. An example of the intervention is reported below.

Excerpts and Responses   *Ratings and Reasons*

COUNSELOR: What do you do when someone cuts in front of you in a line, say, at the supermarket?

CLIENT: I get real mad, but I never say anything.

COUNSELOR: So you do believe that you should say something.

CLIENT: Yes, I know I should.

COUNSELOR: What prevents you?

CLIENT: I don't want to cause a commotion.

COUNSELOR: So, on the one hand, you want to assert yourself and speak up for your rights, but on the other hand, you have this fear that prevents you from doing so.

CLIENT: That's the dilemma I always have, and I get paralyzed.

COUNSELOR: It's not at all unusual to have these two feelings. But we have to change the balance and have your assertiveness become the more dominant one.

CLIENT: That's easy to say, but I always get paralyzed.

COUNSELOR: Learning to express your anger in any situation is hard. Perhaps it's related to your ability to express any of your feelings.

CLIENT: Well, I don't express the way I feel about things very often.

COUNSELOR: Okay, let's first work on having you learn to express your positive feelings.

CLIENT: What do you have in mind?

COUNSELOR: For the next week, I would like you to try to express your positive feelings to one of your children at least once a day.

CLIENT: I think I can do that.

Communication exercises.   The following exercises have been designed to help you gain more knowledge, obtain more experience, and become more competent in using several intervention strategies in the problem-solving role. Each exercise presents some critical information about a client obtained during the early phases of the counseling process. Examine each case as a member of a small group. For each case your group should:

- identify the cognitive, the affective, and the behavioral issues you think may be involved;
- indicate a counseling goal that could be beneficial to the client;
- describe an intervention strategy that you would have selected to reach the stated goal and give the reasons for your choice;
- outline the techniques you would like to use and any difficulties you foresee in employing these techniques.

When you discuss each case, members of your group may express different opinions about a desirable counseling goal. This difference of opinion is understandable since there are different ways to conceptualize a client's concern; hence specific goals may vary. Furthermore, your selection of strategies and intervention techniques may also differ because of the difference of goals and the fact that different strategies may be employed to accomplish the same goal.

After you discuss each case in your group, practice using the selected strategy in a role-playing situation. Have one group member assume the client role, another assume the counselor role, and the other members function as peer supervisors. As the counselor-in-training practices implementing a strategy or trying out a new technique, the entire group should critically observe the process and provide vital feedback.

■ *Client 1:*   Robert is a 13-year-old junior high school student who is not doing very well in school. He is of average height and weight for his age, has a history of good health, and comes from an intact working-class family. He has one older brother and four older sisters; both parents work outside the home.

The assistant principal referred Robert and indicated that he had been accused by the children of stealing money in small amounts from them. There is no proof for this accusation; it is their word against his. Robert is reticent about volunteering information, but seems comfortable when allowed to relax in the counselor's office. He claims everyone picks on him—his family, his classmates, and his teachers—and no one really likes him or trusts him. His academic failures bother him, but he feels he cannot win. He does not appear to have a friend in the school.

■ *Client 2:*   Mary, who is 21 years old, recently came to the United States. She lives with an older sister, her brother-in-law, and their four children. She had an isolated, disciplined childhood, and her parents were extremely protective of her because of a history of epilepsy. She has suffered from petit mal attacks since she was 5 years old. She has another older sister who is also married and lives in the same community. Both of her sisters are college graduates and both are employed in professional occupations; their husbands are both employed in midmanagerial civil service positions.

Mary reports that she gets along very well with her family. However, she feels that she is her sister's housekeeper and baby-sitter. She reports having a poor social life and that she would really like to continue her education and become economically independent. She says that she had a high school average of 92 and loves to read and do crossword puzzles. She admits that she has never had any close friends except for her two sisters. She is active in her local church. The client talks rapidly and is highly verbal.

■ *Client 3:*   Ed is a 53-year-old self-made man who has just lost his job in management with a prominent advertising agency where he worked for 31 years. He appears younger than his stated age, is well dressed, and has the bearing of a very accomplished, successful man. His wife has been moderately successful in the bank where she is employed. They have no children.

His friend, who is also his physician, recommended that Ed see a counselor because he was complaining about migraine headaches, backaches, and chronic fatigue even though he is apparently healthy. Ed admits feeling cheated after all the years of giving his best, but he sees no way that counseling can help him get his old job back or find a comparable position with another prestigious company. He only came to counseling because his physician friend urged him to talk out his feelings about his employment situation.

■ *Client 4:*   Carol is a 16-year-old sophomore who is attending a public high school in a suburban community. Her parents are separated, and her father lives in a city 300 miles away. She lives at home with her mother and her sister, who is 14. Carol is not doing well in school; academically, she is failing two subjects and barely passing the rest. Her deportment is considered awful: she is loud, boisterous, and insolent. She has a strong influence on other students.

As the counselor, you have recently encouraged Carol to stop by for a chat. During the initial interview (the chat) Carol put on a tough-girl act but was open and sincere underneath. She began to relax. It soon became apparent that Carol and her sister are alone a great deal of the time. Her mother is out of town at work about three nights a week. According to Carol, her mother drinks a considerable amount of liquor, and Carol thinks that is the main reason her parents separated. Carol has no other immediate family in town; however, her father's sister lives in an adjoining community.

■ *Client 5:*   Al is a 32-year-old college graduate who has just completed a master's degree in finance. He comes from a prominent family that is active in their community, which is several hundred miles away. Al has never worked in the business field. In college he was active in the college theater group and had several acting jobs in the off-Broadway theater and in summer stock. During a lull in his acting, he took a job in construction and had an accident, which caused a chronic lower back problem. As a result of some vocational counseling, Al went to graduate school and has just finished his coursework. He has a good grade point average.

Because of his lower back problem, Al is reluctant to accept a job that will require sitting at a desk eight hours a day. He is willing to relocate but does not want to return to his hometown to be his father's alter ego.

■ *Client 6:* Patricia is a 14-year-old student in high school. She lives at home with her parents and three siblings, sisters ages 16 and 28 and a brother age 10. Patricia is in good health, currently has a B average in her schoolwork, and enjoys art and music.

The client came to the counseling center because she had difficulty relating to her father. According to her, he has a mental problem. He makes unrealistic statements, verbally degrades her when she disagrees with him, and embarrasses her with his bizarre behavior. The client is very sensitive, has a limited number of friends, and bases her self-worth on what others say and do. Patricia wants to "make something of herself" and feels she needs to learn how to cope more effectively with her father.

■ *Client 7:* Peter is 19 years old and a freshman at the university. He is the first member of his family to finish high school and attend college. He has had an excellent high school education and very good grades but now reports feeling strange and guilty. He lives at home, and his family is emotionally supportive of his going on to college. He senses a feeling of alienation and distancing and a lack of understanding.

He is attracted to the humanities and is thinking of majoring in French or French literature. His family thinks he is not being very sensible and that he should think about a more practical major. Someone told him to stop by the university counseling center and pick up some literature on college majors and occupations. That is why he came to you. It was easy to establish a relationship with Peter. His presenting problem seems to be the real concern.

■ *Client 8:* Martha is a 78-year-old widow who is a resident in an adult home. She worked until she was 70 years old as a secretary to the president of an industrial firm. She lost her right leg six months ago because of vascular problems. She has a married son who visits her once a week.

She was referred to you because she has complained constantly since arriving in the home two months ago. During the initial interviews Martha was quite talkative. She revealed that she was quick to have opinions of others, did not like the home, and was angry at her son because of this placement. Martha is a bright lady who is aware of the current events of the world, and she loves to read and discuss contemporary literature.

■ *Client 9:* Kenneth is 19 years old and finished high school six months ago. He is the middle son in a family of five boys. Both parents work and are in the lower-income range. His two older brothers do not live at home, and he and his younger brothers live in a group home. He has lived in this home for six years, and his two brothers were placed in the home three months ago. All three were placed in the group home by the court because they needed closer supervision.

During the initial interviews Kenneth was fidgety and distracted—he chewed his fingernails and tapped on the table. He has worked in the same unskilled job for the past five years. He manifests poor communication skills, a poor concept of time, and little sense of responsibility or independence. He was willing to come to see you because he thought he might be able to get a better paying job through your office.

■ *Client 10:* Marilyn is a 27-year-old homemaker with two elementary school-age children. She recently lost her job as a salesclerk in a discount department store and was self-referred to your agency because of her desire to seek another job. During your initial interview with Marilyn, you discovered that she was fired from her job because of a drinking problem and that she is having serious marital problems.

Marilyn is responsive and cooperative but is generally reactive rather than proactive. She is anxious to continue with the counseling.

■   *Client 11:*   Anne is a 17-year-old junior in high school. She has a B+ average in her coursework and is on the honor roll periodically. On standardized tests she always scores in the 99th percentile. She lives at home with both parents and a younger sister, age 15. She is tall for her age and in good health.

Anne came to see you because of her lack of assertiveness. She says that every time she goes to the supermarket someone manages to get ahead of her in the checkout line. She has few friends.

■   *Client 12:*   Dan, a handsome 26-year-old, works as a computer specialist in a large corporation. He is married to Eileen, an attractive 23-year-old who works for the same company. Both of them seem happily married, are in good health, and plan to have children and a house in the suburbs within a few years. Dan's parents were divorced when he was 15, and his father remarried a year later. His two older sisters are now divorced and have returned home, each with a young daughter, to live with their mother, who always has a boyfriend but never remarried. Dan's father has young children and what Dan calls an "ideal marriage."

Dan has come to the counseling office because he is touched by nightmares that always focus on losing Eileen in some tragic way. He also wonders what is the matter with his family because no one is happily married. Everyone gets dumped. He realizes he is upsetting his own relationship with Eileen because of his restlessness and his fear of losing her.

■   *Client 13:*   Doreen is a 16-year-old underachieving tenth-grade student who has extremely poor grades and a poor attendance record. She lives at home with her mother and two younger sisters and an older brother. She is of average height and weight and is in good health.

Doreen was self-referred. She came to talk to you because her mother wanted to send her to live with relatives out of town. During the initial interview Doreen revealed that she has little communication with members of her immediate family. She also revealed that she has few friends, is apathetic to schoolwork, and has a poor self-image. Although she's quiet, Doreen appears to be comfortable in the counseling office.

■   *Client 14:*   Charles is 50 years old and employed in an upper-level managerial position. He is married and has two adopted children, who are in junior high school. His wife is an elementary school teacher. He comes from a large family. His father died when he was very young, and he grew up in an economically poor home. Charles has a master's degree and is a CPA. His employment history is stable, and he has worked for the same firm for 20 years.

Charles is pleasant, friendly, and very willing to express himself. He came to the clinic because he is very unhappy about his marital situation. Although he wonders if his feelings of dissatisfaction are a symptom of a midlife crisis, he reports considerable emotional, physical, and social distance from his wife. Both of them are committed to the well-being of the children. However, he reports that "the home is not a sharing, warm refuge but a cold harbor out of the storm of life." Charles pursues his interests, his wife hers. There is cooperation within the family unit and no antagonism. But very rarely is anything done as a family unit.

■ **Client 15:** Susan is 25 years old, a magna cum laude graduate of college, teaching in a private elementary school and pursuing a master's degree in education. She is of average height and weight, comes from a middle-class background, reports having had excellent health, and was married six months ago. Her husband is an accountant and is preparing for his CPA exams.

She came to the university counseling center because she is not pleased with either her professional work or her studies and is convinced that she made a mistake in her career choice. The client has been seen for two sessions. She is outgoing, friendly, and enjoys being in the center of things socially. However, she has also recently begun to question her relationships with others. She feels that, although she has many acquaintances, she has no real friends and that her relationship with her husband is marred by a lack of communication about the deeper issues of their relationship.

Exercises from your own setting. List three personal problems that inhibit, constrain, or otherwise impair individuals in your present setting or may be concerns of potential clients in a setting where you expect to work. For each case, develop an overall strategy for counseling a client who has one of the identified presenting problems. As part of your plan, indicate what issues and concerns need further exploration, and state the counseling goal you would use with each case. Be prepared to discuss each problem with a small group within your class.

SUMMARY

This chapter presented you with the opportunity to study and practice the problem-solving role. Four major topics were covered. First, you were reminded that your effectiveness in using this role depends on your satisfactory completion of the three previous counseling phases: the quality of the relationship with your client; the adequate exploration of your client's concerns; and the identification of an appropriate counseling goal. Then, you were informed about the importance of several factors associated with applying intervention strategies: giving instructions, involving your client in strategy selection, expecting resistance, obtaining supervision, integrating different strategies, monitoring progress, and anticipating termination. Next, the relationship between an identified counseling goal and the type of intervention strategy that could be selected was outlined for you. Finally, you were offered a framework to evaluate the implementation of these strategies.

In addition to covering these four major topics, four different sets of exercises were provided to help you understand how to implement a counseling strategy. First, three cases were illustrated to show you how a particular intervention is related to the counseling goal, how the strategy progresses, and how the process can be evaluated. Then, several cases were presented to enable you to practice understanding and evaluating the problem-solving role. Next, a variety of case situations were provided to encourage you to practice applying these strategies. Finally, you were encouraged to develop your own set of simulated cases and formulate a counseling plan for each case.

Full mastery of the problem-solving skills presented m this chapter will require you to obtain a substantial amount of supervised practice. This practice will give you the opportunity to study these strategies in greater depth, to practice the techniques with actual clients, and to receive constructive feedback from your supervisor.

REFERENCES

Benjamin, A. (1987). *The helping interview.* Boston: Houghton Mifflin.

Cormier, W. H., & Cormier, L. S. (1991). *Interviewing strategies for helpers: Fundamental skills and cognitive behavioral interventions* (3rd ed.). Pacific Grove, CA: Brooks/Cole.

Egan, G. (1994). *The skilled helper: A problem-management approach to helping* (5th ed.). Pacific Grove, CA: Brooks/Cole.

Epstein, L. (1985). *Talking and listening: A guide to the helping interview.* St. Louis, MO: Times/Mirror.

Ivey, A. E., Ivey, M. B., & Simek-Morgan, L. (1997). *Counseling and psychotherapy: A multicultural perspective* (4th ed.). Boston: Allyn & Bacon.

Meier, S. T., & Davis, S. R. (1997). *The elements of counseling* (3rd ed.). Pacific Grove, CA: Brooks/Cole.

Moursund, J. (1990). *The process of counseling and therapy* (2nd ed.). Englewood Cliffs, NJ: Prentice Hall.

Okun, B. F. (1997). *Effective helping: Interviewing and counseling techniques* (5th ed.). Pacific Grove, CA: Brooks/Cole.

Parsons, R. D., & Wicks, R. J. (1994). *Counseling strategies and intervention techniques for the human services* (4th ed.). Boston: Allyn & Bacon.

SUGGESTED READINGS

Burks, H. M., & Stefflre, B. (1979). *Theories of counseling* (3rd ed.). New York: McGraw-Hill.

Corey, G. (1996). *Theory and practice of counseling and psychotherapy* (5th ed.). Pacific Grove, CA: Brooks/Cole.

Corsini, R. J., & Wedding, D. (Eds.). (1995). *Current psychotherapies* (5th ed.). Itasca, IL: F. E. Peacock.

Gilliland, B. E., James, R. K., & Bowman, J. T. (1994). *Theories and strategies in counseling and psychotherapy* (3rd ed.). Boston: Allyn & Bacon.

Gladding, S. T. (1996). *Counseling: A comprehensive profession* (3rd ed.). Columbus, OH: Merrill.

Hansen, J., Rossberg, R. H., & Cramer, S. H. (1994). *Counseling: Theory and process* (5th ed.). Boston: Allyn & Bacon.

Kanfer, F. H., & Goldstein, A. P. (Eds.). (1991). *Helping people change: A textbook of methods* (4th ed.). New York: Pergamon.

Patterson, C. H., & Watkins, C. E. (1995). *Theories of counseling and psychotherapy* (5th ed.). Reading, MA: Addison-Wesley.

Name Index

Subject Index

Applied Electronic Design

D. Joseph Stadtmiller

Mohawk Valley Community College

Prentice
Hall

Upper Saddle River, New Jersey
Columbus, Ohio

Library of Congress Cataloging in Publication Data

Stadtmiller, D. Joseph
    Applied electronic design / D. Joseph Stadtmiller
       p.   cm.
    Includes bibliographical references and index.
    ISBN 0-13-094758-X
       1. Electronic apparatus and applications—Design and construction. 2. Electronic circuit
Design. I. Title.

TK7836 .S728 2003
621.381—dc21   2002029285

Editor in Chief: Stephen Helba
Acquisitions Editor: Dennis Williams
Editorial Assistant: Lara Dimmick
Production Editor: Steve Robb
Production Coordinator: Tim Flem, PublishWare
Copy Editor: Roberta Dempsey
Design Coordinator: Karrie Converse-Jones
Cover Designer: Jason Moore
Production Manager: Pat Tonneman
Marketing Manager: Ben Leonard

This book was set in Century Book by PublishWare. It was printed and bound by R. R. Donnelley & Sons
Company. The cover was printed by Phoenix Color Corp.

Pearson Education Ltd.
Pearson Education Australia Pty. Limited
Pearson Education Singapore Pte. Ltd.
Pearson Education North Asia Ltd.
Pearson Education Canada, Ltd.
Pearson Educación de Mexico, S.A. de C.V.
Pearson Education—Japan
Pearson Education Malaysia Pte. Ltd.
Pearson Education, *Upper Saddle River, New Jersey*

10 9 8 7 6 5 4 3 2 1
ISBN 0-13-094758-X

To Francine, Jes, Joe, Jon, and Ginger

Preface

The purpose of this book is to better prepare students to enter the fast-paced world of electronics by applying the theoretical knowledge learned in their foundation courses on analog and digital electronics. It is a continuation of the premise that prompted my first book, *Electronics: Project Management and Design*, which discussed all the facets of a design project as completed in a business environment. *Applied Electronic Design* offers a different perspective as it discusses the design process and issues relating to a wide range of electronic applications. Following are the underlying strategies of the book:

▶ Expose students to the design perspective from a wide range of electronic applications

▶ Discuss the Six-Step design process, the development of design specifications, and the importance of concurrent engineering concepts

▶ Emphasize general design issues, such as manufacturability, quality, reliability, ease of use, and serviceability

▶ Show methods for dealing with ambient temperature variations, EMI radiation, and noise immunity

The book's main theme is the application of basic analog and digital electronics concepts to actual design problems. This experience will promote a deeper understanding of electronics, better problem-solving skills, and the development of design skills for electronics students.

I developed this text by combining my industrial and academic experiences. Also, comments and reviews from my first book, *Electronics: Project Management and Design*, indicated that there is a general need for capstone-oriented texts and more specifically that a book with a design focus is highly desirable. Reviewers of the early *Applied Electronic Design* manuscript helped to refine the approach used and the topical coverage of the final product.

The book is targeted as a textbook for applied electronics, design, electronic design, senior-project, and electronic project courses. It could also be used as a supplementary text for any electronics program. It is most applicable to the third and fourth year of four-year electronic programs but can also be used in the second year of many two-year electronics programs. It is designed to function completely on its own or side by side with *Electronics: Project Management and Design*.

The book can be segmented into two areas: Chapters 1 through 5 present the design process, and Chapters 6 through 12 cover seven different areas of electronic circuit applications. The coverage of the design process includes defining the design problem, overall design considerations, beginning the design, selecting components, and printed circuit board design. The last seven chapters comprise the following topics: power supplies, amplifiers, oscillators/clock circuits, control circuits, digital logic circuits, embedded systems, and telecommunications. Each of these chapters can be considered a mini-handbook on the topic covered.

Every attempt has been made to simplify the information presented in the book. The book is intended for use at many levels, but a basic knowledge of circuit theory and both analog and digital electronic components is assumed. Each subject area is discussed to a depth that promotes a broad understanding of the underlying design issue. Each chapter starts with an introduction that highlights the topics to be covered. Examples are provided wherever practical, and each chapter concludes with a summary and exercises.

Applied Electronic Design will surely help electronic students take the all-important first step into their professional careers by introducing design problems and applications that represent the major application areas in the electronics field. In many cases, it might also help students determine initial career directions.

Acknowledgments

I would like to thank all of my teachers, professors, and mentors who helped develop the foundation of my knowledge. Thanks also to those whose comments and suggestions regarding my first book helped develop the overall content of this book.

Thanks to Prentice Hall Sales Representative Donna Conroy for supplying me with much reference material, and Acquisitions Editor Dennis Williams for his ongoing direction and support. Steve Robb, the production editor; Tim Flem, the production coordinator; and Roberta Dempsey, the copy editor, were all key players in finalizing and producing this book. It was a pleasure to work with them, and I appreciate the results of their efforts on the final product.

Finally, I thank the following reviewers, whose comments contributed much to the content and character of the book: Don Abernathy, DeVry Institute of Technology–Dallas; Habib Rahman, Saint Louis University; Hesham E. Shaalan, Georgia Southern University; and Sidney Soclof, California State University, Los Angeles.

Contents

7
Amplifier Design   *171*

8
Oscillators and Function Generators   *225*

9
Data Acquisition and Control Circuits   *261*

10
Discrete Digital Design   *311*

11
Embedded System Design 347

12
Telecommunications and Fiber Optics 385

Appendix A
Component Reference Information 419

Index 431

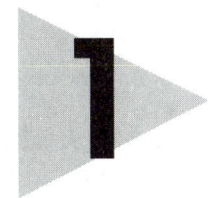

The Design Problem

Introduction

This book applies basic electronics knowledge to a variety of design problems that can be resolved with electronic circuits. The abilities to adapt, design, and create new processes and devices are the skills that promote human survival more than any others. Other hominid species that failed to develop these skills have long since perished while our ancestors persevered. Currently, as we experience the benefits and changes caused by the Internet and the continuing information revolution, we are again realizing the potential of an idea and its resulting design. Beginning as a communication scheme to connect research universities and the defense community, the computer and communications framework that resulted in the Internet began in the mid-1970s. While the computer revolution was causing rapid change and creating many new possibilities, the infrastructure for the Internet was being slowly developed. Roughly 15 years later the personal computer and the Internet would team up to change the way we work and live at a level that rivals the development of the wheel, the printing press, and the atomic bomb. Clearly, the computer, the Internet, and the resulting telecommunications revolution have the potential to change the world as much as any of these historic developments.

Our future as a people, and the future of our businesses and our world, will continue to depend on our ability to design new devices and create new technology. Our most severe technical challenges will involve energy efficiency, natural resource utilization, and pollution. Many of the solutions to these and other problems will be electrical and electronic products and systems, while many will include a combination of technologies. Communication; computing; industrial automation; energy development and efficiency; and medical, entertainment and defense applications of electronics technology will continue to demand creative solutions to design problems. This book will discuss a variety of common electronic design

1

problems and how to approach their solutions as theoretical electronic and circuit concepts are applied in the real world of electronic design.

This chapter begins with a definition of concurrent engineering and discusses the design issues that most projects must address. Then a process called the Six Steps is reviewed as a method for solving design problems. The final topic is the development of design specifications. These represent the formal definition of the design problem for the development team. The specific topics covered in this chapter are as follows:

- ▶ Concurrent Engineering
- ▶ The Six Steps
- ▶ Developing Design Specifications

1–1 ▶ Concurrent Engineering

The design problem is unique because it involves solving a problem with the creation of some device or system. As we create the design, it is important to focus on all of its requirements. During the design process, it is natural to concentrate on a design's central functional requirements, while ignoring seemingly trivial issues such as manufacturability and customer ease of use. However, in the end a design's success will be determined by how well it addresses *all* of the initial requirements.

Concurrent engineering is a design philosophy that promotes the consideration of all the requirements of a design, beginning with the very first step of the design process through to its completion. The concurrent engineering requirements include topics such as reliability, quality, customer use, marketing and sales issues, and manufacturing and financial issues, in addition to the more obvious functional performance specifications. Concurrent engineering is a design process that improves on traditional methods. This process comprises the following strategies, which are summarized in Figure 1–1:

1. Initially develop complete specifications defining the project, and minimize changes to the specifications after the project is started.

2. Consider manufacturing, quality, customer use, field service, and disposal issues at the very beginning of the project.

3. Utilize a project team with representatives from all affected departments. Promote innovation in the team. Empower them and give them incentives to promote their success.

4. Develop detailed schedules with distinct project phases. Deliverables should be defined for the end of each phase, and these must be complete before moving onto the next phase.

5. Include a project verification stage in which the quality, performance, and reliability of the project is verified independently, and the project is utilized in the intended environment.

1. Develop complete specifications

2. Consider manufacturing, customer use, and quality up front

3. Utilize a multifunctional team

4. Develop detailed schedules

5. Include a project verification stage in the project schedule

6. Involve key suppliers

7. Envision the goal

8. Promote continuous improvement

▲ FIGURE 1–1
Concurrent engineering strategies

6. Involve key suppliers very early in the project.

7. Maintain a perspective of the overall project goal and all of the different design issues on a concurrent (simultaneous) basis.

8. Provide for continuous improvement by evaluating the performance of the project when complete and reflecting on what went well and what needs improvement.

When the principles and strategies of concurrent engineering are applied to the design process, good things happen. The most important result is the synergy gained from the team approach to design project management. Concurrent engineering is the application of good common sense to engineering design projects to rectify the situations that evolved as companies became large and departmentalized. The specific results of concurrent engineering are as follows:

1. The multifunctional team ensures that all design issues are addressed up front. Customer, manufacturing, quality, financial, and field service issues are considered equal to other design issues.

2. Design activities are scheduled in an orderly way, taking advantage of parallel paths wherever possible and resulting in minimal linear time for the project. The project team believes the schedule can be achieved.

3. When involved early in the process, key suppliers can provide new and different perspectives that can improve the project results.

1. Manufacturing, customer use, and quality are considered up front.

2. Project schedules are minimized.

3. Key suppliers provide new ideas.

4. Project delays are identified and addressed quickly.

5. Project delays from specification changes are minimized.

6. Project visibility is high.

7. Short ramp-up time to manufacture.

8. Quality is improved.

9. Creativity increases.

10. Team members feel ownership.

▲ FIGURE 1–2
Summary of the results of concurrent engineering

4. Project delays are identified and addressed as they are realized.

5. Delays that result from incomplete or changing specifications are eliminated.

6. The project visibility is very high throughout the company.

7. The ramp-up time for starting manufacturing is planned and minimized.

8. Quality is measured independently.

9. Creativity is maximized.

10. The team feels a joint ownership in the project and its results.

The results of concurrent engineering are summarized in Figure 1–2.

1–2 ▶ The Six Steps of Problem Solving

At this point in your academic career, you have probably solved many problems. Many of them have been homework problems, which you did quickly after skimming the problem write-up and then frantically paging through the book to find an appropriate formula. After plugging in the numbers and performing the calculations, you compared the answer with those in the back of the book. If the answer checked out, you moved on to the next problem. If not, you repeated the process with perhaps a different formula. Only after numerous failures to achieve the book's answer will the average student reread the problem to verify the facts given and confirm what is required in the form of an answer. Very often at this juncture comes the realization that the problem write-up is asking for something completely different from what the student thought initially. A simple change in direction now will often lead to the successful solution. And so it is, with the educational process and life, as the pace of our lives continues to go faster and faster.

The primary role of engineers, technologists, and technicians is to supply technical solutions to problems; design problems, operational problems, and failure problems. As you enter a career in the electronics industry, the pace will continue to be rapid. Today's industry requires superior solutions to a complex set of problems, many of them design problems. In this section we will examine a simple process for solving engineering design problems that works. The Six-Step process is a basic problem-solving process that has been around for a long time. The Six Steps that follow are simple, easy to use, and will solve many types of problems:

Step One: *Research* the problem by gathering information.

Step Two: Completely *define* the problem by studying it and listing as many facts as possible to fully define it.

Step Three: *Plan* the solution. Develop a plan, a list of steps to solve the problem.

Step Four: *Execute* the plan outlined in Step Three.

Step Five: *Verify* the results achieved in Step Four, making sure that they do solve the original problem.

Step Six: *Conclude*. Develop a set of conclusions, and note what is learned in the process.

Figure 1–3 shows a summary of the entire process. Let's look at some examples.

Example 1–1

This problem was posed to a product engineer whose job it is to support the phase-in process for new products as they are turned over to manufacturing. New product phase-in to manufacturing is the process of preparing the company to manufacture a product. The problem is to improve the manufacturability of a new capacitance fuel gauge system for small aircraft. This new product is symptomatic of one designed initially without using concurrent engineering concepts. The details relating to its manufacturability are being addressed as the product is being phased into manufacturing, instead of at the beginning of the project.

Step One: Research and gather information

Step Two: Define the problem

Step Three: Plan the solution

Step Four: Execute the plan

Step Five: Verify the solution

Step Six: Develop a conclusion

▶ **FIGURE 1–3**
The Six Steps of problem solving

The capacitance fuel gauge system uses capacitance sensors to determine the quantity of fuel remaining in a fuel tank. It includes a circuit board, a capacitance sensor, and interconnecting wires all mounted to a stainless steel plate that mounts the unit into the gas tank of small aircraft. The circuit board is totally potted (encapsulated, molded into an epoxy potting compound) to form the shape of small cube. Where the interconnecting wires exit this cube, there is a need to protect the wires from bending or, in engineering terms, provide strain relief for the wires. On the initial prototypes fabricated by engineering, a rubber boot, shaped like a small cylinder, has been glued onto the main body of the fuel gauge to perform the strain relief function. A better solution is needed, one that is more effective as a strain relief and more manufacturable. To solve the problem, the product engineer uses the Six Steps:

Step One—Research the problem: Gather information about the problem. The engineer reviews the assembly process and observes and experiences the installation of the fuel gauge system in an aircraft.

Step Two—Problem definition: To provide a functional and easily manufactured strain relief for the capacitance fuel gauge system. The engineer develops a list of facts about the problem.

1. The interconnecting wires needed mechanical strain relief.
2. The term "easily manufactured" meant a simple, fixturable process that didn't add significant assembly time to the product.
3. The current method was messy, time-consuming, and not reliable.

Step Three—Plan the solution: Develop a plan, a list of steps intended to solve the problem. The engineer has come up with the following steps for solving this problem:

1. Develop two alternative solutions that address all the issues brought up in the problem definition.
2. Prototype and test each of the solutions.

Step Four—Execute the plan: Simply perform the solution plan. The product engineer performs the solution plan.

Step Five—Verify the results: Check the results achieved, making sure that they solve the original problem. The product engineer reviews each solution with engineering and manufacturing and chooses the preferred solution.

After analyzing the problem, the engineer has devised a couple of solutions. One alternative involves changing the tooling (the mold for applying the potting compound) for the potted assembly to include the strain relief and the other utilizes an off-the-shelf strain relief. The tooling change is the most attractive solution because it requires no additional parts or assembly. The strain relief will become part of the main assembly and will be formed at the same time as part of the potting process. When both solutions were built up and tested, the tooling change was the selected alternative. The benefits of this solution were the following:

1. No additional parts were needed.
2. No additional labor time was needed.
3. The strain relief was very secure and functional.

Step Six—Develop a set of conclusions: Take note of what is learned in the process. What the product engineer learned from solving this problem was the advantage of designing all the requirements of a design into any tooled parts included in the design.

This next example discusses how a company might solve the problem of increasing sales and market share of one of its product lines by implementing the Six-Step process.

Example 1–2

A company in the music electronics business desires to develop and market a new innovative electronic guitar tuner. A project manager is selected and a multifunctional project team has been put together to study the project and, if feasible complete it. Here is how the project would be completed using the Six Steps:

Step One: The project team will gather all the information needed to consider this project. The exact information needed will include technical, market, and financial information required to determine if the project is feasible and can proceed to Step Two. Step One will be complete when there is a project proposal that includes all of the technical information gathered on guitar tuners, information on the market for these products, and financial data that estimates the cost and profitability of the project if it is completed.

Step Two: With management approval of the Step One proposal, the project team proceeds to Step Two, where the design specifications are completed. Design specifications define the problem for a product development project, and their development is discussed later in this chapter. The result of Step Two is a set of specifications for the guitar tuner that will allow the project team to determine a solution plan and to develop the product using concurrent engineering concepts.

Step Three: With the design specifications complete, the project team develops a solution plan that is better known as a project schedule for product development projects.

Step Four: Now the Project Team can begin implementing the project, which will begin with the preliminary design stage, in which initial design ideas will be generated, explored, and simulated. Next, components will be selected, procured, and breadboarded to test the design concepts. After testing and modifying the breadboarded circuits, the team will assemble and test prototype circuit boards and a prototype guitar tuner. Step Four includes the preliminary design, component selection, and breadboarding and prototype development, which all involve the implementation of the design.

Step Five: The project team will now verify the design to make sure that it meets the original specifications. Team members will perform product assurance tests on the guitar tuner as well as field tests and a financial analysis. If approved at the completion of Step Five, the guitar tuner will be ready to be released for sale to customers.

Step Six: This step will be completed some time after the project has been released, when the project's performance with regard to sales, profitability, quality, and customer use issues will be reviewed on a monthly basis. The results of the project will be summarized and reviewed to determine what improvements can be made on this product in the future, as well as on the way similar future projects will be managed.

In each of the examples shown, the Six-step process was applied to solve the problem. For solving a design problem, the Six Steps mandate that before beginning work on the design, information must be gathered, the design problem must be completely defined, and a plan or schedule must be created. After the design is complete, it must be verified and then modified for improvement while noting general conclusions. It is most important to understand the significance of Step Two, defining the problem. Failure to complete this vital step results in a higher number of poor design solutions than a mediocre performance on any other step. It is also important to emphasize the last of the Six Steps, developing a conclusion. All too often our desire to complete a design prevents us from taking the time to review and reflect on what we learned from the process. Developing a conclusion promotes the widely used concept of continuous improvement—the ongoing learning that should be part of our everyday life. The next section reviews how to define the design problem formally with design specifications.

1–3 ▶ Developing Design Specifications

What are specifications and why do we need them? Specifications are nothing more than a formal document listing the requirements of a project or product. They are a detailed list of the facts related to the problem definition for a design project. When you construct a house, you follow a set of specifications that define details that must be met upon the house's completion. The general contractor is responsible for satisfying these specifications, but all of the subcontractors (i.e., carpenters, electricians, and masons) must be aware of these requirements to ensure that all aspects of the specifications are fulfilled. Generally speaking, a specification is simply a non-trivial problem definition.

The other benefit of using a formal specification is that a format can be developed that will become a useful guide in completing specifications for similar future projects. This will help ensure that key aspects of a future project are reviewed before the design is started. When one small detail remains unidentified up from, it can result in the project being completely aborted. A better-developed, better-defined set of specifications is more likely to result in a final design that will function and meet the original need.

Before we discuss the development of specifications further, let's again look at what precedes and drives their development. First, there is the need for whatever the design project represents. This results from a desire to meet the strategic priorities set by the company. The strategic priorities drive the specific business reason for the project. During Step One, a significant amount of information is collected about a project and a proposal is put together. This information is developed to determine the viability of the project and provide for the development of the specifications. At this point the multifunctional team will get together and use the Step One proposal information to develop the specifications. This is a critical point for the application of concurrent engineering principles. The specifications must be developed jointly with all of the ultimate requirements of the project in mind.

Marketing representatives are the experts on how the project will be employed as well as the business aspects of its success. The marketing team members are usually not technical experts and are therefore not aware of the technical details, knowledge, and capabilities required to complete the project. Most people that have a house built for them are not experts on building houses, but they are most knowledgeable on what they want their house to be. As they sit down with their contractor to discuss their requirements, they often find that aspects of the home they desire will present difficulties to the contractor. These difficulties will likely increase the price of the house beyond what the owner is willing to pay. The specifications for the house are developed with this give-and-take attitude in mind.

A similar situation occurs in industry. For most new products a company's marketing department, while representing the customer, will define the general requirements for the new product. These requirements are usually called the "market specifications" and are included in the Step One proposal, along with the market/business aspects of the project. Many times the initial marketing specifications are impractical, "pie in the sky" requirements. It is important to discuss the initial market specifications and filter them down to something that is more "real world" before development begins. The marketing, engineering, finance, quality, and manufacturing departments will work together to help develop and review the design specifications. This will ensure that the product not only meets the customer's need, but that it can be developed and manufactured at a cost and quality level that will ensure its business success.

Let's review what might be included in a set of specifications for a new electronic product. In utilizing a general specification, development engineers will look for answers to the following types of questions:

What is the power source for the product being developed?

What is the range in power source voltage over which the product must function?

In what ambient temperature range will the product have to function?

How large can the product be physically?

What are the criteria for the appearance of the product?

What tolerance levels should be selected for the electronic components?

In addition to answering these types of questions, the specifications should also discuss how the product is to operate. In some cases it is possible to be specific up front in defining the product's operation. Yet in other more complicated situations, it may be impractical to state exactly how the product will function. In these cases, the statement of function is handled in a general way.

We can categorize specifications into the following Specification Format:

General Description

Performance

Power Input

Package

Environmental

Operation

Agency Approvals

Cost Specifications

Special Requirements

Following are detailed explanations of each area of the design specifications.

General Description: This features a general write-up for the project describing its purpose, the broad approach to development, and the environment of the end use and the end user.

Performance: This section of the specification deals with the quality or performance level of the project or product under development. To complete this section, it is necessary to identify the key outputs or end result of the project. Next, ideal conditions for parameters that will affect performance should be defined to provide a consistent basis for making the measurements. Then the acceptable range in variation of the outputs must be determined.

Example 1–3

Let's take the example of a digital thermometer. The primary output of the temperature indicator is the displayed temperature. The environmental parameters that affect the displayed temperature are the ambient temperature of the indicator and the quality of the power supplied to the indicator. Following are the ideal conditions for determining this accuracy:

1. The thermometer is connected to a specific temperature sensor that is exposed to a temperature within the operating indication range of the indicator.

2. The thermometer indicator should be maintained at an ambient temperature of 25°C.

3. The input power is within the specification range.

In this case we will say that the operating range of the indicator is 0° to 400°C. We'll define the acceptable accuracy of the thermometer for this application as ±0.5% of range. In degrees, then, the acceptable range of the thermometer display is ±2°C (0.005×400°C). To check this out, the sensor is placed in a temperature within the operating range of the indicator, say 200°C. The acceptable reading on the indicator would be between 198° and 202°C. This is a very simple case because there is only one end result or output from the device, the indicated temperature.

In other projects there may be many outputs with many different variables relating to each one. If we were developing a waveform generator to output a triangle wave, a sine wave and a square wave, we would list each of those outputs in our performance specifications. Each type of output would also have accuracy specifications relating to the frequency, amplitude and overall representation of the waveform. In other words, the specifications analytically define how perfect each waveform must be.

To develop the performance aspect of a project specification, follow these steps:

1. Identify measurement aspects of all of the key outputs of the project or product.

2. Identify the parameters that affect these outputs and their ideal conditions for taking the measurements.

3. Determine acceptable ranges for these parameters.

Power Input: This section specifies the power to be supplied to the device. In most cases this needs to be considered. In others, such as a software-only project, it may be omitted. Much of the time the power supplied is standard 115 V AC, 60-cycle power. Even in this case, it is important to note the range in amplitude and frequency that the device can expect to see and, most important, to verify that the device will operate over that range. Most devices powered from standard 115 V AC use a ±10% variation in voltage level and a range in frequency of 50 to 60 Hertz.

In some projects a device may be capable of accepting power from both AC and DC sources. Specifications should be listed for each case. The load current or power consumption of the device, both typical and maximum values, should be identified also. If the DC source is a battery, then battery size and expected life will be important issues.

To complete the power input section of the specifications:

1. Identify the type and range of all power inputs to the device or project, making sure to include all pertinent parameters, such as frequency and amplitude.

2. Indicate the power (volt-amps) or current requirements on the power input.

Package: This part of the specification relates to the mechanical aspects of the design. The purpose is to define the general package criteria of the project without completing the design. In some cases there already exists a specific package that the project will utilize; that should be stated here. Other times there may be no specific requirement for the package size, and that should be stated here also. Most often, however, specific criteria for the package design is necessary to successfully meet the design goals of the project. The end result of this section of the specifications will identify all the key criteria, completely defining the package design problem for the package designer. Here are the areas that should be addressed:

Mechanical Size Limits: The largest, smallest, or specific volume to which the package must conform.

Environmental Rating: The weatherproof rating for the package—how well it is sealed and its ability to withstand corrosive atmospheres

Shape: The product shape, if important, and any information that will allow the designer to determine the optimum shape

Material: Specific material requirements for the package or any guidelines that will help to determine the proper material for the package

Human Engineering Aspects: All aspects of human interaction that the project will employ must be considered in the design. Are there keys that will need depressed? Does the device mount on a wall? Ease of use in every aspect of the project should be considered, including unpacking, installing, using, servicing, and even recycling and disposing. As we enter the new millennium, we must increasingly appreciate, preserve, and reuse our natural resources.

Environmental: This area of the specifications defines key variables in the environment that are the result of the design process. These primarily include ambient temperature, humidity, vibration, shock, electro-magnetic interference (EMI) immunity, and generation.

Ambient Temperature: This is the range in temperature to which the product will be exposed under normal operating conditions. This is listed as the operating range. It is also necessary to point out the storage temperature range. This is the range of temperature to which the device would be exposed over a normal product life while not operating.

Humidity: Humidity can have a detrimental impact on a variety of products and as such is an important environmental factor. The range in humidity over which the product is expected to operate, expressed as a percent of relative humidity, should be noted here.

Vibration: The vibration levels to which the project will be exposed should be specified. This is usually done in terms of the amplitude of the force applied, the frequency of the vibration, and the direction that the force will be applied to the project.

Shock: The purpose of this specification is to define the one-time shock force that the device should be able to withstand. In most cases this will be the worst-case shock applied during shipment if the device were to be dropped from a certain height on its side or on its corners. Specifications for standard tests used by shipping container manufacturers are often included in this section. In some applications there may be other sources of significant shock forces that can be applied to the device. These levels should be identified to allow development of the appropriate shock specifications.

Electro-Magnetic Interference (EMI) Immunity: The design's immunity to electrical interference of many kinds is an important requirement in many applications. The difficulty here is the creation of a subjective statement that specifies the project's EMI immunity goals in a way that can be verified and tested. Designers are generally concerned with interference such as radiated electrical fields, induced magnetic fields, electrostatic discharges, and power line transients. You can try to develop a set of requirements for each one of these areas or use existing standards, such as MIL-STD-461 (limits) and 462 (test procedures) issued by the U.S. Department of Defense. This standard is very complete and stringent and covers both immunity as well as emission. It may be a simple matter to state in the design specifications "meet MIL-STD-461." However, the actual process of verifying and meeting these specifications is a difficult task. It is best to review the various noise standards and pick the areas most important for consideration in the subject design and include them in the specifications. At the same time you must be able to verify the performance by creating the environment included in the design specifications. This may mean purchasing of some sophisticated and expensive test equipment or using an outside testing laboratory.

Electro-Magnetic Interference (EMI) Emissions: As the operating frequencies and the volume of equipment in operation have rapidly increased, the radiation of electronic equipment has come under increased scrutiny. The best source for this requirement comes from the Federal Communications Commission (FCC), which has defined two levels of requirements and testing, Class A and Class B equipment. Military Standard, MIL-STD-461, also addresses this issue. An appropriate specification statement should be determined and included in the design specifications. To verify the performance, you will need to measure radiated EMI from the design accurately. This may require the purchase of equipment or the use of an outside testing laboratory.

Operation: All of the operational aspects of the device will be addressed in this section. The steps and requirements for operation should be listed, starting with applying power to the unit. All the variables that are provided for adjustment of operation should be shown and discussed. As mentioned earlier, in simpler projects it may be possible to completely define the way the device will operate in the specifications. In cases that are software-intensive with many key depressions and displays, the specific operation is something that may be developed as the project design unfolds. However, it is important to make sure that the hardware requirements will support all of the overall requirements for the project. When the operational requirements are implemented with software, a separate operational specification called "Software Specifications" is usually generated. This details all of the needed software operations and requirements.

Agency Approvals: This area deals with both "recognized testing agencies and recognized specifications" with which the design project is required to comply. These include agencies such as Underwriters Laboratories (UL) and the Canadian Standards Association (CSA). Approval by these testing agencies is increasingly important in markets for a variety of product classifications. The identification of any required agency approvals, along with the corresponding specification, are imperative before beginning the design process.

Cost Specifications: This is one of the most important sections and is often overlooked. This section will determine the potential for the financial success of the project. When considering all the technical details, it is easy to overlook that both the cost of development and the manufacturing cost are crucial to the project's success. As such, they must be identified as part of the specifications. Cost specifications include both project cost estimates and manufacturing cost goals.

Preliminary Project Cost Estimates: This is an estimate of the total cost to develop the project. This step should be saved for last so that a reasonable estimate can be developed from the specifications completed thus far. This estimate should include both direct dollar expenditures and the total man-hours needed to complete the project.

Manufacturing Cost Goal: The manufacturing cost goal includes all manufacturing costs for the product and is the maximum number for the design team. This number should be tied to the profitability of the product and its intended selling price as defined in the Step One project proposal. It should also be tied to the anticipated annual sales volume. It is a goal that, if met, will assure meeting the intended market price for the product. If the sales volume meets or exceeds the projected numbers, the product will be a huge success. The manufacturing cost goal should be itemized to include the following categories: total cost of purchased parts, the labor cost to manufacture, and manufacturing overhead. The projected volume at which these costs are to be achieved should be stated also.

Special Considerations: This is simply a miscellaneous category that is a good place to discuss any design criteria that doesn't fit in any of the other sections already covered.

Following is a sample specification for an electronic digital thermometer.

Digital Thermometer Specifications

General Description: To develop a digital thermometer for use with an RTD (Resistance Temperature Detector) sensor to measure and display the temperature at the sensor location. The input signal to the digital thermometer is the resistance variation of the RTD sensor. The digital thermometer will operate off of 115 V AC, 60 Hz power and will utilize a standard enclosure, available off the shelf. The thermometer will be used routinely indoors and wall mounted. The temperature will be displayed on three seven-segment red LEDs. The accuracy should be within 0.5°F over a maximum range of 0° to 200°F.

Performance Specifications:

Rated Conditions:

> Ambient Temperature = 25°C
>
> Power Voltage = 115 V AC
>
> Indication Accuracy: ± 0.25% of the 200°F range

Enclosure Specifications:

Size: Maximum size of $6'' \times 4'' \times 2''$

Shape: The enclosure will be a purchased component from standard enclosures available on the market. A simple rectangular volume is preferable.

Material: Plastic preferred. Metal acceptable.

Human Engineering Aspects: Following is a list of key requirements:

1. The device shall be easily installed and connected.

2. It should be fail-safe if connected incorrectly.

Environmental Specifications:

Ambient Temperature:

Operation: 32°F to 122°F

Storage: −30°F to 122°F

Humidity: 10% to 90% relative humidity, non-condensing

Vibration: The digital thermometer shall be operable in a vibration environment with a vibration frequency from 0.3 Hz to 100 Hz with amplitudes as high as 0.2 g.

Shock: The digital thermometer shall be capable of withstanding shock that will most likely occur during shipment and must therefore meet the requirements of appropriate ICC specifications.

EMI Immunity: The digital thermometer shall be capable of operation in an environment as follows:

Radiated Electrical Fields:

−1 V per meter from 150 kHz through 25 MHz

−10 V per meter from 25 MHz to 1 GHz

Induced Magnetic Field: 20 A at 60 Hz into the enclosure

Power Line: ± 500 V, 50 ns duration over 360°

EMI Emissions: This design will meet the FCC Class B specifications for emissions.

Power Input: 115 V AC, 50 Hz to 60 Hz, ±10% in amplitude. Current draw a maximum of 100 ma.

Operation: The digital thermometer has no real operational requirements other than the requirement for sensor break protection. The sensor break protection will flash the display when the sensor is out of range. The digital thermometer will simply display the temperature when sufficient power is applied. When the signal is out of range, the display will flash.

Agency Approval Requirements: UL 1092 and equivalent CSA specifications

Special Considerations: None

Digital Thermometer Cost Estimates:

Project cost: $10,000

Manufacturing Cost Goal:

Purchased Parts: $95

Labor Costs: $40

Manufacturing Overhead: $15

Annual Volume: 1000 units

After completing the specifications, it is important that all members of the design and overall project team meet to discuss them. Often the process of putting together the specifications generates questions that had not been anticipated by the project's originators. Any issues should be discussed, resolved, and implemented in the final specifications. The final specifications should be signed off, dated, and distributed to all parties.

During most projects, situations occur that promote some change to the specifications. This is natural simply because it is impossible to foresee everything. One of the principles of concurrent engineering is to minimize or eliminate specification changes during the project. Specification changes that occur after significant project activity has been completed are very detrimental to the timely completion of any design project. If specification changes must be made, they should be implemented formally in writing, noting the revision level and date. The design specification should be a formal document and controlled like any other engineering document, by maintaining revision levels and communicating changes to all affected departments. With the specifications complete and signed off, the design process can begin. The following points are important for emphasis as you proceed with any design project:

1. The Project Specifications are a complete definition of the design problem and as such they are the primary basis for measuring the successful completion of the project.

2. Specification changes should be avoided during the project. If changes must be made to the specifications, they must be discussed and approved by all affected parties and implemented formally in the specifications.

▶ Summary

In this chapter we discussed how concurrent engineering principles promote the success of a design project. We also discussed the six-step process for solving design problems. Step Two of the six-step process involves the definition of the problem in the form of a design specification. The process for completing design specifications was discussed and a sample design specification was presented.

Design specifications define all of the technical and business requirements for the new design. They should include a general description of the project and define its performance, power, and package requirements. They will define the environmental conditions under which the project will operate as well as how it will operate. These environmental conditions include ambient temperature, humidity, vibration, shock, EMI noise immunity, and the amount of EMI-radiated noise allowed. The specifications will also include agency approval requirements, cost goals and any other special requirements.

Once design specifications are developed, it is important that they be recognized as a formal document that is agreed to and signed off by the project team. It is also important to minimize the changes made to the specifications during the project. If changes must be made, the specifications should be formally revised and re-approved by the project team.

When the project is complete, the design specification is the primary document used to measure the success of the design project. Of course the ultimate success of the project will be determined by how well the design functions at its intended task and its financial viability. That is why it is so important that the design specifications reflect the complete requirements of the design up front, for careful consideration by the design team.

▶ Reference

Stadtmiller, D. J. 2001. *Electronics Project Management and Design.* Upper Saddle River, NJ: Prentice Hall.

▶ Exercises

1–1   List all of the benefits that result from a complete definition of the problem as described in Step Two of the six-step process.

1–2   List all of the benefits that result from the conclusion stage of problem solving as described in Step Six of the six-step process.

1–3   You are given a full-wave bridge rectifier that has four connections, all of which are unmarked. Define the problem and develop a solution plan for determining the two AC and DC plus/minus connections.

1–4   You wish to determine the key parameters and connections for a transformer that includes six unmarked connections. Define the problem and develop a solution plan.

1–5   You are given an LED display that includes a decimal point. The device is completely unmarked. Define the problem and develop a solution plan to determine all of its ten connections. There are five dual-in-line connections on the top and bottom of the display. The display's individual LEDs are available wired in either common anode or common cathode configuration.

1–6 List all of the benefits that result from the development of complete design specifications.

1–7 List the general categories that should be included in the design specifications.

1–8 How are modifications to design specifications implemented and controlled?

1–9 Develop a list of the operational parameters that must be considered when designing a +5 V supply.

1–10 Consider the design of a sine wave generator. List the operational parameters that should be considered in this design project.

2 ▶ Design Considerations

▶ Introduction

Any product or system resulting from the design process must ultimately function in the real-world environment of its intended application. It may be a pacemaker that provides the critical pulse of life on a continuous basis in whatever environment the patient might encounter, or it might be a ground fault circuit interrupter that meticulously monitors the current in both legs of an electrical circuit, breaking the circuit upon detection of a minute difference in these current levels. An example of a less critical application is a portable CD player worn by a jogger that must play music while bouncing vigorously, in high or low ambient temperature conditions. From the jogger's perspective, the CD player's unflinching operation under these conditions is no less important and is probably the primary reason for its purchase.

Not only must a design function correctly in the intended environment, but it must also be manufacturable in a practical manufacturing environment. Increasingly demanding customers or users require that products and systems be easy to set up and use. It is expected that the design will function reliably and exude quality over the span of its projected life. In the unlikely event that the product fails, it must be easy to service or replace or represent a low enough cost that it can be discarded in an environmentally conscientious way.

These are design issues that vary significantly from the type of product to its manufacturing environment and application. They are the focus topics of this chapter. While these issues were discussed briefly in Chapter 1, this chapter provides more insight into their consideration at the beginning of the design process. This chapter addresses the following topics:

- ▶ Ambient Temperature
- ▶ Electro-magnetic Compatibility

- ▶ Packaging and Materials
- ▶ Manufacturability
- ▶ Ease of Use
- ▶ Seviceability
- ▶ Quality and Reliability

2–1 ▶ Ambient Temperature

The effects of ambient temperature on a circuit can change the value of a signal, or it can cause a component to fail due to excessive ambient temperature levels. When the value of an analog signal changes, this usually affects the value of some parameter important to the accuracy and/or function of the system. Because of the large margin between 1s and 0s, digital systems are usually not that sensitive to ambient temperature-induced accuracy errors. However, the accuracy of digital systems operated on a marginal basis can be compromised by ambient temperature. Generally speaking, when considering circuit reliability, the higher the ambient temperature, the shorter the operating life of the circuit. The effect of ambient temperature on a component can be determined from its data sheet.

What is most important at this point is the identification of the circuit areas that will be most affected by ambient temperature. The effect of ambient temperature must be considered on each component used in these circuits. To determine the change in analog signal levels that result from ambient temperature changes, review the temperature drift values in the specifications for each component in the circuit. These are usually stated in terms of parts per million per degree centigrade (5 ppm/°C), percent change per degree, or simply volts per degree. The effect of ambient temperature on various passive components is discussed in Chapter 4 along with a description of how to use ppm specifications. The sum total of these effects can be determined analytically by applying the induced ambient temperature changes in component values to the equations for the circuit in question. Circuit simulators, discussed in Chapter 3, can also be used to simulate the ambient temperature effects on all of the circuit components and worst-case scenarios can be developed. To meet the requirements for the design, it may be necessary to select different types or higher-grade components that are less sensitive to ambient temperature. Other approaches are either to control the ambient temperature of the sensitive circuit or to measure ambient temperature and compensate the circuit accordingly. Figure 2–1 summarizes the methods for addressing ambient temperature variations.

To consider the effect of ambient temperature on the reliability of electronic circuits and components, first determine the maximum temperature ratings for all of the components. The most critical are those that will get the hottest, those that dissipate the most power. Voltage regulators, amplifiers, and power switching circuits usually require the most power. Component packages for these devices usually accommodate heat sinks. Heat sinks are metal components designed to mount on electronic component packages for the purpose of dissipating heat. Make sure that high-power components have the proper heat sink to disperse the power they are dissipating.

1. Determine circuit areas sensitive to ambient temperature variations that affect system accuracy.

2. Estimate and/or simulate the net results of ambient temperature variations on these circuits.

3. Resolve unacceptable performance by:

   A. Selecting components with lower temperature coefficients.

   B. Matching positive and negative temperature coefficient devices to minimize the effect of temperature variations.

   C. Monitoring and controlling the temperature of the sensitive circuit to a constant value.

   D. Measuring the temperature of the sensitive circuit and providing some means of temperature compensation to the circuit.

▲ **FIGURE 2–1**
Design for Ambient Temperature Variations

Next, estimate the rise in temperature expected inside the enclosure for the electronic device being designed. Mechanical engineers have more experience with this and can determine this analytically because of their background in thermodynamics. The temperature rise can be estimated experimentally by placing the amount of power (use an appropriate number of miniature lightbulbs) that the circuit will generate in a simulated enclosure fabricated from the design material intended. Measure the rise in ambient temperature that occurs when the circuit goes from a no-power state to full power. Once the rise in ambient temperature is determined, add that number to the ambient temperature range to which the device will be exposed (available from the project specifications). The resulting total is the range in the internal case temperature to which each component will be exposed. Depending on the reliability requirements for the design, each component's maximum operating temperature should be at least 10% less than the maximum temperature allowed. Components that exceed this value can possibly be replaced with those that have a higher maximum operating temperature. Other resolutions involve reducing the power consumption of the electronic device, revisiting the design of the enclosure (its size and material), or adding additional air flow or cooling to reduce the expected internal ambient temperature rise. Figure 2–2 summarizes the methods for addressing ambient temperature reliability.

1. Determine the maximum temperature rating for all components.

2. Determine the circuit components that will dissipate the most power.

3. Estimate the rise in temperature above ambient temperature for any enclosure that houses electronics.

4. Maintain component operating temperatures to at least 10% less than their maximum rating by:

   A. Utilizing proper heat sinks on all high power components.

   B. Selecting components with higher operating ambient temperature ratings.

   C. Providing for as much passive air flow as possible.

   D. Providing active air flow (blowers, fans) or cooling as required.

▲ **FIGURE 2–2**
Design for Ambient Temperature Reliability

2–2 ▶ Electro-magnetic Compatibility

Electro-magnetic compatibility (EMC) is the design of electronic devices that promotes compatibility with electro-magnetic waveforms. It includes both the ability of an electronic device to be immune from electro-magnetic interference (EMI immunity) and the minimization of any generated and radiated electro-magnetic waveforms (EMI emissions).

EMI Immunity

For EMI to be a problem, there must be a source for the noise, a circuit that is sensitive to it, and a means for coupling or connecting the noise to the sensitive circuit. The primary sources for EMI are the AC power grid, radio signals, microprocesser-based equipment, electronic switching circuits, inductive switchgear (relays and contactors), ignition systems, and arc welders. EMI can enter an electronic instrument through external wire connections (conductive EMI), or it can present itself as an electromagnetic signal (radiated EMI). EMI can also be generated within the electronic device that can affect its own operation.

The result of EMI noise presented to electronic circuits is realized either as an analog signal that fluctuates incorrectly or as a circuit that ceases to operate properly in some way. This effect can last for a moment or continuously until the circuit is reset or powered down. One example is a digital display that fluctuates momentarily due to a noise spike on the AC power line. Another is a microprocessor-based circuit that locks up (does not respond to key depressions) due to noise induced from a cell phone transmission.

Conductive EMI is electrical noise that is introduced to the electronic circuit by a circuit connection to an external device. Noise either already exists on the conductor, is picked up by passing through an electromagnetic field, or results from sharing the same power supply or ground with another conductor. The AC power grid contains many noise signals that result from its generation and the frequent switching of large inductive loads. Whenever current flows through a wire, a magnetic field is created around the conductor. When a current-carrying conductor is exposed to another electrical or magnetic field, current can be induced in the conductor from this field. When this current is unplanned and unwanted, it is called noise or EMI that is magnetically coupled onto the conductor. When two circuits share the same ground or power supply, the current flowing through one circuit affects the voltage supplied to the other. In this case it is important to realize that each conductor represents a resistance to the circuit (see Figure 2–3). If the resistance value is made small (by using a larger conductor), the amount of noise voltage induced from one circuit to the other is minimized. This method of inducing noise signals onto conductors can affect external conductors and is a major source for generating noise internal to an electronic device. Radiated EMI occurs when an electronic circuit is exposed to an electromagnetic field directly and some noise current is induced in the circuit.

The methods for promoting EMI immunity in electronic devices combine the following concepts:

1. Minimize the amount of conducted EMI that can enter the electronic circuit.

2. Minimize the amount of radiated EMI the electronic circuit can pick up.

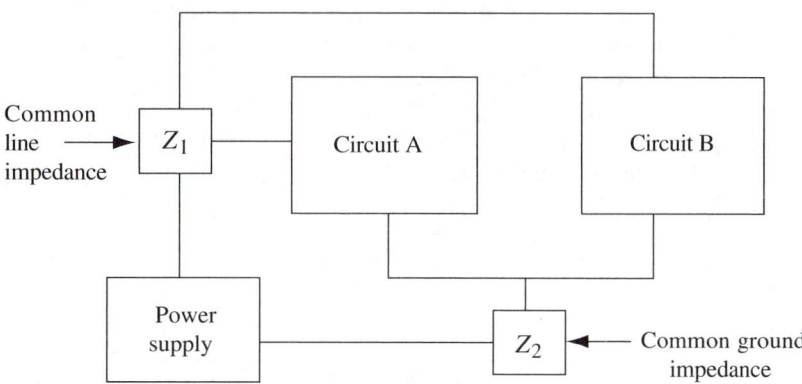

▲ **FIGURE 2–3**
Common ground and power supply

3. Minimize the amount of internal EMI created in the circuit.

4. Minimize the impact of any EMI noise that is presented to the circuit.

These are accomplished by implementing the following techniques:

1. *Elimination of the noise source.* If possible, the simplest and best approach is to eliminate the source of the noise completely. This can be done in a number of ways. If the source of the noise is an electromechanical contactor that is switching an inductive load, then the use of a transient suppressor, such as a metal oxide varistor (MOV) or an RC network placed across the contacts, can eliminate the source of the noise.

2. *Shielding.* The concept of shielding can be applied to conductors or complete electronic devices. It involves placing a conductive material around a conductor or device to pick up noise that would otherwise be induced onto it. The shield is grounded to drain off the induced noise signal with minimal impact to the conductor or device. Shielding works well in minimizing the affects of electrical fields over a wide range of frequencies. Shielding has a lesser effect on reducing noise generated by magnetic fields, especially at higher frequencies, because the current flowing in the shield can be induced on the shielded conductor unless the shield is made from a magnetic material. Shielded cable is available in a variety of configurations to apply the shielding solution to conductors. It is important to connect the shield to the zero signal reference for the signal being shielded. To shield circuits or devices, the entire device should be surrounded by the conductive shield and connected to the zero signal reference. Openings or gaps in the shield should be minimized.

3. *Grounding.* Grounding is the establishment of a zero signal point in the circuit. The basis for good grounding is to separate grounds for circuits where the possibility of noise voltages affecting either circuit exists. Ground loops should also be avoided. When a circuit is grounded in two places that are actually at different potentials, the result is a noise voltage that is the difference in the two ground potentials. This is known as a *ground loop.* Ground loops are also susceptible to noise from magnetic fields (see Figure 2–4).

Good grounding practices involve keeping the grounds from different types of signals separate. The best example is a circuit that includes both analog and digital circuitry. In this case the analog circuit grounds and analog

▶ **FIGURE 2–4**
Ground loop example

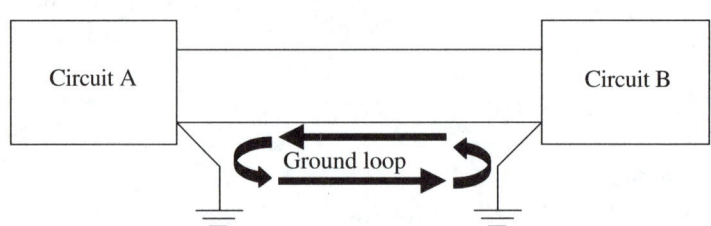

power supplies should be kept separate from digital circuit grounds and digital power supplies. In the case of long ground conductors, avoid the establishment of ground loops. For low-frequency signals, a single-point ground can be used, eliminating the ground loop that results from multiple ground connections.

4. *Impedance matching.* This approach is based upon matching the source impedance with the load impedance to create a balanced situation in a circuit. When this is done, induced noise voltages in the circuit become common mode noise as opposed to differential mode noise. The term *common mode noise* means that the noise is common to both the positive and negative sides of a signal. Differential mode noise is present on only one side of the signal. Common mode noise is easily removed from a signal by using a differential amplifier that amplifies only the differential signal and rejects the common mode signal.

5. *Noise filters.* To eliminate EMI from a circuit, noise filters can be used to attenuate noise from a signal. These are usually designed with capacitors but could be any combination of R, L, and C circuits. The values of the components are selected to attenuate the expected noise-voltage frequencies and pass the signal frequencies.

6. *Physical orientation.* When conductive or radiated noise sources exist, try to keep them as far away as possible from sensitive circuits. On circuit boards locate a switching power supply away from any analog signal amplifiers. In cables and on connectors, locate signals that can interact away from each other and place ground levels in between them. In the case of magnetic fields place circuit runs so that they are perpendicular with the magnetic field.

7. *Circuit isolation.* Transformers are used to isolate circuits for safety reasons, but there is also a benefit for eliminating noise voltages. When a ground loop exists between two circuits, a noise voltage is created between the two circuits if the grounds are at different potentials. Connecting an isolation transformer between the two circuits can break the ground loop (see Figure 2–5)

8. *Ferrite beads.* These are essentially a magnetic shield that serves to attenuate high frequencies without affecting DC or low frequencies. They are installed by passing a conductor through the ferrite beads. The result is a series RL circuit that serves as a high-frequency filter.

▶ **FIGURE 2–5**
Isolation transformer example

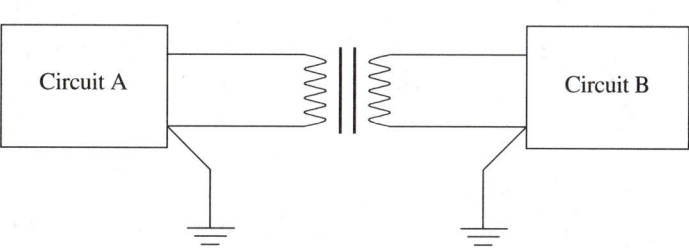

9. *Minimize the EMI effect.* There is always some level of EMI that will be presented to a sensitive circuit. In microprocessor circuits the result of EMI often causes the processor out of the normal program loop. It eventually locks up, unresponsive to any keyboard commands. To prevent this, a watchdog timer can be used to make this invisible to the user. A watchdog timer is a device that is reset at the beginning of every main program loop. The timer value is set at a time that is slightly greater than the maximum time to execute the main program loop. If the timer counts down before being reset at the beginning of the next program loop, then the processor must be out of the program loop. The watchdog timer invokes a reset and the processor will go to the beginning of the main loop. One other detail is that the RAM that contains parameters being used by the program must be preserved for this approach to work well. If the RAM is corrupted by EMI, then operation will not commence properly.

EMI Emissions

An electronic device can emit EMI as radiated waves or as interference that is conducted back into the power supply connections. In an effort to improve EMI immunity, many agencies have established standards to minimize noise emissions. By doing so they are taking the first step in promoting noise immunity—the elimination of noise at the source. The Federal Communications Commission (FCC), the Food and Drug Administration (FDA), and the European Committee (European Union's CE Standards) regulations all specify limits and test procedures to verify that all EMI emissions are held within their published regulations. These requirements are applied generally to any digital device that operates at frequencies of 10 kHz or higher. All of the steps listed previously to promote noise immunity can be utilized to minimize EMI emissions. There are additional measures that can be implemented when the printed circuit board is laid out. These are discussed in Chapter 5.

2–3 ▶ Packaging and Materials

There are a number of issues related to packaging and materials that are important for the electronic designer to consider. While mechanical designers will have primary responsibility for many of these design areas, these areas must be considered by the electronics design team as well. Following are the major packaging issues:

1. *Size and shape.* The overall size and shape of the package are indicative of the type of technology that should be utilized: SMT or through-hole technology.

2. *Material.* The enclosure material affects the EMI shielding, heat transfer capability, and agency approval requirements for the design. Even when plastic is the chosen enclosure material, EMI shielding can be accomplished

with the use of conductive paints applied to the inside surface of the enclosure. Metal enclosures will transfer heat to the outside much better than plastic, which is a consideration when estimating the expected heat rise in the enclosure. Finally, if agency approvals such as Underwriter's Laboratories (UL) or the Canadian Standards Association (CSA) are required, then any materials used should have the appropriate approval ratings. These ratings indicate the flammability of the material, and the safety standards of these approval agencies are a key concern.

3. *Enclosure seal.* The sealing capabilities of the enclosure also determine the amount of heat transfer that is possible from the enclosure's inside to its outside. There are various levels of standards for sealing and moisture-proof enclosures issued by the National Electrical Manufacturer's Association (NEMA). Examples are dustproof, waterproof under normal pressure, or waterproof under high pressure. These specifications might also dictate the need for what is called *conformal coating of the electronics* the entire immersion of an electronics assembly in a waterproof material. This is commonly done with varnishes and epoxies.

4. *Intrinsic safety.* In design applications in which there is extreme danger from any kind of electrical spark, there are requirements for what is called "intrinsically safe equipment." Chemical and petroleum processing plants are good examples of applications for these types of products. There are many levels of instrinsic safety specifications that limit any electronic switching below certain levels and contain any spark within the device.

2–4 ▶ Manufacturability

It is never too early to start thinking about a product's ease of manufacture, even though the lack of any physical form for the design limits visualizing many manufacturing design considerations. The circuit designer must become familiar with the needs and methods of manufacturing and experience the assembly process first-hand. It is also important to involve people in the manufacturing departments, such as manufacturing engineers, floor supervisors, and the assemblers, in the design process. It is the combination of all these sources of knowledge working with the designer that achieves the best results. As discussed in Chapter 1, teamwork and concurrent engineering principles promote the involvement of the manufacturing department early in the project and encourage a feeling of ownership by that department's members. They make the process work, and they will stand behind the product because they had a part in its development.

Manufacturing Process Definition

As the design develops, it is important to review and further define the manufacturing process. The manufacturing department leads this activity, but it needs much assistance from the design engineers. The definition of the manufacturing process involves the determination of the step-by-step assembly process. It also defines the assembly levels to be tested and the test procedures. As the various modules begin to take shape, make a list of the process steps that will be needed to assemble the product. Here are some key questions and issues that should be considered:

1. Can each module be completely tested on its own?

2. Can the final product be completely tested before being installed in its enclosure?

3. Only those manufacturing adjustments that are absolutely necessary should be included in the product.

4. Try to minimize and automate any testing and calibration that must be performed on the product.

There have been many changes in manufacturing ideologies over the last 20 years. The basis for this is a trend away from batch processing to a concept called *one-piece flow.* In batch processing, a large quantity of product is manufactured by assembling a quantity of each succeeding assembly level in different manufacturing areas, until the whole batch is completed. One-piece flow processing promotes the manufacture of a single-end product in a manufacturing cell until it is complete. This is also called *cellurized manufacturing.* Both processes are shown in Figure 2–6, which shows flowcharts for the manufacture of printed circuit boards (PCBs).

Take the assembly of a personal computer as an example. A company desires to manufacture 100 PCs in a week. Batch processing (see Figure 2–6) of these 100 units requires building 100 PC circuit boards on Monday. Testing and doing

▶ **FIGURE 2–6**
One-piece flow vs. batch processing

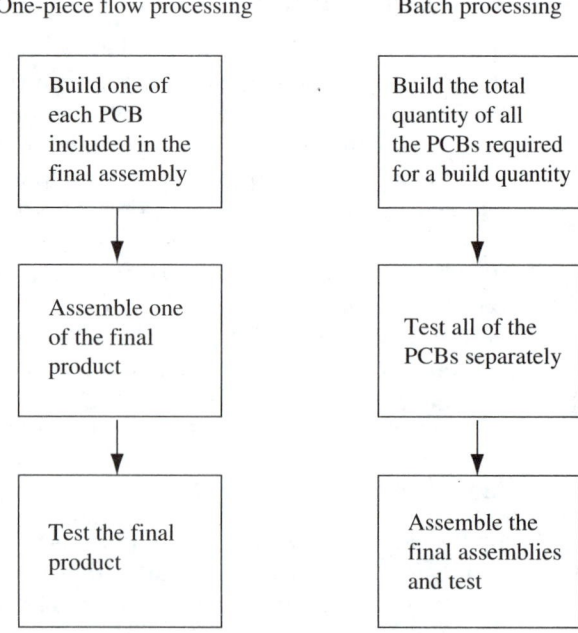

further assembly of those 100 circuit boards would occur on Tuesday. Final assembly of the 100 units would be performed on Wednesday. Then the final assemblies would be tested, calibrated, and burned-in on Thursday. The final assemblies would be packaged and ready for shipment on Friday.

A pure one-piece flow, cellurized manufacturing process (see Figure 2–6) dictates that one set of PC circuit boards be assembled, tested, and completed into a final assembly. Then another and another would be assembled until the 100 units are completed. All of the work would be completed in one manufacturing cell.

The benefits of one-piece flow processing are as follows:

1. Because each unit is completed shortly after all of the operations have been performed, process errors that occur are quickly identified and can be rectified before being repeated in other units.

2. Shipment lead times are reduced because units are available for shipment sooner than if they were batch processed.

3. One-piece flow represents a streamlined process in which the handling and movement of components and subassemblies around the plant are minimized.

4. All of the workers in the cell become cross-trained and are able to perform other cell operations. Because of this, they understand the complete assembly process and are more able to recognize problems in their infancy.

These are all significant benefits over the results experienced with batch processing. The problem with the one-piece flow concept arises with highly automated operations, where expensive equipment is required. Take the soldering operation for the PC example discussed previously. If batch processed, all of the boards would be assembled and then transferred to a wave-solder area for soldering. A pure one-piece flow process would require a wave-solder machine for each manufacturing cell. This is an expensive and space-consuming proposition that usually results in a compromise between batch processing and one-piece flow. The PC assembly process is just one example of the types of decisions that must be made. The manufacturing department or group and the design engineers must work together concurrently to determine the best methods for testing, calibration, and burn-in of all subassemblies and the final product.

Manufacturing Test and Calibration

When the manufacturing process is laid out, the stages in which assemblies will be tested are defined. These are all issues that will be developed later in the design process but should be in the background thought of the electronic designer as the initial design progresses. These stages will depend on the product and the type of process being used—batch processing or one-piece flow. Manufacturing test methods have also seen significant change in the last 20 years. These changes are similar to those discussed for manufacturing assembly.

To better understand this change in manufacturing test philosophy, let us explore the differences between batch processing and one-piece flow as they pertain to circuit board assembly and testing. The following represents a typical batch process circuit board assembly and test operation for a high-volume manufacturer.

Board Assembly and Test—Batch Processing

1. Incoming circuit board components are inspected before assembly.

2. Circuit boards are assembled in lots of 100 with auto-insertion machines. Some components are manually inserted before completing the assembly.

3. The assembled boards are sent to a wave-solder station, where they pass through the wave-solder process. The boards are cleaned and allowed to dry after soldering.

4. The quality department usually inspects each board or sample-inspects the boards for assembly errors and quality defects.

5. The inspected boards are sent to a test station, where an automated tester performs a series of preprogrammed tests on the particular circuit board.

6. If the board passes the tests, it proceeds to the next level of assembly. If not, a printout that includes information about the test failure is attached to the printed circuit board. The circuit board is sent to a test station, where a test technician will troubleshoot and repair the board. The repaired board is sent back to the automated test station for verification.

7. The final product is assembled using the circuit board under discussion in addition to other circuit boards that have experienced the same process. The final product is assembled and tested with a test fixture designed especially for the product. If the unit passes the final assembly tests, it is burned-in and readied for shipment. If not, the circuit boards that possess the malfunctions must be identified and corrected.

This process has been in use for many years. Following are the problems associated and experienced with this process:

1. Assembly or process errors are often repeated throughout an entire lot of boards before being detected during inspection or testing.

2. Because the process is segmented, there are time delays between the operations. There is generally poor communication between the people performing the different operations. Consequently, problem resolution and process improvement are not promoted.

3. Sometimes circuit boards pass their specific automated tests, but they will not function together with other circuit boards when assembled in the final product. Called *dynamic failures*, these result from the inability of the circuit board tests to verify the circuit board's complete operation.

4. In general, because so much time passes between the assembly of a circuit board and its assembly and test in the final unit, there is poor feedback to resolve quality issues as they develop.

In order to address and resolve these issues, cellurized manufacturing for circuit board assembly and test processes utilizing one-piece flow concepts were developed.

Board Assembly and Test—Manufacturing Cells

The following process describes cell manufacturing:

1. Incoming components are batch inspected, organized in assembly kits, and sent to the manufacturing cell.

2. The circuit boards are assembled and soldered within the cell. Small wave-solder machines have been developed for this purpose. If possible, all of the circuit boards included within a particular product are palletized (see Figure 2–7).

3. This means they are all attached to each other, assembled and tested as a unit, and then broken down into individual circuit boards for assembly. The individual boards are held together by a series of small laminate areas that are located between the individual boards. These areas are easily cut away or broken off to separate the boards.

4. Testing is completed with custom test fixtures within the cell. Only minimal testing is performed on the circuit boards until the final level of operation. This is easily accomplished using the palletized board approach. The testing philosophy applied here is to provide testing for a particular assembly only, when the cost of not testing the assembly is greater than the cost of testing it. In other words, an assembly should be tested only if the cost of finding a problem later is greater than the cost of testing the assembly.

The downside of cell manufacturing is realized when automated processes and equipment are applied. Because this type of equipment is expensive, it is hard to justify locating it in every cell, so two or more cells may share equipment by locating them in close proximity to it. The implementation of cell manufacturing has promoted the use of small, dedicated custom-designed test fixtures for testing assemblies and final products.

The test and calibration plan is developed as part of the overall manufacturing process and depends on the degree to which batch processing and cellular manufacturing techniques are applied. The test plan defines all of the assemblies that are tested along with the purpose for the tests.

Test Fixture Development

Once the test plan has been developed, test-fixture development can begin. Consider the test plan to be the specification for the design of the test fixture. When designing test fixtures, the design challenge is making quick and secure connections to points in the circuit where test measurements must be made. Measurement points that are available at the circuit board interconnections are easily accomplished by using a mating connector in the test fixture. For measurement points that are not accessible, a "bed of nails" approach must be used. A bed of nails is simply a test

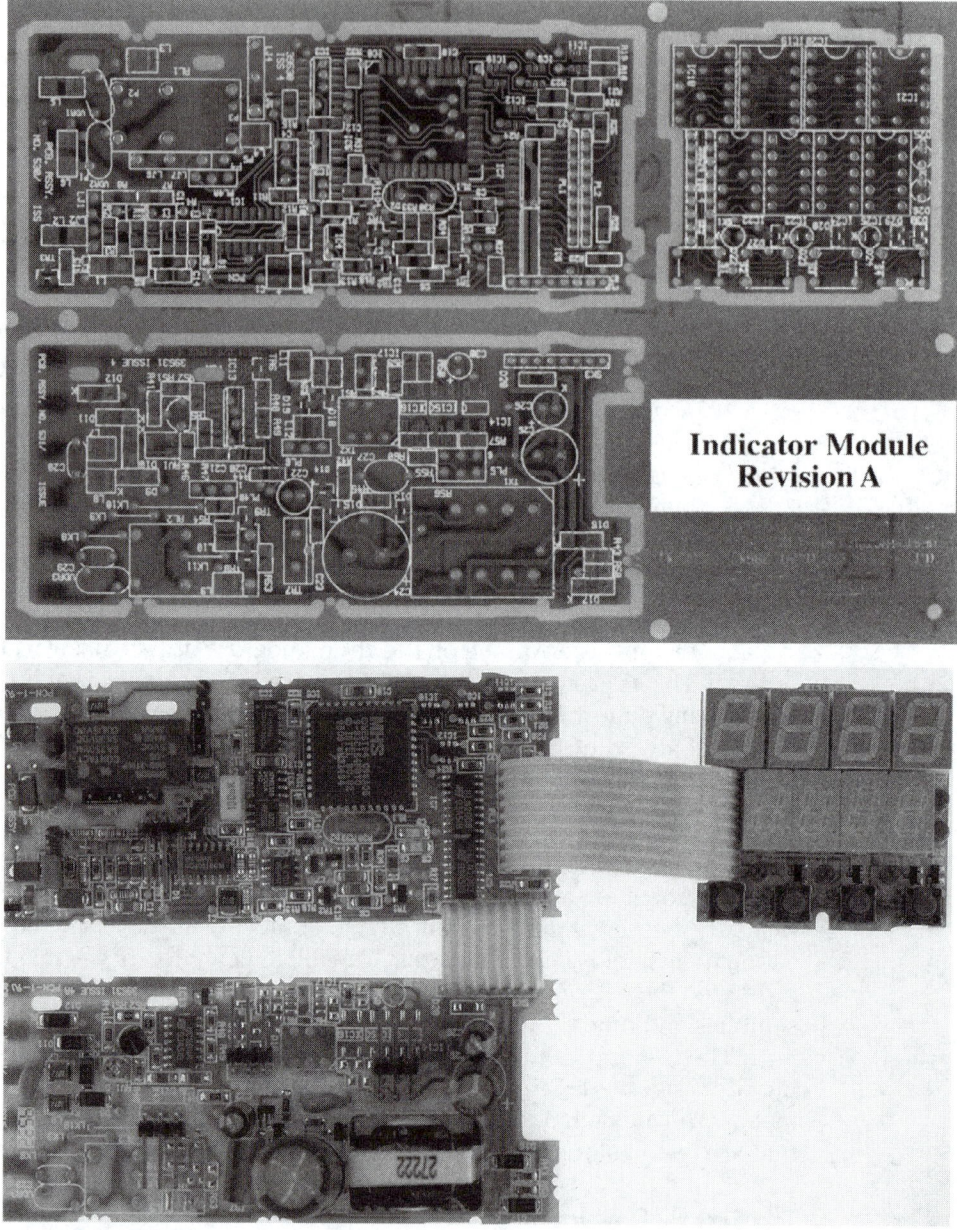

▲ FIGURE 2–7
Palletized circuit board

fixture that includes spring-loaded pogo pins (see Figure 2–8) that are located to make contact with specific pads on the bottom of the printed circuit board. There are two types of bed-of-nails fixtures. In one type the board is pressed down onto the bed of nails and mechanically held against the spring-loaded pogo pins. The other type is called a *vacuum fixture*, where air pressure pushes the pogo pins

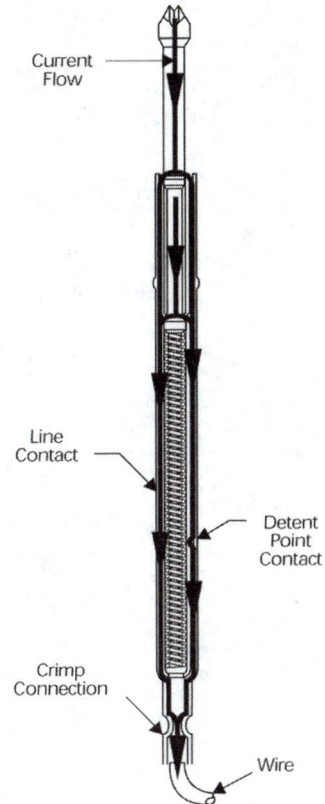

Current
Flow

Line
Contact

Detent
Point
Contact

Crimp
Connection

Wire

▶ **FIGURE 2–8**
Spring-loaded test pin *(Courtesy of
IDI Synergetix)*

against the board that is being tested. Companies that specialize in their design and construction usually develop vacuum fixtures. The design expertise and equipment to fabricate them are usually not available within most manufacturing companies.

Having determined a method for accessing test points, the fixture design can proceed. The test fixture is usually developed with an available programmable tester. Digital, analog, and combination circuit testers are available from a number of manufacturers (see Figure 2–9). Utilizing off-the-shelf automated test systems requires the development of high-level language programs that perform the tests. However, as mentioned previously, cellurized manufacturing has promoted the use of small custom-designed test fixtures for use in manufacturing cells. These custom fixtures can become significant design projects on their own and should be approached as a separate design subproject. Many of these are microprocessor-based designs, for which custom software is developed and circuit boards must be designed and laid out.

Test and Calibration Procedures

Along with any test or calibration fixture, a procedure must be developed to document the process to be followed while using the fixture. These procedures should be concise and accurate. Any changes made to these procedures should be formally

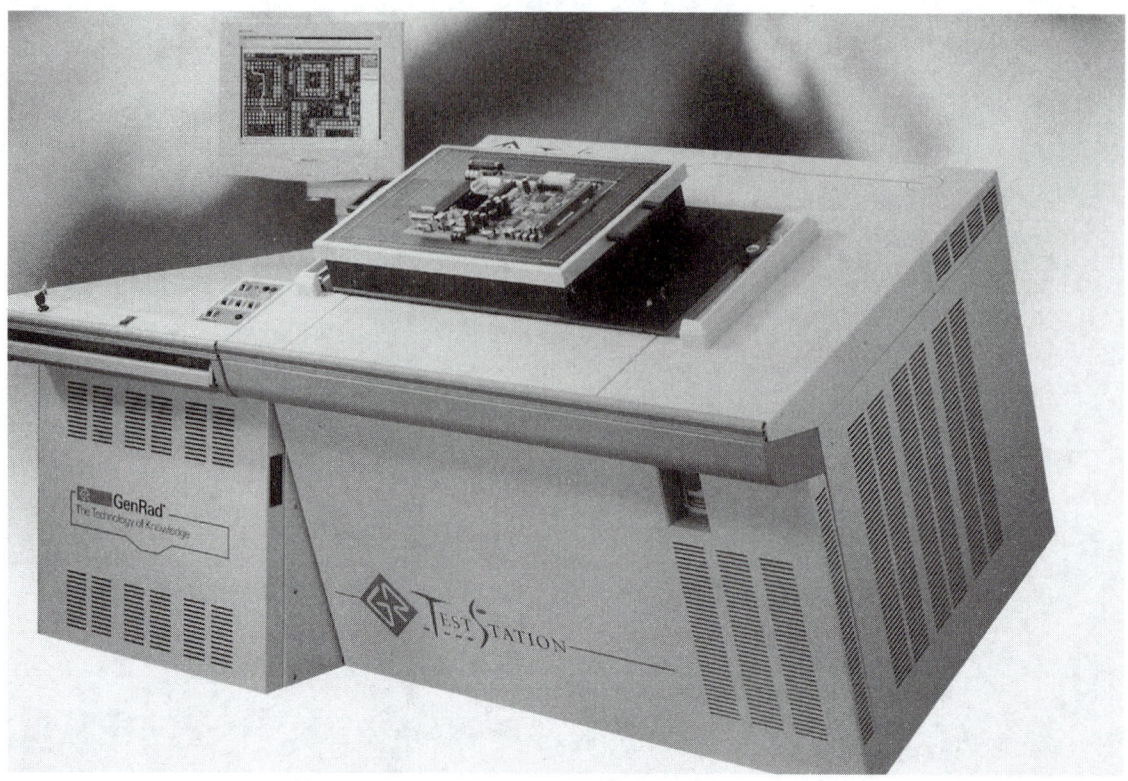

▲ **FIGURE 2–9**
Genrad tester *(Courtesy of Genrad, Inc.)*

controlled as any other engineering document. A test procedure is completed for
each group of tests performed for an assembly and should reference the test fixture
utilized. The test procedure should include the precise, step-by-step description of
the tests to be performed in the sequence that they are to be completed. Completion of a test procedure often includes the compilation of test data and results for
future reference. A blank sample of the test data sheet should be included in the
test procedure. As with any manufacturing process, it is important to streamline
all testing and calibration into a smooth process with minimal repetition of operations while maintaining accuracy and quality goals.

Burn-in

Another manufacturing process often used for electronic products is a process
called *burn-in*. The purpose of the burn-in process is to minimize infantile failures. Infantile failures are premature failures that occur in weak components or
connections. These failures happen shortly after a product is put in use. Many companies define infantile failures as those that occur between 1 and 30 days after a
product is first used in an application. The goal of the burn-in process is to induce
any weak components to fail before shipment to the customer, thereby causing a

pending infantile failure to occur where it can be repaired without any negative impact on the customer.

There are many theories about burn-in and as many different practical approaches to its implementation. In order to induce pending infantile failures to occur, the product should be powered and operated in conditions that equal the customer's actual use. In order to accelerate the wear on weak components and accomplish burn-in quickly, the product is maintained at an elevated temperature. A more efficient burn-in is achieved if the temperature is cycled between room temperature, 25°C, and a temperature around 55°C. This causes the weak component to expand and contract as the temperature is cycled. If the lower temperature is set at 0°C instead of room temperature, the effectiveness of burn-in is further improved. The 0°C setting requires that the burn-in equipment have cooling capability. Finally, the on/off switching of power to the product is an additional stress that can often induce infantile failures.

Infantile failures are the result of weak or inferior components or connections. Many times components or connections are weakened by the manufacturing process. This is the case when a CMOS component is improperly handled and exposed to static electricity, thereby weakening it. Sometimes semiconductor components are weakened by exposure to severe temperature in a wave-solder process. Because components can be purchased pre-burned-in, many companies discontinue the burn-in process, neglecting the fact that the manufacturing process often weakens components.

Many companies believe in burn-in and perform it blindly, while others simply skip the process. The manufacturing department will always have a dim view of burn-in, which consumes much time and space and requires a significant capital investment. If a company has a solid manufacturing process that induces very few weak components, and it purchases top-quality components from quality suppliers and checks the process constantly, then burn-in may not be necessary. Otherwise, burn-in is the only final check to weed out weak components. A sure way to measure the need or effectiveness of burn-in is to monitor the number of infantile failures that occur in customer applications. The burn-in process should be considered at the very early stages of product design and reviewed throughout the project.

2–5 ▶ Ease of Use

"User friendly," a term coined in the 1980s, has been used—and overused—so much that people became tired of hearing it. The concept remains, though, and has increased in significance as a competitive advantage for all products. The primary reason for this is the increased use of microprocessors in products and the resulting increase in the number of features and options included within them. These variations in operation and features require the user to program or set up the product before use. The flashing clock readout on a VCR is a good example of the problem, as most people have a VCR, but few people can remember how to set its clock correctly after a power outage. Ease of use should be a goal for all products. Ease of use should include the sale, installation, set-up, programming, and use of the product. The best way to evaluate the ease of use of a product is to compare it to another competing design. Take every opportunity to compare the ease of use of products and make it a practice to evaluate every product's ease of use. The following areas are a measure of the ease of use of a product:

1. Requirement for an operator's manual. Can the majority of the most common operations be completed without the use of an operator's manual?

2. Quantity and clarity of the required steps. How many steps are required to complete a particular operation, and how clearly are these steps presented?

3. Amount of information to be remembered. How many items in the product's operation must be committed to memory in order to operate it?

To summarize, a product that is easy to use is one that can be operated almost intuitively without an operator's manual. If possible, the product should prompt you through the process. The steps required to set up and use the product should be minimal and clearly presented. Finally, the amount of information about the product required to perform common operations should be minimal and always noted on the product somehow.

2–6 ▶ Serviceability

A product's service requirements should be stated in its specifications. This is an area marketing people tend to gloss over so the service engineering group and the design engineers need to add focus to this topic. Serviceability can range from complete field repairability (repairable to the component level) to no serviceability at all (a throwaway unit). Very seldom are today's products repairable to the component level. Most assemblies are so small and packed together so intricately that disassembly usually damages the product. If the circuit board uses surface mount technology (SMT, explained in Chapter 3) components, it is usually impractical to replace those components. A typical intermediate position is to provide field reparability down to the board level, where circuit boards are changed out and the failed board is deemed not repairable and scrapped. Whichever the case, it is important to consider the serviceability of the product more seriously at this time. If the unit must be repairable to some degree, it must use packaging hardware that will allow disassembly and reassembly in the field. Many times the issues of ease of manufacturability will go against the ease of serviceability.

Example 2–1

A good example of the conflict between ease of manufacture and serviceability involved the method of mounting printed circuit boards to a plastic front panel on an industrial temperature controller. The initial design utilized threaded inserts pressed into plastic tabs that were part of a plastic front panel. The circuit boards were securely attached to the front bezel with screws. As a cost-saving measure, the manufacturing department desired to eliminate both the time-consuming insertions of the threaded inserts as well as the screwing operations. The design of the plastic front panel was changed to include plastic clips that would attach the circuit boards to the front panel. These design changes were integrated into the tooling for the plastic front panel and the change was implemented. The result of this cost-saving measure was a significant reliability and serviceability problem. The plastic clips did not hold the boards in place securely. This made the interconnections between the boards intermittent in high-vibration applications. The plastic clips also made it very difficult to remove the circuit boards once they were attached to the plastic front panel.

The result of this poorly implemented project was an increase in field failures. Also, customers and field service people were very unhappy with the new process for removing circuit boards from the front panel. At a great cost to the company, the design was changed back to the original design that utilized mounting screws.

2–7 ▶ Quality and Reliability

Quality as a measurement is a very broad term that is often made on a relative basis. It includes all aspects of the product, including those previously discussed: manufacturability, serviceability, and ease of use. Reliability on the other hand measures the performance and the time before failure.

Customer Quality Performance

There are a number of ways to measure the quality performance of a product from the customer's perspective. The first and most important is the customer's opinion about its quality. These measurements reflect the customer's expectations and therefore are subject to their point of view. How easy was the product to install? Was the operator's manual helpful and easy to understand? One customer might think that the operator's manual was comprehensive while another might think just the opposite, that the manual did not have enough information—or the right information. These measurements are best taken with a simple questionnaire that allows the customer to comment on the general appearance, function, and ease of use of the product. The performance of the product in these areas should be determined by taking an average of the respondent's replies, developing a rating for the product, and comparing the change in rating as attempts are made to improve weak areas.

The second method for measuring the quality of a product involves its failure and the reason for failure. From the customer's perspective, a failure is a failure. However, failures that occur sooner rather than later leave a less favorable impression. There are four time lengths, or levels of failure, that have important distinctions and are explained next. Figure 2–10 shows a summary of the four levels of failure.

Out-of-Box Failures

These are the most severe failures, because they cause the greatest amount of dissatisfaction for the customer. In these cases, as the name implies, the customer receives the product and unpacks it, and the product fails to perform right out of the box. Out-of-box failures can be induced by rough handling during shipment;

1. Out-of-box failures

2. 30-day failures

3. Within-warranty failures

4. Out-of-warranty failures

▶ **FIGURE 2–10**
Summary of product failure types

otherwise they indicate a complete failure of the manufacturer's quality system. If the failure was induced by rough shipment, then a determination should be made as to the correct use of the packaging and any evidence of improper handling should be reviewed.

When the out-of-box failure is not due to shipment, then the exact nature of the failure must be determined. The most prevalent cause of these types of failures is incomplete testing of the entire assembly before shipment. Once identified, every effort must be made to make changes that prevent any reoccurrence of this particular problem. Another type of out-of-box failure may not involve a failure of the product at all. An example is when an operator's manual does not explain the operation of the product to the customer to the point where the customer believes it is not functional. In this case the product failure is caused by the operator manual.

Failures Within 30 Days of Receipt

These failures are called *infantile* or *premature failures*. The product is received by the customer, set up, and verified for use. After a period of less than 30 days, the product fails. This is a very special case, because the product did function at the customer location and now it has failed. This type of failure is usually caused by a component failure or a weak electrical connection. These failures can occur after routine use or when excessive strain is placed on the product. It is therefore important to determine the failed mechanism, be it a component or connection. The application of the product should be reviewed with the customer for any specifications that are being exceeded. If the failure occurs under normal use of the product, it is a true infantile failure. The only method available to minimize infantile failures is with the burn-in process discussed previously. Infantile failures are almost as aggravating to the customer as out-of-box failures.

Failures Within the Warranty Period

These are similar in nature to infantile failures except that the product operates for a longer period of time (greater than 30 days) but less than the specified warranty period. Of course, some percentage of the product will always fail before the warranty has expired. The actual percentage level of product failures under warranty significantly affects the product's success. These failures are usually due to a weak component, connection, or a design problem. Data indicating the root cause of the failure should be maintained and monitored.

Failures Outside the Warranty Period

These failures are the least bothersome for both the customer and the supplier. From the customer's perspective, that depends on the amount of time after warranty expiration that the failure occurs. A failure that occurs one week after a one-year warranty period is viewed much differently than a failure occurring one year after a one-year warranty expiration. Although these failures are not a financial burden to the manufacturer, they do represent a problem to the customer. Therefore, the reasons for these failures should be determined. Data regarding them should be kept and reviewed regularly while efforts are made to reduce the overall mean time between failure (MTBF, see next section) for the product. These four categories of failures represent four different aspects of the reliability of the product and the quality process that has been put in place to ensure it.

1. Out-of-box failures are a measure of how well a supplier checks out, packages, and ships the product to the customer.

2. 30-day failures are a measure of infantile failures, which can be affected by burn-in.

3. Warranty failures indicate the level of failures within the warranty period excluding 30-day failures. These are usually the result of inferior or misapplied components or other design problems.

4. Non-warranty failures are used in conjunction with all other failures to determine the overall MTBF for the product. These are the result of inferior or misapplied components, other design problems, or the limited life of the product.

Product reliability can be enhanced by a combination of design improvements, test fixture and procedure changes, product packaging, information enhancements, and modified burn-in.

Reliability Projections

When a design is completed, there are always questions about its reliability. The reliability of a design is determined on average by how long it functions properly in the intended application without failure. In industry, the reliability of a design is measured by a term called the *mean time between failure* (MTBF). Statistics theory defines the arithmetic mean as an average. The MTBF is the average time between failures of a product design. There are two ways to project the reliability of a design: accelerated life testing and statistical mathematical reliability projections.

Accelerated Life Testing

Accelerated life tests expose a design to conditions in which failure-prone areas are stressed to accelerate their wear. Take the example of a control relay that is normally cycled on and off five times a day. Accelerated life testing would cycle the relay on and off five times an hour. The net effect of 1 day of testing would simulate 24 days in the intended application. To properly set up an accelerated life test, the design should be reviewed to determine all of the expected failure areas. The test developed should include some component that addresses each of the expected failure-prone areas. Continued exposure to high ambient temperatures is the only way to accelerate wear on many internal electronic components.

Statistical Reliability Projections

The statistical projection of reliability of an electronic design is accomplished by the use of reliability data that is available for many components. This reliability data has been developed with military specifications developed for the purpose of projecting reliability. As discussed previously, military equipment is subject to the most rigorous performance, environmental, and reliability specifications. The data supplied in military specifications lists a mean time between failure for components that is determined by the power, voltage, current, and ambient temperature at which the component is operated. The MTBF for each component utilized in a design is totaled. The grand total is divided by the number of components to determine projected MTBF for the complete design. Software is now available that will take all of the components included within a design and project reliability while considering the operational data supplied. Manual methods for completing these calculations can be cumbersome for a complicated design.

Designers become aware of these are issues as they gain experience in a particular type of design application. Any application can have its own unique set of problems and priorities. What is most important is that circuit designers and software developers become intimately aware of a design's manufacturing and application environment. This can be accomplished by working on the manufacturing floor, going on trips to experience product applications, keeping abreast of trade periodicals and attendance at trade shows. Every attempt should be made to foster these types of activities. Finally, communication amongst engineering, manufacturing, service and quality is critical to the design's ultimate success.

▶ Summary

In this chapter we discussed how to consider and address the most important general design issues that are confronted in most design projects. The issues that most affect the operation of the design are ambient temperature and EMI immunity. The affects of ambient temperature can be minimized by the selection of better grades of components, by temperature compensation, or by temperature control. EMI immunity is generally improved by minimizing the radiated, conducted, and internally generated EMI induced in the product.

The design issues that most affect the end user of the design and/or its manufacture and support are package technology (through-hole or SMT), manufacturing process selection, ease of use, serviceability, quality, and reliability. These issues can gain the most leverage from the concurrent engineering approach described in Chapter 1. In this chapter we discussed the criteria for selecting either through-hole or SMT circuit board processes. We defined the two main variations of manufacturing processes, batch processing and one-piece flow, and how they affect the assembly and testing of a product, as well as their strengths and weaknesses. Methods of automated testing electronic designs were reviewed as methods for making test point connections with either connectors or a bed-of-nails. The manufacturing process called *burn-in* was presented as a method of reducing infantile failures in a product design. Measurements and methods for improving the ease of use and serviceability of a design were reviewed.

Finally, the quality and reliability requirements for a design were discussed. Quality was defined from the customer's perspective in very basic terms while reliability was explored a little more deeply. This chapter presented four basic levels of reliability measures as it defined out-of-box, 30-day, warranty, and non-warranty failures. The significance of each category was discussed as well as methods for improvement. The reliability of design is generally measured in mean time between failures (MTBF). The MTBF can be projected with accelerated life testing or by using statistical methods.

▶ Reference

Stadmiller, D. J. 2001. *Electronics Project Management and Design.* Upper Saddle River, NJ: Prentice Hall.

▶ Exercises

2–1 Name the general types of problems that are experienced by electronic systems when they are exposed to high ambient temperatures.

2–2 What remedies are possible when an electronic component in a system is exposed to ambient temperatures that exceed the maximum temperature ratings of the device.?

2–3 List the four major packaging and material issues discussed in this chapter.

2–4 List the general concepts for maximizing EMI noise immunity.

2–5 In your own words, define what is meant by the term *ground loop.*

2–6 Discuss the main difference between conducted and radiated EMI.

2–7 Why are the grounds from analog and digital circuits kept separate as much as possible?

2–8   What are the two basic types of manufacturing processes from which to select when determining the manufacturing process for a new product?

2–9   Define what is meant by the term batch processing and discuss its advantages and disadvantages.

2–10 Define what is meant by the term one-piece processing and discuss its advantages and disadvantages.

2–11 What is meant by the term *palletized board assembly?* What are the advantages of using the palletized board concept?

2–12 Define what is meant by an *infantile failure.*

2–13 What is the process called *burn-in* and what is its purpose?

2–14 What parameter is used to describe the reliability of a design?

2–15 What are the two primary ways of projecting the reliability of a design?

2–16 List all of the ways discussed in this chapter that the customer quality level of a product can be measured.

2–17 Explain the difference between 30-day failures and out-of-box failures. Which type is more critical and why?

2–18 How can infantile failure levels be reduced?

2–19 How can out-of-box failures be reduced?

3 The Preliminary Design

▶ Introduction

As in life, the first steps made in the design process are often the most difficult ones. Most design problems are complex and actually represent many different design problems all wrapped up into one. The tendency of many first-time designers is to try to design a complete solution all at once. It is extremely difficult for the mind to solve many complex problems simultaneously, so it is necessary to break down the problem into its basic functional components or modules. It is also important to plan the solution (Step Three of the Six Steps) in a logical manner.

As students, we become used to solving problems by analyzing well-defined circuits. Facing a new design problem with a clean sheet of paper is a revealing moment for the beginning design engineer. This chapter will discuss beginning the design process and developing a preliminary design by addressing the following topics:

- ▸ Divide and Conquer
- ▸ Preliminary Design Issues
- ▸ Enhancing Creativity
- ▸ The Initial Design
- ▸ Circuit Simulation Software
- ▸ Breadboarding

3–1 ▶ Divide and Conquer

The best way to start the process is to break down the design problem into smaller blocks or modules, these being the next largest functional modules contained within the overall design. Look at this like a gift-wrapped present that when unwrapped reveals another fully wrapped gift, and then another, and so on. A complex project sometimes has many sub-levels.

Example 3–1

Consider the problem of designing an audio tape deck to play back and record standard audiocassette tapes. In this example the top-level design problem is broken down into subprojects. In order to define the functional requirements inside the tape deck, think about the functional requirements from the operator's point of view. The top-level operational requirements of a standard tape deck are as follows:

1. Power on/off

2. Insert/eject cassette tapes

3. Play tapes

4. Fast forward

5. Rewind

6. Pause

7. Record

8. Stop

9. Adjust record levels

10. View record levels

The operational requirements listed can be categorized into the following common functional circuits in a block diagram:

1. *Tape Deck Control.* This module will control turning the tape deck on and off, all tape deck movement, insertion and ejection of tapes, and the selection of Play/Record.

2. *Audio Signal Playback.* This module includes the audio playback head and amplifiers to the output.

3. *Audio Signal Record.* The audio record head, the signal from the record inputs, the adjustment of the input signals and the display of the record levels reside in this module.

4. *Power Supply.* All of the modules listed previously will need a variety of DC power, which should be centrally developed and supplied by this module to the various circuits.

5. *The Tape Transport.* The cassette tape and the complete mechanism.

The functional requirements for the audio tape deck design have been broken down into five modules that can be approached as separate designs. See Figure 3–1 for the actual block diagram.

After subdividing the project, Step One and Step Two should be re-applied to each module. The level to which this occurs depends on the complexity of the

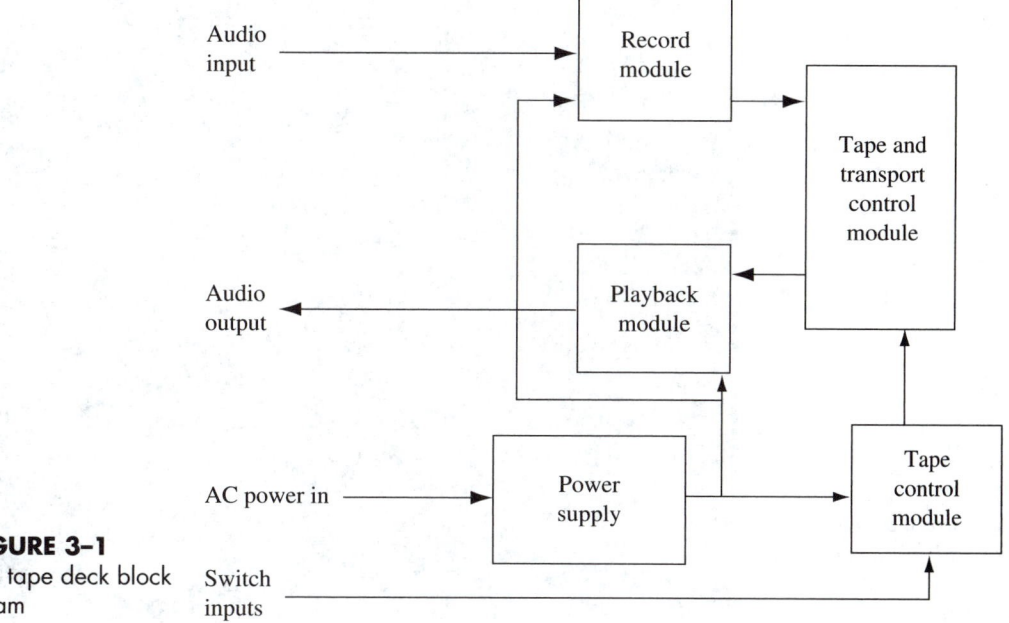

▶ **FIGURE 3-1**
Audio tape deck block
diagram

module. In some projects the modules are highly complicated circuit boards, and
it is appropriate to develop a complete specification for each. For other projects
the requirements can simply be listed as they are designed.

3-2 ▶ Preliminary Design Issues

After the design problem has been broken down into modules, there is more research to be done before actually designing the circuits. This is necessary because
even though data was collected and the design problem was defined for the overall design problem, it has now been broken down into smaller modules. More details about the design of these smaller modules must be determined. In a sense we
are starting the Six-Step process all over again as we attempt to solve the smaller
design problem of the submodules. The research process described in Step One of
the Six Steps should be repeated for the submodule designs. If the module is complex, then Step Two should be completed for the module by developing design
specifications.

Technology Selection

Another important choice to be made is the package technology that will be used
for the project's electronic components. This is important for many reasons that
will become obvious as we discuss them. The primary decision to be made is
whether to use through-hole or surface-mount electronic package technology.
Through-hole technology (see Figure 3–2) is the package technology that requires

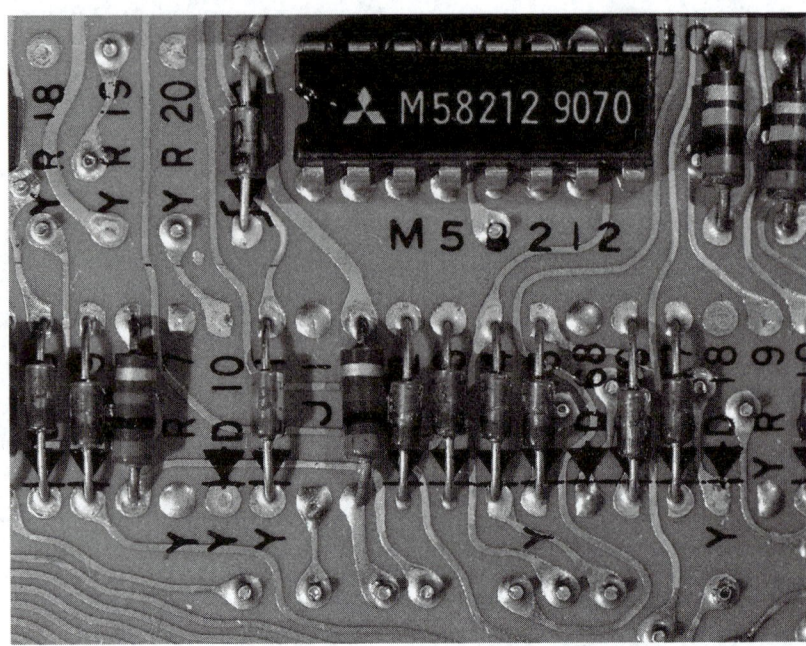

► **FIGURE 3–2**
Through-hole technology
*(Alfred Pasieka/Science
Photo Library/Photo
Researchers, Inc.)*

a hole in the middle of a circuit pad located on the PCB for mounting the component. With surface mount technology (see Figure 3–3), the component solders directly to a pad that is on the surface of the board. Because a hole is not required in the PCB for SMT, the lead spacing can be made much smaller. This allows the reduction of the component sizes as well. The decision between through-hole and surface mount technology is an easy one because of their key differences and their impact. To make this decision, first pose the following questions:

1. Do the product specifications call for very low costs at very high-volume levels?

2. Does the product require an extremely small physical size?

3. Does the company that will manufacture the circuit boards have SMT manufacturing equipment and capabilities?

If the answer to any one of these questions is yes, then SMT should be strongly considered. Otherwise, through-hole technology should be utilized. To get a better understanding of this question, let's review the advantages and disadvantages of SMT:

Advantages:

Very small package sizes are possible.

Low assembly costs are possible in high volume through automated assembly.

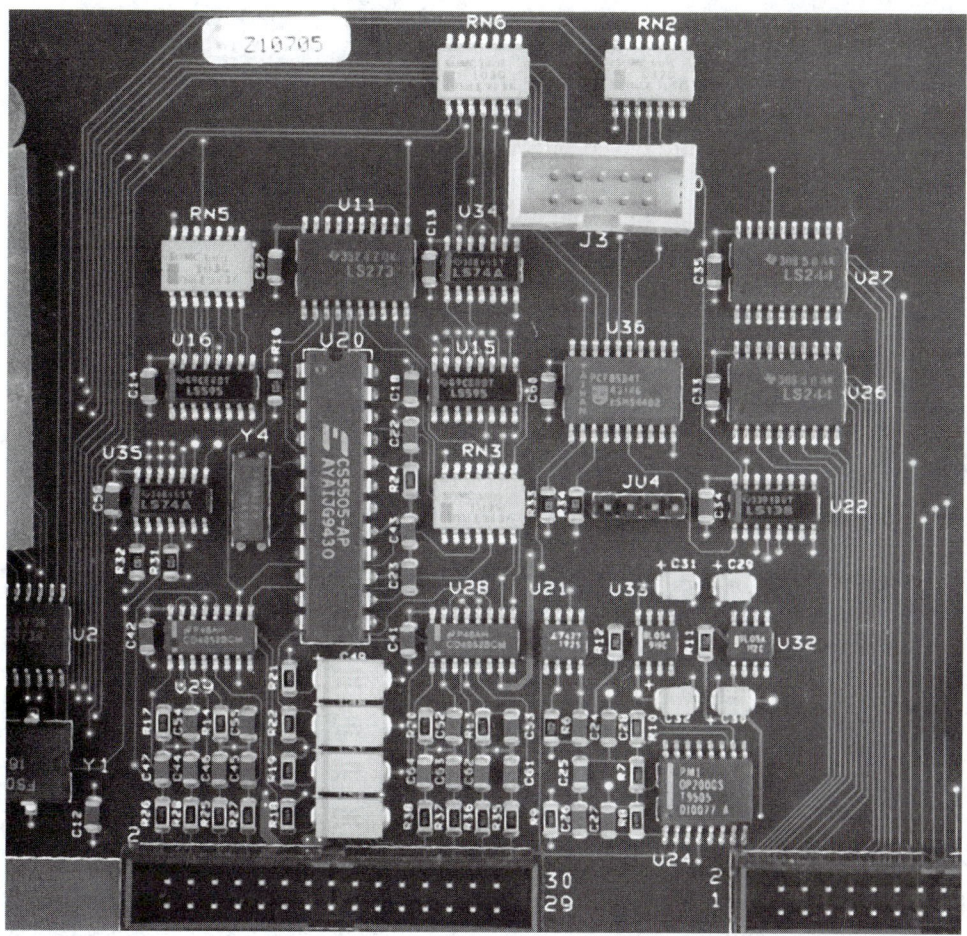

▲ **FIGURE 3–3**
Surface-mount technology

Disadvantages:

SMT boards are difficult to breadboard and prototype.

Components have longer lead times and larger minimum buy quantities.

A large investment in equipment and know-how is required.

These boards are not easily repaired.

The criteria for this decision have been presented. Unless one of the unique advantages of SMT is required (small size or low costs @ high volume) or the company already possesses SMT capabilities, it will not be cost effective to make the investment required for SMT. This situation will change when SMT components cost significantly less than through-hole components, and/or SMT equipment prices continue to decline.

Many times SMT is utilized and all the components needed for the product are not available in SMT packages. This causes a difficult problem because both technologies must then be utilized, which detracts from one of the key SMT advantages: automated assembly. In these cases the SMT components are installed first with an automated pick and place machine. Then through-hole components are inserted manually as a secondary operation. SMT packages are unavailable when the power level is too high to be dissipated in an SMT package or when the volume level is too low for an SMT package to be developed. When using both through-hole and SMT package types, it is advisable to keep the application of the "mixed" technologies as localized as possible. If possible, try to keep all the SMT components on one circuit board. When both technologies are used on the same board, place all through-hole components on one side and SMT parts on the other side.

Manufacturing Cost Budget

At this point it is a good idea to consider the manufacturing cost of the design. A manufacturing cost budget should be developed for each of the functional modules. This is done by dividing up the total manufacturing cost goal for the product among each module, packaging/enclosure costs and total assembly costs. As the design develops, this cost budget should be used as a tool to measure the performance of the design in meeting the cost goals. The total cost of each module will be determined by adding the total cost of the parts and components within that functional module.

3–3 ▶ Enhancing Creativity

Most people are not exposed to a study of creativity in either high school or college. Nevertheless, it is a critical aspect of many careers, especially engineering. Creative thinking is a most useful process, yet it is largely undeveloped in the academic and industrial world. Creative thinking is enhanced when both information gathering and problem definition occur before starting the creative process.

Being creative involves the use of the subconscious, that part of our minds that is a mystery to us because we can't directly access it. Think of the mind's conscious and subconscious parts as being like a computer operating in a multitasking environment, where the background operating system controlling all of the basic functions compares to our subconscious mind and the specific applications programs represent the conscious mind. The applications programs don't appear to directly access the operating system software, but nevertheless, the operating system is there, operating and controlling all critical operations. The operating system in this case actually does a lot of work for the applications programs that are running and is an integral part of their results.

Compare your subconscious mind to the operating system software in your computer. It is a powerful and necessary part of your mind and it can do much good work for you. It differs from software in that it has tremendous creative power. Some of its best work is in the area of producing ideas, novel off-the-wall ideas that can solve problems in unique ways. However, the subconscious mind has some of the same limiting factors as a computer operating system. It has many applications programs running at the same time (i.e., making sure you are breathing and speaking and that your heart is beating) and it has a hard time being creative during busy periods or after a busy day. The best way to put your creative subconscious mind to work is to feed it with all the information and a problem definition and then assign it the task of coming up with some ideas. Relax and let your subconscious mind perform its magic.

Most of us have been troubled by a problem, then "slept on it," only to wake up with a solution right on the tip of our tongue. Many experts believe that the subconscious mind is our most valuable creative tool. When planning daily activities, schedule the review of particularly difficult problems toward the end of the day. Tell your subconscious mind—almost in jest—to figure out a solution. Then relax, sleep on it, and collect the ideas in the morning. The next time you are faced with a significant problem, try giving your subconscious mind a special assignment while you go take a nap. It has been said that the best work flows forth effortlessly. This is true, especially if the preliminary groundwork is done to set the stage.

After your subconscious mind has had time to review the problem, let your mind ramble as you write down the fresh ideas that come to your mind. It is important not to be too critical at this point; turn your discriminating, editing mind off. Now spread out the different ideas and let your mind focus on one idea and see what else your mind comes up with that is an offshoot of the original idea. Let your mind ramble again like this for each of the differing root ideas.

The end result should be a list of different and unique ideas. Many of them will be somewhat ridiculous, but others will surprise you. At this point you should evaluate the list of ideas with only a semi-critical outlook and attempt to combine the positive aspects of one with another. If things don't fit together, try turning one idea inside out, upside-down, or invert it. Play with the ideas until they work for the situation or you are convinced that they won't work. It helps to involve more than one person. Actually, the more people involved, the merrier, and the better chance for a novel idea.

After evaluation, if you don't have an acceptable idea, take note of what you have learned in the process and go back through the cycle again. Figure 3–4 shows a list of the steps to enhance creativity.

Example 3–2

This is an example of brainstorming often used at seminars on improving creativity. With about 20 people in the room, the group is asked to estimate how many different facts they anticipate being able to list about an average pencil. The group discusses this quickly and estimates that they will be able to list between 30 and 40 unique facts about the pencil. The session starts at one end of the room as each person in order is asked to state a unique fact about the pencil. Each fact is written and numbered on a marker board. The brainstorming proceeds quickly for about two complete cycles through the group. Then things slow a bit but still progress. At the end, the group may complete almost six cycles.

1. Gather information.

2. Define the problem.

3. Relax, let your subconscious mind
   work on the problem.

4. Collect the ideas by listing all of them.

5. Categorize the initial ideas.

6. Try combining or modifying the initial list of ideas
   to create more ideas.

7. Edit the list of ideas by excluding the ones that
   obviously do not apply to the problem.

▶ **FIGURE 3–4**
Steps to enhance creative
problem solving

One group developed a list of 114 facts about an average yellow pencil before being unable to continue. The process revealed the power of brainstorming, as one unique idea uncovered a number of other facts about the pencil. Each unique fact fed the process a little longer until, finally, the group could not continue. This exemplifies the creative power that is possible by combining the random thought processes and ideas of a number of people.

3–4 ▶ The Initial Design

We are now ready to proceed with the electronic design, which should proceed in a logical sequence with the input section first. The power supply designs should be completed last, if possible. Many times the designs of the different functional modules will proceed in parallel with different designers assigned to each module. The input and output of each of the functional blocks must be known in order to begin the design. You can usually begin sketching circuits on scrap paper. As the design becomes somewhat firm, you can make a neater sketch on paper with a light grid background.

Example 3–3

Continuing Example 3–1 let's complete the preliminary design of the tape deck control module of the audio tape deck. As shown in Figure 3–5, the inputs to the tape deck control module are the stop, play, record, fast forward, and reverse but-

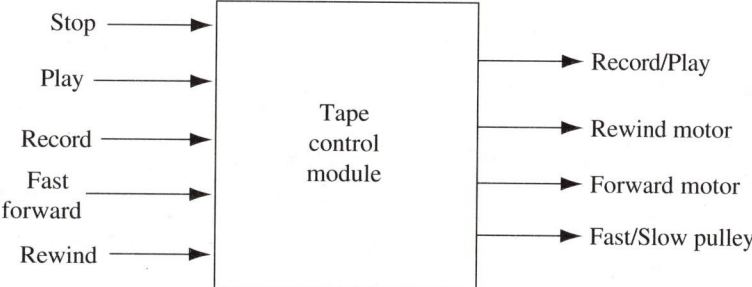

Stop	Play	Record	Fast Forward	Rewind	Record/Play	Rewind	Forward	Fast/Slow
1	x	x	x	x	0	0	0	0
0	0	0	0	1	0	1	0	1
0	0	0	1	0	0	0	1	1
0	1	0	0	0	0	0	1	0
0	1	1	0	0	1	0	1	0

▲ **FIGURE 3–5**
Tape control module block diagram and truth table

tons. The necessary outputs to the tape transport are digital signals that represent the following actions: record/play (1 = Record, 0 = Play), rewind motor, forward motor, and fast/slow speed pulley (1 = Fast, 0 = Slow).

This is a typical logic design problem in which the input and output relationship needed can be shown on a truth table. The truth table for the input and output relationship is also shown in Figure 3–5, which shows that there are four specific input codes that will result in a specific output code. For all other input codes the output code will be all zeros. Using logic circuit design methods, the circuit shown in Figure 3–6 was developed.

3–5 ▶ Circuit Simulation Software

Circuit simulation software has become increasingly effective and easy to use over the last 15 years. Circuit simulators allow the circuit designer to draw a circuit schematic and simulate circuit operation on a personal computer. The simulation allows the examination of any voltage or current in the circuit as a function of time. Circuit simulators provide a very quick and easy way to evaluate a particular design concept without access to expensive test equipment or having to procure parts and assemble a breadboard.

The first widely accepted circuit simulator was SPICE2, which was developed at the University of California–Berkeley in the mid-1970s after having modified its original SPICE program. SPICE stands for *Simulation Program with*

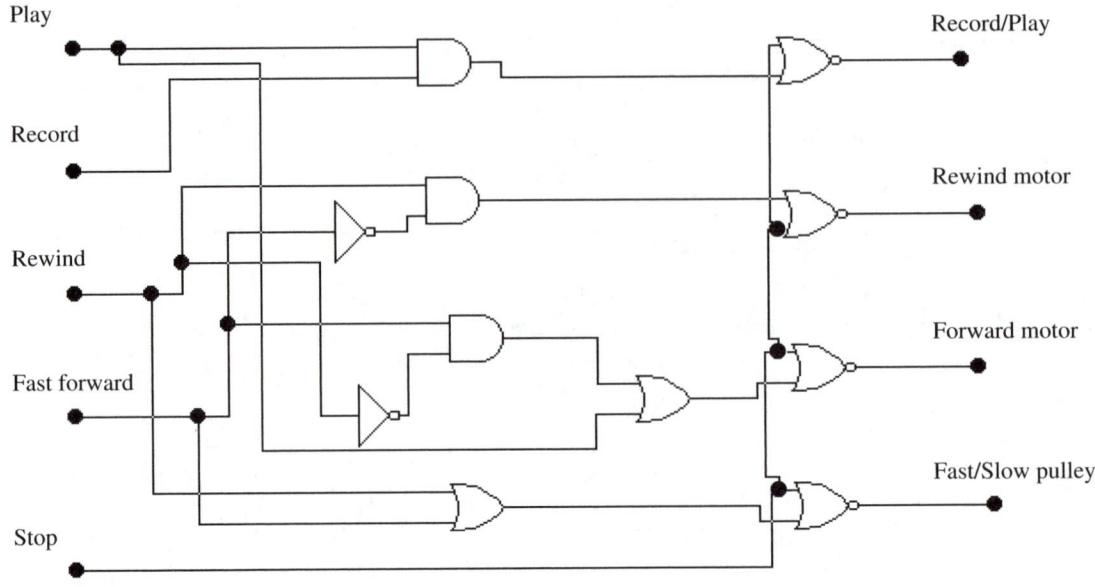

▲ **FIGURE 3–6**
Circuit solution

Integrated Circuit Emphasis. SPICE, SPICE2, and the most current Berkeley version, SPECE3F5 (commonly called BSPICE) are the recognized standard for analog circuit simulation. They were developed with public funds, so the software is in the public domain and available to U.S. citizens. XSPICE, a custom version of SPICE made for the U.S. Air Force, includes special modeling subsystems. PSPICE is a commercial version of SPICE developed by the MicroSim Corporation to operate on personal computers. PSPICE was followed by Electronics Workbench and many other commercially available software circuit simulators that can be run on personal computers. The key competitive differences between these simulators are as follows:

1. The number of device models available—in other words, how many of the available electronic devices have circuit simulation models

2. The allowable circuit complexity. This is usually realized as a limit to the number of components, connections, or circuit nodes.

3. The types of analysis available

4. Functional complexity and ease of use

5. Ability to output schematic to circuit board layout software

The importance of these differences depends on your perspective. Electronics students may be interested in just the basic analysis function, but in industry it is important to have a widely functional software circuit simulator that interfaces directly with circuit board layout programs.

Circuit simulators function by having a computer model for all electrical and electronic components. The circuit designer keys in the schematic diagram for the circuit to be analyzed using the available component models and specifying any parameter values. If a model does not exist for a particular device, one will have to be generated. All currently available circuit simulators allow the schematic to be drawn on the screen, whereas on older SPICE simulators the schematic was defined by specifying the devices to be connected between various circuit nodes. The schematic must be complete in every respect, including all power supplies and ground connections. A wide range of DC and AC power supplies are available as well as input signal sources. The circuit on the screen is almost the equivalent of a software breadboard. The designer then selects the voltages and currents to be analyzed. Some simulators simply plot a graph of voltage/current over time while others allow the connection of a software-driven DVM or oscilloscope to a particular point in the circuit to display the waveform as it would be seen on a real oscilloscope. The circuit simulation described thus far can be classified as basic DC and or AC circuit analysis, nothing more or less than could be accomplished on a circuit breadboard. However, it can be completed more quickly and without any physical components or test equipment. The following discussion covers the many types of analysis provided by state-of-the-art circuit simulators, which provide functions and features that are often impossible to perform on a breadboard.

Transient Analysis

Transient analysis is the determination of instantaneous changes that occur at a circuit node after power up or some other starting point. Transient analysis provides the circuit simulator with a significant functional advantage over breadboards. The analytical treatment of transient analysis often involves rigorous mathematical operations and the definition of boundary conditions. On a laboratory breadboard transient conditions can be difficult to simulate and usually requires a digital scope, storage scope, or some other data-recording device. Circuit simulators accomplish this task with relative ease and control, allowing the precise variation in initial conditions and analysis start and stop times. The transient analysis function provides accurate plots of voltage and or current over the specified time period.

Fourier Analysis

Fourier series analysis is another key circuit simulation tool. Fourier theory says that any non-sinusoidal periodic function can be described by a DC component with some number of sine and cosine functions. With this type of analysis, it is possible to determine the sine and cosine components that make up a complex waveform that exists at any particular circuit node. This information provides the circuit designer with the harmonic frequencies present in a signal as well as their relative amplitude. This can help to filter out unwanted signals by determination of their frequency and their possible source. In many circuit simulators the total harmonic distortion (THD) can also be calculated with the Fourier analysis function.

Noise Analysis

Circuit simulators can also simulate the various types of noise generated by components: thermal noise, shot noise, and flicker noise. Thermal noise is caused by the temperature and its induced effect on the interaction of electrons and ions in a conductor. Shot noise results from the discrete nature of electrons (there can be one electron or two electrons flowing in a circuit, but not 1.5 electrons) flowing in a semiconductor and is the most significant cause of transistor noise. Flicker noise is present in BJTs and FETs at low frequencies. When noise analysis is utilized on circuit simulators, the total noise present at a particular node resulting from these three types is calculated and recorded.

Distortion Analysis

Distortion results when an electronic device such as an amplifier fails to duplicate an input waveform correctly. The causes of distortion are nonlinear gain of a circuit or relative phase variations. Distortion caused by nonlinear gain is called *harmonic distortion*, while phase-induced distortion is known as *inter-modulation distortion*. Both types of distortion can be determined for a circuit and plotted as a function of frequency for a particular circuit node.

DC Sweep Analysis

As discussed in Chapter 1, in the development of specifications, variations in the DC power supply value are always an important consideration affecting circuit accuracy. Many circuit simulators provide a DC sweep analysis function that provides analysis of selected voltages or currents, as one or two DC supply values are varied. When selecting this type of analysis, the designer specifies the particular DC supplies to be varied and the circuit node being analyzed, as well as the beginning and ending supply values and the increment steps. The results will indicate the effect of the DC supply variations on the voltage and current of the particular node.

Sensitivity Analysis

Sensitivity analysis serves to determine the component variations that will most affect the accurate function of a circuit. DC sensitivity analysis includes the variation of all component values, one at a time, in order to determine which component has the greatest impact on a critical circuit voltage value. AC sensitivity analysis, on the other hand, varies the value of just one component, providing the critical variations of the component along with its impact on the circuit.

Parameter Sweep Analysis

The sensitivity analysis just described is usable for determining which component affects the circuit accuracy the most. Parameter sweep analysis provides for the variation of any component parameter value over a range and in increments specified by the user. Semiconductor components will have a number of parameter values that can be varied as compared to passive components, which will have few.

Temperature Sweep Analysis

Chapter 2 discussed the importance of considering ambient temperature effects on circuit performance. Temperature sweep analysis provides a helpful tool in the determination of ambient temperature sensitivity at very early stages in the design process. During this process, circuit operation of selected nodes is recorded for different ambient temperatures. The parameter value for all components that vary with temperature are changed accordingly and the impact on the circuit function is plotted.

Transfer Function Analysis

A transfer function mathematically describes the operation performed on an input signal by a functional circuit block to its output. Circuit simulators can analyze and determine the transfer function for a particular circuit. The designer specifies the inputs and outputs of the circuit to the transfer function analysis feature and then analyzes and determines the transfer function and input and output impedance of the circuit.

Worst-case Analysis

Worst-case analysis is an extremely useful design tool. Often during the design process, it is desirable to know the maximum and or minimum voltage for a particular circuit node. Worst-case analysis can provide this by making sensitivity analysis runs for each component and then plotting the maximum and minimum values found over the course of the sensitivity runs. This is critical information when determining accuracy specifications and selecting component tolerances.

Monte Carlo Analysis

Monte Carlo analysis involves the statistical probability of the variation in the parameter value of a circuit component. In other words, it uses the probability distribution function of a parameter value change to determine its value and the ultimate effect of the circuit node. Each parameter value is selected at random over the range specified using the selected probability distribution function (usually Guassian).

Software Circuit Simulators

Current software circuit simulators offer powerful design simulation tools, and there are many to choose from. There are a number of circuit simulators currently available that offer a wide range in features. There are three distinct levels of performance and application that are apparent: academic, medium-performance, and professional.

Academic Circuit Simulators
These circuit simulators usually are low priced (around $200) and are marketed primarily to high schools and colleges that offer technical and electronic programs. They represent lower-level analysis functions but are a very beneficial educational

tool, primarily due to the ease with which circuits can be built and analyzed. While they may interface with other circuit board layout software, they have no or minimal circuit board layout capabilities themselves.

Medium-performance Circuit Simulators

These usually offer medium- to high-level circuit simulation and analysis and often include mixed signal simulation (analog and digital circuits combined) and programmable logic design. The suppliers usually have functionally limited student versions available for under $200, but the fully functional versions cost between $800 and $1000. There may be additional circuit board layout software that can interface directly with these circuit board simulators offered by the same supplier (at an additional price of between $1000 to $2000), or other circuit board layout software can be used directly. The circuit board layout software for the medium-level circuit simulators usually does not match the performance of the professional circuit board layout packages.

Professional Performance Circuit Simulators

These circuit simulators are usually the most costly, available for around $2000 to $4000. They provide optimum circuit simulation, including mixed signal and programmable logic design, combined with professional circuit board layout capabilities. Circuit board layout features include multilayer circuit boards, surface mount components, powerful auto-routing, and 3D renderings of the final board.

As with all software, circuit simulators are rapidly changing as new features are offered and new suppliers enter the market. There is a significant learning curve required to take advantage of the key features on new products and software versions. This is similar to what occurred with mechanical CAD software and printed circuit board layout software. The market is still developing, but what is desired most is a circuit simulator that is accepted and used widely in industry, that functions directly with professionally accepted circuit board layout software, and that is available as a limited-function student version at a reasonable cost.

3–6 ▶ Breadboarding

Circuit simulators provide powerful functions and are extremely beneficial, but they do fall short in some areas. For example, very few simulators take into account the actual maximum ratings for components. So a circuit might function flawlessly in the simulation but could fail when powered up because it exceeds some component rating. Consequently, it is important at some point to build up a real physical circuit before proceeding too far with the overall design project.

Breadboarding is the process of constructing an experimental schematic circuit from the actual components selected for the design. The purpose of breadboarding is to test the preliminary design of a circuit or module. The breadboard is usually temporary in nature and is more easily modified than a printed circuit board. There are many different methods for completing a breadboard. The method selected depends on the goals of the prototype phase and the complexity and circuit technology of the circuit to be breadboarded. The breadboarding technique discussions that follow do not include all breadboarding methods but do include the methods most viable today.

Solderless Breadboard

The solderless breadboard is one that most electronics students have had experience with in the laboratory. This breadboard consists of groups of circuit connection holes called *points* that are all located on a 0.1″ grid. These circuit points are arranged in groups that are connected together underneath the plastic surface of the breadboard assembly. Horizontal rows of five points are connected together and are arranged into a vertical column. A center channel that is provided for mounting a standard dual in-line package integrated circuit separates two such columns. The integrated circuit straddles the center channel, making connections to connecting points on each side of the channel. With the integrated circuit mounted in place, the laboratory breadboard provides four connection points for each pin on the integrated circuit. Other components, such as resistors and capacitors, can also be mounted across the center channel. There are also separate vertical columns where the points are connected vertically instead of horizontally. These are commonly used for the purpose of bussing power supply voltages and ground to various circuit points. There are a variety of solderless breadboards available, so to be sure about which points are connected to which, use your multimeter to verify the connection scheme of the breadboard you are using.

To construct a circuit with the laboratory breadboard, components are inserted into the connection points so as to implement all the connections shown on the schematic. This is accomplished by connecting two components to the same connection group (i.e., five points that are tied together) if they are electrically connected. The remaining circuit points are connected using 22- to 30-gauge wire that is stripped back about 3/16″ to 1/4″. Precut and pre-stripped wire is available in various lengths for use in these breadboards. The solderless breadboard is limited in the current that can flow in the connections and the wire typically used to make them. The inherent capacitance of the connections and potential crosstalk between conductors also limits the frequency of operation of the solderless breadboard system.

Universal PCB Breadboard

Universal PCB breadboards (see Figure 3–7) are printed circuit boards that have holes all located on a 0.1″ grid system. There are many varieties of these universal boards. In general, some of the holes in the grid system have copper pads to allow for soldering, and some of these pads are connected together. The variations come from the location of the holes that have copper pads and from the combinations of copper pad connections. Some versions are more suited to large numbers of discrete components, and others are geared toward integrated circuit applications. PCB-edge connections are provided on some models. Whichever variety is used, there are areas where the configuration of the universal circuit board requires modification with a hand drill to cut away circuit points that are connected.

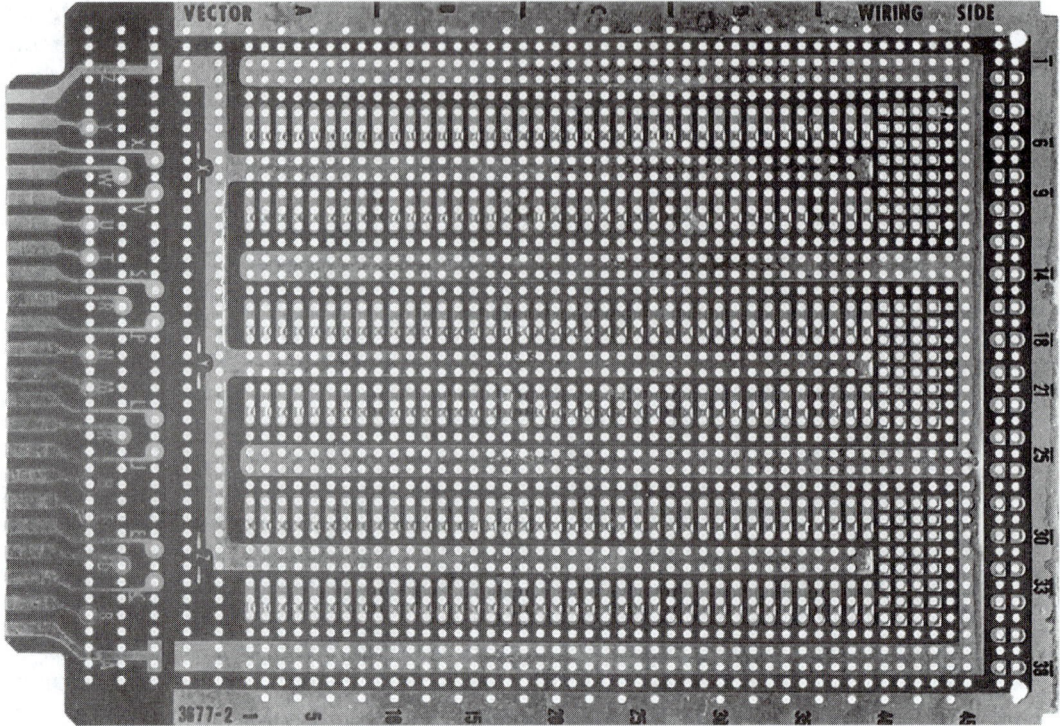

▲ **FIGURE 3–7**
Universal breadboard

Prototyping a circuit with the universal circuit board method is very tedious. After selecting the proper universal circuit board variety, the components are soldered in place. Next, the circuit connections shown in the schematic must be implemented either by soldering wires that connect all the circuit points or soldering together circuit pads with a continuous conductor to make a circuit board run. Finally, some areas of the copper connected pads may need to be disconnected. This can be accomplished by cutting away the connecting copper runs with a razor-blade knife or a hand drill fitted with a slicing tool. If carefully planned out and neatly implemented, the result can be very close to the eventual printed circuit board in function, physical size, and layout. This method can be combined with wire-wrap methods and SMT technology (to be discussed next). Figure 3–8 shows an example of a breadboard circuit that was developed with a universal breadboard scheme. Both the top and bottom views are shown. Notice how the circuit can be made to closely resemble the eventual printed circuit board.

Surface-mount Technology

Surface-mount technology provides unique challenges in breadboarding circuits. Again, there are many choices to be made. The most obvious is to breadboard the circuit with the through-hole equivalents rather than the actual SMT components.

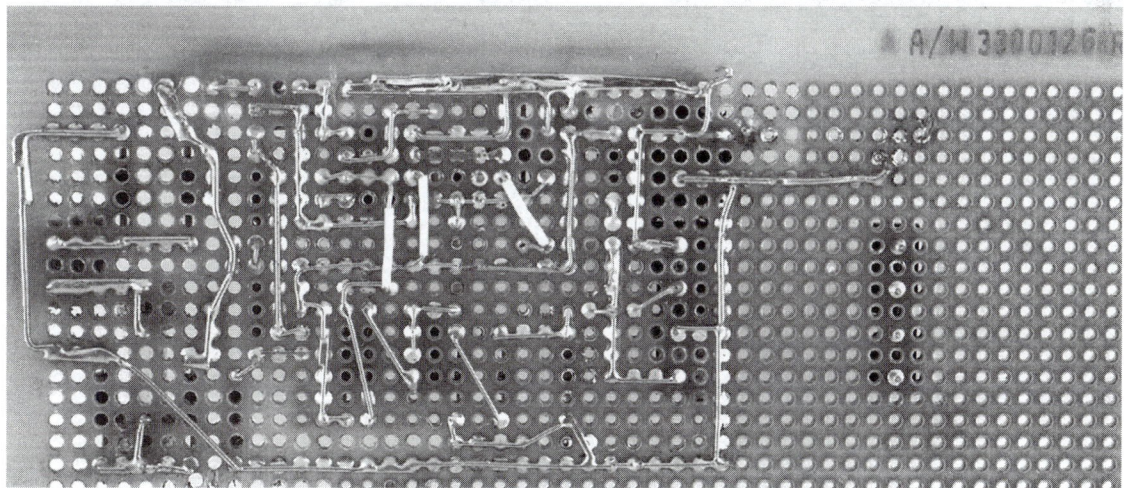

▲ **FIGURE 3–8**
Prototype example using Universal breadboard

If possible, it is best to avoid using of SMT components at the breadboard stage. Most SMT components are available in a through-hole package. If not, the SMT component can either be mounted on an SMT socket or on an SMT "carrier" board. Figure 3–9 shows an example of an SMT socket on a prototype board with extra area allotted for other through-hole circuitry. Figure 3–10 shows an example of an SMT carrier board that can be soldered into a universal breadboard prototype. SMT carrier boards allow the mounting of the SMT components where sockets may not be available or practical. The SMT carrier board can then be mounted to a universal printed circuit board and wired in the circuit with solder connections that go between the two boards. Soldering the SMT component to the carrier board

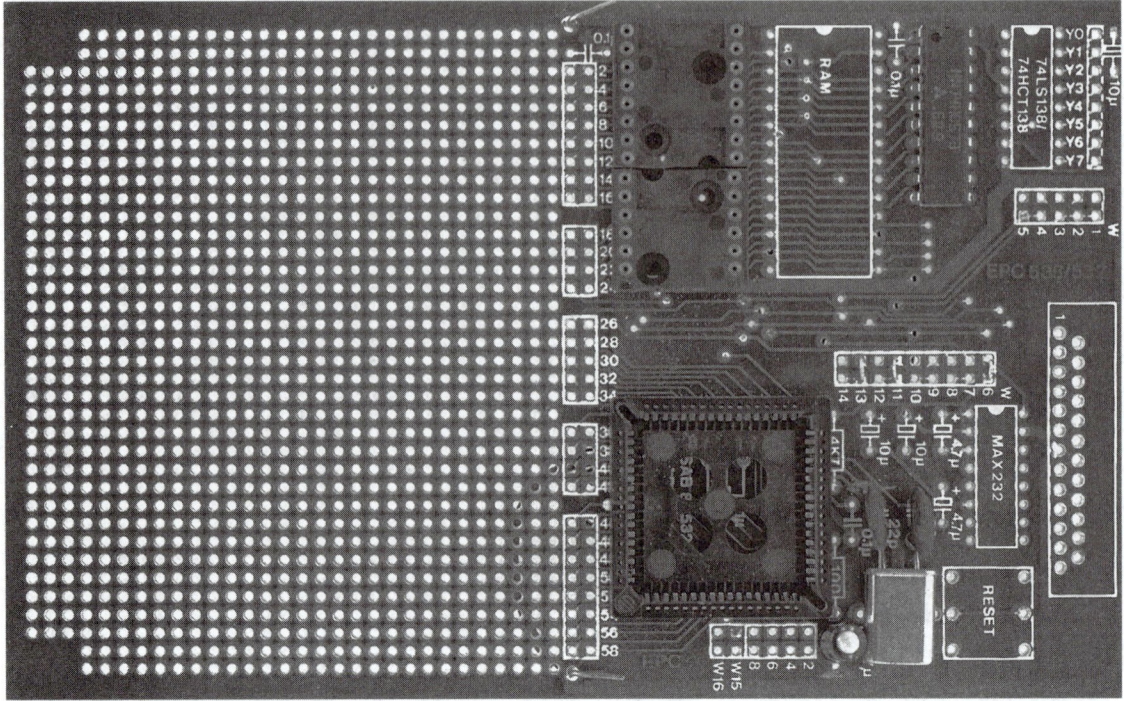

▲ **FIGURE 3–9**
SMT socket board

may take some advanced soldering skills, as the space between connections is small. Use an extra-fine tip for these applications and apply a thin coating of solder to the SMT pads.

It is best to build the breadboard with standard through-hole resistors and capacitors instead of SMT chip resistors and capacitors. The SMT chip components are extremely small, making them hard to handle and solder.

Wire-wrapping

Wire-wrapping is a solderless technique in which circuit connections are made by small wire connections that are tightly wrapped around pins called *wire-wrap pins*. Wire-wrap wire is generally 28- or 30-gauge wire. Wire-wrap pins, which feature right angle corners, are incorporated into integrated circuit sockets or part carriers or used as individual wire-wrap posts. Figure 3–11 shows an example of a wire-wrapped circuit. The wrapping is accomplished with a device called a wire-wrap gun or wire-wrap tool. To develop a breadboard utilizing the wire-wrap process, wire-wrap sockets are utilized for all integrated circuits, and part carriers are used for nonintegrated circuit-type devices such as resistors, capacitors, diodes, and transistors. The wire-wrap sockets and part carriers are lightly glued to a perforated phenolic board. Circuit connections are made point to point, as follows:

▲ **FIGURE 3–10**
SMT carrier board

1. Strip back the wire-wrap wire about 3/8″.

2. Insert the bare-wire end into the outer hole on the wire-wrap gun and bend the wire at a right angle with the axis of the wire-wrap gun.

3. Insert the center hole of the gun over the wire-wrap post to be connected, making sure that the end of the gun is flush with the back of the phenolic board.

4. Squeeze the lever on the wire-wrap gun and the bare wire will be wrapped clockwise around the wire-wrap pin.

Proceed to the other end of the connection and repeat the process. A reliable connection is actually made by the wire and the square edge of the wire-wrap pins as the wire is wrapped around the pins.

The Nonbreadboard

There are many times when the breadboarding process is actually implemented with a printed circuit board. This occurs most often with microprocessor-based digital boards, where the time and complexity of breadboarding is very high. In

▲ **FIGURE 3–11**
Wire-wrap application

this case the engineer ends up with only one wire-wrapped board, which is of questionable value after it is complete and made operational. Usually each software engineer will need a circuit board for software development, so numerous breadboards are often required in the early project stages. This situation promotes going directly to a printed circuit board. In this case the circuit board schematic is checked out and sent directly to the circuit board layout person, usually an electrical designer from the drafting department. (Circuit board layout will be discussed in detail in Chapter 5.) The circuit board is laid out and prototype quantities are ordered with a priority lead-time. When the circuit boards have been received, they are carefully built up and tested one section at a time. When functional problems are encountered, the boards are analyzed and corrected with a combination of "cuts" and "jumpers," component value changes, and additional components. In this case the first generation of the printed circuit board becomes the breadboard. The breadboard stage is not necessarily skipped, but it is replaced with the first version of the printed circuit board. It is desirable to make the prototype board a printed circuit board when one or more of the following is true:

1. The circuit is a complicated circuit board with embedded software.

2. The design is close to being a standard design, like well-known bus-oriented structures for microprocessors. In other words, the schematic has a good chance of being functional.

3. Testing of the prototype is not possible until some basic software is developed, and that is not scheduled to be complete for a couple of weeks.

4. More than one prototype board is required as soon as possible.

5. The prototype board must be reliable.

6. Engineering and technician time is at a premium and drafting layout time is more available.

The high degree of error checking that results from schematic capture software and circuit board layout programs has promoted the use of the nonbreadboard technique. When using complementary schematic capture and board layout packages, the most significant benefit is that the artwork will equal the schematic exactly. If the schematic is correct, then the artwork will be also. With this kind of accuracy, it is a fact that the actual printed circuit board has a higher chance of being equal to the schematic than any breadboard. This does not mean that the prototype board will function as required, which is why breadboards are still favored in many cases. The breadboard is more readily changed or just scrapped when major design problems develop.

Breadboarding Methods

Whichever method of breadboarding is selected, a schematic circuit is put into some physical form. To accomplish this accurately, an organized and methodical process must be implemented. The following procedure produces very good results:

1. Organize all the breadboarding materials and tools on a bench-top area to be used for the duration of the process.

2. It is imperative to start with a neat and orderly schematic. The schematic should be complete and include wire connections for all components that are breadboarded. All of the components on the breadboard should have a component number (e.g., R_1, C_1, and the like). The schematic should be laid out in an easy-to-understand format with inputs on the left-hand side and outputs on the right-hand side.

3. Make two copies of the schematic. One copy will be the breadboard master copy and should be initialed, dated, and filed with all breadboard documentation. As the breadboarding proceeds, use a highlighter marker to highlight each connection as it is made. When this process is used, the most common error, missing connections, is eliminated.

4. Start out wiring power to all points on the board where it is required. Make sure that the power and ground runs are made from heavier wire. Then follow the schematic, left to right, wiring the circuit in logical groups. For example, wire up all the power supply components and check out the power supply. Then wire all data connections from one component to the next component. This tends to minimize errors, because an error, such as wiring to an incorrect pin, will be noticed when an attempt is made to make the correct connection to that pin.

5. Make the connections as short and as neat as possible. Keep in mind to provide easy access for later inspection and the connection of test leads.

6. Many times there are integrated circuits where multiple components are located on one chip. Be sure to note which component on the integrated circuit is used for which schematic function by noting the pins and using a component subdesignation on the breadboard master schematic. Take the example of a Dual 4 Input NAND gate that is given a component designation of U_1. There are two 4 Input NAND gates on U_1, one will be designated U_{1-A} and the other U_{1-B}. Also be sure to properly terminate all unused integrated circuit components as required in their specifications. Unused TTL gates should have their inputs tied high (+5 V), for example.

7. Make a sketch of the assembly showing the relative location of the components with their designation.

By performing this procedure, you may be surprised to find that the circuit will work the first time—that is, if you remember to turn on the power. Of course, the schematic design must be a "working" design to begin with.

▶ Summary

In this chapter we discussed the steps for completing the preliminary design. The steps are listed here as a summary of the preliminary design process:

1. Divide the design problem into smaller modules.
    Complete a block diagram.

2. Define the design problem relating to these modules.
    Develop submodule specifications.

3. Do research on areas relating to each design problem.
    Gather more information.

4. Develop a cost budget.
    Develop cost goals for each submodule.

5. Apply creative thinking!
    Use your subconscious mind, and let your ideas flow.

6. Complete the preliminary design.

    Complete a preliminary design schematic.

7. Perform software simulation.

    Simulate the preliminary design.

8. Complete breadboard and evaluate.

    Breadboard and test the circuit.

When these steps are completed, the preliminary design is complete. A schematic diagram exists that defines the general components selected for the design and it shows their interconnection. The design has been simulated and basic breadboard testing has been completed. The next chapter discusses the selection of the actual components to be used in completing the formal design, the prototype printed circuit board.

▶ Reference

Stadmiller, D. J. 2001. *Electronics Project Management and Design.* Upper Saddle River, NJ: Prentice Hall.

▶ Exercises

3–1 What is the key advantage of utilizing surface mount technology?

3–2 True or false: Surface mount technology is always cheaper to manufacture than through-hole technology. What are the issues that determine which is cheaper?

3–3 What is the key disadvantage of using surface mount technology?

3–4 What is a manufacturing cost budget and how is it developed?

3–5 List the two steps to be completed before trying to utilize creative thinking to solve a problem.

3–6 List the competitive differences between the various circuit simulation software packages.

3–7 List the shortcomings of circuit software simulators in general when compared to the breadboard alternative.

3–8 Explain the concept of transient analysis as described in the section on circuit simulation software.

3–9 Explain the concept of DC sweep analysis as described in the discussion of circuit simulation software.

3–10   Does temperature sweep analysis performed by circuit simulation software do the same general function as ambient temperature testing in an environmental test chamber?

3–11   Explain the process and the result of sensitivity analysis performed on a circuit node by a circuit simulator.

3–12   Explain the difference between parameter sweep analysis and sensitivity analysis as performed by circuit simulators.

3–13   List the four different methods discussed in this chapter for completing breadboards. List one primary advantage and disadvantage of each.

3–14   Explain what is meant by the term *non-breadboard*.

4 ▶ Component Selection

▶ Introduction

In Chapter 3 we discussed the preliminary design process. At this point the design is on paper and the circuits have been computer simulated, breadboarded, and tested. The design includes a variety of active and passive components. Before we start to lay out the printed circuit, we must select and procure the final components for use in developing the circuit board layout and constructing a prototype. Whether you are completing a two- or four-year electronics program, you have seen many resistors, capacitors, and inductors used in circuits. You should possess a solid understanding of their function in a circuit. The discussion that follows summarizes the important aspects of selecting passive components and discusses the many different types available. More importantly, the advantages and disadvantages of each type are reviewed. A method for selecting the right type of component for a specific application is presented. The selection of active components is also discussed in a general way. (Appendix A includes reference information on both passive and active components.) The specific topics of this chapter are as follows:

- ▶ Resistors
- ▶ Variable Resistors
- ▶ Capacitors
- ▶ Inductors
- ▶ Transformers
- ▶ Switches and Relays
- ▶ Connectors
- ▶ Selecting Active Components

4–1 ▶ Resistors

Once we have determined the nominal design value for a resistor in a circuit schematic drawing, we must convert that information into an actual physical resistor that we can connect in the circuit. To select a resistor, the value, the type (material and construction), tolerance, power rating, and temperature coefficient must be defined. The available types of fixed resistors are described in the following list:

1. *Molded carbon (carbon composition) resistors.* These are a common older type of resistor formed by molding carbon, insulating filler, and a resin binder. They are low cost and feature 5% and 10% value tolerances, a wide variety of power ratings, and a negative temperature coefficient of anywhere from –200 ppm to –500 ppm/°C. Example 4–1 describes a simple way to handle coefficients stated in parts per million (ppm).

2. *Carbon film resistors.* These have replaced molded carbon resistors as the most widely used fixed resistor. They are constructed by depositing a resistive carbon film material onto a ceramic rod. They offer smaller size and more stability than the molded carbon resistor and are still low cost. Carbon film resistors come in 1%, 5%, and 10% tolerances with negative temperature coefficients of –200 ppm to –500 ppm/°C and a variety of power ratings.

3. *Metal film resistors.* These resistors utilize the same construction method described for the carbon film resistors but metal film (nickel chromium) is deposited on the ceramic rod instead of the carbon film. Metal film resistors come in 1%, 5%, and 10% tolerances and a wide variety of power ratings and feature a positive temperature coefficient of less than +100 ppm/°C.

4. *Metal oxide resistors.* Tin oxide is deposited on a glass rod to form these resistors. The stability is very high. Metal oxide resistors come in 1% and 2% tolerances and power ratings of 1/5 W and 1/2 W and feature a positive temperature coefficient of less than +60 ppm/°C.

5. *Wire-wound resistors.* These are formed with resistive wire wrapped around an insulating rod. Wire-wound resistors typically have both higher power ratings, and very low resistance values are available. A wide range of values and power ratings are available at medium to high cost. Their temperature coefficient is positive and less than 100 ppm/°C.

Example 4–1

The temperature coefficient of many components is given in a format called parts per million (ppm). This ppm format requires some thought when first trying to apply it. A simple way to use any coefficient given in ppm form follows:

1. Divide the nominal value of whatever the variable in question is by the number 1,000,000. This will be the number of millions that the nominal value represents.

2. Multiply the number of millions calculated in step 1 of this example by the ppm value given.

A practical example would be to determine the resistance variation of a 10,000 Ω carbon composition resistor with a temperature coefficient of –200 ppm/°C from 25°C to 55°C. Follow the steps listed:

1. Divide

10,000 Ω/1,000,000 = 0.01 million Ω

2. Multiply

0.01 million Ω × 200 ppm/°C = 2 Ω/°C

3. Multiply

2 Ω °C × 30°C (increase in temperature from 25°C to 55°C)
= 60 Ω change

Since the temperature coefficient is negative, the 10,000-Ω resistance decreases by 60 Ω to a value of 9,940 Ω.

Resistor Selection

The criteria for selecting the actual resistor for use in a circuit depends upon the nominal resistance value, the level of stability, the tolerance required, the acceptable temperature variation, the power level, and cost. The following process is suggested to select all fixed resistors:

1. Determine which types of resistors have the value and power rating required.

2. Determine the minimum temperature coefficient that is acceptable for the application.

3. Chose the lowest-cost and most available resistor type that will meet the requirements of the circuit.

Figure 4–1 is a resistor comparison chart.

Thick Film Networks

These networks are fabricated with the same technology as metal film and carbon film resistors but are incorporated in a package that allows for multiple resistors of the same value. The packages include dual-in-line and single-in-line as well as SMT packages. For example, you can purchase eight 1000-Ω resistors in one dual-in-line package, and the resistors can all be connected on one side to the same pin or kept completely separate.

Resistor Type	Range of Values	Tolerance	Range of Temperature Coefficient	Power Rating	Cost Factor x = .02	Primary Advantage
Carbon composition	All standard 5% values	+/- 5% to +/- 10%	−200 to −500 ppm	1/8, 1/4, 1/2, 1, 2 W	1x	Cost and size
Carbon film	All standard 5% values	+/- 5% to +/- 10%	−200 to −500 ppm	1/8, 1/4, 1/2 W	1x	Cost and size
Metal film	All standard 1% values	+/- 1%	+100 ppm	1/4 W	2x	Tolerance and temperature coefficient
Precision metal oxide	All standard 1% values	+/- 1% to +/- 2%	+60 ppm	1/4, 1/2 W	4x	Temperature coefficient
Power metal oxide	All standard 5% values	+/-5%	+100 ppm	1/2, 3 W	15x	High power and temperature coefficient
Precision wire-wound	All standard 1% values	+/- 1%	+100 ppm	1, 2, 3 W	100x	High power and tolerance
Power wire-wound	All standard 5% values	+/- 5% to +/- 10%	+200 ppm	1 W on up	75x	High power

▲ **FIGURE 4–1**
Resistor comparison chart

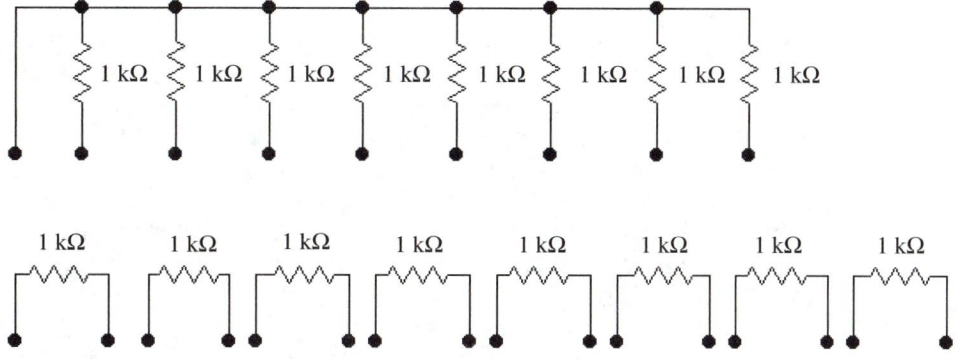

▲ **FIGURE 4–2**
Dual-in-line network configuration

Figure 4–2 shows a schematic diagram of these two configurations. These are handy in situations in which eight of the same value resistors are needed, such as for pull-up resistors on an 8-bit data bus.

Power Resistors

You can classify power resistors as anything over 1 W. These are typically wire-wound or metal film resistors that have the same characteristics as other wire-wound or metal film resistors, except that the packages are physically larger and designed to dissipate heat. Figure 4–3 shows examples of different power resistor packages.

4–2 ▶ Variable Resistors

Variable resistors are also called *potentiometers* and are simply resistors that can be adjusted to many values. These can be full-sized potentiometers or smaller trimming potentiometers called *trimpots*. They come in a variety of packages that can

▲ **FIGURE 4–3**
Power resistor packages *(Courtesy of Vishay Intertechnology, Inc.)*

be circuit-board or panel mounted. Variable resistors are available that are adjustable with circular or linear motion. The circular adjustment types can be single or multi-turn. The multi-turn devices provide a more precise angular adjustment of the resistance value. Inside the potentiometer is either a wire-wound or a continuous film type of resistive element. The wire-wound type is similar to wire-wound fixed resistors and is fabricated by winding fine resistance wire around an insulating bobbin. Each end of the bobbin is connected to a terminal. The resistance between the two end terminals is the maximum resistance of the variable resistor. A third terminal, called the *wiper arm*, is moved along the surface of the resistive windings to achieve the variable resistance value. Wire-wound potentiometers perform much like their fixed resistor counterparts. They are stable and have a good temperature coefficient but are plagued by resolution issues inherent in their construction. As the wiper arm moves across the resistance wire wrapped around the insulating bobbin, the resistance measured will increase in steps as the wiper goes from contact with one "turn" to the next "turn." The number of turns (the number of times the wire is wrapped around the bobbin) will determine the resolution (the smallest resistor value change) of the variable resistor.

Continuous-style potentiometers are fabricated with a thick film composition consisting of metal film on a ceramic substrate. These variable resistors use materials such as cermet, carbon composition, carbon film, and metal film for the thick film compositions. Because they are constructed of a continuous length of conductive material, these potentiometers greatly improve on the resolution problems experienced with wire-wound variable resistors. However, they are limited to smaller power ratings.

Example 4–2

In the op amp circuit in Figure 4–4, determine the proper connection of the potentiometer so that the gain of the circuit increases with a clockwise adjustment of the variable resistor. The gain of the circuit increases as the value of the potentiometer increases. It is important to understand the correct wiring of potentiometers so that they will function properly, which means providing the proper

▶ **FIGURE 4–4**
Op amp adjustment circuit

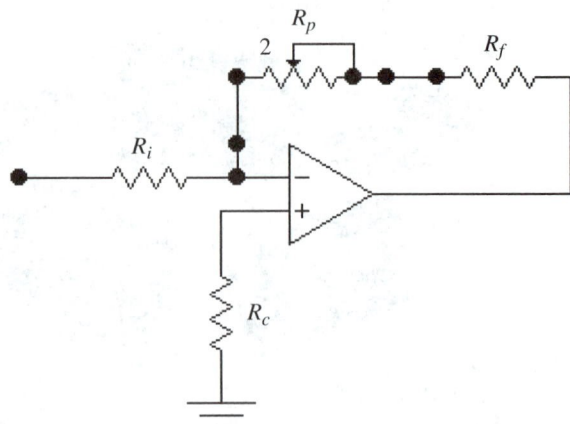

adjustment for the desired direction of adjustment. Potentiometers are three-terminal devices that have their total resistance between end terminals 1 and 3 and a variable resistance between terminal 2 (the wiper) and either of the other terminals. The direction of rotation (or the linear direction for linear adjustment types) that increases the resistance between terminals 2 and 1, and 2 and 3, is the critical point. Notice that the circuit shown has the second terminal connected to one of the end terminals. This is commonly done when the desired effect is to function simply as a variable resistor. In this case there are two common connections to the potentiometer. When a voltage divider function is required, all three connections to the potentiometer are separate.

To solve this problem, we must determine the end terminal (pin 1 or pin 3 of the potentiometer) to which the wiper arm (pin 2 of the potentiometer) should be connected. The solution will come from the answer to one question: When the potentiometer is turned clockwise, between which set of terminals does the resistance increase? This question can be answered by taking resistance measurements on a sample potentiometer or by remembering that for all variable resistors, the resistance between wiper terminal 2 and terminal 1 increases as the potentiometer is turned clockwise. To resolve our example problem, let's list what is known about the problem:

1. We desire the gain to increase when the potentiometer is adjusted clockwise.

2. The gain increases when the potentiometer resistance increases.

To resolve the problem, determine the two terminals where the resistance increases when the potentiometer is adjusted clockwise. The answer is between terminals 1 and 2. To which end terminal should wiper terminal 2 be connected? The answer is terminal 3. Connecting terminals 2 and 3 together shorts terminal 2 to the terminal 3 end. Since the resistance increases between terminal 2 and terminal 1, when the potentiometer is turned clockwise, the desired performance will result.

4–3 ▶ Capacitors

Capacitors are probably the second most utilized passive electronic component, and there are many variations from which to choose. When you are selecting capacitors, your goal will be to find a capacitor with the following:

1. The proper capacitance value

2. An acceptable tolerance rating

3. The proper working voltage

4. A temperature coefficient that is acceptable for the application

5. In some cases insulation resistance, quality factor, and dielectric absorption will also be important

6. Smallest size and cost available

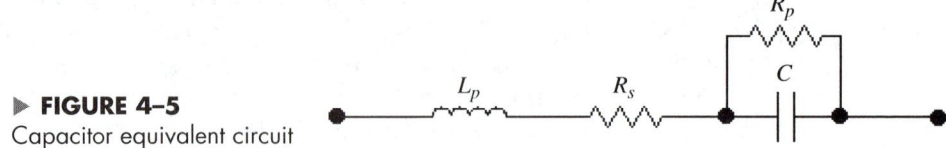

▶ **FIGURE 4–5**
Capacitor equivalent circuit

The physical model for a capacitor is shown in Figure 4–5. Inductance (L_P) and series resistance (R_S) are shown in series with a parallel capacitance (C) and resistance (R_P). The series resistance is a result of the resistance of the leads, plates, and any contact points. The resistance, in parallel with the capacitance, represents the leakage resistance that occurs through the insulation material around the plates. The capacitance shown is the true capacitance of the capacitor.

Insulation Resistance

The insulation resistance limits the capacitor's ability to completely block DC current as, theoretically, it should. That is why it is also called *DC leakage current*. The insulation resistance represents the ability of a capacitor to hold a charge for a period of time. It is an important parameter for capacitors used in integrator, sample hold, and peak detector circuits, which must hold a charge for a long period of time.

Equivalent Series Resistance, Dissipation Factor, and Quality Factor

The equivalent circut shown in Figure 4–5 can be converted to an equivalent series resistance (ESR) and a capacitance (C) as shown in Figure 4–6. The ESR is determined by calculating the equivalent series impedance for the parallel RC network at a given frequency, and adding the resistance component to the series resistance R_S, shown previously. L_P is negligible at low to medium frequencies. The dissipation factor (DF) is a measure of ESR/X_C. As such it is a measure of the AC loss of the capacitor. It is a unitless number that is expressed as a percent. The lower the DF number, the less loss is dissipated by the capacitor at a certain frequency. The quality factor or Q is simply 1/DF. It is the inverse of the dissipation factor. The DF and Q factors are important when precision operation at a certain frequency is required and when sampling a signal. Resonant frequency, precision filters, and sample and hold circuits are a few examples of circuits that require high Q and low DF.

Dielectric Absorption (DA)

Dielectric absorption is the phenomenon that allows a capacitor, which is quickly discharged and open circuited, to recover some of the charge that was discharged. In this case the charge is actually absorbed by the dielectric. In applications such

▶ **FIGURE 4–6**
ESR circuit

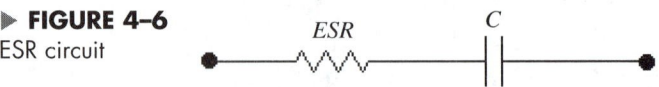

as sample and hold circuits, this recovered charge will add to the signal the next time it is sampled, causing an error. Dielectric absorption (DA) is an important consideration in sampling, timing, and high-speed switching circuits. The characteristic is expressed as a ratio and given as a percent. The higher the percent of DA rating for a capacitor, the greater the amount of DA effect.

Capacitor Types

To meet the circuit's requirements for capacitors, they are selected from many types of construction using different dielectric materials. The key is to find the desired performance characteristics in the smallest package at the least cost.

Ceramic Capacitors

These are widely used because they have a wide range of available values, and they are relatively small and inexpensive. The high dielectric constants available with the ceramic materials used in these capacitors result in large capacitance values for their size. The most common types of construction available for ceramic capacitors are the disc, multilayer, and chip variations. Figure 4–7 shows a typical disc type ceramic capacitor. The performance characteristics have the following ranges:

Capacitance range: 1 pF to 1μF

Working voltage: 25 V to 30 kV

Tolerance: ±5% to as high as +50% and –20%

Temperature coefficient: ±15% over temperature range

Relative size: Small

Relative cost: Inexpensive

Typical use: As medium- to high-frequency bypass, coupling, and filter capacitors

▶ **FIGURE 4–7**
Ceramic capacitors

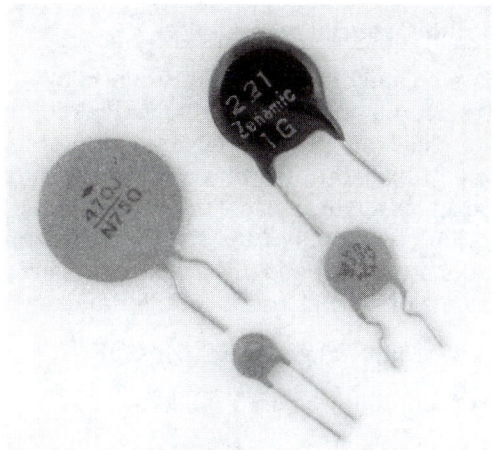

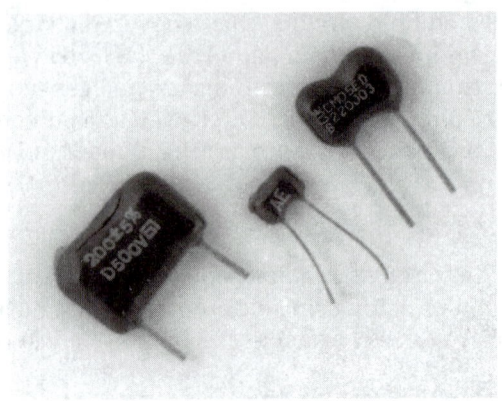

▶ **FIGURE 4–8**
Mica capacitors

Mica Capacitors

Mica capacitors (see Figure 4–8) offer superior performance when compared to the best quality ceramic capacitors when used at frequencies above 200 MHz. They are available in small capacitance values with tight tolerances, high working voltages, and stable temperature characteristics. Their performance characteristics have the following ranges:

Capacitance range: 2.2 pF to 0.01 μF

Working voltage: 50 V to 5 kV

Tolerance: ±0.5% to as high as ±20%

Temperature coefficient: +200 ppm/°C

Dissipation factor: 0.02% to 0.1%

Relative size: Medium to large

Relative cost: Medium

Plastic Film Capacitors

These are a category of many different plastic film dielectric materials that have similar performance characteristics. Plastic film capacitors (see Figure 4–9) are characterized by high working voltages, more stable temperature characteristics, low dielectric absorption, and a higher Q factor. These premiums result in their larger size and higher cost. The most common types of dielectric used to make plastic film capacitors are polyester, polypropylene, polystyrene, polyethylene, polycarbonate, teflon, and mylar. The following performance characteristics are the broad range of specifications for all film capacitors:

Capacitance range: 20 pF to 500 μF

Working voltage: 30 V to 10 kV

Tolerance: ±1% to as high as ±20%

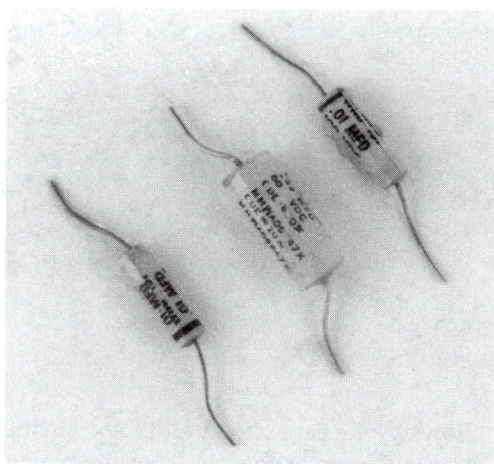

▶ **FIGURE 4–9**
Film capacitors

Temperature coefficient: ±2.5% to ±10% over temperature range

Relative size: Medium to large

Relative cost: Medium to high

Typical use: In low- to medium-frequency ranges where better than average capacitance tolerances, stability, temperature coefficients, and Q factors are required

Next, the individual characteristics that are unique to the different types of dielectric materials used in plastic film capacitors are discussed.

Polyester: These are considered as medium performance plastic film capacitors. They are designed for mounting on printed circuit boards and are available in values from 0.001 µF to 2.2 µF. Polyester capacitors feature low inherent inductance, tolerances of ±5%, ±10%, and ±20%, and a temperature coefficient ±10% change over the rated temperature range. Their size tends to be larger than other plastic film capacitors and they are available at medium cost. They are typically used as coupling capacitors.

Polypropylene: These capacitors (see Figure 4–10) feature very low dielectric absorption (0.001% to 0.02%) in a wide range of values (10 pF to 0.1 µF) and they are inexpensive. Their disadvantages are large case size, an inability to withstand high temperatures, and high inductance. For lower temperature applications, these would be a good choice for sample and hold circuits.

Polystyrene: Polystyrene capacitors offer the highest performance of the plastic film capacitors. They are available in ranges from 10 pF to 0.1µF at tolerances from ±1% to ±10%. Their stability is excellent with a temperature coefficient of around ±1%. The dissipation factor is low, which means the Q factor is high. They also feature a very low dielectric absorption factor.

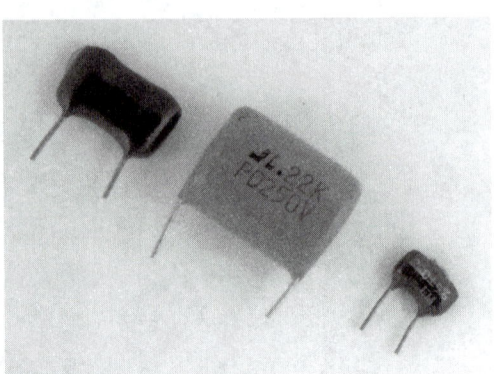

▶ **FIGURE 4–10**
Polypropylene capacitors

Polystyrene capacitors tend to be smaller than other plastic film capacitors and more expensive. They are typically used in filter networks, tuned circuits, and other precision charging circuits in the low- to medium-frequency range.

Polyethylene: These are specialized capacitors designed to suppress transients and noise from the input power connections to many industrial and commercial products. They are available in values from 0.001 µF to 1 µF and temperature coefficients of ±10%. The primary applications are as filter capacitors placed across the primary AC voltage lines.

Polycarbonate: These offer performance almost as good as polystyrene capacitors at a smaller size. If a high-quality capacitor is required in the smallest size, a polycarbonate capacitor may be a good choice. They are available in ranges from 10 pF to 0.1 µF and temperature variations on the order of –2.5%, +1% over the useable temperature range. Their cost is in the medium to high range. Applications include filter networks, tuned circuits, and other precision charging circuits in the low- to medium-frequency range, where small size is an overriding requirement.

Mylar: Mylar capacitors are the general purpose capacitors of the plastic film types. They are available in ranges from 0.001 µF to 0.22 µF and working voltages up to 100 V DC. Their tolerances and temperature coefficients are on the order of ±10%. They are available in small to medium sizes and low to medium cost.

Electrolytic Capacitors

Electrolytic capacitors are designed to achieve high capacitance values in as small a size as possible. The resulting design tradeoffs give electrolytics a lower range of working voltage, and they are polarized. Polarization means that one plate is made positive and the other negative. This polarization is due to the fact that the plates are made of different materials, unlike standard capacitor types. Reversing the polarity of the voltage applied to electrolytic capacitors will destroy them if the voltage is large enough. There are two dielectrics used to make electrolytic capacitors: aluminum and tantalum. Aluminum electrolytics are more common, physically larger, and have a wider range of values. The general range of capacitance values for electrolytic capacitors values goes from 0.1 µF to 5700 µF. Working voltages go from 10 V DC to 500 V DC, depending on the value and type. Tolerances are typically −10% to +50% and temperature coefficients are not usually listed. Their common use is as power supply rectifier filters, so the actual value of capacitance seldom requires high accuracy.

      Aluminum Electrolytics: These feature a cylindrical package with either axial or radial leads (see Figure 4–11). The radial lead is usually preferred for circuit board mounting. There are variations in marking the polarized leads. Some manufacturers will mark the plus lead accordingly. Many others mark the negative lead with a large band with a negative sign embedded in it. There are various grades of aluminum electrolytics available that primarily determine the expected operational life. Their selection will involve using the lowest working voltage and smallest package size combined with the desired package style, grade, and capacitance value.

      Tantalum Electrolytics: These electrolytics are typically smaller and restricted to a narrower range of capacitance and working voltage values. Capacitance values range from 0.1 µF to 100 µF and voltage ratings from 10 V DC to 35 V DC. There are two different packages: cylindrical with axial leads and teardrop shape, as shown in Figure 4–12. The teardrop shape is typically used in circuit board applications.

Capacitor Selection

With all the different types of capacitors to choose from and all the parameters to consider, capacitor selection may seem overwhelming. Yet, with a little experience, the more typical selections become routine. Most of the time the value and function required will result in the use of ceramic disc or aluminum electrolytic

▶ **FIGURE 4–11**
Electrolytic capacitors

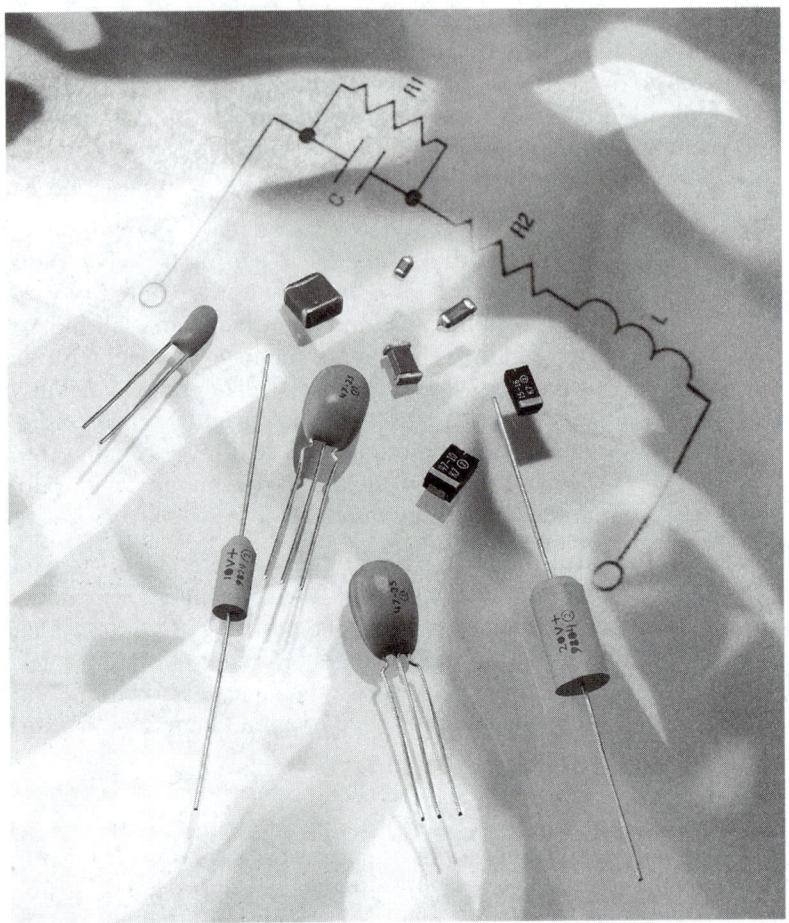

▶ **FIGURE 4–12**
Tantalum capacitors
*(Courtesy of Vishay
Intertechnology, Inc.)*

capacitors. The nontrivial applications will require the most effort. To help in selecting capacitors, use the following steps in conjunction with Figure 4–13:

1. Determine which capacitor types have the value required.

2. Determine the capacitor types that have a working voltage sufficient for the application.

3. Determine those capacitor types that will function over the frequency range of the application.

4. From the application, determine the capacitor types that have an acceptable capacitance tolerance combined with the temperature coefficient.

5. Review any special aspects of the application, such as operation or function at specific frequencies (high Q and low DF), data conversion at low frequencies (insulation resistance), or accurate sampling, timing circuits, and high-speed switching circuits (low DA). Review the insulation resistance,

dissipation and quality factor, and dielectric absorption as required by the application and select the capacitor type that will meet these needs.

6. Review the sizes available of all the remaining capacitor types that meet all the criteria discussed so far.

7. Determine the cost and availability of all the capacitors reviewed in step 6 above. Make the decision based upon the combination of size, cost, and the other key factors defined in steps 1 through 5.

Back-to-back Electrolytics

When large capacitance values and small size are required for voltages that vary both positive and negative, the polarized plates of electrolytic capacitors are a significant limitation. To get around this, it is possible to place two polarized capacitors in series, back-to-back, with the negative plates connected together. Doing this achieves the effect of one nonpolarized capacitor equal to the series equivalent of the two polarized capacitors. Remember that two capacitors in series act like two resistors in parallel when determining the equivalent capacitance. There are some limitations of this practice that relate to tantalum capacitors. These limitations regard the equivalent capacitance value of the back-to-back capacitors and the fact that as the signal level across the capacitor increases, the equivalent capacitance will vary from the value calculated. Also, many manufacturers recommend against using "wet anode" tantalum capacitors in the back-to-back configuration.

Feed-through Capacitors

These are special capacitors for suppressing unwanted signal noise in the form of radio frequency interference (RFI). The purpose of feed-through capacitors is to shunt unwanted noise to ground at the entry or exit of a grounded metal enclosure or cavity. One plate of the feed-through capacitor makes contact with the feed-through conductor and the other capacitor plate is connected to both sides of the enclosure or cavity wall. These are intended for high-frequency applications and the range of capacitance values usually used is between 0.01 µF and 2 µF.

Example 4–3

On many circuit schematics, you will notice the placement of two bypass filter capacitors in parallel with values such as 100 µF and 0.1 µF. The 100 µF capacitor is usually an aluminum electrolytic type while the 0.1 µF value is usually a ceramic disc capacitor. The purpose of both of these capacitors is essentially the same: to bypass any frequency higher than DC, removing them from the power supply output. Why then are both capacitors required? Why can't the 100 µF capacitor filter perform this function alone? In analyzing this situation we will use the equation $X_C = 1/(2\pi fC)$ for capacitive reactance. The larger the value of the capacitance, C, the smaller X_C is at a given frequency, f, which is what is desired: a low impedance value that will bypass the frequency component to ground. The 100 µF capacitor

Capacitor Dielectric	Range of Values	Tolerance	Temperature Coefficient	Range of Working Voltage
Ceramic	1 pF to 1 μF	+/-5% to +/- 20%	+/- 15%	25 to 30 kV
Mica	2.2 pF to 0.01 μF	+/-0.5% to +/- 20%	200 ppm/°C	50 to 50 kV
Plastic film types	20 pF to 2.2 μF	+/- 1% to +/- 20%	+/- 2.5% to +/- 10%	30 to 10 kV
Polyester	0.001 μF to 2.2 μF	+/- 5% to +/- 20%	+/- 10%	30 to 10 kV
Polycarbonate	0.001 μF to 2.2 μF	+/- 1% to +/- 10%	+/- 10%	30 to 10 kV
Polystyrene	10 pF to 0.1 μF	+/- 1% to +/- 10%	+/- 10%	30 to 10 kV
Polypropylene	10 pF to 0.1 μF	+/- 1% to +/- 10%	+/- 10%	30 to 10 kV
Polyethylene	0.001 μF to 1 μF	+/- 1% to +/- 10%	+/- 10%	30 to 10 kV
Mylar	0.001 μF to 2.2 μF	+/- 1% to +/- 10%	+/- 10%	30 to 10 kV
Aluminum electrolytic	0.1 μf to 10,000 μF	−10% to +50%	NA	10 to 500 V DC
Tantalum electrolytic	0.1 μF to 100 μF	−10% to +50%	NA	10 to 35 V DC

▲ **FIGURE 4–13**
Capacitor selection chart

presents a much lower (100 times lower) capacitive reactance at any frequency when compared to the 0.1 μF capacitor. This reinforces the question: Why is the 0.1 μF capacitor necessary? The answer comes from the equivalent model of the capacitor discussed earlier in this section. The equivalent series resistance of the aluminum electrolytic capacitor and the ceramic capacitor also change with frequency. This limits their effectiveness as capacitors as frequency varies. The aluminum electrolytic is not effective above the range of 10,000 Hz. The ceramic capacitor is effective over a frequency range of roughly 1000 to 1 MHz. So neither

Frequency Range	Dielectric Absorption	Quality Factor	Size	Cost	Primary Advantage
High frequency	High	Low	Small	Low	Size and cost
High frequency	High	High	Medium	Low	Tolerance and temperature coefficient
Low to medium	Low	High	Medium to large	Medium to high	High quality factor and low dielectric absorption
Low to medium	Low	High	Medium to large	Medium to high	High quality factor, tolerance
Low to medium	Low	High	Medium to large	Medium to high	High quality factor, tolerance
Low to medium	0.001 to 0.02 %	High	Medium to large	Medium to high	Low dielectric absorption
Low to medium	0.001 to 0.02 %	High	Large	Medium to high	Low dielectric absorption
Low frequency	Low	High	Medium to large	Medium to high	High quality factor, tolerance
Low to medium	Low	High	Medium	Medium	General purpose plastic
Low frequency	High	NA	Small capacitance to size ratio	Low	Large capacitance for small size, polarized
Low frequency	High	NA	Small	Low	Large capacitance for small size, polarized

capacitor by itself can perform the complete needs of the circuit: bypassing all frequencies to ground. Both capacitors together function as a tag team, one taking over where the other one leaves off as the frequency increases.

Example 4–4

In this example we will select a capacitor for use in a sample-and-hold circuit (see Figure 4–14). The circuit requires a value of 0.01 µF and a 20 V rating. The temperature range for the circuit is 0°C to 85°C. A sample-and-hold circuit is

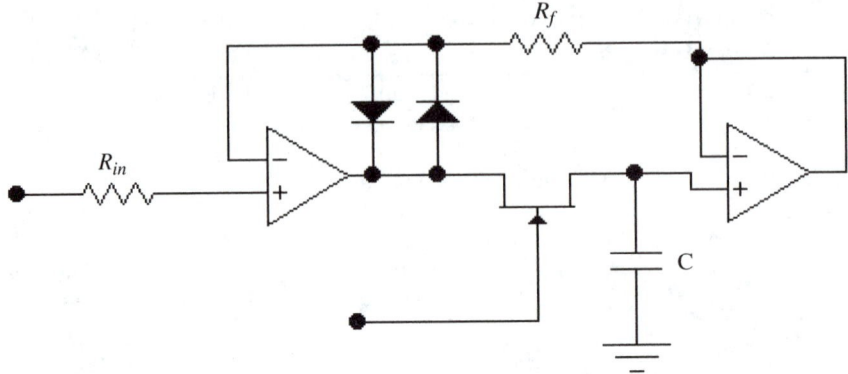

▲ **FIGURE 4–14**
Sample and hold circuit

often used with an A/D converter to sample the signal at one point in time and
save it for the A/D converter to process. In sample-and-hold circuits a capacitor
is connected to the input signal for a brief period of time so that the capacitor will
charge up to the signal value. At the specified sample time, the input signal is
disconnected and the A/D converts the sampled signal. In this case the dielectric
absorption of the selected capacitor, as discussed earlier in this section, is critical. The correct capacitor will have a minimal DA factor. The capacitor types with
the lowest DA factor are polystyrene, polypropylene, and teflon. Polystyrene will
not be used because of its temperature limitations. Either polypropylene or teflon
can be used for this application. Teflon has a little higher DA factor and will be
higher in price. Polypropylene will have a lower DA factor and a larger size and
will be cheaper.

Variable Capacitors

As with resistors, variable and trimming capacitors are available to provide for adjustable capacitance values. There are two basic types: air-variable and trimmer
capacitors.

Air-variable capacitors are used to tune resonance circuits like those utilized
in the front end of a radio receiver. Air-variable capacitors use an interleaved set
of metal plates, with air as the dielectric. Capacitance variations of 1 pF to 200 pF
are available. Trimmer capacitors are fabricated with mica, ceramic, and glass dielectrics and are used for fine-tuning a capacitance value. The key features of the
variable capacitor types are:

Mica: Good stability and low temperature coefficient; good capacitance to size
ratio and can handle moderate shock and vibration; low inductance and
cost

Ceramic: High Q factor with predictable temperature coefficient; good capacitance to size ratio with low inductance; not usable in high shock and
vibration environments; limited to 180° rotation

Glass: Possesses a high voltage capability and can be environmentally sealed, can handle many adjustments with smooth and nearly linear capacitance changes with rotation

4–4 ▶ Inductors

Inductors are the least-used passive electronic components because of their relative size and cost. At low to middle frequencies, the desired effect of the inductance can be achieved with a cheaper and smaller capacitive circuit. This is shown by the fact that we can construct both high- and low-pass filters from either resistor-capacitor circuits or resistor-inductive circuits. The reason that inductors are a more expensive approach for many circuit applications is that at low frequencies, relatively large inductor values are required. As frequency increases, inductors become a more viable approach in ripple reduction and other applications. In Chapter 6 we will see how inductors are combined with capacitors to form effective ripple reduction circuits in higher-frequency switching regulator circuits.

Inductors are used in filter and tuned circuits, as current limiters, and as ripple filters in power supplies. The three principal types of inductors have air, iron, or ferrite cores. The core is the material around which the conductor coil is wrapped. The conductive coil is covered with an insulating layer, usually a varnish, to prevent conduction between the adjacent coils. Magnetic core inductors offer a higher range of inductance values. There are also fixed and variable inductors. Figure 4–15 shows the schematic symbols that correspond to the core materials and fixed and variable symbols.

The equivalent circuit for an inductor is shown in Figure 4–16. R represents the coil resistance and C is the inherent capacitance of the winding. Inductors are classified by their Quality factor (Q) value that equals the ratio of the inductive reactance at a particular frequency to the winding resistance R. A high Q value means that the inductive reactance at that frequency is much larger than the coil resistance and therefore a small amount of power will be lost due to the coil resistance.

▶ **FIGURE 4–15**
Inductor schematic symbols

Air core inductor   Iron core inductor   Variable inductor

▶ **FIGURE 4–16**
Equivalent inductor

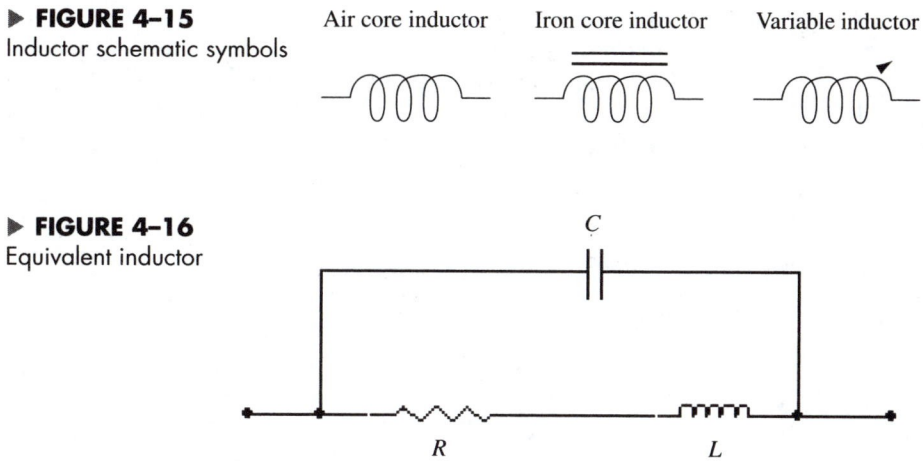

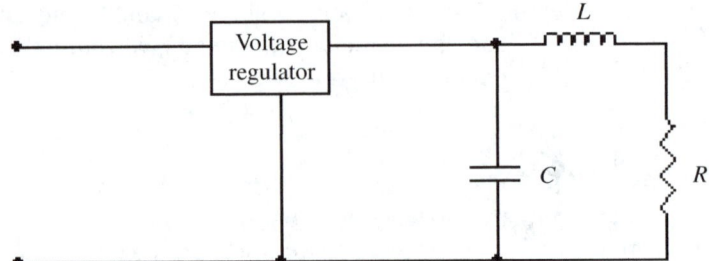

▶ **FIGURE 4–17**
Ripple reduction example

The more common applications of inductors are as follows:

Ripple Reduction: This application involves smoothing the ripple on the output of DC power supplies (see Figure 4–17). The critical parameters in this application are the minimum inductance value, DC current, working voltage, and maximum DC resistance.

Swinging Inductor: Swinging inductors (see Figure 4–18) are applied to the AC input of many power supplies to reduce the ripple input to the supply. The critical parameters in this application are both the minimum and maximum inductance values, DC current, working voltage, and maximum DC resistance.

Current Limiting: As current limiters, the value of inductance and the tolerance becomes important, along with the maximum AC current and maximum AC voltage drop for which the inductor is rated.

Tuned or Timing Circuits: These applications require tighter tolerances of inductance values and consideration of the inductor Q value, current, and DC resistance. Inductor Q value is ratio of the resistance of the inductor to the inductive reactance (R/X_L) at a specific frequency.

The range of inductor values available for the various types are as follows:

Air Core Inductors: Air core inductors are available from a few tenths of a microhenry to several hundred microhenries. These are usually used at high frequencies in the range of 100 kHz to 1 GHz. Very small air core inductors can be fabricated by a few loops of wire or loops on a printed circuit board.

▶ **FIGURE 4–18**
Swinging inductor example

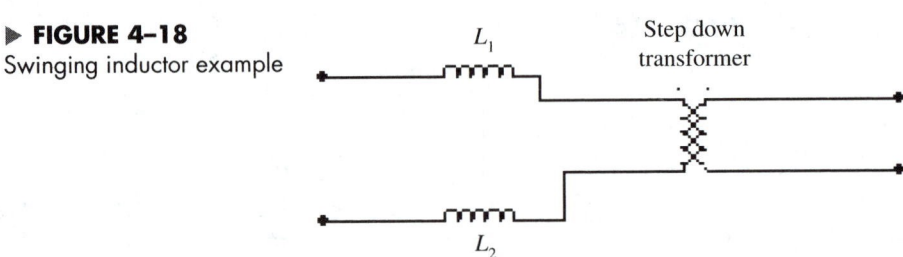

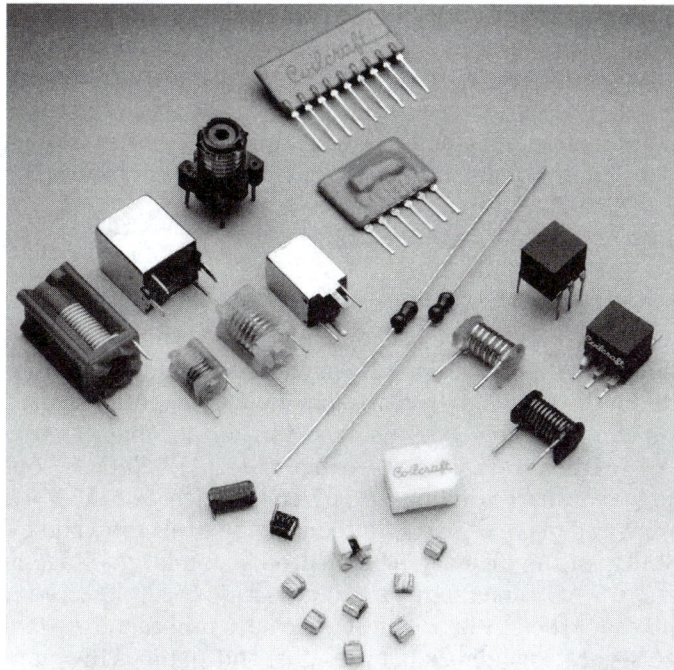

▲ **FIGURE 4–19**
Coilcraft inductor family *(Courtesy of Coilcraft, www.coilcraft.com)*

Iron Core Inductors: Iron core inductors are available from 0.1 to 120 mh with DC resistances ranging from a few to several hundred ohms. Maximum DC currents are on the order of 100 ma with Q values of about 50.

Variable Inductors: Adjustable magnetic core inductors are available that vary inductance by moving the magnetic core in or out of the coil with screw adjustments. Inductors come in a variety of sizes and shapes. Figure 4–19 shows some of the inductor packages available.

4–5 ▶ Transformers

A transformer consists of two separate coils that are wrapped around a closed magnetic circuit. They are used to step down, step up, isolate, and impedance match AC circuits. The ratio of the number of turns on the secondary to the primary turns is called the *turns ratio*, n. The voltage output from the secondary, V_{sec}, is equal to the primary voltage, V_{pri}, divided by the turns ratio. Conversely, the secondary current, I_{sec}, equals the turns ratio multiplied by the primary current, I_{pri}.

$$V_{sec} = V_{pri} \times n$$

$$I_{sec} = I_{pri} / n$$

There are a wide variety of transformer types based on primary and secondary voltages and currents. There are also many variations of primary and secondary windings. In either winding there may be a center tap that is a connection point in the middle of the winding. Center taps are used to create full-wave rectifiers with two diodes or combination plus-minus power supplies. In other cases a winding may actually be two equal windings that can be connected in parallel or series.

Example 4–5

In this example a power supply is designed for use as an industrial product that will operate off of 115 V AC or 230 V AC, depending on which is available to the user. To accomplish this, the product will have to be altered to change the turns ratio of the transformer used. This can be achieved by using a transformer that has two separate and equal windings on the primary side (see Figure 4–20). If 230 V AC operation is desired, then the two primary windings are wired in series. For 115 V AC operation, the windings are wired in parallel, which reduces the turns ratio and increases the current capability of the primary. The desired secondary voltage is 12 V. If the input voltage is 230 V AC, then the required turns ratio is 230/12 = 19.16. For 115 V AC, the turns ratio should be 115/12 = 9.58. Since a half a turn cannot be fabricated, a primary with two separate windings that are equal and 10 times the number of secondary turns will be the best solution. If the secondary has 10 turns, then each of the primary windings should have 100 turns. The turns ratio will vary from 20, when the two windings are wired in series, to 10 with the parallel connection.

The resulting option to the user will be a choice of how to wire the two primaries, in series or parallel. An even easier option is to include a switch in the power supply design that changes the series and parallel wiring of the primaries with the flip of that switch. The primary applications for transformers are discussed next, followed by the criteria for selecting transformers.

Step-down Transformers

This is the most common application of transformers and involves the step down of an AC power supply voltage to a smaller voltage AC voltage for use as a low voltage AC or DC power supply. In this case the turns ratio is greater than one, meaning that the primary has more turns than the secondary.

▶ **FIGURE 4–20**
Transformer example schematic

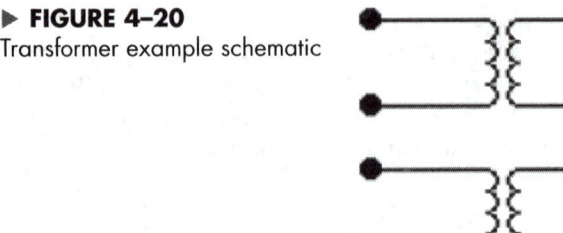

Step-up Transformers

These are utilized whenever it is necessary to increase the voltage level from the AC voltage level available. The best example of this is the development of 230 V AC when only 115 V AC is available. There are many other applications where the AC voltage must be increased slightly. Increasing 208 V AC to 230 V AC is another example. Step-up transformers have fewer turns in the primary than the secondary.

Isolation Transformers

These are used solely to isolate one AC voltage from another AC voltage. Transformers inherently accomplish this because there is no electrical connection between the primary and the secondary. The energy is transferred magnetically. The output voltage and current should be the same as the input voltage and current. The reason for their use is either to eliminate DC noise levels from a signal or to isolate the secondary circuit for safety reasons (see Figure 4–21). In selecting these transformers, the primary issue is finding a transformer that will handle the required power level.

Impedance Matching

Impedance matching involves the matching of a source impedance to the load impedance. This is desirable because maximum power is transferred only when the load impedance equals the source impedance. A transformer can achieve this because of the way the windings reflect the impedance value through the windings. The most common example is the typical 75 Ω source resistance of an antenna lead that is connected to the 300 Ω input resistance of a television receiver. An impedance matching transformer can be used to match these two resistances or, in other words, make the 300 Ω television load appear to the antenna as a 75 Ω load. The selection of impedance matching transformers is most dependent on the ideal turns ratio. The turns ratio can be determined by the formula where $R_{primary}$ equals the value of the source resistance and R_{load} is the actual load resistance. The proper power rating must also be determined by multiplying the maximum secondary output voltage times the output current. This will be the volt-amp requirement for the transformer.

▶ **FIGURE 4–21**

Isolation transformer example

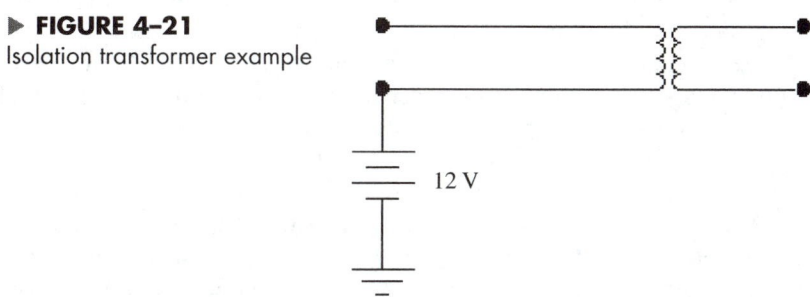

12 V

4–6 ▶ Switches and Relays

Switches are mechanical devices that switch electrical circuits. The two basic types of switches are maintained and momentary. Maintained switches maintain the switch position after they are engaged until they are mechanically repositioned. Momentary switches are spring loaded and revert back to their normal state after being released. Switch contacts are defined as common (C), normally open (NO), or normally closed (NC). The normal state of the contacts are the mechanical "off" state of the switch. Switches are classified by the terms *poles* and *throws*. Poles are merely the numbers of sets of contacts included in a switch. One set of contacts is needed for control of one circuit. If two or more circuits must be controlled, then additional sets of isolated contacts will be needed. The term *throws*, which is derived from the number of positions for old-fashioned "knife" switches, has been carried over to today's switches. A switch that makes or breaks only two points in a circuit is said to have a *single-throw contact*. A switch that makes or breaks one common contact to either a normally closed or a normally open contact is called a *double-throw contact*. To achieve more than two throws, some sort of rotary switch is required that will connect one common contact with potentially many other contacts. Switch selection is determined by mechanical size and style, contact arrangement, and the voltage and current rating of the contacts. Figure 4–22 shows a variety of switches.

Relays

Relays are electromechanical or solid-state devices that can best be defined as voltage-controlled switches. When a voltage is applied to the input, the output contacts change states. Electromechanical relays have been used in control circuits for many years. They continue to be utilized, in spite of the electronic alternative, because of their ease of use, versatility, contact ratings, and relatively low cost. They consist of a coil that, when energized, pulls in an armature, which changes the common contact—or switch position. These relays feature both AC and DC coils and contact arrangements up to four poles in single- or double-throw variations. The poles and throws specification for electromechanical relays is the same as described for switches. Devices called *contactors* are simply large electromechanical relays typically used in motor starter circuits. There are many different packages available for panel mounting, plug-in modules, or direct solder in circuit board variations. Selection of these relays involves the mechanical size and configuration, the coil voltage, the contacts arrangement (number of poles and number of throws), and the contact voltage and current ratings.

Solid-state relays are the electronic equivalent to electromechanical relays. They consist of an input circuit to which an input voltage is applied to change the state of the output contacts. The output contacts are an electronic switch that is either a transistor for switching DC circuits or a triac for AC applications. The input and output circuits are isolated by using opto-isolators. Opto-isolators use an LED and a photodiode to transmit a light signal that turns on the output when the input voltage is applied. Solid-state relays offer a significant improvement in switching life over electromechanical relays. Input voltages are limited to 5 V DC to 15 V

▲ FIGURE 4–22
Switch assortment *(Courtesy of C&K Switch Products)*

DC and only one contact arrangement is available: single pole/single throw (SPST). Care must also be taken to derate the current rating of solid-state relays when they are used at higher temperatures. To select solid-state relays, the input voltage, the output voltage being switched (AC or DC), and the voltage and current ratings of the contact are the key parameters.

Example 4–6

Determine the number of poles and throws for the switches and relays shown in Figure 4–23*.

4–7 ▶ Connectors

Connectors are an important aspect of any electronic design. Connectors involve any device that serves to make an electrical connection from one circuit element to another. There are generally three types of connector situations that occur in electronic design:

Answers: A. DPST   B. SPDT   C. SPST   D. SPDT

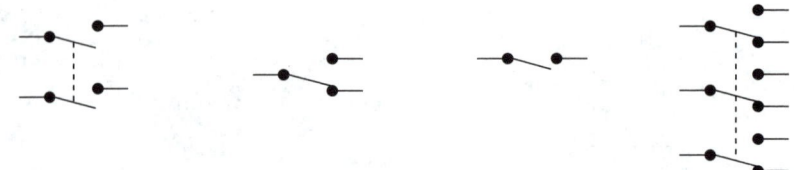

▶ **FIGURE 4–23**
Poles and throws example

Wire-to-wire

Wire-to-PCB (printed circuit board)

PCB-to-PCB

T key aspects that determine the applicability of a type of connector to a specific application are as follows:

1. Application type (wire-to-wire, wire-to-PCB, PCB-to-PCB; wire-to-wire could be flat cable, coaxial cable, or conventional wire)

2. Mounting (none, panel, printed circuit board)

3. Voltage across contacts

4. Current through contacts

5. Size

6. Number of contacts and spacing

7. Termination type (solder or crimp)

8. Environmental aspects (temperature, humidity, seal)

9. Contact resistance, which depends on the contact material; typical contact materials include beryllium copper, phosphor bronze, spring brass, and low-leaded brass. In higher-quality connectors, selective gold or silver plating is used on the specific contact areas. Low-cost connectors utilize an electro-tin plate.

10. Keyed or not keyed; keying prevents incorrect connection

11. Insertion force and pin alignment tolerance

12. Reliability (number of disconnects over life, design life)

13. Cost and ease of assembly

The most common types of connectors will be discussed next, along with their typical applications and advantages.

Printed Circuit Board Edge Connectors

Printed circuit board edge connectors are very cost effective because they form a one-piece connector that either connects a printed circuit board to some wires or to another printed circuit board. They rely on the printed circuit board to substi-

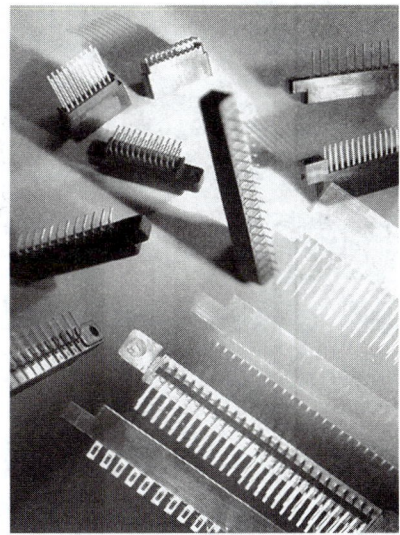

▶ **FIGURE 4–24**
Printed circuit board edge connector
example *(Courtesy of Tyco Electronics)*

tute for the male portion of the connector. Nevertheless, when utilizing printed circuit board edge connectors, care must be taken to ensure that the design and quality of the printed circuit board will provide a secure connection. They are available in both crimp and solder terminations. Typical spacing of printed circuit board edge conductors are 0.156″ centers or 0.1″. Figure 4–24 shows examples of edge connectors.

Flat Cable Connectors

Flat cable connectors are designed to work with standard flat cable and form a termination that pierces and crimps the flat cable wire. This allows a very quick and low-cost connector assembly, which is its primary advantage. Flat cable connectors come in many configurations that include male pin and female receptacles as well as printed circuit board edge connectors. The flat cable connectors are connected to the flat cable by sandwiching the flat cable between the two sections of the connector and carefully pressing them together to pierce the insulation and form a crimp contact between the connector and the wire. The pressure must be applied in a consistent manner and is usually performed with a vice. Flat cable and the corresponding connectors come with many contact arrangements, which can be up to 64 contacts wide. Figure 4–25 shows examples of flat cable connectors.

D-Type Connectors

Connecting data input and output lines between two pieces of equipment is usually accomplished with some sort of D-type connectors. D-type connectors are terminated in a variety of solder lugs, including direct mounting to printed circuit boards. Standard D-type connectors include contact numbers of 9, 15, 25, and 37. Figure 4–26 shows examples of D-type connectors.

▲ **FIGURE 4–25**
Flat cable connectors *(Courtesy of Tyco Electronics)*

▲ **FIGURE 4–26**
D-type connectors *(Courtesy of Tyco Electronics)*

Coaxial Connectors

Coaxial connectors make connection on one axis and are usually restricted to connecting two wires: a signal and ground. These connectors (see Figure 4–27) are typically used for radio frequency (RF) and audio applications. The most popular RF coaxial connector is the standard BNC connector. However, there are many other popular varieties, such as SMA and SMB. Audio-type connectors are usually called phone plugs, phonojacks, and mini- and micro-plugs. The phone plugs are usually $1/4''$ plugs and receptacles. Phono jacks are 3.18 mm in size while the mini-plug is 3.58 mm and the microplug 2.46 mm.

Circular Connectors

These are usually multi-pin connectors of higher reliability. Many military-type connectors are of the circular type. (Military connectors are discussed in the next

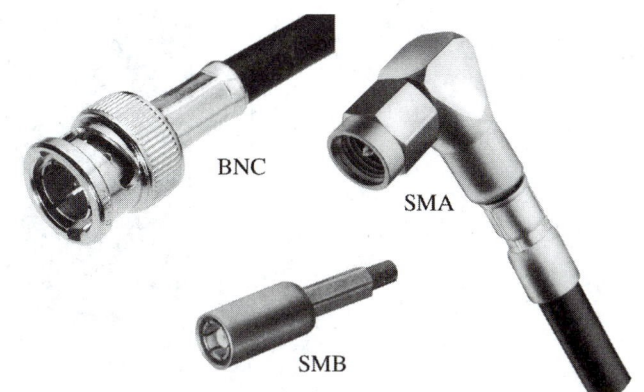

▶ **FIGURE 4–27**
RF Connectors *(Courtesy of Tyco Electronics)*

section.) A good example of a typical circular connector application is the keyboard connector on most personal computers. Figure 4–28 shows examples of circular connectors.

Military Connectors

Military connectors possess extremely high reliability and can withstand extreme environments such as moisture, ambient temperature, vibration, shock, and EMI. There are many different configurations and types and these are used whenever the requirements of the application justify their high cost.

Zero Insertion Force Connectors

Zero insertion force (ZIF) connectors are used whenever there are a high number of contacts—and the number of disconnects is also very high (see Figure 4–29). The primary purpose is to provide superior contact and preclude any damage to the connection point on either side caused by insertion. These connectors mate without any insertion force. The contact force is applied separately after insertion. The most typical application is EPROM programmers.

▶ **FIGURE 4–28**
Circular connectors *(Courtesy of Tyco Electronics)*

▶ **FIGURE 4–29**
ZIF connectors *(Courtesy of Tyco Electronics)*

4–8 ▶ Selecting Active Components

Active components are devices that are fabricated from semiconductor materials. The most commonly used active components are as follows:

Diodes: Rectifier diodes, signal diodes, shottky diodes, tunnel diodes, photo-diodes, zener diodes, light emitting diodes (LEDs), varactor diodes

Transistors: Bipolar junction transistors (BJTs), field effect transistors (FETs), metal oxide semiconductor field effect transistors (MOSFETs)

Thyristors: Diacs, unijunction transistors, silicon-controlled rectifiers (SCRs), triacs

Analog Integrated Circuits: Voltage regulators, voltage references, comparators, op amps, DC to DC converters, A/D converters, D/A converters, multiplexers, filters, drivers, temperature sensors, special functions

Digital Logic Family Integrated Circuits: TTL logic, CMOS logic, ECL logic

MSI, VLSI Digital Integrated Circuits: Microprocessors, microcomputers, memories, programmable memories, programmable logic, drivers, interface circuits, encoders, decoders, multiplexers, and special functions

The selection and use of active electronic components is a broad area that is well covered in most electronic courses and texts. This section is a general review of active components, discussing their critical parameters and summarizing their selection.

The specifications for most active components start out with a section called "Absolute Maximum Ratings," where the maximum ratings for all parameters are listed. It is imperative to review every aspect of these ratings with the intended circuit application to ensure that these ratings are not exceeded. Exceeding these ratings usually means the component will malfunction and may sustain permanent damage. Depending on the application of the design, there should be at least a 10% safety factor between the maximum value of a parameter in a circuit and the absolute maximum value listed in the specifications. The key parameters of concern are usually:

Maximum power supply voltage

Maximum input voltage

Maximum differential input voltage

Maximum output current (source)

Maximum output current (sink)

Maximum operating temperature

Maximum voltage on any pin

Beyond the maximum parameters ratings, the determination of which active component fulfills the functional requirements of a circuit usually comes down to the functional capabilities of the circuit and the speed, tolerance, power consumption, temperature coefficient, reliability, complexity and ease of use of the component. These parameters are realized by a myriad of terms and pages of specifications that the data sheets for active components comprise. To complicate matters further, each semiconductor manufacturer may use slightly different terms for a particular parameter or signal line. This requires that the designer possess a solid understanding of the requirements for the component to be able to understand and sort out the various parameter symbols, names and their corresponding meaning and significance.

Data sheets usually include application hints. These should be reviewed completely as they are the key to the proper function of the active component in a circuit application. Application circuits are also included for many active components and these are often helpful in conveying what might not be so obvious from the rest of the specifications. Most active component data sheets require a lot of reading between the lines. Experience is the only way to develop this important skill. Fortunately, each semiconductor manufacturer has a staff of applications engineers that can be contacted for extra help and support.

▶ Summary

In this chapter we have discussed the variety of components available and the process of their selection for use in an electronic circuit design. In each case the selection of a component involves its quality, size, cost, and labor requirements. This selection procedure is a critical part of the design process. It is important to remember the analogy of the "weak link in the chain" when considering circuit function and reliability. On the other hand, the financial objectives of the design cannot be ignored. This is why it is important to keep track of the cost goals of the project, continuously comparing the latest cost estimates, as they are determined.

The successful completion of any design involves the sound judgments made in the selection of components where the proper combination of function, quality, cost, and size are obtained. In the next chapter we will cover how to implement these components and the circuit schematic into a functioning printed circuit board assembly.

▶ References

Harper, C. A., ed. 1977. *Handbook of Components for Electronics.* New York: McGraw-Hill.

Stadtmiller, D. J. 2001. *Electronics Project Management and Design.* Upper Saddle River, NJ: Prentice Hall.

Warring, R. H. 1983. *Electronic Components Handbook for Circuit Designers.* Blue Summit, PA: Tab Books.

▶ Exercises

4–1   A 1% tolerance, 1 kΩ, metal film resistor is used in an application in which the ambient temperature will go from 0°C to 65°C. Assuming a temperature coefficient of 100 ppm/°C, what is the worst-case resistance range expected for this resistor value after combining the effects of the temperature coefficient and the resistor tolerance?

4–2   For each circuit shown in Figure 4–30, calculate the possible ranges of the voltage V_{OUT}. V_{IN} = 10 V.

4–3   In the circuits shown in Figure 4–31, calculate the smallest resolution values for the voltage V_{OUT}. V_{IN} = 10 V.

4–4   When selecting the actual resistors to be used in a circuit, what are the two key performance parameters that should be used to determine whether to select a carbon film or a metal film resistor? Use the resistor selection chart shown in Figure 4–1.

4–5 Which key design factors promote the use of a wire-wound resistor instead of a metal film resistor in a particular circuit?

4–6 If a design requirement can be accomplished by using higher tolerance resistor values or adjustable trimmer potentiometers, which is likely to be more cost effective?

4–7 Calculate the equivalent series resistance (ESR) for a 0.1 µF capacitor that has an insulation resistance (IR) of 100,000 Ω at a frequency of 60 Hz. Assume that series resistance and inductance equal zero.

4–8 Define in your own words the meaning of the term *dielectric absorption.* When is it an important consideration?

4–9 Define the terms *dissipation factor* and *quality factor.* How are they related?

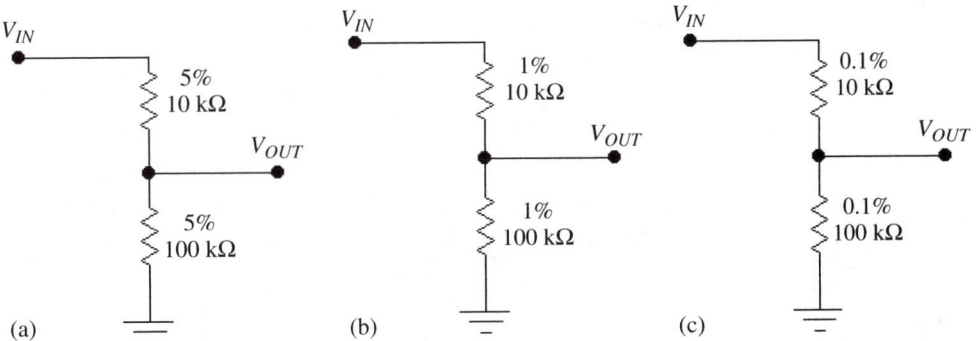

▲ **FIGURE 4–30**
1% and 5% voltage divider circuits (see Exercise 4–2)

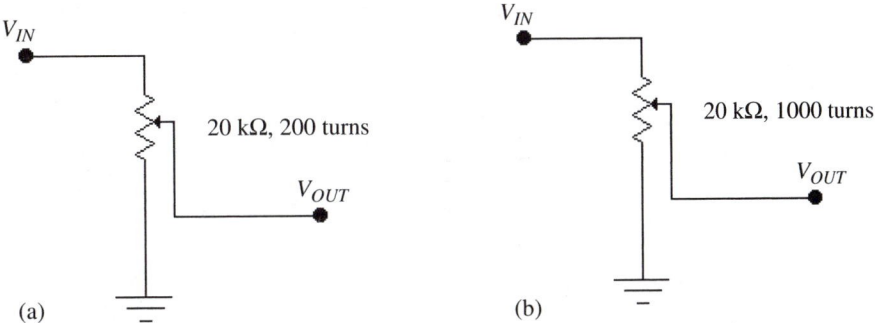

▲ **FIGURE 4–31**
Potentiometer voltage dividers with number of turns (see Exercise 4–3)

4–10   What type of capacitors would you select to perform power-supply decoupling of various integrated circuits on a printed circuit board?

4–11   A capacitor is to be used in a precision low-pass filter circuit for an audio signal. What are the key parameters of concern when selecting the capacitor to be used in this circuit? Based on using the best available capacitor to meet these requirements, which type of capacitor would you select?

4–12   A capacitor is to be used in a 60 Hz, sample-and-hold circuit that is connected up to an A/D converter. What is the most important parameter to be considered in the selection of the type of this capacitor?

4–13   A bipolar capacitor with a value of 10 µF is needed for a circuit. List the different types of capacitors and methods that you can use to achieve this overall capacitance value.

4–14   Show the schematic symbol for the following switches:

   a. SPST maintained switch

   b. SPST momentary switch

   c. SPDT maintained switch

   d. DPDT maintained switch

4–15   What are the three different types of applications for electrical connectors?

4–16   When replacing any type of electrical contact, which two electrical parameters must be known?

4–17   When selecting active components, list the maximum value parameters that should be considered.

5 ▶ Printed Circuit Board Design

▶ Introduction

After the electronic design has been simulated, breadboarded and tested, the circuit is usually developed into a printed circuit assembly. The invention of the printed circuit board (PCB) was a significant factor in the development and growth of the electronics industry. Its development has been just as important as the transistor and the integrated circuit. Over the years the methods utilized to lay out and manufacture printed circuit boards have undergone significant change as large-scale integration and computer technology have been applied to the process. In order to develop a background for circuit board technology, the discussion begins with manual layout and taping methods and then proceeds to the current computer software process. The likelihood of laying out a PCB depends on the career path followed. Students seeking a technology degree are more likely to complete a board layout than students seeking an engineering degree. In any case there is a need to understand the process, as the PCB is a key component in any electronic design. The design engineer will review the PCB layout from an electrical perspective: grounding, component location, bypass capacitors, and the like.

The PCB is an important electronic component. Almost all electronic circuits are implemented with printed circuit boards. Because each circuit is different, the resulting PCB is a custom component designed specifically for a particular circuit. The primary function of the PCB is to make the electrical connections for the electronic circuit, but it also provides for mechanical mounting of the components and the board itself. The circuit conductors, while ideally viewed as 0 Ω conductors, in actuality possess impedance values that include resistance, inductance, and capacitance. In this chapter we will discuss the development and documentation of the printed circuit board as follows:

- ▶ Documentation accuracy
- ▶ Printed circuit board types

- ▸ General printed circuit board design considerations
- ▸ Printed circuit board development—manual
- ▸ Printed circuit board development—computer
- ▸ Printed circuit board documentation

5–1 ▶ Documentation Accuracy

At this point in the design project, there are two documents that define the circuit: the schematic diagram and the parts list. The accuracy of these documents is extremely important as we move into the next phase, because all of the drawings and documents developed later are based on these. Now is a good time to check and update the schematic diagram and the parts list.

It is good practice for whomever has design responsibility for an assembly, module, or system to maintain one set of all the drawings for the design, designated as "Design Master Drawings." The design master drawings—or simply "design masters"—are hard copies of the latest revision of all documents that define the design. They should be labeled in red as design masters with the date and initials of the responsible design engineer. The purpose of design masters is to accumulate all of the modifications to be made to the drawings in one well-assembled document as errors are found and problems resolved. Without drawings designated as design masters, you will soon find yourself with many copies, notes, and scraps of paper listing important changes that may or may not be passed on when final changes are made to the design drawings. Utilizing design master drawings will improve the accuracy of design documents and greatly improve the efficiency of the project engineer. At the beginning of the circuit board layout stage, the schematic and the parts list are checked and modified to correct any errors or implement changes made as part of the design simulation or breadboard testing.

5–2 ▶ Printed Circuit Board Types

Before discussing the layout methods, let us review the makeup of the printed circuit board and the different types currently available.

Circuit Board Laminates

Every printed circuit board starts out with what is called the laminate: the copper-clad material that is etched, plated, and drilled to complete the bare circuit board assembly. The laminate consists of a base material that has a copper foil applied to one or both sides. The typical base materials consist of paper, glass cloth, or glass mat combined with phenolic or epoxy resins. A base material and copper foil are combined to form a particular grade of laminate. Laminate grades have been established by NEMA (National Electrical Manufacturer's Association) and military specifications. NEMA type G-10 (MIL Spec type GE) is a very popular general-use grade of laminate made from glass cloth bonded with an epoxy resin. Other laminate grades include the NEMA prefix FR, which stands for "flame retardant." The FR grades are favored for use on PCBs used in products that must meet approval agency flame retardant requirements. NEMA type FR 4 is also very popular and is similar to the G-10 material with the addition of a flame-retardant epoxy. The mechanical strength, ease of machining, adhesion of the copper foil material, and ability to withstand changing environmental conditions determine the ultimate quality of a laminate material. Laminates are available with single-sided or dual-sided copper foils, and very thin laminates can be layered together to form multilayer circuit boards.

Printed Circuit Board Manufacturing Process

Traditionally, the printed circuit boards have been fabricated from what is called a subtraction process, the removal of copper from a laminate material. Processes that add copper runs have been developed and are becoming increasingly popular. The subtraction process is still predominate and is the process described here. Figure 5–1 shows a flowchart of the process. The basic subtraction process fabrication of a PCB involves the following:

1. The laminate is drilled and the holes are plated with a copper flash process.

2. The laminate material is thoroughly cleaned and dried.

3. The laminate is covered with a thin adhesive-backed sheet of material called a *photoresist* that is applied to the copper foil on the laminate. This photoresist material can be altered with the application of light to resist certain solvents called *developers*.

4. The photoresist material is exposed to fluorescent lights through the negative of the artwork to be etched. Where the negative allows the light to pass through, the photoresist is altered such that a developer solvent removes it from the laminate. Where the negative blocks the light, the photoresist material will not be sensitive to the developing solvent and remains on the laminate.

5. The laminate, with the developed photoresist material attached, is developed by placement in a developing solvent that strips away the sensitized photoresist material.

6. The result is the initial laminate with the remaining photoresist material covering the laminate where the copper runs are desired. The laminate is placed in a copper etching acid solution that strips away the exposed copper areas.

Single-sided Printed Circuit Boards

Single-sided printed circuit boards are the simplest variety, because the copper runs exist on only one side of the laminate. For through-hole technology components, the side of the board with the copper runs is called the *copper side*. The

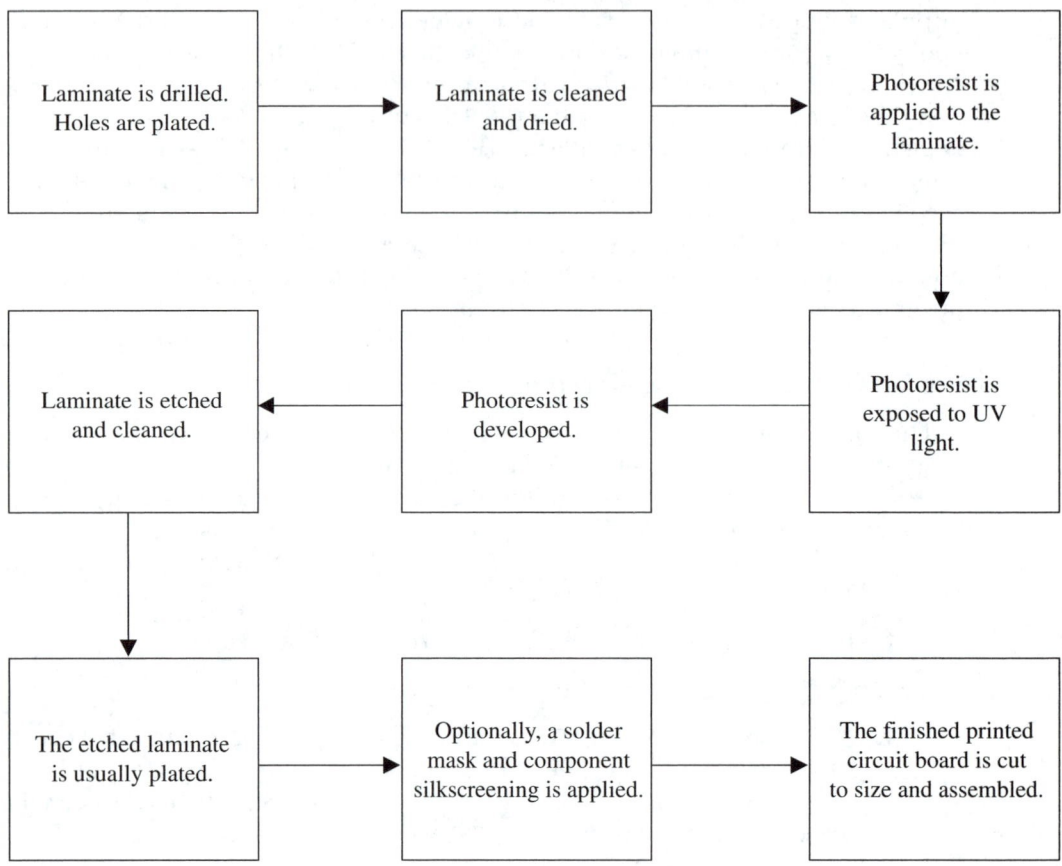

▲ **FIGURE 5–1**
Printed circuit board fabrication process flowchart

other side is designated the *component side.* For surface-mount technology circuit boards, the components and the copper runs are present on the same side. At the present time, single-sided boards are used only for very simple circuits not required to be a minimal size. Because all the connections must be made on a single side, the layout is more complicated, and more space is needed for the copper runs. Also, the holes that are drilled into the printed circuit for mounting through-hole components do not need to be plated through as on double-sided boards. This is because the connection of the component to the copper run can be assured by the solder connection. A single-sided printed circuit board will be cheaper but physically larger than the double-sided alternative.

Double-sided Printed Circuit Boards

The double-sided printed circuit board has copper runs on both sides of the board laminate. The circuit connections can be made much more easily, because there are two surfaces on which to make them. Double-sided boards also provide the ability to transfer a connecting run from one side of the circuit board to the other. This is accomplished through a hole in the printed circuit board called a via or feed-through. The via is a hole in the PCB whose only purpose is to transfer the connecting run from side to side. Consequently, components are not mounted in the via holes. The via hole must be copper plated to ensure connection between both sides of the board. Plating of the holes also improves the solder connection made when the components are installed into the board. Copper runs can be connected to either side of a component hole so circuit connections can be passed from one side of the board to the other through them as well. The double-sided PCB results in a smaller, denser circuit board.

Multilayer Circuit Boards

Multilayer circuit boards have additional thin laminates that provide circuit foils that can make additional circuit connections. Multilayer boards are utilized when complex circuit connections are required in a minimal space. Each layer is aligned with and sandwhiched between the outer layers of the circuit board. Plated-through via holes and component holes are used to transfer connections from one layer to another. If no connection is made at a particular layer, then the via or component hole is isolated from making a connection at that layer. The most typical application of multilayer boards today is the provision of two inner layers to make all the power supply connections. In this case one of the layers becomes power supply ground, and the other makes all the positive power supply voltage connections. This is an optimum situation for noise immunity, as the power supply ground layer is one large ground plane that serves as a ground shield for the entire board. Additionally, with the positive power supply voltage on one side and the ground layer on the other, the inner laminate material acts as a dielectric. With a dielectric between them, the ground plane and the positive supply circuit runs act like a distributed capacitor, providing very noise-free power to the entire circuit.

The four-layer variety of the multilayer printed circuit board is the most common circuit board style currently being utilized. This type of circuit board has two inner layers, one that provides power supply ground and another that supplies the nominal 5 V for most digital systems. The outer component and copper sides of the circuit board make all the other interconnections. These boards cost more than double-sided boards but provide exceptional noise immunity and better circuit densities. The increased utilization of plastic enclosures in the electronics industry has promoted the need for a shielding ground plane in place of the metal enclosures that had once accomplished this. The increased use of plastic electronic enclosures requires that the circuit boards themselves contain some shielding.

5–3 ▶ General Printed Circuit Board Design Considerations

In Sections 5–4 and 5–5 ahead, the specific method of circuit board layout for manual or computer methods is described. In this section the general considerations for printed circuit board design are discussed as they are applied to both methods.

Circuit Board Design Considerations

Following is a list of design considerations for circuit board design

1. *Connecting Runs.*
   a. In general, make all circuit runs (see Figure 5–2 for a summary) as short and as thick as reasonably possible while providing as much space between them as possible.
   b. Provide clearance on all sides of a printed circuit board. An area of about 3.8 mm to 10 mm wide (0.15″ to 0.40″) is recommended. Components and circuit runs should not be located in these areas. These clearance areas are needed to avoid interference with board handling fixtures, guidance rails, and alignment tools.
   c. All circuit pads should be larger than the connecting run to prevent the flow of solder away from the solder connection.
   d. Keep in mind the possibility of crosstalk between long adjacent runs. Insert a O-V potential run between them to minimize the potential for crosstalk.
   e. Try to keep signal and return runs together as they would be in a cable. The equal currents flowing in opposite directions will minimize the inductive effects.

2. *Circuit Board Perspective.* When developing circuit board artworks, negatives, and silk screens and while fabricating prototype boards, be aware of the proper perspective for the situation. (Is the view from the bottom or top side of the board?)

3. *Grounding and Shielding.* The information presented in Chapter 3 on grounding and shielding should be applied to the circuit board layout.

1. Make all circuit runs as short and as thick as reasonable.

2. Do not locate components within 0.15″ to 0.40″ from the edge of the circuit board.

3. Make circuit pads larger than the connecting runs.

4. Insert zero-potential runs between signal runs where crosstalk can occur.

5. Keep signal and return runs adjacent as they would be in a cable.

▲ **FIGURE 5–2**
Printed circuit board circuit runs—layout summary

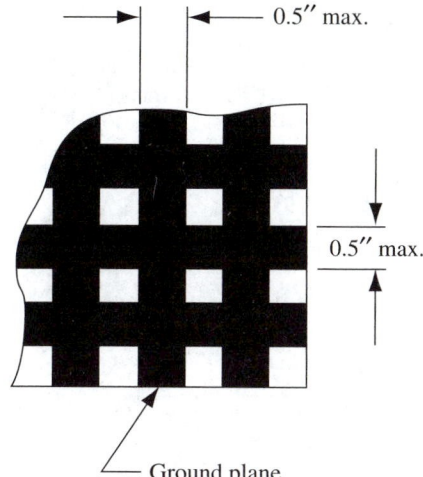

▶ FIGURE 5–3
Crosshatch ground example

Ground plane

a. Ground plane: A ground shield should be utilized wherever possible. This means that the circuit board ground conductor should contain as much copper area as possible. The ideal situation is the one described earlier for multilayer boards, where one entire layer of the board is allocated to ground plane. In single- or double-sided circuit boards, this concept is implemented by making large portions of the circuit board available as a solid copper ground plane. Since most through-hole circuit boards are wave soldered, the ground plane is configured in a crosshatch scheme, as shown in Figure 5–3. This is done because large areas of solid copper absorb heat from the stream of wave solder, resulting in an uneven and lower solder temperature in that area of the board. This degrades the quality of the solder connection. The circuit board with a large exposed ground plane also has a tendency to warp because of the uneven absorption of heat caused by the large mass of exposed copper. The crosshatch ground plane resolves both of these issues.

b. Ground distribution: Ground should be separated and grouped into the following types: low-level analog signal grounds, low-level digital signal grounds, higher-level switched circuit grounds, and a chassis ground (enclosure or card-cage ground). These ground types should be connected at only one point. Within each type of ground, ground connections should be distributed to subgroupings of the appropriate circuitry in parallel as shown in Figure 5–4 and discussed in Example 5–1. This is done to preclude the effect of one long ground loop, where the current return flow from one area of a circuit can affect the operation of another circuit.

c. Guard rings: These are used with operational amplifier circuits to minimize leakage current that can occur at the input terminals to the op amp. The potential error, induced by this leakage current, increases dramatically when the signal source impedance is large. Guard rings are copper traces placed along each printed circuit board surface where the input terminals make contact. On a double-sided PCB with a through-hole

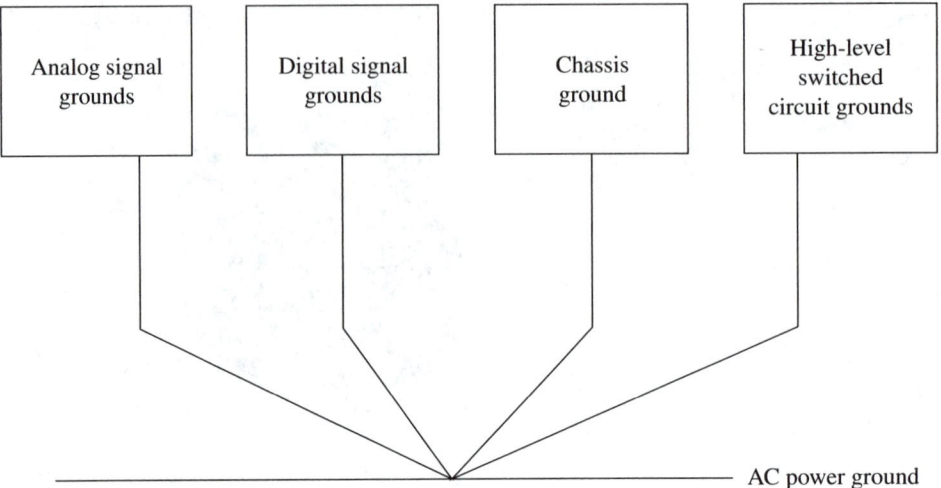

▲ FIGURE 5–4
Ground distribution system

package op amp, the guard ring should be placed on both sides of the board. The guard ring should circle around the sensitive op amp inputs and be connected to the same potential as the positive and negative inputs. See Figure 5–5 for examples of guard rings and their connections for various op amp circuits.

Example 5–1

A circuit schematic shows 15 digital integrated circuits to be laid out on a double-sided printed circuit board. The power supply ground connections are being planned for these integrated circuits. The problem is to determine a practical way

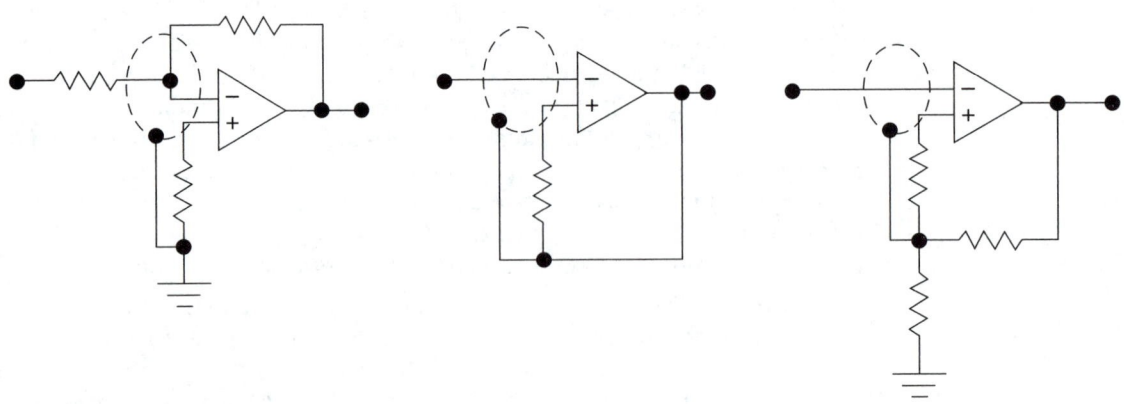

▲ FIGURE 5–5
Guard ring examples

of making these ground connections that will minimize the creation of a ground loop. According to the circuit board design considerations just discussed, ground connections of a similar type of circuitry should be grouped together and a separate ground connection should be made to subgroupings of that type of circuitry. In this example, all of the circuitry is low-level digital circuitry so these circuit grounds should all be kept together. One extreme approach is to have 15 individual parallel runs connecting to the common digital ground. This would require a large amount of circuit board area and make other connections very difficult. The other extreme is to provide one continuous ground connection to all the integrated circuits. A ground loop results when components, attached to the end of the loop, are at a higher ground potential than those at the beginning. Also, ground current flowing from the components at the end of the loop affects the ground level of those components at the beginning. The most practical solution is to break the 15 integrated circuits into three groups of 5 and provide parallel ground connections to each group of 5, as shown in Figure 5–6.

4. *Decoupling capacitors.* As power is distributed throughout a printed circuit board, the circuit runs exhibit some amount of inductive reactance. Inductive reactance will oppose a change in the current flow through the runs. At lower frequencies of operation, the inductive reactance is insignificant because the switched components have enough time to complete their switch transition. They can accommodate a delay in the availability of current caused by the inductive reactance. However, in high-

▶ **FIGURE 5–6**
Ground distribution example

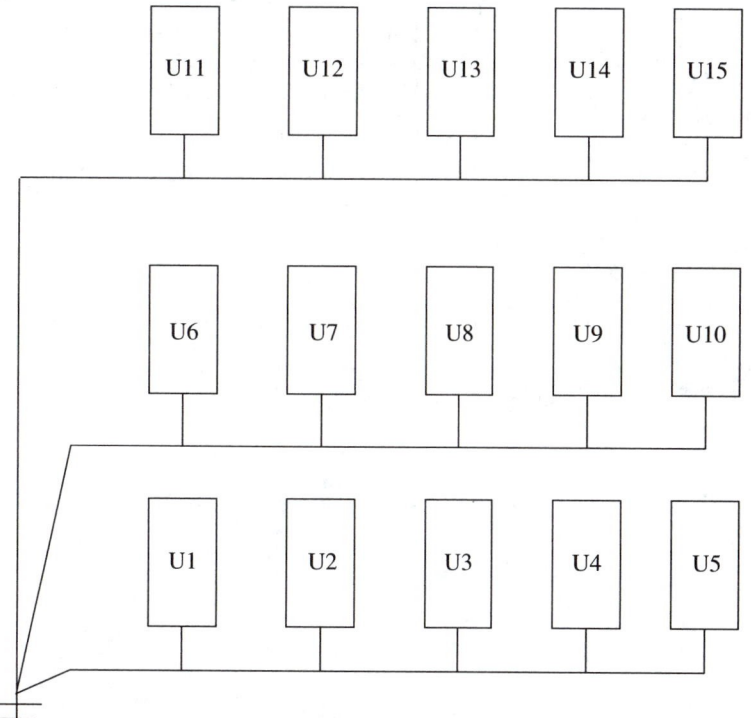

frequency applications, such as typical digital circuits, the inductive reactance of the runs is more critical. It provides a delay of the additional current needed for the device to make the switch transition in time for the circuit to function properly. In these cases, a decoupling capacitor is used to counteract or decouple the power supply run from the effect of the inductive reactance. A 0.1 μF ceramic disc capacitor is typically used for this purpose. The 0.1 μF capacitor stores enough charge in reserve to supply the requirements of the switched component and enable it to switch in the required time. As a rule of thumb, one decoupling capacitor is used for every two integrated circuits. It is important to locate the capacitor as close to the component as possible with thick, short runs. Locating any decoupling capacitor on thin runs away from the component completely defeats its purpose (see Figure 5–7).

5. *Component placement and orientation guidelines.* The orientation and placement of components are important parts of any circuit board layout and varies depending on the type of package technology (through-hole technology or SMT) and the soldering process.

    a. Through-hole Guidelines: Through-hole components are usually either hand soldered or wave soldered. Wave soldering is the method most often used in a manufacturing environment, and it is the process in which component orientation can become important. Wave soldering is an automatic method of soldering in which liquid solder is continuously pumped through a spout to form a well-defined wave. The solder temperature can be tightly controlled over the surface of the wave. The circuit board to be soldered is passed over the wave and all the solder points on that side of the board are soldered. The advantages of wave soldering are as follows:

       1. Short solder times

       2. Reduced temperature distortion of the circuit board. This is because only a portion of the board is exposed to the wave at any time.

▶ **FIGURE 5–7**
Decoupling capacitor examples

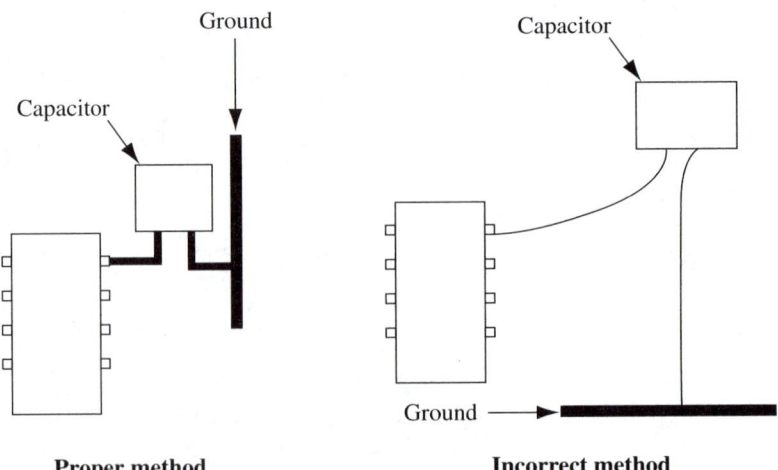

Proper method   Incorrect method

3. There is a continuous flow of fresh solder returned to the wave. Any flux or other residue is filtered out of the process within the solder flow loop. If the circuit board is wave soldered, the orientation of the board as it flows through the wave should be determined. In determining which direction to pass the circuit board through the wave solder machine, the primary concern is the maximum-width circuit board that the wave-solder machine can process. If both dimensions of the circuit board are less than the maximum width for the solder machine, then the board can be passed through the wave in either orientation. If the machine can accommodate only one side of the board, then the longer dimension of the board must be parallel with the direction of flow, as shown in Figure 5–8. If neither dimension of the board fits through the wave, then either a larger wave-solder machine must be used, or the mechanical design must be redone to reduce the board size. This is not the type of information that one wants to learn about during the initial production run. When placing dual in-line packaging (DIP) through-hole packages, the orientation of the main body of the integrated circuits should be perpendicular to the intended flow of the wave solder. The connecting runs on the component side of the board should be in the direction of the wave flow. This is to preclude solder spilling over from one DIP connection to the next. The connecting runs on the component side of the board should be run perpendicular to the runs on the solder side of the board.

b. SMT Guidelines: SMT circuit boards require a lot more planning in their design. The land patterns or circuit pad sizes are critical for the completion of a reliable solder joint. Accordingly, the circuit pads used, either

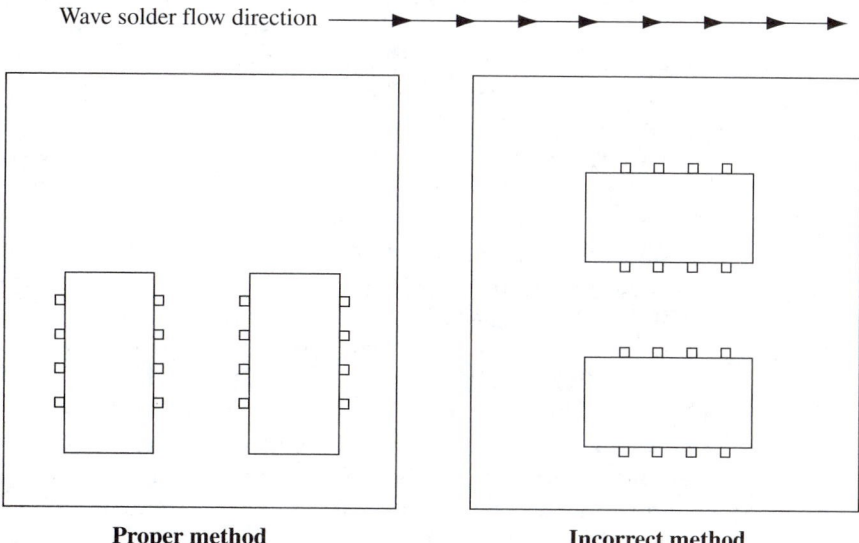

Proper method   **Incorrect method**

▲ **FIGURE 5–8**
Wave solder flow direction

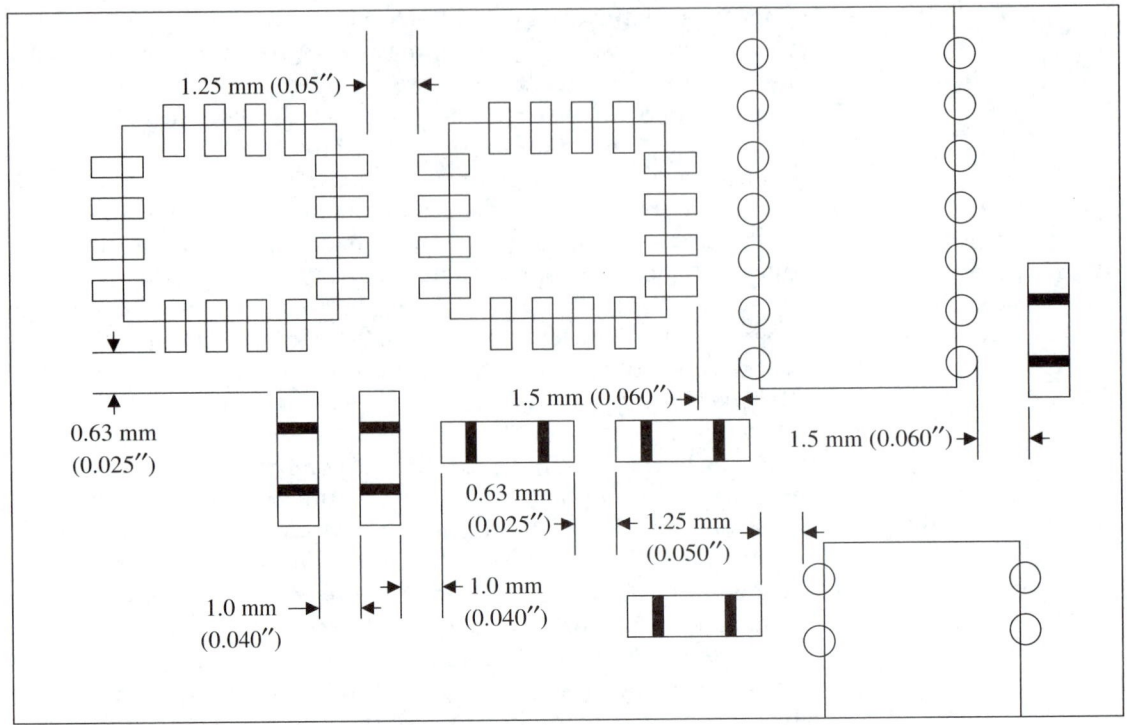

▲ **FIGURE 5–9**
SMT land pattern clearances

computer-generated or stick-on circuit "puppets," should be of the proper sizes as recommended by the Institute for Interconnecting and Packaging Electronic Circuits (IPC) in their standard IPC-SM-872. The clearances between the components, which provide for all manufacturing aspects of the circuit board, are shown in Figure 5–9.

SMT circuit boards can be soldered automatically in two ways: wave or paste-reflow soldering. Because SMT technology has a completely different set of processing issues, the component placement criteria are different. The square SMT packages present a special problem for wave soldering because leads are located on all sides of the package. It is impossible to place these components so that all pads are in the direction of the wave flow. For this reason a solder mask is recommended with most SMT circuits. A solder mask is a coat of epoxy resin covering the entire printed circuit board except where the pads will require soldering. Solder masks are used to eliminate solder bridging between adjacent conductors during wave soldering. Solder masks are currently used with most PCBs of either through-hole or SMT type, as circuit run densities have increased dramatically. Otherwise the placement of SMT components should be as follows:

1. All passive components should be mounted parallel to each other.

2. All integrated circuit packages should be mounted parallel to each other.

3. The longer axis of any integrated circuit package and that of passive components should be perpendicular to each other.

4. The longer axis of the passive components should be perpendicular to the direction of travel of the board through a wave-solder machine.

If paste-reflow soldering is to be utilized, the placement of SMT components is not that critical.

6. *Tooling holes.* To provide for mechanical alignment on any parts placement or testing apparatus, a minimum of two (preferably three) unplated holes should be located in the corners of the circuit board. The actual hole diameters depend on the actual equipment being utilized, but they are generally between 2.5 mm and 3.8 mm (0.10″ to 0.15″). For SMT circuitry, optic targets are needed in addition to the tooling holes to orient and register the component pads to the center of the device. This is accomplished with fiducials, which are optical alignment targets that are silk-screened onto the board. Three fiducials should be placed on a known grid in the corners of the circuit board to form a three-point datum system. Figure 5–10 shows an example of the application of tooling holes and fiducials. This figure shows two different types and sizes of fiducials that can be used.

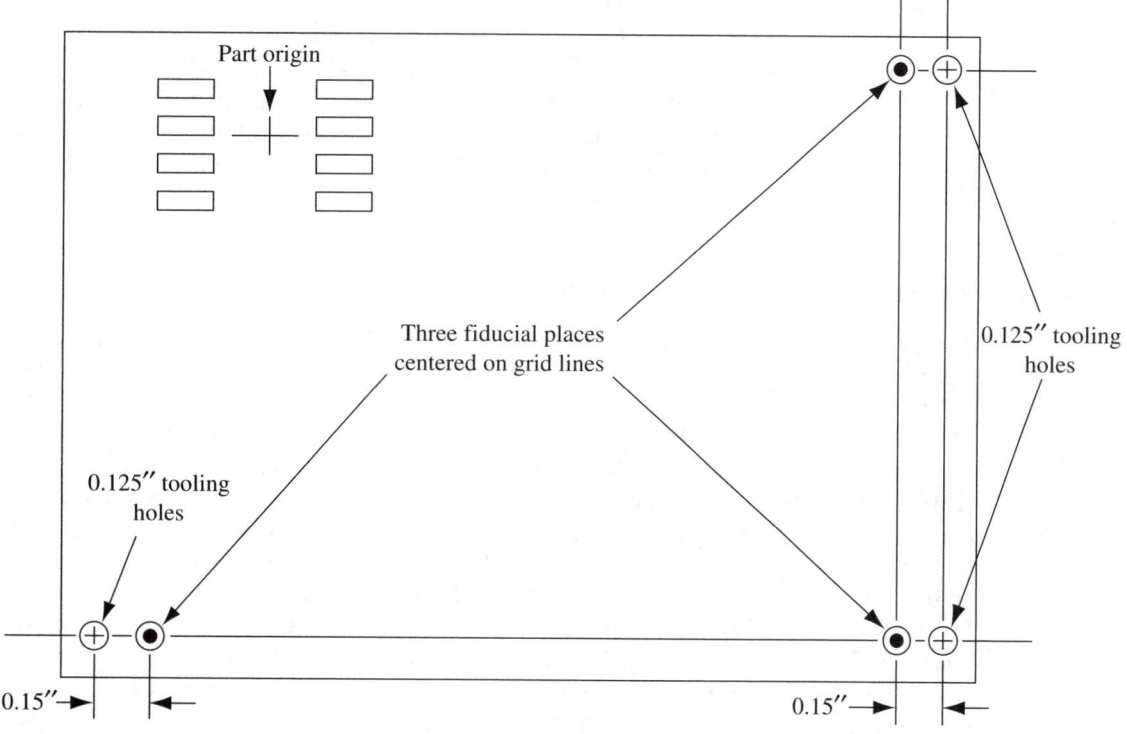

▲ **FIGURE 5–10**
Fiducial tooling hole example

7. *Consider circuit board testing requirements and the need for test points.* Review preliminary circuit board test plans to determine the circuit points that will require access during manufacturing and field-testing. Each point must be accessible for testing and provide a means for attaching meter and oscilloscope test probes. Test points are available as a standard component that can be soldered into the board. Test points are more critical on SMT boards because it is almost impossible to clip probes onto SMT components. With through-hole circuits, test leads can often be attached to component leads without the use of a purchased, assembled test point. If test points are not planned for, it is difficult for manufacturing and field service to test boards and will result in many artwork changes later in the project.

8. *Large or high-power components.* Large or high-power components also require specific attention to design details. It is important to ensure that large components are affixed to the circuit board with the appropriate mechanical strength to support their weight. Most large components designed for circuit board mounting have some means of mechanical mounting incorporated into their design other than the solder connections. Be sure to utilize the manufacturer's recommended circuit board mounting scheme. Do not rely on just the solder connections to mechanically hold a large component onto a printed circuit board.

Components that utilize higher levels of power should utilize heat sinks when necessary. Be sure to determine this before laying out the circuit patterns by providing for the mechanical mounting of any heat sinks. When a component does not require a heat sink, but generates more than 1 W of power (i.e., a 2 W power resistor), be sure to consider its location relative to other temperature-sensitive components. Also, mount the device up off of the surface of the printed circuit board so that heat can radiate evenly in all directions.

5–4 ▶ Printed Circuit Board Layout—Manual

The manual circuit board layout method is one that has been used since the invention of the PCB. The manual layout method is seldom used in industry today, since the process has been, for the most part, replaced with computer software layout programs. However, there is a benefit to understanding this process before discussing the computer methods. Manual circuit board layout involves the use of layout templates to draw the components into position on a layout drawing that is usually a semitransparent medium of some kind. A mylar material is recommended, with one side having a matte finish for the layout drawing, because it erases cleanly and produces a strong, clear pencil image. The layout and the eventual artwork should be done over a precision grid background so that all the holes in the board can be located on the grid. A typical grid background is one with 1 mm spacing. The layout and the eventual taping are usually done at a scale of two times the actual size of the components, although standard 1X, 2X, and 4X templates and circuit puppets are available. A 4X scale, for example, would be used on small, dense circuits. Circuit puppets are adhesive-backed pads that conform to the var-

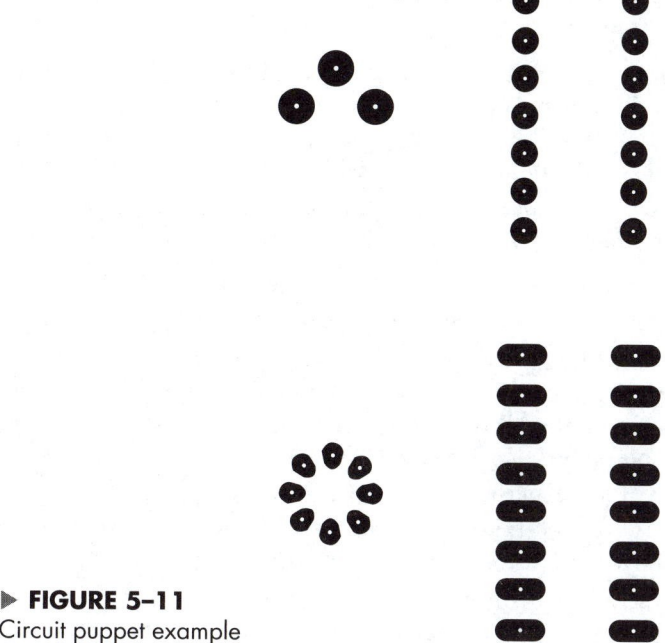

▶ **FIGURE 5–11**
Circuit puppet example

ious circuit components as shown in Figure 5–11. The layout is usually done as a positive. The dark areas define where the copper runs will be. Negative circuit puppets are available if one wishes to develop an artwork directly as a negative.

The Layout Drawing

Developing the layout drawing is the most difficult and critical part of the layout process. Its development will ultimately determine how well the circuit board functions and how easily it is manufactured, tested, and serviced. Completing the layout drawing involves selecting the location of all components on the board and defining the pattern of copper foil connections that will complete all the required connections. To complete the layout drawing, use the following process:

1. *Circuit board mechanical design.* Determine the desired type, size, and mounting configuration of the printed circuit board. This includes the length, width, thickness, and type (number of sides and layers). The choices for mounting usually include using mounting pads or standoffs, card cages, or other specialized hardware that affix to the board edge. These decisions must be made in conjunction with the overall mechanical design for the project as well as the selection of interconnection methods that are discussed below. Be sure the equipment used to process the board in manufacturing can accommodate the circuit board size selected.

2. *Board interconnection.* Determine the method and optimum location of all connections to the printed circuit board. The actual connecting method

must be selected and all relevant information about the connection must be determined.

3. *Component locations.* At this point the mechanical outline of the board and the location and space requirements for its mounting and interconnection have been defined. Next, select the ideal location of the components on the board while considering all of the following:

   a. Keep connections as short as possible. Keep components that have connections between them close together.

   b. Keep the functional blocks of the circuit together.

   c. Maintain an orderly flow of any signal from input to output.

   d. Make the thickness of the runs appropriate for the signal that they carry. Give special consideration to power supply and ground runs. These should always be as direct and as thick as possible. High current runs should be very thick.

   e. At the same time, consider the voltages present on adjacent runs and try to keep the runs as far apart as possible. Approval agencies often have spacing requirements for runs carrying voltages in excess of 30 V.

   f. Leave room for components that will dissipate a lot of power and consider the need for a heat sink.

   g. Attempt to keep component configurations as consistent as possible (i.e., have all integrated circuits going in the same direction, all polarized devices in the same orientation, resistors adjacent and in line, and so on).

   h. Provide access to testing for key circuit areas. Consider the eventual testing method that will be employed and the need for test points.

   i. Consider access to any adjustments or the need to remove any components from the board or the need to remove the board from the assembly.

   j. The board should present a professional and high-quality appearance.

4. *Layout copper runs.* The layout drawing should now include the desired location of all the components in addition to the complete mechanical profile of the board with mounting and interconnection hardware. The process of actually determining the connecting runs is the most difficult part of this process. The process usually takes a number of cycles, so it is recommended to place another layer of matte-finished mylar over the layout drawing that has been completed up to this point. This is done so as not to waste the efforts completed thus far, which occurs when the layout drawing must be redrawn after the first attempt to lay out the connections is abandoned for a better way. One way is to lay out the connections on the top layer of mylar. As the process evolves, simply replace the top layer and start over. The process is an iterative one that involves learning the best way to make the connections for a given circuit. The more experienced designer requires fewer iterations. At this stage, using a light table will make it easier to see through the different levels of mylar.

Draw in the connections with a simple line that will represent the actual circuit run. For double-sided boards, use a red pencil for one side of the board and a blue pencil for the other. For the most difficult connections, utilize a via hole to transfer a connecting run from one side or layer of the board to another. Via holes should not be overused. Each via requires that another hole be drilled in the board, adding a small cost to the board. Also, via hole connections are slightly less reliable than a solid copper run. It is best to make all power supply connections first and then proceed making the other connections.

5. *Layout design check.* After a number of attempts at completing the connecting copper runs, a successful layout drawing is complete. Before starting the taping process, it is important that whoever has design responsibility for the circuit board check all aspects of the layout design. This includes the mechanical size and shape, manufacturing and testing issues, and the location length and size of all circuit connections. This should be done before the taping process is started.

6. *The pad master.* After the layout design is checked, the layout is ready for taping. This involves the use of the circuit puppets, pads, and artwork tape to implement the pencil layout as a taped positive. The taping should be completed on what is called clear taping film. There are usually at least two layers (except for single-sided boards, where there is one) representing the layout so there must be a way to register or locate the sheets of taping film on top of each other. This is usually done with what is called a pin bar, where the pins in the pin bar line up with the taping film that is prepunched to the pin size and spacing on the pin bar. To align the different layers when not on the light table, crosshair puppets are added to each layer of the artwork to allow proper and accurate alignment.

   The taping is started for circuit boards with more than one side by generating what is called a pad master. The pad master is simply one layer of taping film that has pads marking the location of each hole that will be on the board. Generate the pad master by placing one layer of taping film over the layout and placing pads and puppets as appropriate over all of the via holes and mounting pads. Figure 5–12 shows an example of a pad master.

7. *Artwork taping.* The artwork is completed by placing another layer of taping film over the pad master and layout drawing. This layer of taping film represents the copper runs for one side of the circuit board. The copper runs are completed on the taping film by using special artwork tape available in many precision widths. Be sure that the tape overlaps the connecting areas; do not stretch the tape as it is applied. A layer of connecting runs is completed for each side of the board. A completed double-sided circuit board artwork will include a pad master and one layer of connecting runs each for the top and the bottom. A four-layer, multilayer board artwork consists of one pad master and four layers of connecting run taping films. Figure 5–13 shows one layer of circuitry for the same board pad master shown in Figure 5–12. Figure 5–14 shows Figure 5–13 aligned with Figure

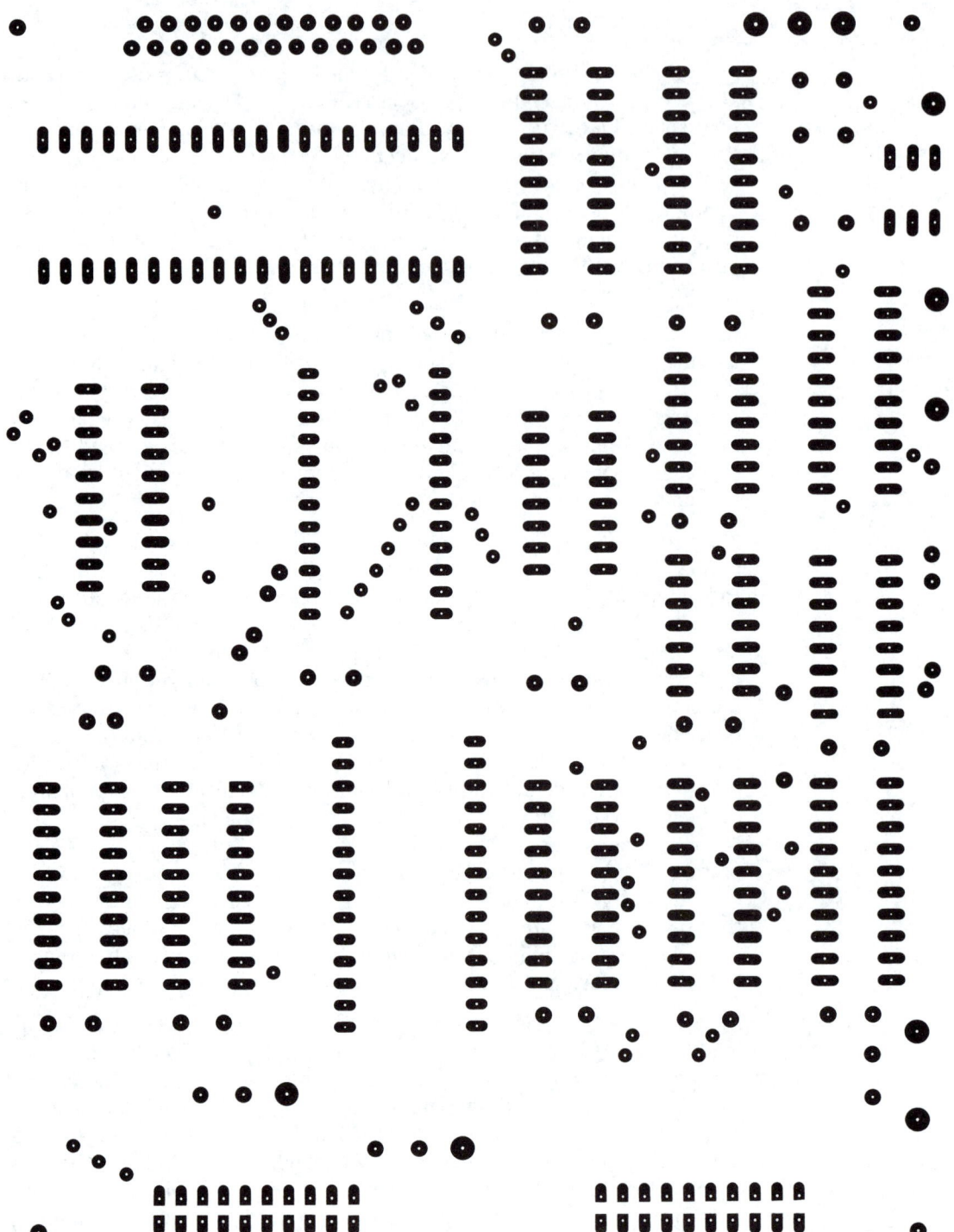

▲ **FIGURE 5-12**
Pad master example

▲ **FIGURE 5–13**
Single-layer taping example

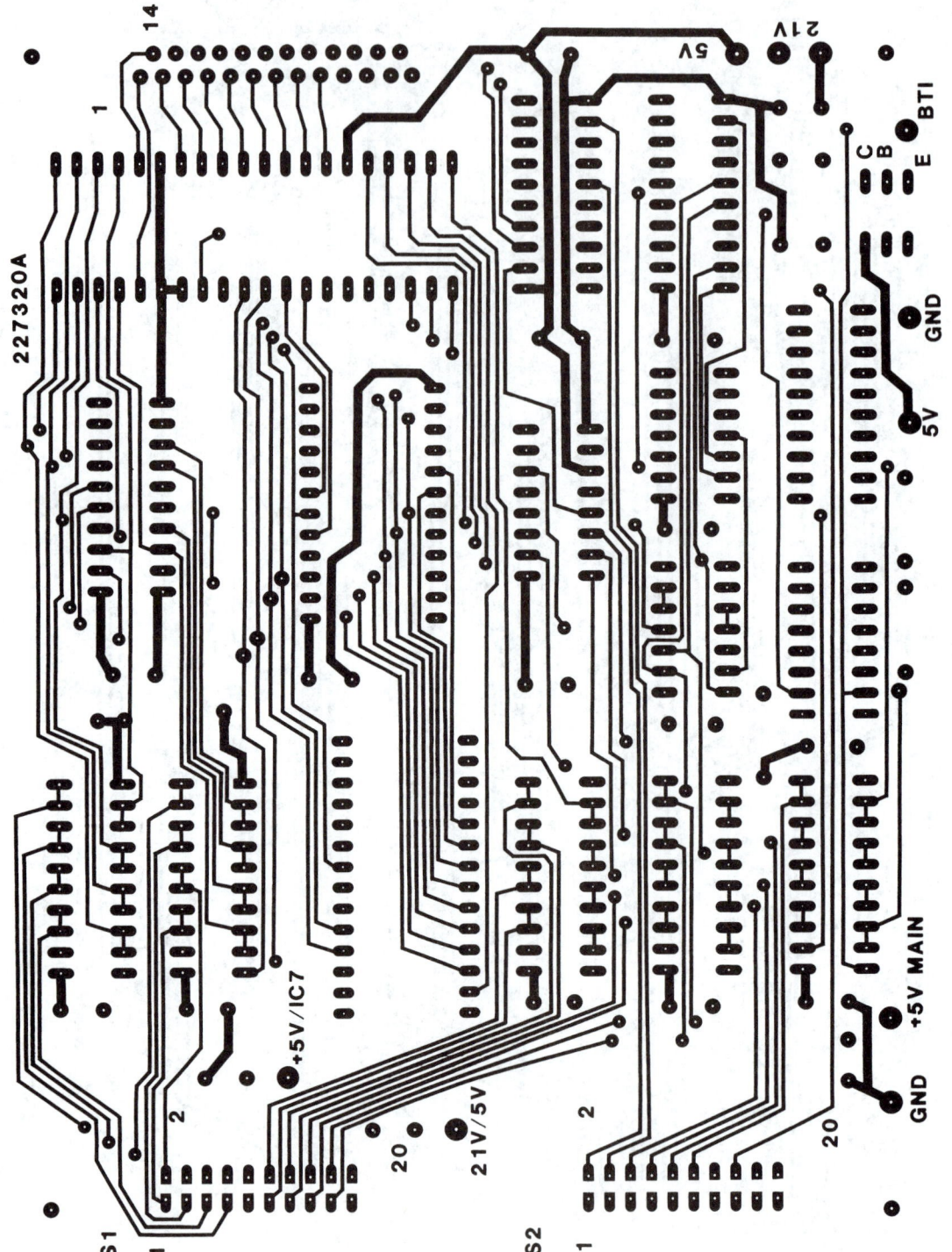

▲ **FIGURE 5–14**
One-side copper artwork (pad master and copper runs)

5–12. Figure 5–14 shows all copper areas on the top side of the circuit board. It represents the complete artwork for that side of the board.

8. *Artwork checking.* The artwork is now complete. If the board design is complex, there is a good chance that there are errors in the artwork. All it takes is one missing bit of tape or one forgotten hole. The detail included in a complex board is incredible. The possibility of an error increases proportionally with complexity. It is best to have two people check the artwork, one who reviews the schematic and another who checks the artwork. The board designer, for example, should review the schematic, while a competent person who is not the designer checks the artwork. This is because the board designer has spent many hours staring at this same artwork, and he or she will have difficulty getting the objective distance needed to see any errors in it. The person reviewing the schematic calls out each connection while the artwork checker verifies the connection. The schematic reviewer highlights each run as it is checked and continues until all of the runs have been verified.

9. *Artwork photography.* The completed and verified artwork is now ready to be photographed for reduction and developing a negative. The artwork is sent to a company that specializes in precision photography and reduction. The pad master is combined with the various layers, reduced, and photographed. This results in a 1:1 negative of each side or layer of the board. The negative and a document called a *fabrication drawing* or a "drill code" are sent to a circuit board manufacturer for fabrication. A drill code defines the mechanical aspects (i.e., size, laminate, plating, and hole sizes) of the circuit board.

5–5 ▶ Printed Circuit Board Layout—Computer

There are two computer methods that can generate circuit board artwork: custom software designed to lay out circuit boards or CAD software to draw the layout of the board. The latter method is identical to the manual process except that the computer is used as a drawing tool. Circuit board layout software packages are most often used today, so this discussion focuses on them. There are many software layout packages available and currently in use. The discussion that follows is general enough to describe the process but may not be entirely accurate when applied to a specific software package. As in the manual layout process, the schematic is the source of defining the circuit connections. The computer layout software requires what is called a schematic capture file to define the schematic. This is simply the schematic keyed into a schematic capture program, which is in a format compatible with the layout software package. All software layout programs have mating schematic capture software, and many accept other schematic capture files as well. When the schematic is created, it may be necessary to add or create a device library for components that may not be present in the standard device libraries in the software. The device library contains all of the pertinent information about the device, the type of component, the number of connections and the label for each connection, and the physical package definition. Make sure the device library is complete for all of the components on the schematic, because the package information is needed to begin the computer layout process.

The computer layout process begins with the same two steps as the manual layout process does: the layout of the mechanical outline and the interconnections. The result is an outline drawing that is the mechanical design of the board and its interconnections. Next, the components are positioned on the board layout by dragging them into position. The result is identical to the pad master drawing generated in the third step of the manual process. The circuit designer has to make a choice at this point whether or not to use the layout program's autorouter feature. An autorouter is a software routine that determines the path of the connections required by the schematic. It is analogous to the trial-by-error process described earlier in the manual layout method. The computer will attempt many circuit paths for making the connections and will choose the ones that its software intelligence determines are the best. The autorouter is a key part of a software layout package. The quality and quantity of the intelligence included in it determine its performance. The price of the software layout package is usually indicative of the amount of intelligence included and the quality of the autorouter, or, in other words, the higher the price the better the autorouter. The decision for using the autorouter is based largely on the experience one has with it. If you have no experience with a particular autorouter, then you can develop some through experimentation. Even the best autorouters are not perfect and cannot possibly possess all of the design criteria for a particular design nor the human insight to make design decisions. There are at least three areas where autorouters produce undesirable results:

1. Power supply and ground runs are not direct or large enough.

2. Connection runs are placed adjacent to areas where there is potential for picking up interference.

3. It utilizes too many via holes.

Many board designers have approached the autorouter decision by connecting up the power supply and ground connections manually. Then they engage the autorouter to make the rest of the connections and modify any undesirable results manually. This is probably the best way to use the autorouter function. There are occasions where an autorouter is unable to make all the connections, and these connections will have to be completed manually.

After completion of the computer layout process, whether it is accomplished manually or with an autorouter, the computer will save files that contain the artwork for each layer of the printed circuit board. The benefit of this process is that the artwork is guaranteed to be accurate and reflect the connections defined in the schematic capture file. If the schematic capture file is correct, then the artwork is as well. There is no need to check and verify that all the connections have been made as was necessary with the manual layout. However, it is still important for the design engineer to review the artwork to make sure that the design will meet the overall requirements for the circuit board. Another real benefit of software layout programs is that they generate the other drawings needed to fabricate and assemble the circuit board. Photography is unnecessary. The artwork and drill code files are simply sent to a circuit board fabricator on a floppy disc or any computer network—including the Internet. While software layout programs are very powerful and offer many benefits, they are somewhat difficult to learn and use. They are as sophisticated as most CAD drawing software programs. Every attempt is made to make the software as easy to use as possible, but there are simply too many complex features and functions that require knowledge and training to use them properly. These are the types of programs that require consistent use to develop expertise in them.

An ideal way to use the electronic design software tools available today—simulators and layout programs—is to have the design engineers perform schematic design on a simulator that is compatible with the layout software being used. When the breadboard and simulation is complete, the file containing the updated schematic is handed over to the board designer. Using the schematic in conjunction with the layout program, the board designer completes the layout and all relevant drawings. The result is a very fast and accurate circuit board development process.

5–6 ▶ Printed Circuit Board Documentation

With the artwork complete, it is time to put together the complete documentation package that will define both the unpopulated and the completely assembled printed circuit board. To define the unpopulated or bare printed circuit board, a document called a fabrication drawing or drill code must be generated.

The Fabrication Drawing

A fabrication drawing is required for each printed circuit board as it defines the board's mechanical requirements. The fabrication drawing, combined with all of the board artwork, completely defines the unpopulated circuit board. The fabrication drawing specifies the mechanical shape and dimensions of the PCB as well as the size and location of any holes. The fabrication drawing must also point out details such as the board laminate material, tolerances, plating, and other optional requirements, such as solder masks and silk-screening. Following is a detailed list of the issues that should be considered to note on the fabrication drawing:

1. The board laminate material

2. Requirements for a solder mask and silk screen

3. Reference to the artwork number and revision level

4. Reproduction of artwork tolerances on the circuit board

5. Plating specifications

6. All mechanical tolerances

Following is an example of the notes included on a typical fabrication drawing:

1. Material: FR4 glass epoxy, 1/16″ thick with 1 oz copper each side per Mil Spec #MIL-P-13949. All holes to be plated through with a minimum of 0.001″ thick copper. After plating the holes, the surface copper should have a total copper thickness of 2 oz.

2. Apply solder mask and silk screen per artwork drawings #12345678, Revision A.

3. For circuit artworks use drawing #12345678, Revision A.

4. Defects:
   a. Circuit run defects such as holes, nicks, and scratches shall not reduce the conductor width by more than ± 0.002″.
   b. Maximum allowable line reduction shall not exceed 0.005″.

5. Plating: The board should be plated with tin/lead 63/37 ± 5% plating to a total thickness of 0.0004″ to 0.0006″. All solder plated areas to be subject to hot oil solder reflow process.

6. Hole diameter tolerances: +0.005″, –0.002″.

Figure 5–15 is a fabrication drawing example.

Solder Mask

A solder mask is a coat of epoxy resin that covers the entire printed circuit board except where solder connections are to be made. The application of a solder mask is optional. Its purpose is to prevent solder from bridging over adjacent circuit runs and pads during automated wave-solder operations. Increasing circuit densities and the use of wave soldering has made the use of a solder mask very common. On through-hole-only technology boards, the artwork for the solder mask can be simply the pad master drawing discussed earlier. When surface-mount technology is used, the pads for all of the SMT components must be included on the solder mask artwork as well. In any case an artwork should be completed and labeled as "Solder Mask" for the subject fabricated printed circuit board. Most computer circuit board layout packages will generate a solder mask on request after the layout has been completed. The circuit board fabricator will apply the solder mask if called for in the fabrication drawing.

Silk-screening

Silk-screening is another optional process that involves the marking of the board with component and other reference numbers. Silk-screening is an aid to manufacturing and service personnel in the field and provides a professional appearance. If silk-screening is required, silk-screen artwork must be completed separately

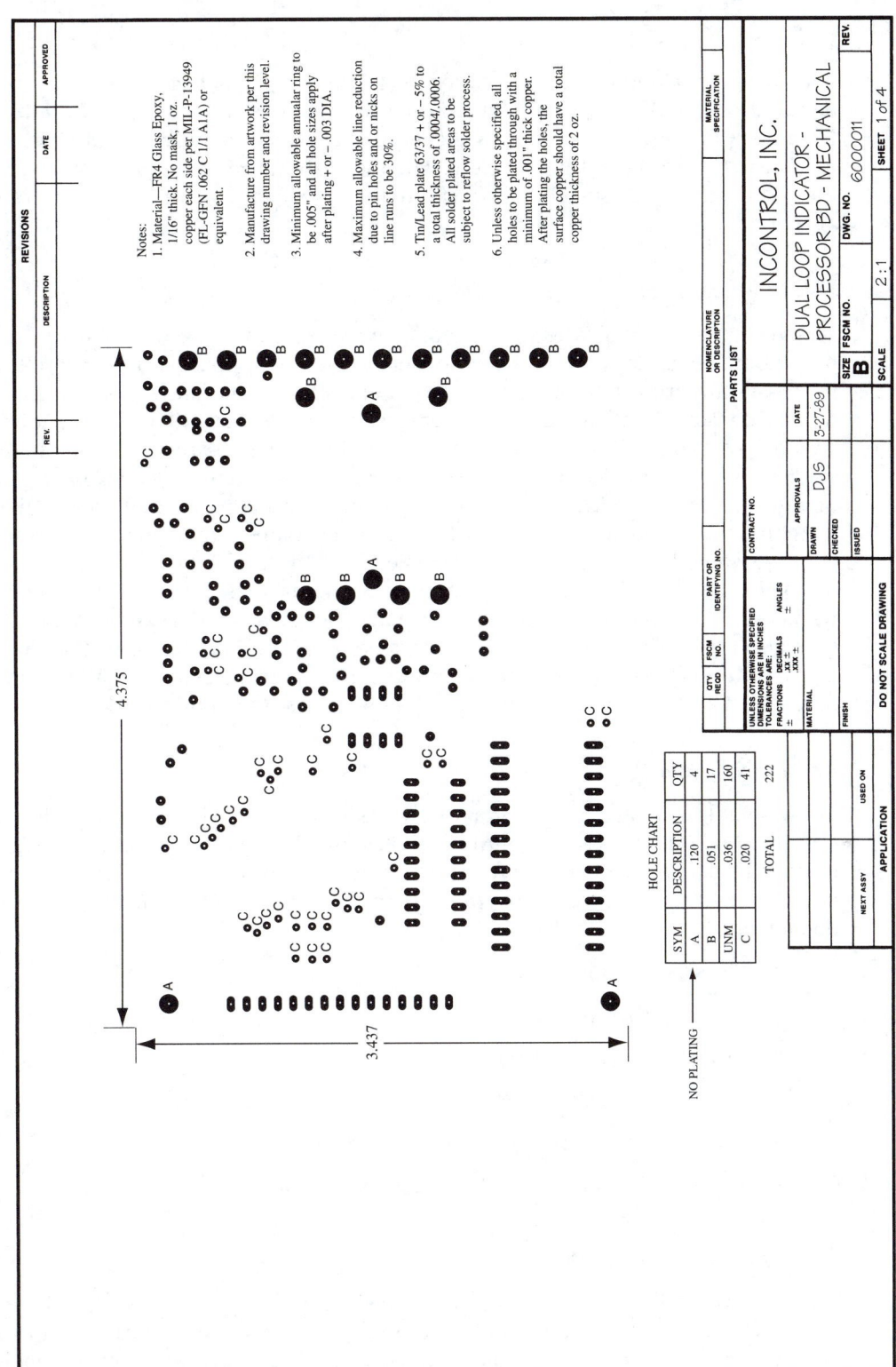

▲ FIGURE 5-15

Fabrication drawing example

that includes the outline and orientation of all component packages, their reference designations, and other pertinent information, such as test points and the like. Most computer layout programs will generate a silk-screen drawing automatically after the board layout is complete. The fabrication drawing must specify that the board is to be silk-screened and refer to the drawing number for the silk-screen artwork.

Solder Paste Screen

The solder paste screen is used as a screen for the application of solder paste to surface-mount technology circuit boards where either vapor phase or infrared reflow processes are utilized to make the solder connections. Therefore, a solder paste mask is necessary only for surface-mount circuit boards that will be manufactured with one of these reflow solder processes. The solder paste screen is similar to the solder mask, except that it includes only the surface-mount pads or connections on a given side of the circuit board. If through-holes exist on the circuit board, they are either vias or used for mounting through-hole components. In either case solder paste should not be applied to these holes. For that reason through-holes should not be included on the solder paste screen. Solder paste screens will be used by whomever assembles the printed circuit board. These artworks can be generated on request by most computer layout programs. The board fabricator will not have any need for the solder paste screen. The actual silk-screen itself will have to be ordered from a silk-screen fabricator per the solder paste screen artwork.

Assembly Drawing

The assembly drawing is a pictorial that will show the physical representation of the circuit board. The assembly drawing will show the location and reference designation of all components that are to be assembled to the board. It will include special notations about the assembly process and refer to the following other related documents:

1. Parts list and bill of material

2. Circuit board specifications

3. Circuit board artworks

4. Circuit board schematic

5. Circuit board assembly and test procedures

Figure 5–16 shows an assembly drawing example.

Parts List and Bill of Material

The circuit board parts list is essentially the same as any other parts list or bill of material. It should include the manufacturer and its part number, the company part number, reference designations, and the quantity used per assembly. The manufacturer's part number is the number assigned to the component by its supplier.

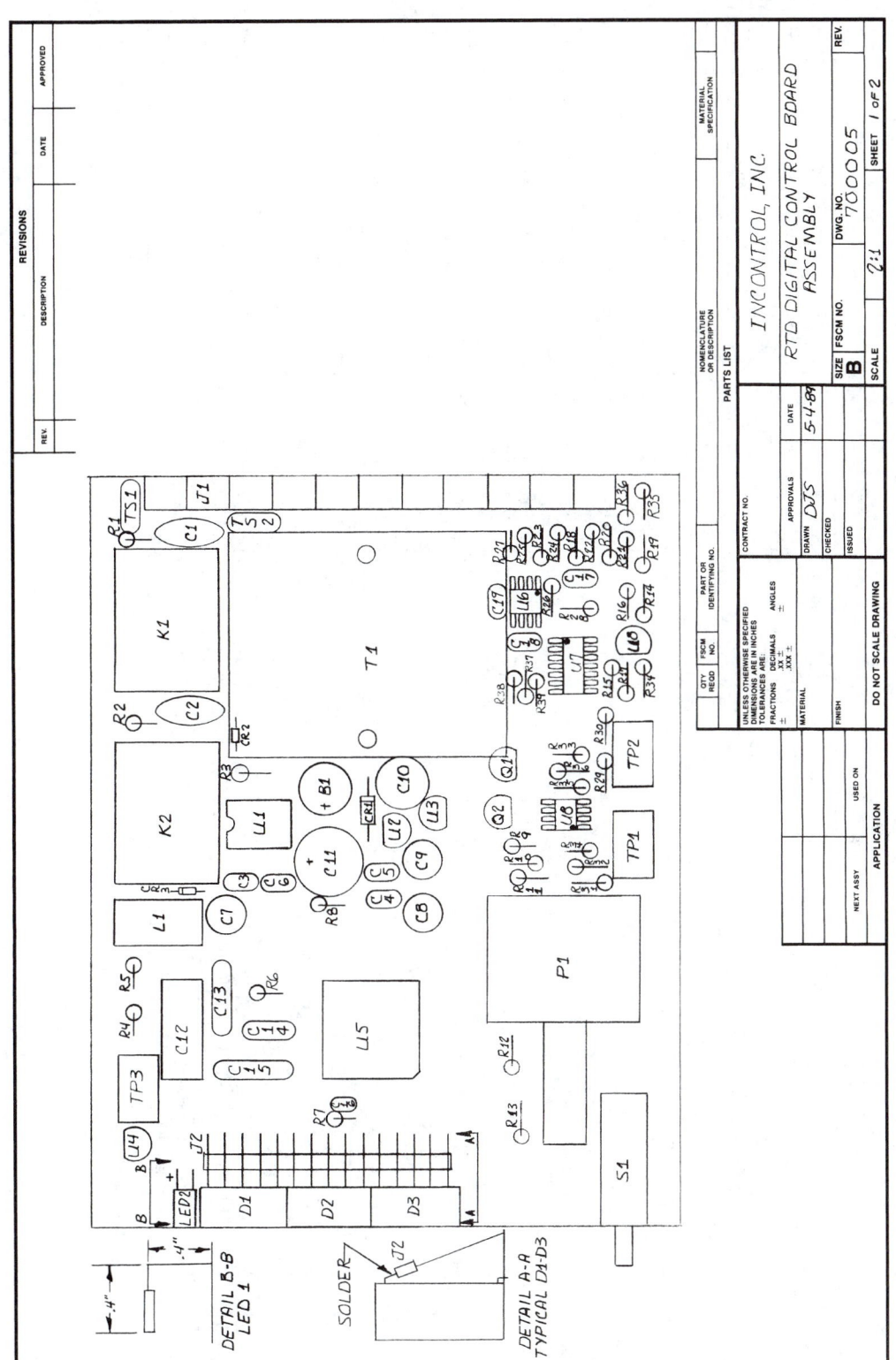

▲ **FIGURE 5-16**

Assembly drawing example

129

Main Printed Circuit Board Assembly

Item #	Description	Company Part Number	Manufacturer	Manufacturer Part Number	Component ID	Quantity
1	2.49 k ohm, 1% Metal Film, 1/4w Resistor	10000000	Res. Inc	2.49kX	R1,R13	2
2	110 ohm, 1% Metal Film, 1/4 w Resistor	10000001	Res. Inc	110X	R2	1
3	100 k ohm, 1% Metal Film, 1/4w Resistor	10000002	Res. Inc	100kX	R3--R6,R15	5
4	26.1 k ohm, 1% Metal Film, 1/4w Resistor	10000003	Res. Inc	26.1kX	R7	1
5	10.0 k ohm, 1% Metal Film, 1/4w Resistor	10000004	Res. Inc	10.0kX	R8,R9	2
6	430 k ohm, 1% Metal Film, 1/4w Resistor	10000005	Res. Inc	430kX	R11	1
7	5.11 k ohm, 1% Metal Film, 1/4w Resistor	10000006	Res. Inc	5.11kX	R10	1
8	1 M ohm, 1% Metal Film, 1/4w Resistor	10000007	Res. Inc	1MX	R12	1
9	470 k ohm, 1% Metal Film, 1/4w Resistor	10000008	Res. Inc	470kX	R14	1
10	1k ohm, 10 turn Trimpot	10000009	TP Inc.	101tp1	RZ	1
11	50 k ohm, 10 turn Trimpot	10000010	TP Inc.	502tp1	RG	1
12	10 k ohm,10 turn Trimpot	10000011	TP Inc.	102tp1	RR	1
13	.1 uF, 50 V, Ceramic Capacitor	10000012	Cap. Inc.	P1101	C1--C4	4
14	.01 uF, 50 V, Ceramic Capacitor	10000013	Cap. Inc.	P1102	C5	1
15	100 pF, 50 V, Ceramic Capacitor	10000014	Cap. Inc.	P1106	C6	1
16	.1 uF, 50 V, Mylar Capacitor	10000015	Cap. Inc.	M1101	C7	1
17	.22 uF, 50 V, Polypropylene Capacitor	10000016	Cap. Inc.	P3224	C8	1
18	.047 uF, 50 V, Polypropylene Capacitor	10000017	Cap. Inc.	P3473	C9	1
19	3300 uF, 16 V, Electrolytic Capacitor	10000018	Cap. Inc.	P5144	C10	1
20	330 uF, 16 V, Electrolytic Capacitor	10000019	Cap. Inc.	P5140	C11, C12	2
21	3 1/2 Digit LED A/D Converter	10000020	IC Inc.	TC7117CPL	U1	1
22	5 V .1 A Voltage Regulator	10000021	IC Inc.	LM320LZ-5.0	U2	1
23	5 V.1 A Negative Voltage Regulator	10000022	IC Inc.	LM340LAZ-5.0	U3	1
24	5 V 1 A Voltage Regulator	10000023	IC Inc.	LM340T-5.0	U4	1
25	Quad Operational Amplifier	10000024	IC Inc.	LM324P	U5	1
26	Voltage Reference- 2.5 Volts	10000025	IC Inc.	LM4040CZ-2.5	U6	1
27	115/20VAC,.3A Center Tapped Transformer	10000026	IC Inc.	MT2111	T1	1
28	Seven Segment .56" Red LED Display	10000027	IC Inc.	67-1463	D1--D4	4
29	Printed Circuit Board	10000028	PCB Inc.	NA	NA	1
30	Terminal Block -5 Position	10000029	Conn. Inc.	W5500	J1	1

▲ FIGURE 5–17
Parts list document example

The purchasing company assigns the company part number to the component. The component will be stocked and tracked by the company part number. Reference designations are numbers that tie a component from the schematic to the parts list and the assembly drawing. For example, a resistor is given a reference designation of R1 on a schematic. That same designation (R1) will be used to show the location of the resistor on the assembly drawing and to specify the resistor on the parts list. Figure 5–17 shows a parts list document example.

▶ Summary

In Chapter 5 we have completed a general review of the printed circuit board: the materials used, types of construction, and their layout and fabrication. The layout of the PCB is as vital to its accurate and reliable operation as the quality of the electronic design. The circuit board layout is usually completed by people who specialize in this area. These specialists usually know the manufacturing process used by the company and are experts at using the chosen circuit board layout program. However, their knowledge and experitise in the theoretical function of a particular design is often limited. Therefore, it is important for all electronic designers to perform a complete review of the circuit board layout before the layout is etched in copper. It is most critical to review areas of the circuit where noise immunity and noise emissions are most significant: power supply, circuits, and signal grounding.

With the completion of this chapter, we conclude the general discussion of the electronic design process. For the remainder of the book, each chapter specializes on a particular area of electronic design and applies those concepts to specific design problems.

▶ References

Coombs, C. F. 1988. *Printed Circuits Handbook*, 3rd ed. New York: McGraw-Hill.

Mardiguian, M. 1987. *Interference Control in Computers and Microprocessor-Based Equipment*. Gainesville, VA: Don White Consultants.

Ott, H. W. 2001. *Noise Reduction Techniques in Electronic Systems*. New York: Wiley.

Stadtmiller, D. J. 2001. *Electronics Project Management and Design*. Upper Saddle River, NJ: Prentice Hall.

▶ Exercises

5–1   What is the purpose of using design master drawings?

5–2   What is the purpose of a via hole? What process is necessary to provide conductivity through a via hole from one side of a circuit board to the other?

5–3   What is a laminate, and what do the different grades of laminate indicate?

5–4   What is the difference between single-sided, double-sided, and multilayer circuit boards?

5–5   On which type of circuit board can components be placed on both sides of the circuit board?

5–6   Compare double-sided and multilayer printed circuit boards as far as cost, size, and noise immunity are concerned.

5–7   How are power supplies and ground usually distributed on multilayer circuit boards?

5–8   What is meant by the term *ground plane,* and why should it be designed in what is called a *crosshatched pattern?*

5–9   Why are the grounds from analog and digital circuits usually kept separate as much as possible?

5–10 What is a guard ring, and why is it used?

5–11 What is a decoupling capacitor, and why is it used?

5–12 When using wave soldering, why is it important to know the direction of the wave when determining component locations on a printed circuit board?

5–13 List and describe the documents and drawings required to completely document a printed circuit board.

5–14 Describe the purpose for a solder mask and what it consists of. How would you develop the artwork for a solder mask?

5–15 What is the purpose of silk-screening a printed circuit board? How would the artwork for one be developed?

5–16 List all of the drawings needed to specify a double-sided printed circuit board to a circuit board fabricator who supplies the bare printed circuit board. Assume that the board will have a solder mask and will be silk-screened.

5–17 Describe the purpose of a computer software board layout autorouter. What are the areas of performance that are a concern when using an autorouter?

5–18 Explain the difference between the two basic types of SMT soldering processes: wave soldering and reflow soldering.

5–19 What is the purpose of test points, and why are they even more critical on SMT circuit boards?

6 ▶ Power Supply Design

▶ Introduction

The design of DC power supplies is a critical aspect of electronic circuit design. The study of power supply design is often viewed as tedious, and even trivial, when compared to elaborate large-scale integrated circuits and high-speed processors. As such, power supplies are often considered just a minor detail, to be worked out later on complex electronic design projects. But the simple fact is that almost every electronic circuit requires a power supply. An appropriate, efficient, and reliable power supply design will largely determine the level of successful operation and reliability of any electronic circuit. Even if power supply design is not in your future, you will be better able to work on a team with power supply designers when you have a basic understanding of their function and the competing design criteria.

Power supplies usually appeal to the analog-oriented individual, and their design is often delegated to someone who specializes in this area. As the performance of power supplies has increased over the years, their design has become more complex with the utilization of more switching circuits to decrease their size and cost. Many new integrated circuits have been developed that include elaborate functions that improve power supply reliability and efficiency and reduce their size. As we continue to deal with reduced energy supplies, the efficiency of power supplies becomes increasingly important. In this chapter we will discuss some of the many types of power supplies, their design concepts, and how to measure and compare their performance. The specific topics covered are as follows:

- ▶ Power supply specifications
- ▶ Linear DC power supplies
- ▶ DC-to-DC converters
- ▶ Switching power supplies
- ▶ Inverters

133

6–1 ▶ Power Supply Specifications

Before we discuss specific power supply circuits, we must first define the power supply design problem with a general set of requirements or specifications. Power supplies provide operating power for electrical and electronic devices by taking an input voltage and converting it to an appropriate output voltage. In order to properly design a power supply, we must define the input and its expected variations along with the output and the acceptable variations for it. The specifications that are developed next will identify all the key power supply design parameters. They are summarized in Figure 6–1.

Input: The input power to the power supply should be completely defined as AC or DC, and the expected frequency range, the nominal input voltage (RMS or peak voltages for AC), and the expected variation in the input voltage level should also be specified.

Output: The output required for the power supply is specified as AC or DC. If the output is an AC voltage, the required frequency range and the ac-

- Input voltage: DC or AC, frequency and range for AC, nominal input voltage and variation

- Output voltage: DC or AC, frequency and range for AC, nominal output voltage and allowable variation

- Dropout voltage: minimum input/output voltage differential

- Output current: continuous and maximum output current

- Ripple voltage: maximum % of allowable peak-to-peak ripple

- Efficiency: output power/input power

- Percent load regulation: % output change/% load change

- Percent line regulation: % output change/% line change

- Noise filter: attenuation shown in dB

- Generated noise: line and radiated, amplitude and frequency

- Failsafe features: current limiting, thermal overload

- Size and cost

▲ **FIGURE 6–1**
Key power supply specification parameters

ceptable variation must be noted. For both DC and AC supplies, the expected output voltage level must be identified along with its acceptable variation. Power supplies also have a maximum current rating that can be safely supplied on a continuous basis. For DC supplies the output voltage will always include some amount of variation around the nominal output voltage DC level called *ripple*. The amount of ripple voltage allowable must be defined in the specifications.

General Power Supply Requirements: These are design parameters that relate to the overall power supply design, such as input/output voltage, current, and ripple.

Dropout Voltage: The specs should include the minimum input to output voltage differential that will provide regulation of the output.

Efficiency: The efficiency of a power supply is measured by comparing the amount of output power supplied to the load to the total input power. The difference between these two numbers is the power consumed by the power supply. Efficiency is specified as a percent and is equal to the output power/input power.

Percent Load Regulation: Most power supplies provide regulated outputs, which means that they control the output to a specified value within the tolerance required. A typical 5-V DC power supply might output 5 V DC within a tolerance of ±1%. The acceptable range of output voltage for this supply is 4.95 to 5.05 V DC. When the supply is connected to a load, the output voltage will change slightly as the load is varied. The percent regulation is the percent of change in the regulated output voltage compared to the corresponding percent change in the load.

$$\text{Percent Load Regulation} = P_{OC}/P_{LC} \tag{6-1}$$

where P_{OC} = the percent change in the regulated output voltage

   P_{LC} = the percent change in the load.

Percent Line Regulation: This is defined as the output voltage change divided by the line voltage change expressed as a percentage.

Noise Filter: The input voltage presented to the power supply often includes noise signals that should be attenuated and filtered. The requirements for this are usually specified as dB levels of attenuation provided over a frequency range.

Generated Noise: Many switching types of power supplies generate noise as they regulate the output voltage. The magnitude of this noise voltage is of concern because of its effect on other electronic devices. It is regulated on certain product categories by the FCC and on all products imported into the European Union, which must meet CE electrical noise standards. These standards include the EMI fields that are radiated by the supply as well as the level of noise that is conducted back into the input power circuit. This input circuit is often the AC line voltage, which can be common to many other electronic devices and is why the noise voltage levels are of concern.

Failsafe Features: There are a variety of other special features that can be specified to make a power supply failsafe. Temperature measurement of the semiconductor regulating device and measurement of the load current or of changes in load current are the most common. In these cases the power supply circuit shuts down or limits the current when excessive load currents are drawn; this precludes damage to the power supply and load circuits.

Size and Cost: All power supply designs will have limits placed on their physical size and the cost of manufacture.

6–2 ▶ Linear DC Power Supplies

Linear power supplies are based on the concept of taking an input voltage and converting it to an appropriate level of DC voltage that exceeds the required output voltage. This voltage is then regulated down to the specified power supply output voltage. If the linear supply is a regulating supply, it monitors the output voltage and varies its resistance accordingly to provide the required output voltage.

There are two basic varieties of linear regulators, series and shunt regulators. Shunt regulators are represented by a series resistance with a regulating mechanism, usually a semiconductor, whose resistance is varied to draw more or less current in a circuit path that is in parallel with the load, thereby adjusting the output voltage to the required level. As the load resistance changes, the shunt regulator diverts more or less current through this parallel path (see Figure 6–2). The efficiency of the shunt type regulator is low when the load current is small (load resistance is high) because a large current is diverted through the regulator. This current isn't doing any work except regulating the output. When the load current approaches full load conditions for the power supply, the efficiency is much higher. A key advantage of the shunt regulator is the fact that when the load is a short circuit, the power supply will not be short-circuited.

Figure 6–3 shows a series regulator with the regulating mechanism in series with the load. The series regulator has the opposite characteristics as compared to the shunt regulator. The efficiency of the series regulator is low when the load

▶ **FIGURE 6–2**
Shunt regulator

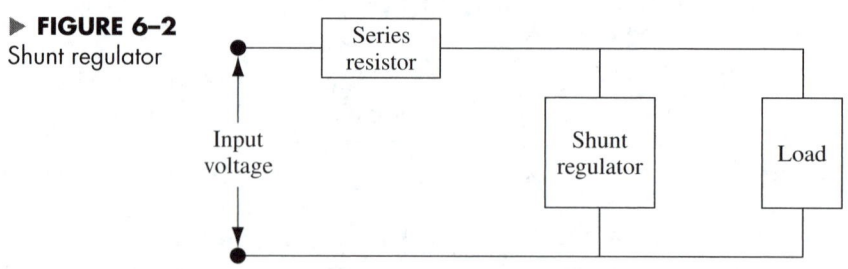

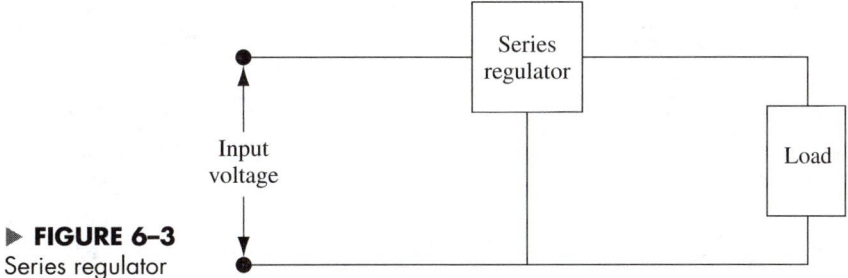

▶ **FIGURE 6–3**
Series regulator

current is at full load levels and high when the load current is low. When the load becomes shorted, excessive current is drawn from the supply. Series regulators are used much more often than shunt regulators. When a regulator is to operate very near full load condition most of the time and there is a possibility of the load becoming shorted, a shunt regulator becomes a viable option.

The block diagram for a general power supply is shown in Figure 6–4. A typical outlet voltage of 115 V AC at 60 Hz powers most power supplies. Accordingly most power supplies include a transformer to step down the AC voltage to a level closer to the ultimate output value. AC-powered linear regulators also require a rectifier circuit to convert the AC voltage to a pulsating DC voltage. DC-powered power supplies will not require the use of a transformer or a rectifier circuit. As shown in Figure 6–4, the primary components of a linear power supply are transformer, rectifier, filter, regulator, and load.

5-V DC Linear Series Regulated Supply

Let's begin by reviewing the detailed operation of a simple 5-V DC linear power supply that utilizes series regulation. See the schematic shown in Figure 6–5. Note that an input filter and output filter are not included in this circuit. The transformer steps the input AC voltage of 115 RMS V AC, 50 to 60 Hz down to a lower AC voltage at the secondary. A full-wave bridge rectifier converts the secondary voltage to pulsating DC with a peak value of 1.4 V less than the peak output of the secondary and a frequency that is twice the input voltage frequency. The rectifier filter capacitor smoothes out the pulsating DC. This produces a DC voltage with a small fluctuating component called the *ripple* riding on top of the DC voltage. The

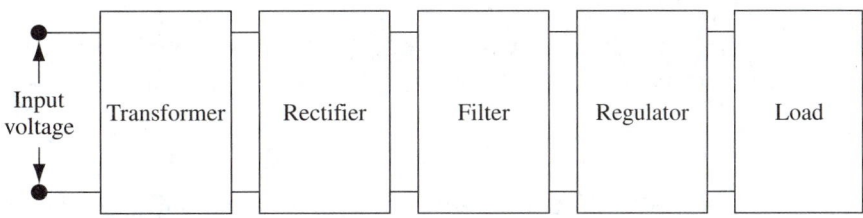

▲ **FIGURE 6–4**
Linear power supply block diagram

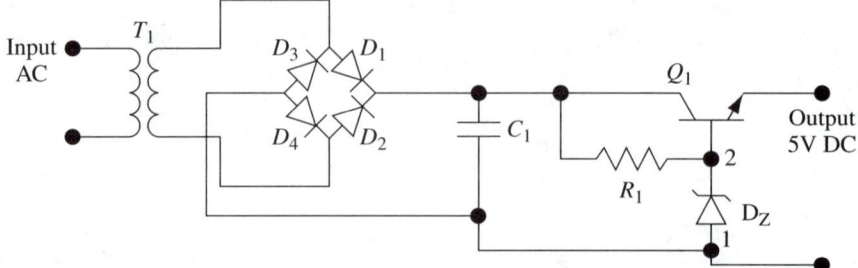

▲ **FIGURE 6–5**
5-V DC linear power supply with series regulation

rectified and filtered DC voltage is then regulated down to 5 V DC and connected to the load.

The regulator circuit is essentially an emitter-biased transistor circuit where the zener voltage maintains a constant base emitter voltage and the emitter voltage is controlled by the transistor to be the zener voltage plus the .7-V drop across the forward-biased PN junction that comprises the transistor base-emitter.

The basic design equations for this power supply are as follows:

$$V_{PSEC} = V_{PPRI} \times n \tag{6–2}$$

where V_{PPRI} = the transformer peak primary AC voltage, V_{PSEC} = the transformer peak secondary voltage, and n = the transformer turns ratio

$$V_{RECT} = V_{PSEC} - 1.4 \text{ V} \tag{6–3}$$

where V_{RECT} = the rectifier output voltage

Note: The 1.4 V is derived from the .7-V drop across each fix forward-biased silicon diode in the rectifier circuit.

$$V_{RIPPLE} \cong V_{RECT}/fC \tag{6–4}$$

where f = the frequency of the pulsating voltage output from the rectifier and C = the value of the filter capacitor

Note: The frequency of the regulator output is equal to twice the frequency of the input frequency for all full wave rectifiers.

$$V_{RO} = V_Z + .7 \text{ V} \tag{6–5}$$

where V_Z = the zener voltage of the zener diode and V_{RO} = the regulated output voltage to the load

Note: This equation is valid only if the zener is in its operating range.

I_O = the rated output current and is dependent on the maximum zener current for the zener to remain in regulation. The other circuit elements, primarily the transformer, diodes and transistor, must be selected to accommodate this current level on a continuous basis. Let's review a specific design example.

Example 6–1

For the power supply circuit shown in Figure 6–5, determine all component values and ratings for the supply to generate 5 V DC ±2% at 100 milliamps with less than 10% ripple voltage. The input voltage is 115 RMS V AC at 60 Hz and can vary in amplitude ±10%.

Solution

The solution of this design problem will require the determination of the following component parameters:

Transformer: primary voltage, secondary voltage, turns ratio and power rating

Rectifier Diodes: current rating, reverse breakdown voltage

C_1: capacitor type, value, voltage rating

Q_1: transistor type, voltage, current and beta

D_Z: zener voltage

R_1: resistor value, tolerance, type, and power rating

The peak input voltage V_{PPRI} is equal to 115/.707 which is 162.7 V. V_{PPRI} can vary ±10% or ±16.27 V, so the peak input voltage input to the primary can range from 146.4 V to 179 V. The 5-V DC output must be maintained within ±2% over this range of input voltage.

To maintain the nominal 5-V output, we will allot 3 additional volts for the series regulator to regulate down to the 5-V level. Therefore, the input voltage to the series regulator circuit, which is the rectifier output V_{RECT}, should be equal to a minimum of 8 V peak. Using the design equation $V_{RECT} = V_{PSEC} - 1.4$ V, V_{PSEC} can be found to equal 9.4 V.

Since $V_{PSEC} = V_{PPRI} \times n$, the turns ratio n is equal to V_{PSEC}/V_{PPRI} or 9.4/146.4 = .064. The primary must be able to handle a voltage as high as 200 V peak and the secondary could see a voltage as high as 20 V. The design equation that defines the zener voltage, $V_{RO} = V_Z + .7$ V is solved for $V_{RO} = 5$ V. The zener voltage $V_Z = 4.3$ V and a 1N749A is selected as the zener diode. The 1N749A has a zener voltage of 4.3 V with a zener test current of 20 mA; the knee current is 6 mA and the maximum current is 85 mA.

The ripple percentage is specified as a maximum of 10%. Ripple is stated as a percent of the nominal output voltage, or $V_{RIPPLE} = .5$ V. Solving, $V_{RIPPLE} \cong \text{LOAD}/fC$ with $I_{LOAD} = 100$ mA and f = 120 Hz. $C = 1666$ µF. The next highest standard capacitor value available is 1800 µF and the closest voltage rating that provides a reasonable margin of safety is 16 V.

The calculation of R_1 is accomplished by establishing a zener current that will be between the smallest (the zener knee current) and largest current (the maximum zener current) for zener regulation. There is a wide range of resistance values that will accomplish this as the nominal 9.4 volts supplied by the rectifier will provide the test current of 20 mA with a 9.4/20 mA = 470 Ω. The range of input voltage that the regulator circuit is expected to see is 8.46 to 10.34 V. With R_1 = 470 Ω the zener currents for this range in input voltage are 18 mA to 22 mA. Considering the possible current flow through R_1, it should be a .5-watt resistor.

There are many transistors that will function in this circuit. The key parameters are the maximum current and voltage ratings for the transistor. The regulator specifications call for a load current of 100 mA and the maximum voltage the transistor should see is 10.34 V. An NPN transistor such as a 2N3904 is selected with a maximum collector voltage of 40 V and a continuous collector current rating of 200 mA. The DC current gain for the 2N3904 ranges from 30 to 100.

Following is a summary of the selected components:

Transformer T_1: primary 115 RMS V AC, secondary voltage 6.6 RMS V AC, with a turns ratio of .064 and a power rating of 2 watts

Rectifier Diodes D_1–D_4, 1N4001 current rating = 1 amp, reverse breakdown voltage of 50 volts, or an equivalent bridge rectifier assembly

C_1: 1800 µF aluminum electrolytic, 16 volts

Q_1: 2N3904, V_{CE} = 40 V_{dc}, I_C = 200 mA

D_Z: 1N749A, V_Z = 4.3 V

R_1: 470 Ω ±5%, carbon composition, .5 watts

Surge Resistor

When selecting the diodes to be used in the rectifier circuit, or a complete rectifier circuit, it is important to consider the surge current that will occur when the power supply is first turned on and the capacitors are all being charged. If the continuous current rating of the diodes is close to the maximum load current output from the power supply, a resistor called a *surge resistor* is often used to limit the flow of initial surge current (see Figure 6–6). The value of the surge resistor should be as small as possible, as it will lower the efficiency of the power supply and reduce the amount of voltage available to the regulator circuit.

Inductive Filters

From previous experience with inductors and capacitors, we realize that it is usually possible to achieve the same results of a capacitor filter with an inductor. This is true with the rectifier filter capacitor, whose job it is to reduce the ripple supplied to the regulator circuit. Theoretically, we could replace the filter capacitor completely with an inductor, as shown in Figure 6–7. However, the inductor required would be very large for a frequency as low as 120 Hz. It would be more practical to reduce the size of the capacitor by using both an inductor and capacitor, as shown in Figure 6–7b, but we will find that even this is not practical or necessary

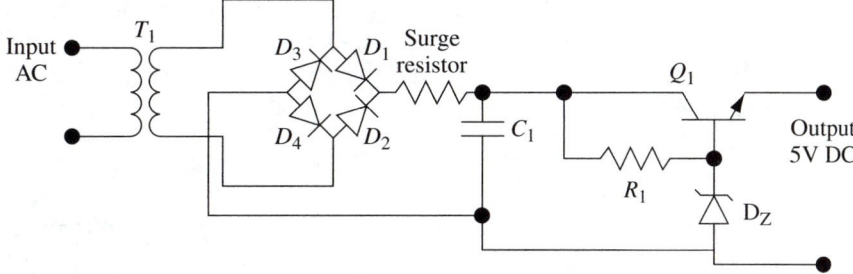

▲ FIGURE 6–6
Surge resistor example

with the integrated circuit regulators that we will discuss next. An inductor used as a filter is called a *choke*. The purpose of the inductor in the filter circuit is to have most of the AC voltage drop across the inductor at a particular frequency. There-fore, the relationship of X_L (inductive reactance) to X_C (capacitive reactance) at a given frequency will determine the AC voltage drop across the two circuit ele-ments. From an AC perspective, the ripple output voltage of the filter is:

$$V_{RIPPLE} = X_C/(X_L \times V_{RECT}) \tag{6–6}$$

(a)

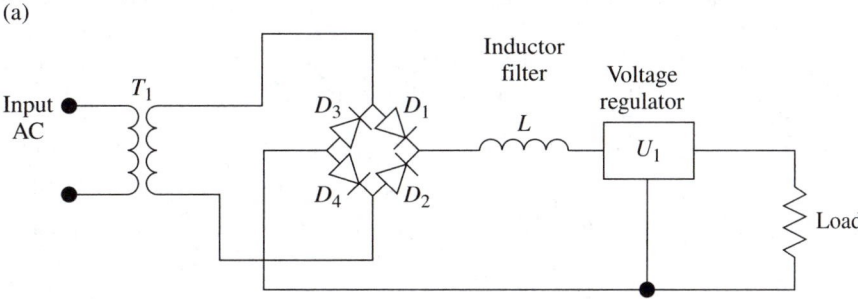

(b)

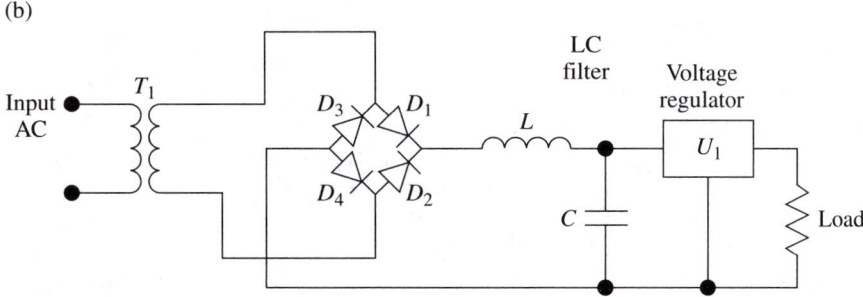

▲ FIGURE 6–7
Inductor rectifier filters

If we let $X_C = 1$ and $X_L = 20$ and $V_{RECT} = 8.4$ volts peak then the $V_{RIPPLE} = .42$ V, which is less than the specified .50 V. Calculating the resulting capacitor and inductor values that would achieve this at a frequency of 120 Hz (the frequency of the rectifier output voltage):

$$X_C = 1/(2\pi fC) = 1 \qquad\qquad C = 1/2\pi 120 = 1326 \text{ μF} \qquad\qquad (6\text{–}7)$$

$$X_L = 2\pi fL = 20 \qquad\qquad L = 20/2\pi 120 = 26.5 \text{ mH} \qquad\qquad (6\text{–}8)$$

The 26.5 mH inductor is still a very large inductance value, and the benefit of reducing the capacitor value such a small amount is not cost effective. We can conclude that using an inductive filter at a frequency of 120 Hz is not practical, especially with the ripple reduction capabilities of today's integrated circuit regulators. Later on when we discuss switching regulators, we will see that their higher frequency of operation provides for the effective use of inductor filters.

Integrated Circuit Regulators

The previous example was worthwhile because it was not only a review of a linear series regulator design, but it also provided example applications of selecting zener diodes and transistors. However, there are many integrated circuit linear regulators available that are popular and easier to use. The simplest varieties are called *three-terminal regulators*, and they perform functions identical to the regulator constructed from resistor R_1, zener diode D_Z, and transistor Q_1 in the previous example. In addition, they provide failsafe features such as current limiting and thermal shutdown. An LM309 linear regulator is a fixed output regulator that can replace the regulator circuit from the previous example directly. Following is a summary of the key specifications for the LM309:

Output Voltage: 5.05 V typical, minimum 4.8 to a maximum of 5.2 V

Output Current: up to 1 amp, depending on the package and heatsink provided. An LM309 in a TO39 package with no heatsink can provide 100 mA up to a temperature of about 50 °C.

Dropout Voltage: The input-to-output voltage difference, where the regulator ceases to regulate with further reduction of the input voltage

Ripple Rejection: 50 dB

Current Limiting: When the peak output current exceeds safe levels, the current is limited to these levels.

Temperature Shutdown: If the IC becomes overheated, the circuit simply shuts down its function as a regulator.

The drop voltage for most of these regulators is between 2 and 3 V. Later we will discuss special regulators that feature low dropout voltages.

Take note of the specifications when you consider the requirement for a heatsink. A heatsink is a thermally conductive device that attaches to a component for the purpose of absorbing heat and dissipating it away. The use of a heatsink is critical for the reliable operation of any component that conducts significant current levels. Heatsinks are often rated in °C/watt. This rating is indicative of the temperature that results when the heatsink is attached to a component that dissipates a certain wattage. A heatsink with a rating of 20 °C/watt will result in a 20 °C rise in temperature for each watt dissipated by the heatsink. The lower the °C/watt rating, the better the heatsink is at absorbing and distributing the heat.

Example 6–2

In this example we will modify the circuit of Example 6–1 to replace the regulator circuit with the LM309. As shown in Figure 6–8, the LM309 replaces the transistor, resistor and zener diode that Example 6–1's regulator circuit comprised. There are some considerations regarding filter capacitors.

Ripple Rejection

Let's examine the 50-dB ripple rejection stated in the specifications for the LM309. The ability of the LM309 to reject ripple is of course frequency-dependent. An examination of the data sheets for the LM309 indicates that the ripple rejection peaks at about 500 Hz (Figure 6–9). The data sheet also shows that the 50 dB specification is met by the device for frequencies ranging from 10 Hz to 100 kHz.

For this design the 50-dB specification means that the remaining ripple will be .003 (a 50-dB loss results in .3% voltage signal remaining) times the input ripple value. It appears like the large filter capacitor is no longer needed to reduce the ripple value. However, it is important to note that the input provided to the regulator must always be 2 to 3 volts higher than the regulated output voltage in order for the regulator to operate properly. So even though the regulator can reduce the ripple significantly on its own capacitor, C_1 is still needed to make sure that the voltage supplied to the regulator is sufficient for its reliable operation. In actual practice C_1 is specified at a value that will reduce the ripple to 10% before input to the regulator circuit. Capacitor C_1 combined with the ripple rejection capabilities of the integrated circuit regulator reduce ripple significantly and very practically.

Recalculating C_1 to provide 10% ripple from the nominal 8.4-V pulsating DC used previously sets the desired ripple at .84 volts. $V_{RIPPLE} \cong I_{LOAD}/fC$ with $I_{LOAD} =$ 100 milliamps, $f = 120$ Hz, and $C = 992$ µF. The next highest standard capacitor value available is 1000 µF and the closest voltage rating that provides a reasonable margin

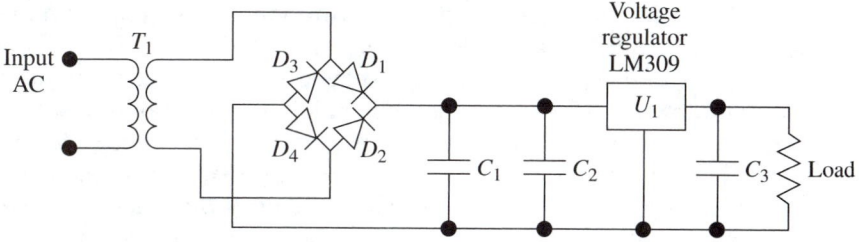

▲ **FIGURE 6–8**
LM309 regulator circuit

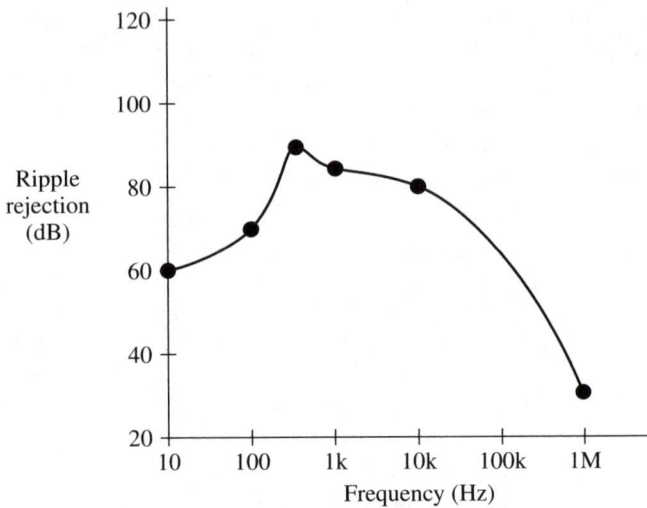

▶ **FIGURE 6–9**
Ripple rejection bode plot

of safety is 16 V. Recalculating the output ripple value for the input ripple value of .84 volts, we have:

$$dB = 20 \, Log_{10} \, (V_{OUT}/V_{IN}) \tag{6–9}$$

$-50 \, dB = 20 \, Log_{10} \, (V_{OUT}/.84 \, V)$
$V_{OUT} = 2.65 \, mV$ of output ripple voltage

C_1 can be reduced or increased in value, depending on the overall ripple requirements of the power supply. C_2, a 1-µF solid tantalum capacitor, is recommended when the regulator is located more than four inches away from the primary rectifier filter capacitor C_1. C_3, also a 1-µF solid tantalum capacitor, is not required to support the regulator's stability but is beneficial in improving the regulator's ability to respond to a transient load change.

Efficiency

The voltage drop across a regulator and its output current determine the power dissipated by a three-terminal regulator. The efficiency of these circuits will determined by how small this voltage drop can be maintained and still provide an input voltage high enough to provide for good regulation.

There are many other varieties of three-terminal fixed-output regulators that are similar to the LM309. They come in a variety of fixed voltage outputs, packages, and power ratings, but functionally they are the same. Current limiting and thermal shutdown features are usually included. In addition to positive fixed-voltage regulators, there are also negative fixed-output voltage regulators available to provide negative voltage supplies. The following list includes some popular three-terminal positive and negative voltage regulators with their basic specifications:

LM78LXX series: +5-V (LM78L05), +12-V (LM78L12), and +15-V (LM78L15) regulators at 100 mA

LM78MXX series: +5-V (LM78M05), +12-V (LM78M12), and +15-V (LM78M15) regulators at 500 mA

LM79LXX series: –5-V (LM79L05), –12-V (LM79L12), and –15-V (LM79L15) regulators at 500 mA

LM79MXX series: –5-V (LM79M05), –12-V (LM79M12), and –15-V (LM79M15) regulators at 500 mA

Adjustable Linear Regulator Circuits

Adjustable voltage regulators can be modified to regulate their output voltage over a range of output voltages. In this type of regulator circuit, the source of the reference voltage used to control the output is provided as an input to one of the regulator inputs. The terminal usually chosen for this purpose is the terminal usually connected to ground on fixed-voltage regulators. Integrated circuit adjustable voltage regulators are available in three-terminal packages. A popular series is the LM317 positive voltage and the LM337 negative voltage adjustable regulators. Their basic specifications are as follows:

LM317: output voltage range, +1.2 to +37 V, up to 1.5 amps output current

LM337: output voltage range, –1.2 to –37 V, up to 1.5 amps output current

A typical circuit application of the LM317 is shown in Figure 6–10. For this circuit:

$$V_{OUT} = 1.25 \, (1 + R_2/R_1)$$

Combination ± Linear Power Supplies

For many analog circuits, ± power supplies are required to provide both positive and negative signals that have a common zero reference point called *analog*

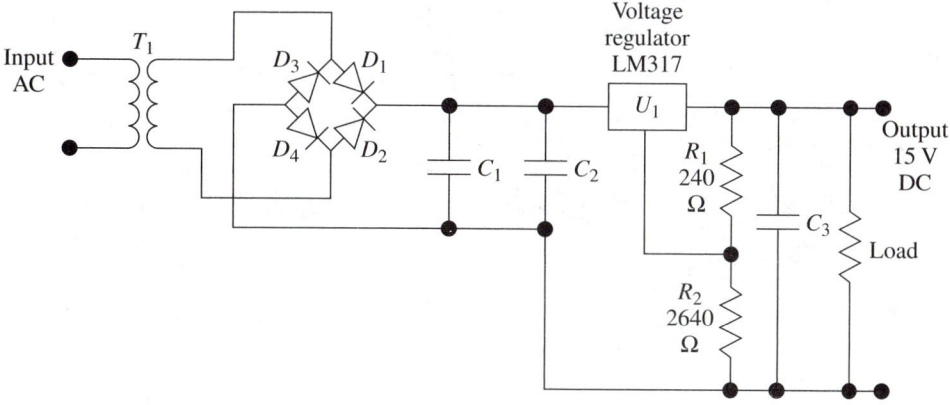

▲ **FIGURE 6–10**
LM317 adjustable regulator circuit

ground. A typical arrangement utilizes a center-tapped transformer and a full wave bridge rectifier connected, as shown in Figure 6–11. This circuit provides one-half of the secondary voltage minus the 1.4-V drop across the rectifier diodes to both the positive and negative rectifier voltage outputs.

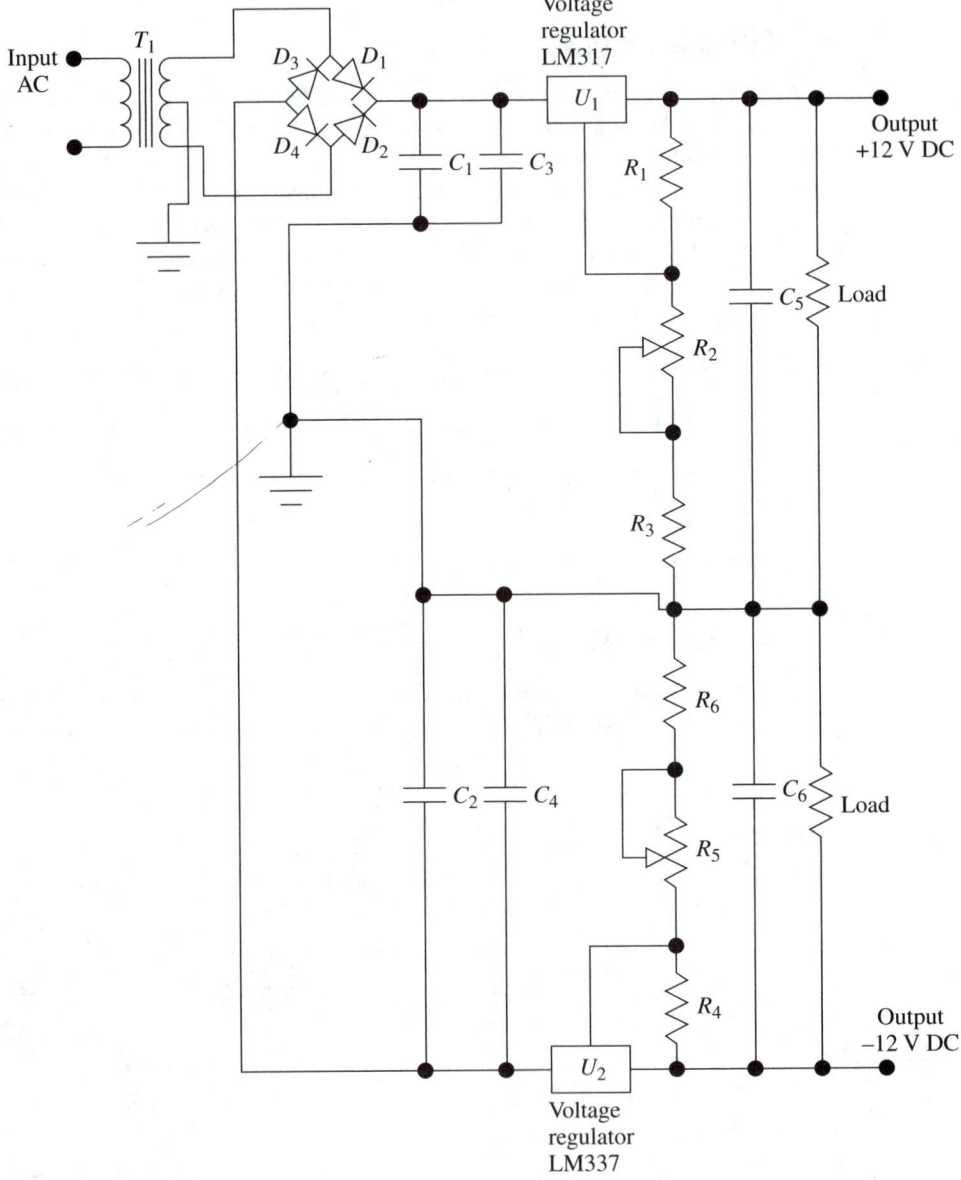

▲ **FIGURE 6–11**
±12 V DC adjustable regulated power supply

Example 6–3

Develop a dual power supply that will develop ±12 V that are adjustable over a range of 11.5 to 12.5 V with an output load current of 100 mA each. Ripple output should be less than .6 mV. The input power is 115 or 230 V AC ±10% at 50–60 Hz.

Solution

The LM317 and LM337 regulators are selected as the integrated circuit regulators for this power supply. The circuit schematic for this supply is shown in Figure 6–10. Since the regulated output is ±12 V the voltage supplied to the input must be ±15 V to allow adequate regulation. Therefore, the output of the secondary must be ±18 V when the input power is at its lowest possible value, 115 or 230 V AC minus 10%, which is 103.5 or 207 V AC. For the 115-V AC input situation, the turns ratio of the transformer must be ±18/103.5, which is 36/103.5 = .35. For 230 V AC the turns ratio must be ±18/207, which is 36/207 = .174. To accommodate either 115 V AC or 230 V AC, we can use two identical primaries with turns ratios of .35 relative to the secondary. When powering the supply with 115 V AC, the primaries will be wired in parallel, making the overall turns ratio .35. For 230 volts AC operation, the primaries can be wired in series to create a turns ratio of .174.

The rectifier filter capacitors should reduce the ripple at each half of the secondary by 10% or down to 1.8 volts. Using the formula $V_{RIPPLE} \cong I_{LOAD}/fC$:

$C = 100$ mA/(120 Hz × 1.8 V) = 463 µF

The next highest standard value capacitor available is 470 µF.

Typical ripple rejection by the LM317 and LM337 regulators is 65 dB; therefore, the ripple that is expected on the output voltage of this supply can be calculated as follows:

$$dB = 20 \, Log_{10} \, (V_{OUT}/V_{IN}) \tag{6–10}$$

-65 dB $= 20 \, Log_{10} \, (V_{OUT}/1.8$ V$)$

$V_{OUT} = .57$ mV

The data sheets for the LM317/337 recommend the use of an input filter capacitor of .1 µF (C_3 and C_4) and a solid tantalum output filter capacitor of 1 µF (C_5 and C_6). In order to calculate the output voltage adjustment resistors, the following equation is supplied by the data sheet for the LM317/337:

$V_{OUT} = 1.25$ V $(1 + R_2/R_1) + 50$ µA R_2

The data sheet recommends that R_1 be 240 Ω. The range of adjustment for the output voltage was specified as 11.5 to 12.5 V. Therefore, when R_2 is near its minimum value, the output voltage should be 11.5 V, and it should reach 12.5 V when it is adjusted close to its maximum value. The output voltage equation is solved for both of these situations:

for $V_{OUT} = 11.5$ V $= 1.25$ V $(1 + R_2/240$ Ω$) + 50$ µA R_2
    $R_2 = 1949$ Ω

for $V_{OUT} = 12.5$ V $= 1.25$ V $(1 + R_2/240$ Ω$) + 50$ µA R_2
    $R_2 = 2140$ Ω

To meet this range of adjustment, R_2 must be about 1949 Ω at its minimum value and 2140 Ω. This can be accomplished with a fixed resistor in series with a trimmer potentiometer. A 1780 Ω 1% resistor (R_3 in Figure 6–11) is selected in series with a 500-Ω trimmer potentiometer (R_2 in Figure 6–11). This will provide more adjustment range than required, but the next smallest standard value potentiometer is 200 Ω, and that would not provide enough adjustment.

Following is a summary of the components selected for Example 6–3 as shown in Figure 6–10:

Transformer T1: primary 115/230 RMS V AC, secondary voltage 36 RMS V AC, dual primary with turns ratios of .35 and a power rating of 3.6 watts.

Rectifier Diodes D_1–D_4, 1N4001 current rating = 1 amp, reverse breakdown voltage of 50 V.

C_1 and C_2: 470 µF aluminum electrolytic, 50 V

U_1: LM317 Regulator

U_2: LM337 Regulator

R_1, R_4: 240 Ω, .5% metal film resistor

R_2, R_5: 500 Ω, 5% trimmer potentiometer

R_3, R_6: 1780 Ω, 1% metal film resistor

C_3 and C_4: .1 µF ceramic disc capacitor

C_5 and C_6: 10 µF solid tantalum capacitor

C_7 and C_8: 1 µF solid tantalum capacitor

Integrated Circuit Shunt Regulators

As mentioned previously, series regulators are used much more often than shunt regulators, which is obvious in any data book on power supply regulators. The key advantages of the shunt regulator are that its efficiency is highest at full load current and it also can handle a shorted load. These are the situations that promote the use of a shunt regulator:

1. The load is a consistent value that is very close to the full load of the regulator.

2. The regulator can be subject to a shorted load.

The LM431 is a three-terminal integrated circuit shunt regulator that is adjustable. If we connect this shunt regulator to the transformer and rectifier circuit of Example 6–2, we have the 5-V DC, 100 mA shunt regulator circuit shown in Figure 6–12.

Resistor R_S is calculated to develop a voltage drop of approximately 3 V to bring the voltage down to the 5-V level where the shunt regulator will maintain this value by adjusting the current shunted in parallel to the load.

R_S = 3 V/100 mA = 30 Ω (the closest standard value is 33 Ω)
$V_O = (1 + R_1/R_2) \, V_{REF}$

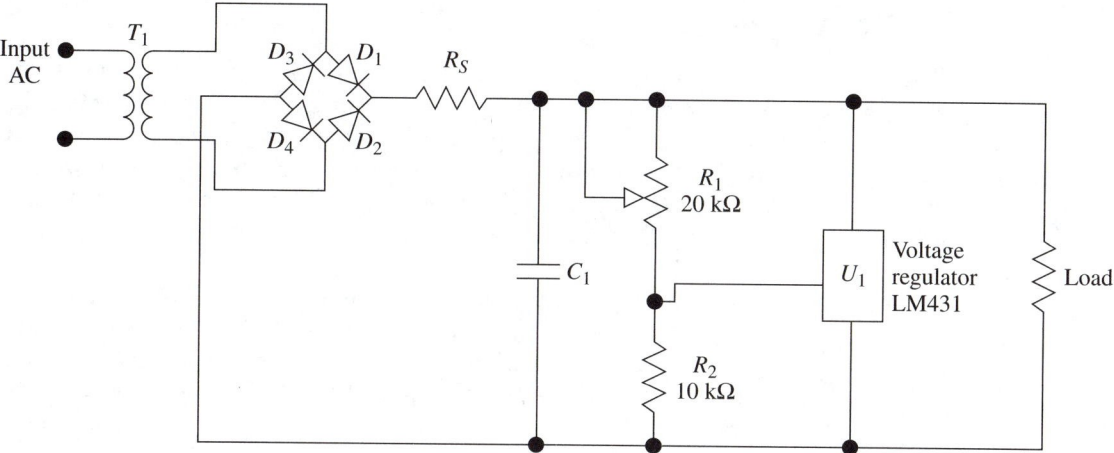

▲ FIGURE 6–12
5-V shunt regulator circuit

Letting $R_1 = 10\text{k }\Omega$ and $R_1 = R_2$ will create the desired operation. R_1 is adjusted to develop the 5-V output when connected to the load.

Low Dropout Voltage Regulators

These are a class of voltage regulators that feature a dropout voltage differential of less than 1 V. The actual range in variation of the dropout voltage differential for these regulators is from approximately .30 to .82 V. In general, these regulators promote better efficiency, because the power consumed by the regulator is a function of the output current times the voltage drop across the regulator. Also, when the input voltage supplied to the regulator comes from a battery, they allow operation of the circuit very close to the minimal battery voltage. Low dropout regulators also include the failsafe features discussed before, such as current limiting and thermal shutdown. Because these regulators are often used in battery-powered circuits, they also provide reverse battery protection and line transient protection. Following is a sampling of some popular low-dropout voltage regulators:

LM2940: fixed outputs of 5, 8, 12, or 15 V at 1 amp, .5-V dropout voltage

LM2926: fixed 5-V output at .5 amps, .35-V dropout voltage

LM2931C: adjustable output 3 to 29 V at 100 mA, .30-V dropout voltage

LM2951C: fixed outputs of 3.0, 3.3, 5 V or adjustable 1.24 to 29 V at 100 mA
with .38-V dropout voltage

It is important to note that the previous discussion about integrated circuit regulators is general. Whenever using a specific integrated circuit in a design, consult the data sheet for that part and use all of the appropriate precautions and application information.

6–3 ▶ DC-to-DC Converters

DC-to-DC converters are a class of devices that convert an input DC voltage to another DC voltage. They are most often used to increase a DC voltage significantly or to generate a DC voltage of opposite polarity. Reducing DC voltage levels are typically accomplished with resistors, zener diodes, and/or voltage regulators in a manner similar to the methods discussed in Section 6–2. There are two basic types of DC-to-DC converters:

1. Switching-type (Step-up or Inverting) Regulators: those that utilize transistor switches to store energy in capacitors or inductors. The stored energy is used to step up the voltage or change its polarity. These regulators are actually a subset of the class of general switching regulators that are discussed in Section 6–4.

2. Push-pull/Flyback Regulators: These regulators convert a lower DC input voltage to AC and then use a step-up transformer to increase the AC voltage, which is converted back to a higher-level DC.

Many times when working on a circuit design, you'll find that there are requirements for special DC voltages to operate particular devices. Vacuum fluorescent displays are a good example. These bright, blue-green-colored displays utilize DC voltages on the order of 200 V for their power. The current requirements are very small. In order to supply this voltage, the circuit designer can use a separate transformer or secondary winding, to develop a larger AC voltage, and then rectify and regulate, as discussed in Section 6–2. An alternative is to use a DC-to-DC converter to step up an available, lower DC voltage to roughly 200 V DC.

Another common application of DC-to-DC converters is in predominately digital circuits that are powered with 5 V DC where a small section of analog circuitry is included that requires either a higher DC voltage and or a voltage with negative polarity. For example, let's say that a small op amp circuit is being added to a predominately digital circuit that has 5 V DC available and the op amp circuit requires = ±12 V DC for proper operation. DC-to-DC converters can be used to resolve both of these issues—generation of both +12 V DC and –12 V from the available 5 V DC. Of course, for this approach to be practical, the current requirements for the ±12 V DC supplies must be minimal.

Switching-type DC-to-DC Converters

The LM1577/2577 is a good example of an integrated circuit switching-type, step-up DC-to-DC converter, otherwise called a *"boost" voltage regulator*. The circuit shown in Figure 6–13 is an LM2577 IC used to convert a +5-V DC input voltage to +12 V DC at 800 mA. The operation of the LM2577 can be understood after a review of its block diagram, as shown in Figure 6–14.

The NPN transistor switch included in the LM2577 is switched at a frequency of 52 kHz. When the transistor is switched on, current flows from V_{IN} through the inductor L. The inductor opposes this attempt to change the current instantaneously by storing energy in its magnetic field, as the current increases over time at a rate of V_{IN}/L. See the simplified circuit in Figure 6–15. At the instant the transistor is switched off, the voltage across the load resistor will be determined by the current flowing through the inductor, multiplied by the quantity of the load resistance minus the voltage drop across the diode. The LM2577 controls this voltage by monitoring the output voltage across the load and adjusting the duty cycle (on time vs. off time) of the 52 kHz oscillator. If the voltage is lower than the desired output (+12 V DC, in this case), the duty cycle is increased. If the input voltage increases slightly, the duty cycle is decreased to bring it back to the desired value. The amplifier and comparator continually monitor the output voltage and make the appropriate changes to the duty cycle. The underlying concept for this circuit is that the output voltage is determined by the amount of energy stored in the inductor during the portion of the 52 kHz clock that the transistor is on. The output voltage is monitored, amplified by the error amplifier, and compared to the desired output. Then the duty cycle is adjusted accordingly.

Inverting, Switching-type DC-to-DC Converters

An inverting DC-to-DC converter is used to convert a positive DC voltage to a negative polarity. For situations where +5 V DC is already available and –5 V DC is also needed, an inverting, switching-type DC-to-DC converter can do the job if the current requirements are small enough. The LMC7660 is an example of this type of DC-to-DC converter. Inverting regulators of this type all use a similar technique to change the polarity of a DC voltage. This process uses two sets of switches that first charge up one capacitor with the input voltage. This charge is then passed on to a

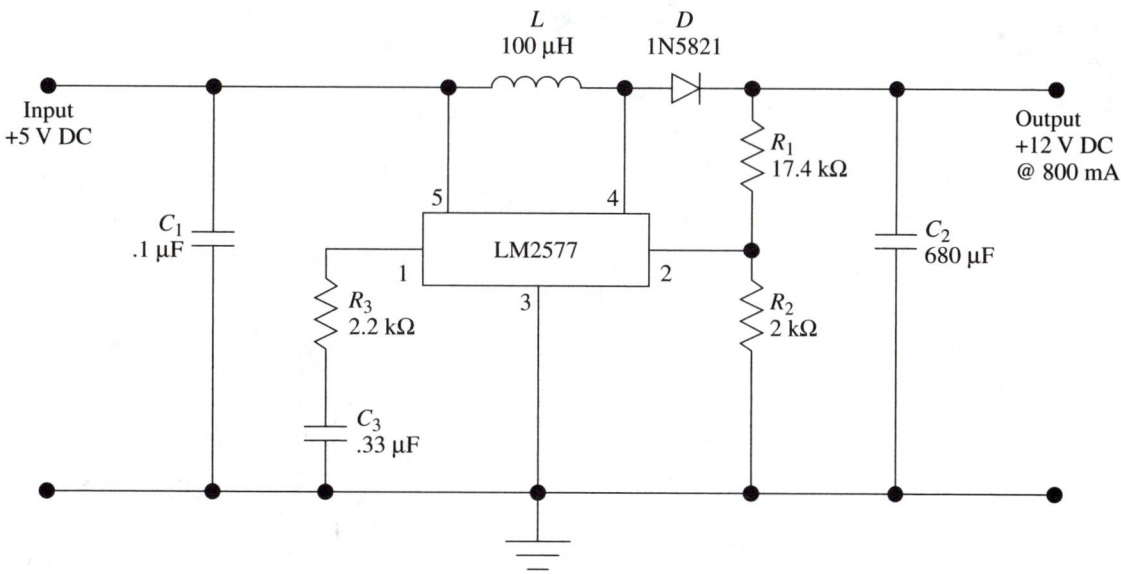

▲ **FIGURE 6–13**
+5-V to +12-V switching-type step-up DC-to-DC converter

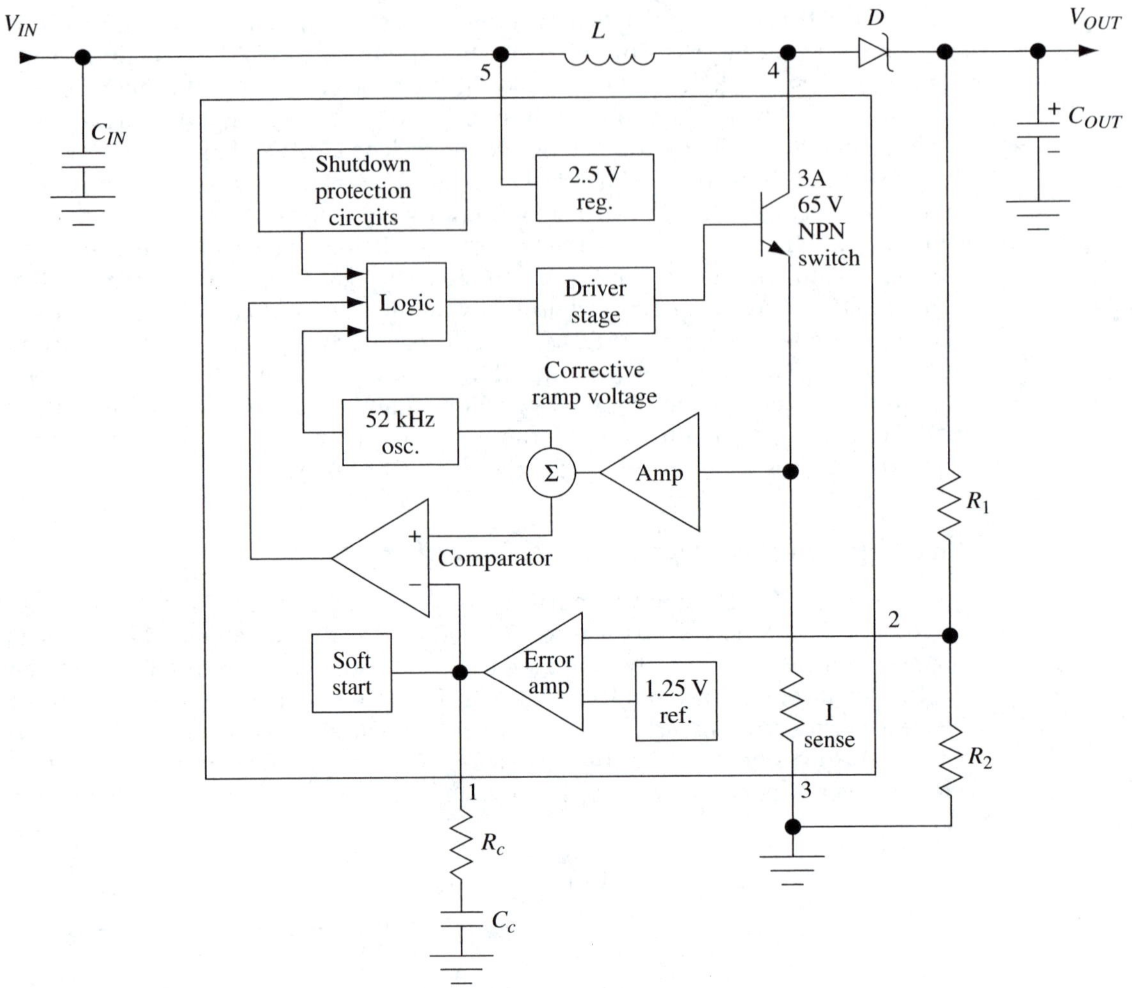

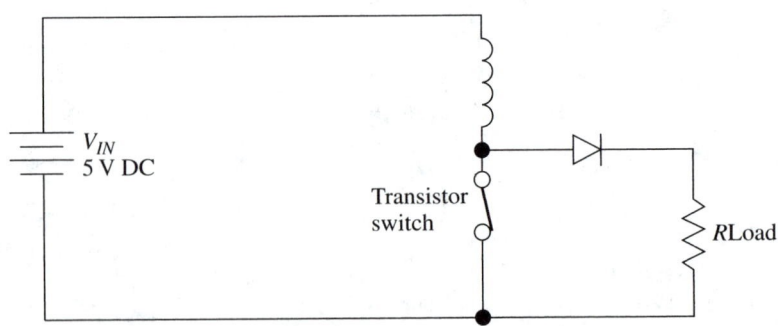

△ FIGURE 6–14
LM2577 block diagram

▶ FIGURE 6–15
Simplified LM2577 switching
circuit

152

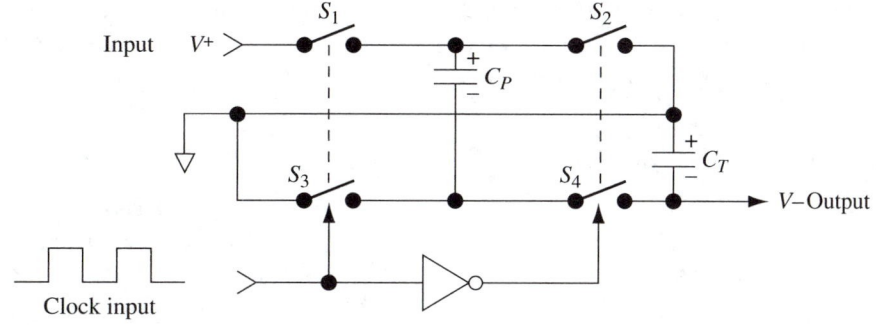

▲ FIGURE 6–16

Inverting, switching-type DC-to-DC converter functional diagram

second capacitor whose positive terminal is connected to ground, reversing the polarity of the output voltage (see Figure 6–16). The LM7660 has an internal oscillator that switches two sets of CMOS switches. The oscillator is connected directly to switch set A, then inverted and connected to switch set B. Therefore, when switch set A is closed, switch set B is open, and vice versa. The frequency of the oscillator is 10 kHz but can be reduced by placing a slow-down capacitor between pins 7 and 8. When a positive input DC voltage (in the range of 3 to 10 V for the LMC7660) is connected to $V+$ and switch set A is closed, the capacitor labeled $C+$ is connected to $V+$ and ground and therefore charges up to $V+$. Then switch set A is opened (which isolates capacitor $C+$ from $V+$ and ground) and switch set B is closed. This connects capacitor $C+$ in parallel with capacitor $C-$, whose positive terminal is connected to ground. $C+$ charges $C-$, initially only up to $V+/2$ but after a number of cycles the voltage across $C-$ becomes equal to $V+$. However, the positive lead of $C-$ is grounded, reversing the polarity of this voltage, the output of this inverting DC-to-DC converter.

Figure 6–17 shows an example application of the LMC7660 converting +5 V to –5 V. The maximum current this device can supply is 400 µA and power efficiency

▶ FIGURE 6–17

+5-V to –5-V DC-to-DC converter

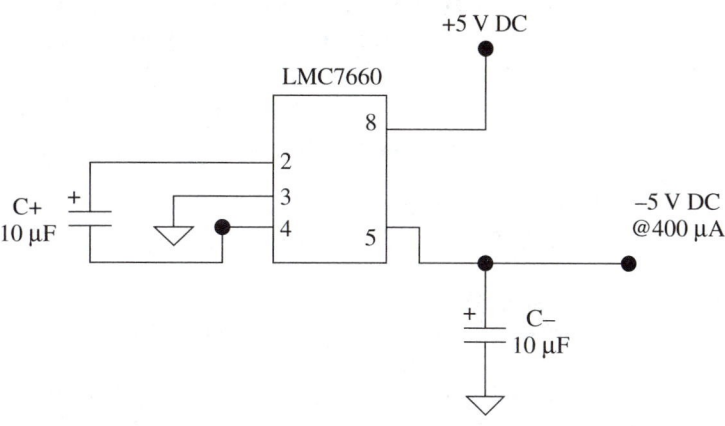

of this conversion is at least 90%. The efficiency can be improved by using a slow-down capacitor, which reduces the oscillator frequency and the quiescent operating current of the device.

Push-pull/Flyback DC to DC Converters

Push-pull/flyback DC-to-DC converters are a class of DC-to-DC converters that convert a DC voltage to AC (usually a square wave) and then use a transformer to increase, isolate, and otherwise modify the output DC voltage. They are usually employed to meet any of the following output requirements:

1. There is a large difference between the DC input voltage and the desired output voltage.

2. The current requirements of the converter output are significant.

3. There is a need for multiple DC output voltages.

4. The DC output voltages must be electrically isolated from the input voltage.

The switching-type DC-to-DC converters described previously do not provide isolation or the possibility of multiple output voltages. Also, because they store energy in the electric field of capacitors or the magnetic field of inductors, they cannot meet high voltage/current requirements without unacceptably high ripple levels. As the current and voltage requirements of DC-to-DC converters increase, so does the stored energy needed to support these increases. At some point the physical limitations of the largest practical inductor and capacitor are reached, and a different approach is needed.

There are two general types of DC-to-DC converters that are capable of higher voltage/current outputs: the push-pull converter and the flyback converter. Both types of DC-to-DC converters resolve the issues of higher voltage/current, isolation and multiple outputs by converting the DC voltage to an AC voltage. Then a step-up transformer is used to increase the voltage and/or change the polarity. This provides the opportunity for multiple outputs with the use of multiple secondary windings. The output voltage and current levels are limited only by the input and the transformer used. Isolation can be achieved by using a separate winding to feedback the output voltage that is measured and used to provide regulation.

Push-pull DC-to-DC Converters

The push-pull DC-to-DC converter consists of two transistors that are configured to operate much like a class B amplifier. One NPN-type transistor conducts current in one direction, while a PNP transistor conducts it in the other. A basic push-pull converter is shown in Figure 6–18. The input DC voltage causes each transistor to switch in succession, generating an alternating square wave input to the transformer primary that is transferred over to the secondary. The frequency of the square wave will depend on the inductive characteristics of the transformer. The turns ratio deter-

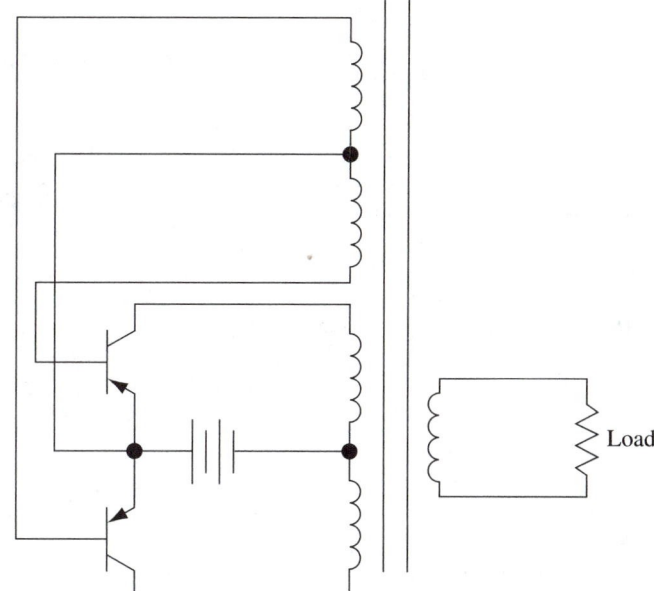

▶ **FIGURE 6–18**
Push-pull DC-to-DC converter

mines the secondary voltage which is in turn rectified, filtered, and regulated like the regulator circuits discussed in Section 6–2. Push-pull converters require matched transistors and the transformer winding must be wound to specifications that determine the proper inductance and output secondary voltage.

Flyback DC-to-DC Converters

Flyback converters eliminate the need for matched transistors and precision transformers by using just one transistor to develop a single polarity pulse waveform that is input to a transformer to be stepped up. The flyback converter is also called a *single-ended converter* because of the single polarity of the generated waveform. While the flyback converter simplifies the converter circuit design, the single polarity waveform fails to utilize the full power transfer capacity of the transistor and transformer. Nevertheless the flyback converter is practical in many situations. An example flyback regulator is shown in Figure 6–19 that utilizes the LM2587-12 integrated circuit flyback regulator. The circuit shown converts a voltage in the range of 4 to 6 V DC to ±12 V DC. A simplified functional diagram for the LM2587 is shown in Figure 6–20. The input DC voltage is connected to pin 5 of the LM2587 and regulated down to 2.9 V internally. The 2.9 V is used to power the internal circuitry, which includes an oscillator, amplifier and comparator. The circuits combine to switch the output transistor on and off appropriately to regulate the output voltage, which is fed back into the LM2587 on pin 2. The compensation connection adjusts the op amp's gain so that it is consistent over the operating frequency range of the regulator.

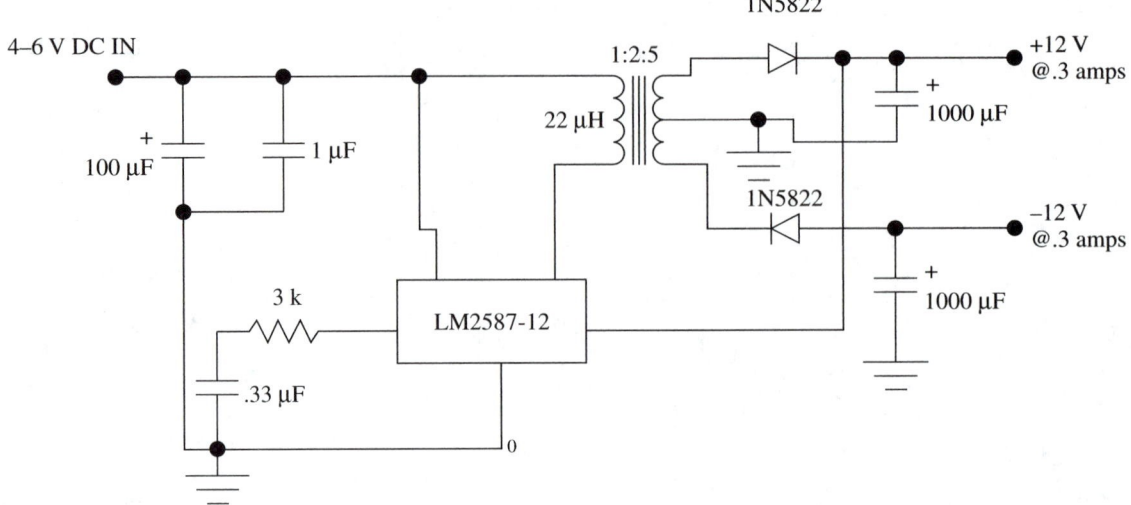

▲ **FIGURE 6–19**
LM2587 ±12-V flyback regulator circuit

Voltage References

A special type of DC-to-DC converter is used to generate precision DC voltages for use as a reference in an analog circuit. Reference voltages are used in analog circuits most often when signal conditioning is being performed. Signal conditioning is when we modify a signal's range, and/or level, to meet some other requirement. Let's say that we have an analog signal with a range of 0 to 2 V that must be converted to a range of 1 to 5 V, a commonly used standard in many instrumentation and control circuits. In this case we are changing the range and the level of the signal and would utilize a signal conditioner circuit to accomplish this. A precision DC voltage is needed to develop the 1-V offset of the 1- to 5-V output signal. A circuit called a *voltage reference* is used for this purpose and for many other applications.

Another common application of voltage references is to supply the reference voltage for analog-to-digital (A/D) converters or digital-to-analog (D/A) converters. In these applications, the voltage reference determines the range of analog values that correspond to the range of digital values. For example, if we supply an 8-bit A/D converter with a 2.5-V reference voltage, a 2.5-V analog input will result in a count of 255 decimal or 11111111 in binary. Conversely, when a digital input of 11111111 binary is input to a D/A converter with a voltage reference of 2.5 V, the analog signal output will be 2.5 V.

A voltage reference must supply a particular voltage value with low noise and a small temperature coefficient. It can be a circuit as simple as a zener diode or an integrated circuit that offers high precision and extremely low temperature coefficients. As was the case with voltage regulators, voltage references are available in a two-terminal shunt configuration or as series references with three or more terminals.

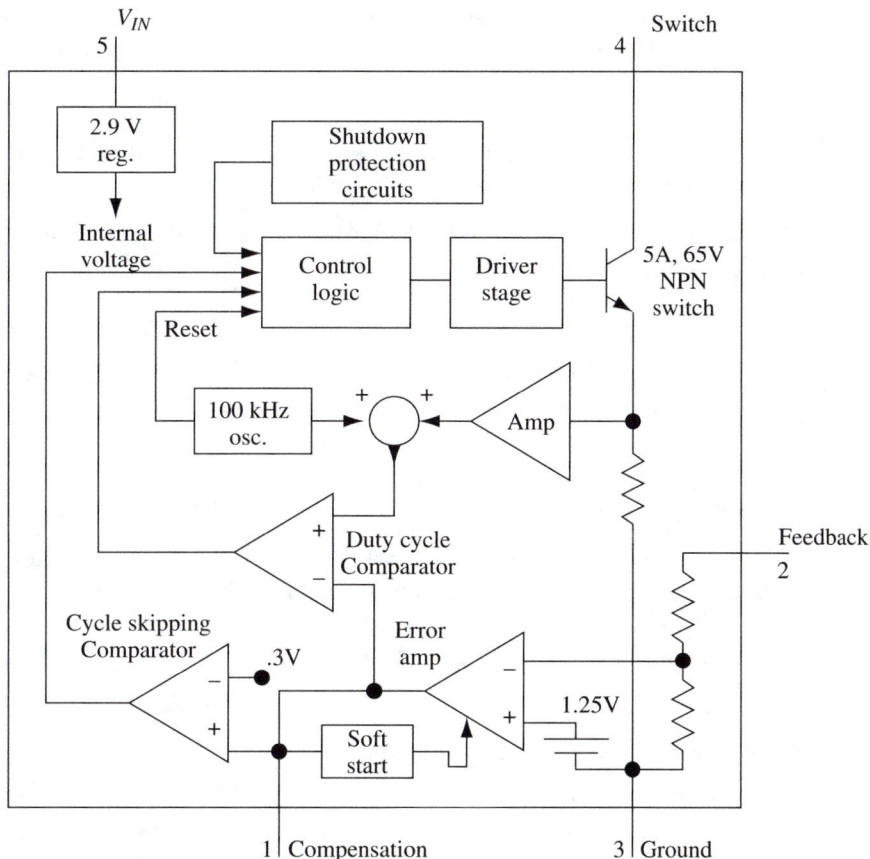

▲ FIGURE 6–20
LM2587 functional diagram

Before solid state voltage references were available, designers utilized various types of batteries that were developed for this purpose. The zener diode was the first semiconductor voltage reference; although it is not quite accurate or stable enough to be used for that purpose without additional circuitry. The voltage stability of the zener diode can be greatly improved by placing a rectifier diode in series with a zener diode. This combination, called a *reference diode*, can result in a temperature coefficient of less than 25 ppm/°C. Reference diodes are combined with op amps to provide voltage references that are highly accurate and offer low temperature coefficients.

Another device that operates in a manner similar to the zener diode is called the *bandgap reference*. Bandgap references are a direct result of integrated circuit technology and include a number of closely matched diodes that are fabricated on a silicon substrate. One of the diodes is connected in series with the combination of all of the other diodes in parallel. When identical currents drive the single and parallel diodes, the result is a stable voltage of 1.2 V across the circuit that exhibits an ideal temperature coefficient of zero.

When selecting a voltage reference the key design parameters, many of which are identical to those discussed previously for voltage regulators, are as follows:

1. Reference Voltage Value: the voltage reference required

2. Specified Reference Tolerance: the expected variation from the ideal voltage reference value

3. Temperature coefficient: the expected variation due to temperature changes

4. Maximum output current

5. Power consumption

6. Drop-out Voltage: the input/output voltage differential where the voltage reference ceases to provide the specified output reference value

7. Line regulation

8. Load regulation

Voltage reference circuits have been simplified greatly by the integrated circuit configurations currently available. But in any design it is important to pay attention to the details. Let's review a few of the varieties of the voltage references available and their typical applications.

A Two-terminal Bandgap Shunt Regulator

The ICL8069 is a very popular shunt type voltage reference that utilizes the bandgap technology discussed previously. It is a two-terminal device that is often shown schematically as a zener diode but offers much better voltage reference performance than a typical zener diode. The schematic shown in Figure 6–21 applies the ICL8069 as an adjustable voltage reference of 1.2 V or less. The output voltage of

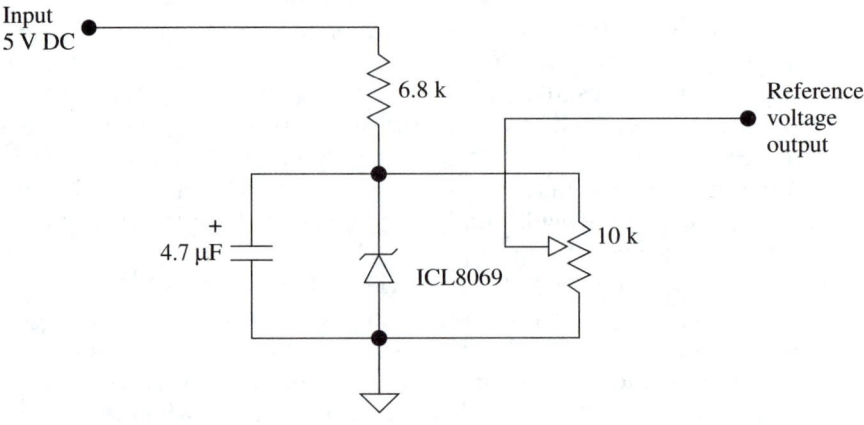

▲ **FIGURE 6–21**
ICL8069 adjustable voltage reference

the ICL8069 is 1.23 V, +20 mV or –30 mV. It is available with temperature coefficients of 10, 25, 50 and 100 ppm/°C. The maximum current that the ICL8069 can shunt is 10 mA in either the forward or reverse directions. This voltage reference is an inexpensive and accurate reference and is available with a low temperature coefficient (10 ppm/°C). However, it suffers the poor efficiency that is inherent with the shunt current reference approach.

A Three-terminal Series Voltage Reference

The MAX6120 is a good example of a three-terminal series type voltage reference that offers accuracy and temperature drift performance similar to the ICL8069 but offers much improved power efficiency. Like the ICL8069, the MAX6120 produces a 1.2-V reference voltage. It can accept input voltages that range from 2.4 to 11 V and offers a 1.2-V reference voltage ±12 mV with a temperature coefficient of 30 ppm/°C. Unlike the ICL8069 and other shunt regulators, the MAX6120 requires typically 50 µA to operate, independent of the input voltage. This offers maximum efficiency and promotes its use in battery-operated equipment and other power-sensitive applications. The typical application of the MAX6120 requires only one filter capacitor as is shown in Figure 6–22. Its maximum output power is 320 mW, which translates to a maximum output current of 320 mW/1.2 V or .266 mA.

Higher Voltage References

The MAX87X series is a group of voltage references that can supply references for 2.5 V (MAX873), 5.0 V (MAX875) or 10.0 V (MAX876). These references are based upon the three-terminal series references discussed previously, except that they have been expanded to include more elaborate functions and therefore require more pin connections. They utilize bandgap reference diodes as the primary reference generator. This voltage is amplified on chip to the desired higher reference value. The connections include the typical input voltage, ground, and output voltage connections that are combined with a temperature output signal, an output

▶ **FIGURE 6–22**
MAX6120 series voltage reference

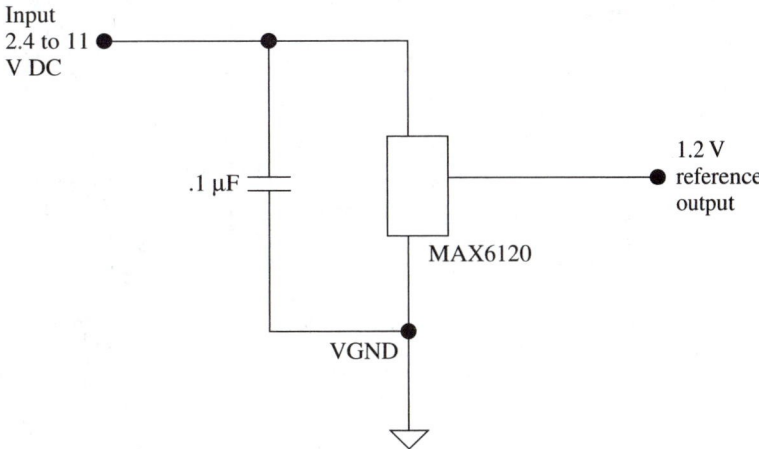

adjust pin, and two test connections. The two test connections are for use only by the IC manufacturer and should be left unconnected. The temperature output signal labeled "TEMP" represents the temperature of the die and can be used to compensate the output voltage over temperature. The TEMP output changes at about +2 mV/°C and is about 608 mV at 25 °C. Since the MAX87X series has a negative temperature coefficient that is fairly linear from 25 to 60 °C, the TEMP output can be used with an op amp circuit to compensate the voltage reference for temperature variations. The output accuracy without trimming is roughly ±.5% and the output can be trimmed with a 100-kΩ potentiometer over 4% of the output voltage range. The temperature coefficient for the MAX87X series is only 7ppm/°C and the maximum power supply current is 280 µA. The maximum output current is 10 mA. An application circuit for the MAX87X family is shown in Figure 6–23.

Kelvin-sensed Outputs

At the high end of voltage reference performance is a class of devices called *Kelvin-sensed voltage references*. These devices use a commonly used technique called *Kelvin-sensing* that minimizes the effect of lead and other circuit resistance (connectors, etc.). Let's examine the three-terminal reference that supplies a reference voltage to the load shown in Figure 6–24. When we consider the lead resistance between the reference circuit location and the load, as symbolized by R_1 and R_2, we see that a voltage drop occurs across each resistor, creating a difference between the sensed and controlled output of the three terminal reference and the load.

A Kelvin-sensed output utilizes separate drive and sense lines to eliminate the error that results from the lead resistances shown as R_1 and R_2. In Figure 6–25 a Kelvin-sensed reference is connected to load with lead resistances R_1 and R_2 as in Figure 6–24. In this case, however, note the separate drive and sense lines available on the reference integrated circuit. What makes this circuit effective is the fact that the input resistance of the sense circuit is very high, so that the current that flows back to the reference through the sense lines is very low. Consequently, only a very

▶ **FIGURE 6–23**
MAX87X voltage reference

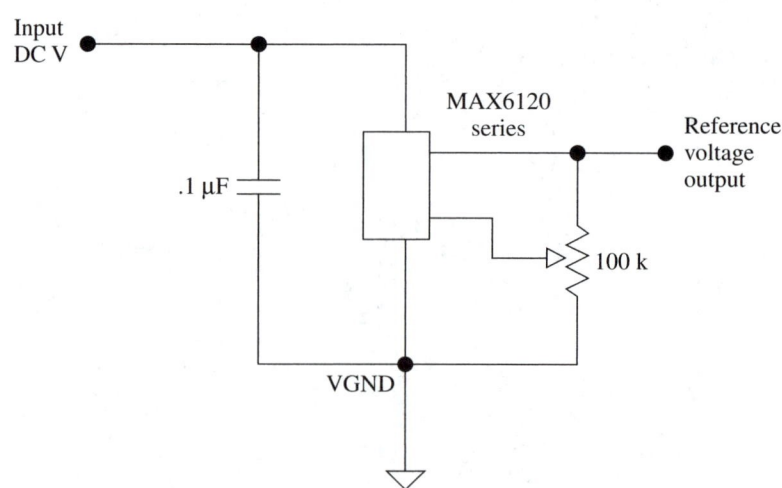

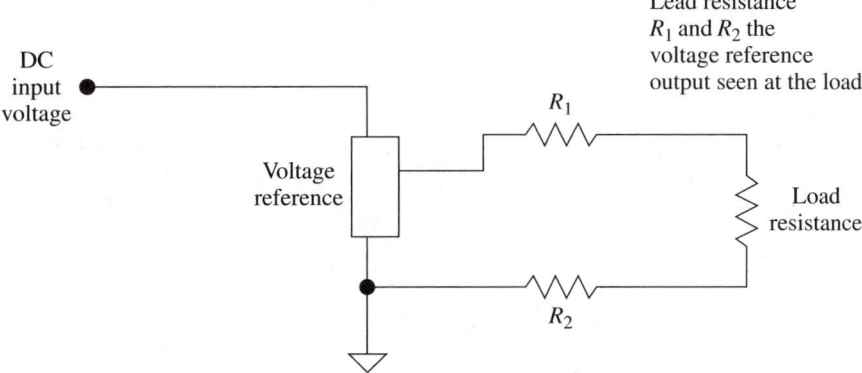

▲ **FIGURE 6–24**
Three-terminal regulator with lead resistance

small voltage is generated across the lead resistance of the sense lines (shown as R_3 and R_4). This means that the reference circuit is receiving a more accurate indication of the reference voltage present at the load and can thereby regulate this value accordingly.

The requirement for a voltage reference is usually the result of a critical circuit function on which the overall accuracy of the circuit is determined. Consequently, proper care must be taken in their selection and application. In the early days of electronics, circuit designers utilized bulky and expensive batteries as voltage reference that barely met their accuracy and temperature drift requirements. Today's technology provides accurate references with low temperature drift coefficients that include the following additional features:

1. Low quiescent current requirements

2. Low dropout voltages

3. Can drive capacitive loads

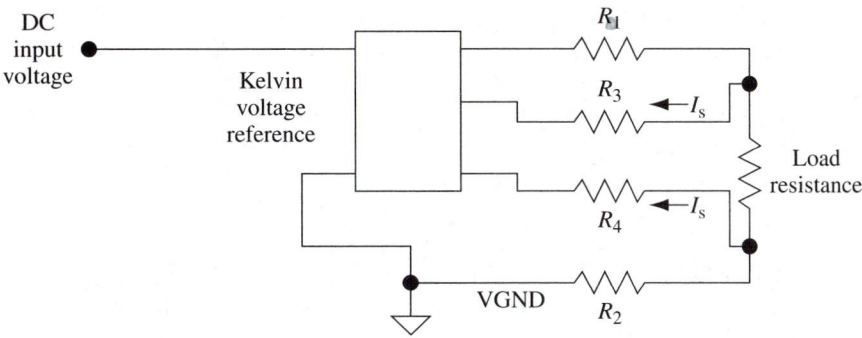

▲ **FIGURE 6–25**
Kelvin-sensing output voltage reference

4. Few external components required

5. Low cost

6. Small size

There are many varieties and choices to be considered in order to match the voltage reference to the cost and space requirements of the design. As with all other design decisions, it is best to make an error in the favor of higher quality and reliability, instead of the alternative.

6–4 ▶ Switching DC Power Supplies

While the linear DC power supplies discussed in Section 6–2 offer superior low-noise performance, they suffer from poor power efficiency. On the other hand, switching power supplies greatly improve power efficiency at the price of increased noise levels. Most digital circuits can accommodate higher noise levels and require higher efficiency as more and more circuitry is squeezed into smaller spaces. Consequently, switching power supplies are often used to generate +5 V DC for digital circuit applications and some less demanding analog circuits as well.

Recall that linear power supplies use the collector-to-emitter resistance of a transistor to attenuate an input voltage down to a regulated output voltage. The voltage drop across the transistor occurs continuously and represents a significant waste of power that results in the relative inefficiency of the linear power supply. Switching power supplies use a different approach. They step down the input voltage by switching the transistor on and off very quickly. The duty cycle of the switching is used to regulate the output voltage and the resulting waveform is smoothed out with inductive and capacitive filters. MOS transistors, which offer very low "on" drain-to-source voltages, are used in these types of supplies. The low "on" voltage across the transistor, combined with the fact that the transistor is switched on for only a portion of the switching cycle, result in significant improvements in power efficiency. Switching power supplies yield efficiencies in the area of 95%. When the switching frequency is made high enough, inductors can then be used for filtering in addition to capacitors, which helps to provide the necessary noise filtering.

Figure 6–26 shows the functional block diagram for a switching power supply. The switching transistor is switched on and off by the control/drive circuit in accordance with the measured value of the output voltage. The switching supply's output voltage is an input to the control/drive circuit, which compares this value with the desired output voltage. If the output voltage is greater than the desired voltage, the control drive circuit will take action to reduce the relative time that the switching transistor is on during the next cycle. For output voltages less than the desired voltage, the control/drive circuit will increase the on time of the switching transistor. The waveform that results at the input to the L-C filter is a pulsed waveform, whose maximum value equals the input voltage value while the minimum value is approximately zero. The L-C filter smoothes out this pulsed waveform and the output voltage is measured by the control/drive circuit, which controls the relative amount of on-time for the switching transistor. The catch diode shown in Figure 6–26 provides a return path for the current when the switching transistor

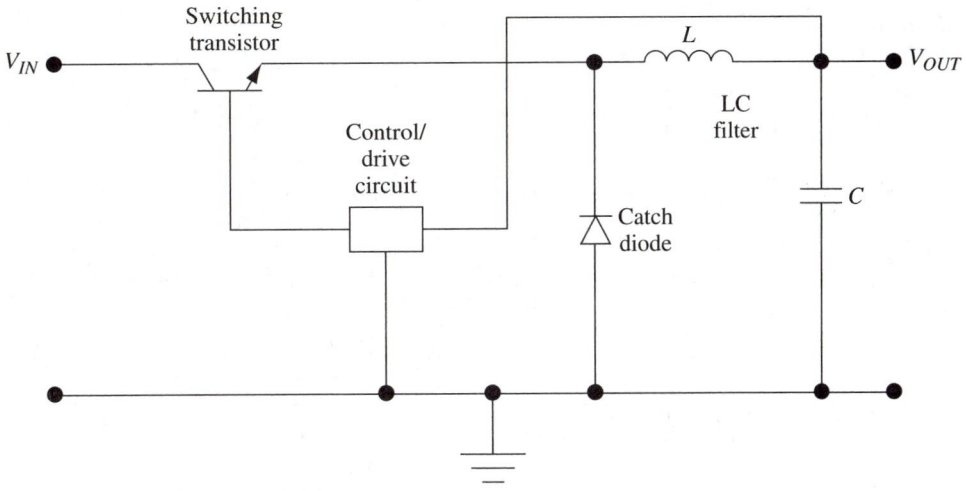

▲ FIGURE 6–26
Switching power supply block program

is off. There are two methods of controlling the switching transistor's relative on-time: using fixed on-time while the cycle frequency is varied or a constant frequency while the on-time is varied. The latter is the approach used most often and is commonly called pulse width modulation (PWM). PWM switching power supplies are used more often today than any other type of power supply.

Switching voltage regulators can be designed to operate in one of two modes: continuous or discontinuous. The current that flows through the inductor causes the operational differences between these modes. In the continuous mode, the current through the inductor never stops flowing during the operating cycle. When the current through the inductor drops to zero for a period of time during the normal operating cycle, the switching regulator exhibits discontinuous operation. Most often the continuous mode of operation is preferred because it offers better regulation and lower ripple. It does, however, require a larger inductor value than would otherwise be necessary for discontinuous operation. Many switching regulators can be operated in either the continuous or discontinuous mode. In this book we will only discuss examples of continuous-operation switching regulators.

The detailed design of a switching power supply can be easily accomplished with discrete components, combined with integrated circuit operational amplifiers for the control/drive circuit. However, there are a wide variety of specific switching regulator integrated circuits that have been developed for this purpose. Many of these ICs require only an input voltage, input filter capacitor and an output L-C filter to operate. Each family of switching regulator integrated circuits will usually offer a range of fixed output voltages and variable voltages, all available at a particular current level. There are also variations between these IC families such as efficiency, noise levels, and features such as thermal shutdown.

The LM2574 series is a good example of a family of switching regulators which offer fixed output voltages of 3.3 V, 5 V, 12 V, and 15 V as well as a variable output version. The maximum output current for the LM2574 is .5 amps. An input

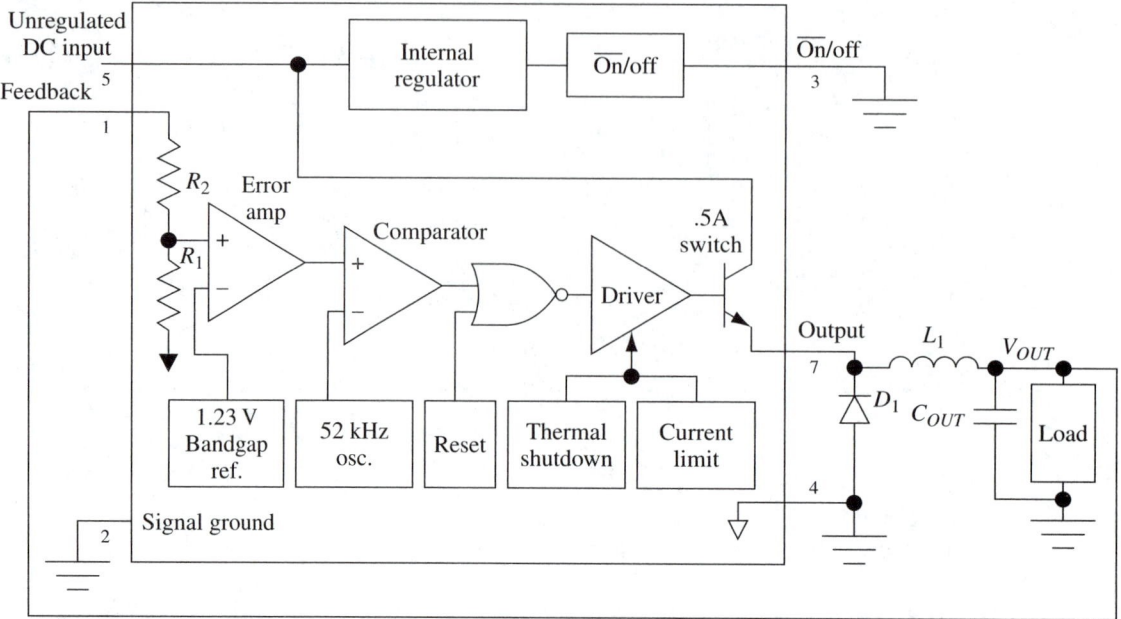

▲ **FIGURE 6–27**
LM2574 switching regulator block program

filter capacitor, catch diode, and output L-C filter are all that is needed to operate the LM 2574 family, switching regulator. The block diagram for the LM2574 is shown in Figure 6–27. This switching regulator operates at a fixed 52 kHz and uses PWM to control the output voltage.

Example 6–4

In this example we will design a 5-V switching power supply with .3 amp current output using the LM2574 family. The input voltage to the regulator is a DC voltage that can range from 8.5 to 10 V and the desired ripple value is 1% of the 5-V output or 50 mV.

Solution

The solution of this design problem requires the selection of the switching regulator IC, the input filter capacitor (C_{IN}), the catch diode (D) and the inductor/capacitor (L/C_{OUT}) that comprise the output filter circuit. See the circuit shown in Figure 6–28.

The fixed voltage output version the LM2574-5.0 is selected as the switching regulator IC. The input voltage range of 8.5 to 10 V is well within the 7- to 40-V input range requirements for the LM2574-5.0 switching regulator. The data sheets for these types of devices always include the design rules for their proper application. The steps outlined for the LM2574 are listed as follows:

1. Select the inductance value for the inductor using the chart shown in Figure 6–29. All of the values on the chart shown in Figure 6–29 assume continu-

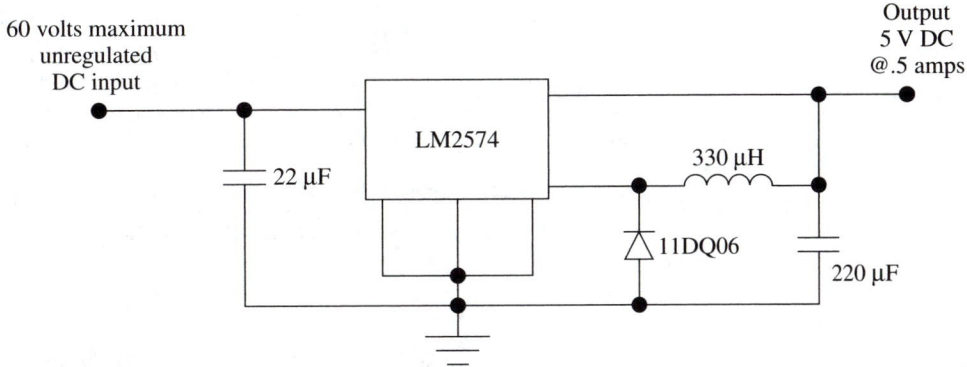

▲ **FIGURE 6–28**
LM2574-5.0 regulator circuit

ous operation of the switching regulator. The value of 220 μH is selected from the chart using the input voltage range of 8.5 to 10 V and the current requirement of .3 amps. The inductor selected shall be rated for operation at 52 kHz and should have a current rating of at least 1.5 times the load current (.3 amps), which is .45 amps.

2. The value of the output capacitor, C_{OUT} can be determined by the following formula:

C_{OUT}: 13,300 ($V_{IN\text{-}MAX}/V_{OUT} \times L$) where L is given in μH and the resulting capacitor value results in μF.

For this example $V_{IN\text{-}MAX}$ = 10 V, V_{OUT} = 5 V and L = 220 μH. C_{OUT} = 121 μF. The application hints for this IC indicate that capacitor values in the range of 100 μF to 330 μF will yield ripple values in the range of

▶ **FIGURE 6–29**
Inductor selection graph

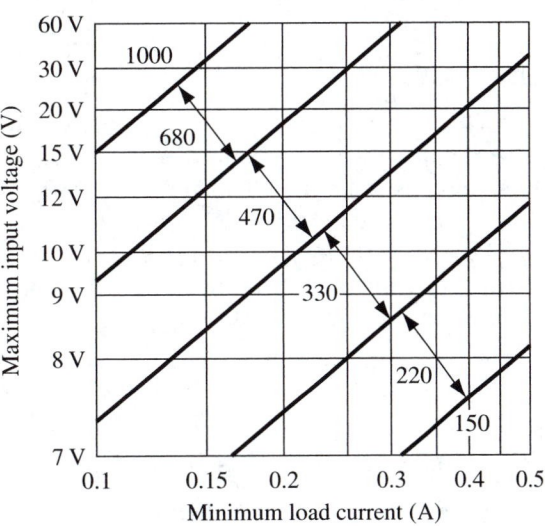

50 mV to 150 mV while larger values will reduce ripple to 20 mV to 50 mV. For this reason C_{OUT} is selected to be 470 µF. The voltage rating for C_{OUT} should be at least 1.5 times the output voltage or 7.5 V. An aluminum electrolytic capacitor with a value of 470 µF and rated at 26 V DC is selected for C_{OUT}.

3. The catch diode can be selected by using the following criteria:

    a. The current rating must be greater than 1.5 times the maximum load current.

       $1.5 \times .3$ amps $= .45$ amps

    b. The reverse voltage rating must be greater than 1.25 times the maximum input voltage.

       1.25×5 V $= 6.25$ V

    c. The diode should be a Schottky or fast-recovery type.

       A 1N5817 Shottky diode is selected with a reverse voltage of 20 V and a current rating of 1 amp.

4. To maintain stability, C_{IN} the input capacitor value must be at least 22 µF and have a voltage rating that will accommodate the maximum input voltage. A 22 µF electrolytic capacitor with a voltage rating of 16 V is selected for C_{IN}.

Switching regulators rapidly switch currents in many parts of the circuit that can cause problems when coupled with wiring inductance and ground loops. Consequently, these circuits are sensitive to the layout of the circuit. When breadboarding or laying out a printed circuit board artwork for a switching regulator, keep the leads to the input filter capacitor, catch diode, and output capacitor as short as possible. Use a single ground point or ground plane for all the ground connections for the circuit.

6–5 ▶ Inverters

An inverter is a device that converts DC power over to AC power, usually at a higher voltage level. In other words, an inverter performs the opposite function performed by a rectifier. This type of inverter is not to be confused with digital logic inverters. The most common inverter application meets the requirement to convert +12 V DC to 120 V sinusoidal AC, at 60 Hz. This is desirable for powering most domestic appliances from automotive or other low voltage DC power supplies. In order to accomplish this feat, the inverter circuit must perform the following tasks:

1. Conversion from DC to AC

2. Development of a fixed frequency

3. Simulation of a sinusoidal waveform

4. Step-up of the voltage

Conversion from DC to AC

The conversion from DC to AC is commonly performed by using the DC voltage to create a square-wave generator by driving two transistors in a typical push-pull arrangement. This was reviewed previously with the push-pull/flyback regulator in the DC-to-DC converter discussion in Section 6–3. See Figure 6–18. The circuit in Figure 6–18 requires some type of starting circuit to initiate oscillation. A self-starting inverter circuit is similar to the one shown in Figure 6–30.

When the DC voltage is connected, current flows through R to the base of both transistors Q_A and Q_B. Because there is always a slight difference between the characteristics of the two transistors, one will always turn on one before the other. If we assume that Q_A turns on first, then current flows through transistor Q_A to ground. While the current flow is changing, a voltage is induced in all secondary windings (N_C, N_{QA}, and N_{QB}) where the dotted end of each winding has a negative polarity. The positive voltage at N_{QA} keeps Q_A on while the negative N_{QB} voltage keeps Q_B off. The current level reaches its peak when the core saturates. At this point, because the current is not changing, the secondary voltages are no longer generated and transistor Q_A will shut off. During the previous time period when Q_A was on, the capacitor, C, maintains a negative voltage across N_{QB}, momentarily holding Q_B off. When Q_A switches off, the current flowing in N_A causes N_A to reverse polarity to maintain current flow. This turns Q_B on, which generates the other half of the AC cycle. The circuit exemplifies the

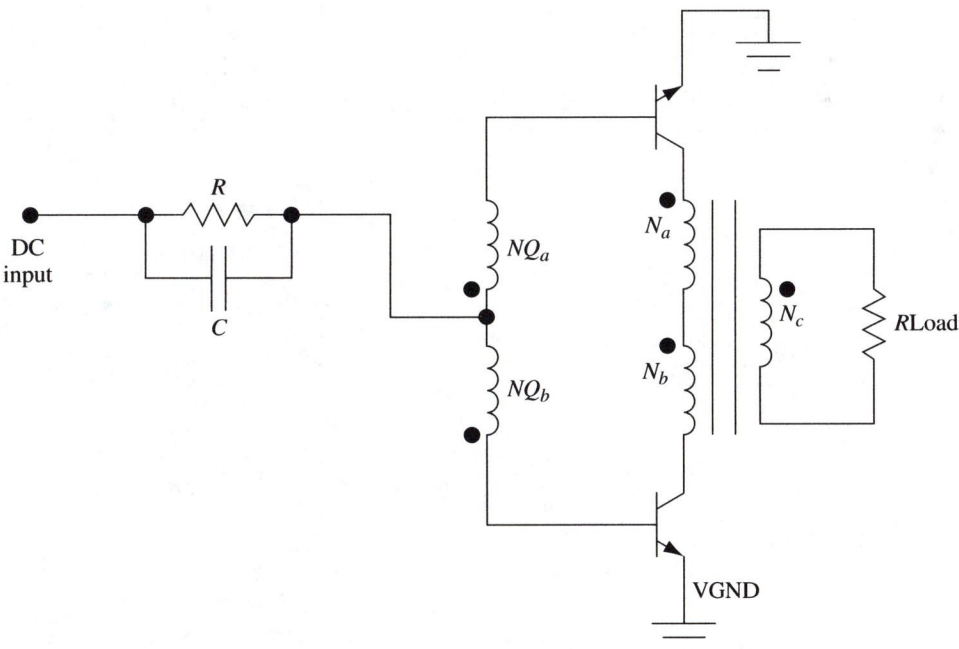

▲ **FIGURE 6–30**
Self-starting inverter circuit

concept of a self-starting push-pull inverter. The resistance, R, and the inductance of the transformer windings determines the inverter frequency.

The amplitude of the AC waveform seen at the load secondary N_C is determined by the turns ratio $N_C/(N_A$ or $N_B)$. The sinusoidal appearance of the waveform is dependent on the load impedance and can be improved by a circuit that matches the inverter output impedance to the load impedance.

There are many ICs available that combine a number of the functions required to build inverters. One of the simplest of these ICs is called simply *a dual output driver*, the CS3706. This IC possesses two output transistor drivers that can be configured to operate in the push-pull mode of operation. In other words, when one transistor is on, the other is off, and vice versa. The input to the IC is a TTL level digital signal that can be a square wave signal at the desired inverter frequency. Figure 6–31 shows the CS3706 connected as an inverter. The input to the circuit can be a square wave at the required inverter frequency. The amplitude of the AC voltage seen at the load secondary is determined by the turns ratio of the transformer. The sinusoidal quality of the AC waveform is determined by the switching frequency and its relation to the inductance of the transformer and the load impedance. There is a significant amount of detail regarding the application of inverters to provide precise sinusoidal waveforms to a wide range of load impedances.

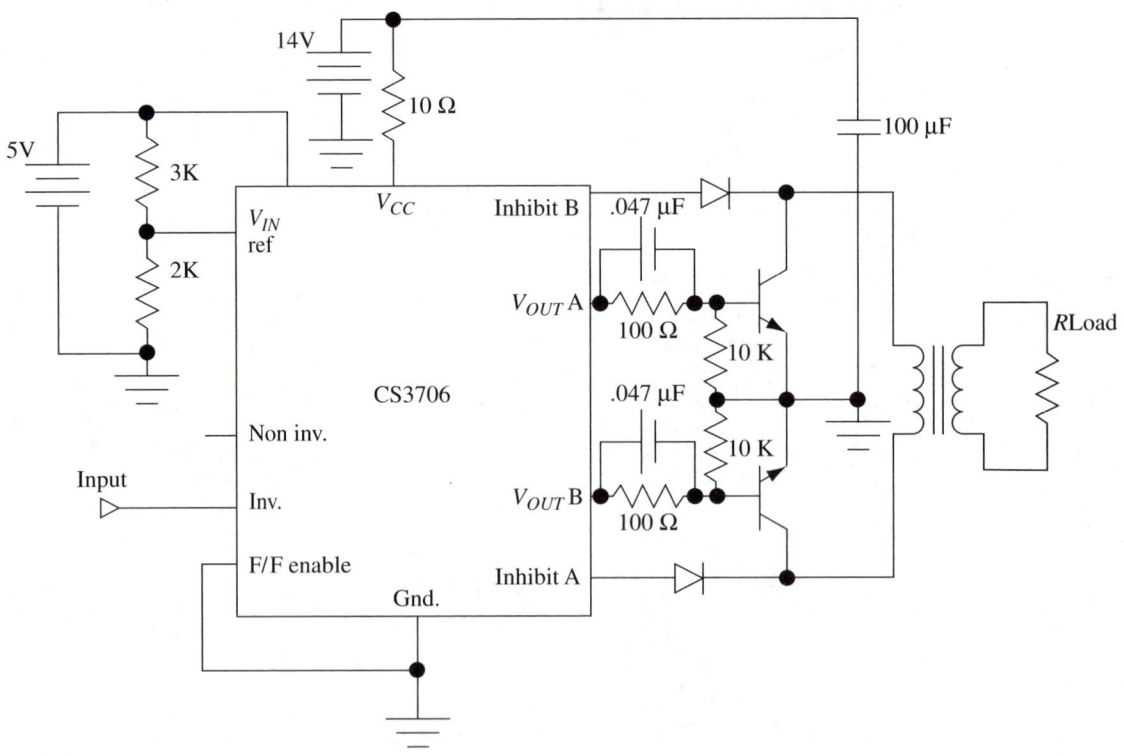

▲ **FIGURE 6–31**
CS3706 Inverter circuit

▶ **Summary**

In this chapter we have reviewed a wide variety of power supply circuits. It should be apparent that power supply and converter circuits require strong circuit analysis capabilities. It should also be apparent that the development of many power supply ICs have simplified the task of the electronic designer significantly. This chapter is by no means a complete discussion of this topic but should be viewed as a starting point for the development of strong power supply and analysis capabilities.

Many of the circuits discussed have been the more simple circuits and applications to make the analysis readily understandable. However, the challenge will continue to be the improvement of power supply and converter circuits in the area of quality and efficiency. The quality of a power supply/converter circuit is determined by how accurately it develops the desired output, without noise, to a variety of load conditions. Its efficiency is determined by the amount of power it uses in the process. Rest assured that the products and applications of the future will require further improvements in both the quality and efficiency of power supply circuits. Based upon the history of electronic development, it appears that we will continue to find new ways of raising the bar of performance yet further.

▶ **References**

Gottlieb, I. M. 1984. *Power Supplies, Switching Regulators, Inverters and Converters.* Blue Ridge Summit, PA: TAB Books.

Hnatek, E. R. 1981. *Design of Solid-state Power Supplies.* New York: Van Nostrand Rienhold.

▶ **Exercises**

6–1 Explain the meaning of the term *dropout voltage.*

6–2 Explain the difference between the terms *percent line regulation* and *percent load regulation.*

6–3 A power supply outputs 5.2 V with a load current of 200 mA. When the load current changes to 220 mA, the output voltage falls to 5.15 V. Calculate the percentage load regulation.

6–4 A power supply with an input voltage of 20 V DC outputs 15 V DC. When the input voltage falls to 19.5 V, the output voltage dips to 14.9 V. Calculate the percent line regulation for this power supply.

6–5 A 620-Ω load is connected to a power supply that generates 6 V DC as an output. The power supply input is 115 V AC RMS, which draws 22 mA. Calculate the efficiency of this power supply.

6–6 Describe the function of a series regulator and an shunt regulator. What load conditions are the most efficient for each of these regulators?

6–7   Design a power supply using the circuit shown in Figure 6–5. Determine all of the component values and ratings for the supply to generate 5 V ±1% at 50 mA and with 10% ripple. The input voltage is 117 V RMS at 60 Hz and can vary in amplitude ±10% and 50–60 Hz.

6–8   Develop a ±12-V DC supply adjustable over the range of 11.25 to 12.75 V with an output load current of 75 mA. Ripple output should be less than .5 mV and the input power is 115 V AC, 50–60 Hz. Use the LM317 and LM337 regulators discussed in Example 6–3.

6–9   Why are inductors impractical to use as output ripple filters in power supplies that have an AC input frequency of around 60 Hz?

6–10   What are the primary functions of DC to DC converters? What is the primary difference between the switching and flyback type of DC-to-DC converters?

6–11   List the most important performance requirements for a voltage reference device.

6–12   Compare the performance of switching and linear supplies in all performance categories.

6–13   Compare the operation of DC to DC flyback converters to the operation of an inverter circuit.

6–14   What is the reason for using Kelvin sensing voltage references over a regular bandgap reference?

6–15   Develop an experimental procedure for determining the efficiency of any power supply. Detail and list each step.

7 ▶ Amplifier Design

▶ **Introduction**

▶ **Introduction**

Even in today's digitally oriented world, there is still a need for amplifiers to increase the voltage and or current level of all types of signals. In spite of the fact that most signals to be stored or transmitted are now digitized, low-level signals must be amplified before being converted to digital in order to achieve reasonable resolution. Also, when digital signals are being converted to analog, their power levels must be increased further for many applications. Then there are the traditional applications of analog signals that are amplified without being digitized, transmitted or stored in the process.

Like every other aspect of electronic technology, amplifier design has changed significantly over the last 30 years. Sophisticated operational, power, and instrumentation amplifiers have been developed and implemented in integrated circuits. High-performance amplifiers are available in small packages at low prices. Like most things today, amplifier technology is available without having to create it. Consequently, fewer and fewer entry-level engineers understand the art of amplifier design and operation. This chapter will focus on developing an understanding of the functional requirements of amplifiers and the application of the current technology available. The particular topics to be covered are as follows:

- ▶ Amplifier performance
- ▶ DC amplifiers
- ▶ AC amplifiers
- ▶ Audio amplifiers
- ▶ Video amplifiers
- ▶ RF amplifiers

7–1 ▶ Amplifier Performance

The general definition of an amplifier is any device that increases the value of some input parameter to a higher level. In the electronic world, amplifiers are designed to increase the level of voltage and/or current of an input signal. An ideal voltage amplifier will have infinite input impedance and zero output impedance. It will accept an input signal and amplify it to the desired level uniformly over the entire range of amplitudes and frequencies possible for the input signal. Consequently, the ideal amplifier should completely reject any frequencies that are outside the possible frequency range of the input signal. An amplifier should have a consistent response time that provides for both an accurate reproduction of the input signal and a minimal delay in its reproduction.

The performance of a real amplifier, as compared to the ideal amplifier described previously, is indicated by the parameters shown in the following specifications, which are summarized in Figure 7–1:

Input Signal: Identifies the range of input signal amplitude that the amplifier can process

Input Impedance: The net input impedance seen by a source connected to the input

Output Signal: Indicates the range of output signal amplitude that the amplifier can supply

Output Impedance: The net impedance seen by a load connected to the output of the amplifier.

Gain: The range in gain that the amplifier is capable of, usually expressed in terms of dB

Bandwidth: The range in frequency that the amplifier can maintain a gain within 3 dB of a reference gain value

Response Time/Slew Rate: This parameter indicates how quickly the amplifier output can change. It is a measure of how well the amplifier can duplicate the input signal from the time perspective.

Distortion: The degree of unwanted, inaccurate signals present in the amplified signal. This is usually due to nonlinearities that exist in areas of amplifier operation. The most common measurement used for amplifiers is called *Total Harmonic Distortion (THD)*, or the distortion factor. This is the classification of the second and higher order harmonic distortion levels that are present in the output.

Noise Rejection: The ability of an amplifier to reject or attenuate input signals outside the range of the specified input signal.

Noise Level: The total noise level output from an amplifier that is either passed through or generated by the amplifier. This can be measured by applying a zero input signal to the amplifier input while replacing the input signal with its source impedance.

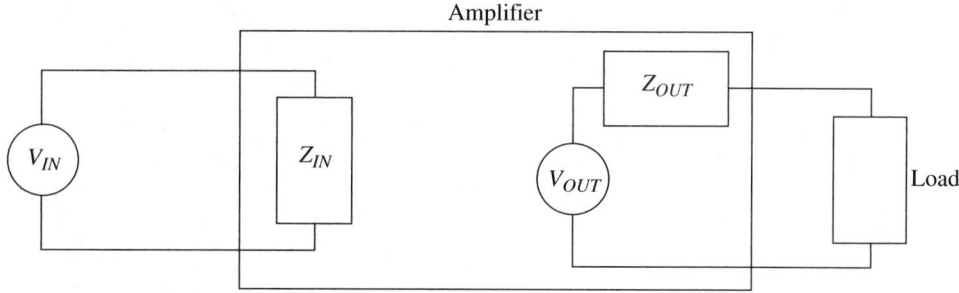

Amplifier

Amplifier specification parameters:

Input signal range	Response time/slew rate
Z_{IN}: Input impedance	Distortion
Output signal range	Noise rejection
Z_{OUT}: Output impedance	Noise level
Gain = V_{OUT}/V_{IN}	CMRR: Common Mode Rejection Ratio
BW: Bandwidth	Efficiency

▲ **FIGURE 7-1**
Amplifier specification parameters

Common Mode Rejection Ratio (CMRR): A parameter applicable to differential amplifiers that measures the degree to which signals common to both differential inputs are attenuated by the amplifier, usually indicated in dB

Efficiency: The output power, divided by the total input power; measures the overall power efficiency of an amplifier

Amplifiers are categorized in a variety of different ways: overall function, frequency range, signal level, and input configuration. Each of these categories are defined and discussed next, as well as a special category of amplifiers called *operational amplifiers*. All amplifiers utilize the concept of negative feedback to achieve gain and bandwidth performance needed to meet the intended application. Gain and bandwidth are opposing performance factors as higher gains result in lower bandwidths, and vice versa.

Amplifier Function

An amplifier can have one of the four following primary functions:

1. Voltage Amplification: a voltage controlled voltage source (VCVS)

2. Voltage to Current Converter or Transconductance Amplifier: a voltage controlled current source (VCIS)

3. Transresistance Amplifier: a current-controlled voltage source (ICVS)

4. Current Amplifier: a current-controlled current course (ICIS)

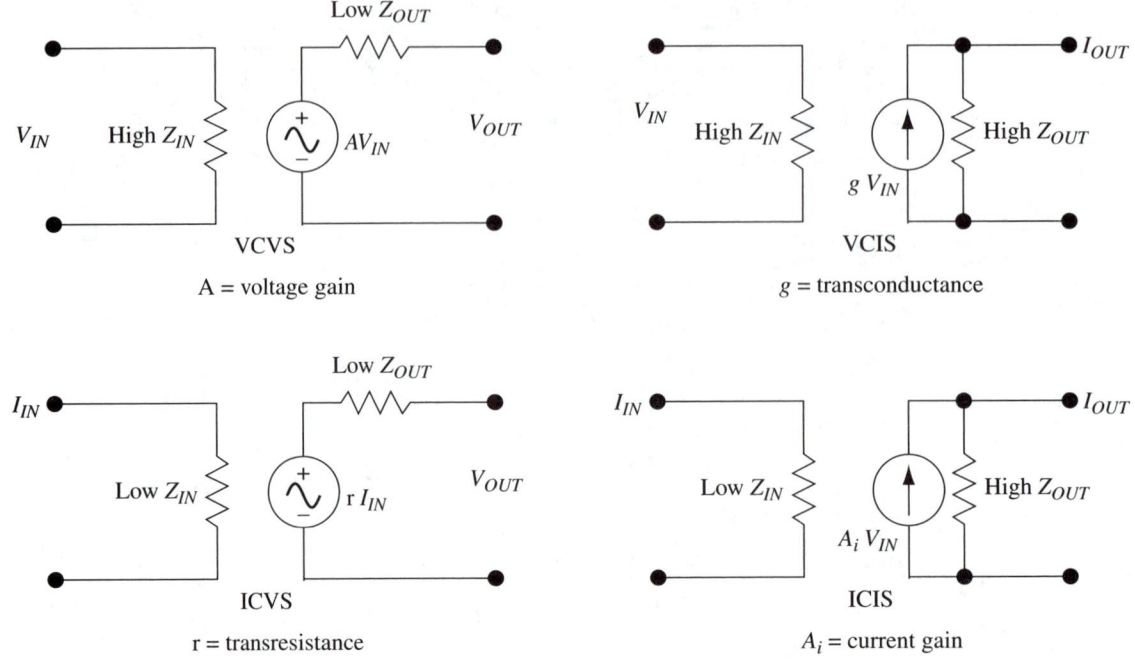

▲ FIGURE 7–2
Functional amplifier block diagrams

Figure 7–2 shows each of these four amplifier functions, along with the desired input and output impedances for each.

Amplifier Frequency Range

The major categories of frequency response are DC, telephony, audio, video, and RF amplifiers. DC amplifiers are used to amplify slowly changing signals from a variety of low-level signal transducers so that they can be indicated, recorded, and controlled. The most common applications are seen in industrial control environments where temperatures, pressures, and flow rates are continually monitored and controlled. Telephony applications include the transmission of voice signals only, which generally cover a frequency range of 100 Hz to 5 kHz. Audio amplifiers are used specifically to amplify signals that cover the human hearing range, roughly 20 Hz to 20 kHz, and are consequently subject to the high-fidelity requirements of our ears. Video amplifiers, also called *wide bandwidth amplifiers* because of their large bandwidth capabilities (20 Hz to 6 MHz), are used to transmit television and other video images. RF amplifiers that are used for most radio communications are designed to amplify signals with frequencies of 30 MHz to 4 GHz.

Amplifier Signal Level

The range of an amplifier's input signal level requires that a different set of design criteria be applied. A small signal amplifier, often called a *pre-amplifier,* must amplify a small signal while rejecting small signals outside the input frequency range while producing minimal distortion. Because the output voltage and currents are at a low level, the efficiency of the pre-amplifier is usually not a key concern. The output power of a pre-amplifier is generally less than 1 watt.

Power amps can have power outputs that range from 500 mW to hundreds of watts, and as a result they have design criteria that emphasizes their efficiency. Power amps are classified into categories that define their design. These categories are class A, B, AB, and C. You probably recall from introductory electronics courses that class A amplifiers establish a quiescent bias point in the middle of the transistor load line. This bias position precludes clipping of the input signal, but also promotes the inefficient operation of the amplifier. This is because when a zero signal input occurs with the class A amplifier, it still consumes power, yet no work is being performed. Class B amplifiers rectify this situation by locating the quiescent bias point at the transistor cutoff point. Operation at the cutoff point causes amplification of only half of the waveform, which is why class B amplifiers use two transistors. Class B amplifiers offer much greater efficiency when compared to class A amps because when the input signal is zero or small, the power consumed is small. Of course class B amplifiers suffer from something called *crossover distortion.* This phenomenon is caused because the cutoff point for two transistors is seldom exactly the same, so there is some distortion when the signal goes from positive to negative and vice versa.

Class AB amplifiers offer a compromise by moving the quiescent bias point slightly off the cutoff point, reducing efficiency slightly, but minimizing crossover distortion.

Class C amplifiers operate below cutoff and offer significant efficiency improvements, but they distort the signal greatly. Class C amplifiers are used to amplify pulsed waveforms where the frequency of the waveform and the presence of a pulse are the primary information carriers.

Amplifier Input Configuration

Amplifiers can be designed to accommodate single-ended or differential input configurations. Single-ended inputs are measured from a circuit common point, so the amplitude of the input signal is the input value referenced to this circuit common. On the other hand, differential input amplifiers have two input connections, neither of which is connected to a circuit common. The input signal processed by the differential amplifier is the difference between these two input points (see Figure 7–3). Differential amplifiers are useful when noise exists that is common to both signals. In this case the differential amplifier can be used to attenuate and practically reject what is called the *common mode noise signal.* The degree to which the amplifier can reject the common mode signal is called the *common mode rejection ratio (CMRR).*

(a)

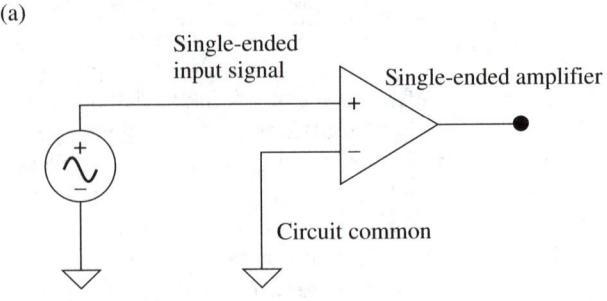

(b)

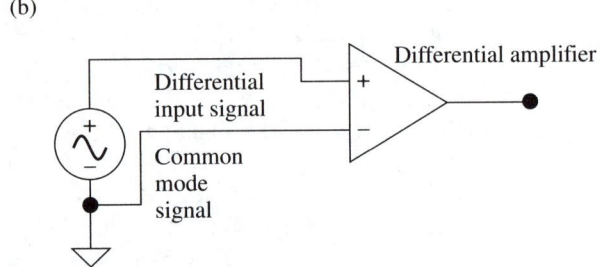

▶ **FIGURE 7–3**
Single-ended and differential
input configurations

Operational Amplifiers

This is a special class of amplifiers that are well covered in most electronics curricula because they have become a primary building block in linear circuit applications. They were named *operational amplifiers* long ago when vacuum tube amplifiers, configured in this way, were used to perform mathematical operations in analog computers. Op amps feature independent positive and negative inputs and a very high open loop gain and provide the ability to develop almost any gain and function by connecting discrete components. Op amps can be configured as single-ended or differential and can perform any of the four amplifier functions (VCVS, VCIS, ICVS and ICIS). Op amps are often configured to function as DC amplifiers with closed loop negative feedback but are also commonly used as AC amplifiers. They can also be used open loop or with positive feedback to create a variety of oscillator and switching circuits.

7–2 ▶ DC Amplifiers

DC amplifiers are used to amplify static or slow-changing signals for the purpose of indication, storage, control, transmission, or to complete some mathematical operation. Integrated circuit op amps are used almost exclusively for these applications, because they offer high performance and are inexpensive and easy to use. This section will discuss the general application of op amps as DC amplifiers and will summarize the key parameters and concerns relative to this application.

V+

Non-inverting input ——— +

Inverting input ——— −

——— Output

V−

▶ **FIGURE 7–4**
Op amp schematic

The basic op amp, shown schematically in Figure 7–4, is a five-terminal device: the negative/inverting input, the positive/non-inverting input, an output and the power connections V+ and V−. The ideal op amp has an infinite gain, infinite input impedance, and zero output impedance and operates over an infinite bandwidth. Real op amps available as integrated circuits approach the ideal op amp definition in a practical sense. They offer a very large gain, high input impedance, low output impedance, and a wide operating bandwidth. The maximum output voltage possible for an op amp is within V+ and V− that power it. Most op amps can only provide an output voltage over the range of V+ minus 2 V to V−plus 2 V. The maximum output current is specified on the data sheet for a particular op amp.

When used as an amplifier, the op amp is connected with negative feedback, realized by a resistor connected from the output terminal to the negative input. The connection of the input signal to either the inverting or non-inverting inputs determines whether the input signal will be inverted or not. Figure 7–5 shows a non-inverting op amp connected to V+ = +12 V and V− = −12 V. The circuit shown in Figure 7–5 is considered to be single-ended, because one of the input connections is shared with the common connection for the op amp circuit. The gain formula for the non-inverting, single ended amp circuit shown in Figure 7–5 is as follows:

$$V_O/V_I = \text{Gain} = 1 + R_F/R_I \qquad (7\text{–}1)$$

$V_O/V_I = \text{Gain} = 1 + R_F/R_I \, R_F = 100 \text{ k} \Omega$ and $R_I = 20 \text{ k} \Omega$ so the Gain = 5

If the input voltage ranges from 0 to 2 V, then the output voltage ranges from 0 to 10 V, which is just within the output range possible for the op amp powered by ±12 V.

▶ **FIGURE 7–5**
Non-inverting single-ended
amplifier

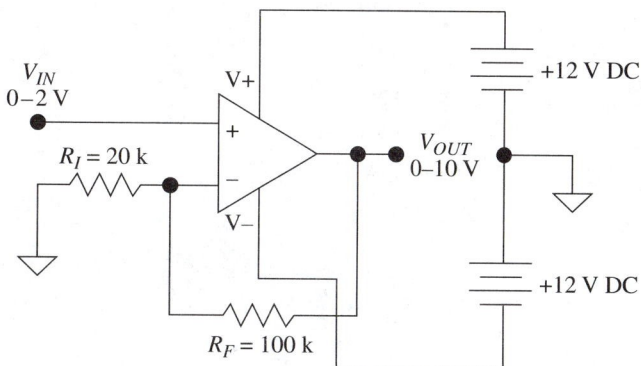

The input impedance seen by the input signal is given by the Formula 7–2:

$$Z_{IN\text{-}NI} = (1 + A_{OL}\,R_F/R_I)Z_{IN} \qquad (7\text{–}2)$$

A_{OL} is the op amp's open loop gain and Z_{IN} is the op amp's input impedance, both of which are available from the op amp data sheet. A review of this formula shows that the input impedance of the non-inverting amplifier is actually much greater than the input impedance of the op amp by itself.

The output impedance seen by the load connected to the non-inverting amplifier is given by the following formula:

$$Z_{OUT\text{-}NI} = Z_{OUT}/(1 + A_{OL}R_F/R_I) \qquad (7\text{–}3)$$

where A_{OL} is the op amp's open loop gain, Z_{OUT} is the op amp's output impedance, and both values are available from the op amp data sheet. This formula shows that the output impedance of the non-inverting amp is actually less than the output impedance of the op amp itself.

The operating bandwidth and the maximum current possible for the non-inverting amplifier are the values provided directly from the op amp data sheet.

A special case of the non-inverting amplifier commonly used is when $R_F = 0$ and $R_I = \infty$ as shown in Figure 7–6. This is called a *voltage follower* because the gain equals 1. It is often used because of the high impedance it presents to an input signal.

A single-ended inverting amplifier is shown in Figure 7–7. The primary functional differences between the inverting and the non-inverting amplifier are as follows:

1. The input impedance presented to the input signal of the inverting amp is usually much less than the input impedance of the op amp. The approximate formula for this is $Z_{IN\text{-}I} = R_I + R_F/A_{OL}$ and if $R_I > R_F/A_{OL}$ then $Z_{IN\text{-}I} = R_I$.

2. The output impedance of the inverting amp is approximately the data sheet value given for op amp's output impedance.

3. The Gain formula $= -R_F/R_I$, so the output is always the negative of the input.

▶ **FIGURE 7–6**
Voltage follower circuit

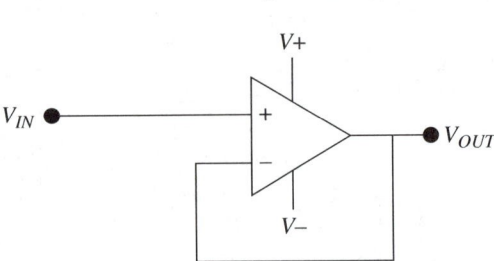

Voltage follower

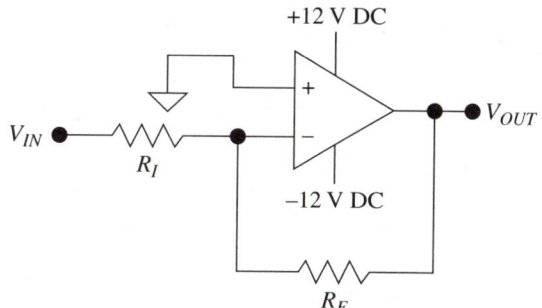

▶ **FIGURE 7–7**
Inverting amplifier

For R_F = 100 kΩ and R_I = 20 kΩ, the gain of the inverting amp is –4. For an input voltage range of 0 to 2 V, the output voltage is 0 to –8 V for the circuit shown in Figure 7–7.

The single-ended inverting amplifier can be converted into an inverting, summing amplifier by simply adding additional inputs through input resistors to the inverting input as shown in Figure 7–8. By varying the value of the input resistor, the gain for that particular input will vary when compared to the other inputs. The gain for each input is equal to $-R_F/R_I$.

Bias Current Values and Compensation

So far we have simplified the application of op amps slightly by ignoring bias currents, those currents that actually flow into the op amp input terminals because the input impedance is less than the ideal value of infinity. Bias currents must flow in each input terminal for the op amp's proper operation. Since the bias currents flow through the input resistors connected to a particular terminal, a voltage drop will occur across the input resistors due to the bias current that flows through them. The value of the voltage drop across the input resistors should be less than one

▶ **FIGURE 7–8**
Inverting summing amplifier

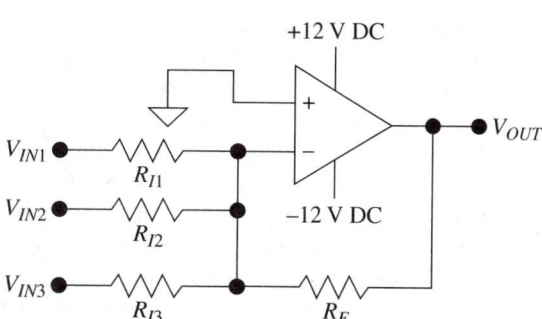

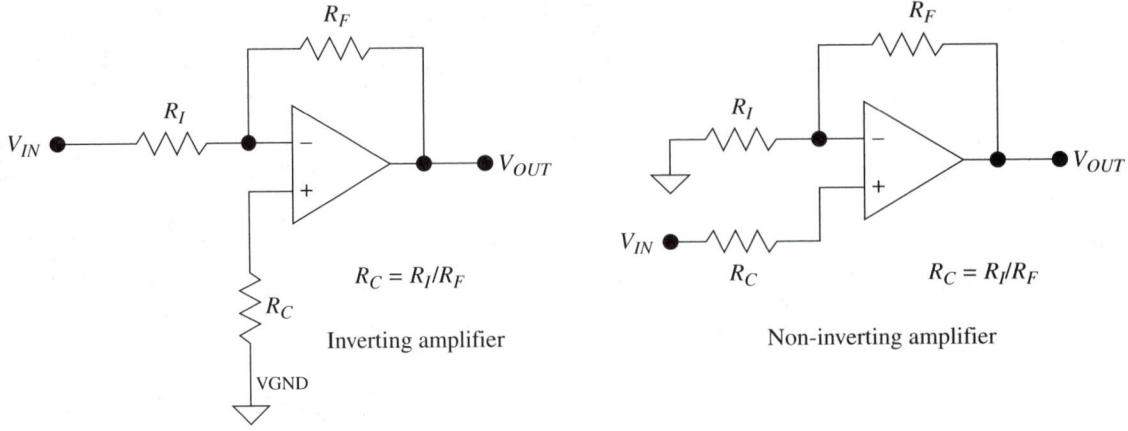

▲ **FIGURE 7–9**
Compensating resistor placement

tenth the value of the base emitter drop (usually V_{BE} = .7 V) across the op amp's input transistors. A particular op amp will also have a maximum value for bias current that is available from the data sheet. The maximum value for any input resistor should be calculated with the following formula:

$$R_{IN\text{-}MAX} = (V_{BE}/10)/I_{BIAS\text{-}MAX} \qquad (7\text{–}4)$$

When the bias currents are not equal, there is a slight error that occurs at the output terminals. A good quality op amp design will try to minimize the difference between the bias currents flowing in the two input terminals. This can be accomplished by using a compensating resistor. Figure 7–9 shows the placement of the compensating resistor for the non-inverting, inverting, and summing amplifiers. The value for the compensation resistor is calculated by determining the parallel combination of all the resistors connected to the negative terminal. If a BIFET op amp is used, the input impedance is sufficiently higher than a BJT op amp and the error due to bias current is negligible.

Input Offset Voltage

Ideally the op amp should have an output of 0 V when the inputs to the op amp are 0. In an actual op amp, a small voltage is present at the output terminal when the inputs are 0. This value is called the *offset voltage*. The op amp circuit will amplify any offset voltage present at the output, so if the value of the offset voltage is significant when compared to the signal level, then some measure must be taken to minimize the value of the offset voltage. Many op amps provide terminals where a potentiometer can be connected to adjust the offset voltage to 0. Figure 7–10 shows a typical offset voltage adjustment circuit.

The value of the offset voltage also changes with the ambient temperature to which the op amp is exposed. So once the offset voltage is adjusted to 0 with the

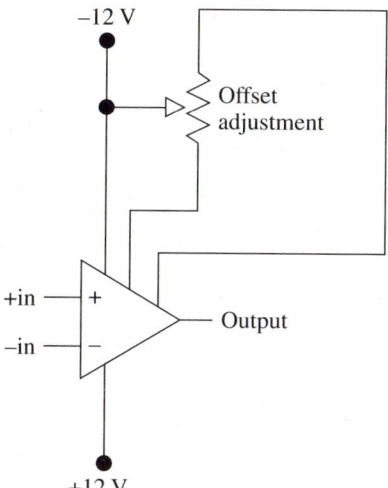

▶ **FIGURE 7–10**
Offset adjustment circuit

potentiometer connection described previously, it will still vary with temperature. The degree to which an op amp's offset voltage varies with temperature is listed in its specifications. Higher-quality, precision op amps have circuitry that minimizes the amplitude of the offset voltage as well as the amount of temperature drift. Care should be taken to review this area of the specs when selecting op amps for use in a particular application, so the impact of the offset voltage and its drift do not affect the op amp's output appreciably.

Differential Amplifier

The differential amplifier is a special amp that amplifies the difference between the two input voltages, as compared to the single-ended amplifier that amplifies the difference between one input voltage and circuit common. The ideal differential amplifier will amplify only the difference between the two input signals. It will reject (completely attenuate) any voltage common to both inputs, called *common mode voltage*. The degree to which a real op amp succeeds in attenuating common mode voltage is given by the specification called *common mode rejection ratio (CMRR)*. CMRR is usually given as a decibel value and the formula is:

CMRR = 20 Log (Common Output Voltage/Common Mode input Voltage)   (7–5)

The CMRR can be measured by making the differential signal zero with the common mode voltage at some value. Any voltage measured at the output under this condition is common mode voltage that has not been attenuated by the differential amp. The circuit for a differential amplifier is shown in Figure 7–11. The CMRR is largely determined by the degree to which the resistors are matched: resistor $R_2 = R_4$ and resistor $R_1 = R_3$. The gain is determined by the ratio of R_4/R_2. Differential amplifiers can be constructed from standard op amps

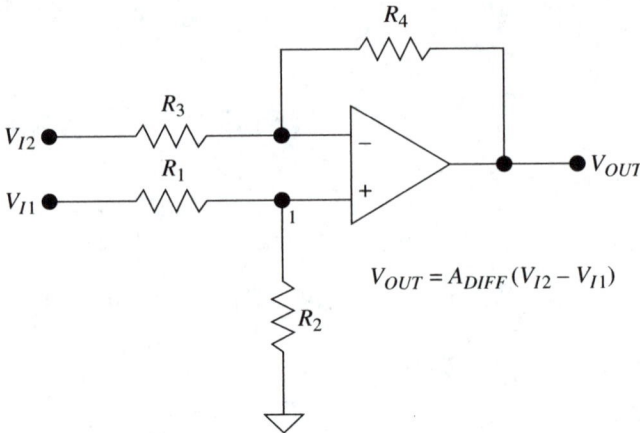

▶ **FIGURE 7-11**
Differential amplifier

or are available as an integrated circuit. The differential amplifier is an improvement over the single-ended amplifier because of its ability to reject common mode signals. However, it does suffer from relatively low input impedance, as does the inverting amplifier. The instrumentation amplifier to be discussed next is an improved differential amplifier that enjoys the high input impedance of the non-inverting amplifier.

An example of an IC differential amplifier is the INA117 shown in Figure 7-12. The INA117 is a precision unity gain differential amplifier. Included on the IC are all of the necessary resistors, implemented on a thin film resistor network. The specifications state a minimum CMRR of 86 dB. More impressively, this amplifier accommodates common mode voltages on the order of ±200 volts. To put this in

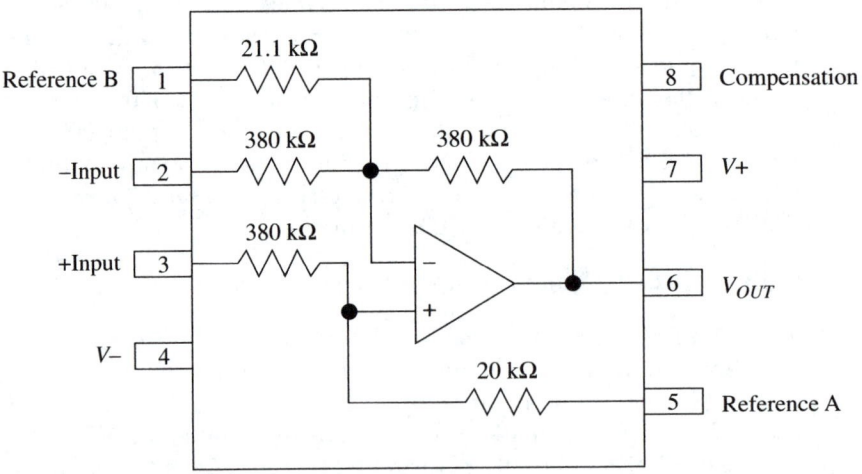

▲ **FIGURE 7-12**
INA117 differential amplifier

perspective, let's say we have a 200-mV DC signal riding on a 120-V AC RMS common mode signal input to this unity gain differential amplifier. The output would be 200-mV DC signal riding on top of a 6 mV AC RMS signal.

Instrumentation Amplifier

The differential amplifier actually possesses a number of design deficiencies: the input impedance is less than desirable, the CMRR is highly dependent on matching the resistor values, and gain adjustment is accomplished by the adjustment of two resistors instead of just one. An amplifier circuit called an *instrumentation amplifier* improves on each of these problem areas. An instrumentation amplifier is shown in Figure 7–13. High input impedance is achieved by using two non-inverting amplifiers on the front end of each input to the instrumentation amplifier. The output stage of the instrumentation amplifier is simply a differential amplifier with a gain of one (all the resistor values equal R). The output of each non-inverting amplifier is connected in a creative scheme that results in the following equation for the instrumentation amplifier's output:

$$V_O = (1 + 2R/R_A)(V_1 - V_2) \tag{7–6}$$

Instrumentation amplifiers can be constructed from discrete components or are available as an IC in many configurations. The INA101 is an example of a high-performance IC instrumentation amplifier. The internal schematic and external connections for the 14-pin DIP package are shown in Figure 7–14. The gain of this amplifier is determined by the value of resistor R_G.

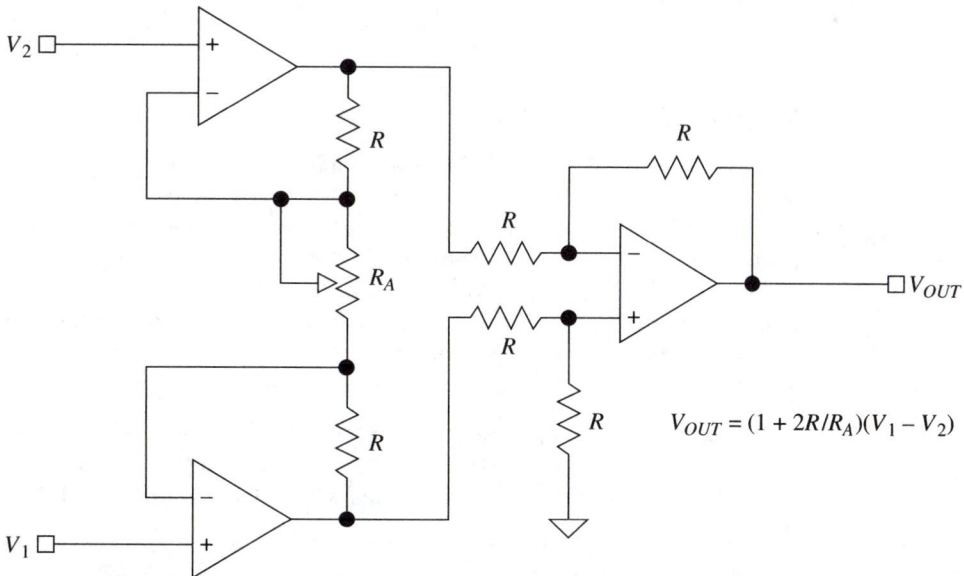

▲ **FIGURE 7–13**
Instrumentation amplifier

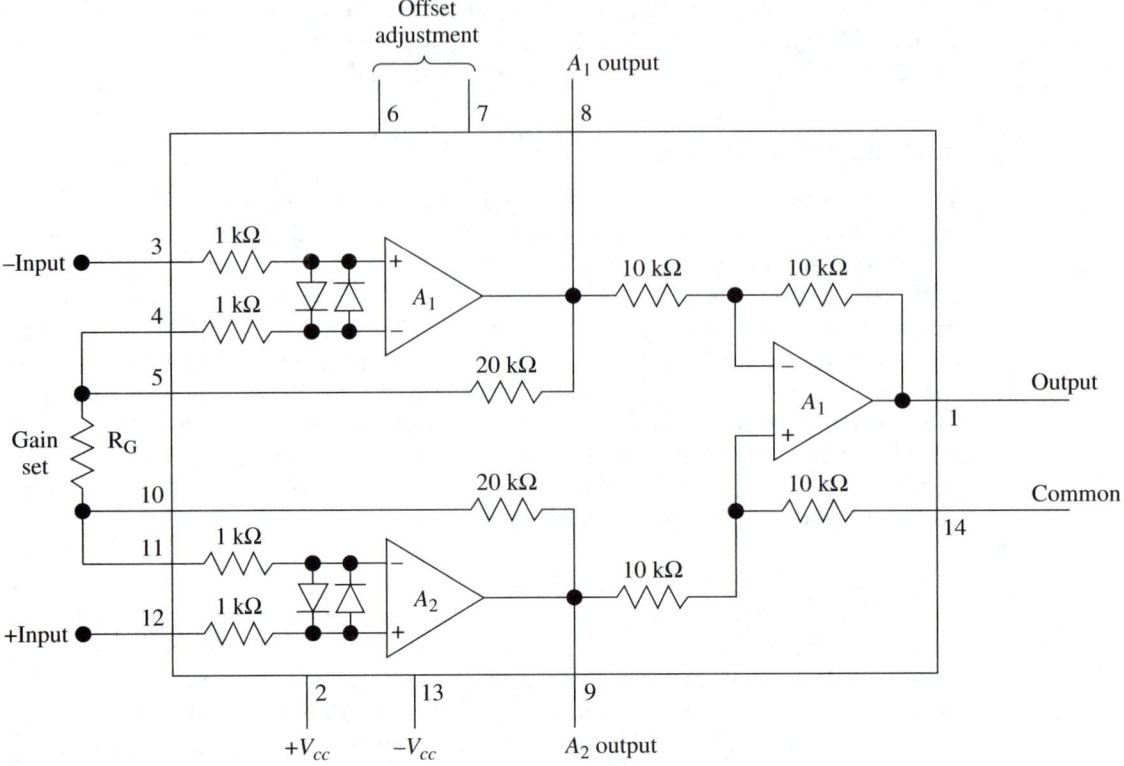

▲ FIGURE 7–14
INA101 Instrumentation amplifier

Single-supply Operation

In all of our discussions using the op amp as a DC amplifier, the power supply connected to the V+ and V– connections has been equal in value and opposite in polarity. All of the circuit examples given thus far have used a ±12-V DC power supply. With a ±12-V DC power supply, the output of the op amp has a maximum range close to ±10 V DC. A dual symmetrical power supply is required when the op amp must output both plus and minus signals, or when the output must have a range that includes 0 under normal operating conditions. The symmetry of dual polarity power also promotes a 0-V output when the input is 0.

> *Note:* There are special function op amps that approach 0-V outputs with 0 input when operated with a single supply, but typical op amps can only drive the output voltage to values within V+ minus 2 V and V– plus 2 V.

In many applications op amps are not required to provide negative or zero output voltages. In these cases, the power supply circuitry can be simplified by using a single-power supply connected to V+ and V–. The voltage for the single supply should be greater than the minimum supply range for the op amp being used, yet

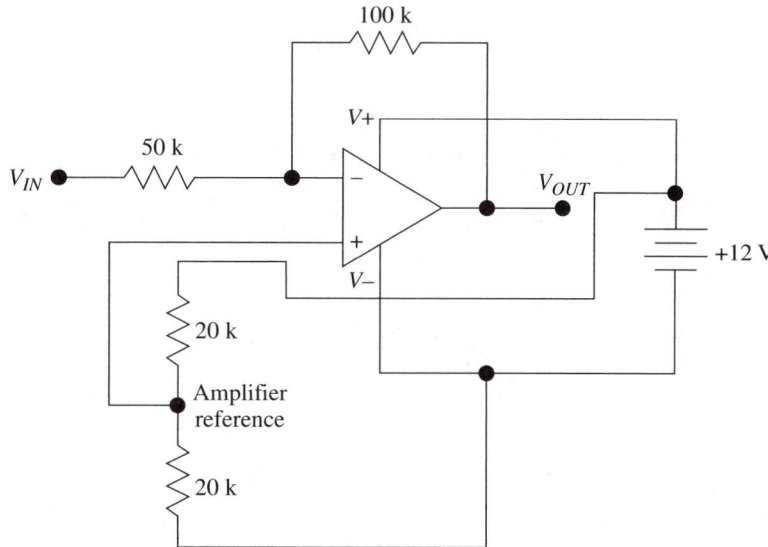

Single-supply inverting op amp

less than its maximum voltage rating. The difficulty presented by this type of circuit is the establishment of circuit common. The dual symmetry power supply develops a circuit common exactly between the $V+$ and $V-$ values. When a single supply is used, the circuit common must be developed, usually with resistor voltage dividers. Figure 7–15 shows an example single-ended op amp, inverting amplifier powered with a single 12-V power supply. The circuit common reference voltage in this circuit is actually $V+/2$, which is 6 V. When the input is equal to 6 V, the output also equals 6 V. If the input increases to 7 V, with the gain of -2 shown, the output will be reduced to 4 V. Likewise, if the input falls to 5 V, the output will increase to 7 V. The overall range of the op amp in Figure 7–15 is 2 to 10 V.

Power Op Amps

A severe limitation of most IC op amps is the low maximum output current specified for most op amps, usually on the order of 25 ma or 500 mW. Connecting an output transistor to the op amp output, as shown in Figure 7–16a, can readily increase the power and current output capabilities of any op amp. In this circuit, the output current flowing through the load resistor R_L is limited only by the current capabilities of the power supply, and the current rating for the transistor. The op amp will drive the collector voltage to a value determined by the op amp input voltage and the gain of the circuit according to the formula $V_O = (1 + R_F/R_1) V_1$ for positive input voltages only. If the op amp input voltage is negative, the NPN transistor in the circuit turns off. In order to drive the output in both polarities, a push-pull arrangement of NPN and PNP transistors could be connected.

There are many varieties of operational amplifiers that have been developed and are available as an IC that increase the op amp's power output. These can take

(a)

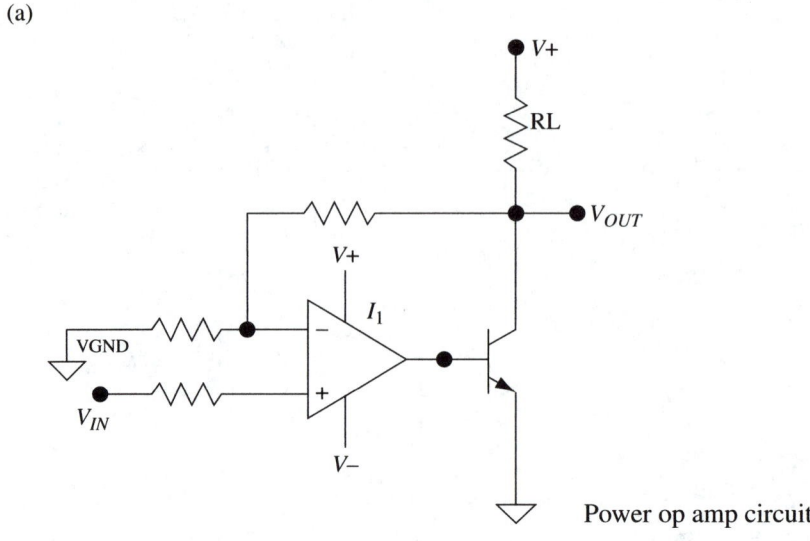

Power op amp circuit

(b)

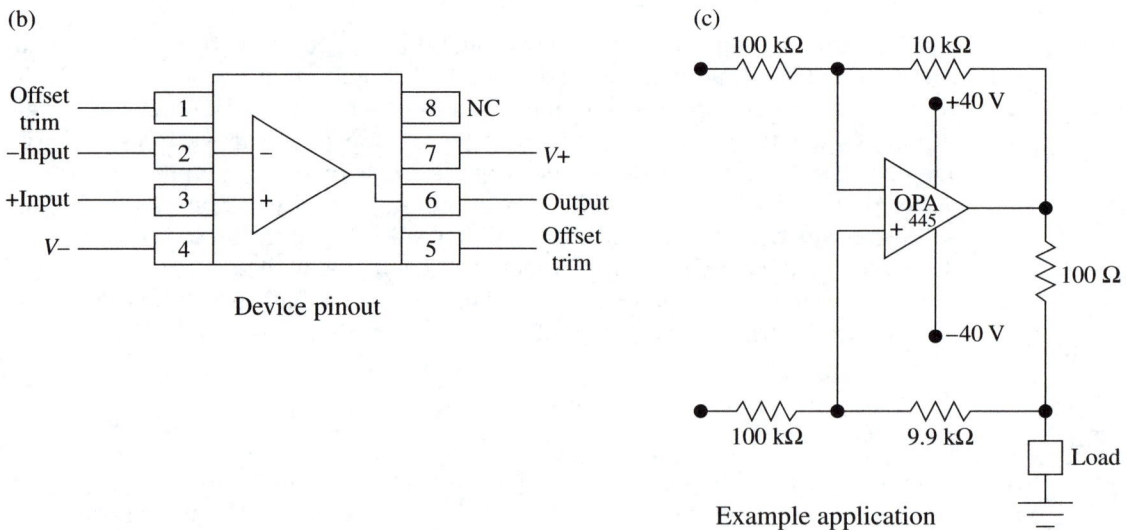

Device pinout

(c)

Example application

▲ **FIGURE 7–16**
Operational amplifier

the form of higher voltage and or current. Most common variety op amps can output about 10 to 20 ma at voltage levels up to ±18 V, or about 500 mW of power. The OPA445 is a good example of an IC that can provide much higher voltage outputs at current levels of 15 ma. The connection pinout for the OPA445 is shown in Figure 7–16b. In the diagram the device appears as a standard op amp but the OPA445 can handle power supply voltages and inputs up to ±45 volts. An example application of the OPA445 is shown in Figure 7–16c.

DC Amplifier Performance

This is a general summary of design and performance factors for DC amplifiers and should be used as a guide in their design and the analysis of their performance:

Input impedance (Z_{IN})

Output impedance (Z_{OUT})

Open loop gain (A_{OL})

Closed loop gain (A_{CL})

Power supply, single, dual, dual tracking

Power supply rejection ratio (PSRR)

Output voltage range

Input voltage range

Output current

Output power

Offset voltage

Offset voltage temperature coefficient

Bias current compensation

Input mode, single-ended or differential

Common mode rejection ratio for differential amplifiers (CMRR)

Type: voltage controlled/voltage source (VCVS)

voltage controlled/current source (VCIS)

current controlled/voltage source (ICVS)

current controlled/current source (ICIS)

7-3 ▶ AC Amplifiers

This section covers the use of the op amp as an AC amplifier over a wide range of frequencies. These circuits will be discussed in later sections where they will be applied to audio, video, and other specific application.

There are two frequency oriented limitations to the function of an op amp used as an AC amplifier. The first is the normal reduction in gain as the signal frequency increases, which is inherent in any amplifier. The other is the speed at which the op amp can change its output, the parameter called "slew rate". The open loop frequency response is available from the data sheet for any op amp. This is usually called the unity gain frequency or simply the bandwidth. The closed loop frequency response for any op amp circuit equals the open loop bandwidth divided by the closed loop gain of the circuit.

$$BW_{CL} = BW_{OL}/G_{CL} \qquad (7\text{--}7)$$

where BW_{CL} = Bandwidth Closed Loop

BW_{OL} = Bandwidth Open Loop

G_{CL} = Gain Closed Loop

The frequency limitation due to an op amp's slew rate is approximated by the following formula:

$$BW_{SR} = S/(2\pi \times V_{PEAK}) \qquad (7\text{--}8)$$

where BW_{SR} = Bandwidth due to slew rate

S = Slew rate from op amp data sheet

V_{PEAK} = maximum amplitude of the signal

Let's start with a simple op amp voltage follower as discussed in Section 7–2. Because the input signal is connected to the positive input, the output will be in phase with the input. To make this circuit an AC amplifier, it is desirable to capacitively couple the input and output of the op amp, as shown in Figure 7–17a. There is a problem with this circuit when compared to the DC voltage follower shown in Figure 7–6. A DC bias current flows into the non-inverting op amp input from circuit common in the DC voltage follower shown in Figure 7–6. The circuit shown in Figure 7–17a will not function because any DC bias current is blocked by the input coupling capacitor. Resistor R_{IN} is added to the circuit shown in Figure 7–17b, for the purpose of providing the bias current needed for the op amp to function.

It is important to note that in the AC circuits to be discussed, where the output of the op amp is capacitively coupled to the load, there is no attempt made to make the bias currents equal, as recommended for DC amplifiers. This is because any offset generated by unequal bias currents will be blocked from the output by the output coupling capacitor.

The circuit formed by C_{IN} and R_{IN} is a high pass circuit whose values should be determined, such that the lowest frequency in the signal range to be amplified is at the 3-dB cutoff point, f_1 for the high pass circuit. At the 3-dB cutoff point the capacitive reactance of C_{IN} should be equal to one-tenth the value of R_{IN}.

$$C_{IN} = 1/(2\pi f_1 (R_{IN}/10)) \qquad (7\text{--}9)$$

R_{IN} becomes the effective input impedance of the circuit, significantly reducing the input impedance of the AC voltage follower from that seen by an input source to the DC voltage follower. It is therefore desirable to make R_{IN} as large as possible, but this is limited by the maximum value for any input bias resistor, as calculated using Equation 7–4. The maximum value for R_{IN} should be determined using Equation 7–4, and the minimum value should be determined for C_{IN} using

(a)

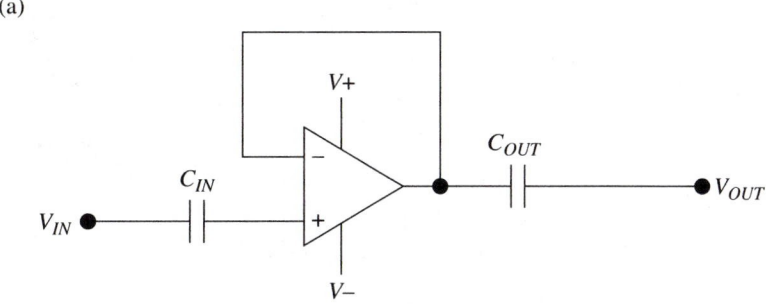

Non-functioning circuit

(b)

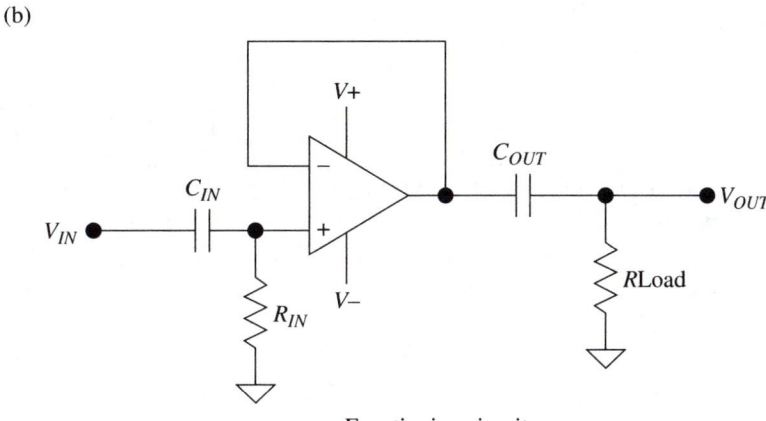

▶ **FIGURE 7–17**
AC Voltage follower

Functioning circuit

Equation 7–8. The input impedance of this circuit can be increased dramatically by using a BIFET op amp, whose bias currents are much lower and can accommodate much larger input resistors, on the order of 1 MΩ. Figure 7–18 shows the AC voltage follower circuit in block diagram form. The output terminal of the op amp also drives a high pass circuit made up of C_{OUT} and R_{LOAD}. The voltage seen across the load resistor can be calculated as follows:

$$V_{LOAD} = V_{OUT} (R_{LOAD}/Z_{LOAD}) \tag{7–10}$$

where Z_{LOAD} = the impedance of C_{OUT} and R_{LOAD}

The voltage across the load is at the –3 dB point when $C_{OUT} = R_{LOAD} C_{OUT}$ can be calculated by equating $X_{COUT} = R_{LOAD}$ at the lowest frequency of the range being amplified.

$X_{COUT} = R_{LOAD}$ at the lowest operating frequency

$$C_{OUT} \doteq 1/(2\pi f_1 R_{LOAD}) \tag{7–11}$$

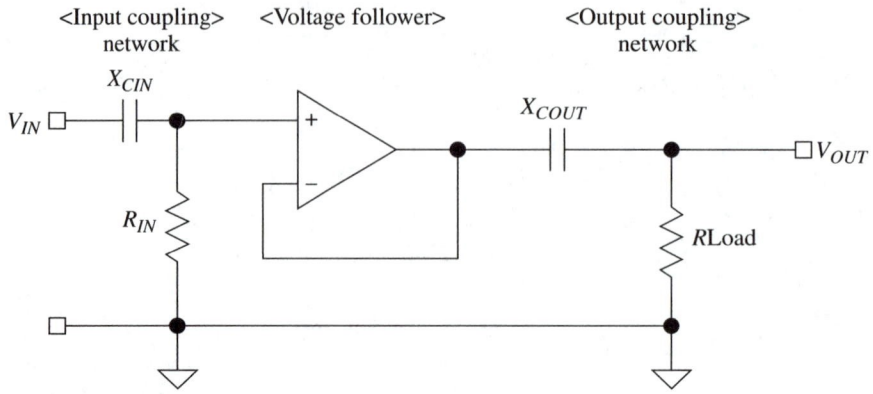

▲ FIGURE 7–18
AC voltage follower block program

Another method for increasing the input resistance of the AC voltage follower is the addition of another capacitor, C_Z, and a resistor, R_Z, to the circuit as shown in Figure 7–19. Capacitor C_Z connects the AC component of the output voltage to the junction between R_{IN} and R_Z. The current flowing through R_Z to ground creates a voltage drop across R_Z that opposes V_{IN} that effectively increases the input impedance. The theoretical input impedance for this circuit is given by the formula:

$$Z_{INPUT} = R_{IN} (1 + A_{OL}) \qquad (7\text{--}12)$$

However, the actual input impedance experienced with the circuit is significantly less than calculated with Equation 7–11, due to the typical stray capacitance that

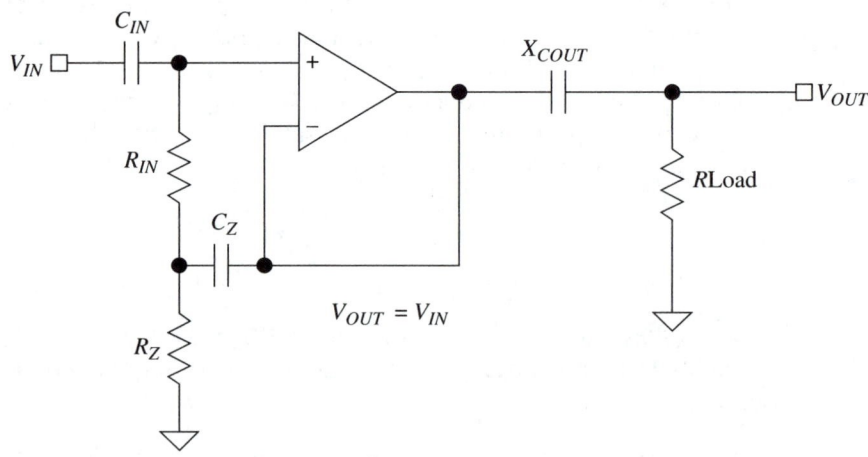

▲ FIGURE 7–19
AC voltage follower with high-input impedance

exists between the op amp terminal and ground. Nevertheless, normal values of stray capacitance will yield input impedances much higher than achieved with the circuit shown in Figure 7–18.

Example 7–1

Calculate all component values for the AC voltage follower circuit shown in Figure 7–17b, which must accommodate a signal with a low-frequency 3-dB cutoff point of 40 Hz. The op amp used in the circuit has a maximum bias current of 500 nA, and the load being driven is 2 kΩ. Also calculate the input impedance of the circuit.

Solution

1. Calculate R_{IN} by determining the largest input resistor value using Equation 7–4.

   $R_{IN\text{-}MAX} = (V_{BE}/10)/I_{BIAS\text{-}MAX} = .07 \text{ V}/500 \text{ nA} = 140,000$
   Use next lowest 1% value of $R_{IN} = 137$ kΩ.

2. The effective input impedance of the circuit is simply the input resistor value $R_{IN} = 137$ kΩ. Calculate C_{IN} using Equation 7.9 with 40 Hz for the lower 3-dB breakpoint and the R_{IN} value just calculated.

   $C_{IN} = 1/(2\pi f_1 .1\ R_{IN}) = 1/(2\pi \times 40 \text{ Hz} \times .1 \times 137 \text{ k}\Omega) = .29 \text{ µF}$
   Use the next largest standard capacitance value, $C_{IN} = .33$ µF.

3. Calculate C_{OUT} using Equation 7–11 with 40 Hz for the lower 3-dB breakpoint and the load resistance value stated.

   $C_{OUT} = 1/(2\pi f_1\ R_{LOAD}) = 1/(2\pi \times 40 \text{ Hz} \times 2 \text{ k}\Omega) = 1.99 \text{ µF}$
   Use the next largest standard capacitance value, $C_{IN} = 2.2$ µF.

Example 7–2

Repeat Example 7–1 for the AC voltage follower circuit with high-input impedance shown in Figure 7–19. The typical open loop gain of the op amp being used is $A_{OL} = 200,000$.

Solution

1. Calculate the largest input resistor value as before using Equation 7–4.

   $R_{IN\text{-}MAX} = (V_{BE}/10)/I_{BIAS\text{-}MAX} = .07 \text{ V}/500 \text{ nA} = 140,000$
   Use next lowest 1% value of $R_{IN\text{-}MAX} = 137$ kΩ.
   Split $R_{IN\text{-}MAX}$ into two equal resistors $R_{IN} = R_Z = 68.1$ kΩ.

2. Calculate C_Z such that $X_{CZ} = R_Z$ at the 40-Hz breakpoint.

$X_{CZ} = 6810 = 1/(2\pi \times 40 \times C_Z)$ $C_Z = 1/(2\pi \times 40 \times 6810) = .584 \, \mu F$

Closest C_Z value $= .56 \, \mu F$

3. Calculate the input impedence of the circuit using Equation 7–12.

$Z_{INPUT} = R_{IN}(1 + A_{OL}) Z_{INPUT} = 68,100 (200001) = 1362 \, M\Omega$

As stated earlier in the section, this is the theoretical value for the input impedance. The actual value will be determined by the amount of stray capacitance in parallel with the op amp inputs. Instead of calculating C_{IN} so that its capacitive reactance is one tenth the calculated Z_{IN}, it is better to use a value for C_{IN} that will be larger than any expected stray capacitance. A good design rule for high-impedance circuits is to use .001 μF.

$C_{IN} = .001 \, \mu F$

4. $C_{OUT} = 2.2 \, \mu F$ as calculated in Example 7–1.

The next step is to turn the AC voltage follower shown in Figure 7–17b into an AC non-inverting amplifier. This can be accomplished with the addition of a feedback resistor, connected from the output to the negative input terminal, as shown in Figure 7–20a. The gain of this is circuit, $A_V = 1 + R_F/R_1$. All other component values can be calculated as in Example 7–1. It is obvious that this circuit suffers from the same low-input impedance, which is effectively equal to the value of R_{IN}, as the voltage follower shown in Figure 7–17b. As before, the input impedance can be increased significantly with the addition of capacitor C_Z and resistor R_Z as shown in Figure 7–20b.

Example 7–3

Calculate all component values for the AC voltage amplifier circuit shown in Figure 7–20b, which must accommodate a signal with a low-frequency 3-dB cutoff point of 60 Hz. The op amp used in the circuit has a maximum bias current of 500 nA, and the load being driven is 1 kΩ. The gain of the circuit should be 20.

Solution
1. Calculate the largest input resistor value as before using Equation 7–4.

$R_{IN\text{-}MAX} = (V_{BE}/10)/I_{BIAS\text{-}MAX} = .07 \, V/500 \, nA = 140,000$

Use the next lowest 1% value of $R_{IN\text{-}MAX} = 137 \, k\Omega$.

$R_{IN\text{-}MAX}$ will be split into two resistors ($R_{IN} + R_Z$) such that their total = 137 kΩ

(a)

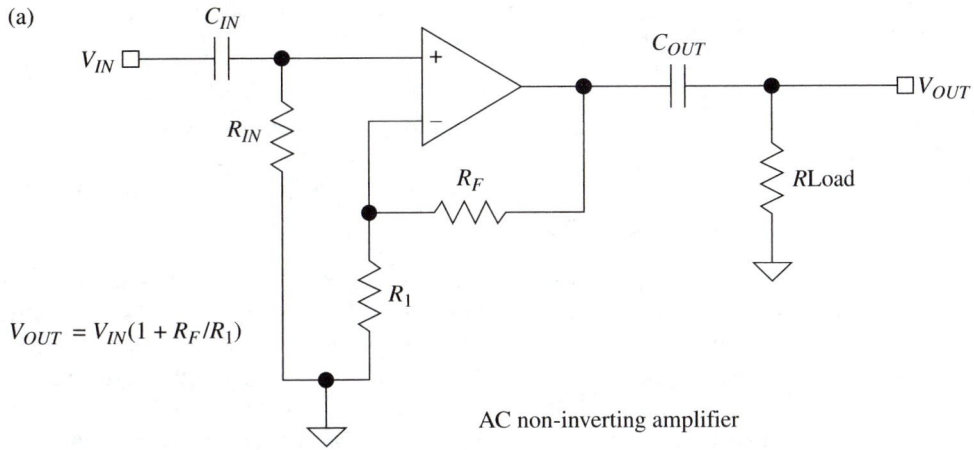

$V_{OUT} = V_{IN}(1 + R_F/R_1)$

AC non-inverting amplifier

(b)

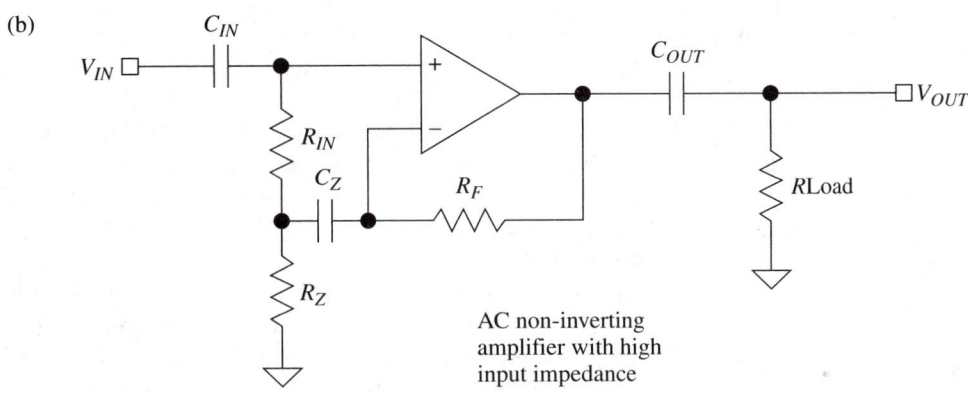

AC non-inverting
amplifier with high
input impedance

▲ FIGURE 7–20
Non-inverting amplifiers

2. Calculate R_Z and R_F to achieve the desired gain of 20.

$A_V = 1 + R_F/R_Z = 20$
$R_F/R_Z = 19$ Let $R_Z = 37.4$ kΩ, then $R_{IN} = 100$ kΩ
$R_F = 710,600$ Ω
Let $R_F = 715$ kΩ, the closest 1% value.

3. Calculate C_Z such that $X_{CZ} = R_Z$ 10 at the 60 Hz breakpoint

$X_{CZ} = 3740 = 1/(2\pi \times 60 \times C_Z)$ $C_Z = 1/(2\pi \times 60 \times 3740) = .709$ μF
Closest C_Z value = .68 μF

4. Using the design rule for high impedance circuits, C_{IN} is selected = .001 μF

5. Calculate C_{OUT} using Equation 7–11 with 60 Hz for the lower 3-dB breakpoint and the load resistance value stated.

$$C_{OUT} = 1/(2\pi f_1 R_{LOAD}) = 1/(2\pi \times 60 \text{ Hz} \times 1 \text{ k}\Omega) = 2.65 \text{ }\mu F$$

Use the next largest standard capacitance value, $C_{IN} = 2.7 \text{ }\mu F$.

AC Inverting Amplifiers

An inverting op amp AC amplifier can be developed from a standard inverting op amp DC amplifier, with the addition of input and output coupling capacitors, as shown in Figure 7–21. As with the non-inverting amplifier, the input coupling capacitor C_{IN} stops the flow of DC bias current through R_{IN}; however, bias current does flow through the feedback resistor R_F. Because the output of this circuit is capacitively coupled to the output, there is no bias current compensation resistor placed between the plus terminal and circuit common. However, if bias current compensation is required, the value of the compensating resistor should be equal to just the feedback resistor R_F, not the parallel combination of R_F and R_{IN} as the case with the DC amplifier. This is because there is no bias current flowing through R_{IN} because of the coupling capacitor.

The value of capacitor C_{IN} is calculated such that its capacitive reactance is one-tenth the value of resistor R_{IN} at the low cutoff frequency. C_{OUT} is calculated so that its capacitive reactance is equal to the load resistance at the low cutoff frequency. The gain of this amplifier equals $-R_F/R_{IN}$.

In situations where an amplifier must process a limited range of frequencies, the low cutoff frequency is determined by the coupling capacitors that a high pass circuit comprises. An AC op amp circuit can create a low pass circuit that will limit the high frequency of operation to something less than the highest frequency the op amp can handle. This is accomplished by adding a feedback capacitor in parallel with the feedback resistor, as shown in Figure 7–22. The upper frequency is set by the capacitive reactance of C_F, relative to R_F, at the desired frequency. The capacitive reactance X_{CF} should equal the value of R_F at the desired upper cutoff frequency. The same approach can be used to limit the frequency of operation of the AC non-inverting amplifier.

▶ **FIGURE 7–21**
Inverting op amp AC amplifier

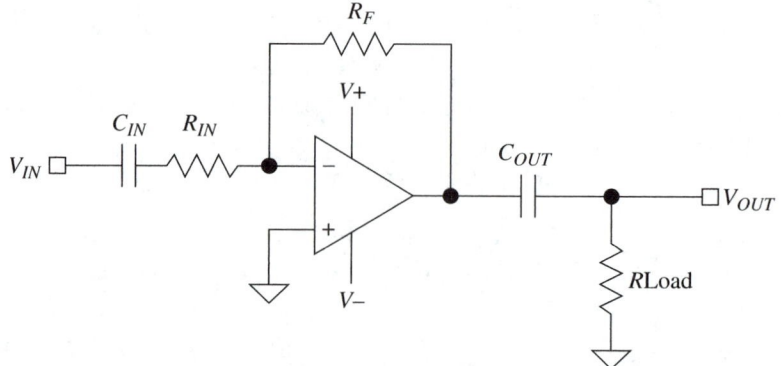

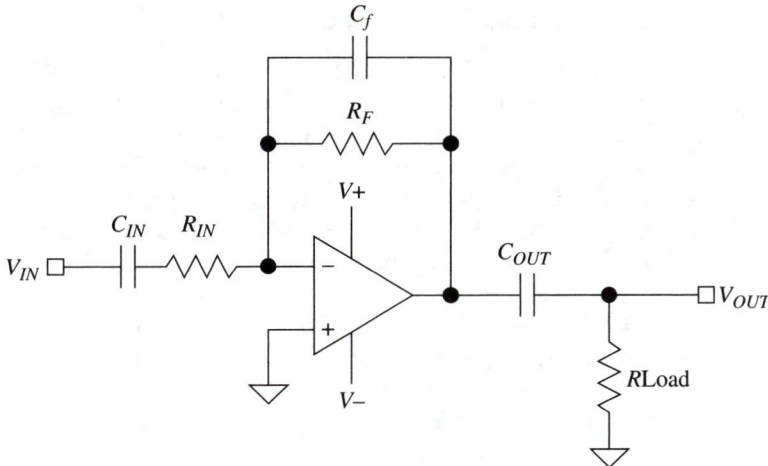

► **FIGURE 7–22**
AC inverting amplifier with
high-frequency limit

Example 7–4

Design an AC inverting amplifier circuit with a gain of –20 that will have an operating frequency range from 40 Hz to 15 kHz and will drive a load resistance of 60 Ω.

Solution

1. The circuit solution for this problem is the one shown in Figure 7–22. All of the resistor and capacitor values must be selected.

2. Determine the value of R_F and R_{IN}. R_F/R_{IN} = 20. Let R_F = 100 KΩ, and then R_{IN} = 5 kΩ.

3. Calculate C_{IN} and C_{OUT} to support the low cutoff frequency of 40 Hz.

   X_{CIN} = .1 × R_{IN} at the low cutoff frequency of 40 Hz

   X_{CIN} = .1 × 5000 Ω = 500 Ω

   C_{IN} = 1/(2π × 40 Hz × 500) = 7.96 μF

   Use the next largest standard value, C_{IN} = 8.2 μF

   X_{COUT} = R_{LOAD} at the low cutoff frequency of 40 Hz = 60 Ω

   C_{OUT} = 1/(2π × 40 Hz × 60) = 66.3 μF

   Use the next largest standard value so C_{OUT} = 68 μF.

4. Calculate C_F so that the circuit will support frequencies up to the upper cutoff frequency of 15 kHz.

   X_{CF} = R_F at the high cutoff frequency of 15 kHz = 100 kΩ

   C_F = 1/(2π × 15 kHz × 100 kΩ) = 106 pF

   Use the closest standard value so C_F = 100 pF.

Single-supply AC Op Amp Circuits

Many AC amplifier circuits are designed to operate off of a single power supply. This is because capacitive coupling eliminates concern about offset voltage errors, plus the fact that the actual value of the amplitude is usually not important, as the output signal should look like the input signal only larger. In Section 7–2, the operation of DC amplifiers with a single supply was discussed, as well as the need to create a circuit common reference in lieu of a ground. The single-supply AC amplifier creates some interesting circuit variations when considering bias current and the creation of a circuit common reference.

The circuit shown in Figure 7–23a shows a low impedance AC voltage follower circuit powered by a single power supply. The bias current flows from the positive supply through R_1 into the positive op amp input. The current flowing through R_2 to circuit common should be on the order of 100 times larger than the

▶ **FIGURE 7–23**
Z_{IN} single-supply AC voltage follower

(a)

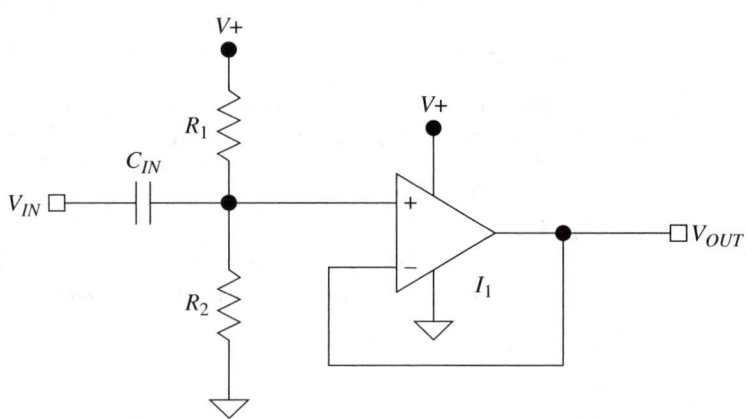

(b)

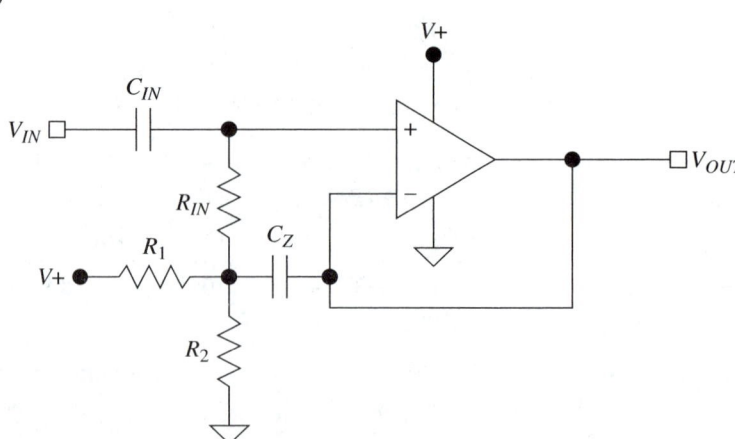

bias current in order to establish a common reference point that is exactly between $+V$ and circuit common. The input impedance of this circuit equals R_1 in parallel with R_2. Therefore, the value of C_{IN} should be one-tenth the value of R_1 in parallel with R_2 at the lower cutoff frequency of operation.

The corresponding single-supply high input impedance AC voltage follower circuit is shown in Figure 7–23b. This circuit is identical to that of Figure 7–19, except for the addition of the positive supply connection through R_I to the junction of R_{IN} and R_Z. In this case, $R_1 = R_Z = R_{IN} = R$ where $2R = .07/I_{BMAX}$. Capacitor C_Z should equal one-tenth the value of the resistance in series with it (R_1/R_Z) at the lower cutoff frequency.

Single-supply AC Non-inverting Amplifier

Figure 7–24 shows an AC non-inverting amplifier operated from a single voltage supply. It is identical to the circuit shown in Figure 7–20a, except for the addition of capacitor C_1 and resistor R_B. Resistors R_B and R_{IN} are equal and create a common reference equidistant between $V+$ and circuit common. A bias current also flows into the plus terminal from $V+$ through R_B. The current flowing through R_{IN} should be 100 times the input bias current flowing into the plus input. The input impedance of this circuit equals R_B in parallel with R_{IN}. Therefore, the value of C_{IN} should be one-tenth the value of R_B in parallel with R_{IN} at the lower cutoff frequency of operation.

A unique situation occurs with this amplifier that is different from DC amplifiers and the AC voltage follower discussed thus far. The DC common reference generated by the voltage divider formed by R_B and R_{IN} equals $V+/2$. This voltage will be amplified, and with even low values of amplifier gain, the amplifier output will

▶ **FIGURE 7–24**

Single-supply non-inverting amplifier

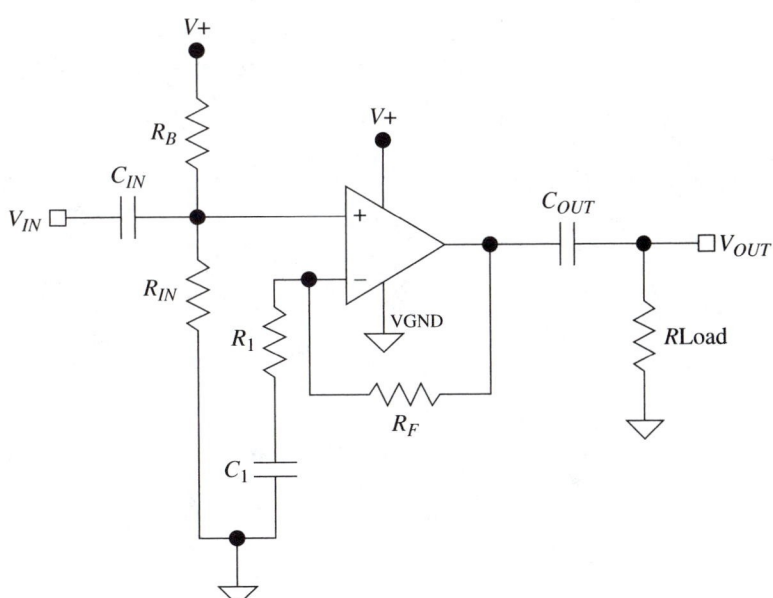

be driven into saturation. Capacitor C_1 causes the circuit to act like a voltage follower for DC voltages and a normal non-inverting amplifier for AC signals. Therefore, the DC output will equal the DC input, while the AC output will result in the AC input amplified by a gain that equals $1 + R_F/R_1$. The value of C_1 is selected so that its capacitive reactance is equal to one-tenth the value of R_1 at the low cutoff frequency.

Single-supply Non-inverting Amplifier with High-input Impedance

Figure 7–25 shows a high input impedance added to the single-supply non-inverting amplifier that is similar to the voltage follower circuit shown in Figure 7–23b, with the addition of resistor R_F that adds gain to the circuit. As with the voltage follower, $R_1 = R_Z = R_{IN} = R$ where $2R = .07/I_{BMAX}$. Capacitor C_Z should equal one-tenth the value of the resistance in series with its AC path to ground ($R_1//R_Z$) at the lower cutoff frequency. The gain of this circuit is also modified such that the gain to an AC signal equals $1 + R_F/(R_1//R_Z)$.

Example 7–5

Let's repeat Example 7–3 for single-supply operation by calculating all component values for the high input impedance AC voltage amplifier circuit shown in Figure 7–25. The desired low-frequency 3-dB cutoff point is 60 Hz. The op amp used in the circuit has a maximum bias current of 500 nA and the load being driven is 1 kΩ. The gain of the circuit should be 20.

Solution

1. Calculate the largest input resistor value as before using Equation 7–4.

   $R_{IN\text{-}MAX} = (V_{BE}/10)/\,I_{BIAS\text{-}MAX} = .07\ \text{V}/500\ \text{nA} = 140{,}000\ \Omega$

   $R_{IN\text{-}MAX}$ will be split into two resistors ($R_{IN} + R_Z$) such that their total = 137 kΩ

▶ **FIGURE 7–25**
Non-inverting amplifier with single supply

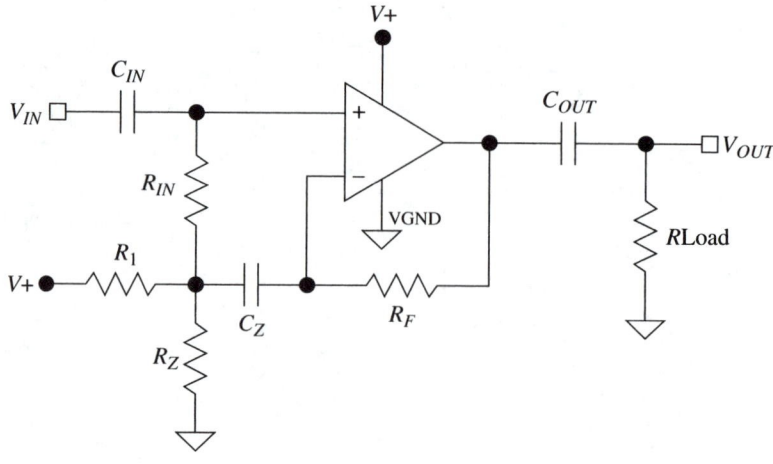

Let $R_{IN} = R_Z = R_1 = 68.7$ kΩ.

2. Calculate R_F that will achieve the desired gain of 20.

$A_V = 1 + R_F/(R_1/R_Z) = 20$
$R_F/(R_I//R_Z) = 19$
$R_F = 652,650$ Ω
Let $R_F = 649$ KΩ the closest 1% value.

3. Calculate C_Z such that $X_{CZ} = (R_I//R_Z)/10$ at the 60 Hz breakpoint

$X_{CZ} = 3435 = 1/(2\pi \times 60 \times C_Z)$ $C_Z = 1/(2\pi \times 60 \times 3435) = .772$ μF
Closest C_Z value = .82 μF

4. Using the design rule for high impedance circuits, C_{IN} is selected = .001 μF.

5. Calculate C_{OUT} as before using Equation 7–11, with 60 Hz for the lower 3-dB breakpoint and the load resistance value stated.

$C_{OUT} = 1/(2\pi f_1 R_{LOAD} = 1/(2\pi \times 60$ Hz $\times 1$ kΩ) $= 2.65$ μF
Use the next largest standard capacitance value, $C_{IN} = 2.7$ μF.

Single-supply Inverting Amplifier

In order to operate an inverting amplifier from a single supply, a circuit common reference is connected to the positive input terminal as shown in Figure 7–26. The component value calculations involve selecting R_1 and R_2 such that the current flowing through R_2 is 100 times the maximum op amp bias current. R_1 must equal R_2 to create V+/2 at the positive op amp terminal. The gain of the circuit is $-R_F/R_{IN}$, and C_{IN} should be selected such that its capacitive reactance is one-tenth the value of R_{IN} at the low-frequency cutoff point.

▶ **FIGURE 7–26**
Single-supply inverting AC
amplifier

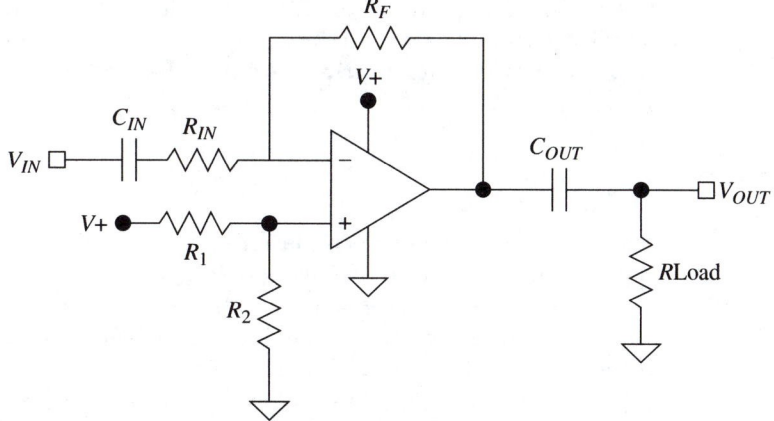

This section has discussed the design and operation of a variety of AC op amp circuits, including voltage followers and non-inverting and inverting amplifiers. Methods were provided to determine proper bias current and the calculation of component values to ensure circuit function over the specified frequency ranges. We discovered that in order to provide a bias current to the AC voltage follower, its input impedance is reduced significantly. The improved voltage follower with high input impedance resolved this shortcoming. The details relating to single power supply operation of AC op amps were also explored. All of these circuits and concepts will be applied to specific AC amplifier applications in the following sections.

7–4 ▶ Audio Amplifiers

Audio amplifiers must amplify signals in the audio frequency range, 20–20 kHz at either the pre-amp (less than 50 mW), medium (50 mW to 500 mW), or power amp (greater than 500 mW) level. As it is with most AC amplifiers, the actual amplitude of the amplified audio signal is usually not as critical as with DC amplifiers. Therefore, design considerations, such as offset voltage and offset voltage drift, are less significant. The goal of the audio amplifier is to provide an output signal that is the duplicate of the input signal except at a higher level.

An ideal audio amplifier will output a perfect duplicate of the input signal, over the entire frequency range of the signal, at the specified higher power level. The input to a practical audio amplifier will include a small noise signal and the amplifier itself will add in some small noise signals, along with the amplifier's power supply, that will also induce unwanted noise signals. The gain of the practical audio amp will vary with the frequency of the input signal. Therefore some frequencies will be amplified more than others.

The rate at which the output signal can change is important when the amplifier must duplicate an isolated fast changing signal. This is called the *slew rate*, and it is an important parameter for any AC amplifier. Stability is also an issue with a practical audio amplifier. It is desirable to eliminate the possibility of positive feedback in phase with the input of the amplifier that will send the amplifier into oscillation. It all comes down to gain, noise, frequency response, and stability. These are the areas where the performance of the audio amplifier is determined, measured either by an array of calibrated test equipment or a discriminating human ear.

Pre-amplifiers

Pre-amplifiers are a class of amplifiers that are designed to take a very small signal and amplify it to a level usually less than 50 mW. Because the pre-amp must work with such small signal levels, the primary design concern is to minimize distortion and provide a flat frequency response. Consequently, high power gain and efficiency are secondary concerns. The types of inputs that are possible for an audio pre-amplifier include a microphone, an instrument pickup, a magnetic tape

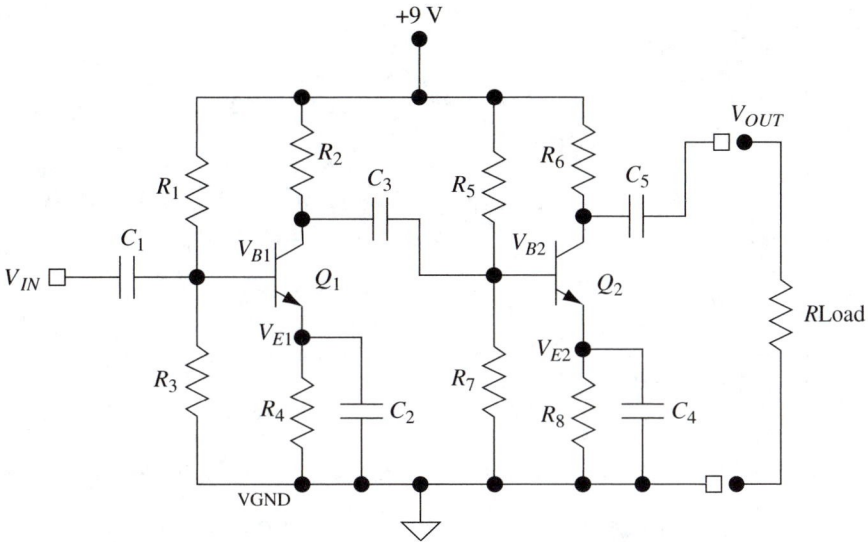

▲ **FIGURE 7–27**
Two-stage BJT audio pre-amp

playback head, a record cartridge and the audio output signal from a frequency selector-demodulator circuit that receives radio signals from an antenna. The gain required of pre-amps handling these many different types of inputs can range from 10 to 10,000, assuming input signal peak-to-peak amplitudes ranging from 100 µV to 100 mV and output signal requirements of 1 to 2 V at low current levels.

    Using current technology, there are three possible ways to develop an audio pre-amplifier: complete a design using discrete transistors, develop a circuit that uses standard low-noise op amps, or utilize special purpose ICs designed to function as audio pre-amps. Let's begin our design discussion with an example of a typical two-stage bipolar junction transistor amplifier shown in Figure 7–27.

Example 7–6

This design problem is to complete a discrete transistor voltage pre-amplifier that will amplify AC signals with peak-to-peak amplitudes as small as 100 µV and frequencies over the audio range of 100 to 20,000 Hz. The peak-to-peak output of the amplifier should be around 1.25 V. DC power is to be supplied by a 9-V battery.

Solution

Since the overall gain of this pre-amplifier is on the order of 12,500, this design will be accomplished in two stages using a voltage divider biased common emitter pre-amplifier, shown in Figure 7–27. The transistors in the design will have β_{DC} = β_{AC} = 150.

    Stage one of the amplifier will have a gain of roughly 62.5 times the gain of stage two, which will approximate 200 (62.5 × 200 = 12500). The AC gain of each stage is equal to the effective collector resistance of the stage divided by the AC emitter resistance $r'e$ $A_V = R_C/r'e$ where $r'e = 25$ mV/I_B for the particular stage.

Stage two design calculations: If I_{E2} is selected to be 1 ma, then the desired $r'e = 25$ Ω and $R_{C2} = A_V \times r'e = 200 \times 25$ Ω $= 5000$ Ω. R_{c2} for stage two is resistor R_6. Since the closest standard 5% resistor value is 5100 let $R_6 = 5100$ Ω.

R_5 is selected to be 10 times the value of R_6 or 51 kΩ. Let R_7 be approximately 20% of R_6. Therefore $R_7 = 10$ k Ω. The DC base voltage V_{B2} for stage two = $(R_7/R_7 + R_5)$ V_{CC}, if R_7 is less than $.1 \times \beta_{DC} \times R_E$. Substituting:

$V_{B2} = (10$ kΩ/10 kΩ + kΩ$)$ 9 V = 1.48 V
$V_{E2} = V_B - V_{BE} = 1.48$ V $-.7$ V $= .78$ V
$I_{E2} = V_{E2}/R_E$ If I_{E2} is desired to be 1 ma, then
$R_E = .78$ V/1 ma $= 780$ Ω
The closest 5% standard resistor value is $R_E = 750$ Ω.

The design for stage two is complete with the following values:

$R_3 = 51$ kΩ, $R_6 = 5.1$ kΩ, $R_7 = 10$ kΩ and $R_8 = 750$ Ω
The actual DC emitter current $I_{E2} = 1.03$ mA.
$r'e = 25$ mV/$I_{E2} = 24.2$ Ω
The actual AC gain for stage two = $R_6/r'e = 5100/24.2 = 210.7$.
This is slightly higher than the design goal of 200.

Stage one design calculations: Since the overall gain for the pre-amp should be 12,500, the new design goal for stage one should equal the overall gain divided by the actual gain of stage two, which is 12,500/210.7 or 59.32.

The emitter current for stage one, I_{E1}, is selected to be 1 ma, which makes stage one's design goal for $r'e = 25$ Ω, which is the same value used for stage two.

$A_{V1} = R_{C1}/r'e$, therefore $R_{C1} = A_{V1} \times r'e = 59.2 \times 25 = 1480$ Ω

However, the effective collector resistor for stage one, R_{C1}, is the parallel combination of the collector resistor R_2 and resistors R_5 and R_7 and the input base resistance of stage two (which $= r'e \times \beta_{AC}$). To achieve the gain of 59.2 the effective R_{C1} must equal 1480 Ωs. Therefore:

$1480 = R_2//R_5//R_7//(R_8 \times \beta_{AC}) = R_2//51$ kΩ//10 kΩ//(24.2×150)
$1480 = R_2//51$ kΩ//10 kΩ//(24.2×150)
$1480 = R_2//2531$ $R_2 = 3900$ Ω is the closest standard value.
For $R_2 = 3900$ Ω the effective $R_{C1} = 1535$ Ω.
Select $R_1 = 51$ kΩ, $R_3 = 10$ kΩ, and $R_4 = 750$ Ω

The design for stage one is complete with the following values:

$R_1 = 51$ kΩ, $R_2 = 3.9$ kΩ, $R_3 = 10$ kΩ, and $R_4 = 750$ Ω
The actual DC emitter current $I_{E1} = 1.03$ ma.
$r'e = 25$ mV/$I_{E1} = 24.2$ Ω
The actual AC gain for stage one = $R_{C1}/r'e = 1535/24.2 = 63.4$.
This is slightly higher than the design goal of 59.2.

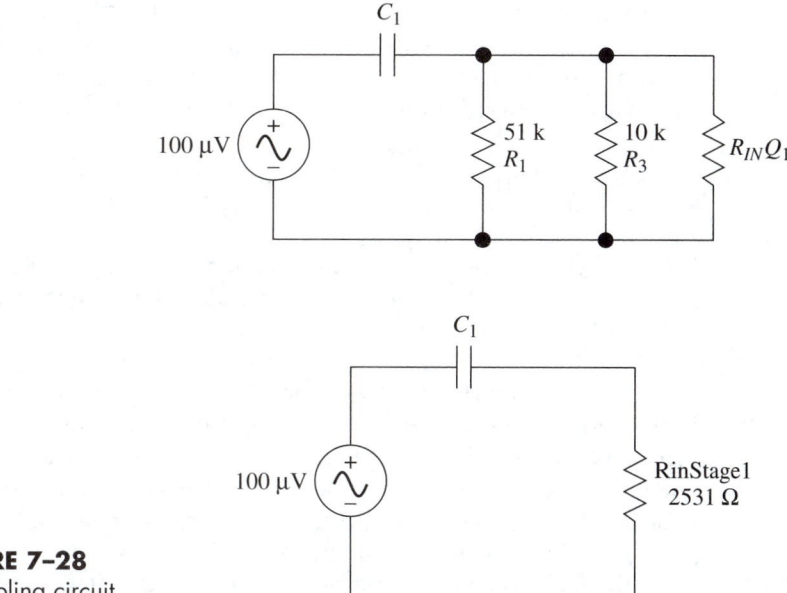

▶ **FIGURE 7–28**
Input coupling circuit

Coupling capacitor calculations: Capacitors C_1, C_5 and C_5 are coupling capacitors that remove any DC component voltage from the AC signal. C_1 and C_3 are input coupling capacitors while C_5 couples the amplifier output to the connected load. The optimum capacitance value for coupling capacitors depends upon the frequency range of the AC signal and the resistance in series with the capacitance. The target value often used is to make the capacitive reactance, X_C, of the coupling capacitor, calculated at the lowest frequency of the AC signal, equal to one-tenth of the resistance in series with the coupling capacitor.

Figure 7–28 shows the effective circuit for the input to stage one. The total input resistance of stage one equals the parallel combination of R_1, R_3, and R_{INQ1}.

$R_{INSTAGE1} = R_1 // R_3 // R_{INQ1} = 51 \text{ k}\Omega // 10 \text{ k}\Omega // 3630 \ \Omega = 2531 \ \Omega$
X_{C1} (at the lowest frequency) $= .1 \times R_{INSTAGE1}$
X_{C1} (at 100 Hz) $< .1 \times 2531 < 253 \ \Omega$
X_{C1} (at 100 Hz) $= 1/(2\pi f C_1) = 1/(2\pi \times 100 \times C_1) = 253 \ \Omega$
Solving for $C_1 > 6.3 \ \mu F$

The input resistance seen by the AC signal going into stage two is essentially the same as the values used for stage one, so the optimum value for $C_2 = C_1$. Since there is no load specified for the amplifier, the value for C_5 will be made equal to C_2 and C_1.

C_5, C_2, and C_1 are all selected to be 10 μF.

Next, the capacitance values for the bypass capacitors C_2 and C_4 must be calculated. The function of the bypass capacitors is to allow the AC signal to bypass collector resistors R_4 and R_8, allowing these resistors to function in their DC bias role of stabilizing the circuit from changes in the transistor beta values. The only consideration in determining the value of the bypass capacitor is the value of the emitter resistor. The capacitive reactance of the bypass capacitor should be less than the one-tenth the value of the emitter resistance.

X_{C2} (at 100 Hz) $< .1 \times R_4 < .1 \times 750 < 75$ Ω
X_{C2} (at 100 Hz) $= 1/2\pi f C_2 = 1/2\pi \times 100 \times C_2 = 75$ Ω
Solving for $C_2 > 21.2$ µF
C_4 bypasses the same value resistance so its value should equal that of C_2.
C_2 and C_4 are selected to be 22 µF. All of the values of the discrete transistor audio pre-amp have been determined.

A significant deficiency of the discrete BJT amplifier is the low value of the input impedance that requires the input coupling capacitance to be fairly large. This is partially a result of the high gain included in the amplifier that requires a smaller emitter resistor. This low emitter resistance translates into a small transistor base input resistance. A much higher input resistance can be obtained with a lower gain BJT amplifier or by using discrete FET transistors.

Example 7–6 shows the process for designing discrete transistor amplifiers as well as the expected performance and limitations. Pre-amplifier design is often accomplished today utilizing low noise op amps or op amps that are customized to perform as IC audio amplifiers.

Op Amp Audio Preamp

An equivalent audio pre-amp can be developed with op amps using the discussion of AC op amp circuits presented in Section 7–3. This particular design uses two op amps to accomplish a net gain of 12,500.

Example 7–7

This design problem is to complete an op amp voltage pre-amplifier utilizing an LM318 op amp that will amplify AC signals with peak-to-peak amplitudes as small as 100 µV and frequencies over the audio range of 20 to 20,000 Hz. The peak-to-peak output of the amplifier should be around 1.25 V. DC power is to be supplied by a single 12-V supply. It is desirable that the input impedance of the amplifier should be at least 1 MΩ and the load being driven has a resistance of 2 kΩ.

Solution

This design uses two op amps connected as shown in Figure 7–29. The first op amp, IC_1, is configured as a non-inverting amplifier with a gain of 50, configured such that it offers a very high input impedance to the audio input. Consequently, this circuit can accept audio inputs with very high source impedances. C_1 is the input coupling capacitor and R_1 supplies bias current to the non-inverting input. R_3 and R_2 serve as a voltage divider to generate a 6-V reference to allow operation

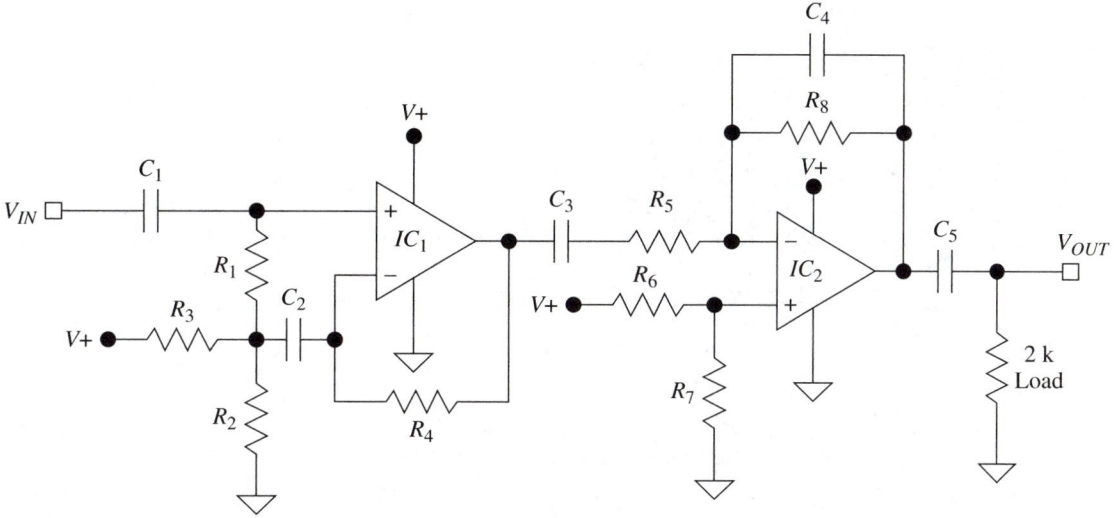

▲ FIGURE 7–29
Op amp audio pre-amp

from a single 12-V supply. IC_2 is an inverting amplifier with a gain of 250, whose input is coupled to the output of IC_1 by coupling capacitor C_3. Resistors R_6 and R_7 form a 6-V reference for C_2 and C_5 is a coupling capacitor for the audio output.

Component Calculations

1. IC_1 is a non-inverting amplifier with a gain of 50 that drives an inverting amplifier with a gain of 250. The net gain of the circuit is 12,500.

2. The maximum bias current for the LM318 op amp is 250 nA.

   $R_{IN\text{-}MAX} = (V_{BE}/10)/ I_{BIAS\text{-}MAX} = .07$ V/250 nA $= 280,000\ \Omega$

   $R_{IN\text{-}MAX}$ will be split into two resistors $(R_1 + R_2)$ such that their total $= 280$ kΩ

   Let $R_1 = R_2 = R_3 = 140$ kΩ

3. Calculate the value of coupling capacitor C_1.

   $X_{C1} = .1 \times R_1$ at 20 Hz

   $C_1 = 1/(2\pi \times 20\ \text{Hz} \times 14\ \text{k}\Omega)$

   $C_1 = .56\ \mu\text{F}$

4. Calculate the value of capacitor C_2.

   $X_{C2} = .1\ (R_3/R_2)$ at 20 Hz

   $C_2 = 1/(2\pi \times 20\ \text{Hz} \times 7\ \text{k}\Omega)$

   $C_2 = 1.14\ \mu\text{F}$ use the closest standard value $= 1.2\ \mu\text{F}$

5. Calculating R_4 to yield a gain of 50 for IC_1.

Gain $= 1 + R_4/(R_2//R_3) = 50$

$R_4/(70 \text{ k}\Omega) = 49$

$R_4 = 3.43 \text{ M}\Omega$ use the closest standard value $= 3.44 \text{ M}\Omega$

6. Calculate the values for the voltage divider resistors R_6 and R_7. The current passing through R_7 should be greater than 100 times the bias current flowing into the positive op amp terminal. The maximum bias current for the LM318 is 250 nA.

$R_7 = V_{R7}/I_7 = 6 \text{ V}/25 \text{ μA} = 240 \text{ K}\Omega$

$R_6 = R_7 = 240 \text{ k}\Omega$

7. Calculate the values of R_5 and R_8 to achieve a gain of 250.

Gain $= 250 = R_8/R_5$

Let $R_8 = 1 \text{ M}\Omega$, therefore $R_5 = 4000 \text{ }\Omega$.

Use closest 1% standard value, $R_5 = 4.02 \text{ k}\Omega$.

8. Calculate the value of coupling capacitor C_3.

$X_{C3} = .1 \times R_5$ at 20 Hz

$C_3 = 1/(2\pi \times 20 \text{ Hz} \times 4.02 \text{ k}\Omega) = 1.98 \text{ μF}$

Use next highest standard value, $C_3 = 2.2 \text{ μF}$.

9. Calculate C_4 to provide a high-frequency cutoff of 20,000 Hz.

$X_{C4} = R_8$ at 20,000 Hz

$C_4 = 1/(2\pi \times 20{,}000 \text{ Hz} \times 1 \text{ M}\Omega) = 7.95 \text{ pF}$

Use the next lowest standard value of $C_4 = 6.8 \text{ pF}$.

10. Calculate C_5 to meet the low-frequency cutoff of 20 Hz.

$X_{C5} = R_{LOAD}$ at 20 Hz

$C_4 = 1/(2\pi \times 20 \text{ Hz} \times 2 \text{ k}\Omega) = 3.98 \text{ μF}$

Use the closest standard value of $C_5 = 3.9 \text{ μF}$.

IC Audio Amplifiers

There are a wide variety of IC audio amplifiers that comprise op amps enhanced for performance in audio applications. These ICs occupy the medium power level between pre-amps and power amps. They can drive speakers directly at power levels around .5 watts. The LM386 is an example of this class of IC. It is called a low voltage audio power amplifier. It is designed for single-supply operation over the voltage range of 4–18 V. The gain is set internally to 20, but with the addition of a

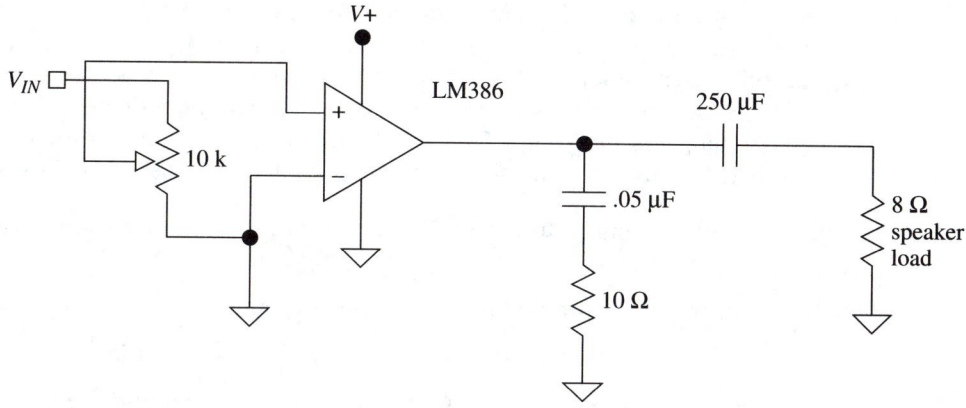

▲ **FIGURE 7–30**
LM386 audio amplifier

resistor and capacitor the gain can be varied between 20 and 200. Figure 7–30 shows the LM386 as an audio amplifier with a gain of 20. Note that to change the gain to 200, a 10 μF capacitor is connected between pin 1 and pin 8. Connecting a resistor in series with the 10 μF modifies the gain between 20 and 200 depending on the resistor value. The distortion rating of this amplifier is .2%.

The LM833 is a dual-audio amplifier with significantly improved distortion levels, about .002%, and a high slew rate, typically 7 V/μs. It functions more as a traditional pre-amp, capable of higher gains and is not intended to drive a speaker directly. Figure 7–31 shows one half of the LM833 connected as a tape deck pre-amp.

▶ **FIGURE 7–31**
LM833 dual audio
amplifier

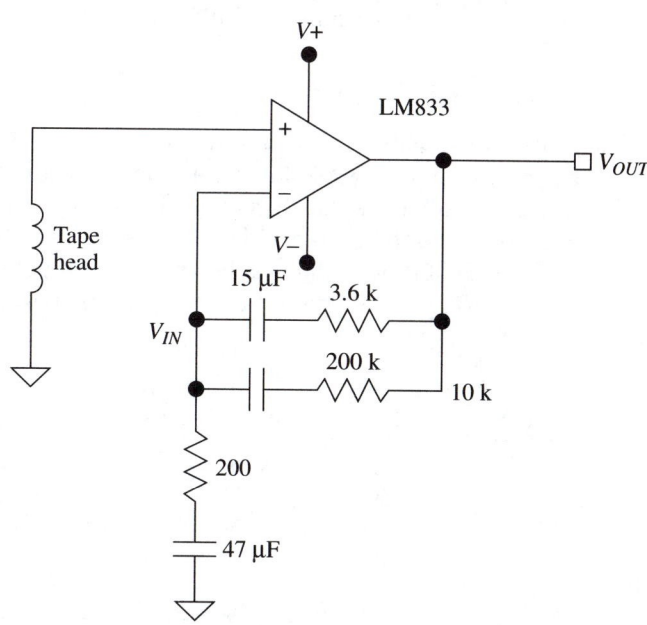

As audio amplifiers are included with personal computers and for operation with other digital circuits, there is pressure for them to improve their performance in these environments. The ability to operate from a noisy 5-V digital supply or low-voltage battery supplies, and an increased emphasis on efficiency and slew rate, are performance issues that relate specifically to desktop and laptop computer applications. Following are the amplifier performance parameters that are affected most:

Power Supply Rejection Ratio: The ability of the amplifier to reject the noise inherent on digital power supply lines

Power Efficiency: Improved efficiency at the .5-watt level

Slew rate: Improved slew rate at low voltage operation

Power Supply Voltage: Operation from low-amplitude, single-voltage power supplies

Output Voltage Swing: Because of the low voltage operation, the audio amp must be capable of driving the output very close to the positive supply value and ground. These are called *"rail-to-rail"* amplifiers and can drive the output to within approximately 55 mV of the positive or negative supply.

The MAX4490 audio op amp exemplifies this type of amplifier. It features operation from a single supply over a voltage range of 2.7 to 5.5 V. The PSRR is typically 100 dB, slew rate equals 10 V/μs, and the output voltage can swing to within 55 mV of either side of the power supply. The MAX4490 is available in a small five-pin surface mount package as shown in Figure 7–32.

The MAX4298 is called a *stereo driver* and it too features a high PSRR and can drive speakers directly to within 55 mV of either supply side. It also features a low noise level of .008%. Figure 7–33 shows the MAX4298 used as a typical headphone stereo driver in a computer application.

Audio Power Amplifiers

Audio power amplifiers have been in use for more than 60 years. Surprisingly, there are relatively few books available that describe the art as well as the science of power amplifier design. Most electronics courses discuss the basic classes of power amplifiers and their typical bias circuits, yet few courses or textbooks deal with the intricacies of their design. In this section we will only scratch the surface but will attempt to take the student a few steps further into this interesting and developing technology.

▶ **FIGURE 7–32**

MAX4490 audio op amp

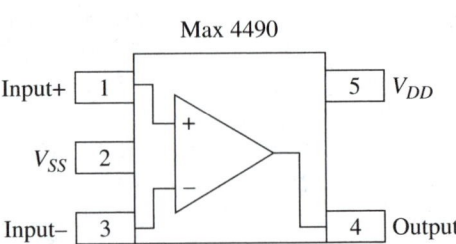

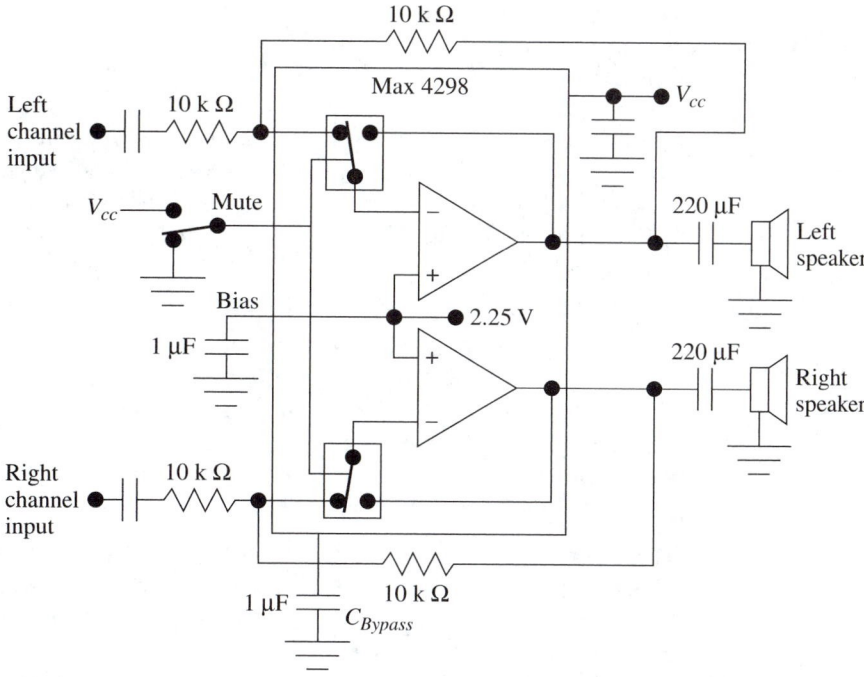

▲ FIGURE 7–33
MAX4298 stereodriver

Audio amplifier designs have progressed through vacuum tubes, bipolar junction and field effect transistors, and most recently the development of custom IC audio power amplifiers. During this process a number of facts as well as myths have been dispersed and widely accepted regarding the design, testing, and analysis of audio power amplifiers. At the center of the controversy is the belief by some that the human ear is such a complex device that it is impossible to qualify audio performance with measured parameters. The degree of disagreement has led to two schools of thought within the audio community: the audio scientists that believe in verified technical measurements as the way to determine audio performance, and subjectivists that accept only certain measured results combined with the sound as it is heard by the human ear.

The limit to which the human ear can detect audio differences is an important part in developing the criteria for amplifier performance. Following is a list of widely accepted limitations of the human ear:

1. Changes in amplitude can generally be detected as small as .5 to 1 dB. For a single frequency, level changes of .3 dB can be detected.

2. The ear is most sensitive to frequency changes in the range of 500 Hz to 2 kHz. Frequency changes can be detected for changes at least .2% in magnitude.

3. The smallest detectable THD level is approximately .2%.

Audio power amplifiers are classified by categories that characterize a particular design philosophy. Following are the various amplifier classes and their general definitions:

Class A: In Class A the transistors are biased in the middle of the load line; therefore, current is flowing at all times through the output connection. When biased in this fashion, the non-linearities associated with turning the transistor on and off are not experienced. Because current is always flowing to the output, these types of amplifiers are usually power inefficient.

Class B: Class B amplifiers use two transistors that are biased at the transistor's cutoff point. The transistors are said to be in a push-pull arrangement, where one transistor is controlling current flow in one half of the AC cycle, and the other transistor controls current flow in the second half of the cycle. Because the transistors are biased at the cutoff point, no current flows when the signal is 0.

This promotes the much-improved power efficiency experienced with Class B operation. However, Class B operation does suffer from something called *crossover distortion*, which is caused by the slightly different bias point achieved for the two transistors. This causes slight distortion when control of the signal is being passed from one transistor to the other.

Class AB: These are essentially Class B amplifiers that have a bias point that is above the transistor's cutoff point. This makes the amplifier operate somewhat like a Class A amplifier with two transistors connected in a Class B amplifier's push-pull configuration, which is the basis for the "AB" classification. This type of operation considerably reduces crossover distortion at the cost or decreased power efficiency.

Class C: The Class C amplifier locates the bias point below the cutoff region for the transistor, which means the transistor conducts less than half of the AC cycle. The Class C amplifier is used in radio signal amplification and is not really suited for audio applications.

Class D: The Class D amplifier is a pulse-width-modulating (PWM) type of amplifier. In other words, it switches a voltage on and off at a high frequency. The average value of the duty cycle (the on time vs. the off time) equals the amplitude of the amplified signal. The benefit of this approach is similar to switching power supplies where efficiency is improved significantly. However, as was also the case with switching power supplies, the PWM process is inherently noisy.

Class G: This is an innovative technique that attempts to improve amplifier efficiency by increasing the power supply voltages in steps as the signal amplitude is increased. This strategy utilizes the fact that less energy is wasted when the power supply voltage is closer to the signal level. Transistor circuits are used to sense and switch in typically three levels of increasing voltage supply. These amplifiers do offer increased power efficiency without significant increases in distortion at a cost of the added circuitry needed to perform the power supply sensing and switching.

Class H: This class of amplifier operates as a Class B amplifier with the added ability to boost, or not boost, the power supply voltage. The goal again is to improve efficiency. This is somewhat similar to the technique that was just described for Class G operation; however, in this case the power supply is simply increased instead of using the Class G approach, in which a different power supply is switched into operation.

Class S: Class S amplifiers are basically Class A amplifiers with a reduced output current drive capability. The Class A amplifier section of the Class S amplifier is backed up by a Class B amplifier section that makes a low resistive load appear to be higher than the minimum load the Class A amplifier section can drive.

Aside from the amplifier classes just discussed, there is also the question of whether an audio amplifier should be AC or DC coupled. AC-coupled amplifiers operate off of a single voltage supply, and with a 0 signal input the output is midway between the power supply rail and ground. A coupling capacitor is used to remove the DC component from the signal provided to the output. DC-coupled amplifiers use equal plus and minus power supplies that bias the input voltage at 0 V, eliminating the need for a coupling capacitor.

AC-coupled amplifiers offer the advantage of single-supply operation. They always provide a 0 DC offset voltage and do not require protection against DC output faults. Also, AC-coupled amplifiers seldom need inductors to provide stability. DC-coupled amplifiers require two power supplies but eliminate the need for large output coupling capacitors. The output coupling capacitors are expensive and they also contribute to distortion levels. By keeping the loads connected to the DC-coupled amplifier's plus and minus power supply voltages balanced, the power supply currents in the ground circuit will be essentially zero. This further reduces the amount of distortion and crosstalk that are inherent in AC coupled amplifiers, because the ground currents include power supply current flow combined with signal current flow.

Audio power amplifiers can be designed using discrete components or custom IC amplifiers. IC amplifiers offer a quick and easier approach but there are some issues that allow discrete amplifiers to still offer a higher performance solution. In IC amplifiers linear resistors are difficult to fabricate, and compensation capacitors are made as small as possible to conserve space and minimize costs. Also, many design techniques are based upon IC fabrication processes instead of focusing directly on amplifier performance. Whether to use IC audio amps or a discrete design will be dictated by the requirements for amplifier performance stated in the design specifications.

A typical audio power amplifier, IC or discrete, consists of three basic functional blocks: the input section, voltage amplifier, and output driver (see Figure 7–34). The input section is a differential type that takes the input signal and subtracts a portion of the output signal fed back to the negative input. The input section is usually a differential transconductance amplifier that takes the voltage difference between the

▶ **FIGURE 7–34**
Audio amplifier functional
block program

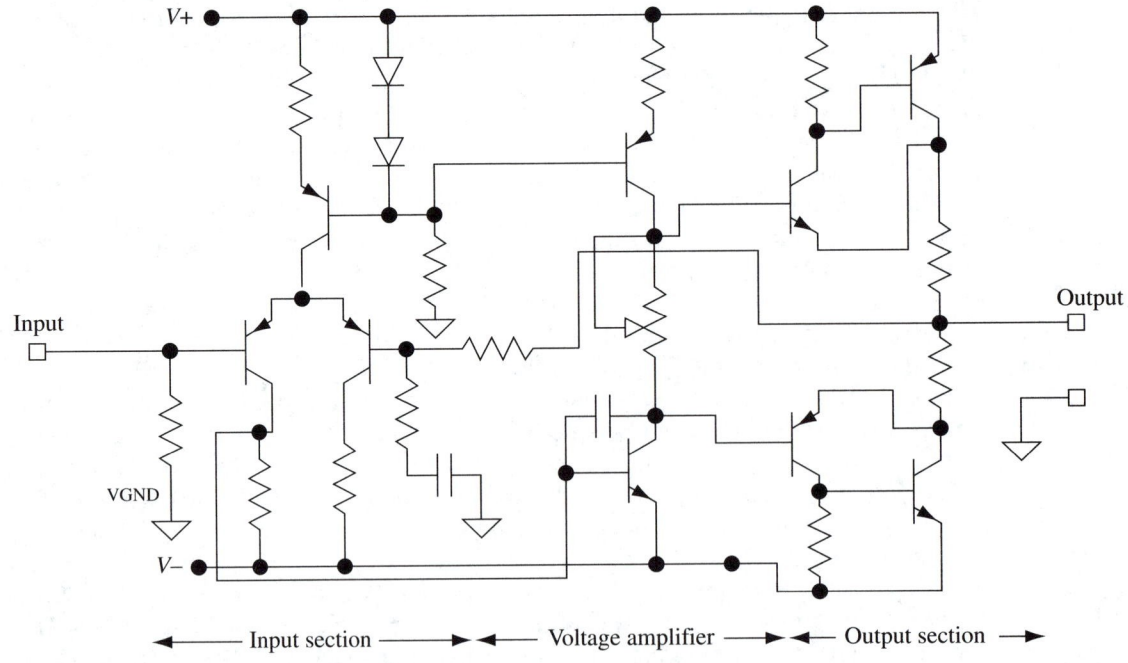

input and the feedback signals and generates a current output. The voltage amplifier
accepts the current signal from the input section and amplifies it to create a voltage
output. This is called a *trans-resistance amplifier.* The output stage takes the amplified voltage signal from the voltage amplifier and supplies the capability to drive a
low impedance load such as an 8- or 16-Ω speaker. Usually the output stage does not
provide any further signal amplification but simply provides the proper voltage and
current level to drive the load. A typical discrete audio power amplifier schematic including all three functional circuits is shown in Figure 7–35.

   The LM1877 is a dual audio power amplifier available on a single IC. The maximum power output of this IC is low, just 2 watts per channel, but it exemplifies this
type of IC power amplifier. This IC is designed to require the minimum number of
external components. It includes internal compensation for all gains greater than
ten and can be operated over a wide range of single or dual power supply voltages.
Figure 7–36 shows examples of both single and dual power supply operation as a
stereo power amplifier.

▲ **FIGURE 7–35**
Discrete audio amplifier schematic

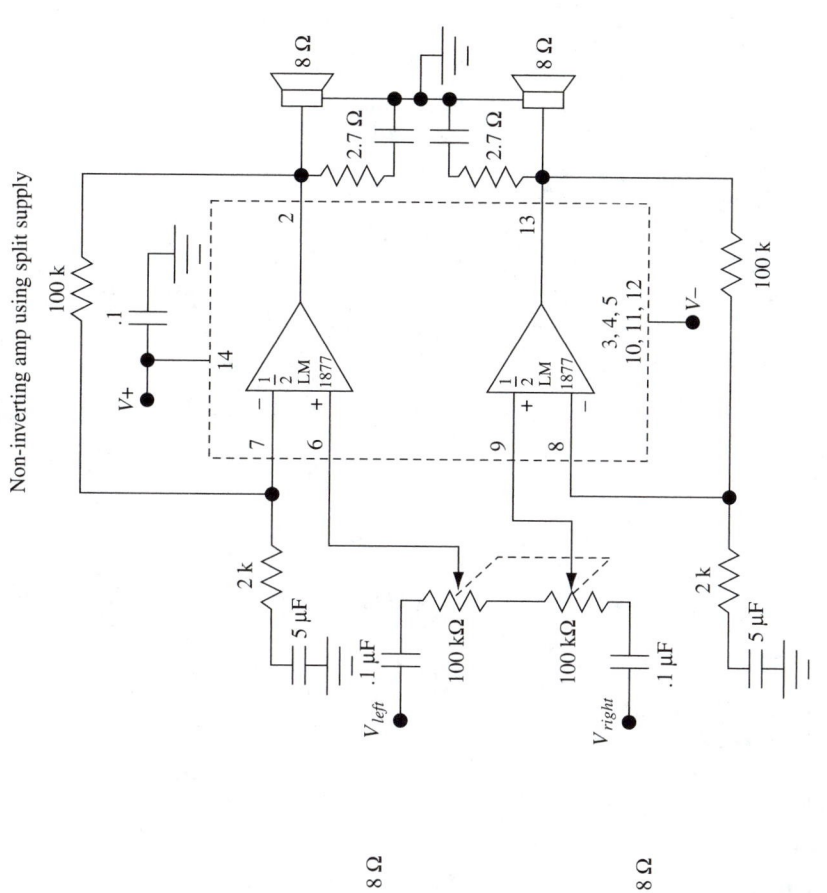

Non-inverting amp using split supply

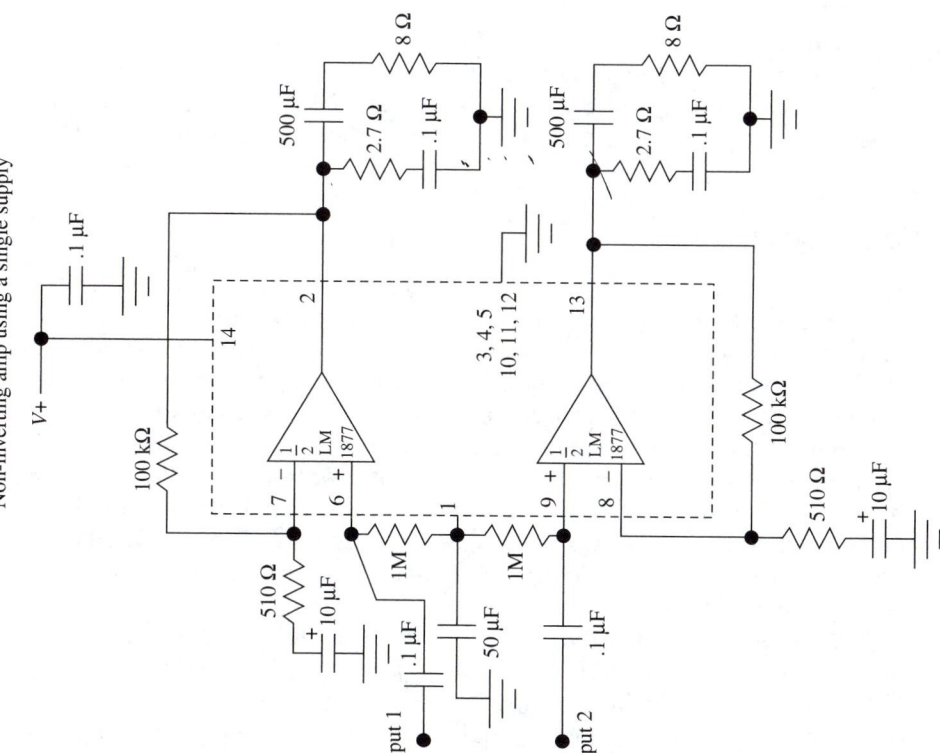

Non-inverting amp using a single supply

▲ **FIGURE 7–36**

LM1877 dual audio power amplifier

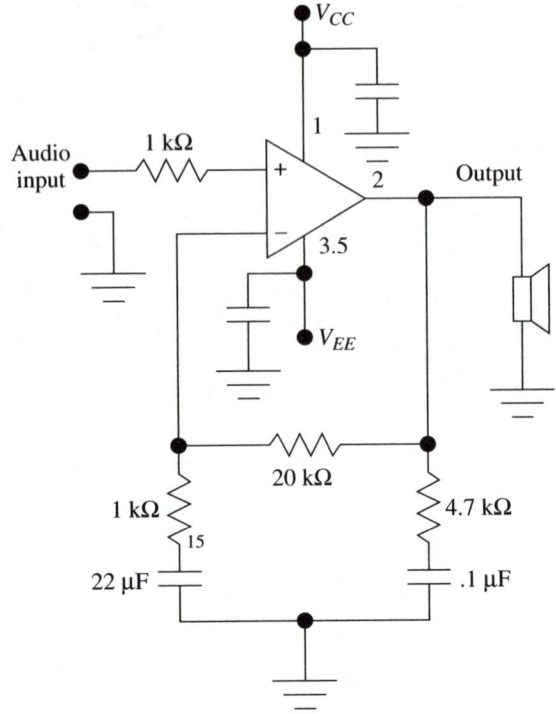

▶ **FIGURE 7–37**
LM4700 audio power amplifier
example

The LM4700 is a single audio power amplifier capable of outputting 30 watts of power into an 8-Ω load with .1% distortion levels. The LM4700 offers a wide range of power supply options ranging from 20 to 66 V either as single or dual supplies. Figure 7–37 shows a typical power amplifier circuit using the LM4700.

7–5 ▶ Video Amplifiers

Video or wideband amplifiers are similar to audio amplifiers except that they must operate over a wider frequency range. The frequency requirements for transmitting video information can range from about 20 Hz up to 6 MHz and greater for other specialized applications. Specific television applications require a narrower operating bandwidth in the range from 4 to 6 MHz. Obviously, the operating frequency requirement for video amplifiers is much more demanding than those seen in audio applications and is why these types of amplifiers are often called *wideband amplifiers.*In order to meet this requirement, the gain level of video amplifiers must be reduced dramatically to provide a wider bandwidth of operation. Also, much effort must be made to consider the inherent capacitance of the transistor as well as source and load impedances.

The coupling and emitter bypass capacitors limit the lower frequency of an amplifier's operating bandwidth. These capacitors will be effective AC shorts at high frequencies and will have no effect on high-frequency operation so they will be ignored in this high-frequency analysis. It is the internal transistor capacitance

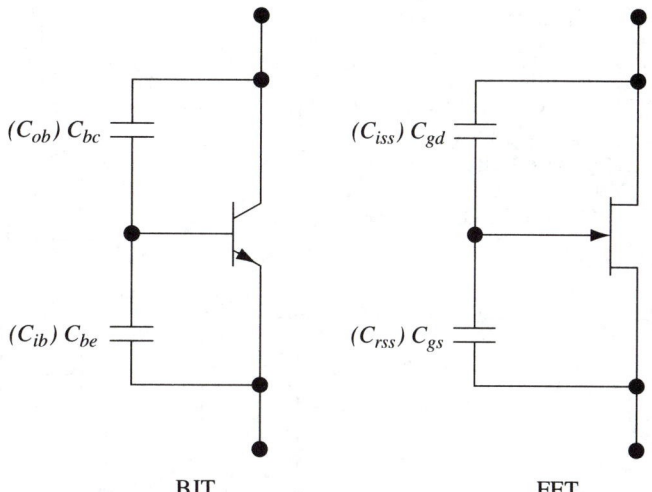

▶ FIGURE 7–38

Transistor capacitance   BJT   FET

that serves to limit high-frequency operation and is of prime concern to video amplifiers. These include the base-to-collector (C_{bc}) and base-to-emitter capacitance (C_{be}) for BJT's and the gate-to-drain (C_{gd}) and gate-to-source (C_{gs}) capacitance for FETs. Data sheets for BJTs often refer to C_{bc} as the output capacitance C_{ob} and to C_{be} as the input capacitance. FET data sheets list the input capacitance as C_{iss} and the reverse transfer capacitance as C_{rss}, from which C_{gd} and C_{gs} can be calculated (see Figure 7–38).

The base-to-collector capacitance is the most difficult to analyze. However, from Miller's Theorem we know that transistor capacitance from the base to the collector (gate to the drain for an FET) can be effectively reflected on the input side of the transistor as well as the output side, while the base-to-collector capacitance (gate to the source for an FET) is only seen on the input side. The amount of base-to-collector (gate-to-drain) capacitance reflected to the input and output side depends on the amplifier gain A_V and is defined by the following Miller's Theorem equations:

$$C_{IN} = C_{bc}\,(A_V + 1) \text{ or } C_{IN} = C_{gd}\,(A_V + 1) \tag{7–13}$$

$$C_{out} = C_{bc}\,(A_V + 1)/A_V\;C_{out} = C_{gd}\,(A_V + 1)/\text{Av} \tag{7–14}$$

Thus C_{IN} is the most significant capacitance value as it results from the base-to-collector (gate-to-drain) capacitance multiplied by the amplifier gain plus 1. The net effect of transistor capacitance can be seen in the AC-equivalent schematic for a common emitter amplifier as shown in Figure 7–39. The impact of this circuit on the operating bandwidth is the generation of two high-frequency break points. The most significant break point is the one resulting from the input side of the circuit.

Looking at just the input side of the circuit we have the equivalent circuit shown in Figure 7–40. The critical frequency for this circuit can be determined by equating the capacitive reactance equal to the total resistance in parallel with it. Therefore:

R_s = Source resistance
R_1 and R_2 are voltage divider bias resistors
rb' = transistor base spreading resistance
$C_{in} = C_{bc}$ reflected at the input
$C_{out} = C_{bc}$ reflected at the output
R_c = Collector resistance
CLoad = Load capacitance
RLoad = Load resistance

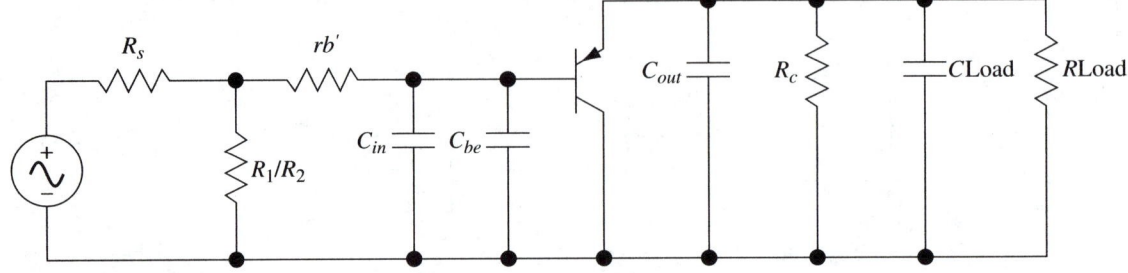

▲ **FIGURE 7-39**
High-frequency AC-equivalent common emitter amplifier

$$X_{CFI} = ((R_S//R_1//R_2) + rb') // \beta_{AC}\, re' \tag{7-15}$$

$$f_1 = 1/(2\pi C_{F1}\, (((R_S//R_1//R_2)+ rb') // \beta_{AC}\, re')) \tag{7-16}$$

where re' is the equivalent emitter resistance = 25 mV'I_E

The design problem for the video amplifier is to make the input circuit critical frequency equal to the highest operating frequency in the bandwidth of operation. To promote this, the following design considerations should be made for discrete transistor video amplifier designs:

1. Minimize the value of re' by making the emitter current as large as possible. This is accomplished by making the collector and load resistances as small as possible.

2. Minimize the net load capacitance.

3. Minimize the source resistance value R_S.

▶ **FIGURE 7-40**
High-frequency AC equivalent
input circuit

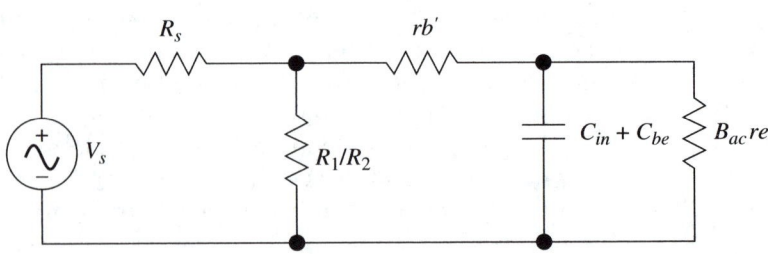

4. Select a high-frequency transistor with the following characteristics: low C_{bc} value, low C_{be} value and low rb' value.

5. Use negative feedback to reduce gain and widen the bandwidth.

A discrete video amplifier can be designed in stages using these design considerations at each stage.

The CLC410 is a specific IC video amplifier. It possesses the wide band required for video applications operating at low gain levels from ±1 to ±8. The CLC410 is available in an 8-pin DIP or surface-mount packages and can be treated as an operational amplifier with inverting, non-inverting output $V+$, $V-$, and offset connections. There is an additional input called a *quick disable* that allows the signal flow to be curtailed within 200 ns of the disable line becoming low. Figure 7–41 shows the recommended non-inverting circuit.

The CLC5602 is a dual video amplifier on one IC that can drive an output with current levels up to 130 mA. The CLC5602 can operate off of single or dual supplies as low as +5 V or ±5 V. The slew rate is 300 V/µs and it is available in an 8-pin DIP or surface-mount package. Figure 7–42 shows the CLC5602 being used as an AC-coupled non-inverting video amplifier operated from a single supply.

▶ **FIGURE 7–41**
CLC410 video non-inverting amplifier example

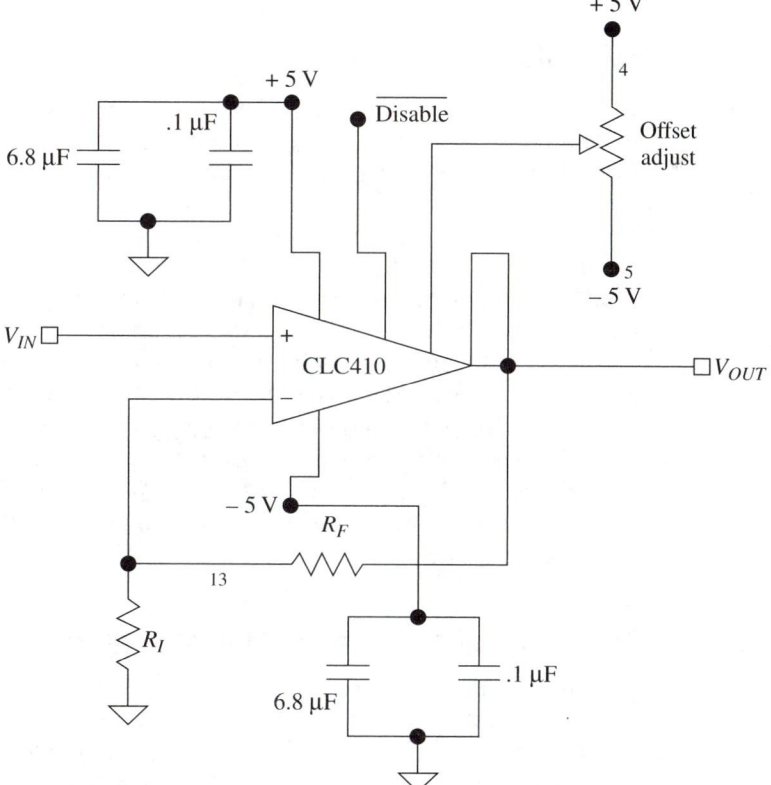

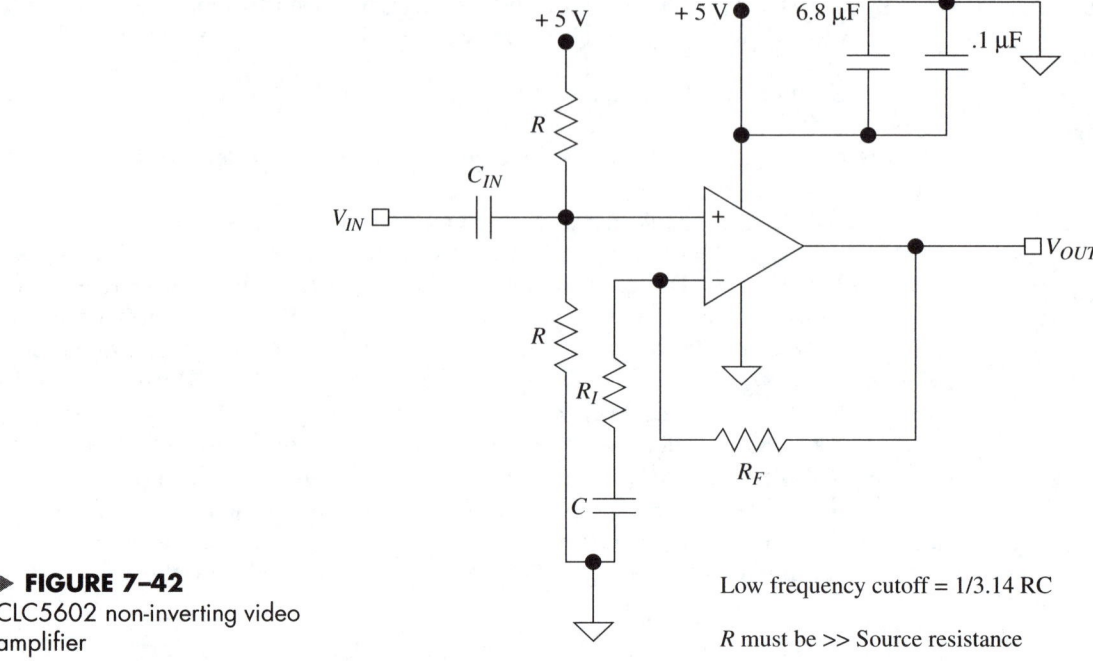

▶ FIGURE 7–42
CLC5602 non-inverting video amplifier

Low frequency cutoff = 1/3.14 RC

R must be >> Source resistance

7–6 ▶ RF Amplifiers

RF amplifiers are increasingly applied in products and systems that involve telecommunications, global positioning systems, and wireless communications. Amplifiers designed for these applications utilize strategies developed for radio frequency (RF) and microwave (MW) circuits. It is important to realize that as transmitting signal frequencies increase, so does the information-carrying capacity of these circuit. This is easiest to see from the digital perspective. Let's say that one bit of information is transmitted for every low to high transition, and we compare the number of bits per second that can be transmitted at 1 MHz versus 1 GHz. At 1 GHz, 1000 times as much information can be transmitted in the same amount of time as a 1-MHz signal. This section will describe only the very basic elements of these strategies, as a more thorough coverage is well beyond the scope of this text. This topic requires a thorough re-discussion of many circuit elements due to the different ways that they react at these frequencies. Figure 7–43 shows the IEEE frequency spectrum. This section covers amplifiers that are designed to function generally at 1 GHz and above.

Passive Component Changes at High Frequencies

Conductors are typically viewed as simply a zero resistance, capacitance, and inductance at low-frequency operation. Actually, we know that conductors do have some resistance to all current flow and also some level of self-inductance for AC current flow. At high frequencies conductors experience significant increases in

Frequency Band	Frequency	Wavelength
ELF (Extreme Low Frequency)	30–300 Hz	10,000–1000 km
VF (Voice Frequency)	300–3000 Hz	1000–100 km
VLF (Very Low Frequency)	3–30 kHz	100–10 km
LF (Low Frequency)	30–300 kHz	10–1 km
MF (Medium Frequency)	300–3000 kHz	1–0.1 km
HF (High Frequency)	3–30 MHz	100–10 m
VHF (Very High Frequency)	30–300 MHz	10–1 m
UHF (Ultra High Frequency)	300–3000 MHz	100–10 cm
SHF (Super High Frequency)	3–30 GHz	10–1 cm
EHF (Extreme High Frequency)	30–300 GHz	1–0.1 cm
Decimillimeter	300–3000 GHz	1–0.1 mm
P Band	0.23–1 GHz	130–30 cm
L Band	1–2 GHz	30–15 cm
S Band	2–4 GHz	15–7.5 cm
C Band	4–8 GHz	7.5–3.75 cm
X Band	8–12.5 GHz	3.75–2.4 cm
Ku Band	12.5–18 GHz	2.4–1.67 cm
K Band	18–26.5 GHz	1.67–1.13 cm
Ka Band	26.5–40 GHz	1.13–0.75 cm
Millimeter wave	40–300 GHz	7.5–1 mm
Submillimeter wave	300–3000 GHz	1–0.1 mm

▶ **FIGURE 7–43**
IEEE Frequency Spectrum

their resistance and inductance due to what is called the *skin effect* and a larger value of self-inductance. The skin effect is a phenomenon that describes the tendency for current to flow in the outer diameter of the wire as the frequency of the current flow increases. Because less and less current flows in the center region of the conductor, the resistance of the conductor increases with the frequency of the current flow. Also, the self-inductance that is always present when AC current flows through a wire is more pronounced at higher frequencies.

Circuits are also affected at high frequencies by the presence of stray capacitance that results from the existing capacitance between two conductors, two components, or between any conductor or component and ground. Stray inductance is also experienced by the parasitic inductance of conductors and components.

Resistors functioning in high-frequency circuits exhibit all three of the passive electrical impedance characteristics shown in Figure 7–44. The resistance is larger than the nominal resistance due to the skin effect, and the lead inductance and parasitic capacitance also are factors. Of course, the magnitude of each parameter value differs for resistors fabricated with different technologies—i.e., carbon composition, wire wound, and metal film. Carbon composition resistors experience a larger capacitance than other resistor types. Intuitively, wire wound

▶ **FIGURE 7–44**
Equivalent high-frequency resistor

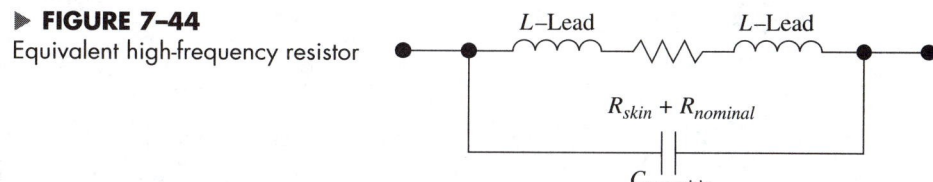

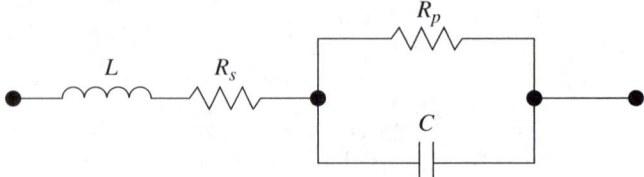

▶ **FIGURE 7–45**
Equivalent high-frequency capacitor

resistors have a higher lead inductance. Thin film chip resistors offer the lowest values of inductance and capacitance. This results in a net decrease in resistance for all resistor types because the parasitic capacitance becomes the predominant factor.

The frequency effect of capacitors was discussed in Chapter 4; however, the high-frequency aspect was not discussed in detail. In this case the lead inductance becomes significant and at some point overtakes the capacitance at the resonant frequency. After this point, the capacitor begins to function like an RL circuit instead of the intended RC function (see Figure 7–45).

The equivalent high-frequency inductor is shown in Figure 7–46. As with the capacitor, there exists a resonant frequency after which the inductor begins to act more like a capacitor instead of the intended resistance to changing current.

It is easy to see that a simple RLC circuit becomes a complicated connection of resistive, capacitive, and inductive elements when analyzed at high frequencies.

Active Component Selection at High Frequencies

The typical pn semiconductor diode is not capable of operation in the RF region. Schottky diodes are a type of diode that can switch much faster than standard diodes and thus are capable of operation at high frequencies. Another style of diode that can operate in the RF region is the PIN diode, which is characterized by an intrinsic semiconductor layer that resides between the p and the n material. The PIN diode is used in RF applications for high-frequency switches and variable resistors. The inherent capacitance that exists between the pn junction is used to fabricate capacitors from diodes. These are called *varactor diodes* and are used in RF circuits as capacitors. Another very fast diode device, called the *tunnel diode*, has extremely high doping levels of the p and n materials that promote fast switching speeds.

Special BJT transistors are capable of operation at RF frequencies. These are called simply *RF transistors* and they feature very low base-to-collector and base-to-emitter capacitance. FET transistors require special changes to promote oper-

▶ **FIGURE 7–46**
Equivalent high-frequency indicator

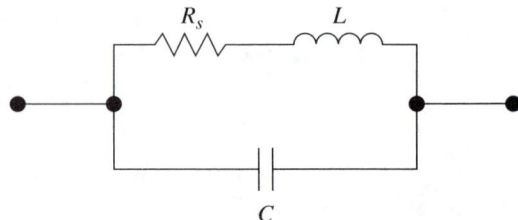

ation at high frequencies because of their inherent gate-to-source and gate-to-drain capacitance. Some of these special high-frequency FETs are called *Metal Insulator Semiconductor FET (MISFET)* and *Metal Semiconductor FET (MESFET)*.

RF Amplifier Design

The design of RF amplifiers is more complex than any other type of amplifier design because, as we have seen already, even a component as basic as a conductor now must be represented as a complex circuit element. A block diagram for an RF amplifier is shown in Figure 7–47.

The signal that is generated by the RF source is input through the input matching circuit because the impedance of the RF source must be matched to the input impedance of the amplifier. This is done to maximize power transfer and minimize signal reflections. After the signal is amplified, the output impedance of the amplifier must be matched to the load impedance again to maximize power transfer and minimize reflections.

The performance of the RF amplifier is characterized by the following parameters:

1. Power output and input

2. Efficiency

3. Operating frequency and bandwidth

4. Gain level over the operating bandwidth

5. Noise levels

6. Input and output power reflections

The design of RF amplifiers involves the development of a particular class of amplifier (A, B, AB, etc.), using a discrete transistor as completed for other transistor amplifiers. However, in this case the complex input impedance of the transistor amplifier is compared to the impedance of the RF source. Then an input matching circuit is developed. This process is repeated on the output side of the circuit.

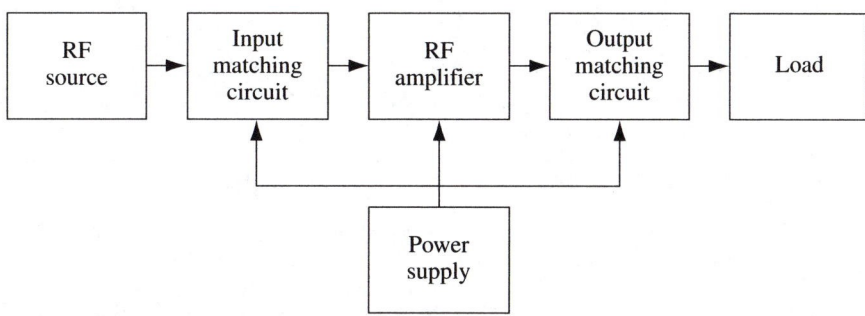

▲ **FIGURE 7–47**
RF amplifier block diagram

▶ **Summary**

This concludes our discussion of amplifier design. The range of amplifier types reviewed in this chapter uncovers many different design criteria—from DC amplifiers, where DC offset and gain accuracy are most important, to RF amplifiers, where impedance matching and minimizing reflections are the most critical. Each amplifier application has its very own agenda, yet there are many aspects of amplifier design that are common to all. The applications for amplifiers range from industrial instrumentation, audio appliances, television, video networks, and telecommunications. The range of operating frequency most often drives the primary difference between the design criteria. Amplifier design concepts will continue development as new technology and applications pushes the frequency, performance, size, and efficiency requirements to even higher levels.

▶ **References**

Bell, D. A. 1990. *Operational Amplifiers: Applications, Troubleshooting and Design.* Upper Saddle River, NJ: Prentice Hall.

Floyd, T. L. 1999. *Electronic Devices.* Upper Saddle River, NJ: Prentice Hall.

Ludwig, R., and Bretchko, P. 2000. *RF Circuit Design: Theory and Applications.* Upper Saddle River, NJ: Prentice Hall.

Malvino, A. P. 1999. *Electronic Principles.* Westerville, OH: Glencoe/McGraw Hill.

Radmanesh, M. M. 2001. *Radio Frequency and Microwave Electronics.* Upper Saddle River, NJ: Prentice Hall.

Self, D. 2000. *Audio Amplifier Design Handbook.* Woburn, MA: Newnes.

Soclof, S. 1991. *Design and Applications of Analog-Integrated Circuits.* Upper Saddle River, NJ: Prentice Hall.

▶ **Exercises**

7–1 Explain the concept of "slew rate" and how it applies to amplifier design. Why is it an important amplifier design consideration? How can the slew rate for an amplifier be determined experimentally?

7–2 What is the relationship between an amplifier's closed loop gain and its bandwidth? In other words, if the closed loop gain of an amplifier increases, what happens to its bandwidth?

7–3 Explain the difference between single-ended and differential amplifiers.

7–4 In your own words, define the term *common mode rejection ratio (CMRR)*. What type of amplifier does it most apply to?

7–5 Design an inverting DC amplifier circuit that will have a gain of –25 and an input impedance of approximately 100 kΩ. Specify the compensating resistor value as well as the feedback and input resistor values.

7–6　Design a non-inverting amplifier that will have a gain of +21. Show all resistor values.

7–7　A voltage follower circuit provides an output that equals the input. What function is provided by a such a circuit?

7–8　Why is it often necessary to have both + and –power supply voltages to power op amp circuits?

7–9　When designing DC amplifiers, why is it important to keep the input bias currents close to the same value?

7–10　Which two op amp characteristics limit their performance as the signal frequency increases?

7–11　Explain the benefits that an instrumentation amplifier offers over a standard differential amplifier.

7–12　Design an AC non-inverting amplifier with high input impedance and powered by a dual supply. See the circuit shown in Figure 7–20b. Calculate all component values that will accommodate a low frequency cutoff point of 40 Hz. The op amp being used has a maximum bias current of 500 nA. The gain of the circuit should be +25 and the load being driven is 1200 Ω.

7–13　Design an AC inverting amplifier with a gain of –30 powered by a dual supply. The operating frequency range is 60 Hz to 18 kHz. The amplifier must drive a load impedance of 32 Ω.

7–14　Design an AC non-inverting amplifier operated from a single power supply. See the circuit shown in Figure 7–25. Calculate all component values that will accommodate a low frequency cutoff point of 40 Hz. The op amp being used has a maximum bias current of 500 nA. The gain of the circuit should be +25 and the load being driven is 1200 Ω.

7–15　Explain the difference between Class A and B amplifiers. List at least one positive and one negative aspect of each.

7–16　Explain the concept of the Class AB amplifier. How does it resolve the negative aspects of both the Class A and B amplifiers?

7–17　What is the basis for disagreement between audio scientists and audio subjectivists, regarding the performance of audio amplifiers?

7–18　List the key design considerations when designing a discrete transistor video amplifier.

7–19　Which parameters most characterize the performance of RF amplifiers?

7–20　Why is RF amplifier design much more complicated than other types of amplifier design?

8 ▶ Oscillators and Function Generators

▶ ## Introduction

There are two basic types of oscillators: relaxation and positive feedback oscillators. Relaxation oscillators are a class of oscillators that use the charge and discharge capacitors to induce the switching of circuit elements to create certain ongoing waveforms. The amplifier circuits discussed in Chapter 7 all use the concept of negative feedback to maintain a constant gain and provide good frequency response. Positive feedback results when an amplifier output signal is sensed at its input in phase with the original input signal. When positive feedback occurs, the amplified output signal is amplified further and further. This can happen in many amplifiers. The most common example is a public address system when the PA system speakers are placed too close and directed toward the microphone input. This is an example of positive feedback, as the amplified output is fed back into the input and then re-amplified. As the process is repeated over and over, the result is a high-pitched squeal most often referred to as, simply, *feedback*. The PA amplifier has become unstable and now functions as an oscillator. Positive feedback oscillators are a class of circuits using the concept of positive feedback to generate a particular periodic waveform, with a DC supply voltage as the only input signal.

It can be said that amplifiers and positive feedback oscillators perform opposite functions: amplifiers must amplify a signal and maintain stability (not go into oscillation) while positive feedback oscillators should generate a periodic waveform at a specific amplitude (without amplification). It can also be said that every amplifier has a tendency to oscillate while every positive feedback oscillator has some disposition toward amplification. In order for a positive feedback oscillator to sustain oscillation, the phase shift of the signal fed back to the input must be 0 and the closed loop gain of the fed-back signal must be 1. If the closed loop gain is less than 1, the signal will eventually attenuate to 0. For closed loop gains larger than 1 the signal increases continuously until limited by the DC power supply.

The simplest oscillator is a clock circuit similar to those used in most digital circuits. There are many other uses for other oscillator waveforms in what are classified as analog type timing circuits. Finally, oscillators are used to develop carrier frequencies in communications circuits. In this chapter we will discuss a variety of oscillator and function generator circuits. The specific areas covered are as follows:

▸ Oscillator and Function Generator Performance
▸ Clock Circuits
▸ Square-wave Generators
▸ Triangle-wave Generators
▸ Voltage-controlled Oscillators (VCOs)
▸ Sine-Wave Generators
▸ Pulse Generators
▸ Integrated Circuit Function Generators

8–1 ▸ Oscillator and Function Generator Performance

Oscillators and function generators produce an output waveform of a particular shape, amplitude, frequency, and duty cycle that is developed from a DC power supply input. The performance of an oscillator or function generator is determined by how well it meets these output signal requirements. In addition, oscillator performance is judged by how much current the output can provide as well as its efficiency relative to developing the output from the DC supply.

Amplitude: The amplitude determines the positive and negative peak values of the output waveform. The oscillator's amplitude accuracy is determined by how closely the oscillator can provide an output amplitude in the range required. In most cases the amplitude accuracy will be determined by the resolution provided for adjusting the oscillator output amplitude.

Frequency: The frequency performance is simply a measurement of how closely the actual oscillator output frequency equals the desired output frequency. This is usually determined by the tolerances and resolution of the circuit elements that the feedback mechanism comprises.

Stability: The amount of variation from the steady state frequency over time

Harmonic Content: The amount of frequencies other than the desired fundamental frequency that are present in the output signal

Waveform: This performance factor is a measurement of how well the output waveform approximates the desired output waveform. Square waves are relatively easy to generate. Triangle and sawtooth waves can be generated by charging a capacitor with a constant current source. Sine waves are developed almost perfectly below 1 MHz with RC components, while LC circuits are used above 1 MHz.

Duty Cycle: Duty cycle represents the amount of time the signal is positive vs. negative for analog signals and high vs. low for digital signals. In most oscillators and function generators, duty cycle is set at 50%. In more advanced function generators and pulse circuits, the duty cycle can be adjusted. In any event the duty cycle performance is determined by how well the oscillator provides the desired output duty cycle.

Output Power: This is usually specified by the output current that the oscillator can provide.

Efficiency: This is a measure of the efficiency of the oscillator—output power divided by the input power from the DC supply.

8–2 ▶ Clock Circuits

Clock circuits are most often used in digital circuits to synchronize their operation or to count real or system time. Digital clock circuits have a positive, peak amplitude around 3 to 5 V and a negative peak amplitude of approximately 0 V. The actual peak values will be defined by whatever type of logic (TTL, CMOS, etc.) is being driven by the clock circuit. The duty cycle will usually be 50%, meaning that the high and low time periods will be equal.

A very basic clock circuit, a type of relaxation oscillator, is shown in Figure 8–1. This type of clock can be constructed from many different types of logic, but we will focus on TTL. On power up, the input to the logic inverter is low; therefore, the initial inverter output is a high logic level. As soon as the inverter output goes high, it begins to charge up capacitor C from the output through the connection to resistor R. When the capacitor charges to a voltage equal to a logical high input, the inverter output will switch to a low logic level. The capacitor will then discharge through resistor R to ground until a logical low input voltage to the inverter is reached. The inverter output will then again become high.

The clock frequency is determined by the RC time constant. The formula is shown as Equation 8–1:

$$\text{Clock Frequency} = .8/RC \tag{8–1}$$

Because the charging and discharging RC values are the same, the duty cycle is very close to 50%. The other constraint placed on the circuit is the maximum values for

▶ **FIGURE 8–1**
Schmitt trigger oscillator

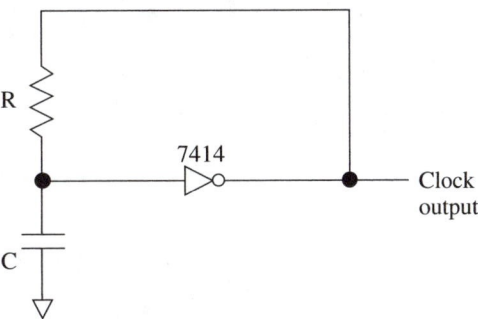

R. For a 74LS14 the maximum value for $R = 2$ kΩ. For a 7414 the maximum value for R = 500 Ω. Because the R and C values determine the clock frequency, its accuracy is determined by the tolerance of these components. While the R value could be adjusted with a potentiometer to compensate for any variations in the C value, this circuit would also be subject to temperature-induced variations in the R and C values and aging of these components over time. The overall frequency accuracy required, combined with the ambient temperature specs for the circuit, will determine the acceptability of this type of RC clock circuit.

A more accurate and temperature-independent clock circuit can be attained with the use of crystal oscillators. Crystal oscillators are constructed with a component called a *quartz crystal*. These crystals are two terminal components that are fabricated from a small piece of quartz crystal. When cut to a specific size and shape, the crystals can be made to resonate at a particular frequency. The frequency of resonance is very accurate, not sensitive to ambient temperature, and does not change over time. Crystals oscillate in either the fundamental or overtone mode. The fundamental mode is its normal listed resonant frequency. Because there is a limit to how small a crystal can be sliced, the maximum fundamental mode frequency for most crystals is 20 MHz. To oscillate at frequencies greater than 20 MHz, the crystal resonates in the overtone mode, which usually involves odd integer multiples of the fundamental frequency.

A variety of crystal-controlled clock circuits using different logic devices is shown in Figure 8–2. All of these circuits are based on the accurate resonant frequency established by the crystal as a feedback device from the output back to the circuit input. Figure 8–2a shows a crystal-controlled clock circuit using a 74LS04 TTL inverter. Figure 8–2b utilizes a CMOS inverter while Figure 8–2c shows a circuit that employs a CMOS Schmitt-trigger.

Up to this point all of the clock circuits discussed have been digitally oriented; their output amplitudes were compatible with digital logic circuits. Clocks, or astable multivibrators, are often needed in analog circuits where the output amplitude must be greater than digital logic levels. These can be developed with transistor or op amp circuits or with the use of 555 counter-timer ICs. A 555 counter-timer is a very versatile circuit that can function as a free-running astable multivibrator (a clock generator) or a monostable multivibrator (a one shot) or a time delay function. The 555 includes two comparators, an open collector transistor, a flip-flop, and an output buffer (see Figure 8–3). The upper comparator has its negative input connected to $V_{CC} \times .666$ and the lower comparator has its positive input connected to $V_{CC} \times .333$. Because the 555 is not designed around TTL or CMOS logic the V_{CC} power connection can be anywhere from approximately 4.5 to 18 V DC, which is the range of the possible output amplitudes from the circuit. Then again, if a digital logic circuit requires a relaxation oscillator, the 555 can be used in this application by making V_{CC} equal to 5 V. Let's look at an example.

Example 8–1

A free-running pulse circuit is needed for an analog circuit that will operate at 100 kHz. The output of the pulse circuit should be +12 V when high and 0 V when low. The duty cycle should be 60%.

(a)

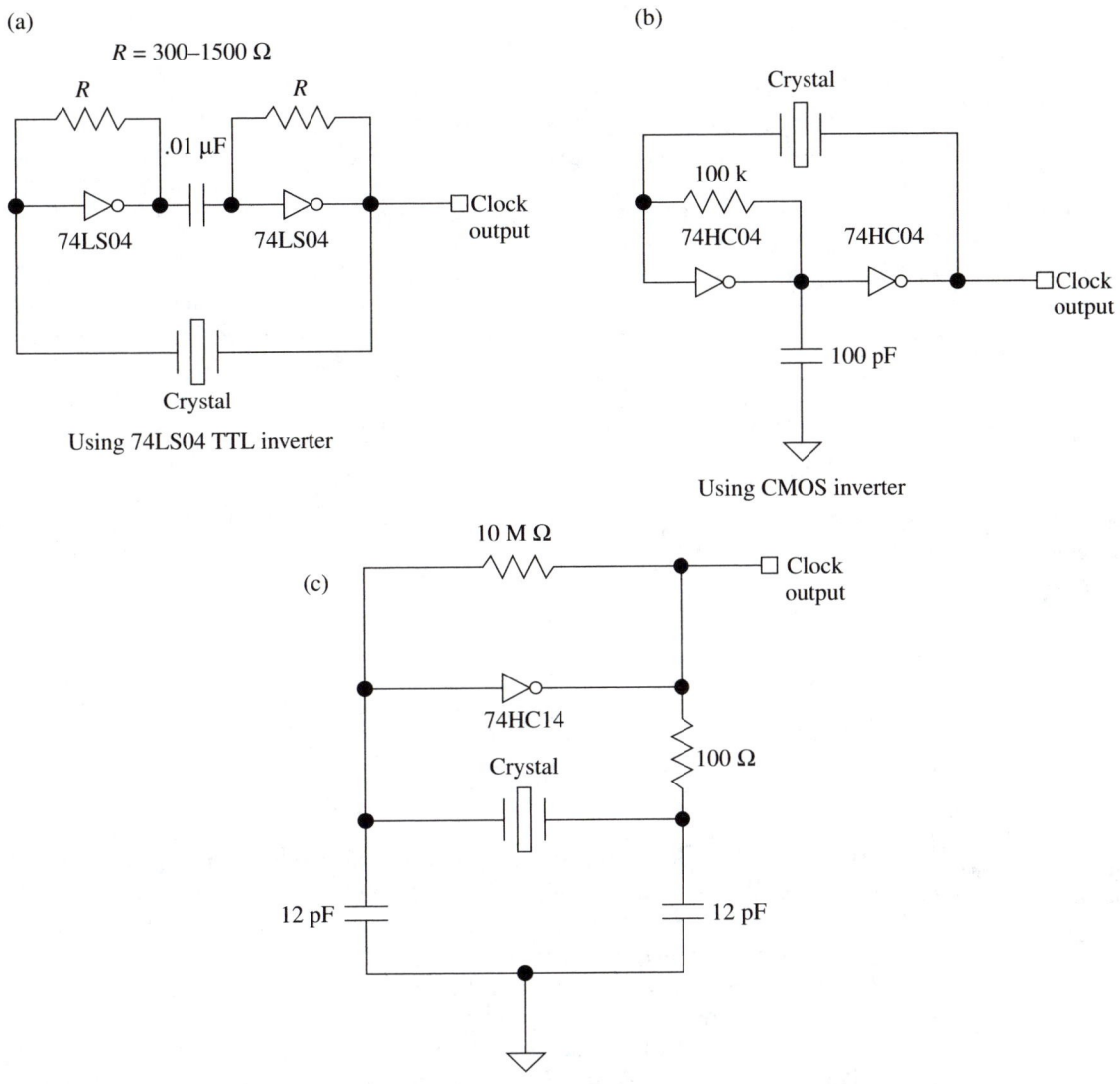

$R = 300{-}1500\ \Omega$

R

R

.01 μF

74LS04   74LS04

☐Clock output

Crystal

Using 74LS04 TTL inverter

(b)

Crystal

100 k

74HC04   74HC04

☐Clock output

100 pF

Using CMOS inverter

(c)

10 M Ω

☐ Clock output

74HC14

Crystal

100 Ω

12 pF

12 pF

Using CMOS Schmitt trigger

▲ **FIGURE 8–2**
Crystal-controlled clock circuits

Solution

Figure 8–4 shows the 555 counter-timer configured to operate in the free-running mode. Notice that both the upper and lower comparators have their available input connected to one side of capacitor C. The upper comparator has a $V_{CC} \times .66$ reference voltage of $12 \times .66 = 7.92$ V. The lower comparator is referenced at $V_{CC} \times .33 = 12 \times .33 = 3.96$ V. Notice that the 555's internal transistor collector is also connected to the same capacitor connection as the comparators.

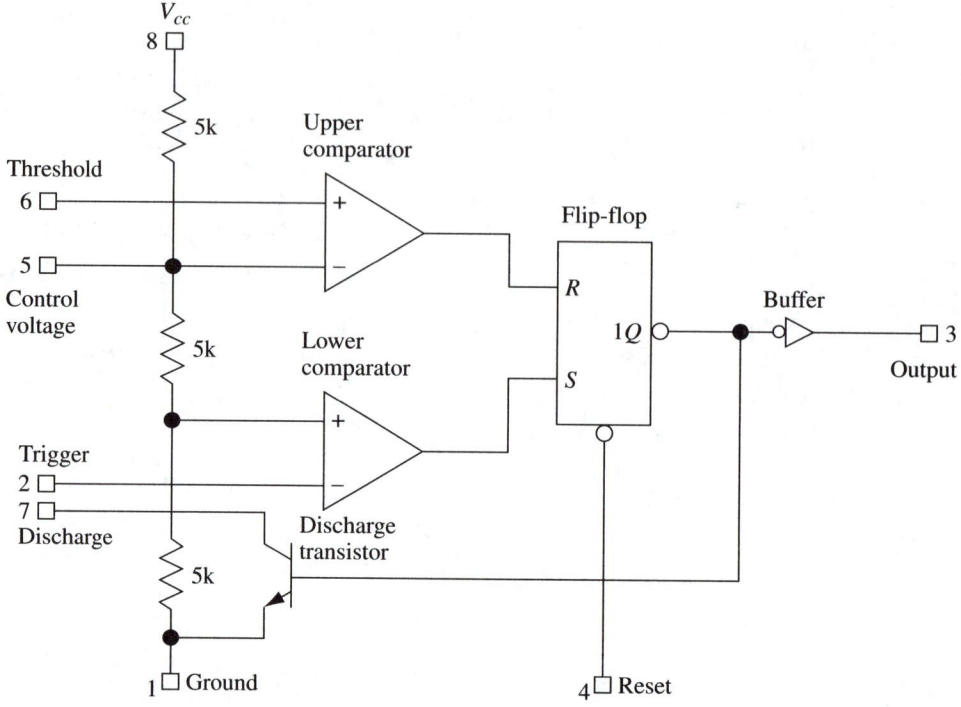

▲ **FIGURE 8–3**
555 counter-timer circuit

Initially the 555 powers up with Q = low and Q' = high. Since Q' is connected to the 555's output terminal, its output is initially high, or in this case, 12 V DC. The Q output from the flip-flop drives the transistor; therefore the transistor is initially off. The circuit begins operation by charging capacitor C through R_A and R_B. When the voltage at C reaches 7.92 V, the upper comparator will switch, setting the RS flip-flop and causing the 555 output to go to 0 V and the 555's internal transistor is turned on. When the transistor is on, it pulls the positive side of R_B to ground. This causes the capacitor to discharge through R_B to ground. When the capacitor voltage discharges down to 3.96 V, the lower comparator resets the RS flip-flop returning the 555 output to +12 V and turning the transistor off. This process repeats itself in time periods determined completely by R_A, R_B, and C.

It is important to note that because the capacitor charges through R_A and R_B, but discharges only through R_B, the 555 by itself can never produce a true 50% duty cycle output. When R_B is > R_A a 50% duty cycle is approached.

In order to provide a +12-V amplitude for the positive pulse, V_{CC} should be +12 V DC. To complete the design, all that is needed is the calculation of the values for R_A, R_B, and C. The formulas are as follows:

$$555 \text{ frequency} f = 1.44/(R_A + 2R_B)C = 100 \text{ kHz} \qquad (8\text{–}2)$$

$$\text{Duty Cycle} = (R_A + R_B)/(R_A + 2R_B) = 60\% \qquad (8\text{–}3)$$

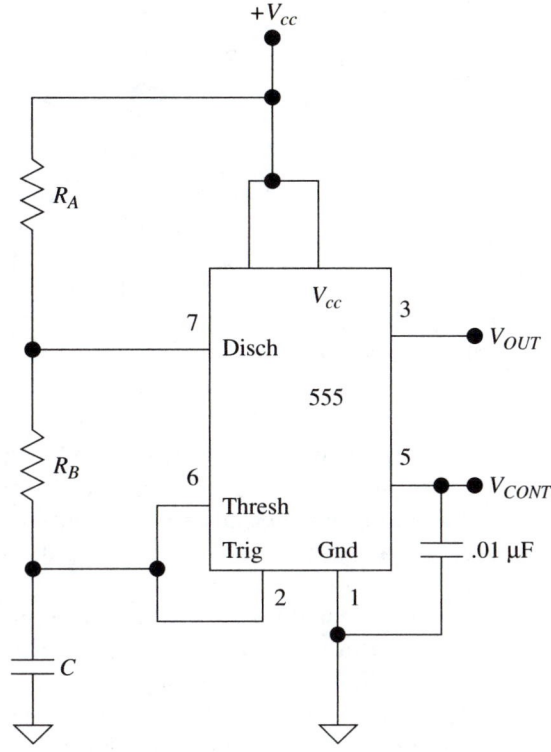

▶ **FIGURE 8–4**
555 Counter-timer in free running mode

There are two equations with three unknowns. First select a standard and available capacitor value and then solve the equations for R_A and R_B. Selecting the capacitors first is the best approach because there are more standard resistor values available, or a trimpot could be used for either resistor value.

Let $C = .001\ \mu F$

Solving the duty cycle equation (Equation 8–3):
$R_A = .5R_B$
Substituting in the frequency equation (Equation 8–2):
$R_B = 1.44/(.001\ \mu F \times 100\ kHz \times 2.5)$
$R_B = 5760\ \Omega$
$R_A = 2880\ \Omega$

8–3 ▶ Square-wave Generators

All of the circuits discussed in Section 8–2 developed waveforms that alternated between a positive high pulse and 0 V. A true square wave is a waveform that possesses positive and negative pulses with equal amplitudes and duration (see Figure 8–5).

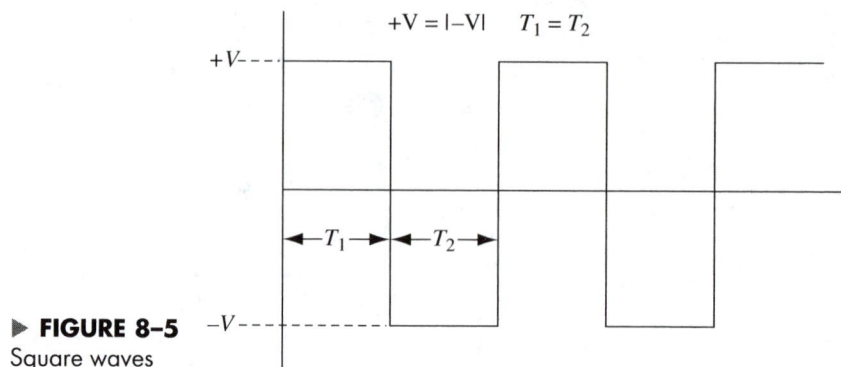

▶ **FIGURE 8–5**
Square waves

Square waves can be generated by a variety of op amp circuits where the op amp is configured as a comparator (with positive feedback), and a capacitor is charged and discharged in a manner similar to the clock circuits discussed in Section 8–2. Figure 8–6 shows an op amp relaxation oscillator that generates a square wave.

The circuit in Figure 8–6 is an op amp with positive feedback, which functions as a comparator. Initially, the capacitor C is uncharged making the negative op amp input equal to 0, so the op amp's output equals the positive saturation voltage, $+V_{SAT}$ for the op amp (usually $V_{CC}-2$ V). The voltage fed back to the positive input is determined by the voltage divider, $R/(R_{FB} + R)$. With the op amp output at $+V_{SAT}$ the voltage at the positive op amp input is $+V_{SAT} (R/(R_{FB} + R))$. The positive op amp output voltage begins to charge the capacitor through R_C. When the capacitor voltage exceeds the voltage present at the op amp's positive terminal, the op amp output will switch to $-V_{SAT}$. The voltage presented to the positive op amp terminal is now $-V_{SAT} (R/(R_{FB} + R))$. The capacitor now discharges through R_C until it becomes less than the voltage at the op amp's positive input, causing the op amp's

▶ **FIGURE 8–6**
Square-wave generator

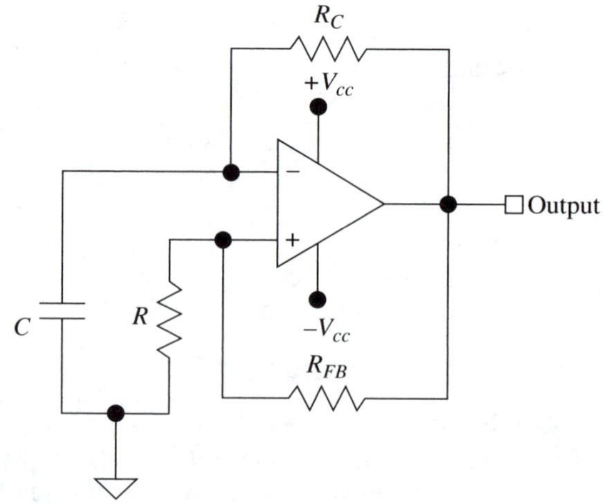

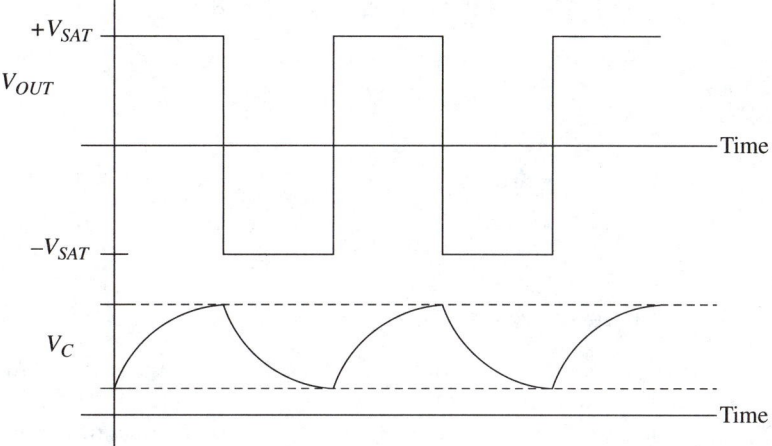

▶ FIGURE 8-7
Square-wave generator
waveforms

output to switch back to $+V_{SAT}$. This represents one complete cycle for this circuit. See Figure 8–7 for the resulting waveforms. This circuit develops a square wave with amplitudes equal to $+V_{SAT}$ and $-V_{SAT}$ at a frequency determined by R, R_{FB}, C, and R_C. The period for the waveform is given by the equation:

$$T = 2R_C C \ln (1 + 2R/R_{FB}) \qquad (8\text{–}4)$$

Example 8-2

Design a circuit that will generate a square wave with ±10 volt amplitudes at a frequency of 50 kHz.

Solution
The circuit shown in Figure 8–6 will perform this function if the proper values of V_{CC}, resistors, and capacitor are chosen.

1. V_{CC} is selected as ±12 V so that $\pm V_{SAT} = \pm 10$ V.

2. Equation 8–4 defines the relationship between the circuit component values and the period of the square waveform. If f must equal 50 kHz, then T = 1/50 kHz = 20 microseconds.

3. Equation 8–4 includes all four of the remaining circuit variables. In order to resolve this problem, some of the component values must be selected arbitrarily. If R and R_{FB} are selected such that $R = .86 R_{FB}$, then the logarithmic function included in Equation 8–4 reduces to $\ln (1 + 2 (.86 R_{FB}/R_{FB})) = \ln 2.72 = 1$. Let $R_{FB} = 33$ kΩ, then $R = 28$ kΩ.

4. For R = .86 R_{FB}, Equation 8–4 reduces to $T = 20$ micro-seconds = $2 R_C C$. Let $C = .01$ μF. Then $R_C = 20$ micro-seconds/.01 μF = 2000 Ω.

The complete design solution is:

V_{CC} is selected as ± 12 V

$R_{FB} = 33$ kΩ

R $= 28$ kΩ

$C = .01$ μF

$R_C = 2000$ Ω

8-4 ▶ Triangle-wave Generators

A triangle waveform increases linearly to a maximum value and decreases at the same rate to a minimum negative voltage equal in magnitude to the maximum voltage. The duty cycle of a true triangle waveform is normally 50%. A common circuit that will generate both a square and triangle waveform is shown in Figure 8–8. This circuit includes two op amps; U_1 is connected as a comparator while U_2 is configured as an integrator. The circuit operation is as follows:

1. Initially assume that the output of U_1 is at $-V_{SAT}$ and the output of $U_2 = 0$.

2. The integrator circuit integrates the constant $-V_{SAT}$ presented to its inverted input causing the output of U_2 to increase linearly until $V_{TRIANGLE}/R_1 = V_{SQUARE}/R_F$. At this point the output of U_1, V_{SQUARE}, switches to equal $+V_{SAT}$.

3. The integrator U_2 integrates the constant $+V_{SAT}$ signal, decreasing linearly again until $V_{TRIANGLE}/R_I = V_{SQUARE}/R_F$, where one cycle of the circuit is complete and it is repeated again and again.

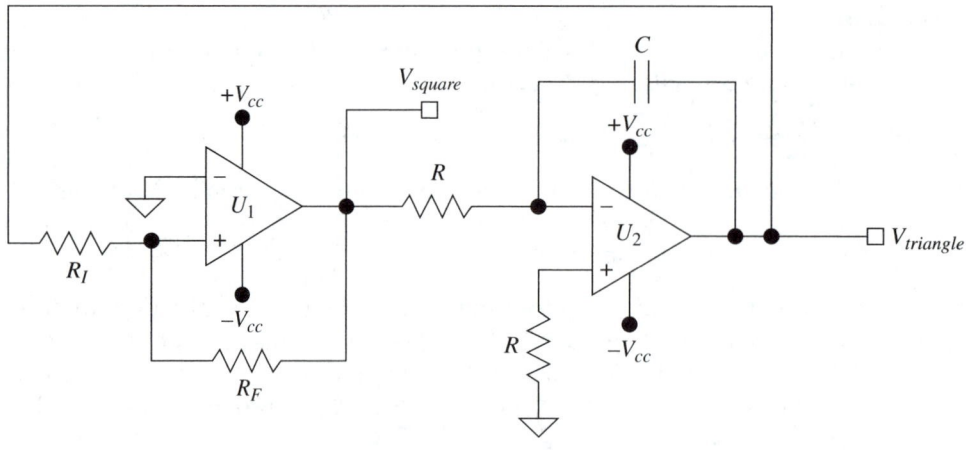

▲ **FIGURE 8-8**
Triangle/square wave generator

The equation that defines the relationship between the components and the resulting frequency for both the square and triangle waveforms is:

$$\text{frequency } f = (R_F/R_1)/4RC \tag{8-5}$$

The amplitude of the square wave equals $\pm V_{SAT}$, while the peak amplitude for the triangle output is determined by $V_{SAT} \times R_I/R_F$.

Example 8–3

Design a circuit that will generate both a square wave and a triangle wave at a frequency of 20 kHz. The amplitude of the square wave shall be ± 8 V and the peak amplitude of the triangle wave should be ± 5 V.

Solution

1. V_{CC} is selected as ± 10 V so that the amplitude of the square wave will be approximately equal to ± 8 V.

2. The peak amplitude of the triangle wave must equal 5 V, which equals $V_{SAT} \times R_I/R_F$. Therefore, $5 = 8 \times R_I/R_F$ or $5/8 \, R_F = R_I$. Let $R_F = 20$ kΩ. Then $R_I = 12.5$ kΩ.

3. Equation 8-5 defines the relationship between the frequency of the circuit and the component values. Substituting in the desired frequency and the results of step 2 above, $5/8 \, R_F = R_I$, we have:

   20,000 Hz $= (R_F/.625 \, R_F)/4RC$
   Let $C = C = .01$ µF
   Solving for $R = 1.6/(4 \times 20,000 \text{ Hz} \times .01 \text{ µF}) = 2000 \, \Omega$

   The complete design solution is:

   V_{CC} is selected as ± 10 V
   $R_F = 20$ kΩ
   $R_I = 12.5$ kΩ
   $C = .01$ µF
   $R = 2000 \, \Omega$

8–5 ▶ Voltage-controlled Oscillators

Sawtooth waveforms are positive voltage waveforms that increase in amplitude at one rate and decrease in amplitude by a much greater rate. Sawtooth generators are a form of oscillator called *voltage controlled oscillators (VCOs)*, because the frequency of the sawtooth generator can be changed by a voltage input to the VCO circuit. An example sawtooth generator is shown in Figure 8–9.

The sawtooth generator shown in Figure 8–9 consists of an op amp integrator, U_1 and an op amp comparator, U_2. A negative voltage V_{IN} is input to the circuit and is the ultimate control voltage that determines the frequency of the oscillator

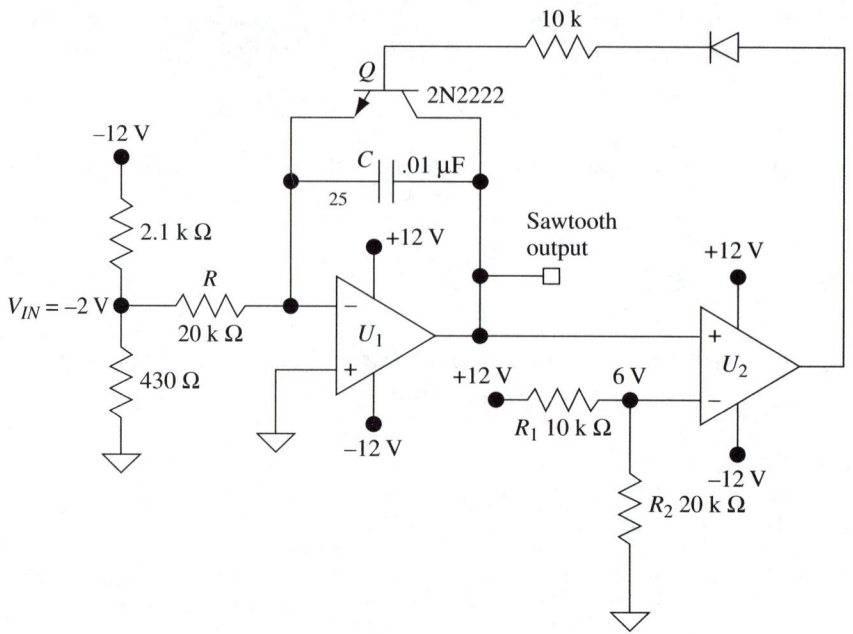

▲ **FIGURE 8–9**
Sawtooth generator

output. V_{IN} is connected to the integrator U_1 through R. Initially the comparator U_2 is at approximately negative rail and transistor Q is off. The integrator charges capacitor C at a rate determined using Equation 8–6:

$$\text{Rate of rise } V_{OUT} = V_{IN}/RC \tag{8–6}$$

Therefore the rate of rise for V_{OUT} is determined by the input voltage V_{IN}, R, and C. Since R and C are usually fixed in the circuit, V_{IN} is the primary voltage for determining the oscillator frequency. V_{OUT} increases until it is equal to the voltage labeled V_{PEAK}, at which point it causes the comparator op amp U_2 to switch bringing its output to approximately positive rail, switching transistor Q on. When transistor Q is turned on, it provides a relative short across the capacitor, forcing it to discharge very rapidly. Consequently, V_{OUT} decreases quickly to 0, which switches the comparator U_2 and transistor Q off. V_{PEAK} determines the peak amplitude of the sawtooth and also has an impact on the frequency. V_{PEAK} is fixed in most circuit applications, making the V_{IN} the exclusive oscillator control voltage. The frequency of the sawtooth waveform is defined by the following equation:

$$f = (1/RC)(|V_{IN}|/V_{PEAK}) \tag{8–7}$$

Example 8–4

Design a sawtooth generator circuit that will output a sawtooth waveform with a peak amplitude of 6 V, with an operating frequency of 10 kHz, when V_{IN} equals

–2 V. Calculate the new oscillation frequency for the circuit designed if the V_{IN} becomes equal to –6 V.

Solution

1. V_{PEAK} equals the peak amplitude of the circuit; therefore, V_{PEAK} = 6 V. R_1 and R_2 must be selected to develop a voltage divider that will divide the +12 V in half.

2. Using equation 8–7:

   $f = (1/RC)(|V_{IN}|/V_{PEAK})$
   10 kHz = $(1/RC)(|-2|/6)$
   30 kHz = $1/RC$ Let C = .01 µF
   $R = 1/(30\ \text{kHz} \times .01\ \text{µF})$ = 3.3 kΩ

   The complete design solution is:

   V_{CC} is selected as ±12 V
   R = 3.3 kΩ
   R_1 = 10 kΩ
   R_2 = 20 kΩ potentiometer
   C = .01 µF

3. For the final circuit the oscillating frequency for V_{IN} = –6 V can be found as follows:

   $f = (1/RC)(V_{IN}/V_{PEAK})$
   $f = (1/3.3\ \text{kΩ} \times .01\ \text{µF})\ (|-6|/6)$ = 30,303 Hz

It should be noted that the sawtooth generator discussed in this section generates a sawtooth waveform with a very steep decline in the output voltage after reaching the peak value. More complicated sawtooth generator circuits provide the capability to specify the rate of decline as well as that of the increasing ramp voltage.

The circuit shown in Figure 8–10 is a very versatile voltage-controlled oscillator circuit that can generate any range of triangle, sawtooth, and square waveforms where the frequency is determined by an input control voltage. The input control voltage V_C is used to generate the increasing ramp integrator input voltage V_{CR} and the falling ramp voltage C_{CF}. V_{CR} can be adjusted with trimpot TP_1, while TP_2 adjusts V_{CF}. The voltage at the trimpot wiper arms are input to voltage follower U_1 to develop V_{CR} and inverting amp U_2 to create $-V_{CF}$. These control voltages are alternately applied to integrator U_5 by the CMOS switches O_1 and O_2. The integrator rise and fall rates are as follows:

$$V_{OUT} \text{ Rise Rate} = + V_{CR}/RC \tag{8–8}$$

$$V_{OUT} \text{ Fall Rate} = -V_{CF}/RC \tag{8–9}$$

The square wave output voltage amplitude V_{SQUARE} is determined by the rating of zener diodes D_{Z1} and D_{Z2}:

$$V_{SQUARE} = (D_{Z1} \text{ or } D_{Z2} \text{ rating}) + .7 \text{ V} \tag{8–10}$$

(a)

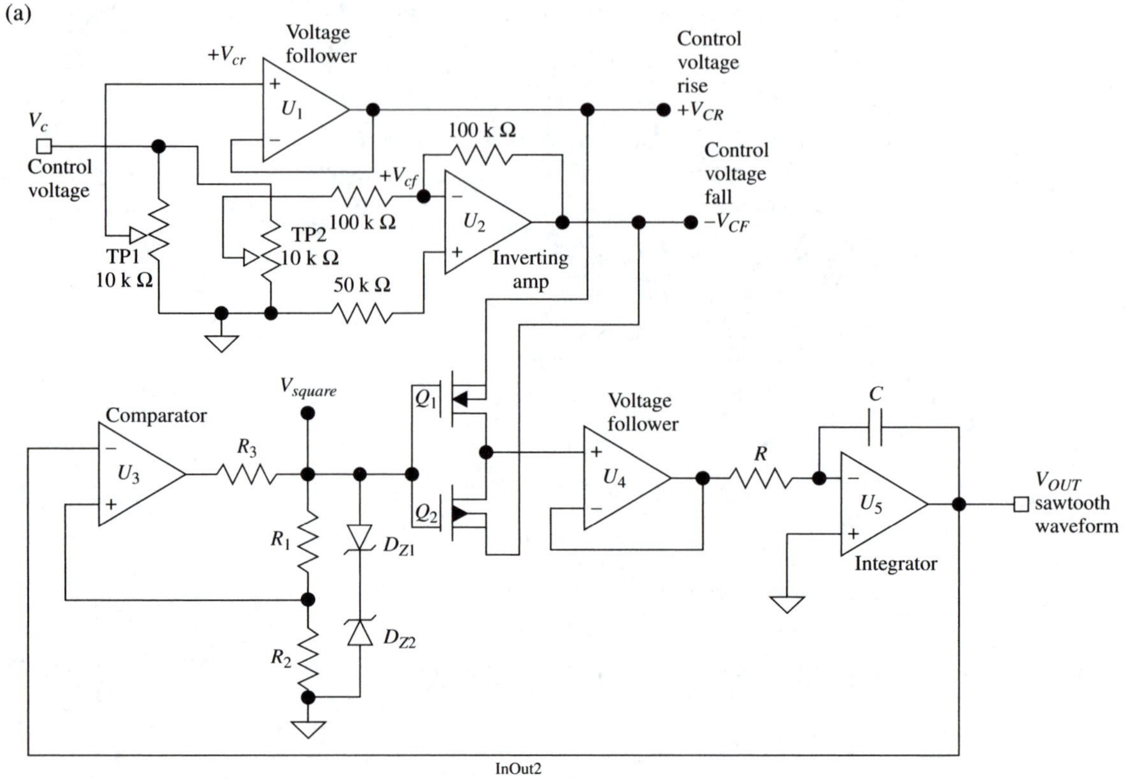

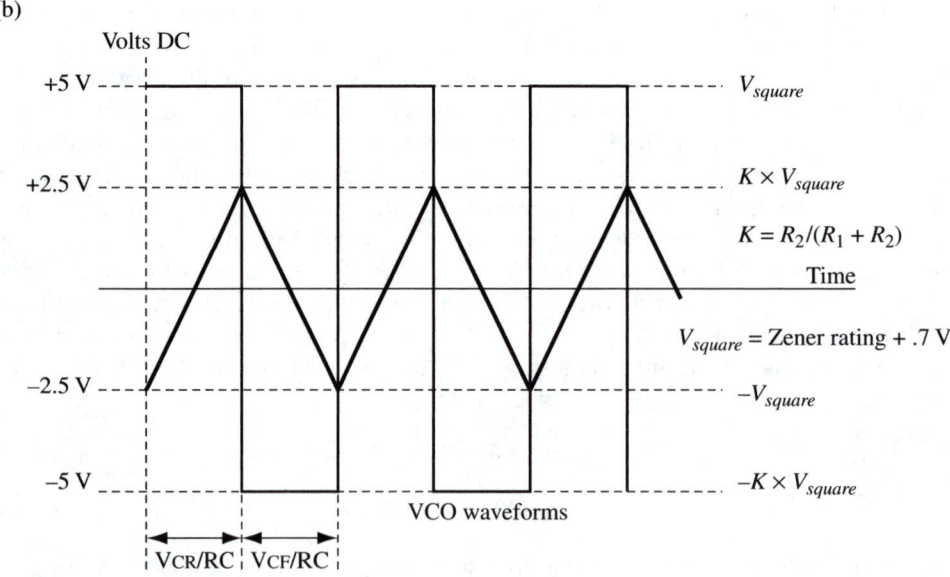

(b)

▲ FIGURE 8–10

Voltage-controlled oscillator circuit

The peak output voltage V_{OUT} is determined by comparator U_3 and the following equation:

$$V_{OUT}\,\text{Peak} = (R_2/(R_2 + R_1)) \times V_{SQUARE} \tag{8–11}$$

The input control voltage will determine the frequency of V_{OUT} while the shape of V_{OUT} is set by V_{CR} and V_{CF}. If $V_{CR} = V_{CF}$, then the waveform is a triangle wave. If $V_{CR} \neq V_{CF}$, the waveform has more of a sawtooth shape. The peak of the output waveform is set by the comparator and is symmetrical if the zener diode ratings are the same. The waveforms shown in Figure 8–10b are for zener ratings of 4.3 V and $R_1 = R_2 = 10\ \text{k}\Omega$. Therefore, the peak voltages of V_{OUT} are ±2.5 V and $V_{SQUARE} = ±5$ V.

The 555 counter/timer discussed in Section 8–2 can also be configured to operate as a VCO. The circuit is almost identical to the circuit shown in Figure 8–4 except that the control pin labeled CONT is not connected through a capacitor to ground, but becomes a voltage control input that determines the frequency of the output pin's pulsed waveform (see Figure 8–11a). When a control voltage is applied to the CONT pin, it determines whether the upper or lower comparators are switched on (refer back to the internal 555 diagram shown in Figure 8–3). The upper comparator will switch off at the value of the control voltage, while the lower comparator switches off half of the control voltage. The waveforms for the circuit are shown in Figure 8–11b. The equation that determine the pulse widths and frequencies for the 555 VCO circuit are as follows:

$$V_{OUT}+ = -(R_A + R_B)C \ln\left((V_{CC} - V_{CONT})/(V_{CC} - .5V_{CONT})\right) \tag{8–12}$$

(a)

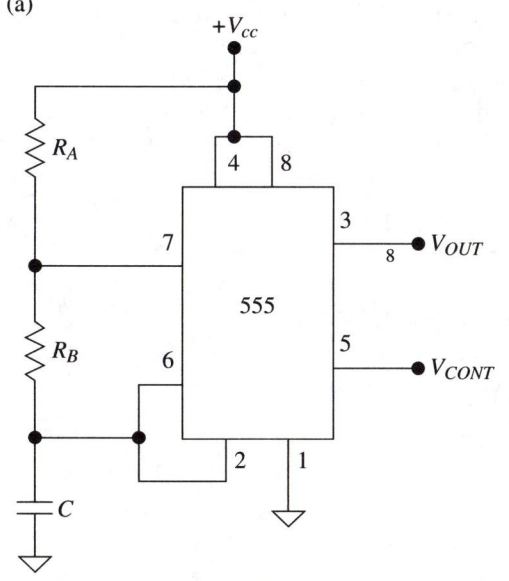

(b)

555 voltage-controlled oscillator with control voltage applied to CONT pin

▲ **FIGURE 8-11**
555 voltage-controlled oscillator

$$555 \text{ frequency } f = 1/(V_{OUT+} + .693R_BC) \qquad (8\text{--}13)$$

where V_{OUT+} = the time the pulse is high.

Another variation of the VCO is a voltage-to-frequency converter. Actually, these two circuits perform the exact same function: both convert a voltage to a frequency. The difference between the two functions really lies in the waveform type and its function. VCOs are circuits that convert a voltage to a waveform operating at a particular frequency where the shape (sawtooth or pulse) of the waveform has some significance. A voltage-to-frequency converter usually converts an analog voltage to a stream of digital pulses that vary in frequency with the analog voltage.

Integrated circuits have been developed to perform voltage-to-frequency conversion on one IC. The pin out and block diagram for the VFC32 voltage to frequency converter is shown in Figure 8–12. The VFC32 is typically powered by ±15 V DC but can handle power supply voltages up to ±22 volts. The input signal is a voltage that is connected to an op amp. The feedback path for the op amp is external capacitor C_2, making it an integrator. The input current to the integrator $I_{IN} = V_{IN}/R_1$. The positive input produces a downward-ramping integrator output voltage. When the integrator ramps down to circuit common, the comparator switches, firing the one-shot. A 1-mA reference current is connected to the integrator while the one-shot is on, which drives the integrator back upscale. After the one-shot has completed one cycle, the integrator ramps downward again, beginning the next cycle. The net result is that the frequency of the output is directly proportional to the input voltage.

Figure 8–13 shows the VFC32 in a circuit that converts a 0–10 V input signal to frequencies ranging from 0–10,000 Hz. The VFC32 can output frequencies as high as 500 kHz. The range of the output frequency is set by capacitor C_1, so its selection (tolerance, temperature drift, and stability, as discussed in Chapter 4) is critical to the accuracy of this circuit. The tolerance, temperature drift and stability of R_1 are also critical. Therefore, metal film type resistors are recommended. The

▶ **FIGURE 8–12**
Voltage-to-frequency
converter block program

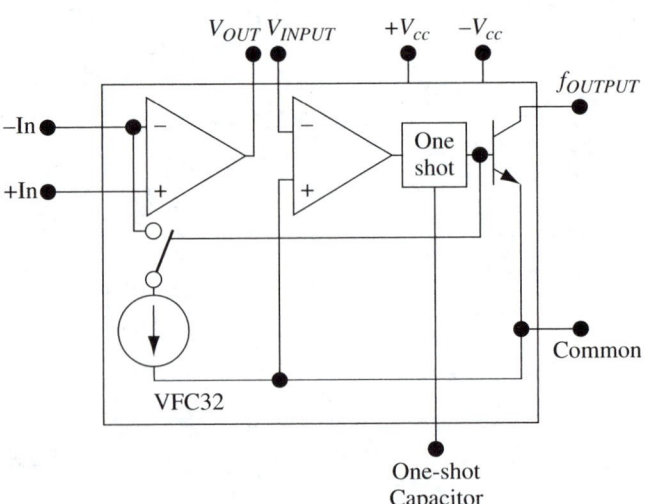

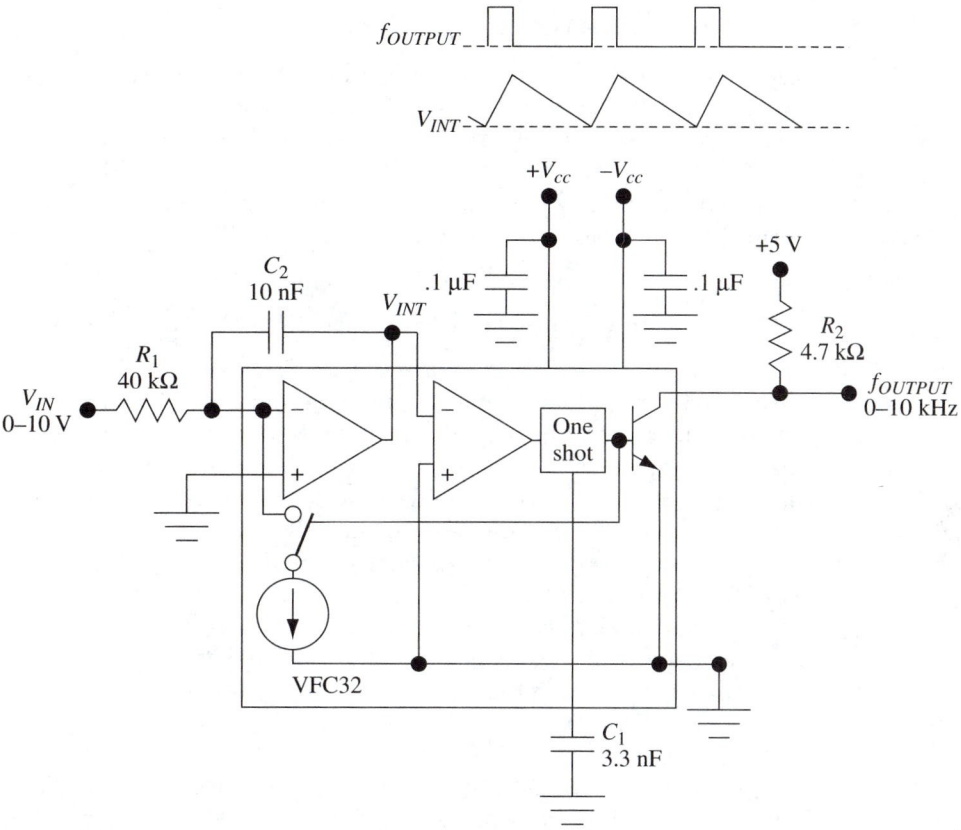

▲ FIGURE 8–13

Voltage-to-frequency converter circuit

data sheet for this chip provides graphs that help select R_I and C_1 so that the duty cycle of the output pulse is generally 25% when the maximum output frequency is less than 200 kHz. For maximum output frequencies greater than 200 kHz, the recommended duty cycle is 50%.

The value of integrating capacitor C_2 is not extremely critical but must be within a range so that the up and down ramping occurs fast enough to accommodate the highest output frequency. The tolerance or temperature stability of C_2 is not important but it should have low leakage and low dielectric absorption (DA). Polycarbonate type capacitors are a good choice for C_2.

Notice that the output terminal is an open transistor collector, which can be connected to a separate power supply or V_{CC} of the VFC32. Figure 8–13 shows the output connected to a 5-V power supply through a 4.7 kΩ pull-up resistor. The pull-up resistor value is selected so that the maximum current passing through the transistor to circuit common, when on, is less than 8 mA. In Figure 8–13 the output is a 5-V pulsed waveform with a 25% duty cycle. The frequency of the output is directly proportional to the 0–10-V input voltage: 0 V in = 0 frequency out, 5 V in = 5,000 Hz out and 10 V in = 10,000 Hz out.

8–6 ▶ Sine-wave Generators

All of the oscillator circuits discussed thus far have been variations of relaxation oscillators; oscillators based on the charging and discharging of capacitors. In order to generate a good-quality sine wave, positive feedback oscillators are the best alternative. Positive feedback oscillators utilize an amplifier whose output is fed back to its input through a feedback circuit. The circuit will oscillate at a frequency determined by the circuit's component values if both of these conditions are met:

1. The net gain around the loop is equal to 1.

2. The phase angle between the feedback signal and the amplifier input is 0.

These condition are called the *Barkhausen criteria* (see Figure 8–14). The net gain around the circuit loop equals amplifier gain, A times feedback gain, A_{FB}. Because the feedback circuit usually consists of passive components, some signal attenuation occurs, which means the amplifier must have some gain to create a net loop gain equal to 1. If the feedback circuit is a resonant circuit, then the maximum feedback will exist at just one frequency, the resonant frequency of the circuit.

In some ways oscillator circuits seem like black magic. The concept of positive feedback is understandable once an input is presented to the amplifier, but where does the signal come from that starts the process? All it takes is some small source of noise voltage, likely thermally generated noise or power-up transients that will cause variations in the input to the amplifier and start oscillation. Once started, the circuit will automatically search out the frequency where the gain is a maximum and the phase shift is equal to zero. If the gain is 1 at this frequency, then oscillation will be sustained. In most sine wave oscillator circuits the initial loop gain is greater than 1 to promote oscillation in a short period of time. Once oscillation has been achieved, the loop gain is automatically adjusted to 1 so that steady oscillation will be maintained. There are two general classifications of sine-wave generators: RC and LC sine-wave generators.

RC Sine-wave Generators (Frequencies < 1 MHz)

Wien-Bridge Oscillators

RC sine-wave generators are used with op amps to generate sine waves at frequencies of less than 1 MHz. A common variety RC oscillator that has become almost an industry standard is the Wien-Bridge oscillator. The Wien-Bridge oscillator

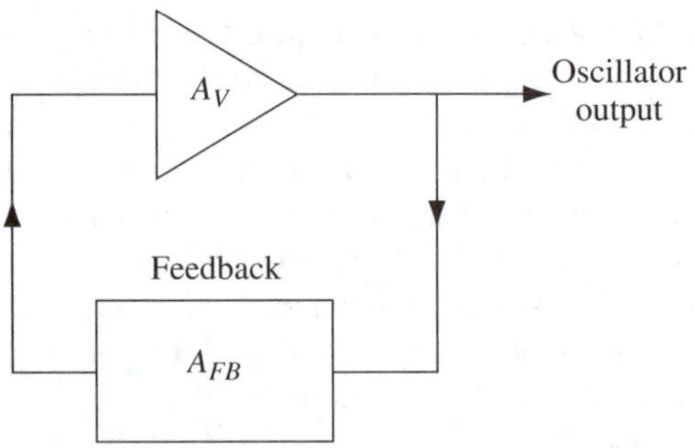

▶ **FIGURE 8–14**
Positive feedback oscillators

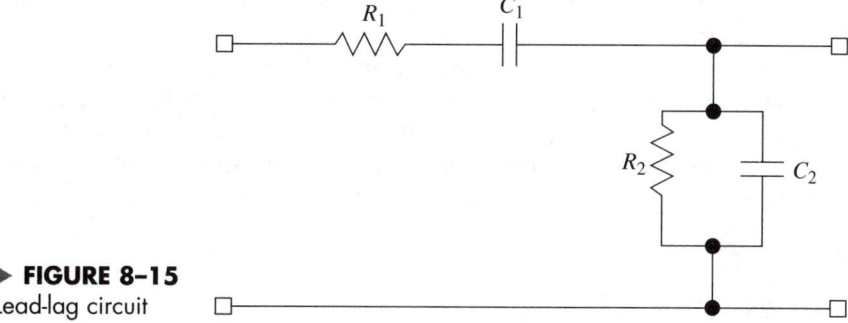

▶ **FIGURE 8–15**
Lead-lag circuit

as shown in Figure 8–17 uses a lead-lag feedback circuit as shown in Figure 8–15. The concept of lead-lag simply means that this circuit element is both a low-pass filter and a high-pass filter at the same time, and that there is a resonant frequency that passes through this feedback circuit with minimal attenuation. At low frequencies both capacitors C_1 and C_2 are open and there is no signal path back from the output to the input. At high frequencies, C_1 and C_2 are both shorts and again there is no signal fed back to the input (see Figure 8–16).

Notice that the Wien-Bridge oscillator has both negative feedback to provide amplification, plus positive feedback to the op amp to initiate oscillation. The noninverting amplifier input provides 0 degrees of phase shift, as does the feedback circuit at the resonant frequency.

If $R_1 = R_2$ and $C_1 = C_2$, then the resonant frequency for the circuit is shown below:

$$f = 1/(2\pi RC) \tag{8–14}$$

It can also be shown that the attenuation provided by the circuit at the resonant frequency is equal to 1/3. In order for the net loop gain to be unity, the gain provided

▶ **FIGURE 8–16**
Lead-lag gain/phase angle plots

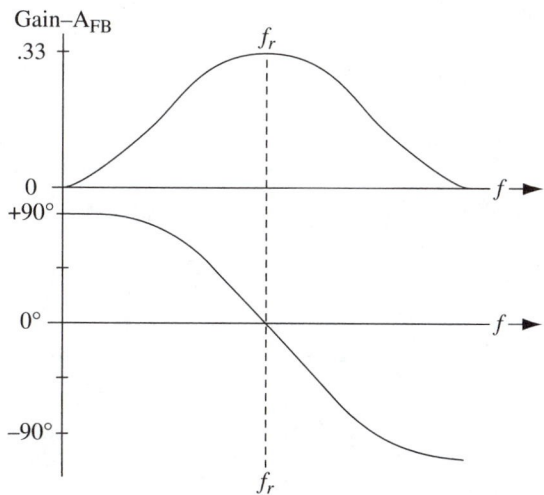

by the amplifier must be 3 to compensate for the attenuation provided by the lead-lag circuit. Once oscillation is achieved, the peak-to-peak amplitude of the sine wave will be close to the saturation voltage of the op amp. This is undesirable; with oscillation very close to the saturation level, some clipping and distortion is likely to occur. Also, when the circuit is powered up, the gain must be higher than 3 in order to cause oscillation to occur in a reasonable period of time. Let's ignore these details for a moment and complete a design example for the circuit shown in Figure 8–17.

Example 8–5

Design a Wien-Bridge oscillator that will generate a frequency of 200 kHz with an amplitude of approximately ±10 V.

Solution

1. Let $C_1 = C_2 = .001$ μF.

2. Solving Equation 8–14 for $f = 200$ kHz:

   $f = 1/(2\pi RC) = 200$ kHz $= 1/(2\pi \times R \times .001$ μF)
   $R = 1/(2\pi \times 200$ kHz $\times .001$ μF) $= 796$ Ω
   Let $R_1 = R_2 = R_4 = 806$ Ωs 1% tolerance resistors.
   In order for the gain to be 3, then $R_3 = 2R_4 = 1612$ Ω.
   Use 1650 Ω 1% tolerance resistor for R_3 to make the gain slightly >3.

▶ **FIGURE 8–17**
Wien-Bridge oscillator

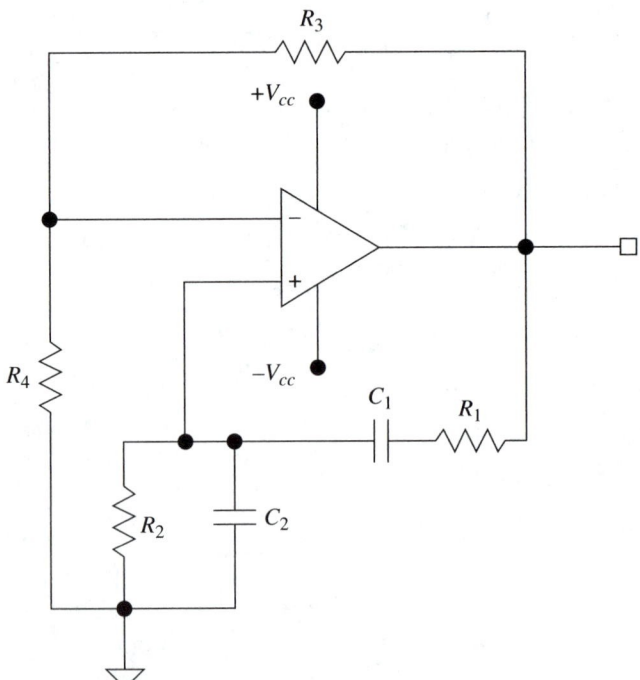

The complete design solution is:

V_{CC} is selected as ±12 V

$R_1 = R_2 = R_4 = 806\ \Omega$ 1% tolerance resistors

$R_3 = 1650\ \Omega$ 1% tolerance resistor

C = .001 µF

The peak-to-peak amplitude of the sine wave will be about ±10 V with $V_{CC} =$ ±12 V.

The circuit in Figure 8–18 shows one method of reducing the peak-to-peak amplitude to a value less than the saturation voltage, and it also provides a higher gain to get the circuit into oscillation. The circuit in Figure 8–14 has taken resistor R_3 and split its value into R_{3A} and R_{3B}. When this circuit is initially powered up, the amplitude of the output is low and the diodes have no effect on the circuit. The gain of this circuit on power up is given by the following equation:

$$A = 1 + (R_{3A} + R_{3B})/R_4 \tag{8–15}$$

When the output amplitude reaches the desired amplitude (as determined by the zener diode voltage rating + .7 V) the diodes will effectively remove R_{3B} from

▶ **FIGURE 8–18**

Wien-Bridge oscillator with gain adjustment

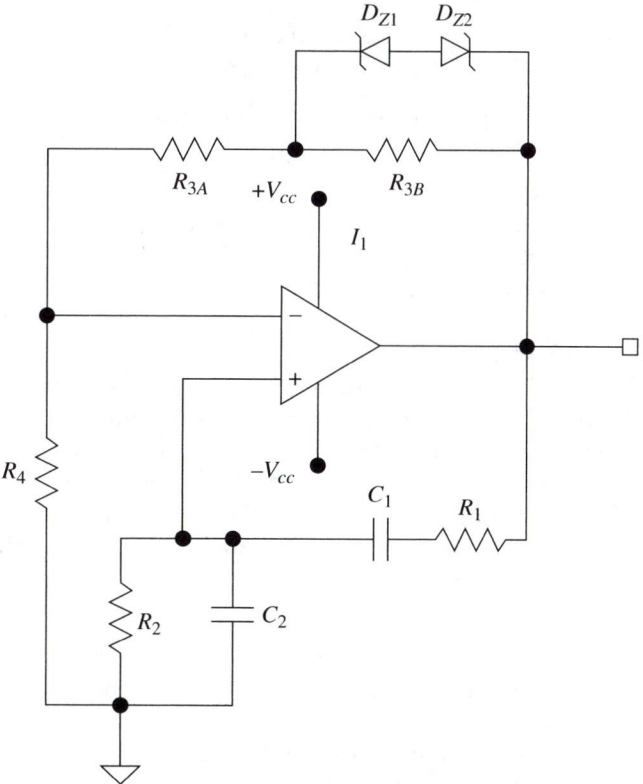

the circuit. The gain of the circuit once the zener diode voltages have been exceeded becomes:

$$A = 1 + (R_{3A}/R_4) \qquad (8\text{–}16)$$

Example 8–6

Modify the circuit developed in Example 8–5 so that the circuit is self-starting and provides a peak-to-peak output amplitude of 6.3 V.

Solution

1. The circuit shown in Figure 8–17 will meet the requirements of this example with the proper component values.

2. Let $R_{3A} = 1650\ \Omega$ and $R_4 = 806\ \Omega$ as before then the gain after the zener voltages have been exceeded will equal:

   $$A = 1 + (R_{3A}/R_4) = 1 + (1650/806) = 3.05$$

3. If $R_{3B} = R_4$, then the gain on power up will be given by Equation 8–15:

   $$A = 1 + ((R_{3A} + R_{3B})/R_4) = 1 + (2456/806) = 4.05$$

4. Zener diodes D_{Z1} and D_{Z2} are selected as 1N4734s with a zener voltage of 5.6 V. The peak-to-peak amplitude of the output will be 5.6 V + .7 V (the forward voltage drop of one zener diode) or 6.3 V.

The complete design solution is:

V_{CC} is selected as ±12 V
$R_1 = R_2 = R_4 = R_{3B} = 806\ \Omega$ 1% tolerance resistors
$R_{3A} = 1650\ \Omega$ 1% tolerance resistor
$C = .001\ \mu F$
$D_{Z1} = D_{Z2} = 1N4734$

Phase-shift Oscillators

This type of oscillator creates a 360-degree phase shift to promote oscillation at a particular frequency. An inverting op amp circuit is used to generate 180 degrees of the needed phase shift, while RC networks that the feedback impedance comprise provide the remaining 180 degrees of phase shift. Each RC network can provide as much as 90 degrees of phase shift (see Figure 8–19).

   If the two resistors are labeled $R = R_1$, then the equation for the resonant frequency of this circuit is as follows:

$$f = 1/(2\pi \times 2.45\ RC) \qquad (8\text{–}17)$$

The attenuation provided by the RC feedback network at resonance = 1/29. Therefore, the gain of the op amp circuit must be slightly greater than 29. The design procedure for the phase-shift oscillator begins by using Equation 8–16 to calculate R and C values that will provide the proper oscillation frequency. Then R_1 is equat-

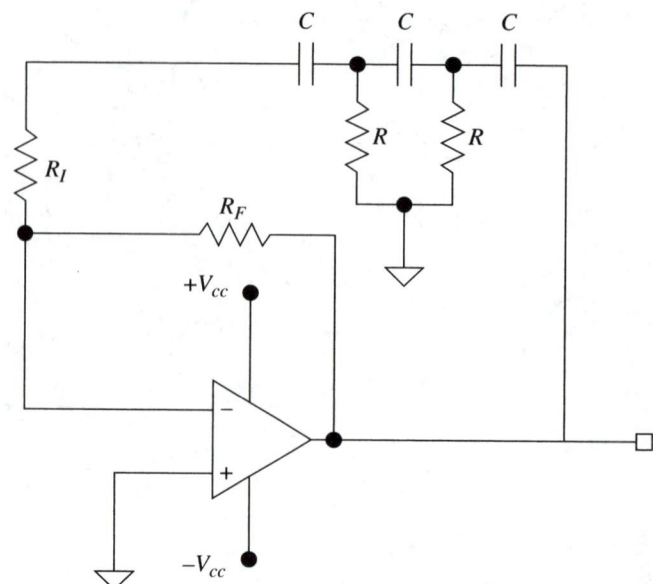

▶ **FIGURE 8–19**
Phase-shift oscillator circuit

ed to the calculated R value and R_F is calculated to provide the inverting input gain $(A = -R_F/R_1)$ which must be slightly greater than 29. However, the phase-shift oscillator has the same amplitude start-up and distortion problem that was discussed for the Wien-Bridge oscillator. The example that follows will show how this problem is rectified in the phase-shift oscillator.

Example 8–7

Design a phase-shift oscillator that will develop a 500kHz sine wave with a peak-to-peak amplitude of ±5 V.

Solution

1. Utilizing the phase-shift oscillator circuit shown in Figure 8–20, solve Equation 8–9 for values of R and C that will promote oscillation at 500 kHz.

   $f = 1/(2\pi \times 2.45\,RC) = 500$ kHz
   Let $C = 100$ pF.
   $R = 1/(2\pi \times 2.45 \times 500\text{ kHz} \times 100\text{ pF}) = 1299\ \Omega$ use 1300 Ω

2. Let $R_1 = R$ and calculate R_F such that the gain $= -29$.

   $-29 = -R_F/\,R_I = -R_F/1300\ \Omega$
   $R_F = 1300(29) = 37{,}700\ \Omega$ use .5% tolerance value of 37,900

3. The gain of the circuit on power up should be higher than 29 to force oscillation to occur quickly. A gain value of 40 is reasonable. The zener diodes

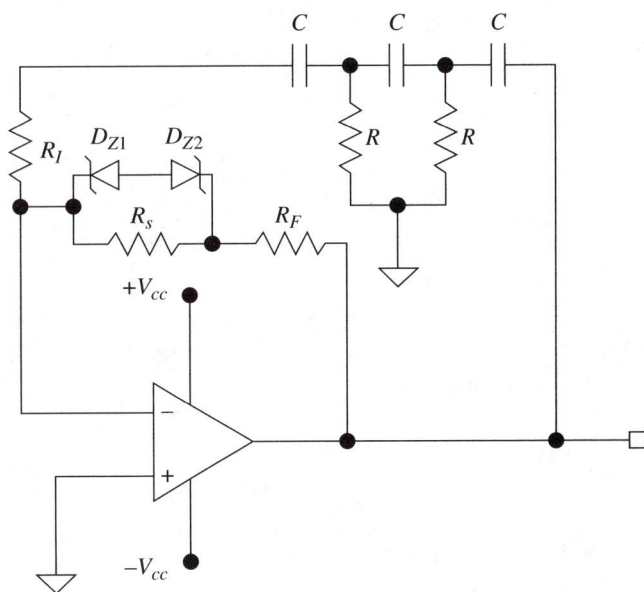

▶ **FIGURE 8–20**
Phase-shift oscillator with gain adjustment

shown in Figure 8–18 function exactly the same as those discussed in Example 8–6. When the oscillator output exceeds the zener voltage rating of the diodes plus .7 V, resistor R_S is shorted out, leaving the gain of the circuit slightly higher than the required gain of 29 to support oscillation. When the oscillator output is low, R_S is added to R_F, increasing the gain of the op amp. Zener diodes D_{Z1} and D_{Z2} are selected to have a zener voltage of 4.3 V that will provide a ±5-V sine wave. To calculate R_S such that the gain is 40 on power up:

$-40 = -(R_F + R_S)/1300$
$R_F + R_S = 52,000$
$R_S = 52,000 - 37,900 = 14,000\ \Omega$
Let $R_S = 14,000\ \Omega$ 1% tolerance value.

The complete design solution is:

V_{CC} is selected as ±12 V
$R = R = R_I = 1300$ 1% tolerance resistors
$R_F = 37,900\ \Omega$ .5% tolerance resistor
$R_S = 14,000\ \Omega$ 1% tolerance value
$C = 100\ \text{pF}$
$D_{Z1} = D_{Z2} = 1N4731\ V_Z = 4.3\ \text{V}$

Twin T Oscillators

A third type of RC oscillator for use at frequencies up to 1 MHz is the Twin T oscillator; so named because of the dual T type filter that is the negative feedback leg of the circuit. Figure 8–21a a shows the Twin T oscillator circuit with the same

(a)

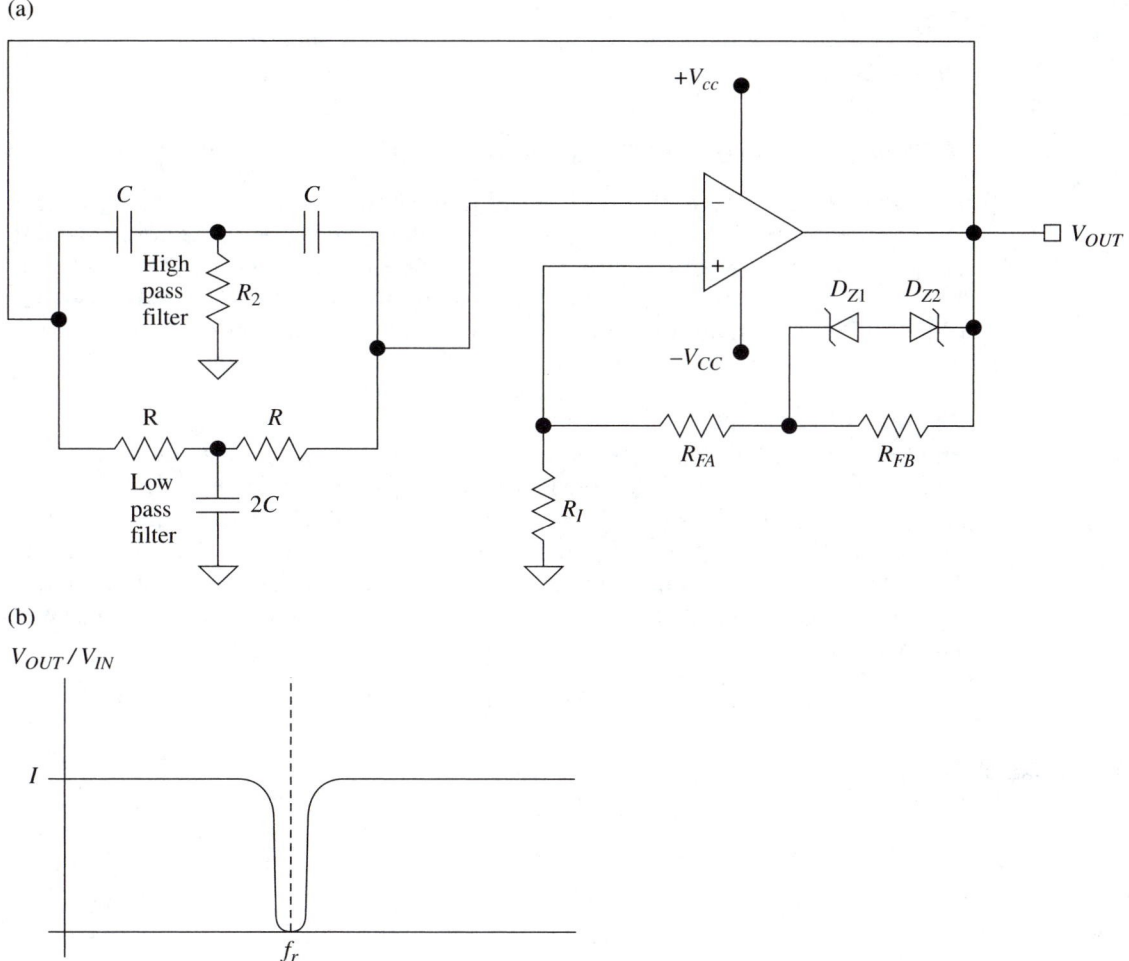

(b)

▲ **FIGURE 8–21**
Twin T oscillator with gain adjustment. (a) Using same gain adjustment as Wien-bridge and phase-shift oscillators. (b) Plot of transfer function.

gain adjustment scheme already discussed for the Wien-Bridge and phase-shift os-cillators. The T filter with two resistors is a low-pass circuit while the dual capac-itor T filter passes high frequencies. Figure 8–21b shows a plot of the transfer function for the Twin T filter, which combines the effects of the high- and low-pass filters to act as a notch filter.

The resonant frequency is given by the following equation:

$$f = 1/(2\pi RC) \qquad (8\text{–}18)$$

The amount of positive feedback is determined by the voltage divided (R_{FA} + R_{FB})/R_I on startup, and after the zener diode ratings are exceeded, this reduces to simply R_{FA}/R_I. R_{FA}/R_1 can range anywhere from 10 to 1000 and as before the peak amplitude of the generated sine wave will be equal to the zener rating of diodes D_{Z1} and D_{Z2}.

LC Sine-wave Generators (Frequencies > 1 MHz)

In order to build circuits that oscillate at frequencies higher than 1 MHz, LC sine-wave generators are most often used. These circuits are usually built out of discrete components because of the closed-loop frequency limitations of most op amps. The design of high-frequency oscillators is complicated by the effects discussed in Chapter 7 on RF amplifiers, such as stray capacitance and inductance and their increased effect on circuit behavior.

Colpitts Oscillator

The Colpitts oscillator is a relatively common LC oscillator whose feedback element, a resonant tank circuit, consists of two capacitors, C_A and C_B, and an inductor, L, as shown in Figure 8–22. The rest of the circuit is simply a voltage divider biased, bipolar AC amplifier. The gain of this circuit equals the effective collector AC resistance divided by the emitter resistance. The AC collector resistance is primarily the impedance of the tank circuit that has a maximum value at resonance. The resonant frequency of the circuit is given by the following equation:

$$f = 1/(2\pi\sqrt{LC}) \text{ where } C = C_A C_B/(C_A + C_B) \tag{8–19}$$

▶ **FIGURE 8–22**

Colpitts oscillator

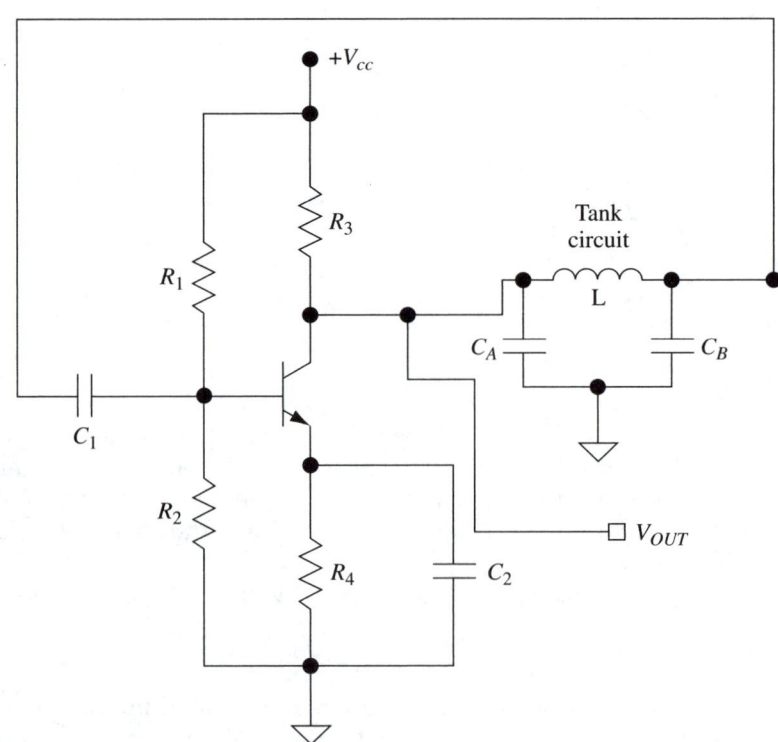

At resonance the amount of signal fed back to the input = C_A/C_B. In order for the circuit to start oscillation, the gain of the amplifier circuit must be > C_B/C_A.

Clapp Oscillator

A variation of the Colpitts oscillator is the Clapp oscillator, which employs an additional capacitor in series with the inductor in the Clapp oscillator's tank circuit (see Figure 8–23). The total capacitance of the tank feedback circuit equals the series equivalent capacitance of capacitors C_A, C_B, and C_C. The equation that approximates the resonant frequency for the circuit is the same as for the Colpitts oscillator:

$$f = 1/(2\pi\sqrt{LC}) \text{ where } C = 1/C_A + 1/C_B + 1/C_C \qquad (8\text{–}20)$$

The advantage of this circuit comes from making the value of C_C significantly smaller than the values of capacitors C_A and C_B. In this case, the value of C_C is the primary determinant of the resonant frequency that eliminates variations caused by stray capacitance between C_A, C_B, and ground.

At resonance the amount of signal fed back to the input = C_A/C_B. In order for the circuit to start oscillation, the gain of the amplifier circuit must be > C_B/C_A.

Hartley Oscillator

Another variation of the Colpitts oscillator is the Hartley oscillator, which interchanges the capacitor and inductor positions in the circuit, so that two inductors are connected to ground in parallel with one capacitor (see Figure 8–24). The

▶ **FIGURE 8–23**
Clapp oscillator

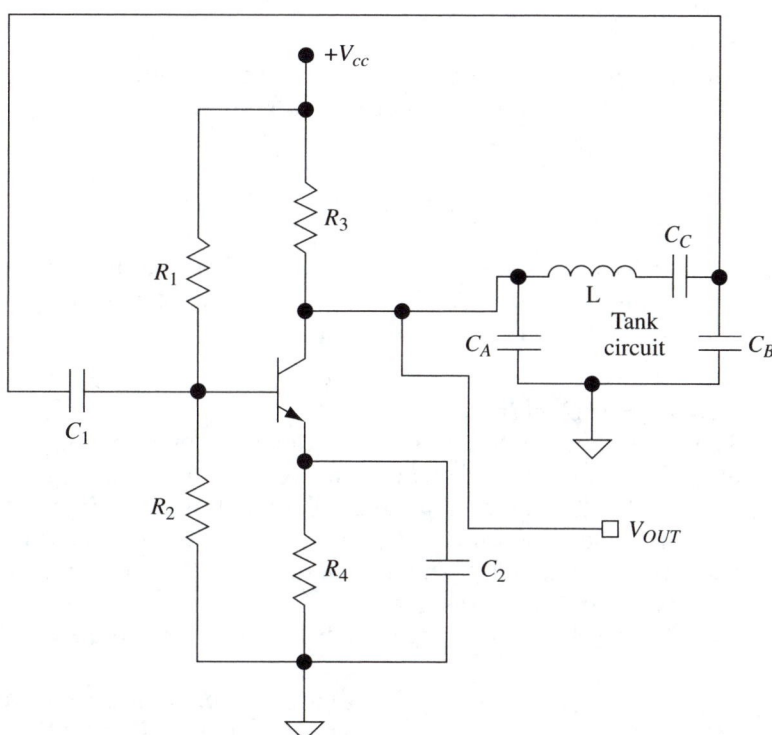

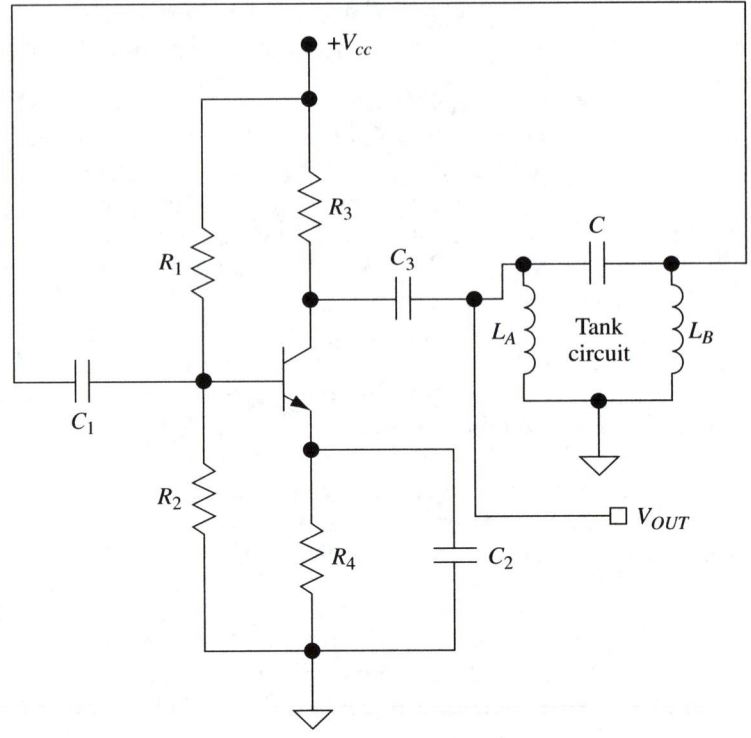

▶ **FIGURE 8–24**
Hartley oscillator

equation that approximates the resonant frequency remains the same as the Colpitts and Clapp oscillators, but inductance value of I is determined by the series equivalent of L_A and L_B:

$$f = 1/(2\pi\sqrt{LC}) \text{ where } L = L_A + L_B \tag{8–21}$$

At the resonant frequency, the attenuation of the output signal fed back to the bipolar amplifier is L_B/L_A. Therefore, the minimum gain of the amplifier required to support oscillation equals L_A/L_B.

Armstrong Oscillator

The Armstrong oscillator uses the primary from a transformer, connected in parallel with a capacitor, as an LC tank circuit. The secondary of the transformer supplies the feedback signal of the bipolar amplifier (see Figure 8–25). The feedback network includes the LC tank circuit and the relationship between the transformer primary and secondary. The inductance L of the tank circuit is the inductance of the primary of the transformer.

The equation that approximates the resonant frequency for the circuit is:

$$f = 1/(2\pi\sqrt{LC}) \text{ where } C \text{ and } L \text{ are the capacitance} \tag{8–22}$$
$$\text{and inductance of the tank circuit}$$

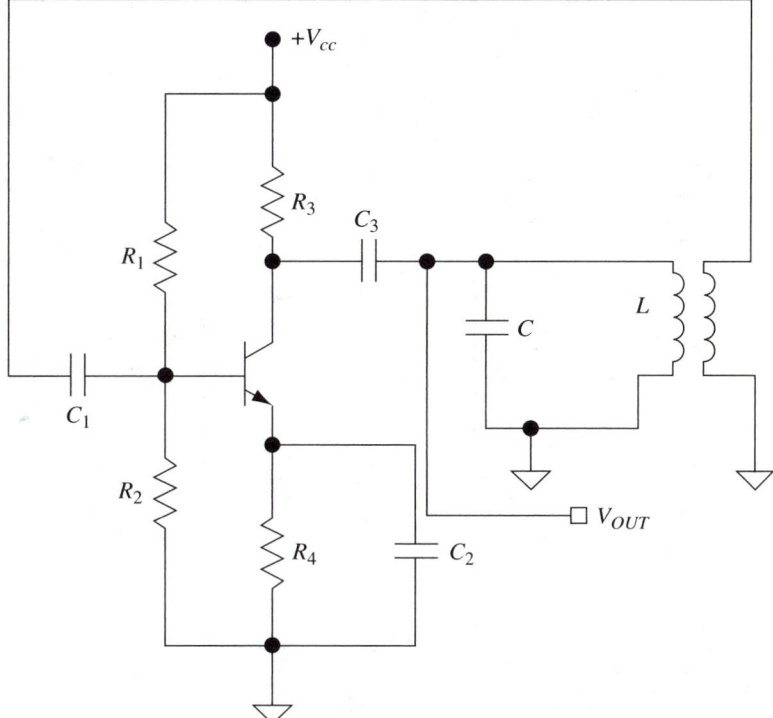

▶ **FIGURE 8–25**
Armstrong oscillator

At the resonant frequency, the attenuation provided by the feedback network equals the mutual inductance between the primary and the secondary M, divided by the inductance L. The gain required to support oscillation equals L/M.

Crystal Oscillator

As discussed for clock circuit generators in Section 8–1, crystals can be used to generate sine waves with very accurate frequencies. A sine-wave crystal oscillator can be developed by replacing the inductor in a Colpitts oscillator with a crystal, rated at the desired oscillation frequency (see Figure 8–26). The resonant frequency of the circuit is the resonant frequency of the crystal. At resonance the amount of signal fed back to the input equals C_A/C_B. In order for the circuit to start oscillation, the gain of the amplifier circuit must be $> C_B/C_A$.

8–7 ▶ Pulse Generators

Pulse generators are very similar to the clock generators discussed in Section 8–2 except that pulse generators can develop a specific positive going pulse and repeat it at the selected frequency. In other words, pulse generators develop a pulse at a selected amplitude, duration, and frequency. Pulse generators can be developed with microprocessor-based circuits under software control or with analog/digital circuits. When using analog/digital circuits, a waveform of some type (usually square or triangle waveforms) is created at the desired frequency, and then a pulse

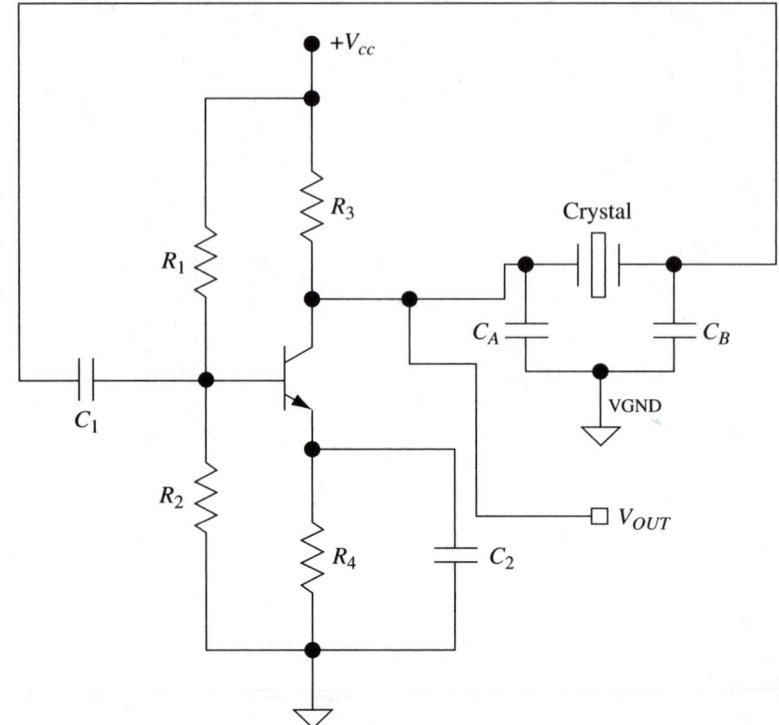

> **FIGURE 8–26**
Crystal oscillator

of the desired amplitude and duration is generated with either a "one shot" or a comparator circuit with an adjustable reference voltage. A "one shot" is another name for a monostable multivibrator, a device that when triggered puts out one pulse with a width that is determined by the RC network connected to it. Let's develop a pulse generator using a comparator circuit.

Example 8–8

Develop a pulse-generator circuit that will output a positive going pulse that is 10 μ seconds in duration with an amplitude of 6 V at a frequency of 20 kHz.

Solution

1. A triangle waveform can be used to develop a specific pulse waveform when it is input to a comparator circuit. Let's start with the triangle-wave generator circuit developed in Example 8–3. This circuit, shown in Figure 8–27, outputs a triangle waveform at 20 kHz with an amplitude of ±5 V.

2. The triangle wave is input to a comparator circuit with an adjustable voltage reference as shown in Figure 8–27. Trimpot TP_1, R_1, and R_2 form a voltage divider that is the reference voltage for the comparator. In order for TP_1 to develop any possible pulse duty cycle, it must be adjustable over the

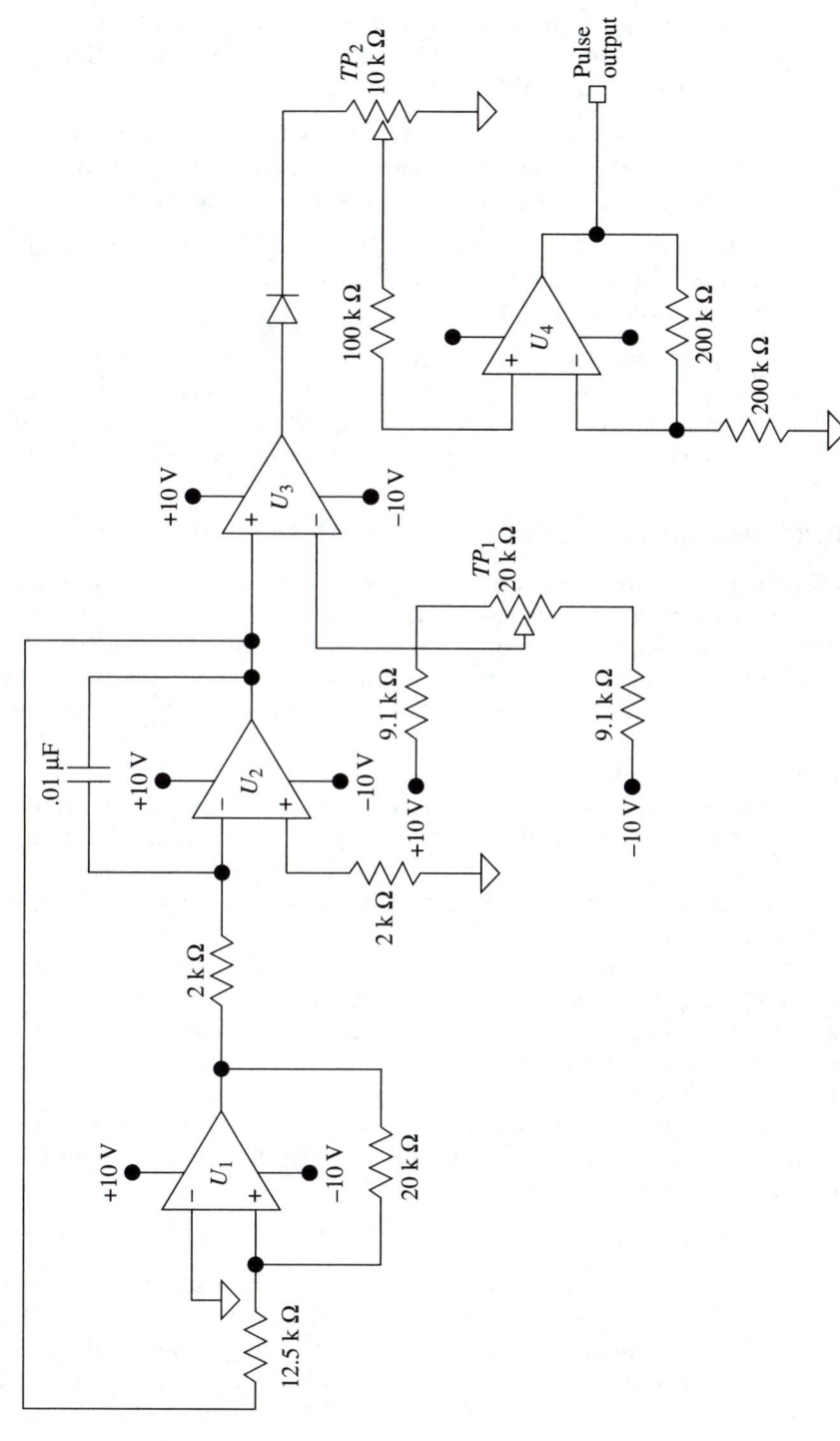

▲ **FIGURE 8–27**
Pulse-generator circuit

entire range of the input triangle waveform (±5 V). Let TP_1 = 20 kΩ while R_1 and R_2 = 9.1 kΩ. When TP_1 is adjusted full CW, the voltage at the wiper arm of TP_1 is +5.2 V. CCW TP_1 = –5.2 V.

3. In order for the output pulse to have a duration of 10 μ seconds, TP_1 must be adjusted to equal +3 V because this is the voltage that represents a 20% duty cycle (10 μ seconds/50 μ seconds = 20% duty cycle).

4. With TP_1 equalling 3 V, the output of comparator U_3 is approximately +8 V for 20 μ seconds and –8 V, for 40 μ seconds. ±8 V is the approximate output saturation voltage for the comparator.

5. The output of U_3 is connected to a diode to remove the negative half of the waveform, which is then input to an attenuation potentiometer TP_2 provided to adjust the amplitude of the peak amplitude down to the specified +6 V. U_4 is simply a non-inverting amplifier that provides the ultimate pulse output.

8–8 ▶ Integrated Circuit Function Generators

There are a number of integrated circuits that have been developed to generate many of the waveforms discussed in this chapter. The first and most common is the 8038 function generator, which is available from a number of manufacturers. The 8038 can create sine, square, triangle, sawtooth, and pulse waveforms with a minimum of external components over the frequency range of .001 Hz to 300 kHz. The sine, square, and triangle waves can be generated simultaneously and the chip can be powered from ±5 to ±15 V.

The block diagram for the 8038 is shown in Figure 8–28. Internally, there are two constant current generators, two comparators, a flip-flop, buffers for the triangle- and square-wave outputs and a triangle-to-sine-wave converter module. The external capacitor C is charged with current source A and discharged with current source B. External resistors RA and RB determine the value for each current source. The constant current sources generate a triangle wave across capacitor C when $R_A = R_B$. The triangle wave switches the flip-flop on and off to generate a square wave. Both the internal square wave and triangle wave are buffered and output to pins 9 and 3, respectively. The internal triangle wave is also sent to the triangle-to-sine-wave converter and then output to pin 2.

To provide 50% duty cycle let, $R = R_A = R_B$ by having just one resistor for both R_A and R_B, and then give the frequency for all of the output waveforms by the following formula:

$$f = .15/RC \qquad (8–23)$$

Figure 8–29 shows the 8038 connected to generate 50% duty cycle, square, triangle, and sine waves at frequencies determined by the values of R and C over the operating frequency range for the device. The amplitudes for the waveforms are approximately equal to the ± power supply values, with the exception of the square-wave output, which can be connected to a different power supply with load resistor R_L. Trimpot resistor TP_1 functions to minimize distortion of the sine-wave output. The optimum value is 82 kΩ, but it is best to make the value adjustable to compensate for potential circuit variations.

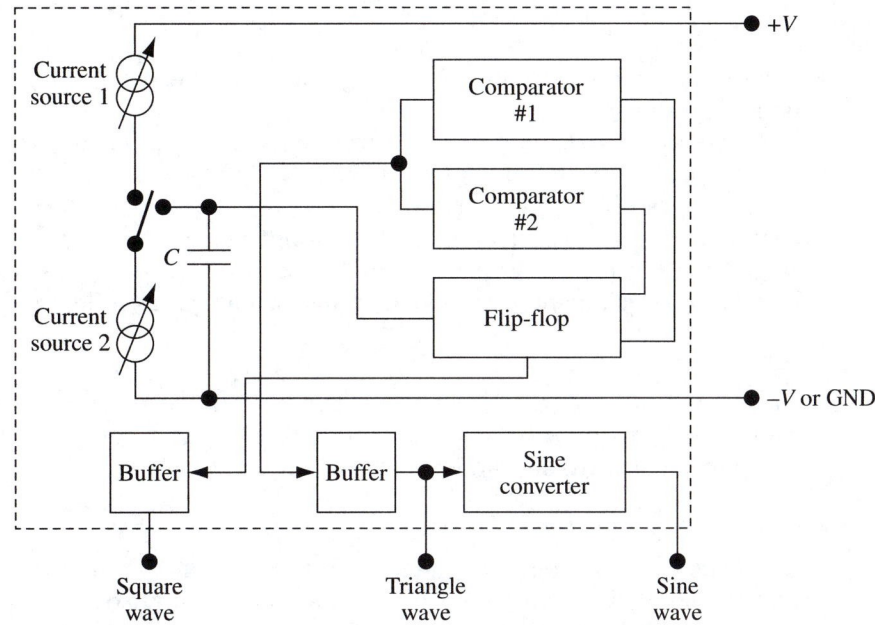

▲ **FIGURE 8–28**
8038 block diagram

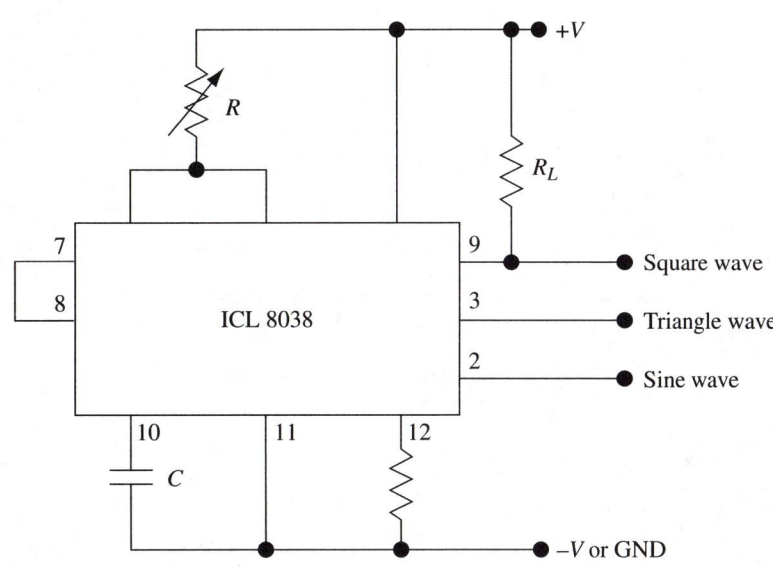

▶ **FIGURE 8–29**
8038 function generator
connector, 50% duty cycle

To create non-symmetrical sawtooth and other waveforms, the values of R_A and R_B must not be equal. This creates a variation in the output frequency whenever either R_A or R_B is varied.

The MAX038 is a newer-function generator IC that operates at a much higher range of frequencies. The MAX038 is similar in operation to the 8038 chip. It uses constant current sources to charge capacitor C, which results in a triangle waveform (see Figure 8–30). The triangle waveform is used to generate both the square and sine waves.

Two logic inputs, A_0 and A_1, determine which of the waveforms are connected to the output through an internal analog multiplexer so the MAX038 can provide only one waveform output at a time. The output frequency is determined by a combination of the current injected into pin I_{IN} and capacitor C. I_{IN} can be an external current source or result from a voltage V_{IN} connected through resistor R. The formula for the fundamental frequency of the oscillator is as follows:

$$f = I_{IN}/C \text{ or } f = V_{IN}/RC \tag{8–24}$$

The MAX038 includes a 2.5-V band-gap reference that can be used for V_{IN}. For example, the frequency of the MAX038 output if the 2.5-V reference signal is connected to a 20-kΩ resistor and $C = 100$ pF is:

$$f = V_{IN}/RC = 2.5 \text{ V}/20 \text{ k}\Omega \times 100 \text{ pF} = 1.25 \text{ MHz}$$

The MAX038 can generate frequencies from less than 1 Hz up to 20 MHz, significantly higher than the 8038 chip. It also possesses separate duty-cycle (DADJ) and frequency modulation (FADJ) inputs that operate independently: duty-cycle adjustments that don't affect the frequency and frequency modulation that does not

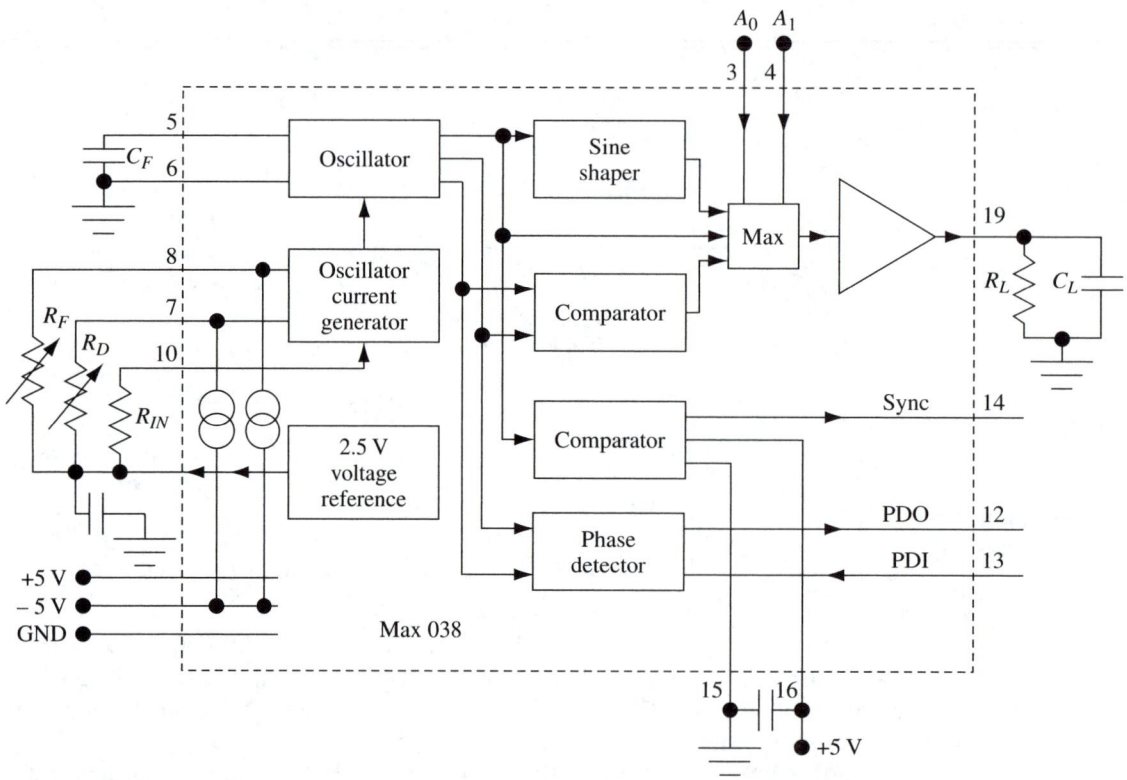

▲ **FIGURE 8–30**
MAX038 block diagram

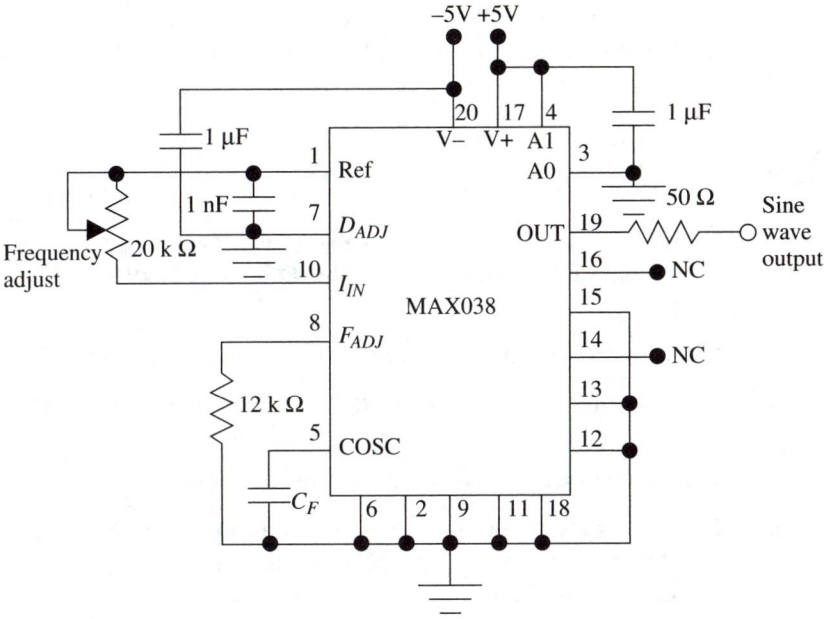

▲ **FIGURE 8–31**
MAX038 function generator circuit

impact the duty cycle. Unlike the 8038, the MAX038 can be powered only by ±5 V DC. Figure 8–31 shows a typical function generator circuit using the MAX038 without the duty cycle or frequency modulation functions.

▶ Summary

In this chapter we have reviewed a wide variety of oscillator and clock circuits that are used in analog and digital circuits that range from computer clocks to RF communications. The two basic types of oscillators are the relaxation type and positive feedback oscillators. Relaxation oscillators function by the charging/discharging of capacitors. Positive feedback oscillators provide positive feedback to an amplifier through a resonant circuit that determines the oscillator frequency. The components of the feedback network are either RC networks, LC networks, or crystals. Voltage-controlled oscillators (VCOs) can be viewed as a subset of relaxation oscillators because they usually use the charging/discharging of capacitors to affect frequency. However, these oscillators all have a primary voltage input that proportionally derives the output frequency. In many ways the VCO is a voltage-to-frequency converter, but there are subtle differences between the two devices.

▶ References

Bell, D. A. 1990. *Operational Amplifiers: Applications, Troubleshooting, and Design.* Upper Saddle River, NJ: Prentice Hall.

Floyd, T. L. 1999. *Electronic Devices.* Upper Saddle River, NJ: Prentice Hall.

Malvino, A. P. 1999. *Electronic Principles.* Westerville, OH: Glencoe-McGraw Hill.

Stanley, W. D. 1994. *Operational Amplifiers with Linear Integrated Circuits.* Upper Saddle River, NJ: Prentice Hall.

▶ Exercises

8–1   Draw two cycles of a pulse waveform that has a frequency of 50 kHz, a peak positive amplitude of 5 V, a peak negative amplitude of 0 V, and a duty cycle of 65%.

8–2   Explain the basic principle of operation for relaxation oscillators.

8–3   What is the benefit of using a crystal as a resonant frequency source as compared to RC or LC circuits?

8–4   What are the three basic types of applications for a 555 timer-counter IC?

8–5   Use a 555 timer-counter to design a free-running pulse circuit that will operate at 50 kHz. The amplitude of the pulse should be +10 V to 0 V and the duty cycle should be 70%.

8–6   Explain why a 555 timer-counter can never achieve a 50% duty cycle without additional circuitry. What additional circuitry can be added to achieve 50% duty cycle?

8–7   Design a circuit that will generate a square wave with ±8 V amplitude at a frequency of 150 kHz.

8–8   Design a circuit that will generate both a triangle and a square wave at a frequency of 50 kHz. The amplitude of the square wave should be ±10 V and the peak amplitude of the triangle wave should be ±6 V.

8–9   Explain the principle of operation of a voltage-controlled oscillator. How can a VCO be used as a voltage-to-frequency converter?

8–10   Design a VCO that will output a sawtooth waveform with a peak amplitude of 5 V and an operating frequency of 20 kHz, when the input control voltage is equal to –2 V.

8–11   Explain the basic principle of operation for positive feedback oscillators. What are the requirements for sustained oscillation to occur?

8–12   Design a Wien-Bridge that will generate a sine wave at a frequency of 100 kHz, at an amplitude of approximately ±6 V.

8–13   Design a phase shift oscillator that will develop a 200 kHz sine wave with a peak-to-peak amplitude of ±8 V.

8–14   What is the benefit of the Clapp oscillator as compared to the Colpitts oscillator?

8–15   What are the major functional differences between the 8038 and the MAX038 function generator ICs?

9 Data Acquisition and Control Circuits

▶ Introduction

Programmable logic controllers (PLCs), micro-based process controllers, and data acquisition systems are widely recognized as the heart of today's industrial control technology. Many advances have been made regarding the inputs to these controllers/systems, as well as the output devices they drive, such as integrated circuit temperature measurement ICs, high-performance A/Ds and D/As, high-resolution encoders and stepper motors, and high power drive electronics. Industrial control and data acquisition circuits utilize a wide variety of the available analog, digital, software and other technologies. Industrial control products are used by a very large group of companies that include manufacturers of all types of products.

Control circuits sense an event or measure a signal level and then generate an appropriate reaction. Sensing an event is usually a digital operation; the event is either occurring or it isn't, the switch is on or off, a photo-switch senses an object or it doesn't. Measuring a signal level is usually an analog operation, at least initially. A variety of parameters are measured with sensors designed to convert their variations into changing voltage/current levels and eventually digital data.

This chapter discusses the application of electronics to many of these control circuit applications. This chapter is subdivided into five major areas:

- ▶ Digital Input Devices: Switches, limit switches, electromechanical relays, proximity detectors, photo-sensors, encoders

- ▶ Analog Input Devices: Voltage/current inputs, temperature measurement, position and liquid level sensing, pressure sensors

- ▶ Data Acquisition and Control Circuits: Timers and time delay functions, voltage/current transmitters, data acquisition and recording, limit devices, ground fault circuit interrupters, on/off controllers, proportional, integral, derivative controllers (PID), PLCs

▶ Output Circuits: electromechanical relays, contactors, solenoids, solid state relays, current voltage outputs, proportional output devices, positioners, triac phase angle fire modules

▶ Data Acquisition and Control Systems: Process control systems, PLCs, SCADA systems

9–1 ▶ Digital Input Devices

Switches and Electromechanical Relays

Switches are very basic circuit components with a wide variety of configurations available. In Chapter 4 we discussed the general switch selection process and the difference between momentary and maintained switches, as well as the concept of poles and throws. Also, the varieties of mechanical configurations were demonstrated: toggle, slide, push, DIP, and so on. All switches are inherently digital in nature because they are either on or off.

Before going much further with the discussion on switches and relays, we must define a special type of schematic diagram commonly used in industrial control systems called ladder logic diagrams. Ladder logic diagrams consist of two vertical rails of the ladder that form the primary voltage that powers the circuit. The rungs of the ladder are drawn horizontally and include circuit elements that are in parallel with all of the other rungs and the rail power supply (see Figure 9–1). The rungs usually include circuit components such as switches, relays, indicator lights, or electronic modules of some kind. Switches or contacts that are considered inputs to the rung are located on the left side of the rung while the rung outputs are located to the right.

It is important to understand that all switches and contacts are shown on a ladder logic diagram in their disengaged, unenergized position. The meaning of the term *disengaged* depends on the type of device being considered. A mechanically engaged on-off switch is disengaged when the switch is in the mechanical OFF position. A float switch that senses the liquid level of fluid in a tank is disengaged when the liquid level is below the location of the float switch. An electro-

▶ **FIGURE 9–1**
Ladder logic diagram example

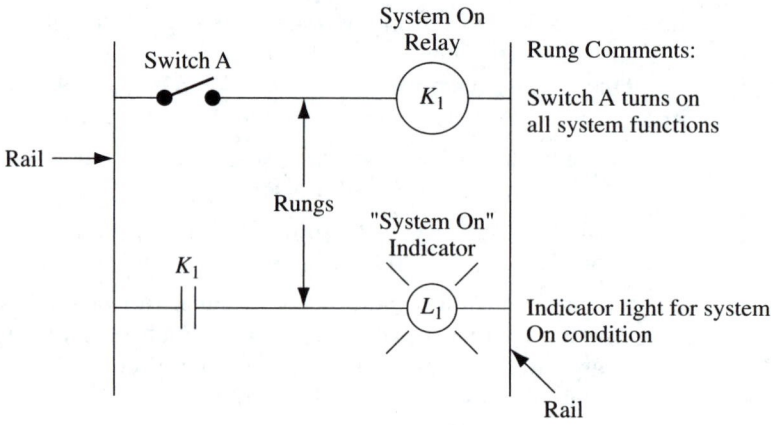

mechanical relay is disengaged when its coil is not powered. Each switch or device can have normally open and or normally closed contacts that are associated with the device. Normally open contacts are those that are open when the device is disengaged and closed when engaged. Normally closed contacts are closed when the device is disengaged and open when engaged.

Each rung is an independent circuit whose output is energized when the switches and contacts on the left side of the rung allow current to flow from the left rail through to the output connected to the right side rail. However, the operation of the rungs are linked together by parallel sets of contacts or contacts that are engaged by relays that are outputs from other rungs. Each rung must have at least one output, or the rung may create a dead short across the power supply. A rung can have more than one output, but they must be in parallel. If two outputs with nominal operating voltages equal to the rail voltage of the ladder circuit are placed on a rung in series, they will split the power supply according to their impedance and will not function.

While any rung theoretically can be placed in any location on the ladder diagram, it makes good sense to position the rungs in order of their sequence of operation and to group rungs that operate together in the same general area. Attaching comments, called "rung comments," is also a good idea to help anyone trying to understand circuit operation. This is analogous to using comments while writing software.

The simple ladder diagram in Figure 9–1 shows switch A as a maintained switch that, when engaged, energizes relay K_1. A normally open set of contacts associated with K_1 close when K_1 is energized, lighting the "system on" indicator light L_1. Figure 9–2 shows a summary of the rules for developing ladder logic diagrams.

1. Two vertically drawn rails represent each side of the power supply.

2. Circuit components are located on horizontally drawn rungs connecting the rails.

3. Inputs are drawn on the left-hand side and outputs are drawn on the right side.

4. A rung cannot have two outputs connected in series and must include at least one output.

5. All contacts are shown in their *disengaged* position.

6. Each rung is an independent circuit but should be located logically close to other interacting rungs and shown in the order of their operational flow.

7. Use rung comments liberally to explain circuit operation.

▲ **FIGURE 9–2**
Rules for ladder logic diagrams

(a)

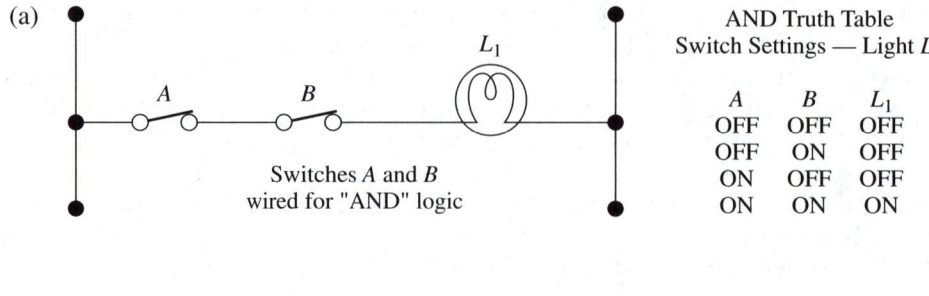

Switches *A* and *B*
wired for "AND" logic

AND Truth Table
Switch Settings — Light L_1

A	B	L_1
OFF	OFF	OFF
OFF	ON	OFF
ON	OFF	OFF
ON	ON	ON

(b)

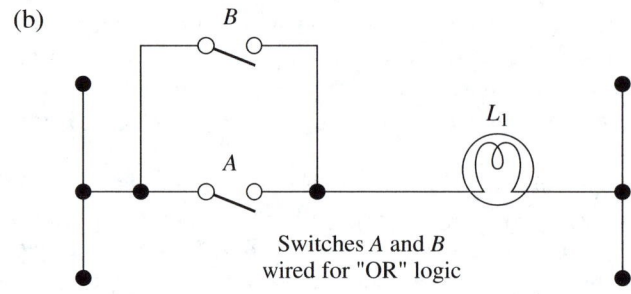

Switches *A* and *B*
wired for "OR" logic

OR Truth Table
Switch Settings — Light L_1

A	B	L_1
OFF	OFF	OFF
OFF	ON	ON
ON	OFF	ON
ON	ON	ON

(c)

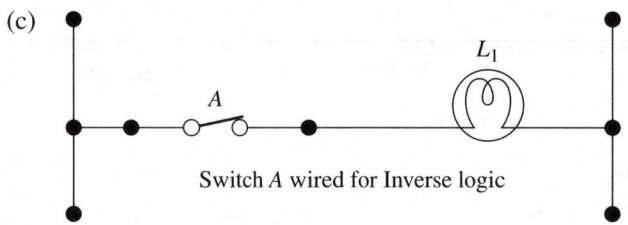

Switch *A* wired for Inverse logic

Inverse Truth Table
Switch Settings — Light L_1

A	L_1
OFF	ON
ON	OFF

(d)

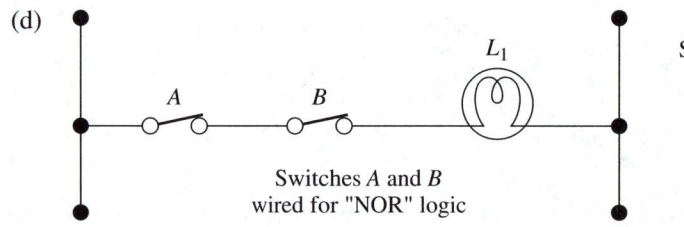

Switches *A* and *B*
wired for "NOR" logic

NOR Truth Table
Switch Settings — Light L_1

A	B	L_1
OFF	OFF	ON
OFF	ON	OFF
ON	OFF	OFF
ON	ON	OFF

▲ FIGURE 9–3
Switch logic ladder diagrams

For industrial control applications it is important to understand how simple switches can be wired together to form the basic logical functions: AND, OR, NOR, and so on. The easiest to reason through are the AND and OR functions. If there are two switches, A and B, where an AND function is required, the normally open contacts for switches A and B should be wired in series. Figure 9–3 shows the lad-

(e)

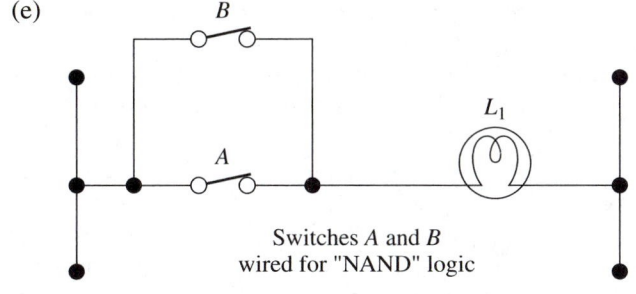

NAND Truth Table
Switch Settings — Light L_1

A	B	L_1
OFF	OFF	ON
OFF	ON	OFF
ON	OFF	OFF
ON	ON	OFF

Switches *A* and *B*
wired for "NAND" logic

(f)

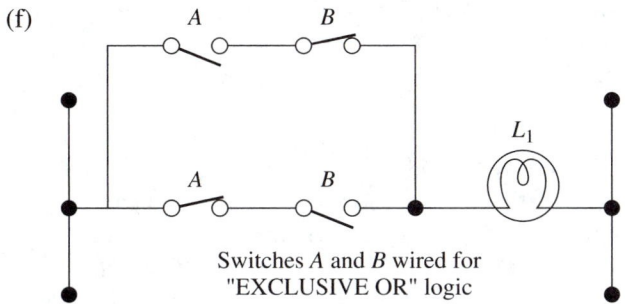

EXCLUSIVE OR Truth Table
Switch Settings — Light L_1

A	B	L_1
OFF	OFF	OFF
OFF	ON	ON
ON	OFF	ON
ON	ON	OFF

Switches *A* and *B* wired for
"EXCLUSIVE OR" logic

(g)

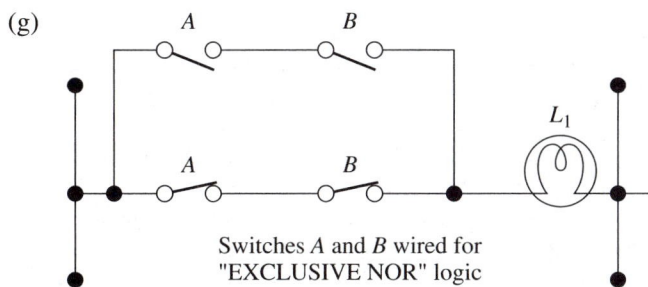

EXCLUSIVE NOR Truth Table
Switch Settings — Light L_1

A	B	L_1
OFF	OFF	ON
OFF	ON	OFF
ON	OFF	OFF
ON	ON	ON

Switches *A* and *B* wired for
"EXCLUSIVE NOR" logic

▲ **FIGURE 9–3** *(continued)*

der diagrams and truth tables for the switch logic functions being described here. If the OR function is required, the normally open contacts for switches A and B are wired in parallel. Invert functions can be achieved simply by using the normally closed set of contacts instead of the normally open ones. In Figure 9–3c the indicator light L_1 will light when switch A is not activated, providing the inverse function of using the normally open contacts.

Figure 9–3d shows the truth table for the NOR function and the ladder diagram. The NOR function is accomplished with switches by wiring the normally closed switch contacts for A and B in series, while the NAND function results from wiring the normally closed contacts from switches A and B in parallel (see Figure 9–3e). The remaining two combinational logic functions are the EXCLUSIVE-OR and the EXCLUSIVE-NOR. These are shown in Figures 9–3f and 9–3g, respectively. Both of these logical functions require using two sets of contacts from each switch; both normally closed and normally open contacts are required for each switch.

Electromechanical relays are contacts that are energized by electromagnetic coils. The contacts are often used as inputs to circuits in the same manner that mechanical switches are. The contacts arrangements and terminology for electromechanical relays are the same as for mechanical switches. (Refer back to Chapter 4 for the discussion of "poles" and "throws" and how they define the contact arrangement for mechanical switches and relays.) On schematic diagrams and ladder logic diagrams the coils for electromechanical relays are shown as a circle with a unique name or identifier shown within the circle. Very often the letters used for identifying relay coils are C, K, R or CR (stands for control relay) but any name scheme can be used. In addition to the basic name, numbers are attached to make the relays unique. For example, if K is chosen as the basic name scheme, the first relay used might be called K_1, the second K_2, and so on (see Figure 9–4). The contacts associated with any relay coil carry the same basic name as the coil. If more than one set of contacts are associated with a particular relay, such as a DPDT arrangement, then various schemes are used. It is most common to see a dash with a number added to differentiate between the physical contacts. For example, if relay K_1 has DPDT contacts, which means that there are two complete sets of contacts with common, normally open and normally closed connections, one set might be labeled K_{1-1} and the other K_{1-2} (see Figure 9–4).

Example 9–1

Review Figure 9–4 and analyze the circuit operation.

Solution

Figure 9–4 is a schematic shown in ladder logic format. On the first rung of the diagram, if momentary switch A is depressed before B, coil K_1 is energized. When K_1 is energized, normally open contacts K_{1-1} close, latching around the momentary

▶ **FIGURE 9–4**
Relay coils and contacts

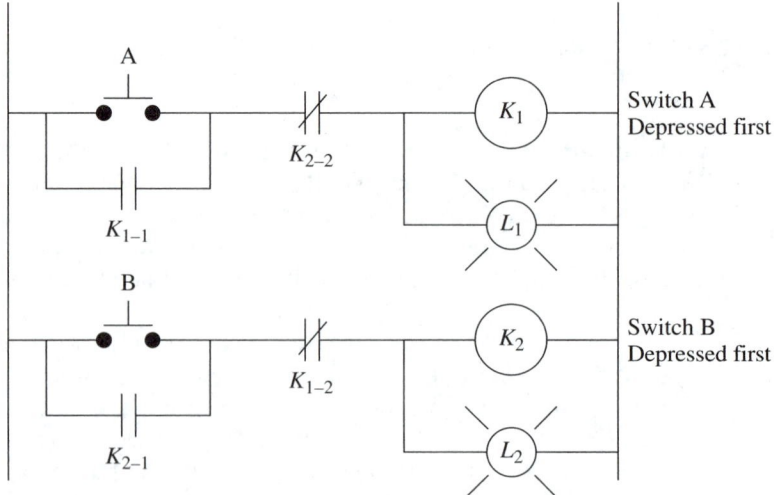

switch A when it is released. (These are called hold-in or seal-in contacts.) At the same time normally closed contacts K_{1-2} open, breaking the connection from switch B to relay coil K_2. Indicator light L_1 is in parallel with K_1 and lights whenever K_1 is energized.

On the second rung of the diagram, if momentary switch B is depressed before switch A, coil K_2 is energized. When K_2 is energized, normally open contacts K_{2-1} close, latching around the momentary switch B when it is released. At the same time normally closed contacts K_{2-2} open, breaking the connection from switch A to relay coil K_1. Indicator light L_2 is in parallel with K_2 and lights whenever K_2 is energized.

The circuit operates to determine which switch, A or B, is depressed first and latches in to maintain this information for use in the system or by a system operator.

Limit Switches

Limit switches are special switches that are engaged mechanically by an object as opposed to being depressed by a person, as regular switches are. In other words, limit switches detect when the degree of mechanical movement has reached a particular level by the switching of the contacts. Limit switches can have a variety of contact arrangements and are identified in the same way as other switches. Figure 9–5 shows a limit switch and its schematic symbol.

Temperature, Pressure, and Float Switches

Temperature switches measure temperature and compare it with a preset or adjustable control point, engaging a set of contacts when the control point is exceeded. The temperature level can be measured mechanically (fluid/gas filled or bi-metallic sensors) or electrically (thermocouples, RTDs, thermistors, etc.). A thermostat is just another name for a temperature switch. The switches incorporated in temperature switches can have contact arrangements like those already discussed for standard mechanical switches. Figure 9–6 shows the schematic symbol for a SPDT temperature switch.

Pressure switches are similar to temperature switches. Pressure can be measured mechanically or electrically to engage a set of contacts when the control

▶ **FIGURE 9–5**
Limit switch example

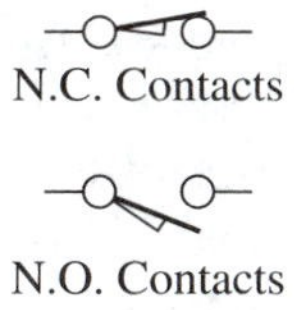

N.C. Contacts

N.O. Contacts

▶ **FIGURE 9–6**
Temperature switch example

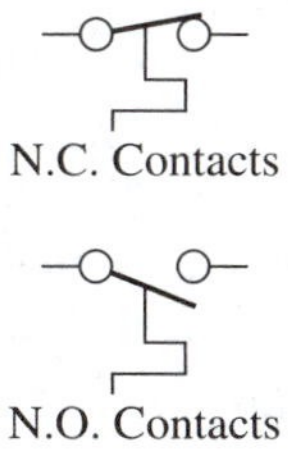

N.C. Contacts

N.O. Contacts

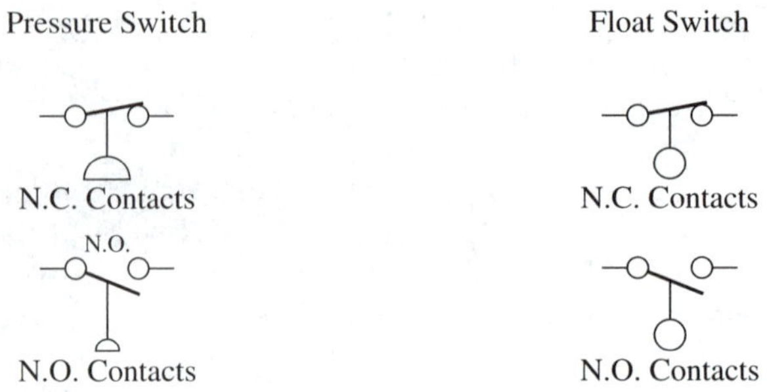

Pressure Switch

Float Switch

N.C. Contacts

N.C. Contacts

N.O.

N.O. Contacts

N.O. Contacts

▶ **FIGURE 9–7**
Pressure and float
switch examples

point is exceeded. Figure 9–7 shows the schematic symbol for a pressure switch. Float switches usually include a mechanical arm with a float that indicates the level of a liquid. When the liquid level exceeds the mechanical trip point, the switch contacts are engaged.

Limit, temperature, pressure, and float switches are those most often used to measure and compare a parameter value to a control point and engage a set of contacts accordingly. However, there are many other varieties of switches that operate in a similar manner.

Proximity Detectors

Proximity detectors detect the presence of an object without making physical contact with the object. They perform the same function as mechanical limit switches except that actual contact between the sensor and the object is not required. There are three classes of proximity detectors: inductive, capacitive, or Hall-effect activated.

Inductive proximity detectors utilize LC oscillator circuits, which are similar to those discussed in Chapter 8, to develop an oscillator signal that is based upon the inductance value of the sensing inductor. The sensing inductor is a coil that is wrapped around a ferrite core. When the ferrite core is not in close proximity to any ferrous metallic materials, the inductance of the coil wound around the ferrite core has a value that equates to the resonant frequency of the LC tank circuit fed back from the amplifier output (see Figure 9–8). Therefore, when the sensor does not detect any ferrous materials, the oscillator will oscillate at the resonant frequency. Detection of ferrous materials causes the effective inductance of the coil to change, forcing the oscillator out of high-level oscillation. This change in the oscillator output is easily detected with a demodulator and comparator that switches on either a transistor or a relay output to indicate the presence of magnetic material.

Inductive proximity sensors are used in applications to detect metal objects, in poor environmental conditions (humidity, temperature, vibration and shock) without any physical contact or contact bounce, and with very quick response time.

Capacitive proximity sensors have the same basic structure as inductive proximity detectors. They include an oscillator, demodulator, comparator, and output stage. However, they overcome the most significant shortcoming of inductive proximity sensors: they can detect the presence of both conductive and nonconduc-

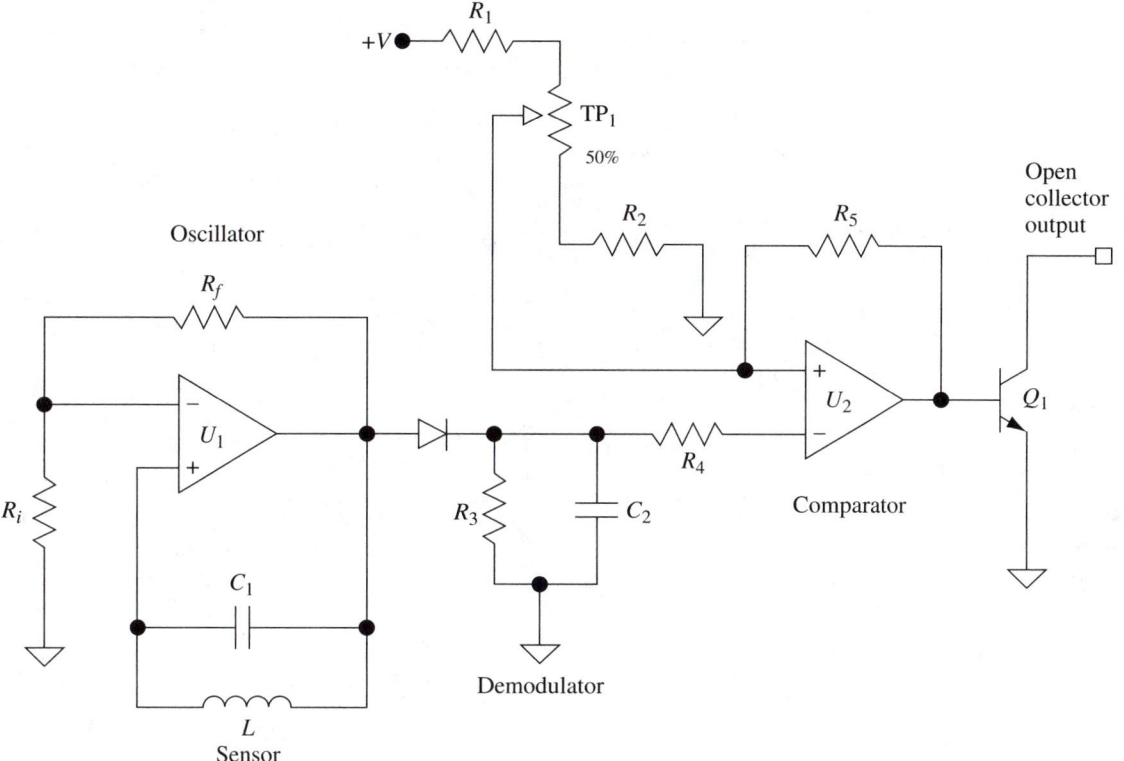

▲ FIGURE 9–8
Inductive proximity detector

tive materials. The sensor is a capacitor, the dielectric of which is either air or the object being sensed. When the object sensed is nonconductive, the capacitance increases because the dielectric constant is greater than one, the dielectric constant for air. When a conductive object is sensed, this effectively creates another electrode for the capacitor, reducing the distance between the plates and thereby increasing the capacitance.

The circuit for the capacitive proximity sensor is based upon an RC oscillator circuit (see Figure 9–9). The capacitance sensor becomes the capacitance value of the RC circuit. It either induces oscillation at the resonant frequency when an object is present or there is low amplitude or no oscillation when no object is detected. This is the opposite function of the inductive proximity detector. As with the inductive proximity detector, the demodulator and comparator detect oscillation and switch the output accordingly. However, the output function is reversed to compensate for the inverted oscillator properties (oscillation occurs when an object is sensed in the capacitive sensor, when no object is detected in the inductive sensor).

Capacitance proximity sensors can be used to detect the presence of solids, powdered materials, or liquids. They can sense both conductive and nonconductive materials as long as their dielectric constant is reasonably high.

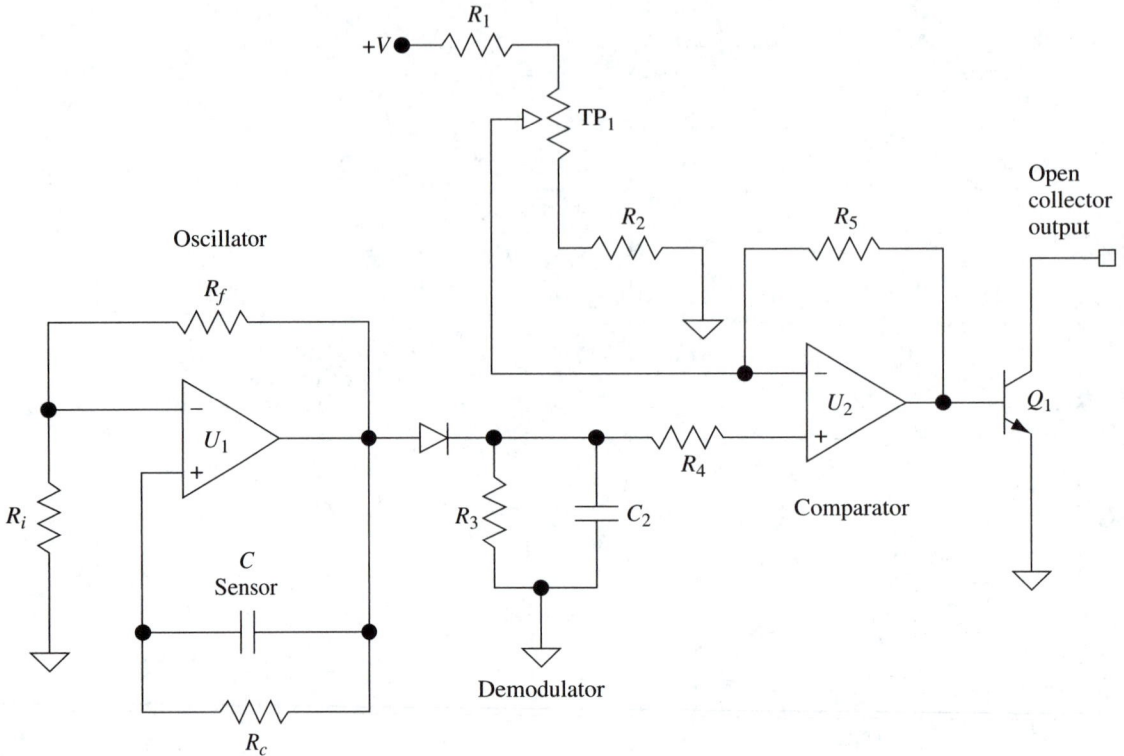

▲ FIGURE 9–9
Capacative proximity detector

Hall-effect sensors detect the presence of a magnetic field. The sensor itself is constructed from P-type semiconductor material. A power supply is connected to two sides of the P-type materials and the opposing sides are the detector connections for the "Hall" voltage. The Hall voltage is generated when a perpendicular magnetic field is in close proximity to the P-type material. A comparator circuit senses the Hall voltage and switches the output transistor on or off accordingly (see Figure 9–10). Hall-effect sensors can only be used to detect permanent magnet or electromagnetic materials. They can function in applications with poor environmental conditions that require fast response times and high frequencies.

Photo-sensors

Photo-sensors use the detection of light to determine the presence of an object. All photo-sensors include both a light source and a light detector. The types of light generated by the transmitters are red, green, or infrared. Red is used for general applications, green for the detection of color marks, and infrared is utilized to detect objects over long distances. There are three different methods for using light to detect objects: through-beam, retro-reflective, and diffuse (also called *reflective*). The performance of photo-sensors is determined by the following specification parameters:

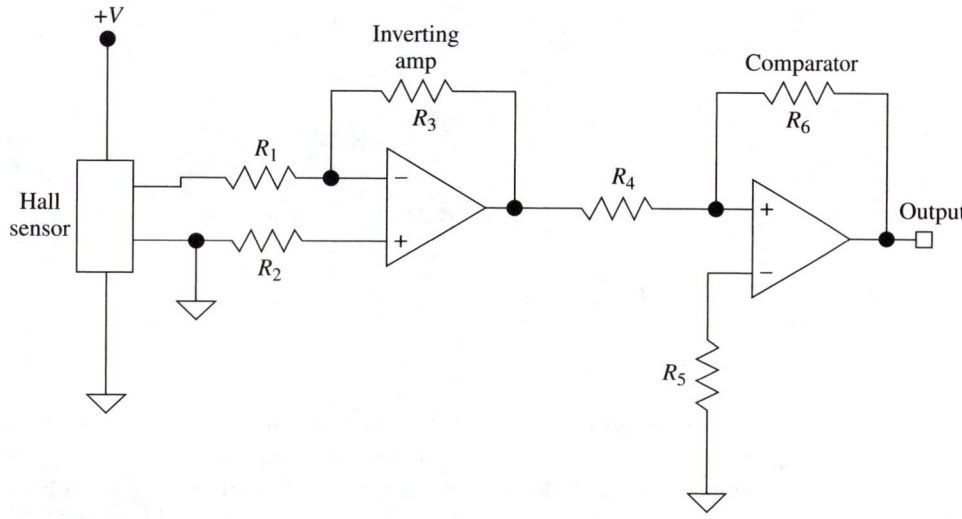

▲ FIGURE 9–10
Hall-effect detector

1. Minimum size object that can be detected
2. Maximum distance over which an object can be detected
3. Immunity to ambient light
4. Minimum amount of light needed for detection

Lenses can be used on either the light source, to reduce the size of the beam, or the detector, to reduce the sensed area.

Through-beam photo-sensors have a separate light source and detector that face each other, as shown in Figure 9–11. The light source and detector are aligned so that the light transmitted from the source is received continually by the detector when no object is blocking its path. Objects are detected when they break the beam, causing the detector to change the state of its output accordingly. Through-beam sensing can detect smaller objects over longer distances and is the most accurate

▶ FIGURE 9–11
Through-beam photo-sensor

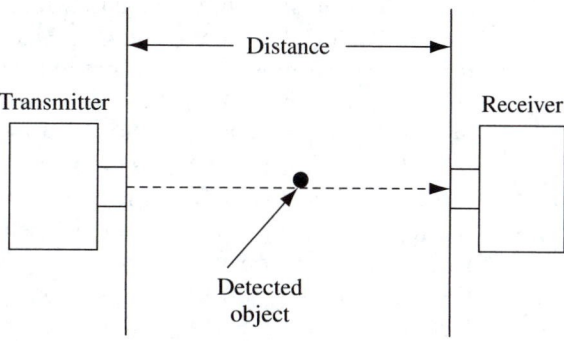

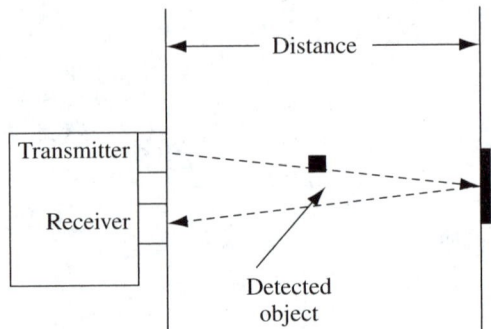

▶ **FIGURE 9–12**
Retro-reflective photo-sensor

photo-sensing method. However, through-beam sensors require two separate packages (light source and detector) that must be carefully aligned.

Retro-reflective sensors contain the light source and the detector in the same package, yet operate in a manner similar to that of the through-beam photo-sensor (see Figure 9–12). Retro-reflective sensors use a reflective disc (similar to a bicycle reflector) to reflect the light back to the detector that resides in the same package as the light source. Objects are detected when they break either the transmitted beam or the returned beam. The angle between the two beams depends upon the displacement between the light source and the detector as well as the distance between the sensor package and the reflector. As the angle increases, the accuracy of the location of the sensed object decreases. This is because the object can break either the transmitted or returned beam, and its location will differ slightly in each instance.

Retro-reflective photo-sensors include the electronics in a single package so they are easier to wire and install. However, the photo-sensor package must still be aligned with the reflector. The amount of light returned to the detector is significantly less than occurs with the through-beam sensor. The lower detected light level combined with the small angle between the transmitted and reflected light limit the size of the object and the range of detection. Retro-reflective sensors are limited to detecting larger objects over medium distances.

Diffuse photo-sensors also have the light source and the detector included in the same package. However, diffuse photo-sensors react to light that is reflected from the object being sensed. This is contrary to the operation of through-beam and retro-reflective photo-sensors, which detect no light when an object is being detected. The light source residing in the diffuse photo-sensor transmits light continuously. When no object is present in the path of the transmitted light, the detector sees only ambient light or the transmitted light reflected from other objects in the area of the sensor. When an object with enough reflective properties is placed in the path of the transmitted light, enough light is reflected back to the detector to cause the output to switch, indicating detection of the object. Diffuse photo-sensors offer the least accuracy and performance when compared to through-beam and retro-reflective photo-sensors, because they are more sensitive to ambient light conditions, and, like retro-reflective sensors, the amount of light reflected from the object is significantly less than the amount transmitted (see Figure 9–13).

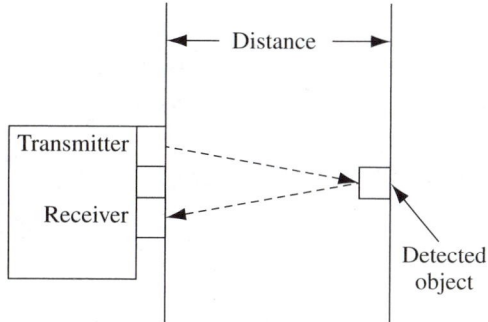

► FIGURE 9–13
Diffuse photo-sensor

There are a variety of schemes to minimize the effect of ambient light on photo-sensor detection. One method is to detect ambient light levels electronically, subtracting them from the total light detected by the sensor. Another method is to strobe the light source and enable the detector simultaneously at a frequency where the ambient light is a minimum. Fluorescent lights powered by 60 Hz AC power actually vary their light intensity at a frequency of 60 Hz, with the minimum light output occurring at the zero-voltage crossing point. A sensor can detect the zero crossing, trigger the light source, and enable the detector simultaneously, creating a situation in which the detector is "looking" for the light signal at a time when the ambient light is at a minimum.

Encoders

Encoders are sensors used to monitor the position of any device attached to the encoder. Encoders can be used to monitor either angular or linear motion, but rotary encoders measuring angular position are the most commonly used. Encoders are included in the digital input category because the output of the encoder is a digital pulse. However, when the device that receives all of the pulses counts them, the net result is a value for the position of the encoder shaft. There are also two other classifications of encoders: relative encoders and absolute encoders. Relative encoders put out a pulse for any relative movement. For example, a relative rotary encoder might output a pulse for every 3 degrees of angular rotation. The net angular position results from knowing the starting position and counting the pulses in either direction. If there is a power outage, the relative encoder loses all previous information. Relative encoders usually employ a zero position sensor for use as a reference for the start position. On system start-up the encoder shaft is positioned at the zero position and relative motion is determined from the zero point. Absolute encoders maintain and provide an output for the actual position of the encoder at all times.

Rotary encoders are constructed using a through-beam photo-sensor concept. Inside the housing there are two light sources, a disk, grid, and two photo-detectors (see Figure 9–14). The disk and grid are attached to the shaft. The light sources and detectors are arranged in through-beam pairs, 90° out of phase with each other. The disk and the grid have opaque and transparent sections etched

▶ **FIGURE 9–14**
Rotary encoder *(Courtesy Omron Electronics, LLC. Used by permission.)*

into them to allow light to pass through to the detector after a particular amount of rotation. The transparent sections are spaced equidistant around the disk, providing an output pulse after a certain amount of angular rotation. Photographic etching processes applied to glass have greatly improved the performance and cost of encoders. These processes provide precision etching of the glass disk and grid, allowing very small transparent areas finely spaced around the disk assembly. This results in encoders with very fine resolution. Relative position, rotary, glass disk encoders offer resolutions in the range of 100–6000 segments per 360 angular degrees of rotation. A 100-segment encoder breaks up the 360° of rotation into 3.6°. A 6000-segment encoder provides one pulse for every .06° of angular movement.

Most encoders provide three output signals that are used by the device receiving the signals to determine the actual position of the shaft. Channels A and B are the signals generated for each transparent segment. The signals output to Channels A and B are out of phase by approximately 90°. The receiving device uses this out-of-phase relationship to determine the direction of angular rotation. If Channel A leads B, then the encoder shaft is moving in a positive (clockwise) direction. Channel B leading A means that the shaft is moving in a negative direction (counterclockwise). (see Figure 9–15). A third signal, called a *control signal*, generates an output pulse after every complete revolution in one direction.

9–2 ▶ Analog Input Devices

Analog input devices convert the value of a physical parameter, such as temperature or pressure, into a voltage or current so that its value can be monitored, displayed, controlled, or recorded. Section 9–3 discusses the devices that perform these operations. There are many types of analog input devices used to measure the following physical parameters:

Voltage/current

Temperature

Position/level

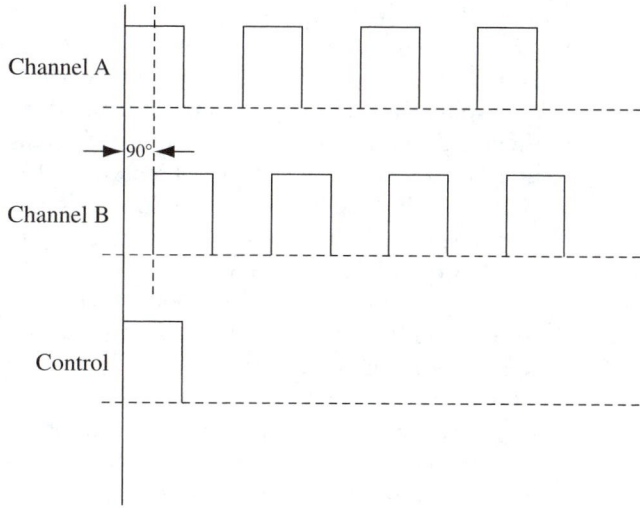

▶ **FIGURE 9–15**
Encoder output signals

       Pressure

       Flow

       Force/weight

       Speed/acceleration

       Humidity, conductivity

       PH, density, viscosity

Many of these signals are fairly slow in changing value, especially temperature. Pressure and flow are examples of fast-changing process variables. Each signal is viewed as a DC or low-frequency input as far as the speed of input changes that occur. This section will review the application of electronics to a few of the more popular types of analog input devices.

Voltage/Current Inputs

Voltage and current are the two most easily measured parameters and represent the starting point for our discussion of analog input devices. Voltage can be easily measured, amplified, digitized, and indicated. Voltage is the most desirable form for any measured parameter to be measured. Current inputs are handled almost as easily; they are simply passed through a resistor to generate a voltage. Currents can also be measured indirectly by measuring the electromagnetic field around a wire carrying current with current "donuts" or clamp-on ammeters.

    Many times after a parameter has been converted to a voltage or current, it is desirable to amplify the signal further before connection to a controller or indicator. This is especially true if the controller or indicator is located some distance away from the sensor. A low-level signal transmitted over a long distance is much more likely to experience significant attenuation and pick up unwanted noise. Because the signal level is smaller, noise levels appear relatively larger and are harder to ignore or reject. To resolve this problem, devices called *transmitters* are used to amplify the input to standard voltage/current signal levels. The most common of these signals for industrial instrumentation are 4–20 mA and 1–5 V. When 4–20 mA or 1–5-V signals are used to transmit analog signal information, the low end of the signal (4 mA or 1 V) represents the minimum range of measured input while the high-end signal (20 mA or 5 V) represents the maximum-input signal value.

For example, if a temperature transmitter uses a thermistor to measure temperature over a range of 0° to 300°F and has a 4–20 mA output, then a 4 mA signal represents 0°F and 20 mA represents 300°F. Otherwise, the 4–20 mA is proportional to the input such that a 12 mA output equals 150°F, 16 mA equals 225°F, 8 mA equals 75°F, and so on. The output of this transmitter would be connected to a device, such as a digital indicator with a standard 4–20 mA input. The digital indicator would need to know the type of signal represented by the 4–20 mA (temperature in °F, pressure, etc.) and the input range vs. the 4–20 mA range. This information is keyed into the digital indicator in the following form: Units, °F; Minimum range, 0; Maximum range, 300. The indicator will then scale the display to show the actual temperature measured by the thermistor.

4–20 mA signals are constant current signals. This means that when the low-end input signal is provided, 4 mA will be the output to any load device as long as its load impedance is below the maximum impedance the constant current source can drive. The 4–20 mA signals are easily converted to 1–5 V by passing the current through a 250-Ω resistor.

Temperature Measurements

Temperature can be converted to an electrical medium by using sensors that vary their voltage or resistance as temperature changes. The most commonly used temperature sensors are thermistors, RTDs, thermocouples, and IC temperature sensors.

Thermistors

Thermistors vary their resistance as temperature changes. There are many varieties and types of thermistors. Most provide a large change in resistance per degree of temperature change and exhibit a negative temperature coefficient (the resistance decreases as the temperature increases). Thermistors are categorized by their resistance value at 32°F (0°C), which is relatively large at 1000 Ω or greater. The relationship between the temperature and the resistance is nonlinear (see Figure 9–16).

In order to convert the resistance change to a voltage, a resistor is placed in series with the thermistor and a voltage applied to the circuit (see Figure 9–17a). Because of the high thermistor resistance value, the relative resistance of the connecting leads is not high enough to cause significant lead length error, as experienced with other resistance sensors. Either an analog or digital circuit that indicates, monitors, records, or controls temperature receives the voltage signal across the thermistor. Another common thermistor circuit is the bridge circuit shown in Figure 9–17b. Thermistors are an inexpensive and simple method for

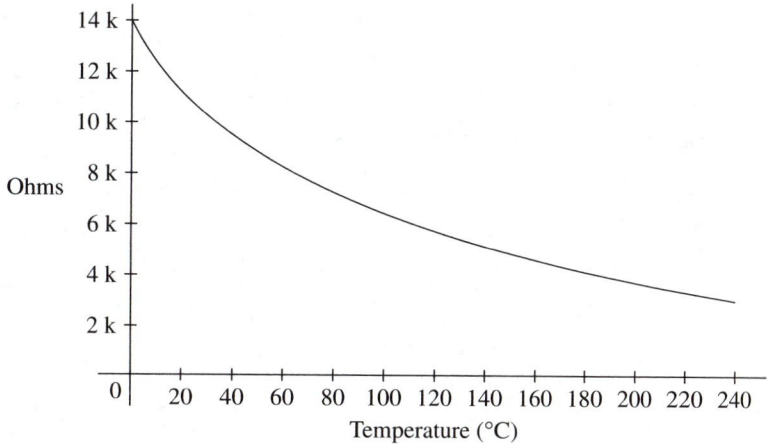

► **FIGURE 9–16**
Thermistor Resistance
vs Temperature

measuring temperature over ranges of approximately 0° to 300°F. Their negative
temperature coefficient, large nonlinear change in resistance, and limited accuracy limit their use to the least critical applications.

Resistance Temperature Detectors (RTDs)

RTDs also vary their resistance with temperature. However, the nature of the resistance change is much different than that experienced with thermistors. RTDs
offer a very linear response and positive temperature coefficient. The amount of
resistance change is small, only about .2 Ω/°F. The nominal resistance value (the
resistance at 32°F) for an RTD is usually 100 Ω. They are fabricated most often
with a nickel or platinum material. Their construction takes the form of wire,
wrapped around a bobbin or thick fim substrates. The resistance values are controlled with great accuracy and RTDs can be used over a temperature range of

► **FIGURE 9–17**
Thermistor temperature measurement
circuits

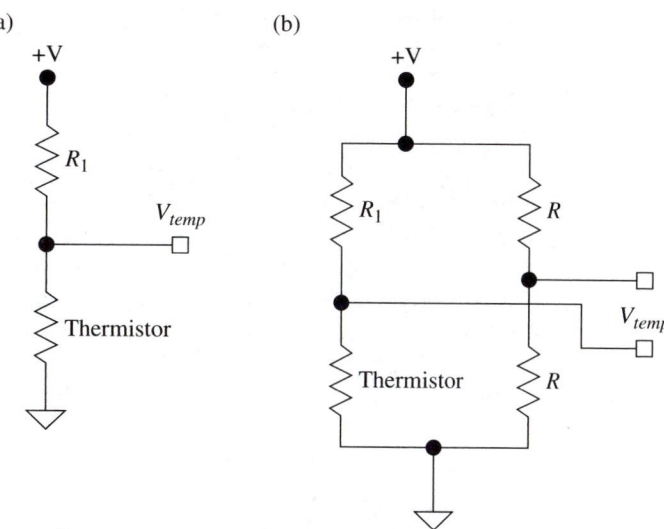

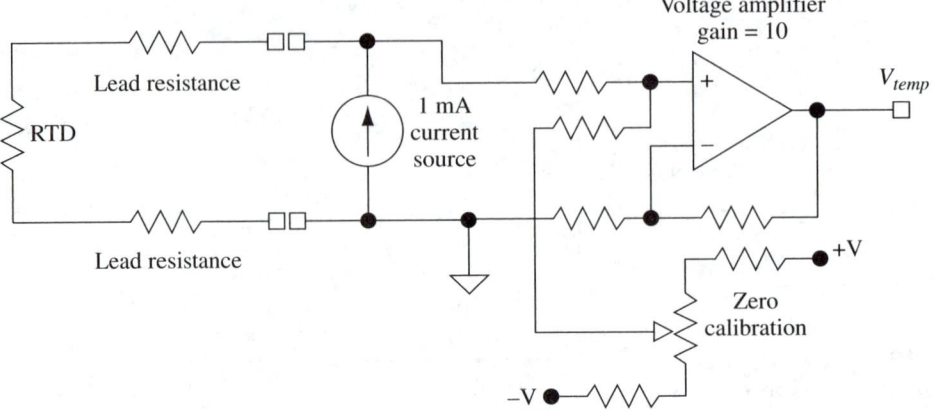

▲ **FIGURE 9–18**
RTD temperature measurement circuit

−100° to 800°F. RTDs are the most accurate temperature sensors available and are commended for use in critical applications. RTDs are linear enough so that further linearization is not required for many applications when the RTD signal is converted to a digital value.

Because both the nominal resistance value and the change in resistance of RTDs are small, the near linear resistance vs. temperature relationship can be preserved by using a constant current source to generate a voltage signal across the RTD. To prevent self-heating of the RTD, the current is usually kept below 1 mA. (see Figure 9–18). Because the resistance value of the RTD is relatively small, lead resistance is more significant. The resistance of the leads adds to the resistance of the RTD, making the voltage seen by the sensing circuit larger than it would be without any lead resistance. The size and length of the connecting leads, as well as the required measurement accuracy, determine whether the amount of lead length error must be compensated for.

The simplest method for minimizing lead length error is to use the shortest lead lengths and the largest conductor size possible, thereby reducing the net lead resistance. A calibration circuit can be added to compensate the circuit for any lead length error. This is shown in Figure 9–18. To calibrate the circuit, the sensor should be placed in a medium for which the temperature value is known. The voltage output from the voltage amplifier is adjusted with the zero adjustment to read the value expected for the temperature being sensed. For example, let's say that the sensor is placed in an ice bath maintained at exactly 0°C. Ideally, the RTD will have a resistance of 100 Ω at 0°C. If the current source is exactly 1 mA and the lead resistance is 0, the voltage across the RTD would be 100 mV. If the voltage gain of the voltage amplifier is +10, then its output is ideally 1 V. Any lead length resistance present in the circuit would add voltage to the output of the voltage amplifier. The zero calibration potentiometer can be used to eliminate the effect of the lead length error.

In some applications calibration is undesirable and a more permanent and automatic form of lead length compensation is needed. This is accomplished by using

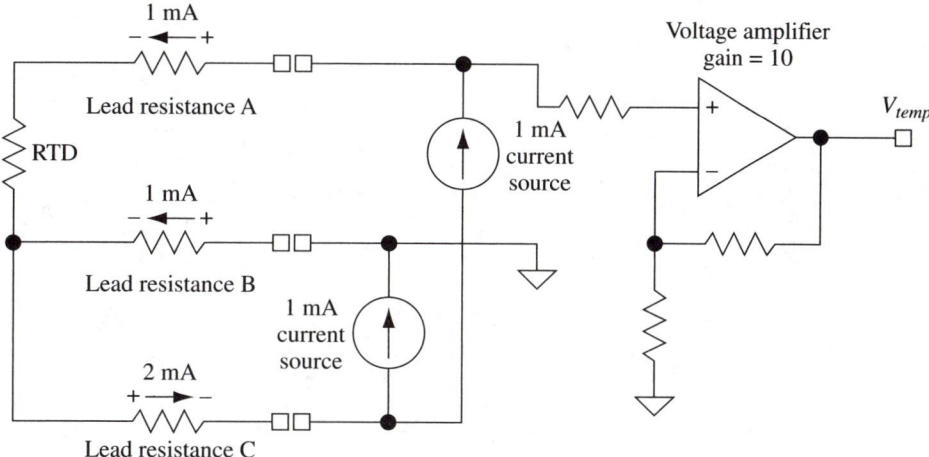

▲ FIGURE 9–19
Three-wire RTD lead length compensation

an RTD with three leads. Two leads are attached to one side of the RTD and the third lead to the other side. A special circuit is developed to drive the three RTD leads. The circuit uses two constant current sources connected to the RTD leads, as shown in Figure 9–19. The trick of this circuit is to connect the voltage amplifier sensing leads to the positive side of each constant current source. By sensing these two points, the voltage drop caused by the lead resistance of lead A and lead B is equal in magnitude and opposite in polarity. The two requirements for this are that the lead resistance must be the same and the constant current source values must be identical. Because neither of these situations is ever completely true, there will always be some amount of lead length error. In actual practice the error is minimal and the system works very well. Three-wire RTDs dictate a higher cost due to the additional lead wire and constant current source required, but the concept is used often to resolve lead length error problems without calibration in industrial appilications. Most industrial instrumentation manufacturers offer both two- and three-wire RTD inputs as a standard feature on their equipment.

An even better method of lead length compensation for RTDs is the utilization of four lead wires. This method employs Kelvin sensing, a concept used on many high-accuracy ohmmeter systems. Current is passed through the resistance being measured and the voltage across the resistor is sensed on two separate lines connected to a high-input impedance amplifier. Because of the very high input impedance, there is very little current flow in the sensing leads and therefore only minute levels of lead length error (see Figure 9–20).

Thermocouples

Thermocouples have been used to measure temperature for a long time. While they might represent old technology, they are still commonly used today because of their accuracy, overall versatility, and the wide range of temperature ranges they cover. Thermocouples are constructed by combining two dissimilar metals together at a

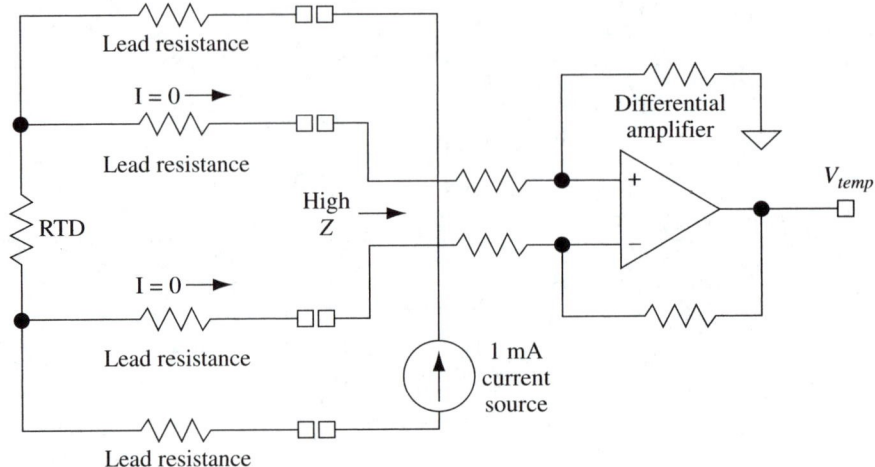

▲ **FIGURE 9–20**
Four-wire RTD lead length compensation

junction point to create a temperature sensor. Whenever dissimilar metals are connected, a small voltage is generated across the junction of the two materials. The value of the voltage is in the millivolt range and varies in a predictable way as the temperature of the junction varies. This is called the *Seebeck effect* and occurs whenever dissimilar metals are connected. When certain dissimilar metals are combined, they create functional thermocouples that have become standard temperature sensors. For example, type J thermocouples are fabricated with iron and constantan and function over a range of 0° to 1400°F. Type K thermocouples are made from chromel and alumel and are used in the range from 0° to 2500°F. There are many other types of thermocouples that have been developed for particular temperature ranges and applications.

Thermocouples are excellent temperature sensors but their use in these applications is complicated by one simple fact: the Seebeck effect is also experienced when sensing leads are connected to the thermocouple to measure the voltage across the junction. Because of this, the wire leads connecting to the thermocouple junction must consist of the same dissimilar metals that make up the thermocouple junction. A type J thermocouple has an iron-constantan junction as a temperature sensor with the iron side of the junction connected to an iron wire lead and the constantan side of the junction connected to a constantan lead. Constantan is a copper-nickel alloy. The sensing iron-constantan junction is often called the *hot junction*. The hot junction is the point where the temperature measurement is being taken (see Figure 9–21).

In order to use the thermocouple as a sensor, a connection to an electrical circuit must be made. A voltage will then be induced by the Seebeck effect at the point of connection, and this must be compensated for. Let's look at what happens when we connect the thermocouple to a DVM. The connection points from the iron and constantan leads to the DVM leads actually create two additional thermocouple junctions (see Figure 9–22a). If the DVM leads are made out of aluminum

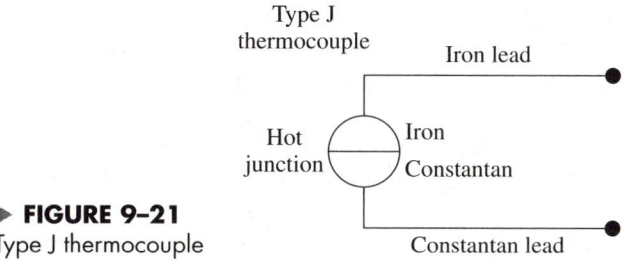

▶ **FIGURE 9–21**
Type J thermocouple

conductors, the created thermocouple junctions are iron-aluminum and constantan-aluminum thermocouples. The connection points to the thermocouple wires are called the *cold junction*. Note that the voltages generated by the cold junction thermocouples subtract from the hot junction voltage. This phenomenon is called *cold junction error* and results from the Seebeck effect that occurs when connections are made to the thermocouple wire. If the connection points to the thermocouple wires are maintained at the same temperature and are made out of the same material, the net effect of the two junctions is one type J cold junction that opposes the hot junction (see Figure 9–22b). The net voltage seen by the DVM is the hot junction voltage minus the cold junction voltage. Let's calculate the DVM reading if the hot junction is placed in a temperature medium of 200°F and the cold junction is at room temperature, 70°F. The table for type J thermocouples shows that at 200°F the type J junction generates 10.777 mV, and at 70°F the voltage is 3.649 mV. The voltage read on the DVM would be 10.777 − 3.649 = 7.128 mV. Converting back to °F

▶ **FIGURE 9–22**
Thermocouple cold junction

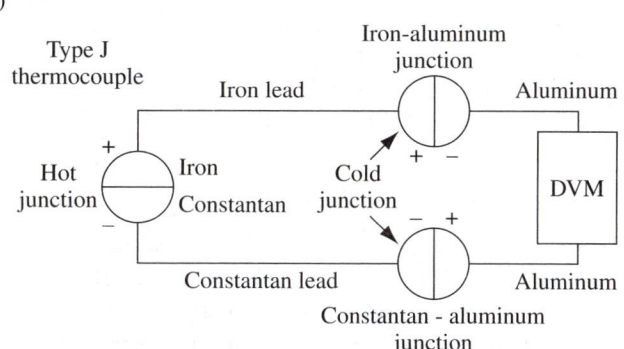

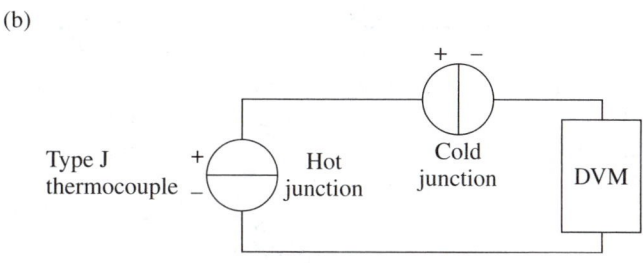

using the thermocouple tables, 7.128 mV is equivalent to 134°F, significantly less than the actual 200°F seen at the hot junction. The cold junction error is not a steady error but varies with the temperature of the cold junction.

In order to use thermocouples to measure temperature, we need some method to compensate for the error induced by the cold junction. Cold junction error can be eliminated by maintaining the cold junction at 32°F, because the voltage generated by all thermocouple junctions at 32°F is 0 mV. However, maintaining 32°F as a cold junction temperature is usually impractical. The preferred method employed on most industrial instrumentation is to measure the cold junction temperature and subtract the equivalent value from the voltage measured for the hot junction. This is done with a small cold junction sensor, usually a thermistor, diode, or IC temperature sensor. Figure 9–23 shows a circuit that measures the thermocouple hot junction value and subtracts the cold junction value.

Because very little current flows in the thermocouple leads, small leads can be used and very little lead length error occurs. Thermocouple types are available to measure temperature ranges that go from approximately –300°F to 4200°F. Some thermocouples are more linear than others but all have areas of significant non-linearity. When thermocouple signals are converted to digital, linearization is required. This is usually accomplished by software linearization tables.

IC Temperature Sensors

Most IC temperature sensors are based upon the variation in voltage drop across the PN junction as temperature changes. Most IC temperature sensors are available in two- or three-pin transistor packages or IC mini DIP packages. The LM335 IC temperature sensor is a very popular IC sensor. The LM335 uses the breakdown voltage across a zener diode as a measurement of the temperature. The LM335 has been configured to provide 10 mV/°K output and operates over the range of –40° to 100°C. The output is very linear and is accurate within 1°C over the central 100°C span. A third terminal is available for calibration of the output. At 0°C the output of the LM335 is ideally 2.73 V (0°C = 273°K, 10 mV/K × 273 K = 2.73 V). Figure 9–24 shows a typical application of the LM335.

Position and Liquid Level Sensors

Analog position sensors output a voltage or current that indicates the absolute position of an object. The most common position sensors are rotary or linear potentiometers. Rotary potentiometers indicate angular position in terms of resistance, while linear potentiometers output a resistance that relates to linear position. Both types of potentiometers offer a multitude of resistance ranges with very linear resistance vs. position relationships. Resolution is an important concern for this type of position sensor. In potentiometers constructed with fine conductive wire, resolution is determined as the number of turns of the conductor used to develop their resistance. Conductive plastic types of potentiometers offer negligible resolution. Potentiometers can be used to develop simple voltage dividers or they can be part of a bridge circuit, as shown in Figure 9–25.

Linear Variable Differential Transformers (LVDTs) are another variety of position sensor. They use basic transformer theory to develop an output that indicates

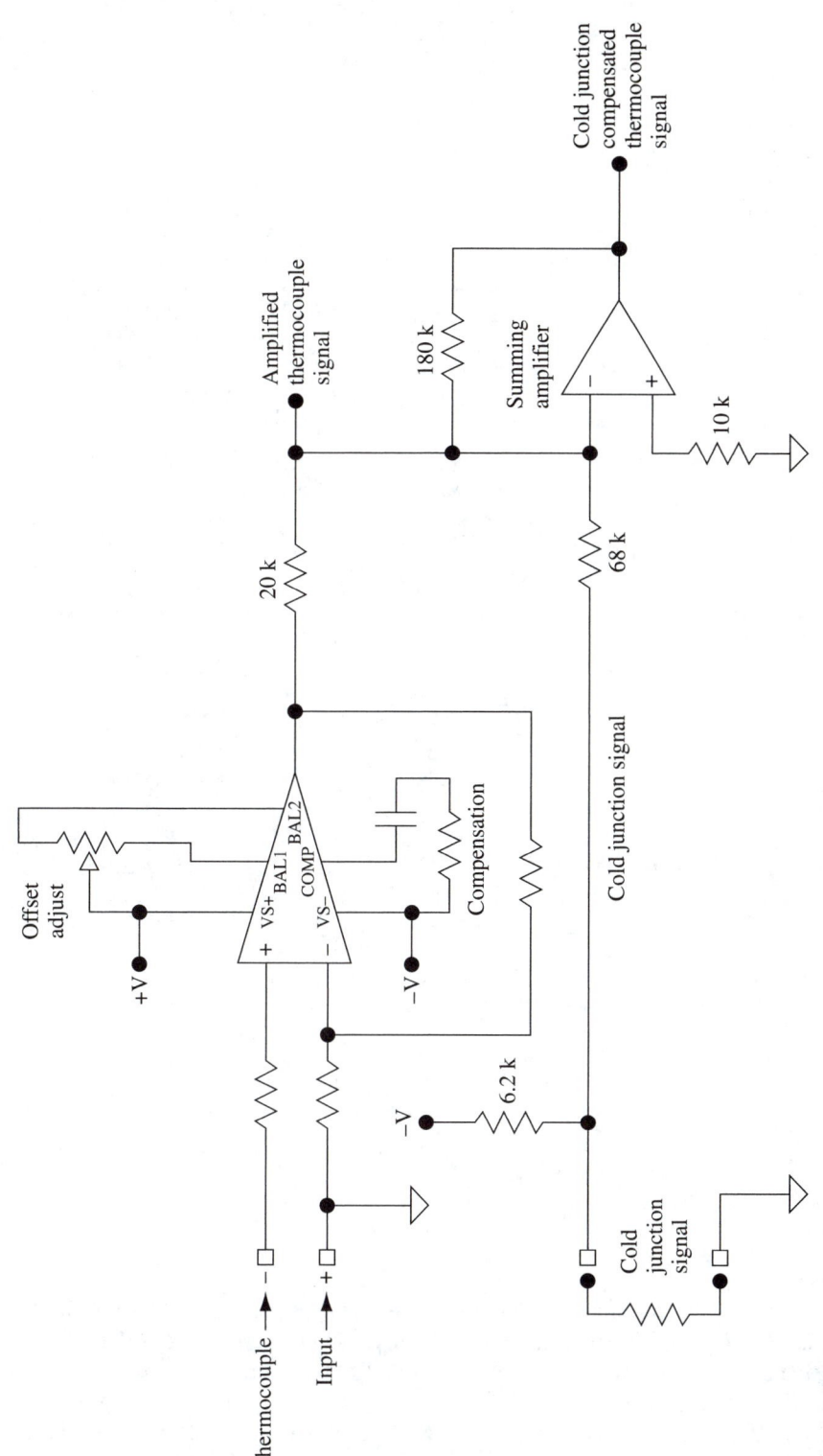

▲ FIGURE 9–23

Thermocouple cold junction condensation

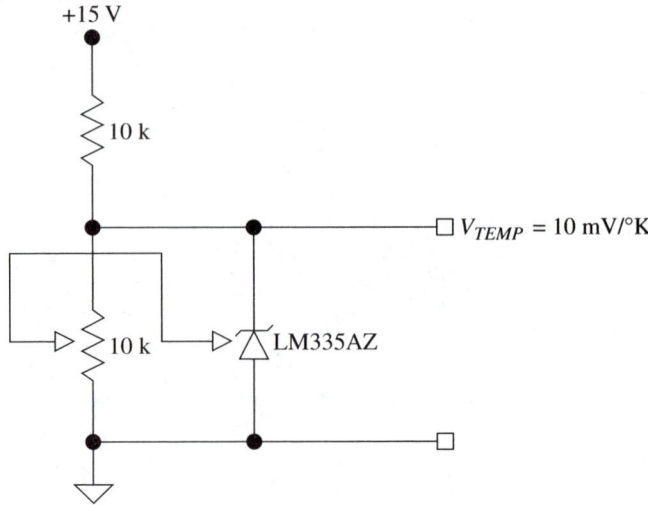

▶ **FIGURE 9–24**
LM335 IC temperature sensor application

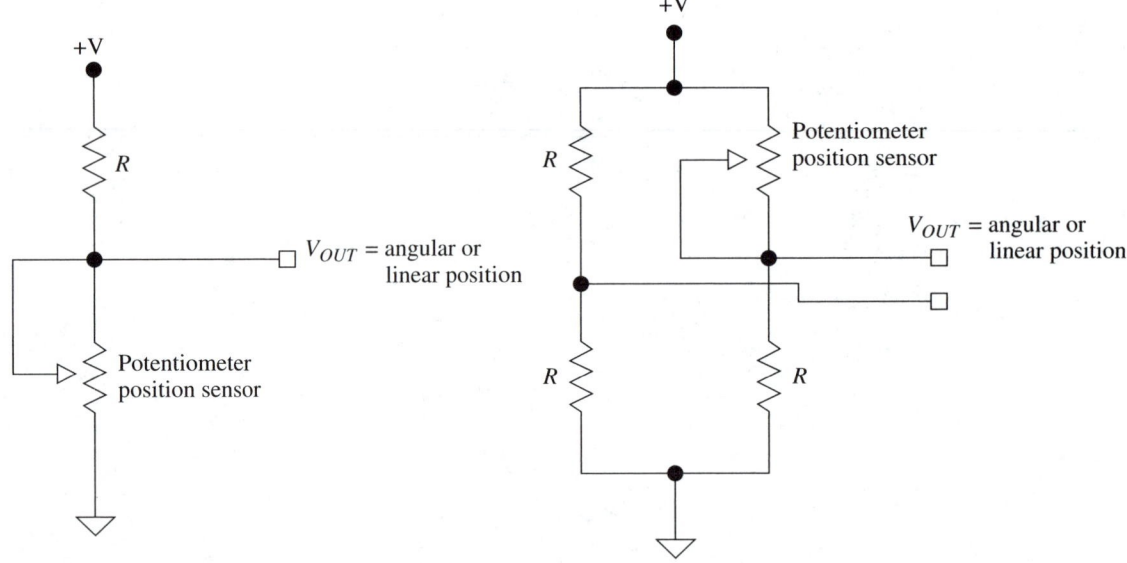

▲ **FIGURE 9–25**
Potentiometer position sensors

position. LVDTs consist of a transformer whose primary and two identical secondaries are wrapped around a tube. A movable core is positioned inside the tube. As the core is moved in and out of the tube, the AC voltage presented to the secondary output is proportional to the position of the moving core (see Figure 9–26).

When a float arm is attached to a position sensor, the result is a liquid level indicator. Sensing the fuel level in a gasoline tank is a very common application of potentiometer position sensors as liquid level indicators. Both potentiometers and

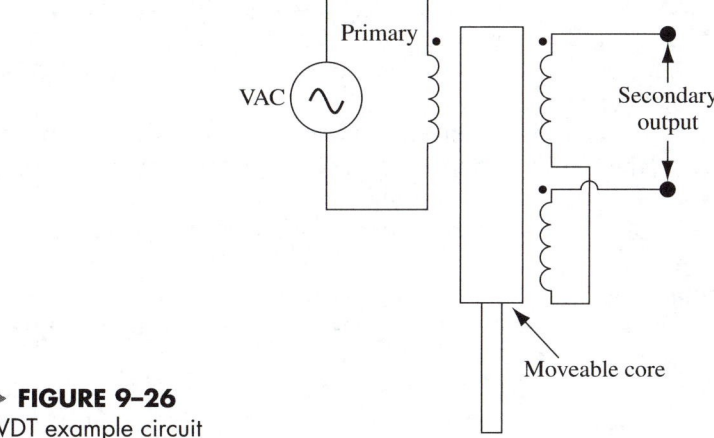

▶ **FIGURE 9–26**
LVDT example circuit

LVDTs can be used as liquid level indicators but potentiometers are the sensors used most often in these applications.

Capacitance sensors can also be used for liquid level detection. Capacitance sensors are constructed by placing two plastic tubes one inside the other. The liquid level being sensed becomes the dielectric in this case, and as the level rises between the two tubes, the capacitance of the sensor changes. If the capacitance of the sensor is used to create a relaxation oscillator as discussed in Chapter 8, the frequency of the relaxation oscillator will be proportional to the capacitance of the sensor and the liquid level being sensed.

The liquid level measurement methods described thus far work well for smaller tanks where relatively small mechanical movement is experienced. However, in large tanks either weight-and-line, differential pressure, or sonic liquid level sensors are used. Weight-and-line sensors are mounted in the top of a tank. They extend a floating weight on a line until the level is detected by the release in tension of the line. The weight is then retracted as an encoder counts the distance of the retraction. Differential pressure level indicators measure the pressure at the top of the tank and the pressure at the bottom of the tank. The differential pressure between these two measurements is proportional to the liquid level. Sonic liquid level detectors use sound wave transmitter/receivers mounted on the top of the tank. The transmitters send out sound waves. The time for the sound waves to be reflected back to the receiver is measured. This time value is proportional to the liquid level in the tank.

Pressure

Pressure can be measured electronically with sensors that vary in resistance, capacitance, or inductance. Piezoelectric sensors output a small voltage when pressure is applied to certain crystal materials. One of the most popular methods for measuring pressure employs strain gages as the principal measuring element. A strain gage is a continuous back-and-forth pattern of fine wire affixed to a flexible surface. As pressure is applied to the surface, the resistance of the wire changes proportionally as the deflection of the surface material. This is readily converted to pressure in units of pounds per square inch (psi). A common nominal strain gage resistance value (with only atmospheric pressure applied) is 120 Ω with resistance changes of 2 Ω/psi.

Capacitance pressure sensors exist where pressure is applied to the plate of a capacitor, thereby changing the capacitance of the sensor. One capacitor plate is made stationary while a moveable plate is attached to a pressure-activated diaphragm. The capacitance of the sensing capacitor varies as the pressure applied to the diaphragm.

Inductive properties can also be used to measure pressure by taking an LVDT, as discussed in this section, and attaching a pressure diaphragm to the moveable coil. These are called *variable reluctance/inductance pressure sensors*.

Because pressure measurement generally requires a mechanical assembly around the sensing mechanism, the sensor is usually converted to what is called a *transducer* or a *transmitter* within the assembly. A sensor is the bare sensing element by itself, such as a strain gage. If the strain gage is connected in a bridge circuit powered by a DC voltage, the result is called a *pressure transducer*. If the output of the transducer is further amplified to develop a 1–5-V output, this device is called a *pressure transmitter* (see Figure 9–27). The same definitions for sensors, transducers, and transmitters are applied to temperature, flow, and other parameter measurement. For example, a thermocouple temperature transmitter includes all the electronics to accept a thermocouple input and develop a 1–5-V cold junction compensated output.

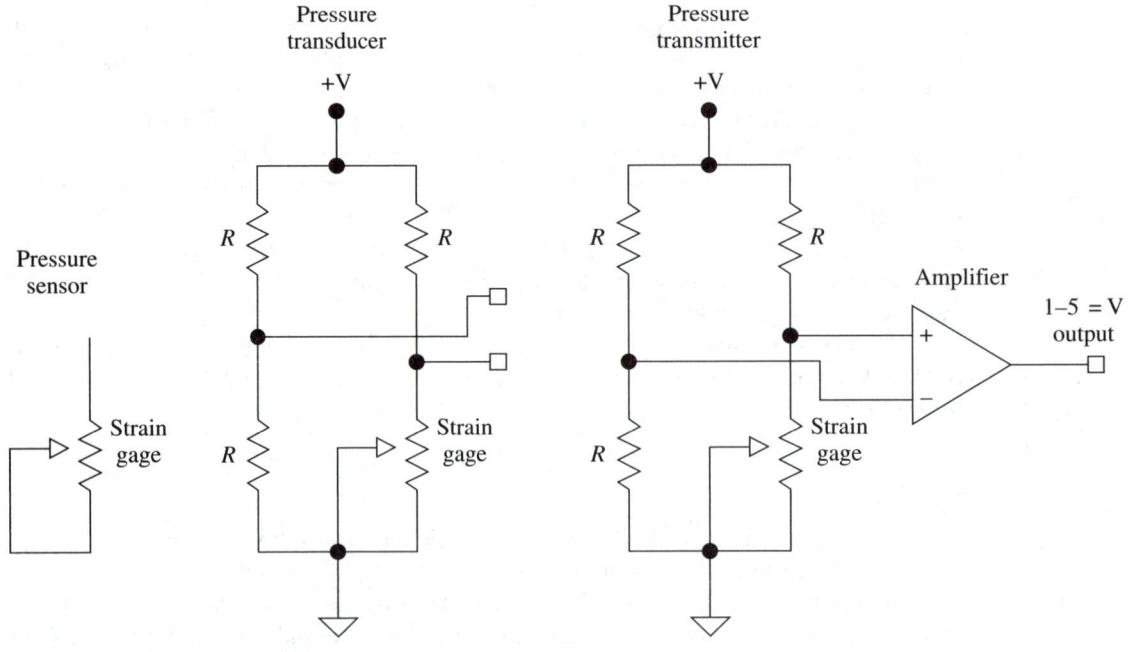

▲ **FIGURE 9–27**
Sensor-transducer-transmitter

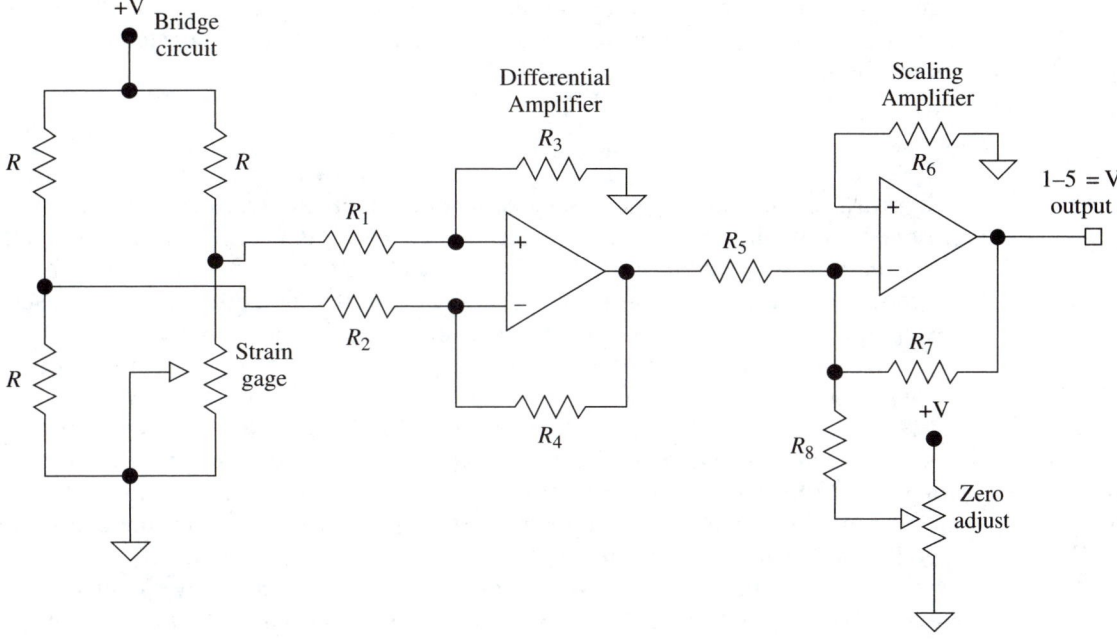

▲ FIGURE 9–28
Pressure transmitter circuit

Pressure sensors are usually converted into pressure transducers or transmitters within the mechanical housing required for mounting the mechanical diaphragm. This is done for two reasons:

1. There is usually room for the electronics in the assembly.

2. The output of a strain gage is a relatively low resistance signal and is subject to the lead length error problem discussed for RTDs.

By including the transducer or transmitter electronics within pressure sensing housing, the lead length problem is resolved with the 4–20 mA or 1–5-V pressure output signal from the pressure transmitter. Figure 9–28 shows the circuit for a very basic strain gage pressure transmitter with a 1–5-V output.

9–3 ▶ Data Acquisition and Control Circuits

Data acquisition and control circuits receive the signals from the input devices described in Sections 9–1 and 9–2. They can either indicate or record the value of the parameter measured, or they can provide outputs that can control its value or the value of some other parameter. Most often these circuits are microprocessor-based and include advanced math functions; timing/counting functions; programmable logic; and proportional, integral, and derivative operations. This section discusses these functions and how they are incorporated in a variety of data acquisition and control products.

Timers and Time Delay Functions

Timers are an important requirement for most control systems. Timers are used to either count the time between events or to engage outputs at an appropriate time. Many times in control circuits, time delays must be incurred to ensure the smooth operation of control systems. There are generally two timing devices that are used to implement timing functions: on-delay timers and off-delay timers.

On-delay timers are available separately as electromechanical devices or as software functions on a variety of microprocessor-based controllers. When powered, each on-delay timer counts the passage of time. As with any other switch or electromechanical relay, there can be a variety of contacts associated with each timer (i.e., SPST, DPDT, etc.). Each timer also has a preset or time set value. When the accumulated time count equals the preset time value, the timer becomes engaged. When engaged, all of the contacts associated with the timer change state. Previous to this, all contacts were in their disengaged condition; normally closed contacts were closed, normally open contacts were open. Once the timer becomes engaged, it remains engaged, still counting time while the outputs are maintained in their energized state. Whenever power is taken from the on-delay timer, it is reset immediately and all outputs revert to their de-energized condition. When energized again, the cycle repeats itself. The on-delay timer is so named because the contacts are delayed from activation after the relay is turned on. They are straightforward in their operation and are the most commonly used time delay function. See Figure 9–29a for a block chart representation of on-delay timer operation.

Off-delay timers are also available as separate electromechanical or software devices. In many ways they operate opposite to the function of on-delay timers. Off-delay timers also can have many different contact arrangements. When the off-

(a)
On-delay timer operating cycle

Coil	Not energized	Energized	Energized
Time	Not being counted	Accumulated time less than preset time	Accumulated time greater than or equal to preset time
N.O. contacts	Open	Open	Closed
N.C. contacts	Closed	Closed	Open

(b)
Off-delay timer operating cycle

Coil	Energized	Not energized	Not energized
Time	Not being counted	Accumulated time less than preset time	Accumulated time greater than or equal to preset time
N.O. contacts	Closed	Closed	Open
N.C. contacts	Open	Open	Closed

▲ **FIGURE 9–29**
On- and off-delay timer function

delay timer is energized, all of the contacts become energized immediately, but time is not counted. The off-delay timer also has an adjustable preset time value. The off-delay counter begins counting time when power is removed from it or it is disabled. At this point, time is being counted and the contacts are maintained in their energized condition. This condition remains until the accumulated time from the point at which power was removed from the timer equals the off-delay timer's preset value. When this occurs, the contacts revert to their disengaged condition. Whenever the off-delay timer is powered up, the cycle repeats from the beginning. The off-delay timer gets its name from the fact that it delays contacts from being turned off for a period of time after the off-delay timer is de-energized. Figure 9–29b shows a block chart of the off-delay timer's operation.

Voltage/Current Transmitters

Transmitters are DC analog devices used in industrial applications to amplify a process parameter such as temperature or pressure and convert it to one of the standard voltage or current ranges used by most data acquisition or control systems. Most common are the 4–20 mA and 1–5-V ranges, but many others are possible. Transmitters are called by the name of the parameter sensor with which they are designed to work. Thermocouple transmitters accept a thermocouple input and develop a standard range signal output that corresponds to a specified range of temperature. There are RTD transmitters, pressure and flow transmitters, and, literally, transmitters for any process parameter typically measured. These transmitters accept the relatively low signal input from a sensor and convert it to a high-level signal that can be sent some distance to a data acquisition or control system. The transmitter will have an input signal range and an output signal range. Sometimes the transmitter will also include a display to indicate the output signal value, either in the units of the parameter (°F for a temperature transmitter) or the output signal (volts, if 1–5 V is the output signal range).

Example 9–2

Determine the temperature value indicated by a thermocouple transmitter that accepts the input of a type J thermocouple over the range of 0° to 800°F and outputs 4–20 mA if the output of the transmitter is 15.6 mA.

Solution

1. Determine the percent of range the output represents.

   The range of a 4–20 mA signal is 16 mA, starting at 4 mA and ending at 20 mA. A 15.6 mA signal is 15.6 mA – 4 mA = 11.6 mA above the 4 mA zero range point.

   11.6 mA/16 mA = 72.5 % of range

2. The temperature value equals the percent of output range times the input temperature range value.

   72.5% × 800°F = 580°F

Data Acquisition and Recording

In many industrial process applications it is necessary to maintain a record of process variables for efficiency and quality control or to meet government regulations. The federal Food and Drug Administration, for example, requires that critical variables be maintained for all processes relating to foods and drugs. An operator of a boiler system desires that the boiler maintain optimum levels of steam pressure. A metal heat-treater strives to maintain accurate and uniform temperatures in their heat-treating processes. Data acquisition systems and recorders provide a means of analyzing and comparing system performance on an ongoing basis.

Before the advent of microprocessor technology, all data acquisition and storage was done on paper. Strip chart or circle chart recorders performed all data storage. Strip chart recorders are available in paper widths from 20 mm to 100 mm and can monitor and record up to 32 channels of data. Circle chart recorders can typically process up to 4 channels of data on circular charts ranging from 6 to 12 in. in diameter. Data loggers and data acquisition systems are available that store all process data in memory and display old or current data on a CRT or LCD screen. The number of channels that can be processed is limited only by the size of the system.

The input capabilities of most of these systems are similar. Most data acquisition systems can accommodate thermocouple, RTD, 1–5-V, and 4–20 mA inputs. The 1–5-V and 4–20 mA inputs can be transmitters for any number of process parameters (temperature, pressure, flow, humidity, PH, etc.). When transmitters are used, the variable must be scaled and the units identified. For example, let's take a pressure transmitter that is connected to channel 3 of a 16-channel strip chart recorder. The pressure transmitter outputs 1–5 V over an input range of 0–300 psi. When configuring the strip chart recorder, channel 3 would be programmed for a zero value of 0, a span (maximum) value of 300 and units selected as psi.

Limit Devices

Limit devices are safety devices that monitor a process parameter and compare its value with a set point. When the set point is exceeded, an output is engaged that either sounds an alarm or shuts down the system. In most cases it is desirable to have the limit device shut down the system. Most limit devices are configured to shut down the system when the set point is exceeded. They maintain the shutdown condition even after the process value goes below the set point. System operation can only commence when the process value is below the set point value and after someone has reviewed the situation and decided that it is all right to continue. That person then depresses a reset button to restart the system operation.

A good example of a limit device application is an environmental test chamber. If the test chamber is designed to function over a temperature range of 0° to 400°F, a safety limit device is added with a set point of 450°F. If a temperature greater than 450°F is sensed, the limit device shuts down the environmental test chamber until the temperature has cooled to less than 450°F and the reset button has been depressed.

Ground Fault Circuit Interrupters (GFCIs)

A very common limit device used in industry and the home is the GFCI. GFCIs work by measuring the current through both the hot and common leg of an AC circuit. If these currents are approximately the same, the operation of the outlet is allowed to continue. However, if a difference of at least 4 mA is detected between the two legs of the circuit, the GFCI trips, which shuts down the outlet. This condition, called a *ground fault*, indicates that current is going from the hot leg back to ground by some other path. This is symptomatic of a human in contact with the hot conductor while grounding some other part of the body. The GFCI breaks the circuit and will maintain this condition until both the ground fault is removed and the reset button has been depressed. Figure 9–30 shows a basic GFCI circuit.

On-Off Control

On-off controllers are similar in operation to limit devices except that their purpose is to control the value of the input parameter so that it equals the value of the set point. A home thermostat is a very simple on-off controller that turns the heat source or air conditioner on or off whenever the temperature goes outside an acceptable temperature band. The inputs to most industrial on-off controls accommodate thermocouple, RTD, 1–5-V and 4–20 mA inputs. When the input is a thermocouple, the on-off control automatically compensates for cold junction error and linearizes the resulting temperature value. For RTD inputs the option of two- or three-wire connections is provided to address lead length error. Soon after the controller receives the signal, its value is digitized and compared to the set point value.

Many outputs can be provided as an option with on-off controls that share either the same or an independent set point. Each output can be selected to operate in either direction: to be activated when the process value is less than the set point (called *reverse action*) or when the process value is greater than the set point

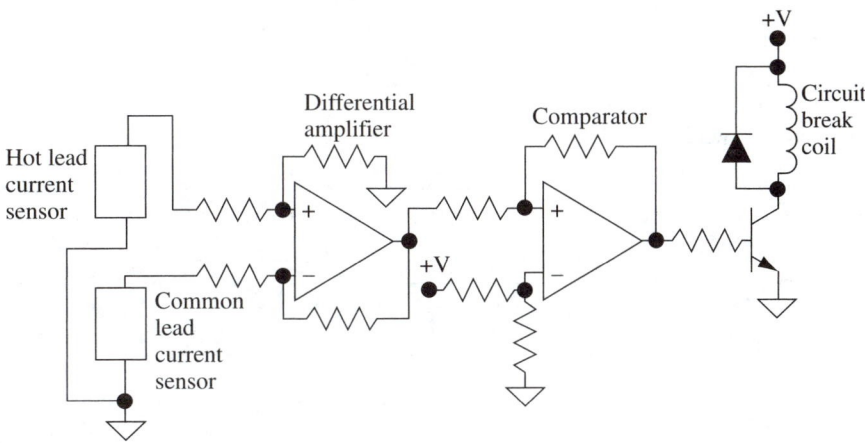

▲ **FIGURE 9–30**
GFCI circuit

(called *direct action*). Each output also has hysterisis, otherwise called *switch differential*, associated with its operation. Hysterisis means that the output becomes engaged and disengaged at different points. Let's take the example of a home thermostat with a set point of 70°F and just one output that operates in the reverse action mode (the output is engaged when the temperature is less than the set point as desired to control heating devices). If the hysterisis value was 0, the thermostat would constantly switch the output back and forth when the temperature was very close to 70°F. If the hysterisis value was set at 2°F, the heat would switch on when the temperature fell to 69°F and switch off when the temperature reached 71°F. The larger the hysterisis, the larger the band of temperature variation allowed by the controller. At the same time, the heating system is cycled on and off less frequently. This is the design tradeoff made when adjusting the hysterisis value of an on-off control: control error vs. on-off cycling of the output. The performance of on-off controls can be seen when recorded on a strip chart recorder as a sawtooth-appearing waveform that shows the hysterisis value (plus system time responses) as the difference between the maximum and minimum control point values as they vary around the set point (see Figure 9–31).

Current technology on-off controls digitize the input signal, linearize and scale the input signal, indicate the process value, and determine all control outputs under microprocessor control. The output devices themselves are either electromechanical or solid state relays driven by analog or digital electronics. Figure 9–32 shows some sample on-off and PID controls.

Proportional-Integral-Derivative (PID) Controllers

PID contollers differ from on-off controllers because they have proportional outputs. Proportional outputs are effectively analog outputs; they can have any value over a defined range of voltage or current. On-off controllers have control outputs that are either on or off and result in either 0% or 100% output to the load. Proportional outputs can have values anywhere from 0% to 100%. Electronic proportional outputs are usually in the standard form of 4–20 mA or 1–5 V, where 4 mA

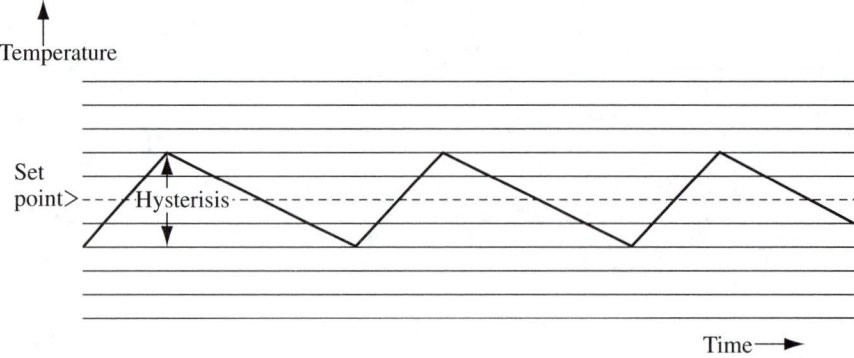

▲ **FIGURE 9–31**
On-off control performance

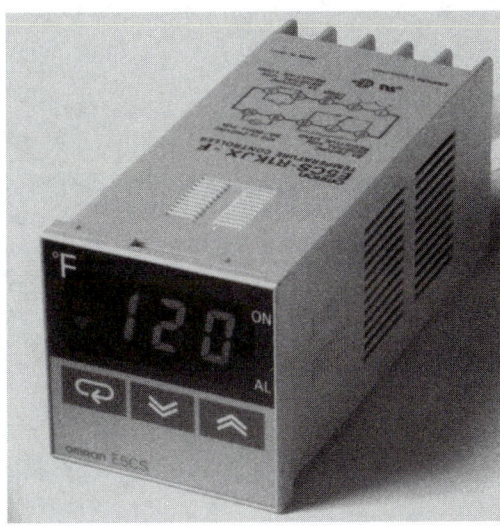

▲ FIGURE 9–32
On-off and PID controllers *(Courtesy Omron Electronics, LLC. Used by permission.)*

or 1 V corresponds to 0% output and 20 mA or 5 V equates to 100% output. A 12-mA signal results in 50% output.

To understand the proportional concept a little better, let's compare the operation of an on-off and proportional controller as it performs in a typical industrial heating application. In a gas-fired industrial oven the temperature is controlled by how much heat is applied to the oven. An on-off control applies either 100% or 0% of the heat capacity by turning the gas valve and heating system on or off. The performance of the system would appear like the jagged sawtooth shown in Figure 9–33a. If the temperature variation shown in the figure is unacceptable, the hysterisis of the controller could be decreased, but the increased on-off cycling of the equipment would also be unacceptable.

A proportional control can be used to control the oven temperature by replacing the on-off gas control valve with a motorized valve positioner. This valve positioner accepts a 4–20 mA signal from the controller and positions the gas valve completely open when the control output is 20 mA, completely closed with 4 mA, and any percentage open between 0–100% for 4–20 mA.

Proportional controls offer smoother and tighter performance because they gradually reduce the heat output as the temperature approaches the set point. Proportional controls are called PID controls because they have three parameters that are adjusted to provide optimum system performance: proportional band, integral action and derivative action, or P, I, and D. The proportional band is the band of process values over which the output is proportioned. It is centered at the set point to provide 50% output. It extends equally in both directions around set point. So if the set point of the oven was 200°F and the proportional band was adjusted to be 100°F, the proportional band would extend from 150° to 250°F. The reverse acting output of the proportional control would begin to reduce the heat into the oven when the temperature just exceeded 150°F by starting to close the gas valve. If the

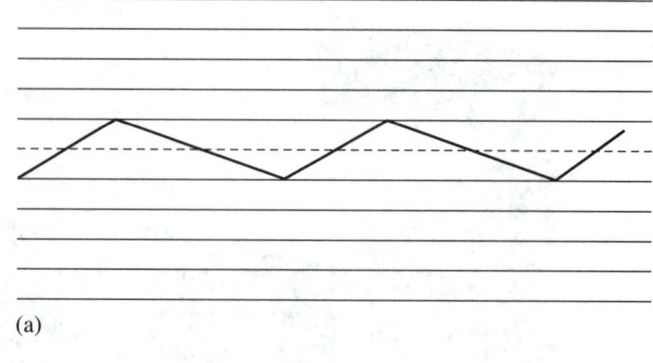

(a)

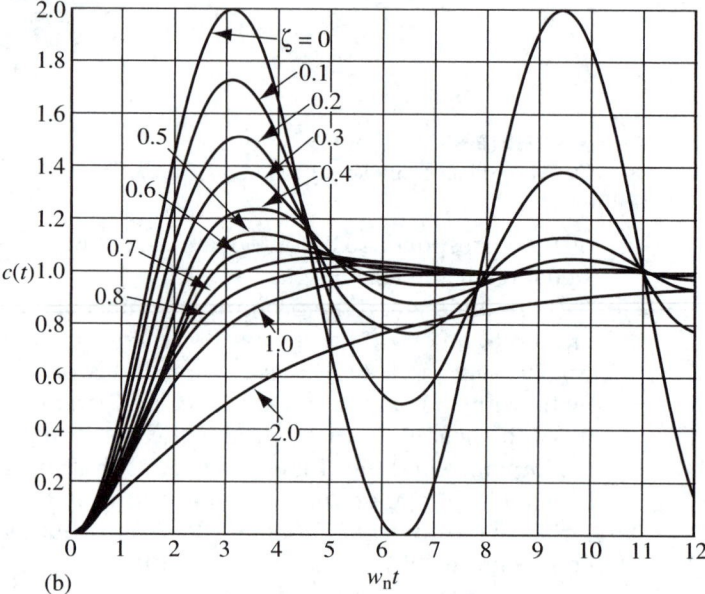

▶ **FIGURE 9–33**
On-off and PID response curves   (b)

temperature exceeded the set point and reached 250°F, the gas valve would be completely closed. You can imagine that as the proportional band is made small, the system will reach the set point faster, but it will have a tendency to overshoot and possibly oscillate, just as discussed in Chapter 7. The larger the proportional band, the slower the system response, but it will have less overshoot and be more stable. The proportional band is the P adjustment provided on PID controls and sometimes is called *gain*, which equals $1/P$. The proportional band adjustment creates a whole family of response curves shown in Figure 9–33b.

Because the proportional band is centered and provides 50% output at set point, the oven will be controlled at the set point only if the load happens to require exactly 50% output. The amount of load on any heating system is determined by the set point, the amount of material in the system, and the ambient temperature conditions around the system. As the load varies, the amount of output required to maintain the set point varies. All proportional controllers need a method for sensing the error from the set point to allow repositioning the proportional band to provide the output value needed to maintain the load at the set point. Integral action performs this function by integrating the set point error. It uses the area under the curve to add to or subtract from the nominal 50% provided by the proportional band at set point. An op amp integrator performs integral action in analog type controls. Software emulates the integrator function in microprocessor-based controls. The amount of integral action is adjustable by changing the gain of the integrator. The integrator gain, the *I* setting, changes the speed at which the proportional band is shifted by the integrator output. If the integrator output changes too fast, the system may overshoot or become unstable. Too low an integrator gain setting causes the system to be slow and unresponsive.

In many applications, system changes can occur rapidly, too rapid for the integrator to respond to them in the short term. This is because the integrator is always working from historical information, continually totaling the area under the error curve over time. Derivative action is used in these situations to provide immediate response to quick changes in the error. Derivative action calculates the rate of change of the error and provides a corrective signal to either increase or decrease the percent output immediately. An op amp differentiator performs derivative action in analog controls while software emulates the function in microprocessor-based controls. The gain of the differentiator, the *D* setting, determines the magnitude of the change induced by a certain rate of change of the error signal.

Programmable Logic Controllers (PLCs)

PLCs evolved after the introduction of the microprocessor in the late 1970s. They are essentially industrial computers that can be programmed to perform logic circuit functions. This is done with a graphical programming language based upon the ladder logic diagram discussed in Section 9–1. The initial PLCs included only digital inputs and outputs. The PLC examines the status of each digital input and stores this in a buffer memory. The PLCs processor then reviews the ladder logic program currently being executed and determines the status of each output as specified by the combination of the input status and the ladder logic program. Once determined, the new output status is loaded in a separate output buffer. Next, the contents of the output buffer are sent to the PLC's outputs. This process represents basically one scan of the PLC, the length of which is determined by the number of inputs, outputs, and the complexity of the ladder logic program.

Let's take an example of a small PLC that has eight inputs and six outputs. The 8 inputs are given address names of I0-I7; the output addresses are O0-O5. The PLC is to be programmed to energize output #1 whenever input 0 is on, and either input #1 or input #2 are on, and input #3 is not on. Figure 9–34 shows the ladder logic program that would be drawn and loaded into the PLC. Note that each input is shown graphically as either an open or closed set of contacts. In each case the graphical symbol shows the status of the unenergized input: open contacts represent an input that is open when not engaged, and closed contacts represent an input that is closed when not engaged. Also, the outputs are shown as an open parenthesis rather than a circle as was done to symbolize a relay.

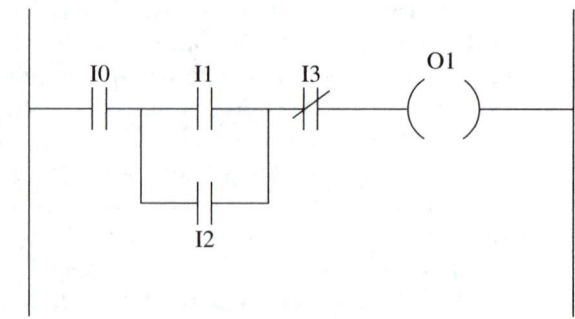

▶ **FIGURE 9–34**
PLC ladder logic diagram

Today's PLCs have been expanded to include analog inputs and outputs, advanced mathematical functions, and PID control as well. They also possess extended communications capabilities and can be configured to function in a variety of networks. An example PLC is shown in Figure 9–35.

9–4 ▶ Output Circuits

Output circuits are used to implement the operational changes determined by the control system. Outputs can be either digital on-off outputs or analog outputs. Analog outputs indicate either the value of a parameter or the relative percent output that should be provided to the controlled process.

Electromechanical Relays, Contactors, and Solenoids

On-off outputs are provided by electromechanical or solid-state relays, contactors, or solenoid valves. All of these devices are either energized or not energized. The schematic symbols and contacts for electromechanical relays were discussed in

▶ **FIGURE 9–35**
PLC example
*(Courtesy Omron
Electronics, LLC. Used
by permission.)*

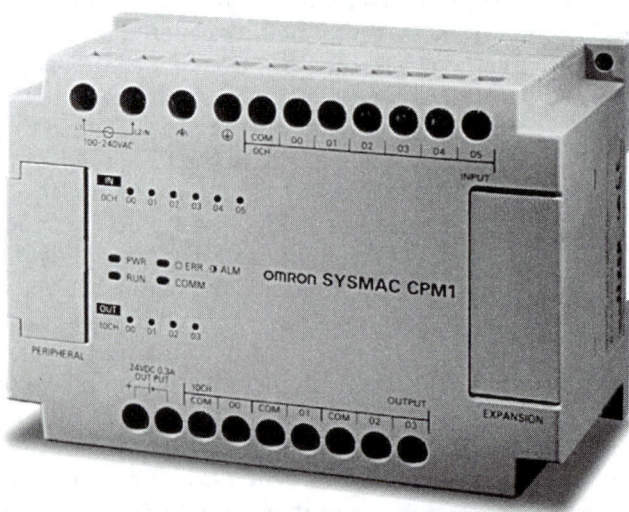

▶ **FIGURE 9–36**
Contactor and solenoid example
*(Courtesy Omron Electronics, LLC.
Used by permission.)*

Section 9–1, which covered control inputs. Electromechanical relay contacts are configured the same as switches (SPDT, DPDT, etc.) and can also represent the input to a circuit. Contactors are simply relays that have contact ratings in excess of 15 amps. Contactors and relays are usually shown by the same schematic symbol, so from an analysis point of view, relays and contactors are viewed the same. Solenoids are simply electromechanical valves that are energized open or closed. Figure 9–36 shows an example electromechanical relay.

Electromechanical relays are available for AC or DC operation and with a variety of coil voltages. A transistor circuit is usually used to energize a DC relay coil. It is common practice to use what is called a *free-wheelin diode* to provide a path for current flow initially after de-energizing the inductive coil of the DC relay (see Figure 9–37). When the transistor turns off, the current flowing in the DC coil will cause a large voltage drop across the collector-emitter of the transistor unless there is a path for this current to flow. The normally reverse-biased free-wheelin diode provides this path for current flow.

▶ **FIGURE 9–37**
DC relay free-wheelin diode

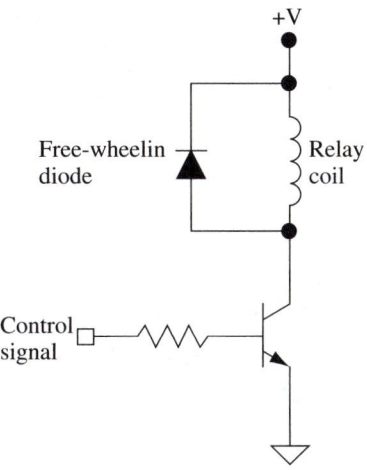

Whenever selecting a device that includes switching contacts, the voltage and current ratings must be considered. The voltage rating indicates the highest voltage that can exist across the contacts without the potential for arcing. The current rating specifies the maximum current that can flow through the contacts. It is also important to protect electromechanical contacts from the wear that occurs with repeated switching. Every time contacts are opened or closed, there is potential for contact damage when the contacts are in close proximity to each other. Damage occurs when there is current flow across the gap between the contacts when they are either just opening or just closing. The EMI generated at this time can also cause electronic systems to fail. Lower-voltage DC circuits (20 to 30 VDC) have the arcing capability of higher voltage (115 V) AC circuits.

The exact calculations for contact protection are rigorous and dependent on the actual load impedances. To protect contacts, RC snubber networks are most often placed across all output contacts from process controls and PLCs. Snubber networks should be applied across contacts of any device when the currents being disconnected are large and there are either capacitive or inductive load impedances. RC networks are commonly placed across contacts for protection, as shown in Figure 9–38. The R value should be equal or less than the load resistance and the resistor should have a power rating of at least ½ watt. The C value can be calculated as follows:

$$C = \sqrt{I_L / 300} \times L \qquad\qquad (9\text{–}1)$$

where I_L = the load current
L = load inductance

Make sure the voltage rating of the capacitor is sufficiently high. A 1000-V capacitor rating is often used for 115/230 V AC applications. Figure 9–38 shows RC values commonly used for 5-amp contacts rated at 230 V AC.

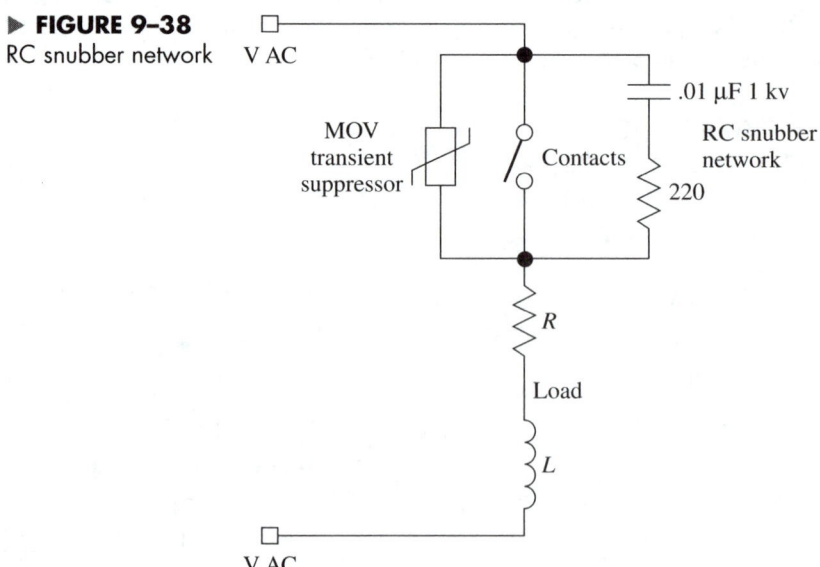

▶ **FIGURE 9–38**
RC snubber network

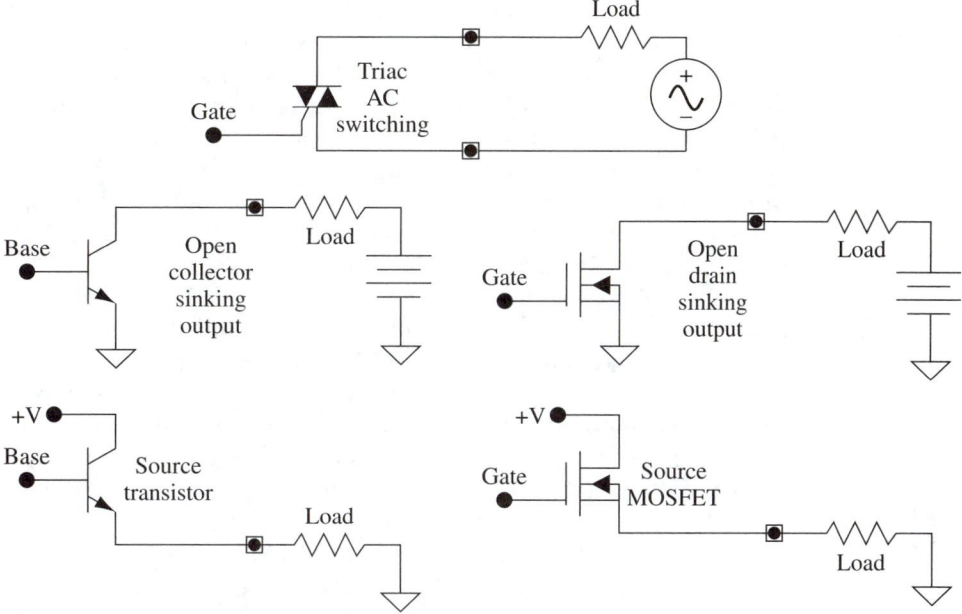

▲ FIGURE 9–39
AC solid-state relay, DC-solid-state relay, open collector transistor, and source transistor

For added protection with inductive loads, metal oxide varistors (MOVs) are also placed in parallel with the snubber network (see Figure 9–39). MOVs are semiconductor devices that reduce their resistance to absorb transient energy when their clamping voltage is exceeded. MOVs have a clamp voltage rating and an energy rating in joules. The clamp voltage rating indicates the voltage where the MOV will begin to absorb transient energy. The energy rating indicates how much energy the MOV can absorb before being destroyed. The key to selecting MOVs is finding a clamping voltage that is close to the highest operating voltage seen by the circuit but is never equal or below it. A MOV can be operative for only short periods of time, or even the highest energy rating will be exceeded.

Solid-state Outputs

Solid-state outputs are simply solid-state equivalents of electromechanical relays. Solid-state outputs exceed the performance of electromechanical relays in the areas of contact life and switching speed. However, electromechanical relays are much more versatile and robust and are easier to apply and troubleshoot.

The devices that make up the switching contacts in solid-state outputs are either triacs for AC circuits or transistors for DC circuits. Triac outputs for AC circuits are often called *AC solid-state relays*. Transistor switches for DC circuits are referred to as *DC solid-state relays, open collector outputs,* or *source transistor outputs* (see Figure 9–39).

Solid-state relays that employ triacs are commonly looked at as replacements for electromechanical relays in 115/230 V AC line voltage applications. Recall that triacs are excellent switching devices that are turned on by a gate voltage. When the gate voltage goes to 0, triacs rely on current flow in the reverse direction to turn off. Because DC circuits usually don't provide any reverse current flow, triacs used alone in DC applications, once energized on, never turn off. There exist commutation circuits that promote the use of triacs for DC switching applications, but they are not commonly used. Consequently, solid-state relays with triac outputs should be generally considered for only AC applications.

Most solid-state relays have inputs, either 3-32 V DC or 9-280 V AC, which, when present, turn the triac on. This results in current flow through the device. These devices use opto-isolators to provide electrical isolation from the input circuit to the output circuit. Figure 9–40 shows an example DC input solid-state relay circuit.

When compared to the electromechanical relay, the solid-state relay is capable of much faster switching speeds and many more contact operations. However, the contacts for solid-state relays are limited to SPST—one set of normally open contacts. Also, much care must be taken with the application of solid-state relays in high ambient temperatures or applications where high voltage spikes are prevalent.

When transistors are used as DC switching outputs, either the DC solid-state relay, open collector, or source transistor arrangements shown in Figure 9–39 are used. The DC solid-state relay is a stand-alone device that employs a MOSFET transistor to achieve low switch resistance. The inputs to the DC solid-state relay are similar to AC solid-state relay, 3-32 V DC. The output switch ratings are usually 0–100 V DC with load currents ranging from 3 to 10 amps.

Open collector or source transistor outputs are often provided as outputs on many discrete sensors or control outputs. For example, the output from a diffuse photo-sensor as described in this chapter is usually an open collector. Also, the outputs from many process controllers and PLCs are optionally electromechanical relays, solid-state relays, open collector, or source transistor outputs. When an open collector is provided, DC power is provided externally (see Figure 9–39). The DC power supply connects to the controlled load that in turn is connected to the open collector output. The transistor completes the circuit to a common circuit con-

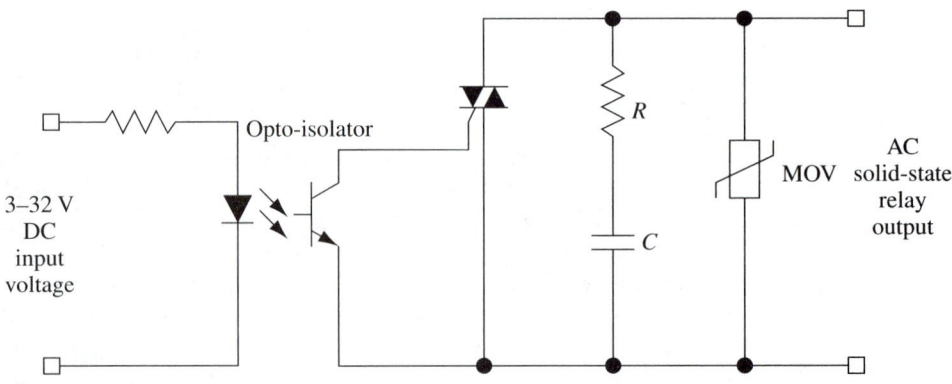

▲ **FIGURE 9–40**

nection when energized. The open collector is viewed as a sinking output. In the source transistor arrangement, the controlling device provides DC power. The load is connected to the transistor emitter and a circuit common connection. When the source transistor is energized, current flows through the load. In this case, the transistor is seen as a sourcing output.

Zero-voltage Switching

Zero-voltage switching is a simple concept that is very useful in eliminating transients that occur when devices are switched on or off in AC circuits. Through the study of transient analysis, we understand that the level of transient voltage spikes that occur when a circuit is powered up depends on the initial conditions present in the circuit. In most cases, the minimum transient spikes occur when the initial voltage is 0.

Because AC circuits offer two points in time, 0° and 180°, when the power voltage is 0, it makes sense that these are the best times for AC devices to be turned on or off. This is the concept of zero-voltage switching. To implement zero-voltage switching, all that is needed is a device that monitors the AC line to determine the zero crossing point. This circuit is called a *zero crossing detector* and can be a comparator connected to a stepped-down AC line voltage. The comparator output triggers a one-shot to output a zero crossing pulse. A microprocessor or other circuit device can use the zero crossing pulse to determine when to turn I/O devices on or off.

Proportional Outputs

Proportional outputs accept the control signals that are output from PID process controllers. They provide the means for controlling the value of some physical parameter that will result in control of the process. In an industrial oven a PID control outputs a 4–20 mA signal to a valve positioner that controls the flow of gas into the burner. This in turn determines how much heat enters the oven and the temperature within the oven. In a gasoline pipeline the flow rate of the gasoline is sensed by a flow meter and compared to the desired flow rate set point. The PID flow controller outputs a 1–5-V signal to a valve positioner, opening a control valve just the right amount to provide the desired flow rate.

The 4–20 mA and 1–5-V signals are the standard electrical signals used by process controllers to communicate to proportional output devices. However, there are many others, such as 0–20 mA, 0–10 V. If you are using an output module that requires a 0–20 mA signal, you must find a process controller with this type of output or develop some circuitry that will accomplish the conversion. In many industrial applications pressurized air signals called *pneumatic signals* are used as an input signal to many types of valve positioners. The standard pneumatic process control signal is 3–15 psi, where 3 psi = 0% output and 15 psi = 100% output. Many times a process controller with a 4–20 mA output must send a control signal to a pneumatic valve positioner. In this case a current to pressure (I to P) converter is used to convert the 4–20 mA electrical control signal over to a 3–15 psi pneumatic signal.

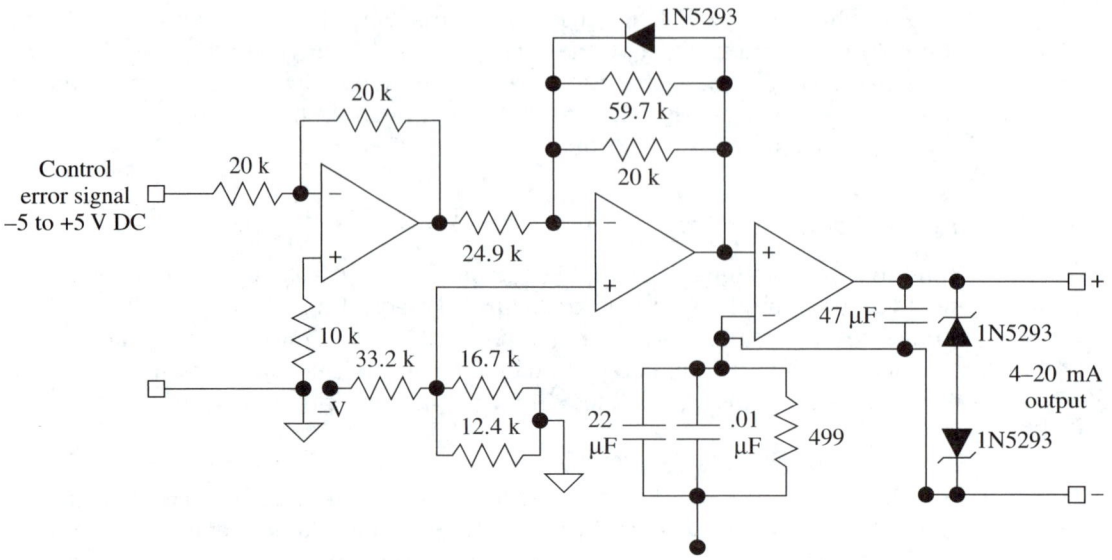

▲ **FIGURE 9–41**
4–20 mA output circuit

The circuit shown in Figure 9–41 uses an op amp to convert a ±5-V error sig-nal over to a 4–20 mA signal capable of supplying a constant current to a load re-sistance up to 750 Ω. The 4–20 mA signals are easily converted to 1–5 V by passing a 4–20 mA current signal through a 250-Ω resistor. The voltage drop across the re-sistor is a 1–5-V signal.

Motorized Positioners

Motorized positioners are used to proportionally position all types of devices: valves, dampers, doors, hydraulic cylinders, and so on. These devices are actual-ly a control system within a control system. The output from a PID process con-trol requests that a certain percentage of some variable be added to the system under control. This control signal becomes a set point to the motorized position-er that moves the motor while sensing its position with a position sensor. The types of motors used to perform the positioning are servomotors, stepper motors, or any common fixed-speed electric motor. For each type of motor, the position of the motor shaft is fed back to the motor control circuit by a potentiometer, an LVDT, an encoder, or possibly photo-sensors.

Stepper motors are the opposite of encoders; they move the shaft of the motor a certain number of degrees for each input pulse to the motor and can be stepped in either direction. The key parameters for stepper motors are the step angle and maximum stepping rate. The step angle determines the amount of angular rota-tion that occurs for each pulse. The maximum stepping rates indicates the highest speed at which the stepper motors can be stepped. In a stepper motor positioner system, the motor is stepped while sensing its position with a potentiometer or encoder. The actual position is compared to the desired position and the motor is pulsed to correct its location if necessary.

Servomotors accept a voltage signal and position their output shaft according to this voltage, moving in either positive (clockwise direction) or negative (counter clockwise direction). Servomotors can be viewed as motorized analog indicators where the position of the meter pointer represents the position of the motor shaft. A potentiometer or encoder usually senses the shaft position, and a control circuit provides the correct output voltage signal to position the shaft properly.

Common variety fixed-speed electric motors are often used as positioners for slower changing outputs, such as dampers in temperature control systems. In these systems, the output of the controller is the input to the motor positioner control circuit. The control circuit senses the position of the motor shaft and compares it to the desired position. If the shaft position is in error, it energizes a relay to turn the shaft in either a clockwise or counterclockwise direction.

Triac Phase-angle Fire Outputs

Triac phase-angle fire devices are used to provide proportional amounts of heat, generated electrically with resistance, to a temperature-controlled system. These are complete electronic proportional output devices. They proportion the amount of power dissipated across resistance heating devices by switching a triac on and off at various times in an AC voltage waveform. Two SCRs, connected in parallel in reverse polarity, with a common gate are used to construct a triac. When the gate receives a pulse during the AC waveform, whichever SCR is currently forward biased turns on. The SCR stays on until the AC current flow reverses direction where it turns off. Another pulse, applied during the second half of the waveform, causes the other SCR to turn on and off in the same manner. The triac phase-angle fire output device is so named because it controls the amount of power applied to a resistive load by varying the phase angle at which the triac is fired or triggered.

If the signal sent to a triac phase-angle fire output calls for 50% output, the triac will be fired at 90° and 270°, as shown in Figure 9–42. The triac will conduct current only during the portions of the AC waveform between 90° to 180° and 270° to 360°, exactly half of the area under the sine-wave curve. A 75% output requirement requires the triac to be fired at 45° and 225°. Again, the signals used to communicate from the process controller to the triac output module are either 4–20 mA or 1–5 V, where 4 mA and 1 V represent 0% output and 20 mA and 5 V call for 100% output. Figure 9–43 shows a basic circuit that implements the phase-angle firing concept. As the voltage across the capacitor C becomes large enough, the gate of the triac is triggered. The resistance value adjusted for R determines the phase angle at which the triac will be triggered.

9–5 ▶ Data Acquisition and Control Systems

Data acquisition and control systems use all of the components discussed thus far to provide acquisition and control of one or more system variables. We have discussed a variety of digital and analog input and output devices as well as the concepts

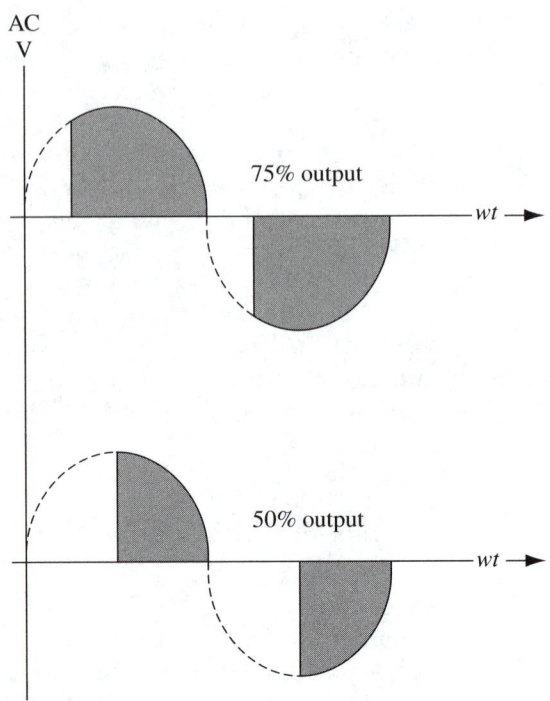

▶ **FIGURE 9–42**
Triac phase-angle fire waveforms

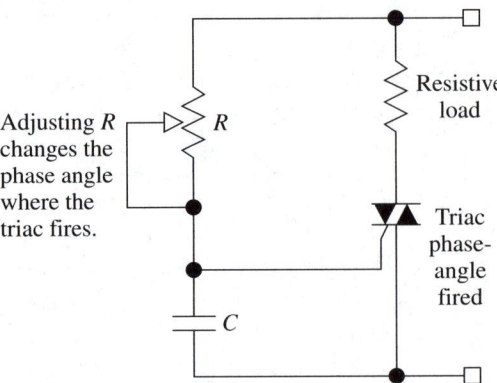

▶ **FIGURE 9–43**
Triac phase-angle fire circuit

of the process (PID) controllers and PLCs. All of these devices can now be connected to a personal computer in networks that result in very powerful data acquisition and control systems.

Process Controller Systems

A basic process control system includes just one control loop. A control loop consists of one process controller, an input measuring device, and a control output. There is just one set point and therefore one parameter under control. In many industrial applications it is necessary to control many parameters or take many different measurements of the same parameter at different locations in the system. These applications are called *multi-loop systems* because there are many control loops that monitor and control the system. Multi-loop systems can be developed in two ways: stand-alone controllers can be connected together in a network, or a multi-loop process controller or data acquisition system may be used. Figure 9–44 shows the block diagram for stand-alone controllers configured into a multi-loop network. A multi-loop block diagram is shown in Figure 9–45.

Process controllers used to accept only one analog input and provide up to three control outputs. These three outputs provided control of two output devices per controlled parameter and an alarm output. As more microprocessor power and surface-mount packaging technologies have been applied to these products, many additional inputs and outputs, both analog and digital, have been added to these controllers. There have been many added features as well: advanced math functions to manipulate and combine measured variables, many digital I/Os to implement ladder logic commands, and fuzzy logic algorithms to self-adjust PID values.

PLC Systems

PLCs are available as fixed or as rack-mounted units (see Figure 9–46). The fixed PLCs include a standard number of inputs, outputs, and control capabilities that cannot be expanded upon later. Rack-mounted units feature a card cage that provides almost limitless expansion. While the early PLCs offered only digital I/O, their capabilities have now been expanded to include a variety of analog I/O, which means that the PLC can actually measure an analog variable and output a proportional control output. In order to use the added analog I/O, PLCs have software

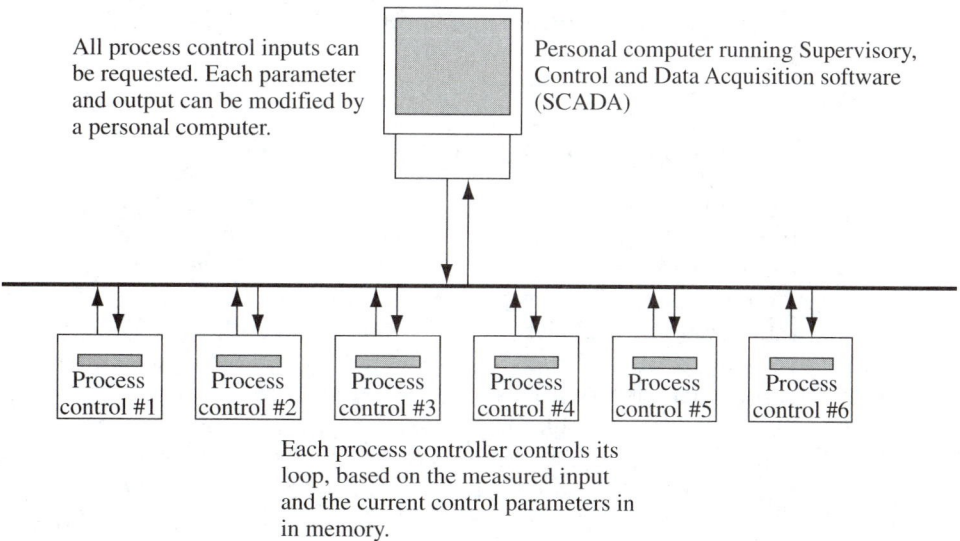

▲ **FIGURE 9–44**
Single-loop process control network

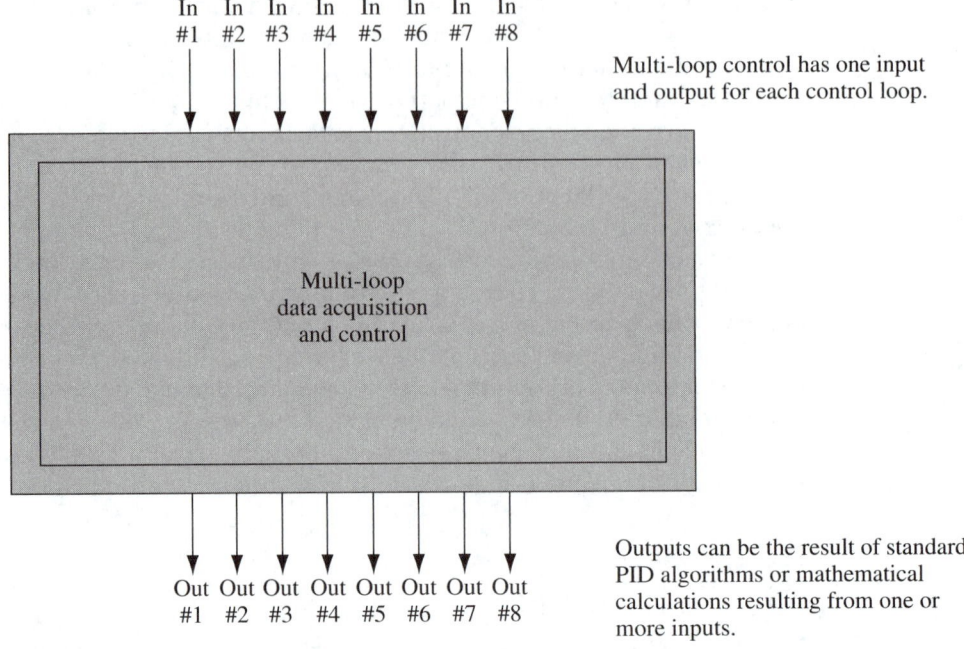

Multi-loop control has one input and output for each control loop.

Outputs can be the result of standard PID algorithms or mathematical calculations resulting from one or more inputs.

▲ **FIGURE 9–45**
Multi-loop process control network

PID control modules with full proportional control capabilities. Today's PLC also includes advanced digital communications capabilities and can be connected in a variety of network configurations.

Process Control and Data Acquisition Software

As process controllers and PLCs became larger and acquired additional capabilities, the personal computer became a standard device with the capability to tie all these devices together as a process control and data acquisition network. Beginning in the mid-1980s, personal computer software was developed with protocols that communicated with process controllers and PLCs. There are many high-level software packages available today that run on a personal computer and provide advanced data acquisition and control capabilities. Most of this software allows the user to create custom display screens that are pictorial representations of the process being monitored and controlled. The measured variables are displayed within the process screen at appropriate locations. For example, if the temperature of a chemical product processed in a tank is measured at various locations in the tank, this would be shown as a picture of the tank with the temperature values located at the appropriate locations on the tank.

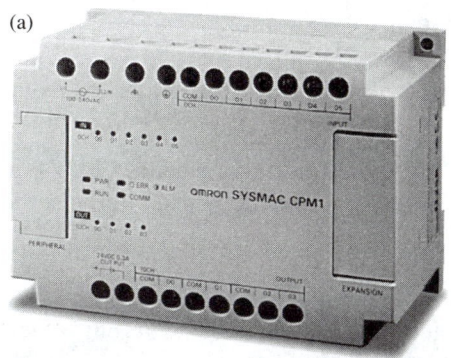

▶ **FIGURE 9–46**
PLC fixed (a) and rack-mounted (b) units. *(Courtesy Omron Electronics, LLC. Used by permission.)*

▶ Summary

In this chapter we have discussed a wide variety of the technology associated with industrial control and data acquisition systems. We have also reviewed much of the history and witnessed how the old world of industrial control has evolved from electromechanical relays, timers, and controllers to advanced process controllers, PLCs, and process control software. As we look back on all these advances, we can now see that the process controller has evolved to include many PLC (digital I/O and logic function) features while the PLC has acquired many process control (analog I/O and PID) capabilities. In many ways, when viewed strictly from an operational point of view, these two classes of products are difficult to tell apart.

We have also seen examples of old technology that continue to be used in spite of many efforts to replace them with faster, smaller electronic alternatives. At this point, we are unable to develop electronic alternatives to devices that are as rugged, versatile, and as easy to use as the electromechanical relay and the thermocouple. This chapter is just a snapshot of the industrial data acquisition and control world. It represents a broad combination of old technology and state-of-the-art embedded systems, software, and networks.

▶ References

Bartelt, L. M. *Industrial Control Electronics: Devices, Systems and Applications.* Albany, NY: Delmar, 2002.

Kissel, T. E. *Industrial Electronics.* Upper Saddle River, NJ: Prentice Hall, 1997.

▶ **Exercises**

9–1   When reviewing ladder logic diagrams, how can you determine whether a set of contacts is energized or not?

9–2   When using one set of SPDT contacts (C, NO, and NC), can both the NO and NC contacts be used in the same control circuit?

9–3   How can you tell if a rung on a ladder logic diagram operates completely independent of all other rungs in the diagram?

9–4   Does the location of a rung affect the operation of the rung in any way? Explain.

9–5   Why does each rung require at least one output device? Why can't two output devices be connected in series? Can two output devices be connected in parallel?

9–6   Draw a ladder logic diagram that will operate as follows:

Output relay K_1 will be energized when either maintained switch A is on or momentary switch B is depressed. If switch B is depressed, a set of contacts from K_1 will seal-in momentary switch B until switch C, a normally closed momentary switch, is depressed, shutting off K_1. Whenever switch A is on, relay K_1 is energized.

9–7   What is the primary difference between a limit switch and a proximity detector?

9–8   What is the primary advantage of using capacitive proximity detectors instead of inductive proximity detectors?

9–9   List the three primary types of photo-sensors. List and discuss one advantage of each type.

9–10 List and discuss one disadvantage of each primary type of photo-sensor.

9–11 What technological developments have led to the development of high-resolution optical encoders?

9–12 Explain the difference between relative and absolute encoders.

9–13 A pressure transmitter converts a pressure signal from 0 to 400 psi to a 4–20 mA signal. If the transmitter outputs 6.5 mA, what is the pressure input to the transmitter?

9–14 When does an analog process signal require linearization?

9–15 What is lead length error and which sensor is most susceptible to it?

9–16 Discuss the three methods for resolving lead length error associated with RTDs.

9–17 What is cold junction error and what type of sensor is most affected by it?

9–18 What is the most important advantage of IC temperature sensors when compared to thermistors, thermocouples, and RTDs?

9–19   A thermocouple sensor is placed in a medium of 220°F. The leads are connected to a cold junction compensated temperature indicator. The ambient temperature in the area where the thermocouple leads are connected to the indicator is 66°F. What temperature does the indicator read?

9–20   An LM335 IC temperature sensor measures the temperature in an environmental test chamber. The output of the sensor is 3.23 V. What temperature is the LM335 measuring?

9–21   What determines the resolution of wire-wound potentiometers used as position sensors?

9–22   Explain the difference between a sensor, transducer, and a transmitter.

9–23   Why are pressure sensors usually combined in one assembly, with all the electronics necessary to make them a complete pressure transmitter?

9–24   Explain the difference between the on-delay and off-delay time delay functions.

9–25   How do GFCIs protect people from electrical shock?

9–26   If someone touches the hot side of a GFCI-protected AC circuit with one hand, and the common side with the other hand, will the GFCI shut down the circuit? Will the person receive an electrical shock?

9–27   Define the term *hysterisis* as it is applied to on-off control output devices.

9–28   Define the difference between proportional and on-off outputs.

9–29   Explain the main concepts behind the proportional, integral, and derivative functions that make up PID control.

9–30   Explain the basic function of a PLC with digital I/O only.

9–31   What is the difference between an electromechanical relay and a contactor?

9–32   Explain the function of a device called a *solenoid*.

9–33   List and explain the two methods for protecting the life of electromechanical contacts.

10 Discrete Digital Design

► Introduction

Digital circuit design has also experienced rapid growth and change since the initial development of digital ICs. Overall speed, chip densities, and power efficiency continue to increase, providing a basis for increasingly complex functions in smaller packages. TTL, which was developed in the 1970s, represents mature technology that has seen great expansion and improvement over the years. Mature TTL devices are still used in many modern applications. CMOS technology has provided the foundation for significant improvements in the area of power efficiency and has also experienced much development. BiCMOS technology, which combines the speed capabilities of TTL with the power efficiency of CMOS, is providing the path for the future with further performance enhancements. There also is a push for lower logic voltage levels to help attain further speed and efficiency improvements. Lower voltage technology (LVT) reduces the nominal power for digital logic circuits from 5 V to 3.3 V, 2.5 V and even as low as 1.8 V. These lower power supply voltages reduce power consumption while increasing speed. In other application areas, the need for user programmable logic has increased. The variety and complexity of programmable logic devices (PLDs) has expanded to accommodate this need.

This chapter summarizes the circuit design concepts and considerations covered in most digital electronic courses. These concepts are then reviewed in light of the current digital devices available. Following are the specific topics covered in this chapter:

- ► Discrete Design Considerations
- ► Logic Families
- ► Package Considerations
- ► Programmable Logic Devices

10–1 ▶ Discrete Design Considerations

Digital components are often classified by their level of sophistication. Small-scale integration (SSI), medium-scale integration (MSI), large-scale integration (LSI), and so on, are terms used to classify ICs by their complexity. Basic digital electronic devices can also be classified as combinational, sequential, or bus-oriented. Combinational logic includes logic gates that are connected together to achieve a particular Boolean logic function. The outputs of combinational logic are determined by the inputs at any point in time. Combinational logic circuits are a combination of one or more of the following logic gates: AND, OR, NAND, NOR, INVERTER, EX-OR, EX-NOR. Figure 10–1 shows all of the logic symbols and truth tables as a reference.

Sequential logic utilizes digital components that can have three kinds of inputs: a clock, synchronous, and asynchronous. The clock input initiates changes to the outputs dictated by the synchronous inputs. Asynchronous inputs affect the

AND

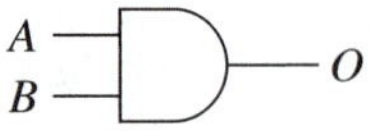

AND Truth Table

Inputs		Output
A	*B*	*O*
0	0	0
0	1	0
1	0	0
1	1	1

OR

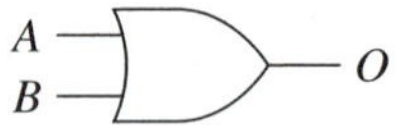

OR Truth Table

Inputs		Output
A	*B*	*O*
0	0	0
0	1	1
1	0	1
1	1	1

NAND

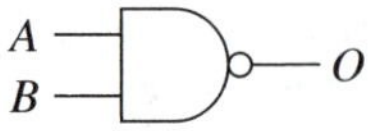

NAND Truth Table

Inputs		Output
A	*B*	*O*
0	0	1
0	1	1
1	0	1
1	1	0

NOR

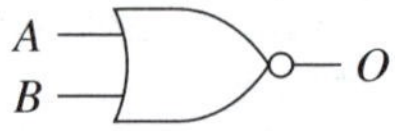

NOR Truth Table

Inputs		Output
A	*B*	*O*
0	0	1
0	1	0
1	0	0
1	1	0

Inverter

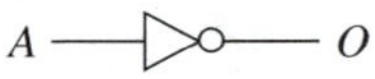

Inverter Truth Table

Inputs	Output
A	*O*
0	1
1	0

Exclusive-OR

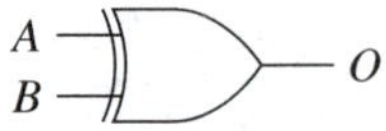

EX-OR Truth Table

Inputs		Output
A	*B*	*O*
0	0	0
0	1	1
1	0	1
1	1	0

Exclusive-NOR

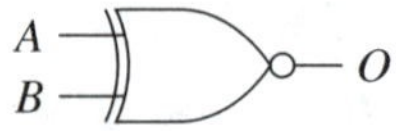

EX-NOR Truth Table

Inputs		Output
A	*B*	*O*
0	0	1
0	1	0
1	0	0
1	1	1

▲ **FIGURE 10–1**
Logic symbols and truth tables

output independent of the clock. The outputs from sequential circuits often depend on the state of the outputs prior to the clock. Sequential circuits form the basis for electronic memory and include devices such as flip-flops, monostable multivibrators (one-shots), and counters. Figure 10–2 shows the symbol and truth tables for two basic sequential circuits: the D flip-flop and the J-K flip-flop.

In many modern circuit applications, bus configurations are used to communicate signals to different areas of the circuit. A bus allows two or more devices to communicate with other devices over a common connection. Access to the bus is controlled so that only one device can output data at any one time. This is coordinated with the receiving device so that it receives only the data destined for it. The outputs from both standard combinational and sequential circuits are not designed to function with more than one output connected together. This precludes the use of these circuits in a bus environment. Tri-state logic was developed to resolve this problem. Logic devices with tri-state outputs can have their outputs connected together. Each tri-state device includes an enable input that, when active, connects the output of the device to the bus. When disabled, the tri-state device appears as a high input impedance to the bus, making it, essentially, electrically invisible to all devices on the bus. Figure 10–3 shows two commonly used tri-state logic devices: the 74LS373 and the 74LS374. Each of these ICs also has a clock input, so they are considered sequential, tri-state devices. As integrated circuits progress from SSI to MSI, LSI and so on, their classification and overall function usually becomes a mixture of combinational, sequential, and bus-oriented devices.

▶ **FIGURE 10–2**

Sequential circuit logic symbols and truth tables

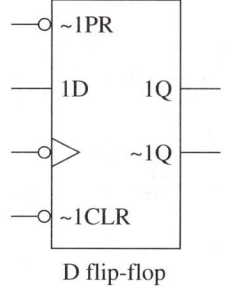

Truth Table

D	Clk	Pre	Clr	Q
0	Active	1	1	0
1	Active	1	1	1
×	×	0	1	0
×	×	1	0	1

D flip-flop

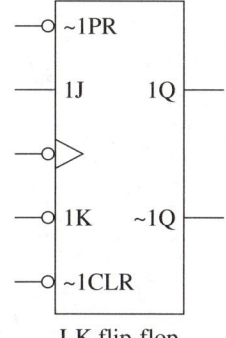

Truth Table

J	K	Clk	Pre	Clr	Q
0	0	Active	1	1	0
0	1	Active	1	1	1
1	0	Active	1	1	1
0	1	Active	1	1	0
×	×	×	0	1	0
×	×	×	1	0	1

J-K flip-flop

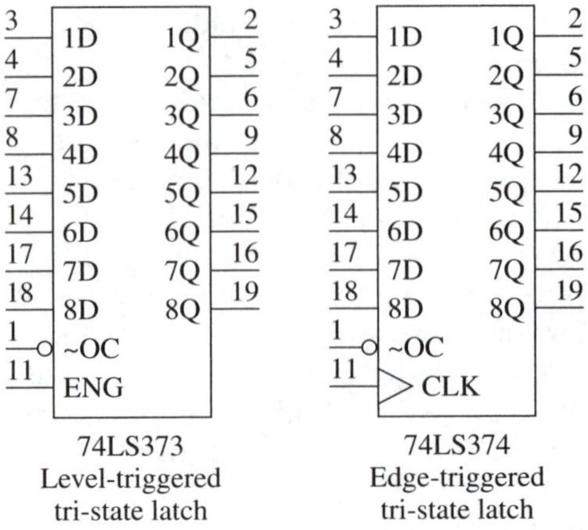

3	1D	1Q	2
4	2D	2Q	5
7	3D	3Q	6
8	4D	4Q	9
13	5D	5Q	12
14	6D	6Q	15
17	7D	7Q	16
18	8D	8Q	19

► FIGURE 10–3
74LS373 and 74LS374
tri-state logic devices

74LS373
Level-triggered
tri-state latch

74LS374
Edge-triggered
tri-state latch

Design specifications vary significantly between the various logic families that are included within the standard TTL and CMOS categories. All of the logic families and subfamilies are listed in Figure 10–4 to serve as a reference for the discussion of each specification category.

The design considerations for digital devices can be simplified by focusing on their inputs and outputs. Let's consider a digital device as simply having logic inputs and outputs, with power inputs and power outputs as well, as shown in Figure 10–5. The basic design considerations for all digital devices can be summarized as follows:

1. The voltage levels of all inputs, including both the logic and the power supply inputs, must be within the range of values defined in the subject specifications.

2. The rise time, width, and fall time of all input signals must be slower and wider than the specification values. For the case of sequential circuits, the relative time relationship between synchronous and clock inputs must also be met.

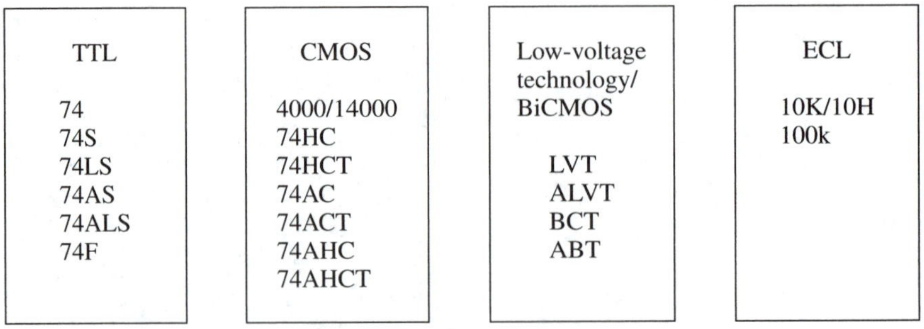

TTL	CMOS	Low-voltage technology/ BiCMOS	ECL
74	4000/14000		10K/10H
74S	74HC		100k
74LS	74HCT	LVT	
74AS	74AC	ALVT	
74ALS	74ACT	BCT	
74F	74AHC	ABT	
	74AHCT		

▲ FIGURE 10–4
Digital logic families

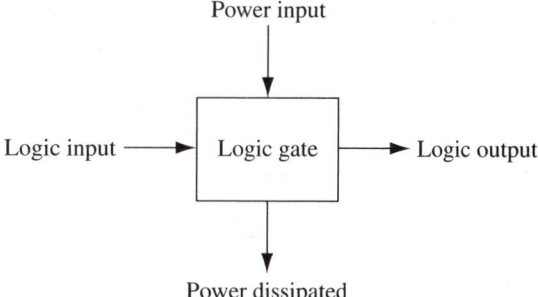

▶ **FIGURE 10–5**
Digital device functional diagram

3. The voltage and current levels of all logic outputs must be less than the specification values that are noted as "Absolute Maximum Values."

4. The power dissipated by the device must be less than the maximum power dissipation allowed.

5. General considerations such as ambient temperature, noise immunity, shock, and vibration must also be considered (see the discussion included in Chapters 4 and 5).

Power Supply Voltage Requirements

The most important input voltage level is that of the power supply. Any logic device ceases to function properly if the power supply voltage is not maintained within an acceptable range. Digital ICs are unforgiving of power supply voltage levels higher than the *absolute maximum values* specified. The result is usually permanent damage to the IC. For standard TTL, the required operating range for the power supply input is 4.75 to 5.25 V. The absolute maximum power supply input must be less than 7.0 V. For CMOS the 4000/14000 and 74C devices will operate on power supply voltages that range from 3 to 15 V with an absolute maximum value of about 18 V. The 74HC/HCT, 74 AC/ACT, and 74AHC/AHCT will operate over a power supply range of 2 to 6 V with an absolute maximum value of 7 V.

Input Logic Levels

The input requirements for logic circuits are presented in data books and textbooks in the form of V_{IL} and V_{IH}. V_{IL} is the maximum input voltage that is considered a logical low or 0. V_{IH} represents the minimum input voltage that is a 1 or logical high. There is also the entire range of inputs that will be recognized as either logical highs or lows. To ensure reliable operation, the input logic levels provided to a digital circuit must be within these levels. The acceptable range of inputs, V_{IL} and V_{IH} for TTL and CMOS families, are shown in Figure 10–6.

When one logic device drives another, it serves as a current source to the input of the device being driven when its output is high; low outputs are a current sink for the input being driven. The value for the current flowing to an input when the input is a logical high is denoted as I_{IH}; I_{IL} is the current that flows back to the

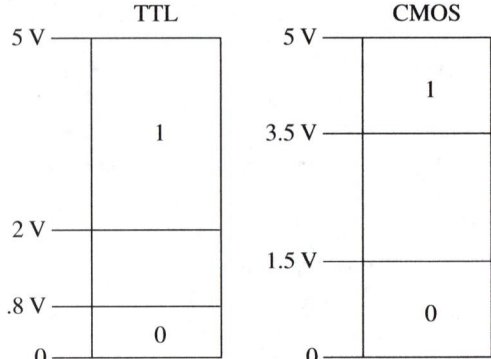

▶ **FIGURE 10–6**
Input and Output logic requirements
for TTL and CMOS

output when it is low. Both of these values can be obtained from the data sheet for
any logic device.

It is often necessary to bias a logic device to a logical high or logical low voltage when connecting switches and other devices as inputs. In these situations the
input is either pulled high or low when the switch is open; when the switch is
closed, the opposite logic level results (see Figure 10–7).

To calculate the proper pull-up resistor, determine the largest resistance value
that will develop an input voltage larger than the minimum value for high logic
($V_{IH(MIN)}$) while supplying the input current for a logical high (I_{IH}). If the resistor
value is too large, the voltage seen at the logic input will not be above the required
minimum logic high input; too small a resistance results in excessive current flow
and wasted power.

Example 10–1

Calculate the pull-up resistor value for the circuit shown in Figure 10–7b.

▶ **FIGURE 10–7**
Switch inputs

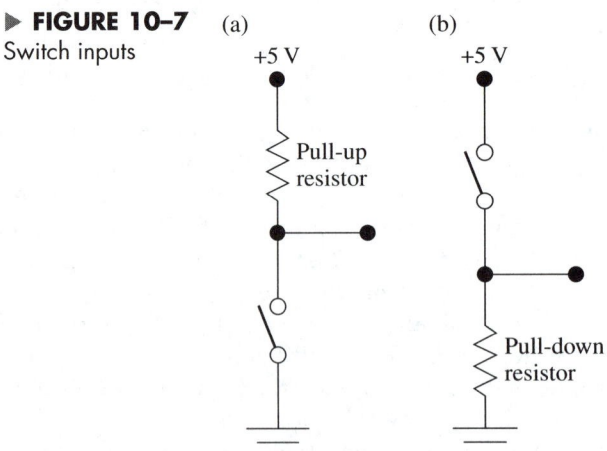

Solution

1. $V_{IH(MIN)} = 2.0$ V and $I_{IH} = 40$ µA for the logic device shown.

2. Let's select an input voltage of 4.6 to the logic device.

3. The voltage drop across the resistor when the switch is not depressed is:

   $V_R = 5.0$ V $- 4.6$ V $= .4$ V

4. Calculate the resistor that will develop a .4-V drop while 40 µA is flowing through it.

   $R = .4$ V/40 µA $= 10$ kΩ

5. 10 kΩ is commonly used as a pull-up resistor value.

To calculate the pull-down resistor values, determine the largest resistance value that will develop an input voltage less than the minimum value for low logic ($V_{IL(MIN)}$) while supplying the input current for a logical low (I_{IL}). If the resistor value is too large, the voltage seen at the logic input will be above the maximum logic high input; too small a resistance results in excessive current flow and wasted power.

Example 10–2

Calculate the pull-down resistor value for the circuit shown in Figure 10–7.

Solution

1. $V_{IL(MAX)} = .8$ V and $I_{IH} = -1.6$ µA for the logic device shown.

2. Let's select an input voltage of .16 to the logic device.

3. Calculate the resistor that will develop a .16-V drop while 1.6 µA is flowing through it.

   $R = .16$ V/1.6 µA $= 100$ Ω

4. 100 Ω is commonly used as a pull-down resistor value.

Timing Requirements

Sequential circuits have a clock input with time requirements for synchronous inputs relative to the clock. Input signals present at the synchronous inputs must be at a logic level for a period of time prior to the active clock transition, called the *setup time* or t_S, in order for the output to respond to the input. The input signal must also remain at that logic level for a period of time, called the hold time or t_H, after the active clock transition.

Propagation delay defines how quickly the output responds to input conditions that require the output to change state. Propagation delay is present in all logic devices. It is specified as propagation delay low-to-high, or t_{pLH}, and propagation delay

t_S – setup time
t_H – hold time
t_{PHL} – propagation delay high to low
t_{PLH} – propagation delay low to high
$t_W(\text{L})$ – clock low time
$t_W(\text{H})$ – clock high time
$t_W(\text{L})$ – low pulse width required at
set and clear inputs

▶ **FIGURE 10–8**

Logic device timing specifications

high-to-low, or $t_{p\text{HL}}$. Sequential devices can have different propagation delays for synchronous inputs and asynchronous inputs (e.g., SET and CLEAR).

Sequential devices also have timing requirements for the clock input signal. The clock signal must remain low for a time denoted as $t_W(\text{L})$ and high for a time $t_W(\text{H})$. There is also a maximum frequency specification for the clock, called f_{MAX}. Asynchronous inputs such as SET and CLEAR have minimum pulse widths for these input signals for their active state. Active low asynchronous inputs have a specification, $t_W(\text{L})$, while active high inputs specify $t_W(\text{H})$. Figure 10–8 summarizes all of the timing requirements for logic devices.

Output Levels and Loading

The output from any logic device is in the form of a voltage that signifies either a logical 1 or 0. Of course, each logic family has different specifications for these voltages, which are designated $V_{\text{OH(MIN)}}$, the minimum logical high output voltage, and $V_{\text{OL(MAX)}}$, the maximum logical low output voltage. The values for these output voltages must be within the range of acceptable input voltage for the logic device being driven.

The logic output either sources current to or sinks current from the device being driven. It is important to make sure that the current in either case does not exceed the maximum ratings for the device. These specifications are listed with the other *recommended operating conditions* and are denoted as output current logical high, I_{OH}, and output current logical low, I_{OL}. The specification values for these two parameters will differ by a large amount.

The outputs of two or more conventional TTL and CMOS devices should never be connected together. Open collector outputs can be connected together to implement what is called a *wired-and* configuration. Otherwise, tri-state outputs should be utilized to allow the connection of multiple logic device outputs for the purpose of sharing a connection.

The output current specifications can easily be met when driving logic devices of the same family by verifying that the fan-out specification has not been exceeded. Fan-out is an indication of how many standard logic devices of the same logic family can be driven by the logic device. Standard TTL has a fan-out specification of 10. This means it can drive 10 standard TTL devices without exceeding the output current specifications. The fan-out specification varies for each logic subfamily and is discussed in the next section.

Noise Margin

One major advantage of digital devices is their relative immunity to input signal noise. The degree to which a device is immune to noise is known as the *noise margin*. The noise margin is defined for high and low outputs as follows:

$$\text{Noise Margin High Outputs} = V_{NH} = V_{OH(MIN)} - V_{IH(MIN)}$$
$$\text{Noise Margin Low Outputs} = V_{NL} = V_{IL(MAX)} - V_{OL(MAX)}$$

Noise margin varies between the different logic families and is usually higher in CMOS devices when compared to TTL.

Power Requirements

The total power dissipated by a logic device is the sum of the output power and the power consumed to bias all of the internal transistors. In both cases the amount of power dissipated varies for logical high- and low-output conditions. I_{CCH} is the amount of current drawn from V_{CC} for a high output and I_{CCL} is the value for a logical low output. Both of these parameter values are listed in the spec sheets for digital devices. In order to estimate the average power dissipated over time, an estimate of the percentage of time the output is high and low must be made.

It is important to estimate the amount of power dissipated by each device in a circuit because the net power of the entire circuit must be calculated. This is done for two reasons:

1. To provide guidelines for designing the power supply

2. To ensure that proper heat dissipation is provided for in the design of the enclosure

A summary of the design considerations for digital logic circuits is shown in Figure 10–9. The actual specification numbers for the parameters discussed in this section, as they apply to a specific logic family, are reviewed in the next section.

10–2 ▶ Logic Families

The two primary types of logic families are TTL and CMOS. TTL has always been noted for high speed and poor power efficiency. The small bias currents and inherent capacitance associated with CMOS logic devices have given them better power efficiency and slower speeds. Many different subsets of these two logic families have been developed over the years and new initiatives continue that include combining

1. Verify that power supply voltages are within acceptable operating ranges.

2. Verify that all input/output logic voltages are within the required levels for the respective high/low conditions of the logic device.

3. Verify that all timing requirements have been met — specifically, setup and hold times for all sequential circuits.

4. Verify that all clock signals meet minimum width and maximum frequency requirements.

5. Consider the effects of propagation delays using worst-case scenarios in all areas of the logic circuit.

6. Verify that all output currents are within acceptable ranges for all logic devices.

7. Estimate the power dissipation for each device and compare that with its maximum power rating.

8. Estimate noise levels at key circuit inputs and compare to noise margins to determine circuit noise immunity.

▲ **FIGURE 10–9**
Summary of digital design considerations

the best of TTL and CMOS to lowering logic voltage levels. These strategies serve to improve both speed and power efficiency at the expense of noise margin. These new design innovations have resulted in new logic families, such as BiCMOS and low voltage technology and many variations, combinations, and extensions to each of these. The part numbers for the digital devices currently available include an array of letters that indicate the type of design philosophy utilized. The variations seem endless as the older, mature technologies still available are flanked with newer high-performance devices.

TTL Logic Family

TTL logic devices were the first widely accepted logic ICs and they still enjoy broad use today. These devices are recognized by their 74xx designation. The 54xx devices function the same as equivalent 74xx devices except that they meet extended military specifications. It is important to note that the power consumed by TTL devices is relatively constant as the switching frequency changes. We will see that this is not the case with CMOS devices. Following is a summary for each currently available TTL logic subfamily that includes the typical performance specifications for 74xx00 devices:

74xx Series—Standard TTL:

	Propagation Delay	Power	Max Frequency	Fan-out
Standard TTL	9 ns	10 mW	35 MHz	10

74Sxxx Series—Schottky TTL: This series includes a Schottky barrier diode that is connected between the base and collector of all transistors in the circuit. This serves to reduce the propagation delay to 3 ns, which is one-third the propagation delay of standard TTL.

	Propagation Delay	Power	Max Frequency	Fan-out
S Series	3 ns	19 mW	125 MHz	20

74LSxxx Series—Low-power Schottky TTL: The LS series includes the Schottky barrier diodes but has larger resistance values that serve to reduce power consumption at the expense of reduced speed.

	Propagation Delay	Power	Max Frequency	Fan-out
LS Series	9.5 ns	2 mW	45 MHz	20

74ASxxx Series—Advanced Shottky TTL: As devices represent a major improvement in the design if the TTL circuit that still uses the Schottky barrier diodes on all transistors. These design improvements make the AS series the fastest TTL family.

	Propagation Delay	Power	Max Frequency	Fan-out
AS Series	1.7 ns	8 mW	200 MHz	40

74ALSxxx Series—Advanced low-power Shottky TTL: These devices are identical to the AS series but include larger resistors that reduce power consumption and increase propagation delays.

	Propagation Delay	Power	Max Frequency	Fan-out
ALS Series	4 ns	1.2 mW	70 MHz	20

74Fxxx Series—Fast TTL: F series devices feature new fabrication technologies that reduce the inherent coupling capacitance between circuit devices. These innovations yield performance that make the F TTL series as fast as the TTL S series, while consuming about one-third of the power.

	Propagation Delay	Power	Max Frequency	Fan-out
F Series	3 ns	6 mW	100 MHz	33

Good design practice calls for connecting all unused TTL inputs to a logical high or low voltage that will allow proper function of the device. All unused TTL devices should have their inputs connected to yield a logical low output all the time.

CMOS Logic Family

The CMOS logic family was actually developed before TTL. However, because of fabrication problems it was not commercially developed until well after bipolar TTL devices had become standard. CMOS logic devices typically feature better power efficiency at lower speeds. However, design enhancements have led to many CMOS subfamilies that have improved on the inherent weaknesses of CMOS technology. One of the inherent advantages of CMOS has always been its better power efficiency. It is important to note that the power consumed by CMOS devices increases with the switching frequency. This is because the internal capacitance must be continually recharged; the faster this occurs, the more power is lost.

Following is a summary for each currently available CMOS logic subfamily that includes the average performance specifications:

4000/14000 Series—CMOS: Series 4000/14000 devices were the initial CMOS families marketed. The 4000 series was developed by RCA while Motorola designed the 14000. For the most part, the 4000 and 14000 devices are equivalent to each other. However, they are not electrically or pin compatible with TTL devices. Series 4000/14000 devices are not usually used in new designs but can be found in many older products.

	Propagation Delay	Power (Static)	Max Frequency	Fan-out
4000/14000	100 ns	.3 mw	4 MHz	2

74Cxxx Series—CMOS, pin/function compatible with TTL: These are second-generation CMOS devices that featured pin compatibility with TTL devices. The C designation indicates that an IC is a CMOS device that is pin-for-pin and functionally compatible with TTL devices. This means that a 74C00 has the same pin-out and logic devices, which perform the same function as a 7400 or any other TTL series device (74LS00, 74ALS00, etc.). However, 74C devices are not electrically compatible with TTL, which means that their definitions of logical high and low voltages are different. The 74C series was discontinued after the 74HC/HCT series, which is discussed next, was introduced.

	Propagation Delay	Power (Static)	Max Frequency	Fan-out
74 C Series	100 ns	.3 mw	4 MHz	2

74HCxxx Series—High-speed, pin/function-compatible CMOS: This series improved upon the performance of the C series, which was discontinued after the HC series was introduced. The H stands for *high-speed*. HC-series propagation delays were reduced by a factor of ten when compared to the C series. Power consumption is also reduced. The HC series is pin and functionally compatible with TTL devices, but the two families are not electrically compatible. The HC series uses the standard CMOS logic voltage levels, as shown in Figure 10–6.

	Propagation Delay	Power at 100 kHz	Max Frequency	Fan-out
74HC Series	9 ns	.068 mw	55 MHz	11

74HCTxxx Series—High-speed, TTL-compatible CMOS: This family was introduced with the HC series. The primary difference is that the HCT series is also electrically compatible with TTL. In fact, the CT designation signifies that a device features CMOS technology that is functionally, pin-for-pin, and electrically compatible with TTL. The performance specifications for the HCT series differ slightly from the HC devices.

	Propagation Delay	Power at 100 kHz	Max Frequency	Fan-out
74HCT Series	10 ns	.050 mw	50 MHz	11

74 AHC Series—Advanced high-speed CMOS: This series features design enhancements made to the 74HC series that improve both speed and efficiency. The AHC and the TTL-compatible AHCT series discussed next represent the latest in CMOS technology and the highest performance levels. The AHC series also can operate from 3.3- or 5-V power.

	Propagation Delay	Power at 100 kHz	Max Frequency	Fan-out
74 AHC Series	5.2 ns	.073 mw	100 MHz	11

74AHCTxxx Series—Advanced high-speed, TTL-compatible CMOS: The TTL compatibility requirement affects the performance slightly, but for all practical purposes the AHCT and HCT series perform the same except for the logic voltage levels accepted and output by each.

	Propagation Delay	Power at 100 kHz	Max Frequency	Fan-out
74 AHCT Series	5.5 ns	.075 mw	100 MHz	11

IC manufacturers continue to seek performance improvements in the form of higher functionality, smaller packages, and quicker switching speeds with better power efficiency. To accomplish this, both power supply and logic level voltages

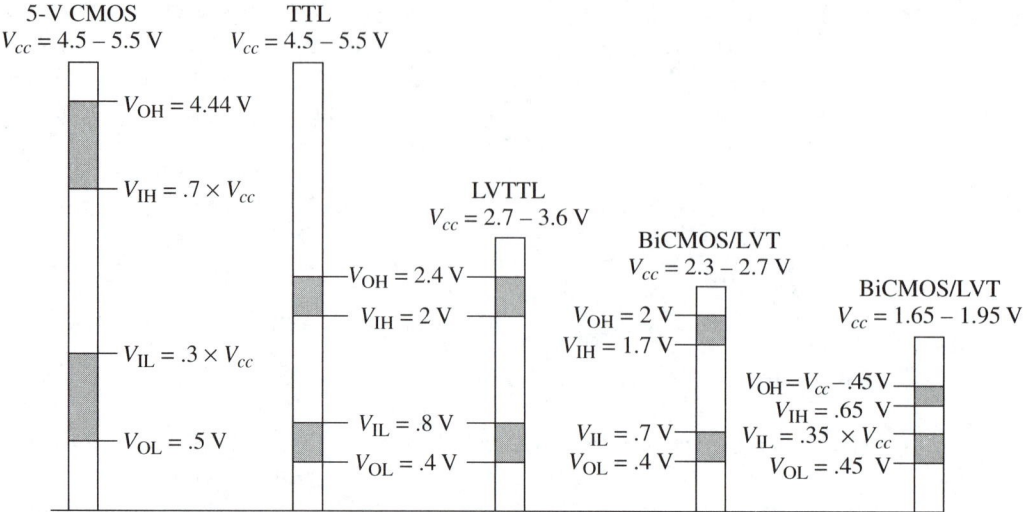

▲ FIGURE 10–10
Logic level definitions for standard and low-voltage logic families

have been decreased on new logic families. As transistor geometries become smaller, they can no longer withstand voltages in the 5-V range. Decreasing power supply voltages helps support performance improvements by allowing circuits to be placed closer together. Lower power supply voltages mean less current and therefore less power consumption. Propagation delays are reduced slightly because logic voltage levels are lower; the output can go from a logical zero to one quicker because the voltage margin is smaller.

Future plans call for three low-voltage standards powered by these power supply voltages: 3.3 V, 2.5 V and 1.8 V. New devices will be developed to operate at these logic levels and released in stages. Logic level standards for these low-voltage families are shown in Figure 10–10.

The following logic families represent the low-voltage families that have been developed most recently.

74LVxxx—Low-voltage series: This is a TTL low-voltage series and includes devices that are powered by 3.3 V. It features many of the more common SSI and MSI logic devices.

	Propagation Delay	Power at 100 kHz	Max Frequency
74 LV Series	5.4 ns	.11 mw	60 MHz

74LVCxxx—Low-voltage CMOS: This series is the CMOS version of the 74LV series; however, there is a broader range of devices available. Also, the 74 LVC series can accept regular 5-V logic inputs and it can drive 5-V logic inputs as long as the maximum output current specification is not exceeded.

	Propagation Delay	Power at 100 kHz	Max Frequency
74 LVC Series	5.4 ns	.05 mw	60 MHz

74ALVCxxx—Advanced low-voltage CMOS: This series features higher performance in the area of propagation delay and can be used with 3.3-V logic only. It is intended for tri-state bus-oriented applications.

	Propagation Delay	Power at 100 kHz	Max Frequency
74 ALVC Series	2 ns	.22 mw	180 MHz

74AVCxxx—Advanced very-low-voltage CMOS: these are the latest in pure CMOS devices and are designed to operate from power supplies over a range of 1.8 to 3.3 V.

	Propagation Delay	Power at 100 kHz	Max Frequency
74 AVC Series	1.9 ns	.22 mw	200 MHz

Special CMOS Considerations

When designing or working with CMOS circuits, there are special limitations that must be considered. These limitations include the sensitivity of CMOS to static electricity, requirements for unused CMOS inputs and devices, the effect of switching frequency on power consumption, and the impact of the load output on propagation delay.

CMOS inputs must always be connected to some voltage or device. If there is no need for an input, tie it to a logic voltage (low or high) that will allow the device to function properly. If a device is not being used at all, connect the inputs to fixed logic voltages that will yield a logical low output all the time.

The silicon dioxide layer that insulates the inputs of all CMOS devices is the primary mechanism for the high-input impedance and low-bias currents that are associated with CMOS technology. At the same time CMOS devices are known for their sensitivity to static electricity capable of generating thousands of volts at very low currents. These high-voltage shocks can destroy or seriously degrade the silicon dioxide layer to the point of failure or marginal operation. Consequently, the following considerations should be made when utilizing CMOS devices:

1. Handle CMOS devices only when using grounded wrist straps on conductive bench pads, and make sure that all test equipment and powered tools are properly grounded.

2. CMOS devices and circuit boards should be stored in anti-static tubes, anti-static bags, or other appropriate (conductive) containers. Styrofoam is not an acceptable storage medium.

3. Power up CMOS devices before signals are applied to their inputs and remove signal sources before taking power away.

4. Power down CMOS devices before inserting or removing them from a circuit.

CMOS Power Consumption

While it is true that CMOS generally exhibits better power efficiency when compared to TTL, it is important to note that increases in switching frequency also increase the amount of power consumed by a CMOS device. TTL devices consume relatively constant levels of power as the switching frequency increases up to frequencies around 3 MHz. Above 3 MHz, TTL power consumption also increases with the frequency. Therefore, it is critical that the digital designer review the specifications completely in regard to power consumption and switching frequency. It is conceivable that at a particular frequency, a TTL device may offer equal or better power efficiency when compared to a CMOS device operating at that same frequency.

Output Load Effect of Propagation Delay

The fan-out stated in the specifications for CMOS and TTL devices indicates the number of gate inputs that can be driven safely by the device's output. The number of CMOS devices driven can affect the propagation delay of the driving device. This is caused by the capacitance associated with the input of a CMOS circuit. The designer must review the specifications to determine the actual propagation delay expected for a given fan-out situation.

Latch Up

In the early development stages of CMOS technology, CMOS devices were highly susceptible to a condition called "latch-up." Latch-up occurred as a result of transistors mistakenly fabricated on the CMOS substrate as part of the fabrication process. Transient voltage spikes and noise can permanently switch on these parasitic transistors. Current CMOS devices have internal circuitry that minimizes the possibility of latch-up, but it is good design practice to use power supplies that are well regulated and filtered and feature current limiting.

BiCMOS Logic

BiCMOS is the result of combining the best aspects of bipolar TTL and CMOS technologies to develop devices that are fast and power-efficient. It was developed for microprocessor and bus-oriented applications in which speed and efficiency are most critical. BiCMOS devices are available in standard 5-V and 3.3-V power configurations.

> **74 BCTxxx—BiCMOS bus interface technology:** This operates with standard 5-V logic and generally offers significant reduction in power consumption while maintaining low propagation delays. The BCT series operates off of 5-V power and is pin compatible with TTL devices and includes primarily bus interface devices.

74 LVTxxx—Low-voltage BiCMOS technology: This series includes mostly bus-oriented devices that can accept either 3- or 5-V logic level inputs where the outputs are compatible with TTL.

	Propagation Delay	Power at 100 kHz	Max Frequency
74 LVT Series	5.4 ns	.6 w	95 MHz

74ABTxxx—Advanced BiCMOS technology: This is the second generation of BiCMOS devices that operates off of 5 V and is also bus-oriented.

The 74ABT245 is a good example of the ABT series of devices. It is an Octal Bus Transceiver with tri-state outputs. This means that it can interface asynchronously with an 8-bit data bus, bi-directionally. The 74ABT245 is powered by 5 V, $V_{IH} = 2$ V and $V_{IL} = .8$ with propagation delays in the area of 4 nanoseconds. Power consumption is a maximum of .6 watts for all 8 transceivers. The pin-out and logic diagram for the 74ABT 245 is shown in Figure 10–11.

74 ALVTxxx—Advanced low-voltage BiCMOS technology: This series features high-performance BiCMOS devices capable of operation with power inputs of 3.3 or 2.5 V. ALVT devices offer low propagation delay, low static power consumption, and 64 mA current drive capability. They can interface with 5-V logic devices on a mixed-mode basis. This means that the input can be 5 V while providing a 3.3-volt output.

The 74ALVTH16244 exemplifies the ALVT series as it provides fast and efficient communications with 16-bit data buses. Propagation delay for this device is about

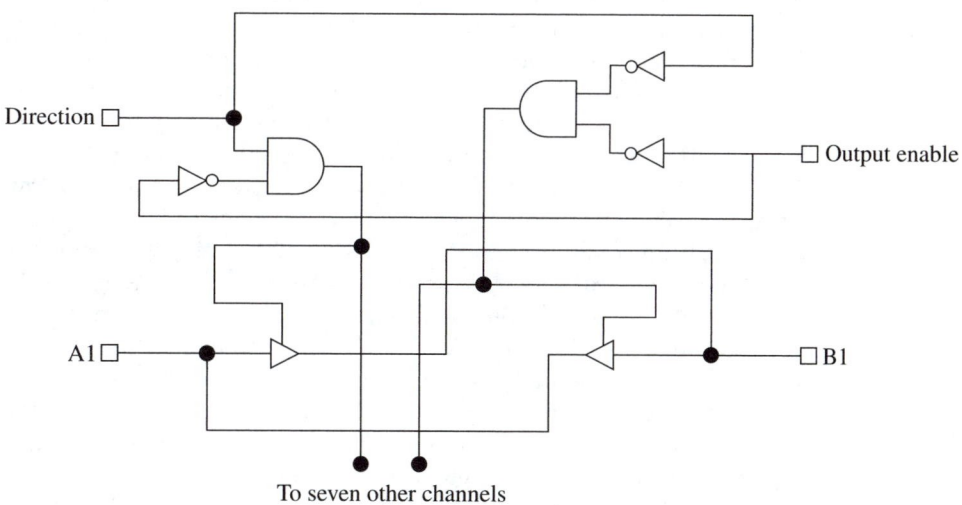

To seven other channels

▲ **FIGURE 10–11**
74ABT 245 pin-out and logic diagram

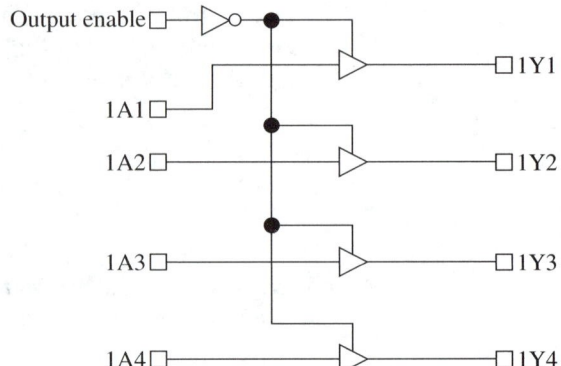

▶ **FIGURE 10-12**
74ALVTH16244 logic diagram

4 ns and it is available in a Widebus (a Texas Instruments trademark) package that allows all 16-line connections to be made in line, one-on-one through the device. The pin-out and logic diagram for the 74ALVTH16244 are shown in Figure 10–12.

74ALBxxx—Advanced low-voltage BiCMOS: This series features bus-oriented devices that operate with 3.3-V logic levels.

Emitter Controlled Logic (ECL) Family

The ECL family was developed to provide very high switching frequencies that surpass the switching capabilities of all other logic families developed thus far. The ECL family utilizes bipolar transistors that are configured to select between one of two paths of current flow, depending on whether the input is high or low. This configuration, called *current mode logic* (*CML*), is a drastic change from the totem pole arrangement of the transistors used in both TTL and CMOS logic families. ECL can be viewed as a differential amplifier, where the current levels that define ECL high and low logic levels do not require the saturation of the transistors. This is the key to fast switching times that also results in a smaller difference between the logic high and low levels and high power consumption. Consequently, ECL is used only in applications where extremely high data rates are experienced and power efficiency is a much lower priority. These applications include large mainframe super computers and communications equipment that interfaces with fiber optic transceivers for gigabit Ethernet and ATM networks.

The difference between a logical high and low is generally less than 1 volt for the ECL family, so the noise margin provided is smaller than TTL or CMOS. To improve noise performance, ECL was designed to use a negative power supply. This was done because ground lines are usually more noise free than the positive supply side. Since ECL logic is referenced to the most positive voltage, it uses the more noise-free ground line as the most positive reference, with a negative power supply.

The CML structure of the ECL family provides another unique result: ECL devices have outputs for both the true logical output and the inverted output. In other words, ECL devices provide complementary outputs.

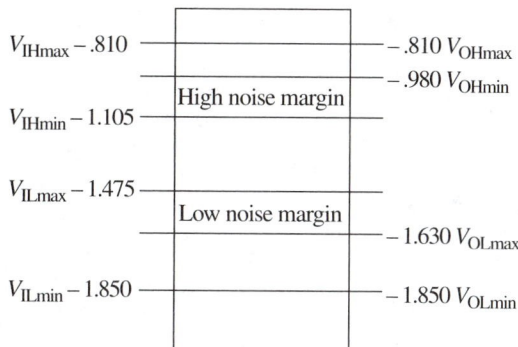

▶ **FIGURE 10–13**
ECL 10K logic levels

ECL 10K/10H Series—Emitter coupled logic with 10xxx designations:
This is the most popular ECL family that is identified with a five-digit number with the first two digits fixed at 1 and 0, respectively. This series is powered with $V_{CC} = 0$ V and $V_{EE} = -5.2$ V. The logic voltage levels for ECL are shown in Figure 10–13. The 10H designation means that these devices are compensated to operate from voltages other than –5.2 volts.

Internally, both TTL and CMOS logic devices incorporate a pull-up resistor within their totem-pole circuit arrangement. Because the switching times for ECL are so fast, circuit connections longer than a few inches must be viewed as a transmission line. In ECL devices a pull-down resistor is necessary because the outputs are emitter coupled. The value of the pull-down resistor should match the effective impedance of the connection and minimize power consumption. For this reason the selection of the pull-down resistor value (270 to 2 kΩ) is left up to the circuit designer. These pull-down resistors consume a lot of power, which is why the power consumed by ECL devices can vary so greatly.

	Propagation Delay	Power
ECL 10K/10H Series	2 ns	35 to 175 mw per gate

ECL 100K Series—Emitter coupled logic with 100xxx designations: The 100K series is identified with six digits, with the first three digits fixed as 1, 0, and 0. The numbers have no significance relative to the 10K/10H series. The 100K series offers improved speed performance at the price of lower power efficiency. The propagation delay for ECL 100K is in the area of .7 ns with approximately 40 mw/gate of additional power consumption. This series uses $V_{CC} = 0$ and $V_{EE} = -4.5$ V, which changes the logic level voltages also.

Positive emitter coupled logic: These are ECL devices designed to operate from positive power supplies. This promotes their interfacing with TTL and CMOS logic families.

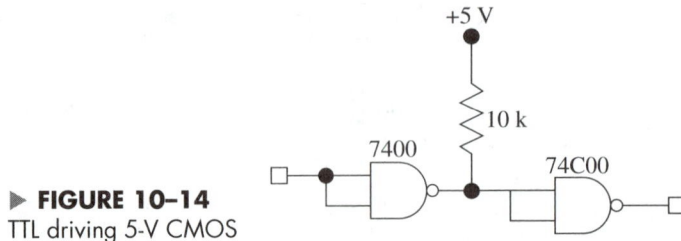

▶ **FIGURE 10–14**
TTL driving 5-V CMOS

Interfacing Logic Families

TTL to 5-V CMOS

TTL is very capable of supplying enough current to drive CMOS devices. When interfacing any TTL family device to a 5-V CMOS device, care must be taken to insure that the high output voltage is high enough to register as a logical high with the CMOS device. The minimum high output voltage, $V_{OH(MIN)}$ for all TTL devices is too low when compared to the minimum high input voltage, $V_{IH(MIN)}$ for most CMOS devices. The proper method for TTL driving CMOS is to connect a 10-kΩ pull-up resistor on the output of the TTL device. This will pull the high output voltage of the TTL device well within the acceptable range for CMOS devices (see Figure 10–14).

TTL to High-voltage CMOS

A TTL device with an open collector output is often used to drive CMOS logic powered by voltages greater than 5 V. The voltage rating for open collector outputs is usually around 30 V DC, greater than the maximum power supply voltage for CMOS logic. The open collector output is pulled up to the power supply voltage being used, as shown in Figure 10–15.

5-volt CMOS to TTL

Most 5-V CMOS families can drive TTL directly. It is important to review the specific data sheet in question to determine how many TTL devices can be driven safely. However, the early 4000 and 4000B series of CMOS devices cannot sink enough current when driving a TTL device to a logical zero. In order to cover this situation, the 4000 series includes special buffers. Two devices, the 4050 buffer and the 4049 inverting buffer, have higher current sourcing and sinking capabilities that resolve this interface problem. Figure 10–16 shows a 4000 series logic device driving TTL with a 4050B device acting as a buffer/driver.

▶ **FIGURE 10–15**
TTL driving high-voltage CMOS

$V_{cc} = 5$ V   CMOS buffer
7404   4050B   4011B
$V_{cc} = 15$ V
$V_{cc} = 15$ V

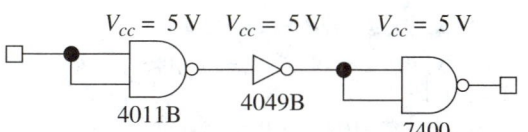

▶ **FIGURE 10–16**
4000 CMOS driving TTL

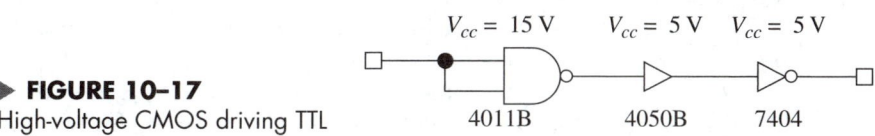

▶ **FIGURE 10–17**
High-voltage CMOS driving TTL

High-voltage CMOS to TTL

When high-voltage CMOS circuits must drive TTL, a CMOS buffer can be used to translate high-voltage CMOS levels down to 5-V CMOS. In this case either the 4049B or 4050B can be used, as was discussed previously for CMOS driving TTL devices. Figure 10–17 shows an example circuit in which high-voltage CMOS drives a TTL logic gate.

Interfacing with ECL

IC manufacturers have addressed the difficult problem of converting ECL to TTL and vice versa. ECL 10k series devices have been developed especially to accomplish this task. The 10125 interfaces ECL to TTL while the 10124 accepts TTL inputs and drives ECL outputs (see Figure 10–18).

▶ **FIGURE 10–18**
ECL and TTL interfacing

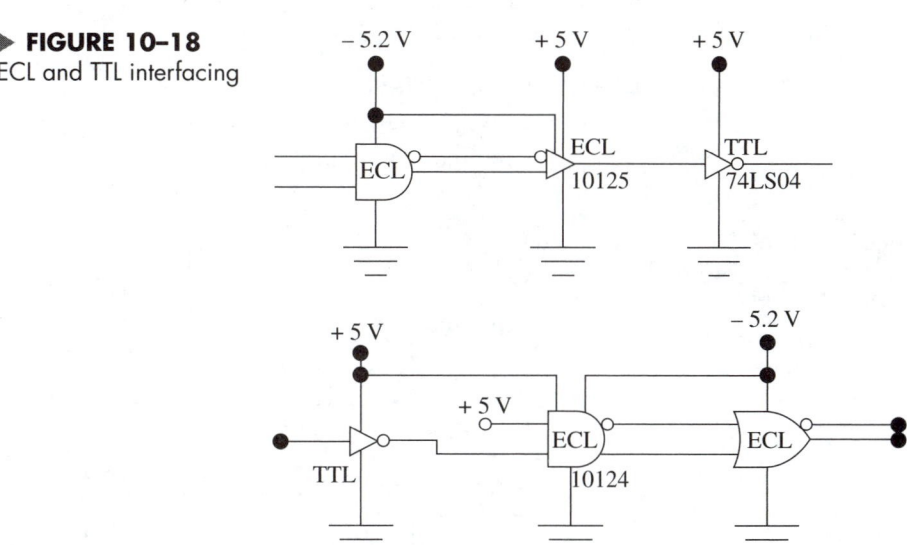

5-V to Low-voltage Logic

The development of low-voltage logic devices has brought about the need to translate between 5-V and 3.3-V logic systems. Most devices cannot tolerate input voltages higher than their power V_{CC}. Special circuitry must be added to 3.3-V devices to make them tolerant of 5-V inputs. Even though many 5-V and 3.3-V devices provide TTL-compatible interface levels and are 5-V input fault tolerant, some devices lack these capabilities. For example, there are certain CMOS devices that can drive to 5 V but cannot tolerate a 5-V input. These devices require 5-V to 3.3-V translation when the two logic levels must be interfaced.

A common design requirement is the interfacing of low-voltage microprocessor and memory circuits with 5-V I/O devices and memory (see Figure 10–19). The 74CBTD3384 is a special device that has been developed to provide translation between these two logic levels. The bus switches included for each bit of the 74CBTD3384 consist of an N-channel MOSFET. The inherent voltage drop across the drain and the source of the MOSFET serves to drop the 5-V levels that are input to the 3.3-V devices down to a maximum of 3.3 V (see Figure 10–20).

10–3 ▶ Package Considerations

The original package configuration for digital ICs was the dual-in-line package (DIP). DIPs are consistent with older through-hole package technology, where all electronic components are mounted to printed circuit boards by inserting their connecting leads into holes in the PCB. Copper pads present on the surface of the PCB surround these holes. The component lead is soldered to the copper pad, making the electrical connection and securing the component to the circuit board. The spacing between DIP leads, called the *lead pitch*, is .1 in. There are two rows of leads with an equal number in each row. The .1-in. lead spacing is the minimum dimension practical, when considering minimum hole and pad sizes for fabricating PCBs.

Early TTL and CMOS IC families were founded on the DIP. DIP packages are available in two package widths, .3 in. or .6 in. between lead rows. Following are the standard DIP configurations:

Mini-DIP—8 pins, .3-in. width

14-pin DIP—14 pins, .3-in. width

16-pin DIP—16 pins, .3-in. width

▶ **FIGURE 10–19**
5-V to 3.3-V interfacing (TI data sheet 74 CBTD3384)

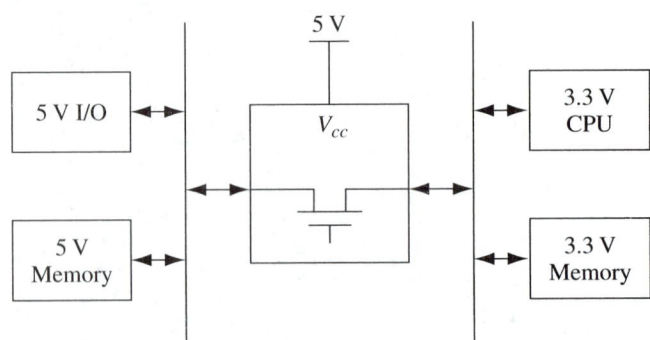

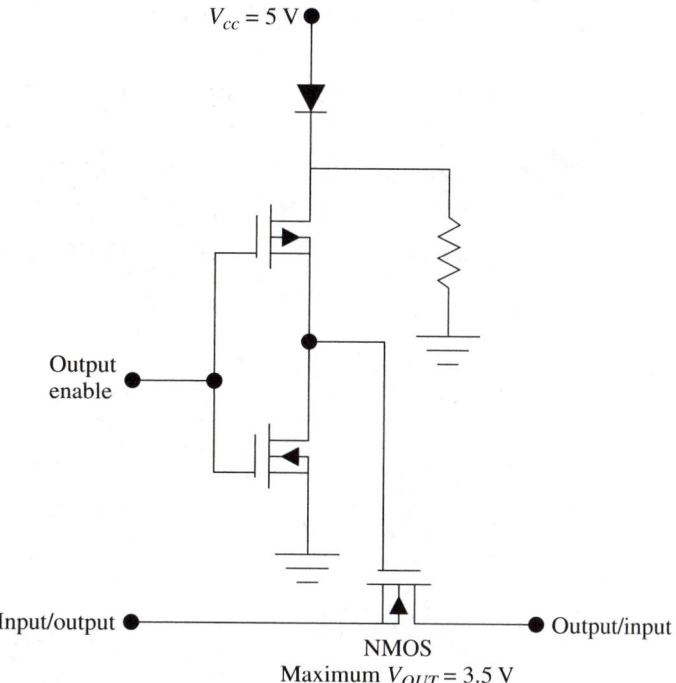

$V_{cc} = 5$ V

Output enable

Input/output

Output/input

NMOS

Maximum $V_{OUT} = 3.5$ V

▶ **FIGURE 10–20**
NMOS Switch of 74CBTD3384
(TI data sheet 74 BTD3384)

20-pin DIP—20 pins, .3-in. width

24-pin DIP—24 pins, .3-in. width

24-pin DIP—24 pins, .6-in. width

28-pin DIP—28 pins, .6-in. width

40-pin DIP—40 pins, .6-in. width

As integrated circuit densities increased and package sizes decreased, there was a need to decrease lead pitch as well. A new method was needed to make component electrical connections and affix the component to the circuit board. Surface-mount technology (SMT) was the result. The first surface-mount package style to be developed was the Small Outline (SO) package developed for the watch industry. SMT quickly became the standard for circuit connections made on the surface of PCBs. SMT connections are made with small pads etched onto the surface of the PCB. Surface-mount devices (SMDs) have leads that fit circuit board pads. SMDs are placed on the circuit board pads and soldered into place, making electrical connections and affixing the component to the board. SMT does not require holes in the PCB and supports lead pitch as small as .4 mm.

Surface-mount devices incorporate different lead styles dependent on the overall package configuration. SMD lead styles include gull-wing, J-lead, and contact ball and pin. These lead styles are combined with the following package styles:

Small Outline Integrated Circuit (SOIC): gull-wing leads arranged in equal rows similar to DIP with lead pitch of 1.27 mm

Shrink Small Outline Package (SSOP): a small outline package with more dense gull-wing leads arranged in equal rows with a lead pitch of .65 mm

Thin Shrink Small Outline Package (TSSOP): a shorter height SSOP package with gull-wing leads arranged in equal rows and a lead pitch of .65 mm

Thin Very Small Outline Package (TVSOP): a more dense TSSOP package featuring gull-wing leads with a lead pitch of .4 mm

Plastic Leaded Chip Carrier (PLCC): square packages with J-leads on each side; lead pitch is 1.27 mm and standard package sizes are 28, 44, and 68 pins

Quad Flat Pack (QFP): square packages with gull-wing leads on each side; lead pitch is .635 mm with standard packages of 48 and 96 pins

Thin Quad Flat Pack (TQFP): more dense QFPs with gull-wing leads and a lead pitch of .5 mm

Low-profile Fine Pitch Ball Grid Array (LFBGA): feature contact ball leads placed on a grid along the bottom surface of the IC; lead pitch is .8 mm

Pin Grid Array (PGA): identical to the LFBGA except the ball leads are replaced with pins that are designed to mate with a surface-mount socket that is soldered into the circuit board; PGA ICs are easily removed and replaced. Most of the currently available personal computer motherboards feature PGAs for connecting the processor to the board.

Whichever package technology is used, it is important to review all specifications for the particular device package being utilized. For example, when using a 74 AHC triple, three-input Nand gate IC in a DIP package, its performance specifications when packaged as a SOIC surface-mount device may differ in some key areas. There are two areas where the differences in performance between through-hole and surface-mount technology are significant: high-frequency signal operation and maximum power dissipation levels. SMDs offer better high-frequency operation over DIPs because the IC is physically smaller, containing less inductance and capacitance. On the other hand, the small size of SMDs means there is less surface area to dissipate heat. Consequently, DIPs usually have a greater power dissipation capacity.

10–4 ▶ Programmable Logic Devices

In digital electronics courses, the various methods of circuit minimization are studied at length. Boolean algebraic manipulation and Karnaugh maps are the two methods discussed most often. Software tools are also available that simplify this process by allowing the circuit designer to enter a Boolean logic function. The software then determines the minimum combinational logic circuit that will perform that logic function. One well-known example of this type of software is the logic converter included with Electronics Workbench and MultiSim programs. Once the minimum circuit is known, the designer can implement the circuit with discrete logic devices.

Another approach to digital circuit design is to employ the use of programmable logic devices (PLDs). PLDs are a collection of logic devices that are connected as general logic circuits configurable to generate any possible logic function. PLDs have seen rapid development over the last decade as the requirements for complex programmable logic have increased dramatically. While PLDs usually require using more than the minimum logic circuit, they can often be the most versatile and economical design solution that consumes the least space. *PLD* is a general term that is used when conversing about combinational logic devices that are programmable with fuseable links or memory cells. The field of PLDs seems confusing and overwhelming because of all the different terms that are used and the complexity of these devices. SPLDs, PALs, PLAs, GALs, CPLDs, and FPGAs are some of the more common terms that define various PLDs.

PLDs are derived from sum-of-the-product logic circuits where the various combinations of input logic variables are ANDed together, then ORed to form the final output. There is one AND gate for each possible input combination. The standard logic circuit schematic for a sum of the product circuit is shown in Figure 10–21a. Figure 10–21b shows the simpler PLD method for representing the same circuit. The output from each AND gate is called a "product-line" because it represents the Boolean product of the inputs to the AND gate.

Generally, PLDs have programmable links located either at the inputs to the AND gates called Programmable Array Logic (PALs), or at the AND gate's inputs

▶ **FIGURE 10–21**
(a) Standard sum of the product logic circuit. (b) PLD format.

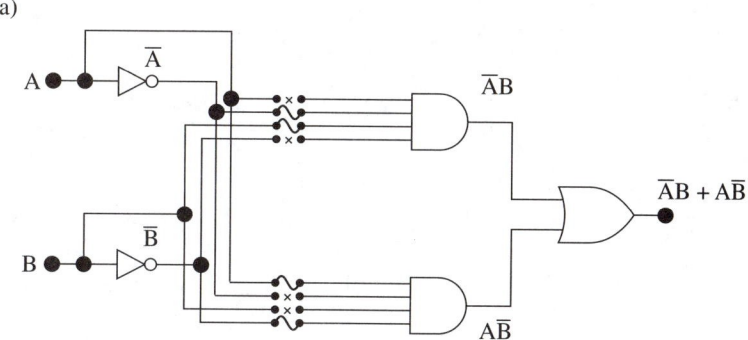

(a)

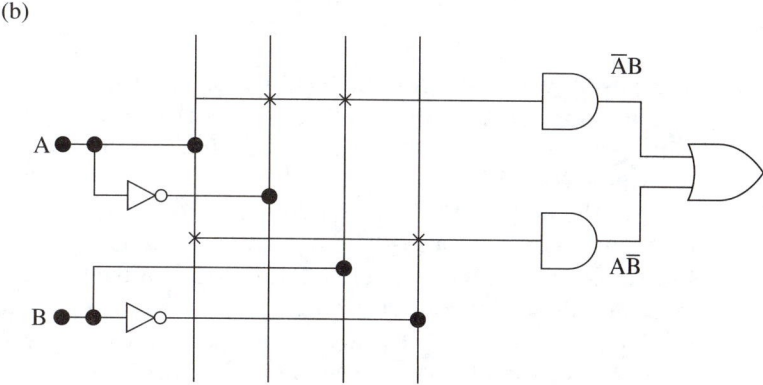

(b)

(a)

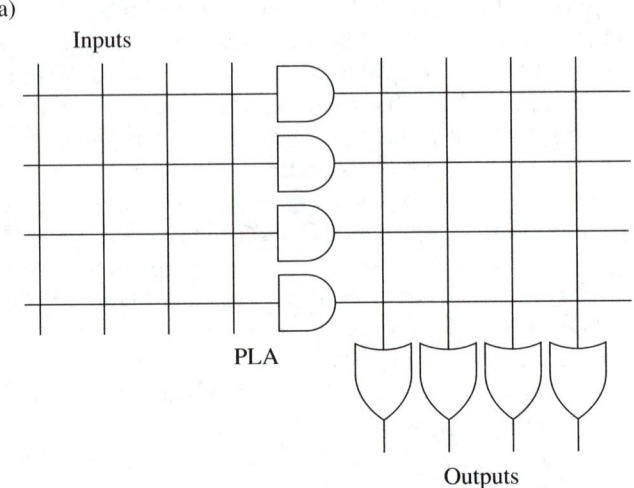

PLA representation

(b)

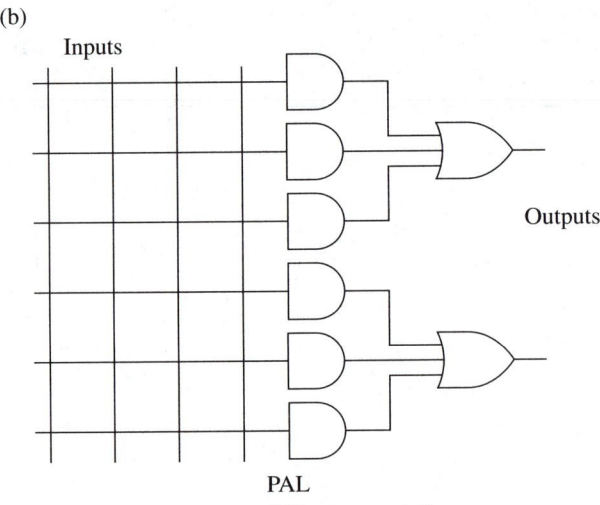

▶ **FIGURE 10–22**
PLA and PAL representations

PAL representation

and outputs called Programmable Logic Arrays (PLAs). These are the two distinct variations in the structure of PLDs: PALs that have a programmable AND array with fixed OR connections or PLAs that have both a programmable AND and OR array (see Figure 10–22).

In PROM-type PLDs, fuseable links provide the logic circuit programmability. Nonvolatile memory cells can also be used as a way of implementing logical functions where each cell reflects the status of each fuseable link position. Both PALs and PLAs can configure each AND gate to provide an output for any combination of inputs to output a logical one for any truth table combination. The output OR gates for a PAL are fixed and have a maximum number of inputs that limit the AND gate combinations available to provide the desired logical output function. When using a PAL, it is important to select one that provides enough OR gate inputs to allow implementing the desired logic function. Programming the PAL is like programming a one-time programmable PROM, unless an EPROM version with an erase window is available.

The outputs from PALs can also be configured in a variety of different ways: active high logic, active low logic, complementary, programmable, and versatile. Higher-level PALs include the programmable and versatile output features by using Output Logic Macro Cells (OLMCs). OLMCs allow the output of the PAL to be programmed as active high or low, programmable or synchronous. Flip-flop "registered" outputs can also be selected.

Generic Array Logic (GAL) devices are similar to PALs, but they are electrically eraseable. They usually include OLMCs and the complete output programmability that they allow. Simple Programmable Logic Devices (SPLDs) include PLDs, PLAs, PALs, and GALs; the name is just a way of differentiating this group of devices from other, more complex devices such as CPLDs and FPGAs. SPLDs are on the low end of the PLD family of devices and include anywhere from 4 to 22 output cells that can replace a limited amount of discrete logic devices.

PALs were the first PLDs to be developed and marketed. The PAL16L8 is well known and has been in use for years; considered a mature product by some and by many others, retired. The structure of the part number system often used to identify PALs, GALs, and other PLDs is shown in Figure 10–23. The part number identifies directly the number of inputs and outputs, as well as the type of output. Note the variety of output types shown in Figure 10–23. The major variations in output configurations include those that simply determine the active logical state (L, H, P, and C designations), those that have "registered" outputs (R designations), or more complex variable output modules (V designations). PLDs with an "R" designation have registered outputs that include some type of flip-flop on the output to allow clocking the change in output to coincide with system timing requirements.

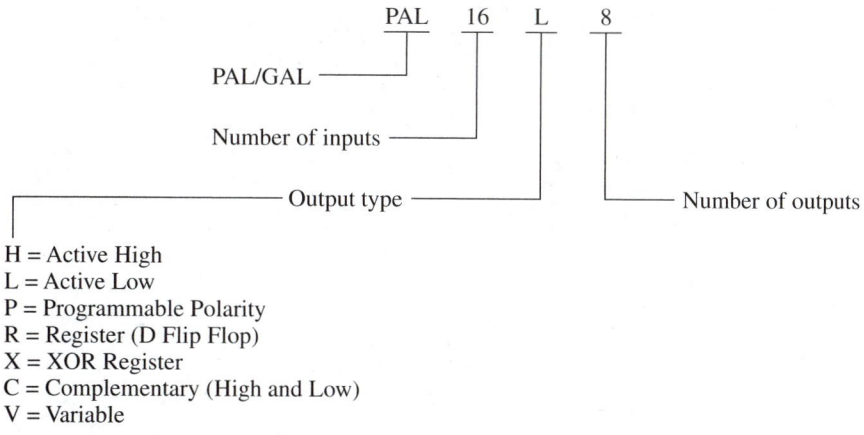

H = Active High
L = Active Low
P = Programmable Polarity
R = Register (D Flip Flop)
X = XOR Register
C = Complementary (High and Low)
V = Variable

▲ **FIGURE 10–23**
PAL part numbering system

Variable or versatile architecture PLDs, denoted with a "V," have complex output module circuits.

Let's review the operation of the PAL16L8. It is designated as a PAL, and therefore only the inputs to the AND gates are programmable links. Figure 10–24 shows the logic connections to the PAL16L8. The part number scheme indicates that the

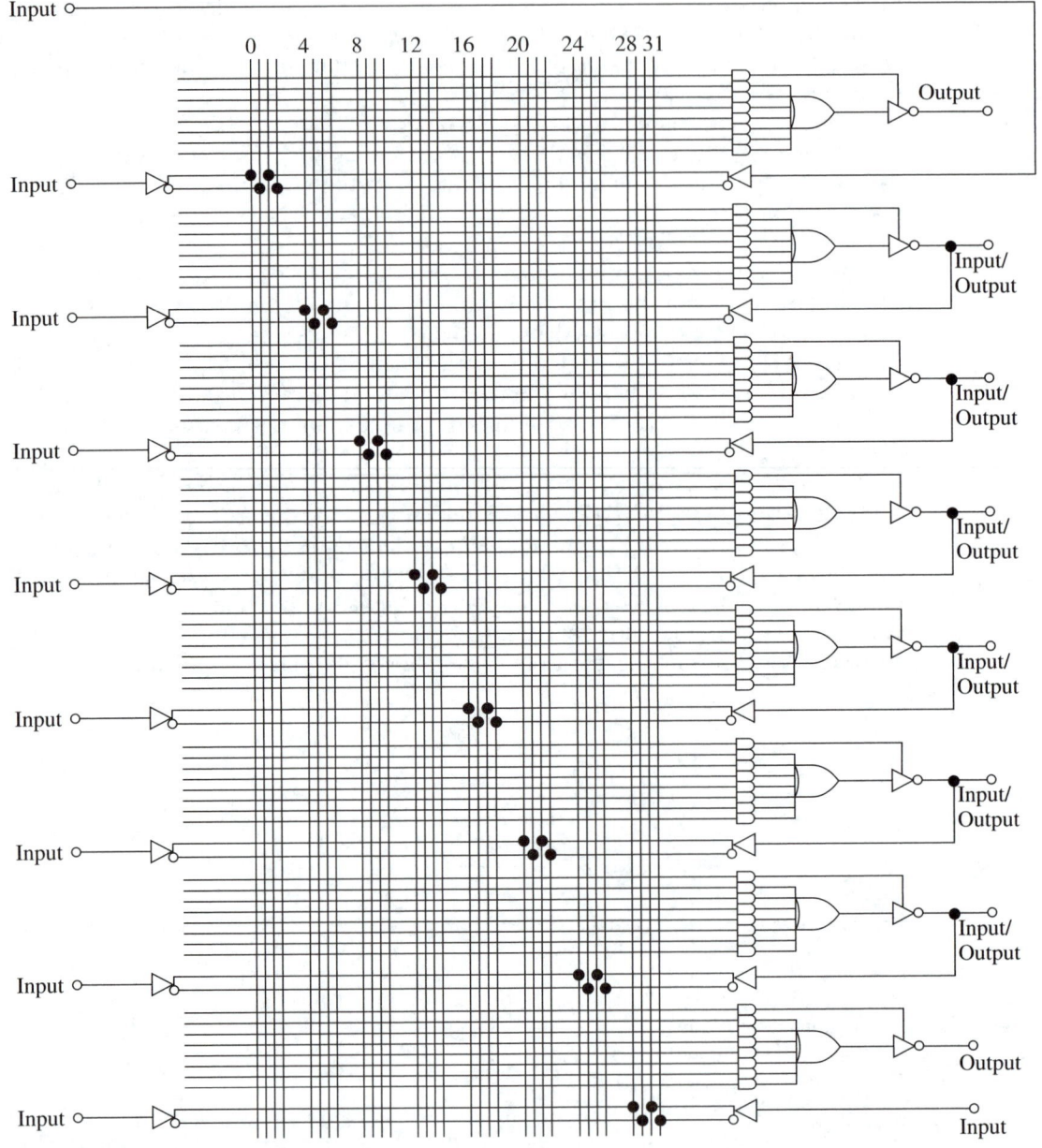

▲ **FIGURE 10–24**
PAL16L8 schematic diagram

PAL16L8 has 16 inputs with 8 outputs. While this is possible, 6 of the pins can be used as either inputs or outputs, so it is more correct to say that the PAL16L8 has a maximum of 16 inputs or 8 outputs. The PAL16L8 has 10 dedicated inputs and 2 dedicated outputs, with 6 pins that can be used as inputs or outputs.

The outputs from a PAL are generally tri-state so that some form of output enable is needed to connect the logic output to the output pin. The PAL16L8 has an inverter between the ORed product lines and the output pin that is enabled by a separate product line. The enable connection is active high. When disabled, the output reverts to its high impedance state. If all connections on the enable product line are blown, the inverter is always enabled because the inputs are all seen as high. If all connections are left in place, the AND gate always has both logical states for each variable, which causes the output to be low, disabling the inverter.

The GAL16V8 is a step up from the PAL16L8, because it is electrically erasable and it has versatile outputs, as denoted by the V located between the maximum inputs and maximum output designations. GALs can typically be erased and reprogrammed about 100 times and will retain their memory for at least 20 years. The GAL has 8 pins designated as inputs and 8 that are selectable as inputs or outputs. There are also 2 pins that can be dedicated inputs or clock and output enable pins, depending on the operating mode selected. With power supply and ground, the GAL16V8 requires 20 pins that accommodate a 20-pin DIP, a 20-pin PLCC, or a 20-pin SOIC package.

The key to the extensive output variability of PALs and GALs is the output logic macro cell (OLMC). The GAL16V8 includes eight OLMCs. Each can be selected to function globally in one of three modes: simple, registered, or complex. The functional diagram for the GAL16V8, configured for operation in the simple mode, is shown in Figure 10–25. When programming the GAL16V8, the operating mode of all eight OLMCs available on the device is accomplished by selecting the status of the global architecture cell. This cell consists of two programming bits called SYN and AC0. The bit combination selected by the operating modes is shown below:

SYN	AC0	Operating Mode
0	1	Simple Mode
1	0	Registered Mode
1	1	Complex Mode

GAL16V8—Simple Mode

When selected to function in the simple mode, six of the eight OLMCs of the GAL16V8 can be programmed to function as either a dedicated input or as an always active, combinatorial output. The remaining two OLMCs (pins 15 and 16) can only be dedicated outputs. Pins 1 and 11 become dedicated inputs to the AND array in this operating mode. Each cell designated as an output has a maximum of eight product terms with programmable polarity. There are two bits for each OLMC that determine whether it is an input or an output and the output polarity, XOR and AC1. The XCOR bit determines the output polarity for any cell designated an output— XCOR = 0 means the cell has an active low output and XCOR = 1 signifies active high

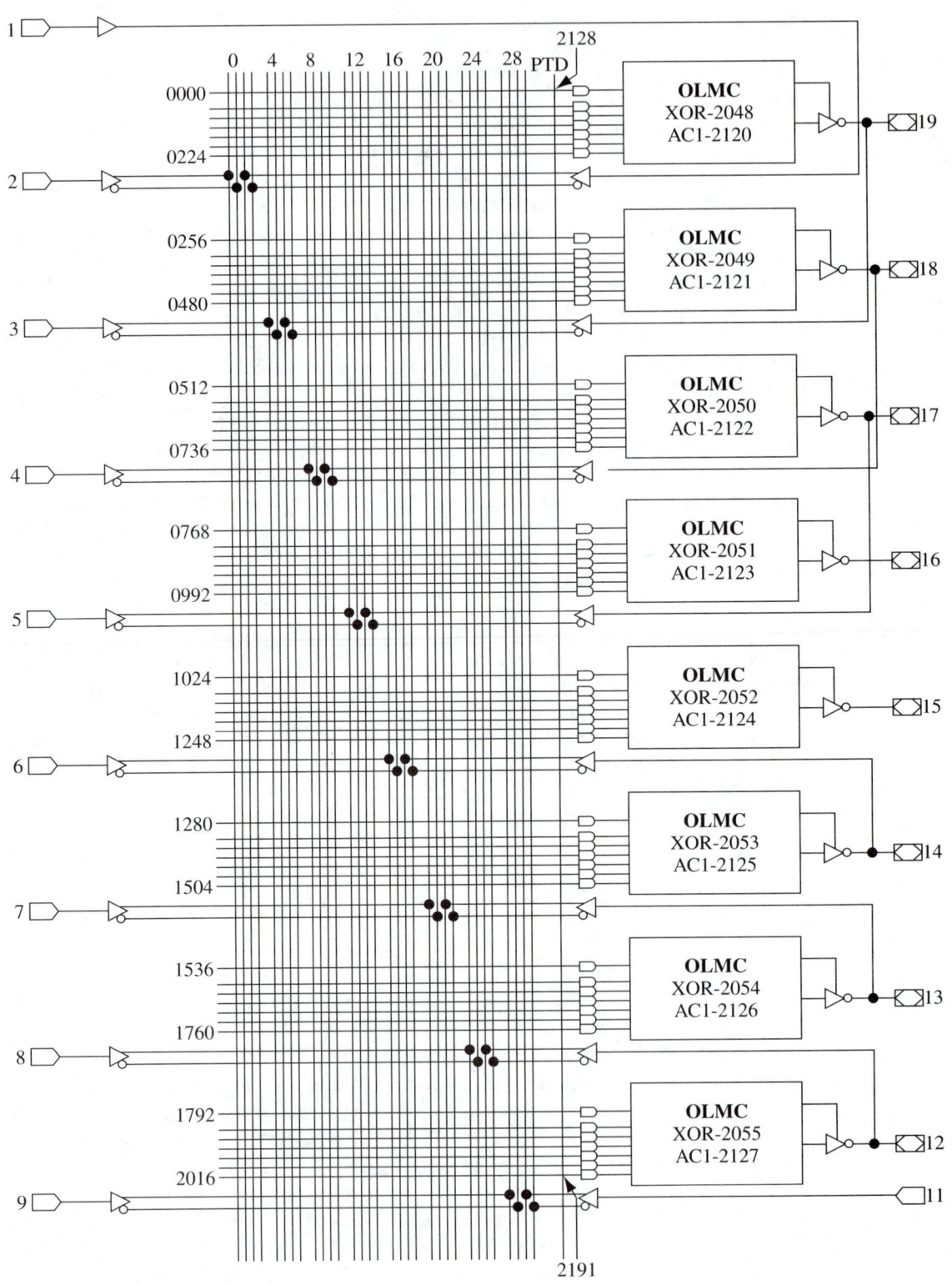

▲ **FIGURE 10–25**

GAL16V8 in simple output mode

operation. AC1 = 0 selects the OLMC to be an output while AC1 = 1 means input. The development software, as programmed by the circuit designer, configures the status of these bits for each OLMC.

Example 10–3

Set up the GAL16V8 to function in the simple mode. The three OLMCs associated with pins 12, 13, and 14 are to be configured as dedicated inputs. Pins 15 and 16 are to be dedicated as always active low outputs with no feedback, while pins 17, 18, and 19 will be always active high outputs that can be fed back to the inputs.

Solution

1. Select the Simple Mode of operation by making AC0 = 0, SYN = 1.

2. Set up the OLMCs as follows:

   OLMC pin 12—AC1 = 1, XOR = X = don't care these are inputs
   OLMC pin 13—AC1 = 1, XOR = X = don't care these are inputs
   OLMC pin 14—AC1 = 1, XOR = X = don't care these are inputs
   OLMC pin 15—AC1 = 0, XOR = 0
   OLMC pin 16—AC1 = 0, XOR = 0
   OLMC pin 17—AC1 = 0, XOR = 1
   OLMC pin 18—AC1 = 0, XOR = 1
   OLMC pin 19—AC1 = 0, XOR = 1

GAL16V8—Registered Mode

In the registered mode each OLMC can be configured either as a dedicated registered tri-state output or a combinational tri-state I/O pin. Registered operation simply means that a flip-flop register buffers the output. The polarity of the logic output is selectable for each output. In this mode pins 1 and 11 become fixed as the clock and output enable inputs, respectively, for the registered operation.

The same two bits, XOR and AC1, discussed for the simple operating mode select the variations of operation provided for in the registered mode. The XOR bit determines output polarity—0 = active low and 1 = active high. AC1 = 0 selects a tri-state registered output for a particular OLMC. AC1 = 1 selects a combinational tri-state output for the OLMC.

GAL16V8—Complex Mode

The complex mode allows six of the eight OLMCs (pins 13 through 18) to function as tri-state combinational I/O while the remaining two OLMCs associated with pins 12 and 19 operate as dedicated tri-state outputs. AC1 = 1 selects this configuration while the XOR bit defines the polarity of the outputs. Each OLMC in this mode has seven product terms per output as one of the product terms is always used as an enable output control. Pins 1 and 11 are always data inputs to the AND array.

Example 10–4

You are developing a logic circuit that includes mostly combinational logic with a synchronous output. You wish to implement the circuit with a GAL16V8. The general requirements for the circuit are as follows:

> **Inputs:** eight logic level inputs, one clock input and an output enable input.

> **Outputs:** one registered output and four combinational tri-state logic outputs. All outputs are active high.

Develop the global and local configuration bits for the GAL16V8.

Solution

1. To provide even one registered output, the GAL16V8 must be configured in the registered mode. Therefore $AC0 = 1$ and $SYN = 0$ define the registered mode of operation. The clock is connected to pin 1 and the output enable line to pin 11.

2. The OLMC connected to pin 19 is configured as a registered active high tri-state output—$XOR = 1$, $AC1 = 0$.

3. The OLMCs connected to pins 15, 16, 17, and 18 and are configured all in the same way—$XOR = 1$ and $AC1 = 1$.

As with all digital devices, the selection of PALs and GALs should include the consideration of speed (total propagation delay through the device), power consumption, package, and the overall grade (commercial, industrial, etc.). PALs and GALs are often used for the control of Direct Memory Access (DMA), state machine control, high-speed graphics processing, and simply replacing existing logic functions with smaller and cheaper alternatives.

Complex PLDs (CPLDs) include a number of PALs on one IC that can be connected together to provide complex logical functions. A CPLD can contain a few hundred macrocells. CPLDs are usually divided into logic blocks that include a portion of the macrocells. The logic blocks can then be connected through a switch matrix. The degree to which the logic blocks are connected varies from CPLD family to the manufacturer. One hundred percent connection is not always provided. Each of the macrocells includes an OLMC as discussed for the GAL and PAL devices.

An example CPLD is the Xilinx XC9500 family. This family of CPLDs includes anywhere from 36 to 288 macrocells. The product designations indicate the number of macrocells available on each device. For example, the XC9536 is on the low end of the product family with 36 macrocells. The XC9536 contains 800 usable gates and 36 registers. The general structure if the XC9500 family is shown in Figure 10–26.

Field Programmable Gate Arrays (FPGAs) are a class of PLDs that are significantly different from the devices we have discussed so far. They offer the highest logic capability. FPGAs have logic blocks or cells that are located in the center of groups of programmable interconnections. Around the outer edge of the chip are programmable I/O blocks. The general functional diagram for a FPGA is shown in Figure 10–27.

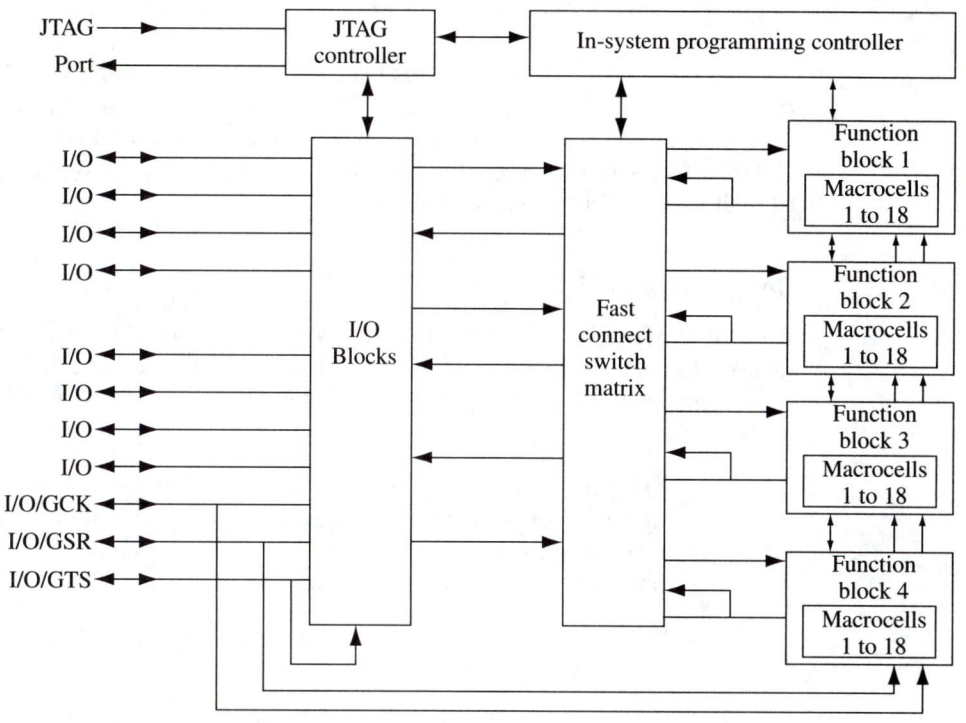

▲ **FIGURE 10–26**
XC9500 CPLD family

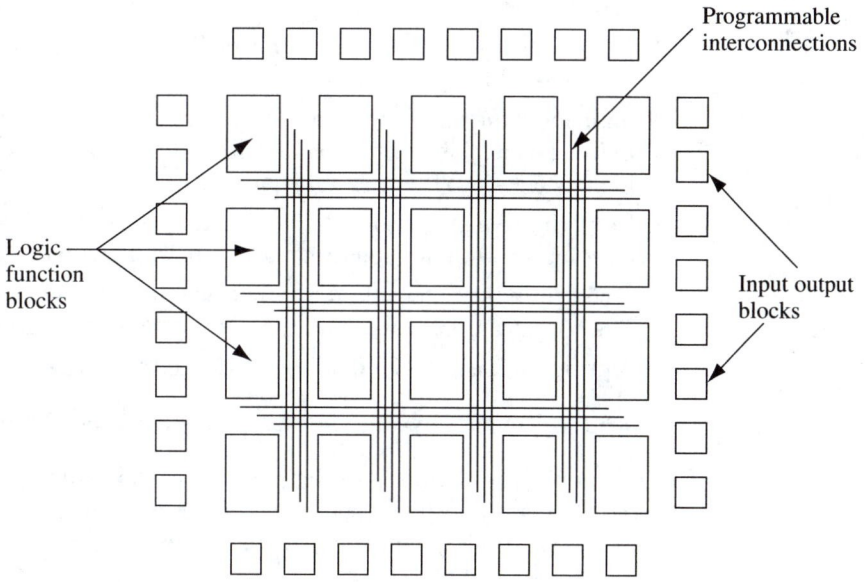

▲ **FIGURE 10–27**
Gate array functional diagram

There are two different classes of FPGAs that categorize the size and quantity of the logic blocks. Coarse-grained FPGAs contain relatively few large-sized logic blocks. FPGAs classified as fine grain have a larger number of smaller blocks. FPGAs offer a lot of design flexibility and are most often used in the development of high-level processor-based systems.

Designing with PLDs

Designing with PLDs involves the use of development software that translates the desired logical function into the program that will implement it. Let's use the Six Steps discussed in Chapter 1 to outline this process of developing logic circuits with PLDs.

Step One: *Research and gather information* about the various types of PLD devices that are available. Search out periodicals and books on the subject. Determine the manufacturers and accumulate data on the various product lines that are available.

Step Two: *Define the problem.* Develop a complete definition of the design problem in the form of a specification.

Step Three: *Plan the solution.* Develop a plan for completing the PLD design.

Here is a typical plan for PLD development:

1. Develop either a schematic or Boolean logic statement for the logic function required. Develop the logic design either as a schematic capture file or in hardware description language (ABEL, Versilog, or VHDL).
2. Review the requirements with the available devices and select the appropriate PLD for this application.
3. Implement the design with the development software that corresponds to the device being used. The development software will translate the logic design into the available hardware.
4. Next, the design rules for the device are checked against the translated solution. Modifications are made consistent with these design rules.
5. Logic circuits are partitioned and fitted into the available logic blocks. The blocks are allocated and the connections are routed.
6. A program file is created and loaded into the device.

Step Four: *Implement the plan.* The plan outlined in Step Three is completed.

Step Five: *Verify the design.* The performance of the resulting circuit is measured against the original specifications. Key performance target areas are function, timing, power, cost, and space.

Step Six: *Develop a conclusion.* What was learned in the process? What would be done differently next time?

▶ Summary

In this chapter we have gathered the current information about digital logic design. We have reviewed the practical aspects and requirements for successful design implementation. With many logic families and devices from which to choose, the designer is faced with a maze of decisions and considerations: CMOS, TTL, BiCMOS or Low-voltage technology, and PLDs or discrete logic devices. These decisions are more easily made when reliability, cost, and availability considerations are made. Devices considered mature will dictate increasingly higher prices and be harder to procure. Those that represent the newest technology usually have the least field experience and may also have longer lead times, initially. Unless the latest technology is required to make the design feasible, the more prudent approach is to use those devices that are still in their growth phase, yet have been applied enough to develop a track record of performance in a variety of application areas.

The continued development of PLDs into CPLDs and FPGAs has moved logic design closer and closer to on-chip integrated circuit design. As data, address, and control buses become wider and more intricate, the designs and design tools have expanded to fulfill this need. But in the end the design will be judged as digital designs have always been judged: speed, accuracy, efficiency, reliability, size, and cost.

▶ References

Dueck, R.K. *Digital Design with CPLD Applications and VHDL*. Albany, NY: Delmar, 2001.

Klietz, W. *Digital Electronics: A Practical Approach*. Upper Saddle River, NJ: Prentice Hall, 1999.

Tocci R. J., and Widmer, N. S. *Digital Systems: Principles and Applications*. Upper Saddle River, NJ: Prentice Hall, 2001.

Wakerly, J. F. *Digital Design: Principles and Practices*. Upper Saddle River, NJ: Prentice Hall, 2001.

▶ Exercises

10–1   Why do TTL devices tend to consume more power than CMOS devices?

10–2   Why do CMOS devices tend to be slower than TTL devices?

10–3   Explain the difference between combinational, sequential, and bus-oriented logic devices.

10–4   List the general digital design considerations discussed in this chapter.

10–5   Describe the 74HC and 74HCT logic families. What is the primary difference between these two families?

10–6   List three special considerations for designing and working with CMOS devices that are different from other logic families.

10–7   What is the basic premise behind the development of BiCMOS technology?

10–8   What performance benefits are there for lowering both power supply voltages and logic levels of digital logic devices?

10–9   What are the design criteria for calculating the value of pull-up resistors in digital logic circuits?

10–10 What are the design criteria for calculating the value of pull-down resistors in digital logic circuits?

10–11 What is the primary purpose behind the development of the emitter coupled logic (ECL) family?

10–12 Explain what is meant by the term *current mode logic*. To what family of logic devices does it apply? How does it compare to a totem pole arrangement?

10–13 Why are the logic levels associated with ECL defined as negative voltages? What noise margin does ECL provide?

10–14 What is meant by the term *lead pitch*?

10–15 List the four different lead styles currently available for SMDs.

10–16 Explain the difference between a PAL and a PLA.

10–17 How does a GAL differ from a PAL?

10–18 Describe what is meant by the term SPLD. Describe what is meant by the term CPLD. Explain the differences between them.

10–19 When using a GAL, describe the purpose of the global selection bits. What functions do the local bits select?

10–20 Describe the structure of a FPGA. What are the different classes of FPGAs, and how do they differ?

Embedded System Design

▶ Introduction

In the early 1970s the world's first microprocessor, the Intel 4004, was introduced. It was a four-bit microprocessor with a very limited instruction set, but it was unique in the fact that it was a central processing unit (CPU) contained on one integrated circuit. The 4004 was followed by its eight-bit counterpart, the 8008, and then the 8080. This began a long chain of expanded data/address buses and processor capabilities that continues today. At the time the 4004 was introduced, CPUs consisted of multilayer circuit boards that contained complicated and extensive circuits, including many combinational logic and sequential devices. These CPU boards were physically large and expensive to manufacture. Consequently, they were confined to applications that included medium-level minicomputer or large mainframe computer applications. The introduction of the microprocessor initiated an entirely new way of thinking about computer applications. Engineers and scientists began thinking about how to apply microprocessors to many products already available, and, more importantly, how to create new products that became practical with the availability of a one-chip CPU.

Today it is hard to find a product that does not include a microprocessor embedded within it. Microwave ovens, electric ranges, VCRs, stereos, and CD players all are likely to rely on a microprocessor as a central control device. The microprocessor has offered many new features, versatility, reduced cost, and smaller size to products available before its introduction. The personal computer, electronic games, Palm Pilots, and MP3 players are just a few examples of products that became possible with the availability of the microprocessor.

Embedded systems are systems in which a microcomputer or microprocessor is embedded as a controlling device. This chapter discusses the design considerations that are important when designing low- to medium-level embedded systems. Following are the specific topics covered:

347

- Design Considerations
- Central Processing Units
- Memory
- Serial Communications
- Parallel I/O and Special Functions
- Signal Conversion

11-1 ▶ Design Considerations

The design process always begins with preliminary research and gathering information about the design problem. Then the design problem is defined completely by design specifications. Because embedded systems include microprocessors, there should be two sets of specifications: one for hardware and one for software. With embedded systems there are many critical design decisions that must be made in the initial stages of the project. For example, an estimate must be made of the time it will take to process a certain amount of data, well before it is determined exactly how the data will be processed. These are the types of decisions that warrant serious consideration up front. It is much like beginning the construction of the foundation for a new building when you are not sure exactly how large the building must be to fulfill its intended purpose. In this case decisions are weighted more heavily toward overdesign; yet if the system is overdesigned, its cost and size might be unworkable.

In order to study the design problem and develop hardware and software specifications, the following analysis steps should be taken:

1. Develop an overall flowchart for the top level of processor operations.

2. Develop preliminary flowcharts for all key data-processing activities or any activity that is expected to take a significant amount of processor time.

3. Determine a realistic estimate of the quantity and type of instructions required to complete all software operations identified on the flow chart.

4. Identify the time constraints that are inherent in the design problem. Is this a real-time application for which data must be processed within a certain time period in order to be ready for the new data? If so, what is the required time period? In applications that are not real-time, what are the time requirements for performing the identified software operations?

5. Develop estimates for the amount and type of data memory required. Will the data memory requirements be volatile or nonvolatile?

6. Develop estimates for the amount and type of program memory required. Will the program memory requirements be volatile or nonvolatile?

7. Study the requirements for functions that will be programmable or selectable by the intended user of the device. Determine a preliminary process for providing this programmability.

8. Identify the quantity and type of input/output operations needed to support all operations.

9. Define the operational environment where the embedded system will be used: consumer, industrial, military, or hazardous atmosphere. These translate into ambient temperature, moisture proof, vibration, and shock requirements stated in the environmental specifications.

10. Complete the development of hardware and software design specifications.

The completion of these steps will result in enough data to allow consideration and completion of the following:

1. Develop a preliminary hardware block diagram for the embedded system.

2. Determine a range of microprocessors that provide the proper operational structure for the task at hand.

3. Identify a clock speed with significant safety factor for all operations.

4. Estimate the amount of data memory required, along with the access time and volatility requirements.

5. Estimate the amount of program memory required, as well as the access time and volatility.

6. Identify parallel and serial I/O operations and develop preliminary selections for the devices that will carry out these operations.

A summary of the analysis steps and the resulting design decisions is shown in Figure 11–1.

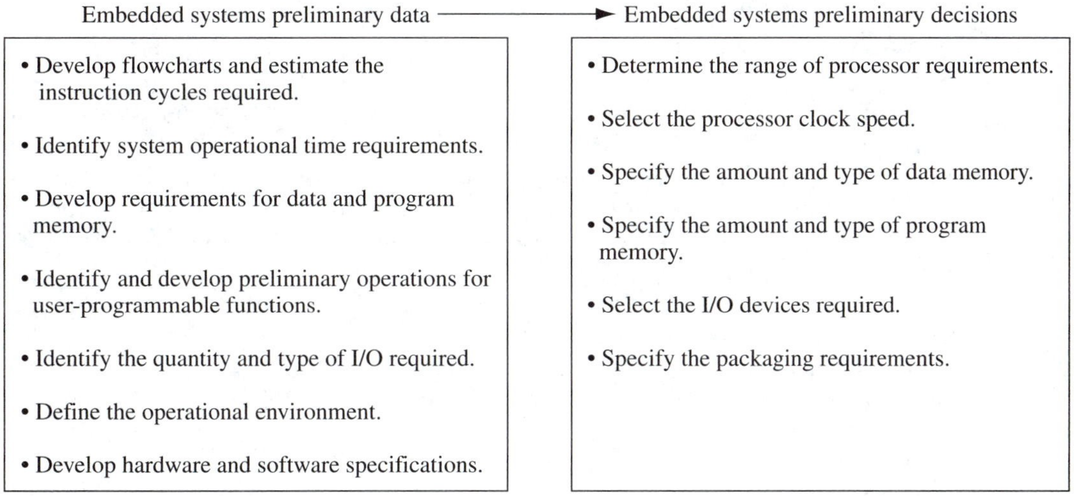

Embedded systems preliminary data ⟶ Embedded systems preliminary decisions

Embedded systems preliminary data	Embedded systems preliminary decisions
• Develop flowcharts and estimate the instruction cycles required.	• Determine the range of processor requirements.
• Identify system operational time requirements.	• Select the processor clock speed.
• Develop requirements for data and program memory.	• Specify the amount and type of data memory.
• Identify and develop preliminary operations for user-programmable functions.	• Specify the amount and type of program memory.
• Identify the quantity and type of I/O required.	• Select the I/O devices required.
• Define the operational environment.	• Specify the packaging requirements.
• Develop hardware and software specifications.	

▲ **FIGURE 11–1**
Preliminary considerations for embedded systems

Along with the selection of the CPU, memory and I/O, the embedded system will require at least consideration for the design or procurement of an adequate power supply and a system clock. (The design and application of power supplies is discussed in Chapter 6 and clock generators are covered in Chapter 8.) In many cases the I/O will be analog in nature and the signals may require amplification and scaling. (Chapter 7 covers the design and application of amplifiers and scaling circuits.)

EMI Immunity

EMI is always a prime consideration in any electronic circuit and is a significant source of failure in an embedded system. (The topics of EMI immunity and EMI emissions are discussed in general in Chapter 2.) In embedded systems there are some additional methods that can be utilized. As discussed in Chapter 2, it is always best to eliminate the source of the noise. If this is not possible, then shielding and grounding can be used to keep the noise signal from entering the operational circuit of the device in question. Once present in the circuit, filtering can be used to keep EMI noise from affecting sensitive circuits. While high levels of noise immunity can be achieved, there is always the possibility of noise with a large enough amplitude, at just the right frequency, which can affect the operation of a particular circuit.

In embedded systems there are additional steps that can be taken to minimize the effect of noise on the processor circuit. EMI noise can disrupt the processor operation by causing erroneous operations resulting from:

1. Control lines that are driven high or low to cause improper functions—for example, the processor performs a memory read instead of a write

2. Address lines that are driven to incorrect addresses, causing the processor to look for its next instruction at the wrong location

3. Data lines read incorrectly, resulting in the failure of the processor

These all can result in the processor accessing incorrect memory locations for instructions that are, most likely, completely invalid. One incorrect instruction can easily knock the CPU out of its proper program loop, causing it to become hopelessly lost. This can be seen on your personal computer when it ceases to respond to any key depressions and is hopelessly locked up until you press CTRL-ALT-DEL or restart the system.

Because they are usually developed for one specific purpose, embedded systems have a well-defined, top-level program loop. In this situation there are additional measures that can be taken to minimize the impact of any EMI. Let's say that a CPU is part of a data acquisition system that examines and processes an input signal 60 times a second. In order to keep up with the data flow, the data acquisition and processing must occur faster than 16.7 ms (1/60 cycles/sec). If the processor always performs this task in less than 10 ms, we can use this fact, with the addition of a watchdog timer to the CPU operation, to minimize the effect of any EMI. A watchdog timer is a separate timer that is reset every time the CPU

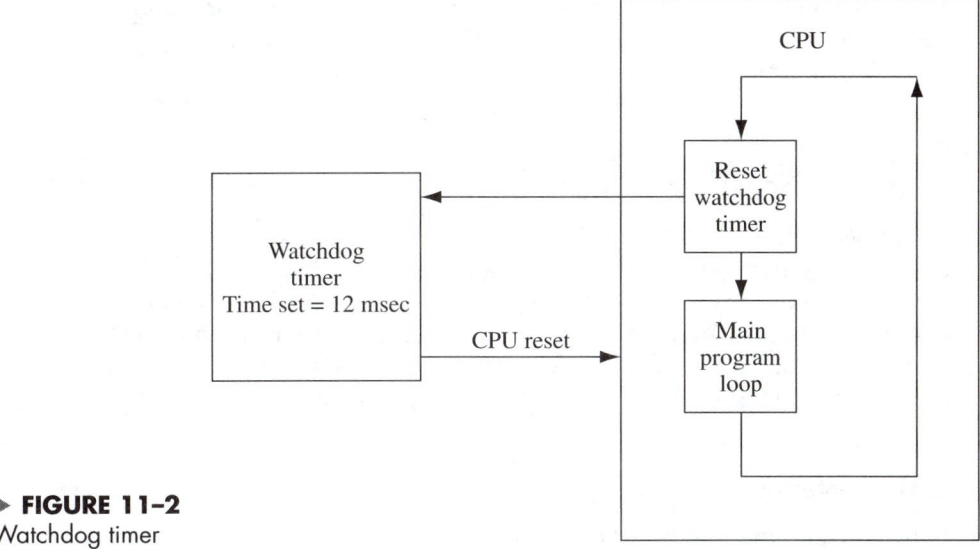

▶ **FIGURE 11–2**
Watchdog timer

starts in the main program loop. The timer is set to a time—in this case, let's say 12 ms. The timer counts down, starting at 12 ms, while the processor is performing its normal program loop operations. If the timer is allowed to count down to zero, this means that the CPU took much longer than its normal 10 ms to complete the main program loop and has likely been knocked out of its program loop. If the CPU completes its operations as usual, it resets the watchdog timer to 12 ms and the process is repeated. If the timer is allowed to count down to zero, its output resets the CPU to start over as if initially powered up (see Figure 11–2).

For this to be an acceptable solution, the process must be one in which the loss of one program loop operation is not critical to the system. It is also important that critical program and data memory locations are protected from corruption during the time that the CPU may be functioning outside its normal operating loop. If program memory locations are corrupted, they will have to be restored before proper operation can commence. Many systems that use watchdog timers use elaborate memory locks to prevent erroneously writing to program memory. As a last resort, correct program memory is verified and corrected after a watchdog timer-induced reset occurs.

Embedded systems can enjoy significant improvements in EMI noise immunity by using watchdog timers combined with methods that preclude writing to program and key data memory locations.

Ambient Temperature

Discussed in general in Chapter 2, ambient temperature is a serious consideration for embedded systems. Because embedded systems are inherently digital, variations of voltage levels with ambient temperature are not generally a concern. However, the large number of power-hungry components often included in embedded systems requires the maintenance of operating temperatures well below the absolute maximum levels for all devices. In order to accomplish this, elaborate heat sinks, cooling fans, package considerations, and judicious selection of components (speed vs. power) may all be necessary.

11–2 ▶ Central Processing Units

Selection of the CPU is a critical decision for any embedded system design. The CPU decodes instructions that are contained in memory, completes arithmetic and logic operations, transfers data to and from memory and I/O, and coordinates all system operations. There are many technical, manufacturing, and business issues that impact this decision. It is best to start with the technical issues, because if they are not met, the business issues become inconsequential.

CPU Architecture

Before discussing the different classes of CPUs, it is important to discuss some key CPU architecture variations. The first is the von-Neumann vs. the Harvard approach for transferring data between the CPU and program/data memory. The traditional method has been the von-Neumann approach, which provides one data bus for sending program and data information to and from the CPU. The Harvard method provides separate data busses for program and data memory CPU information transfers (see Figure 11–3). The von-Neumann approach provides much greater versatility and flexibility, but the fact that program and data memory transfers use the same data bus decreases CPU throughput for one operating cycle. Because of its separate program and data memory busses, the Harvard approach is set up to read the next instruction while it executes the current instruction.

Another key concept is called *pipelined data flow*. Non-pipelined data flow occurs when a CPU transfers data and only deals with one transfer at a time. Pipelined data flow breaks down the transfer process into steps that can occur at the same time. Therefore, pipelined data is transferred in concurrent steps that allow for data

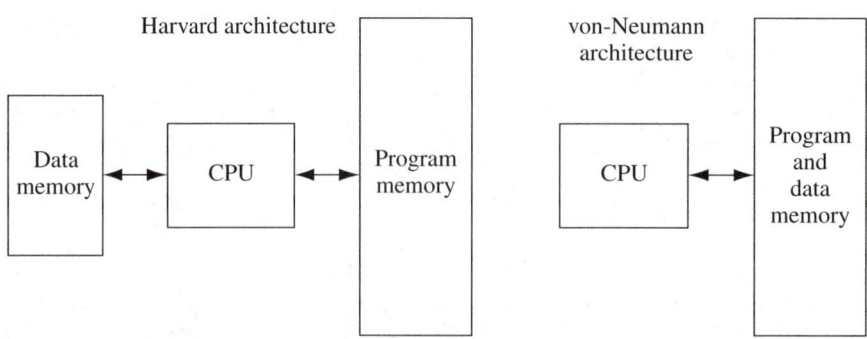

▲ **FIGURE 11–3**
Data memory transfers: von-Neumann vs. Harvard

to be sent and received at the same time. Pipelined data flow increases CPU throughput significantly but requires extra registers and limits flexibility.

There are two basic varieties of central processing units: the complex instruction set computer (CISC) or the reduced instruction set computer (RISC). These terms are general categories that are used to classify processor units. A CISC is a traditional CPU in which the instruction set is relatively extensive, variable, and can be located anywhere in memory. A CISC generally uses von-Neumann architecture and the data path flow is said to be non-pipelined. Most middle- to high-end CPUs are considered to be a CISC.

The RISC type of CPU features a reduced instruction set, Harvard architecture, and pipelined data flow, which all serve to increase throughput significantly for relatively simple and repeated operations. The reduced instruction set means that fewer bits are needed to decode the instruction. RISC CPUs often feature instructions that provide enough extra bits to include the address for a data transfer within the instruction itself. So not only is the instruction read from a separate data bus using a pipelined process (while other instructions are being executed), but all of the information about the transfer (the instruction plus the memory location of the data to be transferred) is included in the instruction itself.

RISC processors also feature a concept called *register file architecture*. Register file architecture allows for CPU registers to be addressed either directly (by their direct name or address location) or indirectly (as a relative address).

Defining CPU Requirements

The following questions help to define the requirements for the CPU and help to identify those CPUs that can potentially meet the application's requirements. A number of CPUs that meet these overall requirements should be identified. The final decision is made by selecting the CPU that best meets overall short and long-term objectives of the project or product.

1. Is the application best served with one CPU or can a number of distributed processors better meet the requirements? For applications in which data must be acquired, converted to digital, and processed in real time, it is often better to have a front-end processor that performs these tasks. This allows the main processor to handle the more central operations. Other examples are updating displays or printing data. These tasks are repetitive and time-consuming, and are often best left to a dedicated low-end processor.

2. What are the input and output data requirements? How many bits per data word? How many different types of data are there? How much calculation and sorting must be done to the data? How fast must the data be processed? After answering these questions, determine the ideal data bus size and clock speed for this application.

3. What is the complexity of the instruction set required to perform CPU operations? What is the estimated size of the application program? After answering these questions, determine the ideal address bus size for this application.

4. Review the instruction set for potential CPUs. Do the necessary instructions exist for the software development of the application? Are compilers and assemblers available for the CPU under consideration and the development software to be used? Is adequate documentation available?

5. Determine whether the application is a low-, medium-, or high-end application. There is no definite way to discriminate between these application levels other than to review the results of the previous questions combined with other facts about the application process. Low-end applications have less data and variability and therefore smaller programs that can be executed quickly, even with relatively slow clock speeds. High-end applications have a lot of data with much variety and complex long programs that require fast clock speeds to meet the speed requirements of the application. Medium applications fall somewhere in between. Later we will categorize some common CPUs into these same categories to aid in matching the processor to the application.

6. What type of memory will contain the program—RAM, ROM, EPROM, or EEROM? Will the program memory be maintained off-chip or must it be part of the CPU IC?

7. What type and how much memory will be required for read/write purposes? Will this memory be on- or off-chip?

8. What are the interrupt requirements of the application? Do the CPUs under consideration fulfill the basic requirements for interrupts?

9. What are the package requirements for this application? Is SMT or through-hole technology a requirement? Does the application require a microcomputer where all I/O, memory, and clock circuits are available on-chip or a microprocessor where they are provided off-chip?

10. Determine the power supply and environmental requirements for the CPU.

11. Determine the cost and size criteria for the CPU and select only those available CPUs that meet these criteria.

12. What is the degree of reliability for the CPU under consideration? Is it a tried and tested product or new and unproven? This is an important quality and reliability issue for the CPU.

13. Does the company have any experience or background with a CPU under consideration for this project? Identify this expertise and its relevance to the project in question.

14. What is the current lead-time for receipt of the CPU after it is ordered? What is the minimum order quantity? Is the CPU available from another source? The advantage of a second source is critical for the manufacturing and procurement departments. Single-source components must be managed much differently than those with two or more sources. Figure 11–4 shows a summary of the CPU requirements that must be identified to select the proper CPU.

Level of operation: Low-Medium-High

Variation of user program: Low-Medium-High

Program memory size and type

Data memory size and type

Quantity and type of I/O

Instruction set requirements: Simple-Complex

Package requirements

Power requirements

Environmental specifications

Reliability requirements

Cost/Leadtime/Minimum order quantity

▶ **FIGURE 11–4**
CPU requirements

Integrated-circuit central processing units can be segmented into four categories: 8-bit microcontrollers, 8-bit microprocessors, 16-bit microprocessors, and 32/64-bit microprocessors. Notice the distinction made between the term *microcontroller* and *microprocessor.* Microcontrollers are typically low-end microprocessors that include memory and I/O circuitry on-chip that make them fully functional without any peripheral ICs. Microprocessors are CPUs that require off-chip memory and peripheral ICs. Let's review the variety of microcontrollers and processors that are currently available.

8-bit Microcontrollers

PIC Microcontroller

Low-end processors are often called *microcontrollers.* The PIC microcontroller is manufactured and sold by Microchip Technology. PIC stands for *p*eripheral *i*nterface *c*ontroller. This name implies that its main purpose is to provide an interface with peripheral devices, so it is a prime candidate for performing this task in multiprocessor environments. The PIC microcontroller represents an entire product line of processors that are available with optional features in a variety of packages and memory types. The applications range from low end to medium levels. Options include serial ports, parallel ports, and analog-to-digital converters.

The PIC microcontroller features many aspects of the RISC processor structure that serve to provide high throughput for highly repetitive processes. These RISC oriented features are as follows:

- ▶ Harvard architecture
- ▶ Long, single-word instructions
- ▶ Single-cycle instructions
- ▶ Instruction pipelining
- ▶ Reduced instruction set
- ▶ Register file architecture

There are four distinct families of PIC microcontroller devices with distinguishing features:

PIC12CXXX: 12-bit instructions, 8-pin package, CMOS microcontroller, DC to 4 MHz operation for extremely low end applications

PIC16C5X: 12-bit instructions, CMOS low-end microcontroller, DC-20 MHz operation available with one-time programmable or ROM program memory

PIC14C000: 14-bit instructions, mixed signal microcontroller, DC to 20 MHz operation, one-time programmable program memory with built-in analog-to-digital and digital-to-analog converters; mid-range applications

PIC16CXXX: 14-bit instructions, CMOS mid-range microcontroller, DC to 20 MHz operation; variations include combinations of one-time programmable or ROM with optional analog and comparator functions

PIC17CXXX: 16-bit instructions, CMOS mid- to high-end microcontroller, DC to 25 MHz operation; variations include combinations of one-time programmable or ROM with optional mixed signal functions.

The discussion that follows focuses on the PIC16 and PIC 17 product lines. These are the mid-to-high range of the PIC product line and they are available with many options. The lower-level products merely represent a subset of the PIC16/17 product capabilities discussed here. The basic block diagram for the PIC16/17 products is shown in Figure 11–5.

Clock: The fastest clock speed for the PIC processor family is 25 MHz. With the reduced instruction set and other RISC features, the PIC executes most instructions in .2 µsec. The user determines the internally generated clock speed with the selection and connection of two capacitors and a crystal oscillator. If desired, the PIC can operate from an externally generated clock or a less-expensive RC network oscillator.

Program Memory: The program memory is contained internally on the PIC microcontroller. Up to 8K words are available. The size of the word varies with the PIC processor being used. The PIC 16 uses 14-bit instructions so its maximum program memory is 8K × 14 bits. The PIC 17 uses 16-bit instructions with a maximum program space of 8K × 16 bits. The program

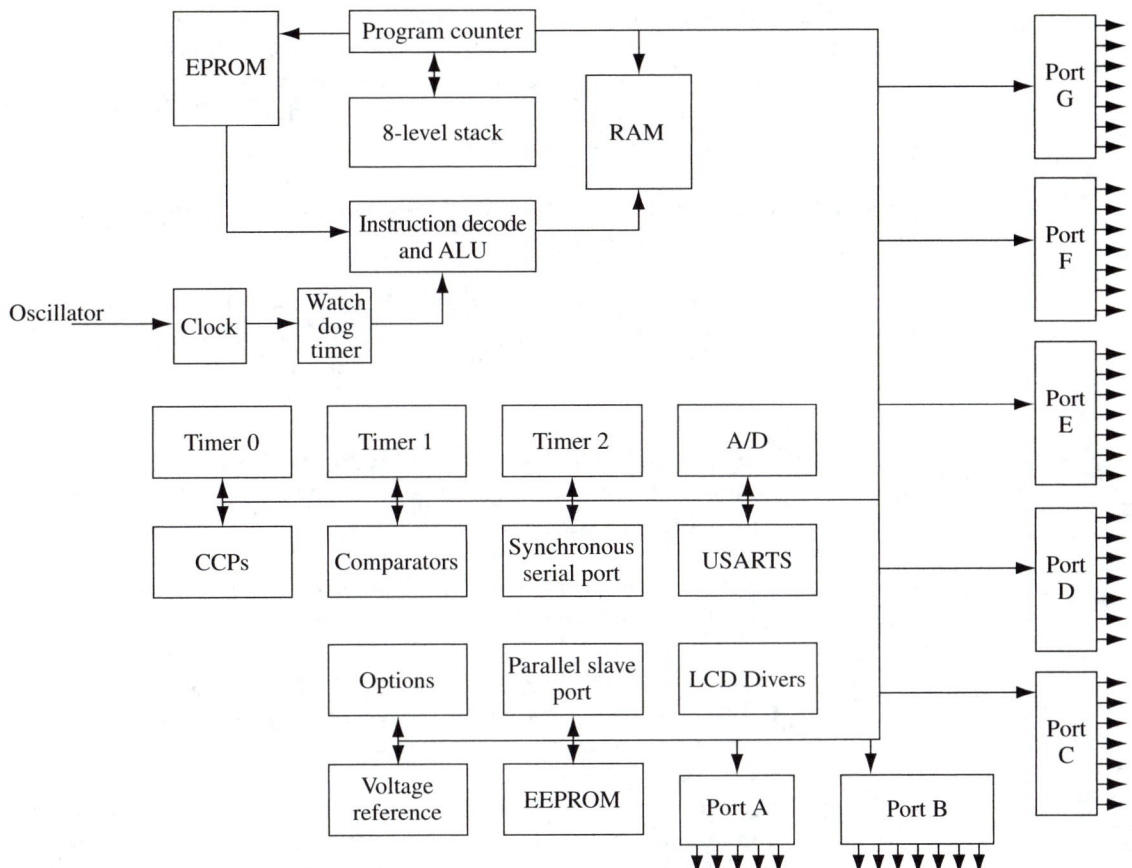

▲ **FIGURE 11–5**
PIC processor block diagram

memory can be one-time programmable (OTP) PROM, EPROM, or EEROM.

Instruction Set: The PIC processor uses a reduced instruction set that includes just 35 instructions, most of which operate in one machine cycle.

Data Memory: This is RAM that is available as a maximum of 256 bytes located on-chip. RAM is available in two banks, 0 or 1. Each bank includes 96 bytes of RAM plus 32, 8-bit special-function registers. The memory used for the stack to save addresses when calls are executed is separate and eight levels deep.

I/O Ports: The PIC features up to 56 I/O pins, most of which are individually configurable as inputs or outputs. The number of I/O pins available depends on the version PIC selected, including the package size. Some of the I/O pin functions are also multiplexed with special functions that are included on the chip. When these functions are being used, the I/O pins become dedicated to that function. These special functions include a compare/capture/pwm (CCP) module, a synchronous serial port (SSP), a universal serial asynchronous receiver transmitter (USART), and A/D and D/A converters.

Special Functions: The following describes the special functions optionally available on PIC microcontrollers:

Compare/Capture/Pulse Width Modulation Function (CCP): This is a variable-function block whose function is selected by bit values in the control registers. The CCP module can operate in one of the following ways:

Compare Mode: A 16-bit register associated with CCP function is compared to timer 1's register values. If they are equal, an output pin can be driven high or low.

Capture Mode: When an event triggers an input pin to the PIC, timer 1's value is captured and saved for further use.

Pulse Width Modulation (PWM): The CCP module operates to output a pulse on an output pin whose duty cycle and frequency depends on the value of registers in the PIC microcontroller.

Synchronous Serial Port (SSP): This port provides synchronous serial communications that can take the form of a serial peripheral interface (SPI) or to provide inter-IC communications (I^2C).

SPI: When operating in the SPI mode, the SSP allows 8 bits of data to be synchronously transmitted and received simultaneously. This is accomplished with the use of three I/O pins labeled serial data out (SDO), serial data in (SDI), and serial clock (SCK). This mode is ideal for communicating with one peripheral device.

I^2C: This is a standard two-wire serial communications protocol developed by Phillips Semiconductor that allows many serial IC devices to communicate with each other. I^2C can support communications ranging from 100 Kbps to 400 Kbps. Any device connected to the bus can initiate communications. The sending device becomes the master device and all listeners act as slave devices. Each device connected to the bus has a unique address. The PIC microcontroller implements the I^2C bus with two I/O pins labeled *SCL* for serial clock and *SDA* for serial data. These pins are multipurpose, open-drain outputs that are labeled RC3/SCK/SCL and RC4/SDI/SDA. This operating mode supports serial communications with many peripheral devices.

USART: The USART provides a second serial communications module that can operate either synchronously or asynchronously. Synchronous communications are half duplex while asynchronous communications are full duplex. The USART module utilizes two output I/O pins, transmit Tx and receive Rx.

Voltage Reference Module: This functional module provides a programmable voltage reference that is specified by values placed in the voltage reference control register. The output reference voltage connects to one I/O pin labeled V_{REF}.

Comparator Module: This module includes two analog comparators whose inputs can be connected to the analog input channels or V_{REF}. The comparator outputs can be connected to two separate I/O pins.

A/D Converter Module: Various PIC microcontrollers include A/D converters with either 8- or 10-bit capabilities. In each case the A/D converter can process any where from five to eight different analog input channels connected to the I/O pins. A variety of clock sources are possible. The internal voltage reference can be used to scale the analog signal range or an external reference can be utilized. The A/D module can be programmed to generate an interrupt when the A/D conversion process is completed.

LCD Driver: The PIC microcontroller can include an LCD driver module on certain versions of the product line (PIC16C9XX series) that is capable of driving up to 32 LCD segments.

Parallel Ports: Some of the PIC microcontrollers feature an 8-bit-wide Parallel Slave Port (PSP) that is multiplexed onto one of the device's normal I/O ports. Where available, this port is made functional by setting a control bit called *PSPMODE*. In this mode the PSP is asynchronously readable and writable from the external devices.

Watchdog Timer: PIC microcontrollers include an on-chip RC oscillator that can be used as a watchdog timer. A register is associated with the watchdog timer that serves to scale the timer setting. As discussed previously, watchdog timers provide a method of invoking a reset if the processor strays from the main program loop.

Timer 0: There are three timers available on PIC processors. Timer 0 is 8 bits wide and can be used to cause interrupts that are generated by dividing either the internal clock or an external clock connected to bit 4 of output port A. A prescaler register determines the amount to divide the input clock by. Timer 0 generates an interrupt when it overflows from FF Hex to 00 Hex.

Timer 1: This timer is a 16-bit timer/counter that is more versatile than Timer 0 or 2. It can be used as a timer in conjunction with the CCP module. When configured to work together, Timer 1 and the CCP module can drive an output pin at specific times without intervention by the processor.

This is ideal for applications such as starting A/D conversion at a precise time on a continuous basis. Timer 1 can also be used as an external event counter, both synchronously and asynchronously.

Timer 2: This is another 8-bit timer that is either used as the time base for the PWM function or as a separate 8-bit timer. Typical uses for Timer 2 are the generation of baud for serial communications. When used as a counter, Timer 2 can be set up to count the program loop time or other similar internal operations.

68HC11/12

The 68HC11/12 series is a good example of the next level up in processor complexity and capabilities. The 68HC11 was the first in this series of microprocessors and was introduced in 1985. The 68HC12 is the most recent version and was released for sale in 1997. The 68HC11/12 series fits the CISC processor model. It uses von-Neumman architecture, so program and data memory are accessed through the same data bus. Its instruction set is relatively large and the processing of instructions is not a pipelined process. The 68HC11 features approximately 145 instructions, while the 68HC12 offers an additional 40 instructions for an approximate total of 185.

All the 68HC11/12 products include a watchdog timer (WDT), a serial peripheral interface (SPI), an asynchronous serial communications interface (SCI), and a 16-bit timer. As with the PIC microcontroller, there are many varieties of the 68HC11/12 that include different amounts of memory and I/O as well as optional modules and features. Figure 11–6 shows some of these variations for the 68 HC11.

This processor can operate on instructions and data that are included in on-chip memory, or operations can be extended to multiplexed operations that provide access to external memory. This is called the *expanded mode*, which allows a selectable 8-bit or 16-bit data bus to be connected to ports C and D while a 16-bit address bus is provided through interconnections with ports A and B. Also, the 6 bits associated with port G can be used to extend memory addressing to a full 22 bits. Figure 11–7 shows the general block diagram for the 68HC12A4. The following describes the function of the various optional 68 HC11/12 modules:

Parallel I/O: For each of the parallel port I/O lines, there is a data register as well as a data direction register. The data direction register selects each

▶ **FIGURE 11–6**

68HC11 microcontroller options

Part	ROM/EPROM	EEPROM	RAM	A/D	I/O Pins
68HC11A8	8 k	512	256	Yes	38
68HC711D3	4 k	0	192	No	32
68HC711E9	12 k	512	512	Yes	38
68HC711K4	24 k	640	768	Yes	62

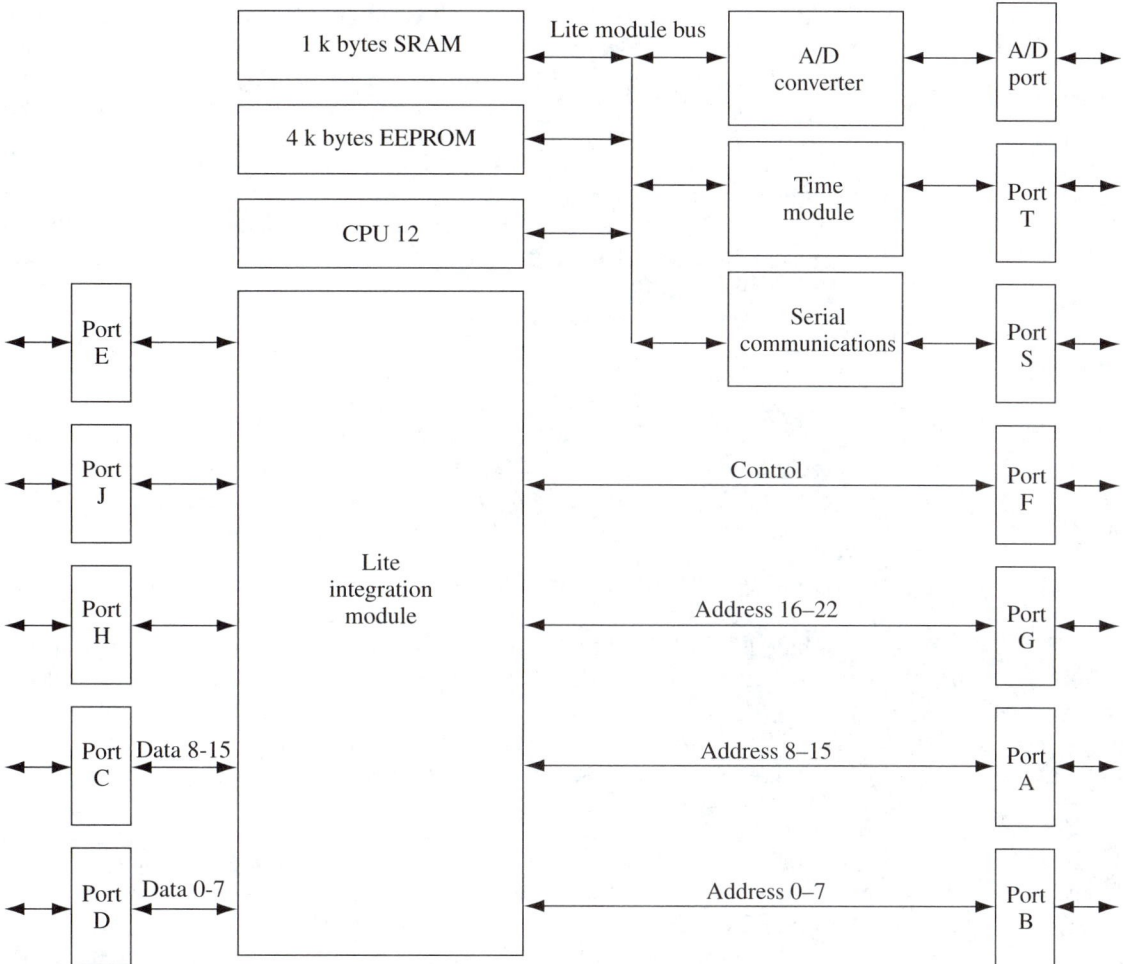

▲ FIGURE 11–7
68HC12 block diagram

individual I/O line as an input or output. When the output direction is selected, the data register contains information to be sent out. Otherwise the data register contains data that has been input. All of the ports are bidirectional except for the port for the A/D converter called *PORTAD*, which is input only. Many of the ports have alternate functions that they are intended to perform. For example, ports A and B are used as the data bus in the normal expanded mode, while ports C and D function as the address bus. If this mode is selected, these ports, which add up to 32 I/O lines, are not available as parallel I/O. Up to 85 I/O lines are available on the most complete versions of the product, with eight more lines available as analog inputs for the A/D module.

Serial Peripheral Interface (SPI): This is the synchronous serial interface for the 68HC11/12. It is used to communicate synchronously with other serial devices or processors through the serial data in (SDI) and the serial data out (SDO) pins. The serial clock I/O pin labeled *SCK* is the clock for the synchronous communications.

Serial Communication Interface (SCI): Some versions of the 68HC11/12 have two of these asynchronous serial communications ports (SCI0 and SCI1) while others have just one. These ports provide the proper start and stop bits and generate baud rate and parity information to support formal RS232 serial communications.

Analog to Digital Converter (ADC): This module is available on some versions of the 68HC11/12 series product line. The A/D module supports up to eight analog channels of 8-bit successive approximation type A/D conversion. On the 68HC11 product there are no interrupt capabilities, but the 68HC12 can generate an interrupt when the A/D conversion is complete.

Timer: The timer-generated features that are included in the 68HC11/12 family are all based on the operation of one free-running 16-bit up counter labeled *TCNT*. The timer operates in conjunction with a fairly complicated timer system that connects to port T. The timer module utilizes eight 16-bit capture/compare registers to initiate interrupts when the TCNT counter value is equal to the register value. The time for certain outside events can also be determined by capturing the event with port T's I/O pins.

The PIC and 68HC11/12 microcontrollers were covered with some detail because they represent two distinctively different and popular microcontroller operational philosophies. There are many other 8-bit microcontroller devices available, such as Intel's MCS51 family, the Zilog Z8 microcontroller, and the Atmel AVR series.

8-bit Microprocessors

Intel Corporation developed the first 8-bit microprocessor, the 8008. In 1974 it was replaced by the Intel 8080, which represented a significant improvement in performance. About the same time, Motorola introduced its 6800 8-bit microprocessor, Fairchild produced the F8, and Advanced Micro-Devices released the 6502. A few years afterward, the newly founded Zilog Corporation released its first product, called the Z80. For many years these five 8-bit microprocessors were the workhorses behind many computer and embedded system products and systems.

The 8-bit microcontroller has taken over many of the applications of 8-bit microprocessors while high-end requirements have pushed microprocessor development up to 16-, 32-, and now 64-bit systems. Once the only microprocessor product available, now the 8-bit microprocessor market is one with few players that covers the middle ground between 8-bit microcontrollers and higher bit processors.

Z80 Microprocessor

The Z80 was developed and released in the late 1970s. It was developed by Zilog Corporation, a new venture company at the time. The Z80 utilized the same basic instruction set as the Intel 8080, with some additional powerful instructions and features. The Z80 could be used for existing 8080 applications and offered many programming improvements. After the Z80 was released, Zilog developed many peripheral ICs that supported the Z80 and increased its popularity even further. Consequently, the Z80 is one of just a few still available from the era when the 8-bit microprocessor was king.

The Z80 is available in 40-pin DIP or 44-pin PLCC packages. It features an architecture that was common at the time of its introduction. An external 16-bit address bus, 8-bit data bus, and numerous control bus signals. Dependent on the particular model, the operating clock frequencies range anywhere from 2.5 to 8 MHz. The input/output diagram for the Z80 is shown in Figure 11–8.

The Z80 includes six general-purpose registers in addition to its accumulator and flag registers. There is a mirror set of all eight registers (general purpose registers plus accumulator and flags) that cannot be directly accessed by the programmer but can serve as an easy way to save the contents of registers during the execution of interrupt service routines or other subroutine calls. The instruction set includes 158 different types of instructions that are categorized into the following groups: data transfer, logic, arithmetic, bit manipulation, and branch and control operations.

In order to develop a functional embedded system using the Z80, external program and data memory, and serial and parallel I/O may be needed, as well as data conversion or counter/timer peripherals. The Z80 appears as a very simple device today when compared to the microcontrollers and high-end microprocessors that have been developed since its initial release.

▶ **FIGURE 11–8**
Z80 I/O diagram

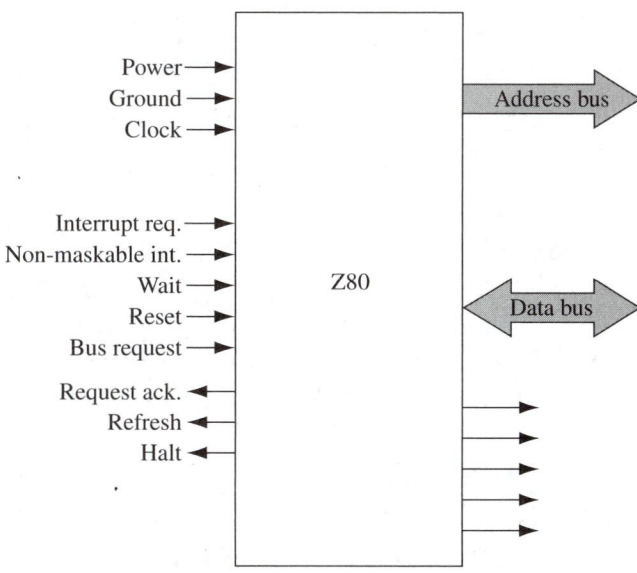

Zilog has enhanced the Z80 with numerous product enhancements such as the Z180. The Z180 is an 8-bit microprocessor built on Z80 architecture with an advanced processor core that improves performance by 33%. The Z180 also includes on-chip two asynchronous serial ports and an ISA bus interface.

Rabbit 2000

Another 8-bit microprocessor is the Rabbit 2000, which was developed by Rabbit Semiconductor Corporation. The Rabbit 2000 is a modern 8-bit microprocessor that possesses a unique combination of features. The Rabbit 2000 was developed from the basic Z80/Z180 architecture with improvements that offer higher performance. It possesses all of the capabilities that would classify it a microcontroller except for on-chip memory. It includes on-chip parallel and serial I/O as well as timers. The Rabbit 2000 is packaged in a 100-pin rectangular PQFP surface-mount package. Following are most of the Rabbit 2000's features:

- ▶ Clock speeds up to 32 MHz
- ▶ 40 pins for parallel I/O
- ▶ Four asynchronous serial I/O ports, two of which can function as synchronous serial ports
- ▶ Two sets of timers: one that includes five 8-bit reloadable down counters and a second group that has a 10-bit free running counter with two 10-bit match registers. These timers are typically used for providing baud rate clocks for the serial ports and for generating interrupts.
- ▶ Slave port that allows the Rabbit 2000 to be used as an intelligent peripheral device
- ▶ 20-bit address bus that can access up to 1 Mb of memory
- ▶ Enhanced Z180 instruction set
- ▶ Battery-backed-up internal real-time clock
- ▶ Watchdog timer
- ▶ Unique sleep mode with a current draw of about 200 μA
- ▶ Software developed using Dynamic C development software

Figure 11–9 shows the block diagram for the Rabbit 2000 microprocessor.

16/32/64-bit Microprocessors

Just as integrated circuit designers were continuing to find ways to pack more circuitry and features into smaller microcontrollers, they applied these same innovations to high-end processors as the race to increase processor speed and throughput was just beginning. The result has been the continuous development and application of the following strategies:

1. Increase circuit densities by increasing process resolution and exploring unique geometries.

2. Increase power efficiency.

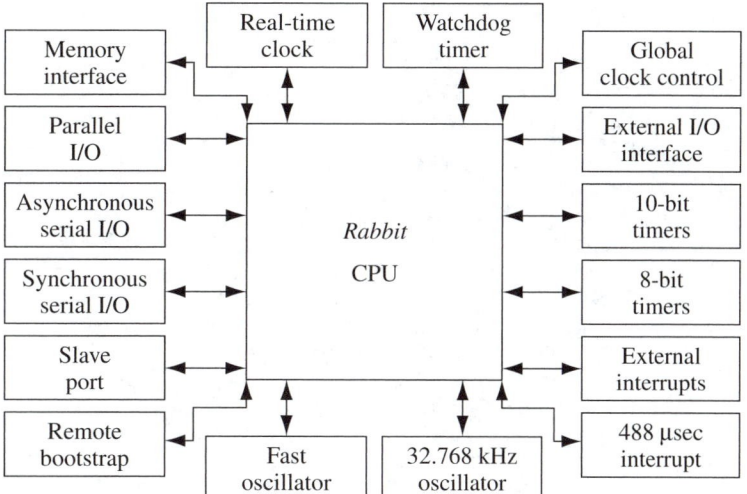

▶ FIGURE 11–9
Rabbit 2000 microprocessor

3. Increase clock speed by further minimization of inherent capacitance levels and signal lead lengths.

4. Increase throughput with the use of pipelined processes and increasing the size of parallel data busses.

These strategies have led to the ongoing release of improved high-performance 16/32/64-bit processors, starting with the 8086 and culminating most recently with the Intel Pentium IV. Intel released the 8086 in 1978 as a significant improvement in performance over the microprocessors available at the time. It could address 1 Mb of memory and its data bus and internal registers were all 16 bits wide. The 8086 also featured pipelined processing. The ongoing improvements that began with the 8086 have led to 32- and then 64-bit data busses, 36-bit address busses (can address 64 Gb of memory) and clock speeds up to 2 GHz. Package sizes have now expanded to 478 pins. The Pentium IV represents the latest in microprocessor development with 64-bit data, 36-bit address, a 2 GHz clock, and 478 electrical connections. It requires a large heat sink attached to the chip to dissipate power. Figure 11–10 shows the general trend in microprocessor advances over the last 25 years. Most of these processors are aimed at the personal computer market or for other high-end computer applications.

11–3 ▶ Memory

Semiconductor memories have undergone developments similar and as significant as those employed in microprocessor technology. The densities of memory cells have increased substantially and power efficiency has also been improved. Pipelined processes are used to increase effective access times and wider data

Intel microprocessor developments

Processor	CPU clock	Internal register size	Data I/O bus width	Memory address width	Maximum memory	Number of transistors
8088	100M	16-bit	8-bit	20-bit	1M	29,000
8086	100M	16-bit	16-bit	20-bit	1M	29,000
286	100M	16-bit	16-bit	24-bit	16M	134,000
386SX	100M	32-bit	16-bit	24-bit	16M	275,000
486SX	100M	32-bit	32-bit	32-bit	4G	1,185,000
486DX2	200M	32-bit	32-bit	32-bit	4G	1,100,000
486DX4	300M	32-bit	32-bit	32-bit	4G	1,600,000
Pentium	300M	32-bit	64-bit	36-bit	64G	5,500,000
Pentium II	500M	32-bit	64-bit	36-bit	64G	7,500,000
Pentium III	1G	32-bit	64-bit	36-bit	64G	28,000,000
Pentium IV	2G	32-bit	64-bit	36-bit	64G	42,000,000

▲ **FIGURE 11–10**

Microprocessor development

words can be stored in one location. Semiconductor memories are categorized as either volatile (data is lost after the power is removed) or nonvolatile (data is retained when the device is not powered).

Volatile Memory

Volatile semiconductor memory is usually called *random access memory* (*RAM*). The term *random access* actually means that each location is accessible with the same access time. This name came about because older volatile memory was called either *RAM* or *sequential access memory* (*SAM*). Sequential access memory is an older style of memory in which the access time for each location depended on its location in the memory. All currently available volatile semiconductor memory is RAM, although the distinction *random access* is no longer important. Volatile memory is sometimes called *read-write memory* (*RWM*), which would be a better name for it today.

There are two distinct categories of RAM: static RAM (SRAM) or dynamic RAM (DRAM). Static RAM retains its data as long as power is applied. Dynamic RAM retains data while power is applied if each location is refreshed every few milliseconds. This refresh is necessary because the charge that is stored in the dynamic memory cells leaks out and must be refreshed.

DRAMs

DRAMs are MOS-type devices that provide high chip densities and power efficiency with average access times. This means that more memory cells can be located on a single DRAM memory device than any other type of memory. Information that is stored in a DRAM is actually stored in a small MOS capacitor. The charge can leak out of the capacitor over a small amount of time so the DRAM must be refreshed every few milliseconds. This refresh requirement complicates the use of DRAMs because circuitry must be included on the DRAM chip itself to implement refresh, or it must be done with external circuitry. In spite of the refresh requirement, DRAMs are still the most popular choice where large amounts of memory must be provided in a small space with less power and the lowest cost. DRAMs typically have four times the density of SRAMs. Consequently, DRAMs are most often used as the main memory in personal computers.

DRAMs contain such large capacities that the number of address lines required to address them would increase the package size to an unpractical size. To resolve this, DRAMs share or multiplex their address lines. Usually, each address line is multiplexed into two different address bits and the data for each is sent and latched into the DRAM during different parts of memory transfer cycle.

Because the inherent advantage of the DRAM is capacity, power efficiency, and low cost, the challenge for DRAM manufacturers is to develop DRAMs that can keep up with the ever-increasing clock speeds offered by computer manufacturers. Many innovations are being developed that help to solve this problem:

Fast Page Mode DRAMs (FPM DRAMs): These provide faster access to data that is on the same page.

Synchronous DRAMs (SDRAMs): SDRAMs were developed in the early 1990s. These memories offer a simpler synchronous interface between other system components and an internal process that is similar to the pipelined approach discussed for processors. SDRAMs internally have multiple banks of DRAMs that can perform operations simultaneously. All the address and control inputs are sampled synchronously on the same rising edge of the clock input.

Double Data Rate SDRAMs (DDR SDRAMs): This is an improved SDRAM that performs memory read or write operations on both the rising and falling edges of the synchronous clock.

SRAMs

Static RAMs are read/write volatile memory devices that retain data as long as power is applied. SRAMs can be fabricated with bipolar, MOS, or BiCMOS processes and the access speeds of the SRAM are directly related to the type of process used. Fast SRAMs are often used in personal computers to support operations that require very fast access time. The SRAMs used in these applications are called *cache memory.*

The older standard type of SRAMs are now referred to as *asynchronous SRAMs* because SRAM manufacturers have now developed a new type of synchronous SRAM (SSRAMs). The SSRAM is similar to what was done to speed up SDRAMs discussed previously. SSRAMs use a synchronous clock to set up the memory read/write operations into a pipelined process in which many operations are performed at the same time.

Nonvolatile Memory

Most embedded systems require a large amount of memory that is maintained when the power is removed. Even a personal computer maintains its BIOS program, with instructions of what to do when the power is first turned on, in nonvolatile memory. The program memory for embedded systems is usually maintained in ROM, PROM, EPROM, EEPROM, or Flash ROM. In addition, embedded systems usually employ many user-selected parameters that must be maintained when the power is shut off. These parameters must be retained in some type of nonvolatile memory.

Read Only Memory (ROM): This type of memory is programmed by the IC manufacturer per the user's program. The user pays a masking charge of a few thousand dollars to set up the proprietary program. ROMs are much cheaper in volume than other nonvolatile memories but the data cannot be changed once programmed. Masking charges preclude their use in low volume or with new programs that expect some change.

Programmable Read Only Memories (PROMS): These are a type of ROM in which the user can program the PROM using a device called a *PROM programmer*. The PROM programmer blows fuseable links inside the PROM to store the information permanently. Once programmed, the PROM functions just as a ROM; it retains the data under all conditions and it cannot be modified. PROMs provide low-volume users with an affordable alternative to the ROM because there is no masking charge. However, PROMs are significantly more expensive than ROMs. Another name for a PROM is "one time programmable" or OTP.

Eraseable Programmable Read Only Memories (EPROMs): similar to PROMs, EPROMs are programmed by the user with an EPROM programmer. The EPROM programmer functions much differently than the PROM programmer. An EPROM is programmed by the application of a voltage to each cell where a binary 1 is to be stored. The charge used to program the cell remains after the voltage is removed because there is no path for discharge. The EPROM includes a window that is positioned over the semiconductor chip. An EPROM can be erased by exposing it to ultra violet light. The ultraviolet light causes current to flow through a photo transistor, allowing the programming charge to dissipate, erasing all the cells in the EPROM. Because the EPROM can be erased, it provides a significant advantage over the PROM. However, in order to erase an EPROM, it must be removed from the circuit. EPROMs also cost more than ROMs or PROMs.

Electrically Eraseable Read Only Memories (EEROMs): EEROMs have the same basic structure as an EPROM except that they have a small oxide layer above the drain of the MOSFET memory cell. When 21 V are applied between the MOSFET's gate and drain, a charge flows into the gate that can program the cell. This charge is retained even after power is removed from the device. The voltage applied to a cell can be reversed to erase the cell. EEROMs offer ease in programming and erasing. Both can be accomplished in-circuit and only the cell to be modified need be erased and reprogrammed. EEROMs offer significant advantages over all other types of nonvolatile memories. However, they are much more expensive than other nonvolatile memory types and memory density is also much lower.

Flash Memory: Flash memory is a newer style of EEROM that provides erasure of large sections of memory or the entire memory at one time. True EEROMs can program and erase a particular word or byte in the memory. Flash memory can program individual words but must erase large blocks of memory at one time. While flash memory is not as versatile as EEROMs, there is a benefit to the bulk erasure requirement of flash memory. In the EEPROM, two MOS transistors are required to maintain the data and erase each memory cell. Flash memories only require one transistor; a second transistor is used to erase many cells. Consequently, flash memories can achieve a much higher memory density when compared to EEROMs and they are available at a much lower cost.

There are two basic varieties of flash memory devices: NOR and NAND architectures. The NOR-type flash memory is named because it resembles NOR logic. NOR-type flash memories provide fast read times and slow write/erase cycles. NAND-type flash memories, whose architecture resembles the NAND gate, exhibit the opposite features—slow read times with fast write/erase cycles.

Direct Memory Access (DMA)

In many embedded systems it is necessary to transmit large amounts of data from peripheral devices to memory and vice versa. In a basic microprocessor-based system, this data must be read in through the processor. To accomplish this, the processor must fetch an instruction to read in the data, fetch an instruction on where to send it, and then fetch another instruction to repeat the process for the next location. For large amounts of contiguous data, this represents a significant amount of processing time. If the task of moving the data is repetitious, or if the amount of data is large and located together in memory, then the application of a DMA controller may offer significant savings in processing time.

The DMA concept, as the name implies, is to give direct access to memory locations without having to pass data through the processor. A DMA controller IC is a specialized chip that is designed to accomplish this task. A DMA controller connects to the system control, address and data busses. Additional inputs to the DMA are the DMA Request and Hold Acknowledge; the outputs are DMA Acknowledge and Hold Request. Their function and interconnection is as follows:

DMA Request Input: Connects to external I/O devices and is used to request DMA transfers

Hold Request Output: Connects to the system processor and requests permission from the processor to use the system busses. The Hold Request line must remain high for the entire time that the DMA is using the system bus.

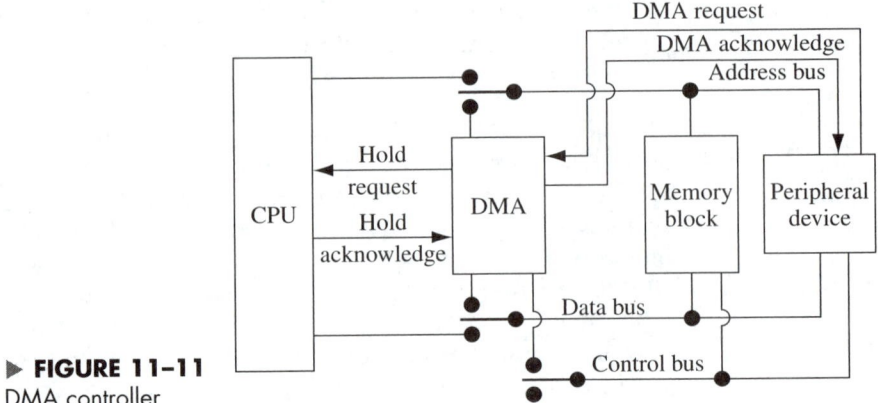

▶ **FIGURE 11–11**
DMA controller

Hold Acknowledge Input: Connects to the system processor line that is used to grant permission to the DMA to take over the system bus. When the processor is ready to relinquish control of the bus, it drives this pin high.

DMA Acknowledge Output: Connects to the peripheral device that requested the DMA transfer. When the DMA takes over control of the system bus, the DMA signals the peripheral to begin transmission by driving this pin high.

A DMA chip can have multiple channels for controlling the transfer of data. It will have a DMA Request and DMA Acknowledge pin for each channel, but only one Hold Request output and Hold Acknowledge input (see Figure 11–11).

When a DMA transfer is to be performed, the device that initiates the transfer activates the DMA Request input on the DMA chip. The DMA follows by forcing its Hold Request line high. The processor receives the Hold Request and, after finishing the current instruction, drives the Hold acknowledge high, indicating to the DMA that it can proceed. The DMA follows by driving the DMA Acknowledge line high, which signals the peripheral device to begin the transfer.

Each DMA channel is programmed by the processor to set up its data transfer task before the DMA Request is made. The initial data required is twofold: the starting memory location and the number of locations to be transferred. Each DMA channel also has a control word location written to by the processor that dictates the type of operation to be performed and the address of the device to which or from which the data is being transferred. DMA operations can consist of transfers from I/O to memory, memory to I/O, or memory to memory.

The 8237 is a specific DMA controller that was used in the early personal computers. It includes four DMA channels and can transfer up to 64k bytes of data. The 40-pin DIP version of the 8237 is shown in Figure 11–12. Note that there are only eight address lines available on the 8237. These eight lines will support only 256 memory transfer operations. The additional eight bits required to support 64k data transfers are multiplexed through the data bus. The ADSTB line is used to indicate that the high byte of the address bus is present at the data bus pins. An external chip must be provided that will latch the high order address byte. A 74LS373 is often used for this purpose because of its tri-state outputs.

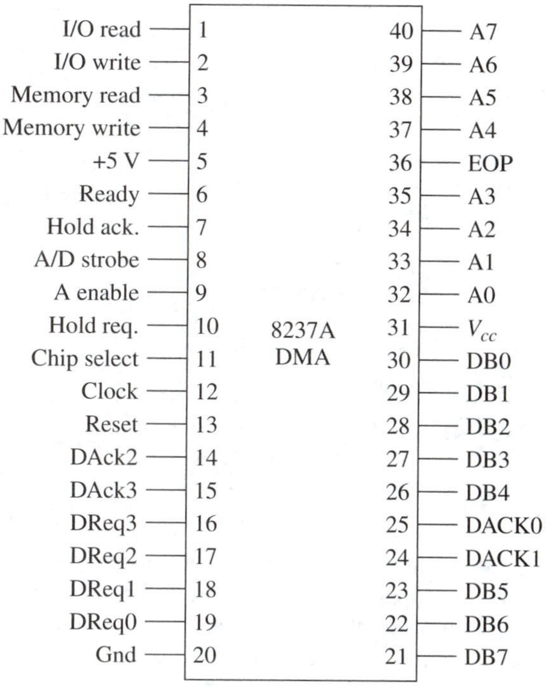

▶ **FIGURE 11–12**
8237 DMA

11–4 ▶ Serial Communications

Many of the microcontrollers discussed in Section 11–2 included serial communications ports on-chip. Most microprocessors do not include serial communications ports on-chip because of all the circuitry required to process massive amounts of data quickly. Many serial communications ports are available as stand-alone ICs that interface with the microprocessor as an I/O port and handle all serial communications. This saves space on the processor chip and gives the user the flexibility to decide which and if any serial communications peripherals are needed.

All serial communications require a method for synchronizing the transmission and receipt of the information. There are two types of serial communications: synchronous and asynchronous. Synchronous communication requires a separate hardware clock line to synchronize communications between the transmitter and receiver. Asynchronous serial communications embed the clock within the data being sent.

Synchronous I/O ports are often called a *serial-peripheral-interface (SPI)*, as seen with many of the microcontrollers discussed in Section 11–2. Asynchronous serial ports are usually called *universal-asynchronous-receiver-transmitters (UARTs)*. Most serial communications ICs are completely programmable and can function either as synchronous or asynchronous serial peripherals. These are often called *universal-serial-asynchronous-receiver-transmitters (USARTs)*.

The Zilog Z85C30 is a prime example of a modern serial communications peripheral often called a *serial communications controller (SCC)*. It is fabricated with low-power CMOS technology and features two independent full-duplex

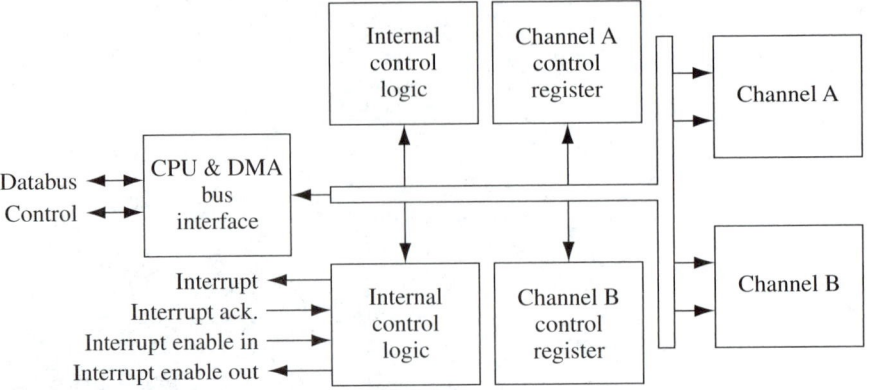

▲ **FIGURE 11–13**
SCC functional block diagram

(can send and receive at the same time) serial ports. These ports can be programmed to operate synchronously or asynchronously at transmission rates of up to 4 Mbits/Sec. They can encode data in NRZ, NRZI or FM formats and also provide for error checking. Each of the ports included in the Z85C30 can connect to separate crystals to generate the baud rate. The block diagram for the Z85C30 is shown in Figure 11–13.

11–5 ▶ Parallel I/O and Special Functions

Programmable parallel I/O devices are also available for connection to high-end microprocessors or to expand microcontroller parallel I/O capabilities. The 8255 IC is one of the oldest and still popular devices used for this purpose. The 8255 connects to microprocessor data and control busses. The 8255 can be connected to function as memory-mapped I/O (I/O that is located at unused memory addresses) or as peripheral I/O (I/O addresses). It includes three 8-bit parallel I/O ports. Port A can be programmed so that all 8-bits are inputs, outputs, or bi-directional. Port B can function with all 8-bits as inputs or outputs. The bi-directional capability is not provided for ports B or C. Port C is the same as port B except that it can be broken down into two 4-bit nibbles, and each nibble can be used as an input or an output.

The 8255 is connected to the processor data and control busses. The software programs ports A, B, and C in the 8255 to function as required by the program. The processor then writes the appropriate data to the ports, which present the data to their output pins. Any 8255 pins that are selected as inputs receive data that is input to them. The 8255 signals the microprocessor via the interrupt request line that it has data to be read. The interrupt priority status of this particular I/O will determine how quickly the processor will respond to answer this request. Eventually the processor will read the data that the 8255 is holding in one of its ports. The block diagram for the 8255 is shown in Figure 11–14.

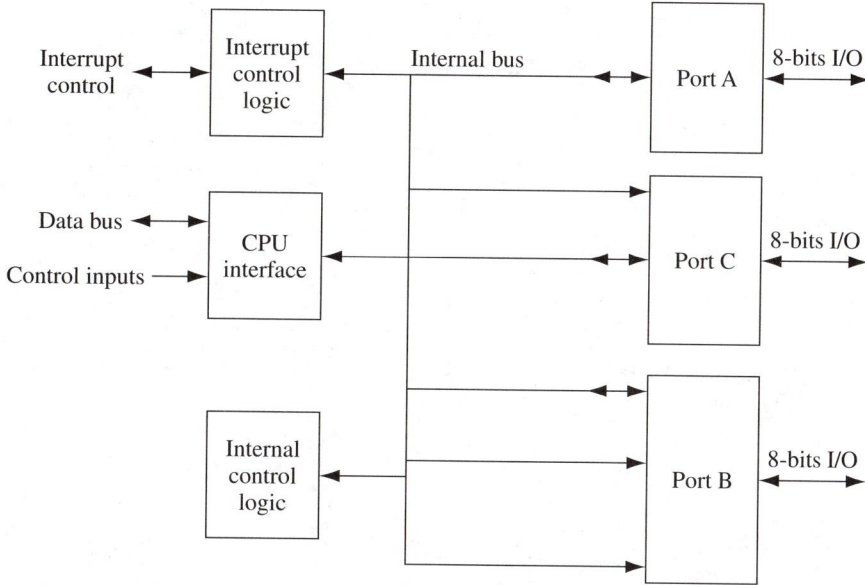

▲ FIGURE 11–14
8255 block diagram

Counter-Timer Circuits

Many of the microcontrollers discussed in Section 11–2 also included counter-timer modules on-chip. Counter-timers are useful in creating software time delays and in generating baud rates for serial communications. These devices are also available as standalone ICs for connection to microprocessors.

Counter-timers are simply counters that divide down an input signal by a scaling factor. The range of the scaling factor depends on the size of the counter. The 8-bit counters can divide the input frequencies over a range of 1 to 256, while 16-bit counters have a scaling range of 1 to 65,536. The output of the counter-timer usually connects to some output device and supplies an output frequency as determined by the input frequency divided by the scaling factor programmed into the counter-timer IC.

The Intel 8253 is a counter-timer IC that was utilized on the initial IBM PC computers. It includes three 16-bit counter-timer functional blocks that must be programmed separately. The block diagram for the 8253 is shown in Figure 11–15. Each counter in the 8253 has an input clock, a gate, and an output. Once programmed and selected, each counter divides down the input clock signal by the scaling factor programmed into the counter-timer scaling register. The gate signal is used as an external hardware inhibit for any one of the three counter-timers.

The Zilog Z8536 CIO, called a *counter-timer and parallel I/O unit*, is a newer device that combines the functions of the counter-timer and parallel I/O all on one IC. The Z8536 includes two independent 8-bit, bi-directional I/O ports, a 4-bit special purpose I/O port and three independent 16-bit counter-timer modules. The block diagram for the Z8536 CIO is shown in Figure 11–16.

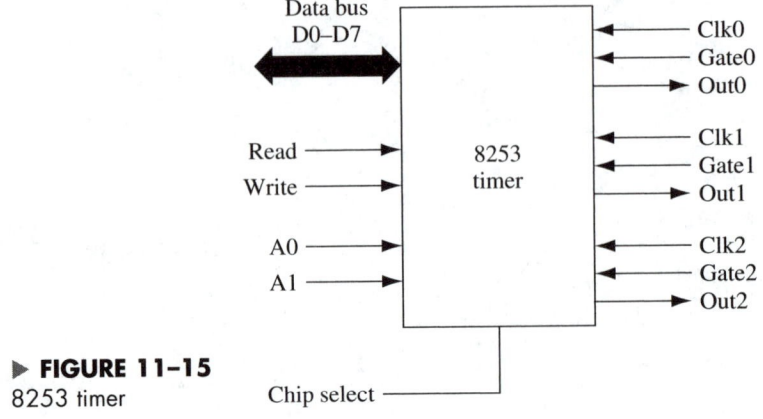

▶ **FIGURE 11–15**
8253 timer

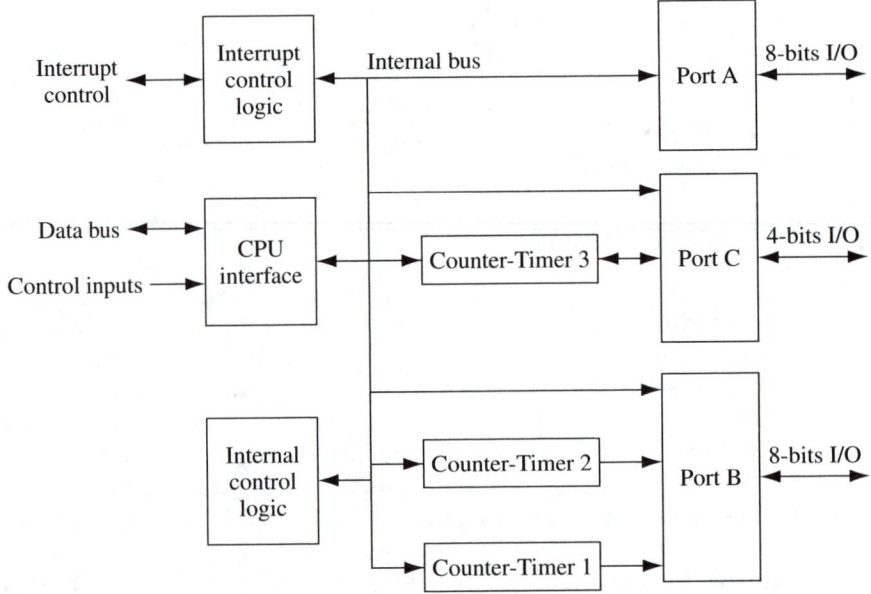

▲ **FIGURE 11–16**
Z8536 CIO block diagram

As the diagram shows, Ports B and C can be used to provide external access to the counter-timer modules. Port A does not interface with the counter-timers. Ports A and B can be configured to function together as one 16-bit I/O port. Each of the three ports includes pattern recognition logic that can be used to generate an interrupt when a certain pattern is input to the port. The three 16-bit counter-timers are all identical down counters. As many as four I/O lines can be dedicated to each of the counter-timers to provide an input, gate, trigger, and output. Each counter-timer can output either pulse, one-shot, or square-wave outputs. The Z8536 is available in a 40-pin DIP package or a 44-pin PLCC package.

Real-time Clock

In many applications it is desirable to maintain and record real time on an ongoing basis. Real-time clock ICs have been developed for use with microprocessors or microcontrollers that do not include this function on-chip. Most real-time clocks are stand-alone devices that require only DC power and an external crystal to operate. If the real-time clock is to operate when the rest of the system is powered down, a battery backup must also be connected. Real-time clocks maintain the date and time for all personal computers as well as a host of other embedded systems.

Real-time clocks like the 3285 RTC shown in Figure 11–17 simply count and maintain a calendar and time based upon a crystal input. The 3285 utilizes a 32.768 kHz oscillator. One cycle of this clock represents 30 µsec. Real-time clocks connect to the microprocessor data and address bus so that the microprocessor can program and read the current time value. The real-time clock can also act as an alarm clock for the processor by generating an interrupt to initiate real-time operations. The calendars for most real-time clocks are set up for a hundred years and feature automatic correction for leap year and daylight savings time changes. The 3285 RTC also provides a programmable square-wave output that can be used as a synchronous clock source for external devices.

11–6 ▶ Signal Conversion

Signal conversion circuits are needed for any embedded system in which there are analog inputs or outputs. Many of the microcontrollers discussed in Section 11–2 include analog-to-digital (A/D) converters on-chip that convert analog voltages to digital signals as inputs to the microcontroller. Digital-to-analog (D/A) converters convert digital signals back to analog signals to drive devices that require analog voltages. Much development effort has been applied to the development of faster conversion devices with higher levels of resolution.

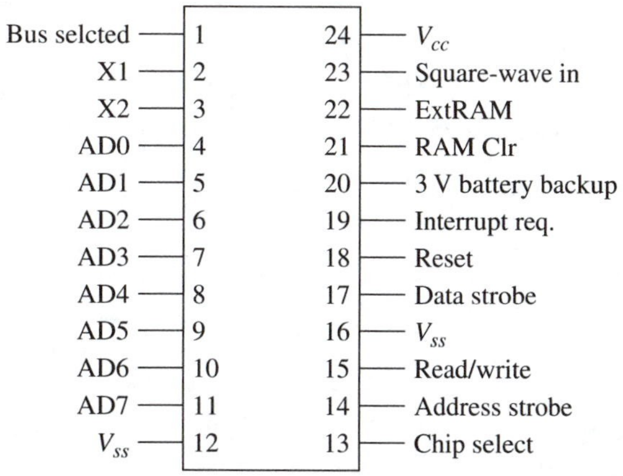

▶ **FIGURE 11–17**
3285 real-time clock

Bus selcted	1	24 — V_{cc}
X1	2	23 — Square-wave in
X2	3	22 — ExtRAM
AD0	4	21 — RAM Clr
AD1	5	20 — 3 V battery backup
AD2	6	19 — Interrupt req.
AD3	7	18 — Reset
AD4	8	17 — Data strobe
AD5	9	16 — V_{ss}
AD6	10	15 — Read/write
AD7	11	14 — Address strobe
V_{ss}	12	13 — Chip select

A/D Converters

A/D converters are used whenever an analog signal must be converted to a digital signal for processing by some digital system. The key functional requirements for any A/D converter are its resolution, conversion time, and voltage range. Other important details are the power supply requirements, power efficiency, package size, and cost.

There are many different types of A/D converters but they all essentially perform the same basic operations: the input signal passes through a low pass filter; and a sample and hold circuit holds the sampled value, which is then converted to digital bits that represent the analog voltage sampled. The low pass filter is designed to filter out any signal that is higher than the highest frequency expected as an input signal. Sample and hold circuits serve to take a snapshot of the input signal and hold it constant while the conversion process takes place. The conversion process is where the many different types of converters are created. The most common types of A/D converters are successive approximation, integrating, and flash converters.

Successive Approximation A/D Converters

Successive approximation converters test each bit of a digital signal pattern, starting with the most significant bit down to the least significant bit, in order to develop the digital number that represents the input analog signal. The block diagram for an 8-bit successive approximation A/D is shown in Figure 11–18. This figure shows the control logic, D/A converter, and comparator that are the key component in the successive approximation converter. A sample conversion is requested by setting an input sample request signal to the A/D converter. The input is sampled, held, and converted to a representative digital signal. The A/D converter first sets the MSB of the digital word—in this case, D7. The D/A converter converts this digital number (10000000) to analog and it is compared to the sampled analog value being converted. If the sampled input signal is greater than the D/A output, then D7 will remain a 1; otherwise, it becomes a 0. Next the A/D control logic loads the result, D7 = 0 or D7 = 1, and sets D6 = 1. The process is repeated using the comparator to indicate whether the D/A output is greater than or equal to the sampled input signal. The converter continues through all 8-bits, testing the resulting D/A output

▶ **FIGURE 11–18**

Successive approximation A/D Circuit

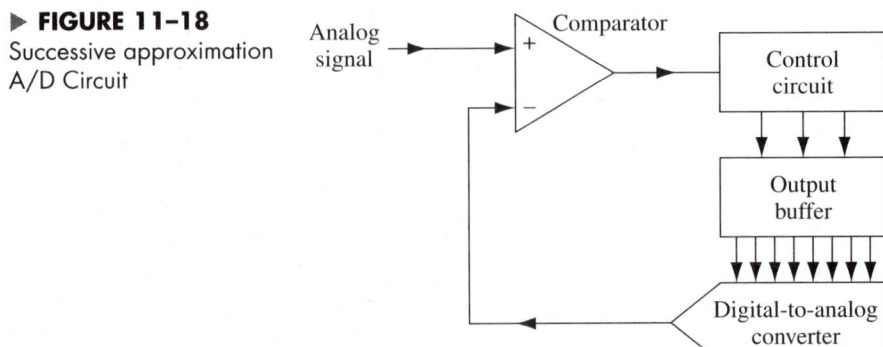

while compiling the digital word that most closely represents the amplitude of the sampled input. The number of comparisons to be made is determined by the number of bits included in the output digital word. In this case the 8-bit word will require that eight comparisons be performed.

Successive approximation converters are reasonably fast, require relatively few components, and are very versatile. Their conversion time and resolution are directly related to the number of bits, which determines the number of comparisons that must be made. Obviously, the conversion time increases with the number of bits that are output because the number of comparisons increases.

The ADC0841 is an example of a successive approximation converter that is designed to interface easily with a microprocessor. The chip pin out and block diagram are shown in Figure 11–19. The digital outputs of the ADC0841 are tristate so they can connect directly to the processor's data bus. The processor can initiate a conversion by toggling both the chip select (CS) and read (WR) lines. When the converter is complete it signals the processor by pulling the interrupt request line (INTR) low. The processor can then read the digital outputs by pulling the read (RD) line low. The analog input connects to the V_{IN+} and V_{IN-} connections and V_{REF} determines the range of the analog signal.

Integrating A/D Converters

Integrating converters are useful for conversion of lower frequency or DC types of signals. This is because they suffer from very slow conversion times, which means that they will not be able to accurately represent a higher-frequency waveform. Consequently, this type of converter is used extensively in digital multimeters and in instrumentation circuits for slowly changing signals, such as temperature. There are some variations in the types of integrating converters. Single- and dual-slope are the two most popular.

The block diagram for the single-slope converter is shown in Figure 11–20. These converters begin conversion by integrating a voltage reference signal with

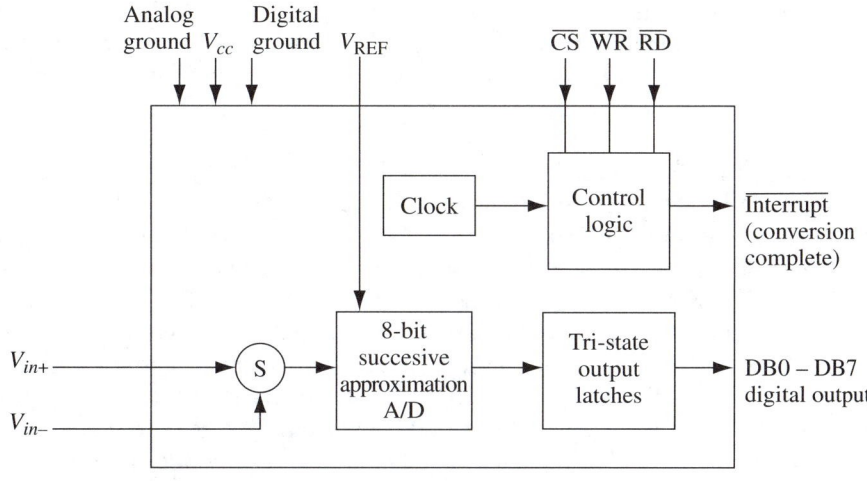

▲ **FIGURE 11–19**
ADC0841 A/D converter

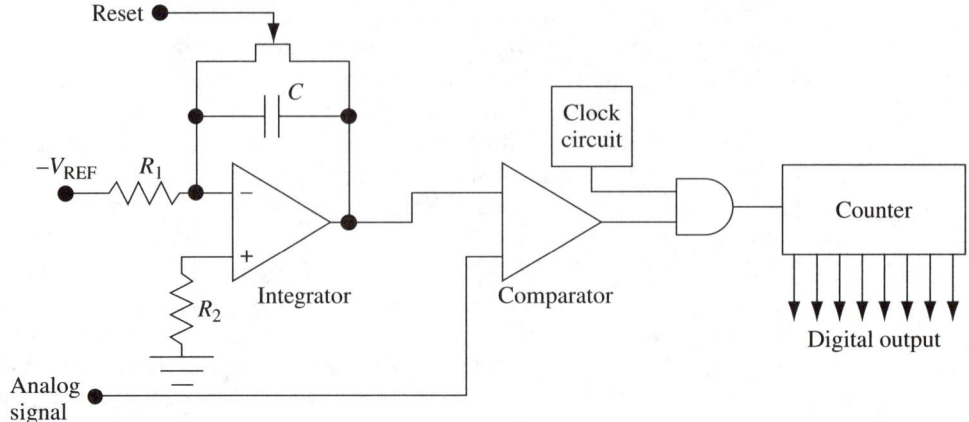

▲ **FIGURE 11–20**
Single-slope A/D converter

an op amp integrator circuit. At the same time, a clock is started that counts while the integration proceeds. The output of the integrator is compared to the analog signal being converted. When the integrator output equals the input signal, the comparator switches, stopping the counter and the conversion process. The counter value is the digital representation of the analog input. The single-slope converter is sensitive to changes in the reference voltage, the integrating capacitor, and the clock circuit.

A dual-slope integrator block diagram is shown in Figure 11–21. It improves on the performance of the single-slope converter significantly. The dual-slope converter initiates conversion by starting a counter and integrating the analog signal for a period of time such that the counter counts through all states. When this happens, the integrator is connected to the reference signal, and the counter starts again until the integrator output goes back to 0 V. At this point the comparator switches, signaling the end of conversion. The end result of this process is that the digital value is proportional to the two cycles of integration, and it is independent of the RC values of the circuit as well as clock variations.

Flash A/D Converters

Flash A/D converters are the fastest A/D converters available. The block diagram for a Flash converter is shown in Figure 11–22. In a flash converter the input analog signal is connected to comparators that represent each combination of digital outputs. For an 8-bit flash converter, there are 255 (2^{n-1}) comparators. The reference inputs to these comparators are the analog voltages that are coincident with the combinations of digital outputs. The internal analog reference voltages are created by dividing down the reference voltage with 255 equal resistor values. The flash converter is fast because all the comparisons take place in parallel at the same time. The comparator outputs are fed to a decoder that interprets them and outputs the appropriate digital word. Flash converters approach conversion times of 20 ns and are practically limited to 8 bits.

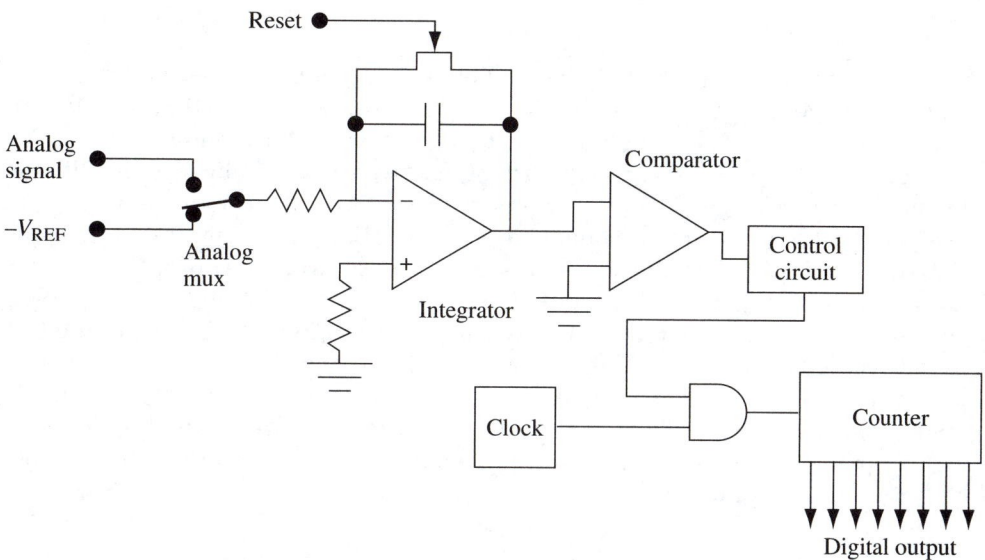

▲ **FIGURE 11–21**
Dual-slope A/D converter

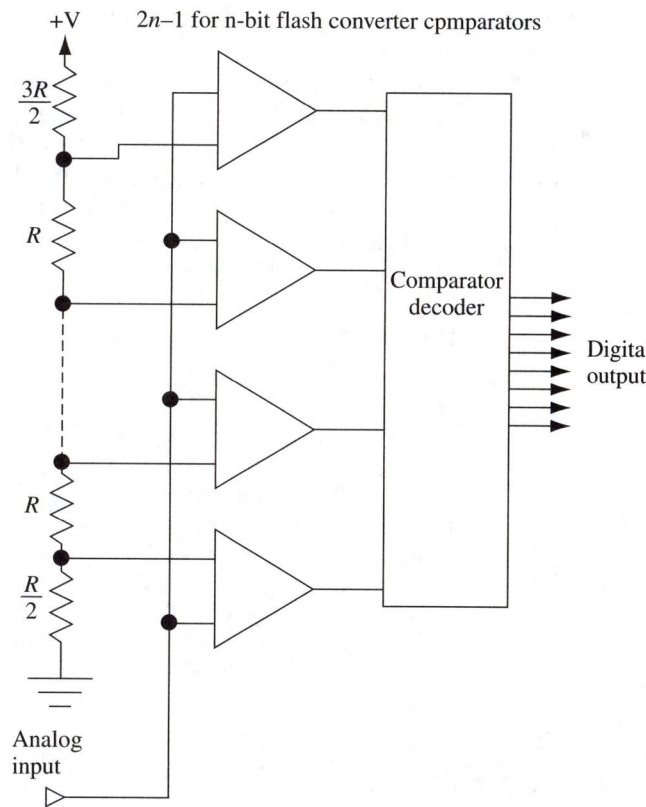

▶ **FIGURE 11–22**
Flash A/D converter block diagram

D/A converters

D/A converters take an input digital number and output the corresponding analog output voltage. The most popular type of D/A converter is called the R-2R D/A circuit. Figure 11–23 shows the functional block diagram for the R-2R circuit. The name of the circuit comes from the use of just two resistor values, R and 2R. The result is that the digital bits that connect the various 2R resistor segments are weighted according to their labeled bit position. The op amp output becomes the net sum of all these weights and represents the desired analog output.

The accuracy of the D/A converter is tied to the weighting resistors tolerances and the op amp and the reference voltage variations. The speed of the D/A is determined by the speed of the analog switches that switch in the resistors and the overall op amp frequency response. The performance of a D/A is typically noted on the data sheet by the settling time required after conversion and the slew rate of the op amp. The block diagram and pin out for the ever popular DAC08 D/A converter is shown in Figure 11–24.

▶ Summary

Think about all of the appliances and devices that you use every day. Begin with the thermostat that automatically warms the house before you get out of bed and the alarm clock that stirs you from your sleep. Perhaps you listen to an MP3 player while you take a morning walk. The microwave oven, electric range, television, satellite TV, or cable selector are all devices you will likely use before heading out for the day. Then perhaps you will drive your car while listening to the car radio or use your cell phone. While at work in an office, you use a personal computer, advanced calculators, fax machines, copy machines, and possibly computer projection devices. Working in more specialized fields almost always involves the use of some specialized equipment or devices. While you are at work, your VCR records your favorite television program for later viewing and your answering machine records messages from important callers. If you need cash for shopping, you access an ATM; then when you spend that cash, the product is scanned with a bar

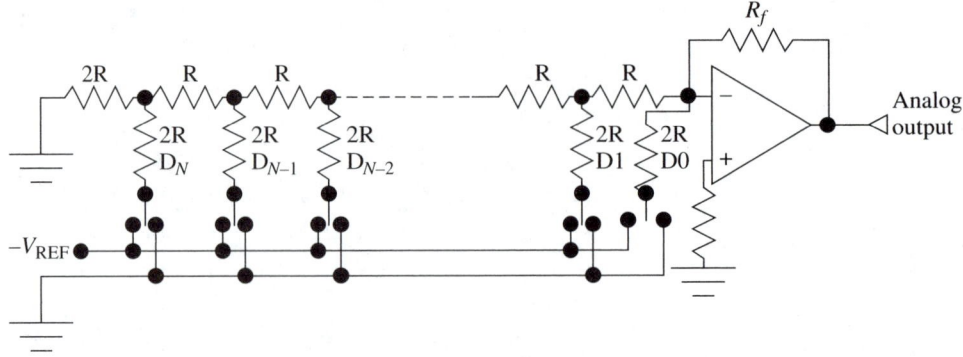

▲ **FIGURE 11–23**
R-2R D/A converter block diagram

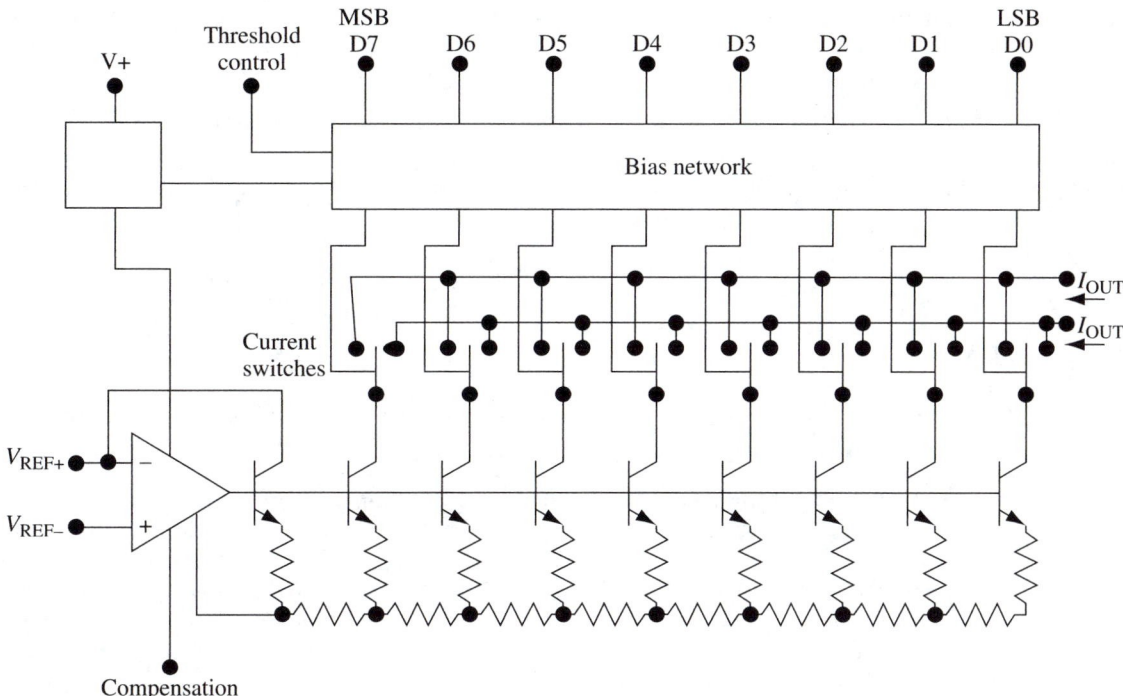

▲ FIGURE 11–24
DAC08 Digital-to-analog converter block diagram

code reader, processed on a terminal, and printed on a printer. These devices are just some of the examples of embedded systems. A microcontroller or microprocessor is inside controlling the device as it has been programmed to operate.

Embedded systems products must be both reliable and easy to use. Accomplishing this goal while maintaining a competitive price is a goal that's accomplished only with thorough planning, a high level of innovation, attention to detail, and teamwork. The raised bar of performance for embedded systems demands that they are easily set up and used. They must be impervious to electrical noise while not radiating excess EMI. They must withstand vibration and temperature variations while using little power and operating at high speeds—all of this while the average product development cycle is made shorter and shorter. Embedded system design usually requires an extended team of specialized hardware and software professionals. These goals can only be achieved by managing the project on a concurrent engineering basis.

▶ References

Gaonkar, R. S. *The Z80 Microprocessor.* Upper Saddle River, NJ: Prentice Hall, 2001.

Haskell, R. E. *Design of Embedded Systems Using the 68HC12/11 Microcontrollers.* Upper Saddle River, NJ: Prentice Hall, 2000.

Mazidi, M. A., Mazidi, J. *The 80X86 IBM PC and Compatible Computers: Design and Interfacing of IBM PC; PS and Compatible Computers.* Upper Saddle River, NJ: Prentice Hall, 2000.

Peatman, J. B. *Design with PIC Microcontrollers.* Upper Saddle River, NJ: Prentice Hall, 1997.

Stanley, W. D. *Operational Amplifiers with Linear Integrated Circuits.* Upper Saddle River, NJ: Prentice Hall, 1994.

▶ Exercises

11–1 List the key design decisions to be made before starting the design of an embedded system.

11–2 What additional steps can and should be taken to promote noise immunity in embedded systems?

11–3 What two primary processor architectures provide uniquely different schemes for transferring program and data information from memory to the processor? Describe each of these architectures and highlight the difference between them.

11–4 List the primary characteristics of an RISC processor system.

11–5 List the primary characteristics of a CISC processor system.

11–6 Explain what is meant by the term *pipelined processing*. What is the net effect of pipelined processing on system performance?

11–7 List three examples of microcontrollers.

11–8 List the major categories of volatile memory.

11–9 List the key differences between DRAMs and SRAMs.

11–10 List the various types of improved DRAMs and discuss the advantage of each.

11–11 Explain the meaning of the term *cache RAM*. What type of RAM is usually used as cache RAM in a computer system?

11–12 What enhancements are used in the development of memories called *Static Synchronous RAMs (SSRAMs)* and what are the benefits?

11–13 List the major categories of nonvolatile memory.

11–14 Explain the primary differences between EEROMs and Flash memory.

11–15 List the two different types of Flash memory and the characteristics of each.

11–16 What is the purpose of a DMA controller? Explain the basic steps of a DMA data transfer.

11–17 List and explain the two major categories of serial communications ports.

11–18 Describe the basic functions included on a counter-timer IC and list some typical applications.

11–19 List the three different types of A/D converters and explain the operation of each.

11–20 What is the fastest type of A/D converter available and what characteristics are the basis for its speed?

12 ▶ Telecommunications and Fiber Optics

▶ Introduction

In the early stages of the electronics revolution, people became aware of new discoveries by their application in audio and video products, transistor radios, and solid-state television. After the development of the microprocessor, the application of state-of-the-art electronics to all types of products became more visible. All along, some advances in electronics had been applied to telecommunications products. However, the monopolistic environment that existed in the industry at that time kept many innovations in the laboratory. During this time, the telecommunications industry enjoyed stable growth. This would all change as the breakup of AT&T became law and many new market opportunities emerged. The telecommunications revolution is the result of the following contributing factors:

- ▶ The breakup of AT&T and the technical ramifications of the legal directive
- ▶ The development of the microprocessor and its application in many telecommunications products
- ▶ The development of a computer network that provided for communications between various research universities and defense programs. This network evolved into the Internet.
- ▶ The rise of many other communications protocols, which improved the efficient use of the existing telecommunications infrastructure
- ▶ The development of the personal computer and the ensuing information society
- ▶ The development of fiber optics as a new vehicle for transmitting telecommunications information
- ▶ The development of a variety of wireless communications technologies

These developments positioned many companies to compete in this rapidly growing and profitable business. The capabilities made possible by the technology created new demand that provided paths of opportunity. In the background, the Internet and the protocol TCP/IP were becoming a reality. During the last two decades, the telecommunications industry expanded at such a rate it was considered, on its own, a revolution.

Today, high-speed computerized routers, bridges, and switches all send packets of data to their assigned destinations through the quickest path available, either as pulses of light or electricity. In this chapter we will look at modern telecommunications systems and how new electronics and fiber-optic technology have been applied to make it all work. The specific topics of this chapter are as follows:

- ▶ Defining Telecommunications
- ▶ Telecommunications System Design Considerations
- ▶ Modulation
- ▶ The Public Switched Telephone Network
- ▶ Modems
- ▶ Error Detection and Correction
- ▶ Protocols
- ▶ Computer Networks
- ▶ The Internet
- ▶ Fiber Optics in Telecommunication

12–1 ▶ Defining Telecommunications

Telecommunications can be defined simply as the communication of information from one location to another. Typically, the two locations are some distance apart. Initially, the information to be transmitted is electrical in nature and its form is either analog or digital. The most common methods for transmitting this information are as electrical signals transmitted on a wire cable, light information sent down an optical fiber, or wireless radio signals transmitted through the atmosphere and space. This broad definition of telecommunications includes radio transmissions, television, telephone lines, and computer networks.

Because the two locations communicating on a telecommunication network are some distance apart, it is always desirable for the communication medium to require as few connections as possible. This is because each connection requires more electrical or fiber cable or radio frequencies to complete the connection. This also requires the information to be sent in serial verses parallel form. To make the system even more efficient, the ability to share the transmitting medium with many users is a significant advantage. A basic telecommunications system is shown in Figure 12–1. It includes inputting information, encoding the information, and transmitting the encoded signal down the communication medium. On the other end the receiver accepts the information, decodes it, and converts it back to its original form. The signal is encoded so that many users can transmit information

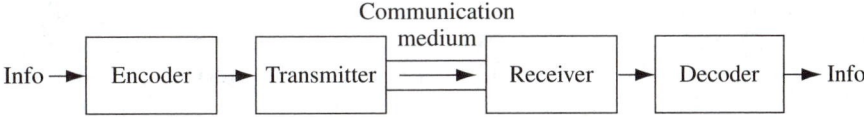

▲ FIGURE 12-1
Telecommunications system block diagram

over the communicating medium at the same time. Encoding provides a way of identifying the signal so that it can be decoded on the other end.

Typical residential telephone system communications today consist of land-line telephone, microwave, or cellular telephone communications. Television signals are transmitted either as local wireless signals, via cable TV, or as directed satellite communications. Audio radio information is transmitted either as a local wireless signal or on cable TV mediums. Computer communications can be performed through the telephone system by using a modem, through dedicated local area networks (LANs) or metropolitan area networks, (MANs) or the Internet.

The performance of any method of telecommunication is always based upon the amount of information that can be sent; how far it can travel; the cost of installation, maintenance, and transmission; and the quality of the information that is received. The requirements for quality largely depend on the type of information that is being transmitted. Voice telecommunications are the least demanding, while audio, video, multimedia and computer data require higher levels of accuracy and quality.

12-2 ▶ Telecommunications System Design Considerations

The design considerations for telecommunication systems are closely tied to the performance measures already mentioned in the last section—how much data can travel how far, and at what cost and quality level. The basic types of transmission mediums to be compared are conductive electrical cable, fiber-optic cable, and wireless communication.

Bandwidth

The various methods of information encoding are discussed in the next section. However, each encoding scheme uses a carrier frequency of some type. In each case either an analog or digital communication channel is encoded onto a carrier frequency. The next channel is encoded on the next available carrier frequency. The frequency bandwidth required for a communication channel depends on the type of signal being transmitted by that channel. Digital signals require significantly more bandwidth than analog signals. The amount of information that can be carried over the communications medium is determined by its overall frequency bandwidth. The bandwidth capability of the medium determines how many communication channels can be transmitted at the same time. In telephony, this converts to the number of voice channels that can be transmitted at the same time, which equates to the number of phone calls that can take place simultaneously on the same phone line. The greater the bandwidth of the medium, the more data can be transmitted simultaneously over the medium.

Each communication medium has a bandwidth limitation just as any electronic circuit. The physical basis for this limitation differs for the medium in question. For electrically conductive communication cable, the sources of these limitations are usually linked to the inductive and capacitive properties that are inherently part of the conductor. Conductive communication cables offer the lowest bandwidth because of their inductive and capacitive properties. Fiber-optic cable and wireless communications offer much higher bandwidths because neither have limiting factors as significant as the affect of inductance and capacitance on electrical signals.

Attenuation

Attenuation is a measure of the loss of signal that occurs as the signal passes through a component. In telecommunications, attenuation measures the signal loss over a length of the communications medium. Attenuation experienced on a transmission line is usually measured in dB per unit length. Again, the physical basis for attenuation differs significantly for the communication mediums. In electrically conductive cable, attenuation results from the resistance and inductance of the cable. The higher the signal frequency, the greater the loss due to the inductive reactance (X_L) of the cable $(X_L = 2\pi fL)$. Wireless communications offer the next highest attenuation while fiber-optic cable offers the lowest. Attenuation is important because it determines how far a signal can be transmitted down a certain medium before regeneration of the signal is required.

Quality

The perceived quality level of a transmitted signal depends greatly on the transmission mode (analog or digital) and the type of signal being transmitted (voice, audio, video, data). Voice telephone communications have the lowest quality requirements while computer data has the highest. In voice communications the quality level can be determined by the following criteria:

1. Amplitude level: Can the voice be heard?

2. Clarity: Is the voice clear and distinct without the presence of background noise?

3. Recognition: Can the voice be recognized as that of the caller?

Audio and video signal quality is usually a function of transmission method. Electromagnetically transmitted radio and television signals are always subject to noise and interference. Routine audio and video signals transmitted digitally are usually subject to the same quality requirements as voice communications.

Critical computer communications have only one measure of signal quality: they require that the data be received accurately. Because perfect transmission and reception cannot be guaranteed, error detection and correction circuits and algorithms are required for important computer data communications.

Cost

The cost of sending information includes the cost of installing telecommunication facilities and the cost of operation and maintenance. This varies greatly for the differing telecommunication methods. Fiber-optic cable requires more elaborate equipment to complete splices when compared to electrical wire. Expensive and more intricate laser light sources are used as fiber-optic transmitters in many telecommunications applications. However, fiber optics offers much less signal attenuation, so the need for amplifiers or repeaters to rejuvenate the signal is much less than the quantity required for electrical signals. Also, the increased bandwidth of fiber optics means that each fiber can carry more information. The least costly method is selected to resolve the telecommunication problem. Figure 12–2 summarizes the design considerations for telecommunication system design.

12–3 ▶ Modulation

Encoding is defined as the process of placing information on what is called a *carrier*. The carrier for this book is the paper on which it is printed. The encoding format is the English language printed on the pages. When you speak, the carrier is the air around you. Your vocal cords modulate a signal onto the air, which carries the signal to whom you are speaking. Your listener's ear decodes the signal and hopefully understands your message. In telecommunications, the carrier is an electromagnetic waveform. The electromagnetic waveform takes the form of either

Bandwidth: How much data can be transmitted?

Attenuation: How far can the data be transmitted without rejuvination?

Quality: How accurate is the received signal when compared to the transmitted signal?

Cost: What are the installation, operation, and maintenance costs?

▲ **FIGURE 12–2**
Telecommunications design considerations

an electrical waveform transmitted down a wire, electromagnetic radio waves, or as light passing through fiber-optic cable.

The purpose of encoding is to identify the signal uniquely, as it is transmitted through a medium where many other signals travel. The best example of this is radio signals transmitted from a radio station. The radio broadcast is encoded on the frequency assigned to the station, either as an amplitude modulation (AM) or frequency modulation (FM) encoded signal. The desired station is selected by tuning in the carrier signal frequency of the station on your radio dial. Your radio receiver blocks out all other frequencies and decodes the signal from the carrier signal.

Amplitude Modulation

Amplitude modulation and frequency modulation are two common ways to encode analog signals. Amplitude modulation simply changes the amplitude of the carrier frequency as the amplitude of the signal waveform changes. Amplitude modulation is usually used to encode signals within the audio frequency range (20–20 kHz). The carrier frequencies utilized for AM encoding are in the middle of the radio frequency ranges, typically 300 kHz to 3 MHz. The modulation index, m_a, is the relative magnitude of the peak voltage of the modulated signal, V_m compared to the peak carrier signal amplitude, V_c. Figure 12–3 shows an example of an input signal that is amplitude modulated onto a carrier signal.

$$m_a = V_m/V_c \qquad (12\text{--}1)$$

AM transmissions are relatively simple to complete, but they suffer from sensitivity to noise. Noise is easily picked up and added to the AM transmitted signal, but it is difficult to detect and remove. If the amplitude of the noise is large enough and it is within the frequency band of the receiver, it has to be considered as part of the modulated signal. AM also suffers from power inefficiency. This is because the information being transmitted is actually contained in the portion of the signal above and below the carrier signal amplitude. These are called the *upper* and *lower sidebands*. The power used to transmit all of the carrier frequency is wasted because it contains no information.

▶ **FIGURE 12–3**
Amplitude modulation

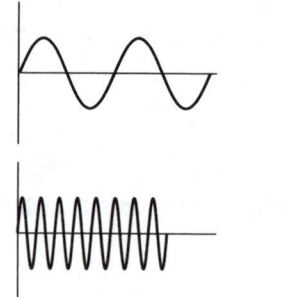
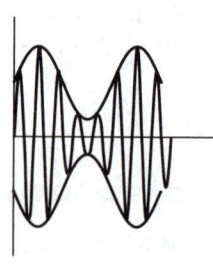

Frequency Modulation

Frequency modulation offers a significant improvement over both of the inherent weaknesses experienced with the AM system. FM systems encode the signal waveform onto a carrier signal by varying the frequency of the carrier waveform as the amplitude of the modulating signal. The difference of the carrier frequency from the unmodulated value is proportional to the amplitude of the modulated signal. The largest frequency variation induced by the amplitude of the modulated signal, δ determines the modulation index, m_F for the FM system. The modulation index m_F is given by the formula:

$$m_F = \delta/f_m \tag{12-2}$$

where f_m = the frequency of the modulated signal
and δ = frequency deviation/amplitude

Following are the key performance differences between AM and FM:

1. Noise usually couples onto the modulated carrier waveform by increasing its amplitude. Because the amplitude of the carrier signal does not contain information about the input signal, noise is easily detected and rejected.

2. The encoded information is included as part of the primary carrier waveform; therefore, the power used to transmit the combined FM signal is used more efficiently.

3. The frequency band needed for FM is obviously greater than AM because the signal inherently varies around the center carrier frequency.

The commercial FM broadcast band is from 88 to 108 MHz. An example of FM is shown in Figure 12–4.

Pulse Code Modulation

Both AM and FM are considered to be analog encoding methods. Pulse code modulation (PCM) is essentially a digital method for encoding an analog signal and is the preferred method of telecommunications. In order to encode an analog waveform with PCM, the input signal is sampled by a sample-and-hold circuit, which connects to an analog-to-digital converter (A/D). The A/D develops a digital number that represents the amplitude of the analog waveform at the instant it was sampled.

▶ **FIGURE 12–4**
Frequency modulation

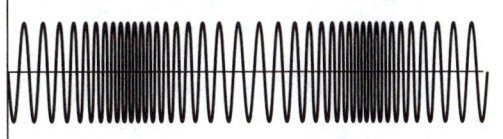

The number of bits provided by the A/D converter determines its ability to break down the input signal into small pieces. The resolution of the A/D, $R_{A/D} = 2^n$, where n is the number of A/D bits. An 8-bit A/D can break down an input signal into 256 pieces. The bit pattern representing the amplitude of the input signal is converted to serial pulses and is ready to be encoded further and then transmitted over the communication medium.

The other half of the PCM process is the method by which the pulses are sent over the communication medium. The communication of digital signals requires that the transmitter and receiver be synchronized. This is because the amplitude of the received signal is used to determine whether the received signal is a digital 1 or a 0 at a specific time. The synchronization signal indicates when the receiver should sample the transmission. Synchronization can be provided with a separate clock transmission or a clock signal can be encoded within the information to be transmitted. For most telecommunications applications the requirement for a separate clock is not practical because an additional communication line would be required. Therefore, a self-clocking encoding method for PCM signals is highly desirable. Self-clocking encoding means that the clock signal is embedded in the transmission signal. This is accomplished by causing a transition of some type (0 to 1 or 1 to 0) to occur during each clock cycle. The transition is used as the synchronizing clock. Self-clocking also resolves the problem of nonchanging voltage levels resulting from strings of 1s and 0s that occur with many encoding schemes. Certain encoding schemes require a wider-channel bandwidth than others because of the method used to include the clock in the transmission. When selecting the encoding scheme, the important considerations are the required channel bandwidth, whether the encoder is unipolar or bipolar, and the expected bit error rate (BER).

Unipolar signals are those that have only one polarity: the signal is either a peak high level or zero. Bipolar signals utilize two polarities: the signal is either a peak positive value or a peak negative value. Unipolar signals are simpler and easier to develop and encode. However, long strings of high or low levels affect the net DC level seen by the receiver. Receivers use the DC level to help develop a threshold for defining the high and low logic levels. Because the DC component varies with the nature of the data being transmitted, recovering the unipolar signal is more difficult. Bipolar signals offer a constant zero DC component, which promotes the establishment of a consistent and accurate logical threshold. In addition, bipolar signals can have twice the differential between logical highs and lows as unipolar signals.

Non-Return-to-Zero Encoding

The various serial encoding schemes define a binary 1 and 0 differently. Figure 12–5 shows examples of various encoding schemes using the same data and clock segments. Unipolar Non-Return-to-Zero (NRZ) encoding is referred to as standard digital encoding because a binary 1 is defined simply as the high logic level and a binary 0 equals the low logic level. This is the same definition used in standard logic representations. Bipolar NRZ defines a binary 1 as a positive logic

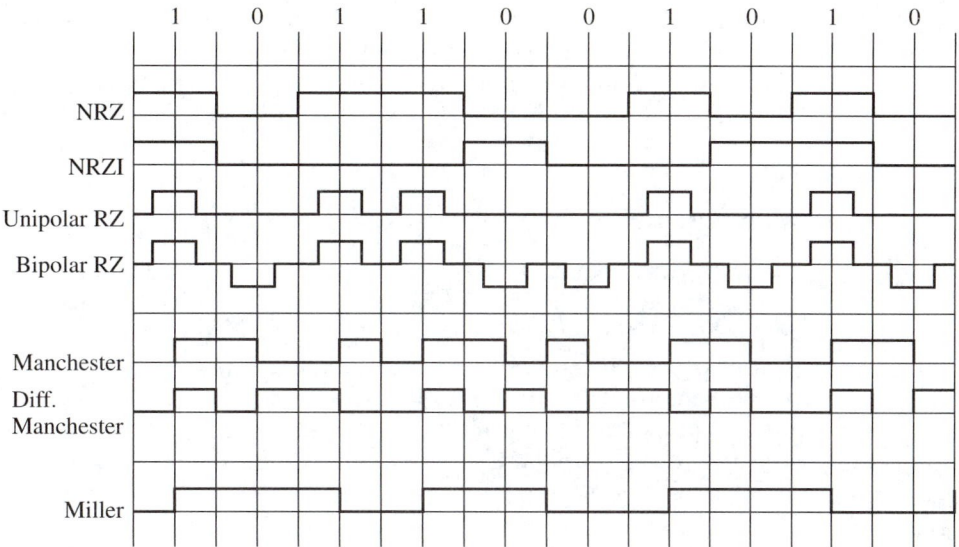

▲ **FIGURE 12–5**
Digital serial encoding schemes

voltage and a binary 0 as a negative logic voltage. NRZ code does not include a clock signal within and therefore requires a separate hardware clock signal. Notice that with long strings of binary 1s or 0s the NRZ does not change for many clock segments.

Non-Return-to Zero-Inverted Encoding

Non-Return-to Zero-Inverted (NRZI) encoding defines a binary 0 as any transition at the beginning of the clock cycle; a binary 1 equates to no transition. NRZI eliminates part of the problem experienced with NRZ code; long periods of low logic levels for a string of binary zeros. However, continuous binary 1s still result in a string of nonchanging transmission levels. NRZI is a differential encoding technique because its definition of binary states is determined by voltage transitions as compared to voltage levels. NRZI also does not include a clock within the transmission. Unipolar NRZI and bipolar NRZI signals are the same except that a negative voltage level represents a logical 0 (see Figure 12–5).

Return-to Zero Encoding

Return-to-Zero (RZ) code results in significant variations when applied to unipolar or bipolar signals. RZ code splits the clock cycle into two half periods. Unipolar RZ defines a binary 1 as a transition to a high level in the first half of the clock signal with a transition to low level in the second half. A binary 0 is interpreted when there is no transition. Note that unipolar RZ results in strings of nonchanging signals with successive binary 0s. Bipolar RZ results are quite different because of the negative logic level used for a binary 0. Bipolar RZ still defines a binary 1 the same as unipolar RZ; however, a binary 0 requires a transition from 0 V to the negative logic level and back to 0. The resulting encoded bipolar RZ signal changes state during each clock period and is therefore considered to be self-clocking.

Manchester Encoding

Manchester encoding is a self-clocking code that is used in many LAN systems and is specified for Ethernet LANs. A binary 1 is defined as a transition from 0 to 1 in the middle of the clock period. Binary 0 is interpreted as a 1 to 0 transition in the middle of the clock period. The transition in the middle of the clock period is used as the synchronizing clock. Bipolar Manchester encoding results in the same waveform as unipolar Manchester encoding except for the different levels seen for the low logic level (unipolar 0 = 0 V, bipolar 0 = negative voltage level).

Differential Manchester Encoding

Differential Manchester encoding is used in many token ring computer networks. The definition of a binary 1 is no transition at the beginning of the clock period. A binary 0 is read when a transition does occur at the beginning of the clock cycle. Differential Manchester is self-clocking and unipolar and bipolar waveforms look the same.

Miller Encoding

Miller encoding is a unique scheme that defines a binary 1 as any transition that occurs during the middle of the clock cycle. A binary 0 is interpreted when there is no transition at the middle of the clock period. In order to keep the signal changing for a string of binary 0s, Miller encoding inserts a transition at the end of the clock cycle if the previous bit was a zero. The result is a self-clocking waveform that changes at least every other clock cycle. The resulting clock is one-half the frequency of other encoding schemes, so Miller encoding requires less overall bandwidth to transmit a given amount of data.

Data Rate vs. Signal Rate

It should be noted that whenever an encoding scheme defines a binary 1 and 0 that requires more than one transition, the actual data or number of bits transmitted is less than the number of transitions. The data rate (bit rate) of a communication link is defined as the number of bits transmitted per unit time, usually stated in bits per second. The signal or baud rate is defined simply as the frequency of the signal transitions. The baud rate equals the bit rate for encoding schemes such as NRZ, NRZI, and Miller, because each transition equates to a bit being transmitted.

Manchester, differential Manchester, and RZ encoding require two transitions for each bit of data transmitted. Therefore, the actual bit rates for these codes are one-half of the signal or baud rate.

Binary Data Codes

In addition to the serial encoding, there is the issue of which binary code the data represents. Transmitted digital data can represent any one of the following codes:

Standard binary code

Binary coded decimal (BCD)

ASCII—Standard Keyboard Character

Baudot—older code that was used for Telex machines

Excess-3 Code—number code similar to BCD

EBCDIC—Extended Binary-Coded Decimal Interchange Code, used extensively in IBM mainframe computers

The most common digital codes transmitted are standard binary code for voice communication and ASCII for text information.

Bandwidth Requirements for PCM vs. Analog

As discussed earlier, AM and FM are considered to be analog methods of encoding information onto a carrier. Since FM requires more bandwidth than AM, let's use the bandwidth requirements of FM encoding to compare the bandwidth needs for PCM. For most telecommunications applications, we are concerned with the transmission of voice information. Since the very beginning, the telecommunications industry has used a bandwidth of 4000 Hz for voice signals. FM encoding therefore requires 4000 Hz of bandwidth for each voice channel transmitted down a transmission line or a wireless link. This means that the carrier frequencies must be at least 4000 Hz apart.

The bandwidth requirements for PCM encoding of voice information are dependent upon the A/D converter used to convert the analog data to digital and the rate at which the data is sampled. The standard used in the telecommunications industry is 8-bit A/D conversion at a sample rate of 8000 samples per second. 8-bit A/D conversion offers reasonable resolution of the signal amplitude for voice signals. The sample rate of 8000 samples per second is determined by communication theory that calls for sample rates of twice the expected highest signal frequency (2 × 4000 Hz). If an 8-bit A/D converter samples an analog voice signal at a rate of 8000 samples per second, it will create 64,000 bits of data for every second of the voice signal. Therefore the bandwidth required for PCM of voice signals is 64 kHz, which is one PCM voice channel.

Example 12–1

Let's take an example of a telephone cable that has a maximum bandwidth of 200,000 Hz. Determine the location of the carrier frequencies and the number of voice channels for both FM and PCM encoding. Compare the results.

Solution

1. The bandwidth requirements for FM = 4000 Hz = 1 voice channel

   200,000 Hz bandwidth of the telephone line/4000 Hz/voice channel = 50 voice channels

2. The voice channel carrier frequencies would start at 2000 Hz and be spaced every 4000 Hz up to 198 kHz (2000 Hz, 6000 Hz, 10,000 Hz, and so on).

3. The bandwidth requirements for PCM = 64 kHz = 1 voice channel

   200,000 Hz bandwidth of the telephone line/64,000 Hz/voice channel = 3.125 = 3 voice channels

4. The voice channel carrier frequencies would be 32 kHz, 96 kHz, and 160 kHz.

5. The results of these calculations indicate that the telephone cable in question can carry either 50 FM-encoded voice channels or 3 PCM-encoded voice channels at the same time. The bandwidth requirements for digital PCM encoding are 16 times those needed for analog FM encoding.

This example indicates that the bandwidth requirements are significantly greater for digitized signals compared to analog signals when they are transmitted over a communications medium. Why, then, has digital PCM become the preferred method of telecommunication? The answer to this question has many facets.

From the study of digital systems, we know that they possess inherent noise immunity that comes from their differential input and output voltage levels. Therefore, digital system noise immunity offers a significant advantage over any analog encoding scheme. When analog and digital signals are transmitted over a telecommunication line, the signal is attenuated over the long distance of the wire. After a certain distance, the signal must be rejuvenated in order to travel further and be recognized at its final destination. Analog signals are rejuvenated with amplifiers. The problem is that any noise picked up on an analog signal is also amplified. As the analog signal progresses, its signal to noise ratio actually becomes smaller, and the quality of the signal decreases.

Digital signals also experience attenuation and must be rejuvenated. The information encoded onto the digital signal is contained in the bits (whether a bit is a 1 or a 0). Therefore, digital signals can be reconstructed if the proper level for the signal can be interpreted. Devices called *repeaters* reconstruct digital signals. Repeaters sample the signal much like a receiver, determine the binary level, and output a reconstructed signal at that binary level.

Because telecommunications now includes the communication of much digital computer information, voice telecommunication systems must also be capable

Advantages of Digital Encoding

• Inherent noise immunity
• Ability to reconstruct the signal
• Need to transmit digital data
• Error detection and correction
• Digital signals are easily transmitted with fiber optics

Advantages of Analog Encoding

• Lower bandwidth requirements

▶ **FIGURE 12–6**
Advantages of digital vs. analog encoding

of transmitting digital signals. If noise is picked up by a digital signal, error detection schemes can be used to detect the error and correct it.

One last benefit of digital encoding is that digital signals are very easy to transmit using light. When the light is on, it represents a binary 1; off, a binary 0. Fiber optics readily accommodates digital signals. The increased bandwidth capability of fiber optics more than makes up for the higher bandwidth requirements of digital signals.

A summary of the advantages of digital vs. analog encoding is shown in Figure 12–6.

Digital Transmission Levels

Bipolar digital signals are the most popular for use in computer networks because of the enhanced noise immunity created by the greater difference between logical 1 and 0. The older RS-232 standard requires bipolar digital signals and defines a logical 1 as –3 to –15 V and a logical 0 as +3 to +15 V. The newer RS-422 and RS-485 standards use lower voltage levels and define a logical 1 as –2 to –6 V and logical 0 as +2 to +6 V.

12–4 ▶ The Public Switched Telephone Network

The Public Switched Telephone Network (PSTN) represents the telecommunications connection for most of our voice telephone, cell phone, and computer communication. It begins with a connection of twisted pair cable that runs from our homes to a location called the *central office* (*CO*). The connections made to the CO are called the *local loop*. If a phone call is made to another party that is also connected directly to the same CO, the phone call is connected through the CO. Otherwise, the call must be passed on to another CO. The signals transmitted to the central office are most often analog signals with a bandwidth of 300 to 3400 Hz. If it is a long distance call, it will most likely be converted to a digital signal and then

Class 1 — Regional center
Class 2 — Sectional center
Class 3 — Primary center
Class 4 — Toll center
Class 5 — End office

▶ **FIGURE 12–7**
Switching exchange classifications

transmitted on a trunk line to the CO closest to the final destination. Then it is converted back to analog and received at the destination phone number. There are five classes of offices that develop a hierarchy of telephone switches within the PSTN. Figure 12–7 shows these classes of switching exchanges.

Today, computerized switches route phone calls from one exchange to the other. These switches determine the shortest route for a call, depending on the available circuits. The criteria used is to have the call travel the shortest route and use the smallest number of switching centers.

Trunks

Trunks provide the interconnection between the various switching exchanges. Trunks can take the form of twisted-pair, coax cable, microwave or satellite links, or fiber-optic cable.

Twisted-pair trunks are used for short distances with bandwidths under 1 MHz. Twisted-pair cable used for this purpose suffers from crosstalk and high signal attenuation per unit of distance. Coax cable is used for longer distances at frequencies higher than 1 MHz and can be buried underground or protected for underwater (submarine) applications.

Microwave radio links are often used instead of coax cable trunks. These links can carry several thousand voice channels over long distances with repeater stations located every 20 to 30 miles. Microwave links require a line-of-sight transmission and must be located high above any possible obstructions. Satellite communications are essentially microwave links with repeater stations located in space. These satellites are in orbit at approximately 22,300 miles in space above the equator. At that distance the satellite is said to have a geosynchronous orbit, which means the satellite maintains a fixed relative position to the same 40% segment of Earth. These satellites allow line-of-sight tracking 24 hours a day.

Most long-distance telecommunications are carried over fiber-optic trunk lines. (Fiber optic telecommunication is discussed in Section 12–8.) Fiber optics offers exceptional bandwidth capabilities because optical fiber does not possess the inductance and capacitance that limits the bandwidth of twisted pair and coax cable. This means that fiber-optic signals can be switched at much higher frequencies than electrical signals carried over conductive mediums. Fiber-optic fiber is also very small so many fibers can be placed in a fiber-optic trunk line. Fiber optics offers increased bandwidth in much smaller and lighter cables.

Multiplexing

Trunk lines must carry many voice channels of telecommunication signals. Modulation is applied to the signal to provide distinction for one voice channel from another. When analog signals are sent over a trunk, the method used to multiplex voice channels on the medium is called *frequency division multiplexing (FDM)*. (This is the same as frequency modulation as described in Section 12–3.) The number of voice channels that can be transmitted over the trunk is determined by the bandwidth of the signals that can be transmitted on the trunk. The trunk bandwidth is simply the highest possible transmission frequency minus the lowest. The number of voice channels possible equal the overall bandwidth of the trunk, divided by the bandwidth required for one voice channel (4000 Hz for analog voice signals). FDM can be used to send many voice channels of analog signals over twisted-pair cable, coax cable, microwave, or satellite trunks.

The preferred method used today is the multiplexing of digital PCM signals using a method called *time division multiplexing (TDM)*. TDM splits a transmission in specific time slices, allowing one slice for each voice channel that is input. For example, let's review a 10-channel TDM line that carries 1 second of data for each channel at any given time. The TDM circuit places the first second of data for channel 1 followed by channel 2 and so on until the data for channel 10 is the last data transmitted for the first second of the transmission. As the data arrives at the end of the trunk, it is demultiplexed and separated back into channels 1 through 10. TDM provides an added delay to the transmission because each channel shares transmission time. However, if the overall transmission bandwidth is high enough, the delays experienced will not be discernible.

12–5 ▶ Modems

The local loop for most PSTN connections is made up of twisted-pair telephone lines designed to carry the analog signals that are output from a typical telephone set. In order for a computer to communicate over these lines, the digital signals transmitted by a computer must be converted to a digitally encoded, analog signal. A modem (short for *modulator-demodulator*) is a device designed to accomplish this. Modems convert and transmit digital data to an analog signal that contains the digital information. A modem on the receiving end reads the digitally encoded analog signal and converts it back to its original digital format. There are five commonly used methods for encoding digital information on an analog signal: amplitude shift keying, frequency shift keying, phase shift keying, differential phase shift keying, and quadrature amplitude modulation.

Amplitude Shift Keying (ASK)

ASK is a simple scheme that applies a frequency with a defined high-level amplitude to transmit a binary 1 and a low-level amplitude for a binary 0. The low level amplitude usually selected is 0 V. ASK by itself is usable at very low transmission rates because of its inherent sensitivity to noise and the low bandwidth signals that are possible. Figure 12–8 shows examples of modem encoding methods.

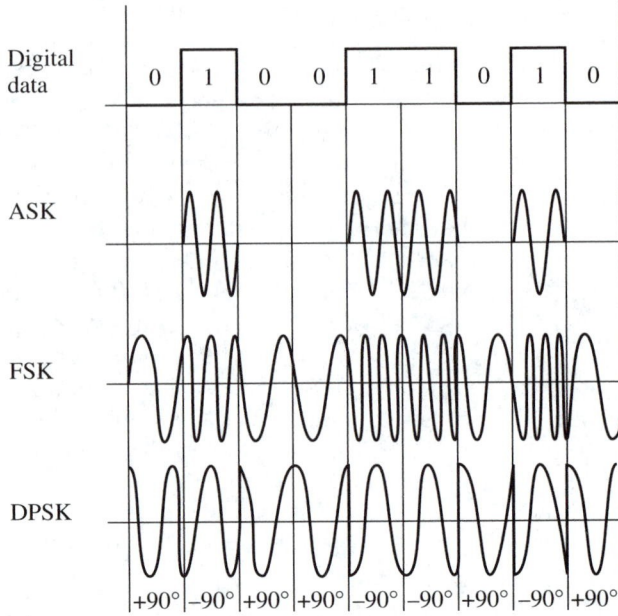

▶ **FIGURE 12–8**
Modem modulation examples

Frequency Shift Keying (FSK)

FSK is FDM applied to digital signals. FSK uses an upper frequency to encode a binary 1 (called a *mark*) and a lower frequency to indicate a binary 0 (called a *space*). Recall that the bandwidth allotted for each analog voice channel is 4000 Hz. The actual transmitted frequency range is 300–3400 Hz. The frequencies used to implement FSK that equate to the mark and space must be within this 300–3400 Hz band. FSK is used for asynchronous communication at relatively low transmission rates with a maximum rate of 1800 bits per second (bps).

Phase Shift Keying (PSK)

PSK modulates the phase relationship of each succeeding portion of the waveform as compared to a reference waveform. A number of different phase shifts can be used. When only two phase shifts are encoded, this is called *binary phase shift keying*. The binary 1 waveform is 180 degrees out of phase with the binary 0 waveform. When more than two phase shifts are used, it is possible to encode more than one bit into each phase shift. For example, let's say that the following phase shifts are used to encode two bits:

0° phase shift—represents binary 0–0

90° phase shift—represents binary 0–1

180° phase shift—represents binary 1–0

270° phase shift—represents binary 1–1

This is possible because each phase shift is unique for all of the possible combinations of the two binary bits.

Differential Phase Shift Keying (DPSK)

DPSK is similar to the two-bit scheme just described for PSK. The primary difference between DPSK and PSK is the fact that the phase shift decoded is the difference between each succeeding waveform. Typically, DPSK is used to encode up to eight differential phases to achieve data rates up to 4800 bps. Each of the eight phase shifts encodes 3 bits of binary data, all the possible combinations for 3 bits.

Quadrature Amplitude Modulation (QAM)

QAM is an even more complex scheme that achieves yet higher data rates. QAM is a combination of the ASK and DPSK. QAM can encode more data bits into one waveform transition because it combines the phase shift information with differing amplitude levels. If we take a DPSK signal with eight phase shifts and then encode these signals with three different amplitudes, 24 different binary combinations are possible. Because 24 is not an incremental power of two and to allow maximum separation of the encoding requirements, the eight phase-shift and three amplitude QAM signal is structured as shown in Figure 12–9 to achieve data rates of 9600 bps.

▶ **FIGURE 12–9**
QAM phase diagram

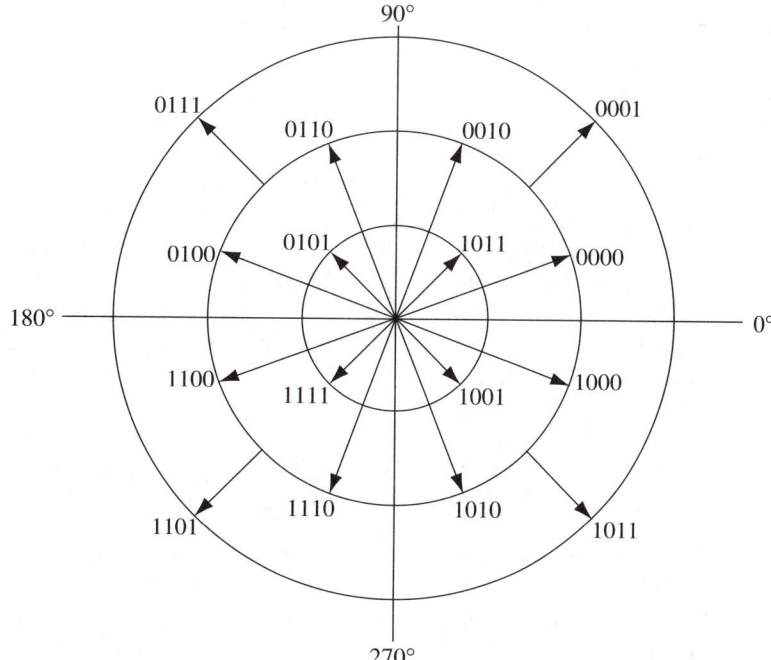

Modems were initially developed for teletype and telex communication over the Bell Telephone system. Consequently, Bell Telephone developed many of the older modem specifications. As the personal computer was introduced, the need for higher data rates was realized globally. The International Telecommunications Union (ITU) develops international standards for modems and other global telecommunications issues. Their specifications are issued as ITU-TS (Technical Specifications). There are many ITU-TS documents that technically define modem communication. In general, communication over the existing analog twisted-pair telephone wire is limited to 56 kbps. However, it is well recognized that 56 kbps significantly stretches the capabilities of twisted-pair telephone cable. The ITU-TS V .34 is the specification for most often used data rate for home personal computers. Data rates on the order of 28,800 and 33,600 are possible with QAM encoding schemes that use a greater number of amplitude levels and differential phase angles to encode more bits into each signal transition.

Cable Modem

Another type of modem is called the *cable modem*. This type of modem utilizes the high bandwidth capability available from coaxial cable that is already in place as part of the cable TV (CATV) network. Cable modems perform the same function as telephone system modems described previously; however, they are capable of much higher data rates. A typical CATV subscriber enjoys data rates on the order of five to ten times the data rates achieved on telephone lines with the additional benefit of not blocking phone communications. Television signals are transmitted over separate frequency channels and are transparent to any modem communications.

ISDN Modems

In order to be competitive with CATV cable modems, the telephone companies have developed the integrated services digital network (ISDN) or digital subscriber lines (DSL). These are telephone lines that connect to a home that provide direct digital communications to the phone system. This system provides much higher bandwidth. It also serves to allow a separate channel of communication for digital computer data that can occur simultaneously with voice communication. The net effect is that digital subscriber lines provide increased data rates and the ability to separate voice and data communication so that they can occur simultaneously.

Transmission Modes

Whenever two serial devices are communicating, the mode of the transmission must be defined. There are three levels of transmission modes: simplex, half-duplex, and full-duplex. Simplex mode is communication that takes place in one direction. Half-duplex mode is the transmission and receipt of data shared on one medium.

Transmission and reception occurs alternately. Full-duplex operation allows both of the communicating devices to send and receive data at the same time. This occurs over two separate lines or by splitting the frequency of communication in half over one line.

12–6 ▶ Error Detection and Correction

The performance of telecommunications systems is truly amazing when you consider the amount of information that is transferred in any one-second period of time. The bit error rate (BER) provides a measurement of the number of incorrect bits per total correct bits sent in a transmission. The BER depends on many factors, including signal bandwidth, distance traveled, signal-to-noise ratio, and the transmission medium and environment. The acceptable BER depends upon the type of communication. A missing bit or two from a voice communication will not make a significant difference in the result of the transmission. Computer data transfers of your bank account information are likely to require a greater level of accuracy and security. The BER is a measure of how accurately a transmission medium is transmitting data. There are many systems that offer extremely low BERs, but none is perfect. Therefore, whenever critical data is being transferred that must be received correctly, a means of detecting and correcting transmission errors is needed.

The oldest and most simple method of detecting errors is the parity method. Parity is an error detection scheme that adds one bit, called a *parity bit*, to any bit pattern being transferred. There are two types of parity detection: even parity and odd parity. In even parity, the parity bit is selected to make the entire transmitted bit pattern have an even number of 1s. Odd parity selects the parity bit so that the bit pattern possesses an odd number of 1s. When parity error detection is used, the sending and receiving device must be set up to operate on the same parity mode, even or odd parity.

In a system that uses parity, the transmitting device attaches a parity bit according to the parity mode that is selected. Let's say that odd parity is selected and that a 7-bit ASCII number of 40 HEX is being transmitted. Because the data 40 HEX transfers to the binary bit pattern 100 0000, the parity bit is made a 0 so that the transmitted number includes an odd number of ones. The bit pattern transmitted becomes 0100 0000, or an 8-bit binary number that still translates to a 40 HEX. On the other end, the receiver examines the received data using odd parity error detection. The receiver expects that all data received will have an odd number of binary ones; otherwise the transmission must be in error. When an error is detected, the receiver requests that the data be retransmitted.

Parity error detection can be implemented easily. The only overhead added to the transmission is the added parity bit and the small time required to add and transmit it and check for correct parity on the receiving end. Its shortcoming is that it can only detect errors with one or an odd number of bit changes in a transmission. An even number of bit changes cannot be detected for either even or odd parity detection. Parity error detection was developed to detect single-bit errors, and it performs this task very well. Higher levels of error detection require more sophisticated methods and greater overhead.

Cyclic Redundancy Checks (CRC)

The CRC concept provides a much better method of error detection and correction and is commonly used in block data transfers. CRC achieves performance levels of 99.9%. CRC functions by calculating a binary number that reflects the value of the data included in a block transfer. This number, called a *block check character* (*BCC*) is added to the data to be transmitted. The BCC represents the remainder of the binary division of the data by a CRC polynomial generator. The receiver performs the same division on the block of data received. The result of the receiver calculation should yield a zero remainder. Otherwise, the data is incorrect and must be resent or corrected by analyzing the remainder calculated by the receiver.

The key to the CRC process is the method used to calculate the BCC. Cyclic codes prescribe a specific number of BCC bits for a certain message size. CRC codes are also called *polynomial codes* because they view a bit string as a polynomial where the coefficients of each polynomial term are the 1s and 0s contained in the bit string. International standards have established 8-, 12-, 16-, and 32-bit BCCs, which are called CRC-8, CRC-12, CRC-16, and CRC-32, respectively. The size of the BCC corresponds to the size of the block being transferred; for example, CRC-8 is used to protect the 5-byte header on ATM data blocks.

The BCC is calculated by dividing the entire block of data to be transferred by what is called the *polynomial generator*. Polynomial generators are defined for each CRC standard. The standard for CRC-16 is $X^{16} + X^{15} + X^2 + 1$, which equals the binary number 1100000000000101. The BCC is generated by dividing the binary representation of the entire data block by the polynomial generator. The quotient resulting from the division is discarded and the BCC becomes the remainder of the binary division, which is added onto the data block. The resulting data plus BCC represents a binary number that is evenly divided by the polynomial generator. The receiver can verify the data transmitted by dividing the entire data block (including the BCC) by the polynomial generator. If the result is zero (no remainder), then the data is accepted. Otherwise, any remainder indicates that there is an error within the block of data. CRC-16 develops a 16-bit BCC. This concept can detect any odd number of bit errors as well as bursts of the number of BCC bits + 1 (17 bits for CRC-16).

Checksum

Checksum is another method used to detect errors in binary data. Checksums are often used to verify the content of programs and other variable data blocks. Checksums are also used in the transfer of data, usually to verify large blocks of transmitted data. There are a variety of different checksum methods that are used.

Single Precision Checksum

Single precision checksum is the most common. It results from the simple addition of succeeding words of data while ignoring any overflow of the MSB. The addition can be performed on any number of data words. After the last data word is added, the remaining word is the single precision checksum result. Any device receiving or reading the successive data words calculates its own single precision checksum for the data received or read. If the checksum values are the same, then the data is assumed to be correct. Single precision checksums are deficient because they allow one particular error to pass undetected. If the MSB of the data word is erroneously always a 1, the result is always the same as any other combination of 1s and 0s in the MSB positions. To test this theory, take the following hexadecimal numbers and add them, keeping only the least significant eight bits:

$$42H + 2DH + 17H + 34H = 6AH = \text{single precision checksum}$$

Now make the MSB of all of the previous numbers a 1, add the resulting numbers, and then compute the single precision checksum:

$$C2H + ADH + 97H + B4H = 26A, \text{the single precision checksum} = 6AH$$

Single precision checksums allow this constant high MSB error to exist because the result of the overflow operation of the MSBs are excluded from the result.

Residue Checksum

The residue checksum resolves the constant high MSB problem just described for the single precision checksum. Residue checksum is calculated just as the single precision checksum except that the carry from the addition of the MSB column is wrapped around and added onto the LSB. This step corrects for the MSB locked high problem because the carry information resulting from the MSB additions is included in the ongoing sum instead of being ignored. Every high MSB will impact the result of the checksum process uniquely. Calculating the residue checksum of the two hexadecimal numbers 87 H + BA H would follow like this:

87 H + BA H = 41 H with a carry
the carry is added to the 41 H to develop the residue checksum of 42 H

Double Precision Checksum

Double precision checksums double the width of the data words being added. With this method the carry-overs from the MSB additions are included in the extended width sum of the data. Consequently, this method also corrects for the MSB locked high problem as well as improving the performance of the checksum error detectors. Any carry that results from the overflow of the double-wide sum is ignored. The double precision checksum is calculated as follows:

$$D3 \ H + C5 \ H + F4 \ H + AB \ H = 27A \ H$$

It is not until the checksum total for a group of data exceeds the hexadecimal number FFFF H that the carry operation is ignored.

Error Correction

When errors are detected while transmitting information, there are two obvious alternatives: resend the information or correct the error. Resending the information is called *automatic repeat request* (*ARQ*), while correcting the error is known as forward error correction (FEC). The factors that dictate the use of ARQ or FEC are the size of the data block being transmitted, accuracy requirements for the data, the amount of time required to retransmit, and the error detection method being utilized.

The use of the ARQ method requires that the transmitter and receiver maintain bi-directional communications. The transmitter sends a block of data and the receiver either acknowledges the receipt of the correct information (no errors detected in the block) with an acknowledge (ACK), or replies with an ARQ indicating that an error was detected in the block of data.

The FEC method is often used when there exists only one-way communication between the transmitter and receiver. In this situation retransmission is not an option. FEC requires the use of more elaborate schemes that provide not only a method of error detection but a way of locating and correcting the error. This is called *redundant error-correction encoding*. These encoding methods insert redundant bits into a block of data to be transmitted. The location of these bits are pre-determined and made known to the transmitter and the receiver. The most commonly used redundant error correction code is called the *Hamming code*. A discussion of the Hamming code and other redundant error correction codes is beyond the scope of this book.

12–7 ▶ Protocols

Whenever two devices are communicating, there must be a set of rules that coordinate this communication. These rules are called *protocols* and they define the process of communication between devices. The simplest protocols are used to define the communication between two devices that interface directly over a dedicated connection.

For example, communication between a personal computer and the printer connected to it. This communication can be either serial or parallel format. The software driver for the printer used by the computer makes sure that the information being transmitted is in a code and format that will be understood by the printer. The protocol for this communication could be as follows:

1. The computer sends a message to the printer indicating that it has data to be sent to the printer.

2. The printer replies that it is ready and also sends back an identification number that specifies its manufacturer and model number.

3. The computer uses the appropriate software driver to encode and format the data, sending a block of data to the printer.

4. The printer either acknowledges the receipt of the data (ACK) or requests a retransmission (ARQ).

When communication involves two computers that are located across the country and connected by telephone lines and the Internet, the protocols required are much more complex. This is because this type of communication includes many layers of communication requiring many layers of protocols. In order to standardize global communications, the International Standards Organization (ISO) works with other global communication committees to establish standards for protocols. These studies have evolved into seven layers of protocols called the Open System Interconnect (OSI) model. The seven layers of the OSI are as follows:

1. Physical. This is the lowest of the layers and it defines the specific electrical and mechanical details of the interface and protocol between two devices.

2. Data Link. The data link layer defines the format of the data being sent, which includes the data code (ASCII, BCD, etc.), the framing characters (header and trailer), and the error detection/correction scheme.

3. Network. This layer determines the method for sending data throughout a communications network. The network can be the PSTN or a small LAN.

4. Transport. The transport layer deals with the communication over the entire path between the transmitter and the receiver. It promotes the efficient and reliable transmission of information.

5. Session. This layer manages the log-in and log-out procedures when the communication is part of a defined session.

6. Presentation. This deals with the conversion of data being transmitted from one type of code over to another.

7. Application. This layer defines the type of application software that the communication is related to. E-mail is a common application used on most PCs. If someone sends out an e-mail, the application layer information included with the transmitted data indicates to the receiving computer that the data is an e-mail message.

The seven-layer OSI model includes all the possible layers currently available in telecommunications. However, just five layers—application, transport, network, data-link, and physical—apply to the majority of computer communications. The session and presentation layers apply only to more specialized telecommunications applications. The transport, network, data-link, and physical layers all define hardware aspects of the communication while the application, session, and presentation layers deal only with software.

Let's discuss the application of the five layers of the OSI model to a typical e-mail communication between two people. A person named John@ABC.com writes a message to Sue@XYZ.edu, sending the message as e-mail to her given Internet address. John's computer is a home computer connected to the PSTN and he uses the Internet service provider called ABC. Sue is a college student at XYZ university, and her computer is connected directly to the school's network, which connects to the Internet.

When John writes the message as an e-mail, the application layer protocol used is called the *simple mail transfer protocol* (*SMTP*). The SMTP message is given a code number equal to 25, called the *port number*, which identifies it as an

SMTP transmission. The computer John is using sends out the message over the telephone connection to his computer with the SMTP port number 25 attached, along with other information about the application. The transport layer determines the information about the actual physical location of the address where the message is being sent, which in this case is XYZ university. It also attaches the physical address of the sender.

Next, the message is sent from John's computer through the PSTN to John's ISP ABC.com. Along the way, this message may be transmitted over a variety of communication links. Most likely the message will be sent through the local loop to the closest central office as an analog signal. Then it might be converted to a digital signal and sent over a trunk line to the central office closest to the ISP, ABC.com. ABC.com most likely retains a high bandwidth link with the central office because of the high volume of transmissions that they handle. Whatever path the message travels, the network layer of OSI is used to format and control the transmission from one end of the branch to the other. In other words the network layer identifies the method of communication from end-to-end of a particular branch of the path.

The data-link layer identifies the type of data being sent as well as the use of any error detection and correction schemes to be used with the transmission. The data-link layer would indicate that the data included in the e-mail is ASCII characters with parity error detection. The physical layer identifies the actual physical connection that exists over each step of the transmission, starting with the telephone wire to the central office, the trunk connection from John's central office to the central office closest to John's ISP, and so on.

The five OSI levels discussed serve to guide John's e-mail along the proper path (see Figure 12–10). Each level attaches information to the original message that is important to the transmission of the message. First is the message itself, which was written as an e-mail. The message plus its application (SMTP) are then readied for transmission and the transport layer adds the actual physical destination address. The data-link layer identifies the type of data and error detection/correction, while the network layer specifies details about the branch of the connection through which the message is currently passing. The physical level is where the signal is actually transformed to have the correct physical properties for transmission through a medium. The signal may be converted from FDM-modulated analog signals to TDM digital signals to fiber optics over the course of its transmission.

▶ **FIGURE 12–10**
The OSI layers

1. Physical
2. Data-link
3. Network
4. Transport
5. Application

12–8 ▶ Computer Networks

The enhanced capabilities of computers and telecommunications systems have been applied to allow the interconnection of computers in ways that would not seem possible. Computer networks are the interconnection of computers for the purpose of communication to share information and peripherals (printers, ISPs, etc.). Computer networks are called *local area networks* (*LANs*) when the system components are located in relative close proximity to each other within a building or a group of buildings. Broader networks located within an area of approximately 100 miles are called *metropolitan area networks* (*MANs*). The method of communication between computers and peripherals is largely determined by the network topology, the method used to interconnect them. The most common network topologies are star, bus, and token ring.

Star Topology

The star topology was one of the first topologies developed and forms the basis for the existing PSTN. A diagram for the star topology is shown in Figure 12–11. A star topology network consists of a number of devices that connect to a central device that resides in the center of the star configuration. All communications must pass through the central node: data destined for a device within the star network as well as data to be sent to devices outside the network. The star configuration is the best alternative when most communication comes from the central node to some other network. When most of the communication is between devices located within the star topology, communication is limited by the overburdened central node. The function of the central node is critical to the operation of the star network; however, the malfunction of just one device within the star network does not render the entire network nonfunctional.

▶ **FIGURE 12–11**
Star topology

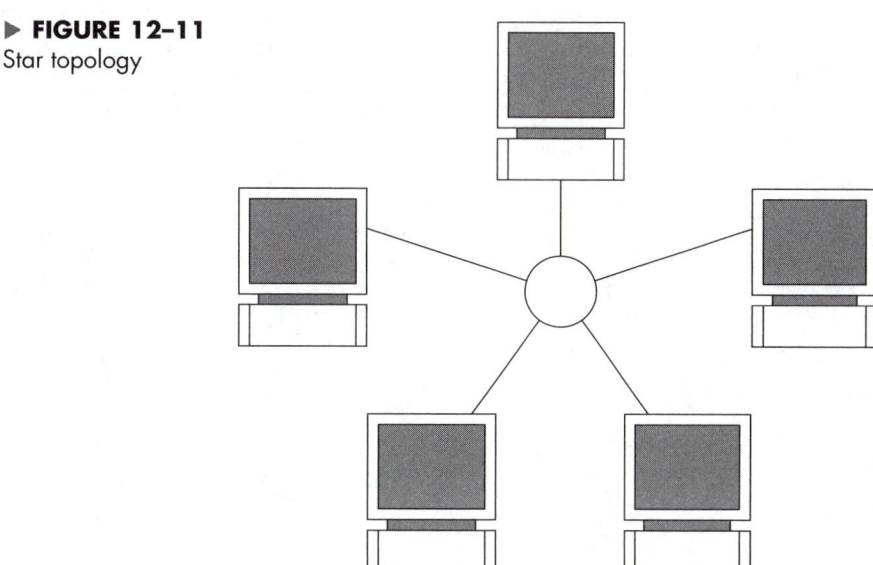

Bus Topology

A bus network is a very simple and commonly used topology for interconnecting computing devices. The bus topology consists of a common group of connections that exist between each device connected to the network (see Figure 12–12). These connections are referred to as the *network's backbone*. Each device connected to the bus can communicate with any other device on the bus; however, only one communication can be sent at one time. Therefore, the number of computers connected to the bus largely determines network performance. Bus topologies are often referred to as passive, because the devices connected to the bus simply listen to bus communications to determine if they should receive the information. They have no responsibility for passing data onto other devices. If one computer fails, the rest of the network continues to operate.

When a device wishes to communicate on the bus, it listens for a quiet period and then proceeds to transmit data. If by chance another device transmits at exactly the same time, there is a collision of the data. The transmissions are garbled and both devices, sensing the collision, retreat while selecting a random number that is counted down before attempting a re-transmission.

Token Ring Topology

The token ring topology is one in which the devices are connected serially in a ring, as shown in Figure 12–13. Communication commences only in one direction around the ring and each device is responsible for passing on the transmission. For this reason the token ring topology is classified as an active network. A data word called a *token* is passed around the ring in the direction of communication. When a device possesses the token, it has the opportunity to transmit data on the network. It modifies the token by adding the address of the device it is transmitting to and the data being sent. The data is sent around the ring until it reaches its intended destination, where the receiver acknowledges receipt by sending an acknowledge signal back to the sender. The failure of just one device in the token ring renders the entire network nonfunctional.

▶ **FIGURE 12–12**
Bus topology

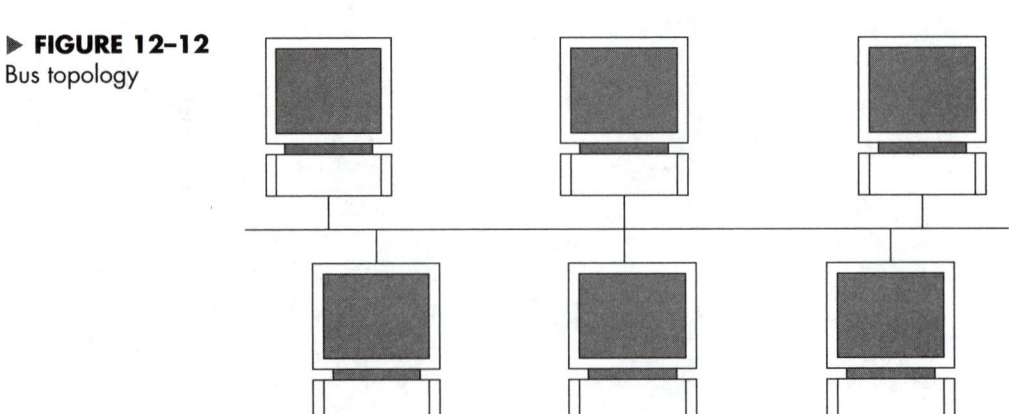

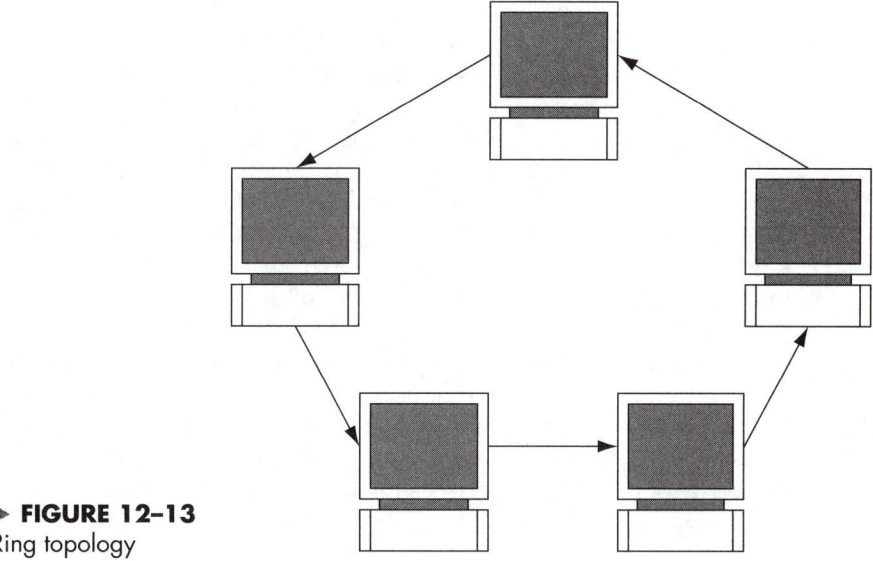

▶ **FIGURE 12-13**
Ring topology

Ethernet Technology

Ethernet is an example of a protocol that is widely used today. Ethernet can be implemented in either a bus or star topology and is defined by the IEEE specification number 802.3. The Ethernet standard essentially fits into the data-link and physical layers of the OSI model, defining the physical connection between the network components as well as the method for communication between all devices connected to the network. There are a number of Ethernet variations that specify the interconnection cable, transmission codes, network topology, and data rates.

10 Base 2 Ethernet is a commonly used network connection for businesses and schools. It uses thin coax cable, has a maximum data rate of 10 Mbps, and uses a bus topology and Manchester encoding. Another Ethernet version, called 10 Base T, utilizes twisted-pair cable wired in a star configuration that also has a 10 Mbps data rate and uses Manchester encoding. 100 Base T is an extended data rate version of 10 Base T with a 100 Mbps data rate. It is wired in a star configuration with twisted-pair cable but uses a more efficient encoding scheme called 4B5B.

Gigabit Ethernet is the latest version of the Ethernet standard that pushes data rates up to 1 Gbps. It is used as a backbone for many larger networks to eliminate the bottleneck in communications that occurs when various devices from one branch of a network communicate with other branches of the network. Gigabit Ethernet uses a star topology just the 10 Base T and 100 Base T Ethernet.

Network Devices

Three basic devices are used to interconnect computers that are part of a network: hubs, bridges, and routers. These devices are similar in nature because they all accept an input and provide a number of outputs. However, each function at a different layer of the OSI protocol hierarchy.

Hubs operate at the physical layer and are essentially repeaters or level-changing devices. The frames or bit patterns input to a hub are the same as those sent to all of the hub's outputs. The hub makes no decisions about the data transmitted and does not route the data to a particular output port. It simply passes on the information. The purpose of the hub may be to rejuvenate the signal or to change the physical output such as conversion from electrical to optical signals.

Bridges are devices that route data according to the link layer destination address of the frame transmitted. Bridges are used to interconnect networks of any kind. The networks can be of the same or different topologies. Data input to the bridge is routed to the link layer address of the network that is connected to a particular bridge output terminal.

Routers are switches that perform the same function as a bridge, yet they operate within the network, functioning at the network layer of the OSI protocol. Routers connect devices that are all part of the same network. Data input to the router is processed and routed to the output connection that will send the data to the network destination address included in the data frame.

12–9 ▶ The Internet

The Internet has evolved as an important communications device over the last 20 years. Also called the World Wide Web (WWW), the Internet can be defined as a global group of interconnected networks that all use the network layer protocol called, appropriately, the *Internet Protocol* (*IP*). Some of the networks that the Internet comprises are publicly owned while some are owned privately. Special-access networks provide connections to the Internet through companies called *Internet service providers* (*ISPs*). A unique aspect of the Internet involved the development of the Web page. A Web page is simply a document that can be published on the Internet that contains information as well as links to other Web pages. When a Web page is published, it is maintained as a file in the Internet network memory and can be read by anyone with Internet access. Links from the main Web page to other Web pages can be controlled with passwords and other security methods.

Another aspect of the Internet that is now part of many computer networks is an innovation in the way information is transmitted, called *packet switching*. In order to define packet switching, let's first define what is called a *connection* between communicating devices. A connection is a maintained continuous path for communication between two devices. The best example of a connection is a telephone call. Telephone calls all develop a maintained and ongoing connection between two parties until one party hangs up.

A packet is a small group of data that is sent out together that represents only part of the information to be transmitted. Each packet travels toward its intended network address destination separately along the shortest and quickest route available at the time of transmission. Therefore, it is entirely possible for the packets to arrive out of order. The packets include information that indicates the order of transmission, so the receiving device is able to reassemble the data in the correct order. The use of packets allows for the optimum utilization of the existing transmission mediums. If traffic is busy down one path, then the packet is diverted around the bottleneck over the next shortest and quickest path.

When dedicated connections exist between two devices, the communication is very secure and reliable; the transmitter can send data and the receiver can respond directly with an acknowledgement or request a retransmission. With packet switching there are two approaches to the transport level program: connection-oriented protocols and connectionless protocols. Connection-oriented protocols are used for packet-switched information where reliability is desired. In other words, we want to make sure that the data reached its destination and that it is received accurately. Connection-oriented protocols establish handshaking much the same as maintained connections, even though the data packets transmitted may travel completely different paths. The connection-oriented protocol used on the Internet is called the *transmission control protocol* (*TCP*). The cost of reliability is realized with the overhead needed to setup the handshaking between the two communicating devices. This overhead slows down TCP significantly.

Connectionless protocols send out packets of data blindly and hope the data is received accurately. The connectionless protocol used for Internet communication is called *user datagram protocol* (*UDP*). UDP is a simple and very fast protocol because it does not carry the overhead of establishing a virtual connection.

Communication over a network can utilize a maintained connection, connection-oriented packet communications or packets sent on a connectionless basis.

The Internet uses only five layers of the seven-layer OSI model described earlier in this section. The five layers used are application, transport, network, data-link, and physical. There are a number of application programs that are used for Internet communication but the most common are the hypertext transfer protocol (HTTP), simple mail transfer protocol (SMTP), and the file transfer protocol (FTP).

HTTP is the application layer protocol used to transmit Internet information that is published as Web pages. All Web pages and other Internet resources have a distinct uniform resource locator (URL), which is the Internet location of the resource. FTP is the file transfer protocol used by the Internet, and SMTP is the application protocol used for e-mail. The next OSI layer is the transport layer. The Internet transport protocol is either TCP or UDP. TCP is used for Web pages and other communications that require reliable transmission. UDP is used when higher data rates are necessary and the reliability of the data is not critical. Such applications include real-time audio, video, or multimedia communications.

The network layer protocol for Internet communications is called the Internet protocol (IP). The IP protocol works together with either TCP or UDP to complete the protocol needed for Internet communication. The IP protocol by itself establishes a connectionless link between the sender and receiver and relies on TCP to establish reliability. The data-link and physical layers vary for each branch of the packet's journey and are invisible to the sending and receiving devices. Figure 12–14 shows the five layers of protocols used for Internet communication.

12–10 ▶ Fiber Optics in Telecommunications

Nothing has had a larger impact on the nature of the telecommunications industry than developments in the field of fiber optics. Fiber optics uses light to transmit information instead of electrical signals. The primary advantages of fiber optics result from two facts:

1. Physical
2. Data-link
3. Network   IP
4. Transport   TCP/UDP
5. Application   HTTP/FTP/SMTP

▶ **FIGURE 12–14**
Layers of OSI for Internet applications

1. Light can be switched on and off at a much higher frequency than electrical signals.

2. Light signals are attenuated only slightly (as compared to electrical signals) as they travel down the highly pure optical fiber available today.

Consequently, light signals that are sent over fiber-optic cable can be transmitted at much higher frequencies and can travel much further before requiring rejuvenation. A common misnomer is the thought that fiber optics provides more capacity because light travels faster than electrical signals. Electrical signals travel almost as fast as light does down a glass fiber, and the difference is not significant enough to warrant the capacity increases experienced with fiber optics. Fiber optics offers increased capacity simply because light can be switched on and off much faster than electrical signals.

Fiber-optic communications are implemented with a light source, either an LED or a laser that is connected to a fiber cable. The data to be transmitted is sent to the light source that switches according to the data stream input. On the receiving end of the fiber-optic cable, an optical sensor, usually either a PIN photodiode or an avalanche photodiode (APD), converts the light signal back to an electrical output signal.

The fiber cable itself consists of pure glass that includes two sections: an inner core with an outer cladding. The core has a higher index of refraction than the cladding, which means that light injected into the core is reflected off the border between the core and the cladding. The light is reflected according to a principle called *total internal reflection*. This results when the light is incident to the core-cladding border by an angle greater than what is called the *critical angle*. The critical angle is determined by the difference between the index of refraction of the core and the cladding. Light that is incident at angles less than the critical angle passes on through the cladding and is lost (see Figure12–15).

The increased bandwidth and attenuation performance of fiber optics happens because fiber cable lacks limitations such as the resistance, inductance, and capacitance effects on electrical signals as they travel down a conductive cable. All electrical cables offer resistance to current flow—the smaller the cable, the larger the resistance. Also, the inherent inductance and capacitance of wire limits the highest frequency that can be transmitted on the cable.

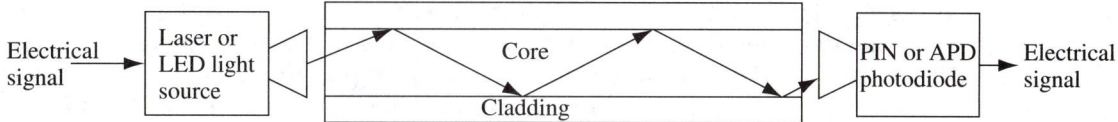

▲ FIGURE 12–15
Fiber-optic communication

A summary of the advantages of fiber optics is as follows:

▸ High bandwidth

▸ Low attenuation

▸ Small physical size

▸ Light in weight

▸ Noise immunity—insensitive to electrical noise

▸ Secure—does not radiate or easily tapped into

▸ Increased safety in hazardous atmosphere due to absence of potential for electrical spark

Fiber-optic cables do attenuate light signals as they pass through the cable. There are also frequency limitations due to properties of the cable and the way light is transmitted down the fiber. The attenuation of light signals is due to impurities that are present in the fiber that absorb the light instead of allowing it to pass through. The amount of attenuation is determined by the amount of impurities present and the size of the core.

The frequency limitations of fiber are caused by a property called *dispersion*. In general, dispersion results when the light injected into the fiber reaches the end of the fiber at different times. There are two distinctly different types of dispersion: the light can take different paths, which is called *modal dispersion* (modes = paths in fiber-optic terminology), or the light has a range of wavelengths that all travel at different speeds, which is called *chromatic dispersion* (see Figure 12–16).

Modal dispersion is the most significant bandwidth limitation affecting basic fiber-optic cable, called *step-index multimode cable*. Step-index multimode cable is the lowest performing grade of fiber cable. It suffers from limited bandwidth due to its large core size. This results in many paths (modes) for the light to travel down, therefore causing more dispersion of the light signal. As the input pulses

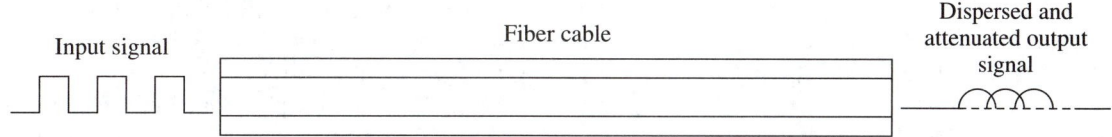

▲ FIGURE 12–16
Dispersion in fiber-optic cables

are dispersed on the other end of the fiber, the receiver cannot detect the 1-to-0 transition that indicates a binary low signal. Graded-index multimode cable improves the performance of step-index multimode fiber by graduating the index of refraction difference between the core and the cladding instead of the step-change in the index of refraction seen on step-index fiber. This gradual change in the index of refraction slows down the light that travels the shortest path through the fiber, thereby reducing modal dispersion significantly.

Single-mode fiber has been developed that, for all practical purposes, eliminates modal dispersion. Single-mode fiber has a core size that is much smaller than multimode cable, which effectively limits the number of paths to one. With only one path to travel, the light reaches its destination at the same time. With modal dispersion virtually eliminated, chromatic dispersion becomes the bandwidth-limiting factor for single-mode fiber. The level of chromatic dispersion is highly dependent on how wavelength consistent the light signal is.

Ideally, light transmitted down a fiber cable is just one wavelength. In practice, the spectral width (range of wavelengths) created by light sources varies significantly between the various types of light sources. LEDs have a spectral width of 30 nanometers while laser light sources can achieve narrow spectral widths of 2 to 3 nm. Because chromatic dispersion is based upon the varying speeds that wavelengths travel through fiber, it stands to reason that the wider the spectral width of the light source, the greater the level of chromatic dispersion. Therefore, the amount of chromatic dispersion experienced with single-mode fiber is highly dependent on the light source used (LED or Laser). The effect of using a wide spectral width light source (an LED) on the bandwidth of single-mode fiber is so dramatic that single-mode fiber is only used with laser light sources.

The applications of fiber optics can be separated into three categories: high bandwidth telecommunications applications, high-speed network backbones, and routine network applications. Telecommunications applications for fiber are usually trunk connections that require a very high bandwidth and throughput with low attenuation. Single-mode fiber cable and laser light sources are used almost exclusively in telecommunications applications. High-speed network backbones such as gigabit Ethernet can benefit from the application of fiber optics. These also use single-mode fiber cable with laser light sources. General application networks that interconnect with fiber cable will use graded-index multimode fiber and LED light sources because the bandwidth requirements are not as severe.

▶ Summary

Telecommunications is a complicated area for electronic applications that now includes computer communication, voice, audio, video, multimedia, and wireless communications. Each application includes many levels of protocols and codes all symbolized with an ever-increasing multitude of acronyms. Yet there is a feeling that we are still just beginning to explore the many possibilities. The bandwidth potentials of fiber optics are yet to be fully utilized. Video conferencing and other multimedia communications offer more potential for change at a time when it seems like we have already experienced so much change. Sometime in the future, fiber-optic cable will connect every home to a global network that will offer all the potentials for telecommunications.

The growth opportunities for telecommunications are promising and the need for creative and knowledgeable technical professionals continues to be high. The telecommunications industry requires people with a range of knowledge that includes digital electronics, microprocessors, software development, fiber optics, general telecommunications, and business operations. The work can range from the design of telecommunications equipment (routers, hubs, bridges, telephone switches, peripherals, etc.), to laying out communications networks and trunks, to managing operations, field-service, or new construction. The skill levels required are high and the rewards are many.

▶ References

Hioki, W. *Telecommunications*, 3rd ed. Upper Saddle River, NJ: Prentice Hall, 1998.

Kurose, J., and Ross, K. *Computer Networking*. New York: Addison Wesley, 2001.

▶ Exercises

12–1   Explain how the bandwidth capability of a communication link determines the amount of information that can be transmitted at one time.

12–2   Explain the process of amplitude modulation, frequency modulation, and pulse code modulation.

12–3   Explain the difference between unipolar and bipolar digital telecommunications signals.

12–4   Draw the waveform that represents the digital bit stream 1100101101 when encoded with Manchester encoding. Repeat for Miller encoding.

12–5   Explain the difference between data rate and signal rate.

12–6   A communication link operates at a bit rate of 100 kbps. If NRZ code is used, what is the baud rate? What is the baud rate if RZ code is used?

12–7   When comparing the bandwidth required for digital PCM signals verses analog FDM signals, which type of signal requires the most bandwidth? Explain the reason for the large difference in bandwidth requirements.

12–8   What advantages do digital PCM signals offer over analog FDM signals?

12–9   Explain the purpose of multiplexing and the differences between time division multiplexing (TDM) and frequency division multiplexing (FDM).

12–10 What is the purpose of a modem? List the five different types of analog telephone line modems discussed in this chapter.

12–11 Explain the performance and functional differences between cable modems and telephone line modems.

12–12 Describe the function of simplex, half-duplex, and full-duplex serial transmission modes.

12–13 Define the term *bit error rate* (*BER*). What are the factors that determine the BER for a telecommunication system?

12–14 Explain the parity method of error detection. What types of parity detection are there? What types of errors can and cannot be detected with this method?

12–15 Explain the operation of CRC error detection. What performance level does CRC error checking achieve?

12–16 Explain the general process of checksum error detection methods and list the types of checksum error detection discussed in this chapter.

12–17 What is the limitation of single precision checksum error detection? How do residue checksums and double precision checksums overcome this problem?

12–18 When errors are detected in a transmission, what methods are available to correct them?

12–19 Explain the purpose behind each of the five layers included in the five-layer protocol used for Internet communications.

12–20 List and describe the three types of bus topologies discussed in this chapter.

12–21 Explain the difference between a hub, a bridge, and a router.

12–22 By what process does light travel down a fiber-optic cable?

12–23 Explain why fiber optics offers superior bandwidth performance when compared to communication using electrically conductive wire.

12–24 What are the three different types of fiber-optic cable? Which offers the lowest and highest bandwidth performance?

12–25 What characteristics of fiber-optic cable limits it bandwidth performance?

12–26 Describe what is meant by dispersion in fiber-optic cable. List and describe each type of dispersion discussed in this chapter.

Appendix A ▶ Component Reference Information

A–1 ▶ Resistors

Resistors limit the flow of current and divide voltage in electrical circuits. If the current through a resistor is known, the voltage drop across it can be calculated using Ohm's Law ($V = I \times R$). Resistors are not frequency dependent, so they have the same resistance value for AC and DC voltage.

Resistor color codes are shown in Figure A–1. Included in Figure A–1 are the four-band code used for 5%, 10% and 20% tolerance resistors and the five-band color code used for 1% tolerance resistors. Figure A–2 shows the standard value resistors that are available at different tolerance values.

A–2 ▶ Capacitors

Capacitors store electrical charge on plates separated by a dielectric material. Capacitors oppose any changes in the voltage across them by giving up previously stored charge if the voltage is decreasing or storing more charge if the voltage across them is increasing. Current never actually flows through a capacitor (except a small leakage current), but with AC voltages it appears to because the current is constantly changing direction. In AC circuits, the capacitor is continually charging and discharging as the current flows in one direction, and then it reverses. Capacitive Reactance, X_c, is the impedance that the capacitor offers resisting the flow of AC current and is equal to:

$$X_C = 1/(2\pi f C)$$

where f = frequency
C = Capacitance value

419

Resistor Color Codes

0 = Black	7 = Violet	Gold Multiplier = 0.1
1 = Brown	8 = Gray	Silver Multiplier = 0.01
2 = Red	9 = White	
3 = Orange	1% = Red	
4 = Yellow	5% = Gold	
5 = Green	10% = Silver	
6 = Blue	20% = No Color	

Four Band—5%, 10%   Five Band—1%

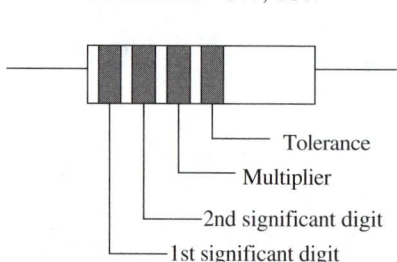

▲ **FIGURE A–1**
Resistor color codes

As frequency increases, the Capacitive Reactance decreases. For DC circuits then, $f = 0$ so the Capacitive Reactance is theoretically infinite. In DC circuits capacitors completely block DC current flow (again, except for leakage) and charge up to the DC voltage. The capacitance value determines its ability to store charge. The larger the value, the more space it has to store charge. It makes sense that capacitance is added when you connect two capacitors in parallel. Conversely, it follows that two capacitors in series will react like two resistors in parallel and can be calculated by the formula, $C_t = C_1 \times C_2/(C_1 + C_2)$. This is because the effective plate area is reduced and the distance between the plates is increased.

Capacitors are rated by their value, dielectric type, and the voltage they can withstand. These values are either stamped on the capacitor or color codes are used. The standard capacitor values available use the same multipliers as for 10% tolerance resistors. Figure A–3 shows the standard capacitor values. It is important to note that not all of the values are available for a particular dielectric type or a specific manufacturer. For example, aluminum electrolytic capacitors are usually available only in multiples of 10, 22, 33, 47, and 68. Figure A–3 also shows the voltage ratings that are usually available for capacitors.

Capacitor color code locations are dependent on the type of dielectric used. The location and meaning of the color codes are shown in Figure A–4.

Standard Resistance Values
(the following values are available in powers of ten)

0.1% / 0.25% / 0.5%	1%	2% / 5%	10%
10.0	10.0	10	10
10.1			
10.2	10.2		
10.4			
10.5	10.5		
10.6			
10.7	10.7		
10.9			
11.0	11.0	11	
11.1			
11.3	11.3		
11.4			
11.5	11.5		
11.7			
11.8	11.8	12	12
12.0			
12.1	12.1		
12.3			
12.4	12.4		
12.6			
12.7	12.7		
12.9			
13.0	13.0	13	
13.2			
13.3	13.3		
13.5			
13.7	13.7		
13.8			
14.0	14.0		
14.2			
14.3	14.3		
145			
14.7	14.7		
14.9			
15.0	15.0	15	15
15.2			
15.4	15.4		
15.6			
15.8	15.8		
16.0		16	
16.2	16.2		
16.4			
16.5	16.5		
16.7			
16.9	16.9		
17.2			
17.4	17.4		
17.6			
17.8	17.8		
18.0		18	18
18.2	18.2		
18.4			
18.7	18.7		
18.9			
19.1	19.1		
19.3			
19.6	19.6		
19.8			
20.0	20.0	20	
20.3			
20.5	20.5		
20.8			
21.0	21.0		
21.3			
21.5	21.5		
21.8			
22.1	22.1	22	22
22.3			
22.6	22.6		
22.9			
23.2	23.2		
23.4			
23.7	23.7		
24.0		24	
24.3	24.3		
24.6			
24.9	24.9		
25.2			
25.5	25.5		
25.8			
26.1	26.1		
26.4			
26.7	26.7	27	27
27.1			
27.4	27.4		
27.7			
28.0	28.0		
28.4			
28.7	28.7		
29.1			
29.4	29.4		
29.8			
30.1	30.1	30	
30.5			
30.9	30.9		
31.2			
31.6	31.6		
32.0			
32.4	32.4		
32.8			
33.2	33.2	33	33
33.6			
34.0	34.0		
34.4			
34.8	34.8		
35.2			
35.7	35.7		
36.1		36	
36.5	36.5		
37.0			
37.4	37.4		
37.9			
38.3	38.3		
38.8			
39.2	39.2	39	39
39.7			
40.2	40.2		
40.7			
41.2	41.2		
41.7			
42.2	42.2		
42.7			
43.2	43.2		
43.7		43	
44.2	44.2		
44.8			
45.3	45.3		
45.9			
46.4	46.4		
47.0			
47.5	47.5	47	47
48.1			
48.7	48.7		
49.3			
49.9	49.9		
50.5			
51.1	51.1	51	
51.7			
52.3	52.3		
53.0			
53.6	53.6		
54.2			
54.9	54.9		
55.6			
56.2	56.2	56	56
56.9			
57.6	57.6		
58.3			
59.0	59.0		
59.7			
60.4	60.4		
61.2			
61.9	61.9	62	
62.6			
63.4	63.4		
64.2			
64.9	64.9		
65.7			
66.5	66.5		
67.3			
68.1	68.1	68	68
69.0			
69.8	69.8		
70.6			
71.5	71.5		
72.3			
73.2	73.2		
74.1			
75.0	75.0	75	
75.9			
76.8	76.8		
77.7			
78.7	78.7		
79.6			
80.6	80.6		
81.6			
82.5	82.5	82	82
83.5			
84.5	84.5		
85.6			
86.6	86.6		
87.6			
88.7	88.7		
89.8			
90.9	90.9	91	
92.0			
93.1	93.1		
94.2			
95.3	95.3		
96.5			
97.6	97.6		
98.8			

▲ FIGURE A–2
Standard resistor values

Standard Capacitance Values

Picofarads	Picofarads	Microfarads	Picofarads	Microfarads	Microfarads	Microfarads	Microfarads
1.8	120		12,000	0.012	1.0	120	1800
2.2	180		15,000	0.015	1.2	180	2200
2.7	220		18,000	0.018	1.8	220	2700
3.3	270		22,000	0.022	2.2	270	3300
3.9	330		27,000	0.027	2.7	330	3900
4.7	390		33,000	0.033	3.3	390	4700
5.0	470		39,000	0.039	3.9	470	5600
5.6	560		47,000	0.047	4.7	560	6800
6.8	680		56,000	0.056	5.6	680	8200
8.2	820		68,000	0.068	6.8	820	
10	1000	.001	82,000	0.082	8.2	100	
12	1200	.0012	100,000	0.1	10	120	
15	1500	.0015		0.12	12	150	
18	1800	.0018		0.15	15	180	
22	2200	.0022		0.18	18	220	
27	2700	.0027		0.22	22	270	
33	3300	.0033		0.27	27	330	
39	3900	.0039		0.33	33	390	
47	4700	.0047		0.39	39	470	
56	5600	.0056		0.47	47	560	
68	6800	.0068		0.56	56	680	
82	8200	.0082		0.68	68	820	
100	10,000	.01		0.82	82	1000	
					100	1200	

Standard Voltages

6.3	250
10	400
16	450
35	500
50	1000
63	2000
100	3000

▲ FIGURE A–3
Standard capacitor values

422

Capacitor color code designations are the same as for resistors:

0 = Black	7 = Violet	Gold Multiplier = 0.1
1 = Brown	8 = Gray	Silver Multiplier = 0.01
2 = Red	9 = White	
3 = Orange	1% = Red	Band 1 = 1st digit
4 = Yellow	5% = Gold	Band 2 = 2nd digit
5 = Green	10% = Silver	Band 3 = Multiplier
6 = Blue	20% = No Color	Band 4 = Tolerance
		Band 5 = Temperature coefficient
		or voltage rating

The location and meaning can vary with the manufacturer but generally the following are used for color bands:

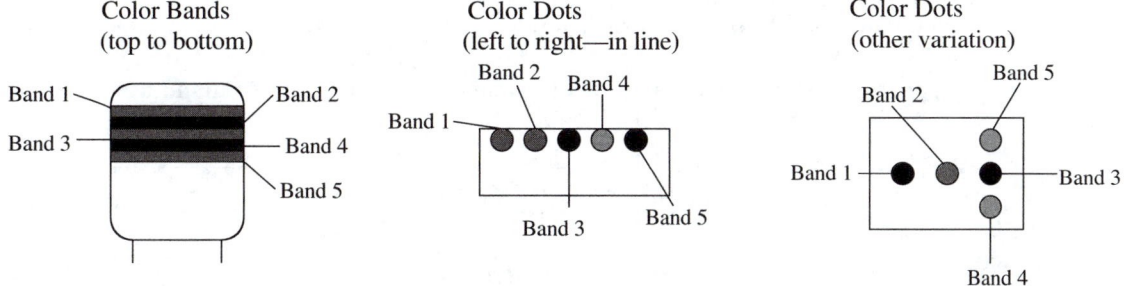

▲ **FIGURE A–4**
Capacitor color codes

A–3 ▶ Inductors

An inductor is a coil of conductive material that stores electrical energy in the magnetic field created by the *changing* current passing through the inductor. Inductors oppose any change in the current passing through them. They accomplish this by giving up previously stored energy if the current is decreasing or storing more energy in the magnetic field if the current is increasing. In AC circuits the inductors continually store and release energy as the current increases, reaches a maximum, then declines and eventually flows in the other direction. Inductive Reactance, X_L, is the impedance that the inductor offers to resist the flow of current and is equal to:

$$X_L = 2\pi f L$$

where f = frequency and L = Inductance

As frequency increases the inductive reactance, X_L increases. This is exactly opposite of the way capacitors function (X_C decreases as frequency increases). For DC circuits, $f = 0$ so inductive reactance is = 0. In DC circuits inductors are a steady state short circuit. The inductance value, L, is given in units called *henrys* and determines the inductor's ability to store energy. Practical ranges of inductance are millihenries (mH) or microhenries (μH). The larger the inductance value, the greater the capacity to store energy. Inductors are similar to resistors in that the equivalent of two inductors in series is simply the total of the two inductances. The equivalent of two inductors in parallel can be calculated by:

$$L_1 = L_1 \times L_2/(L_1 + L_2)$$

It is impossible to have a pure inductive component because of the resistance of the conductor used to make up the coil. The quality factor Q is a measure of this fact and is a ratio of the inductive reactance over the DC resistance:

$$Q = X_L/R_{DC}$$

Inductor values are given in henries. Inductors are rated by their value, tolerance, and maximum current. Inductor values are determined from the same standard number set as resistors and capacitors. Available inductance values range from nanohenries, microhenries, and millihenries. The nominal inductance values available are shown in Figure A–5. The actual values available depend upon the magnetic material used, the type of package, and the inductor manufacturer.

Standard Inductance Values					
Nanohenries	Nanohenries	Microhenries	Nanohenries	Microhenries	Microhenries
1.0	120	0.12	12,000	12	1000
1.2	180	0.18	15,000	15	1200
1.8	220	0.22	18,000	18	1800
2.2	270	0.27	22,000	22	2200
2.7	330	0.33	27,000	27	2700
3.3	390	0.39	33,000	33	3300
3.9	470	0.47	39,000	39	3900
4.7	560	0.56	47,000	47	4700
5.6	680	0.68	56,000	56	5600
6.8	820	0.82	68,000	68	6800
8.2	1000	1	82,000	82	8200
10	1200	1.2	100,000	100	
12	1500	1.5		120	
15	1800	1.8		150	
18	2200	2.2		180	
22	2700	2.7		220	
27	3300	3.3		270	
33	3900	3.9		330	
39	4700	4.7		390	
47	5600	5.6		470	
56	6800	6.8		560	
68	8200	8.2		680	
82	10,000	10		820	
100					

▲ **FIGURE A–5**
Standard inductance values

A-4 ▶ Diodes

There are many different types of diodes designed for use in specific applications. Each type of diode will be discussed along with the key parameters involved in its selection. The available package designations are shown in Figure A–6.

Rectifier Diodes

The primary purpose of rectifier diodes is simply the conduction of current in one direction, most often for the purpose of converting AC voltage to DC voltage. Generally, the key parameters for rectifier diodes are the forward-biased current and the peak inverse voltage. The switching speed and reverse-bias leakage are also important.

Zener Diodes

Zener diodes are commonly used to regulate or clamp voltages and as such are connected reverse-biased. The key parameters are the zener voltage, zener current, and power rating. The tolerance and variation of the zener voltage and zener current with temperature are also important considerations. The most significant parameter for their selection is the zener voltage.

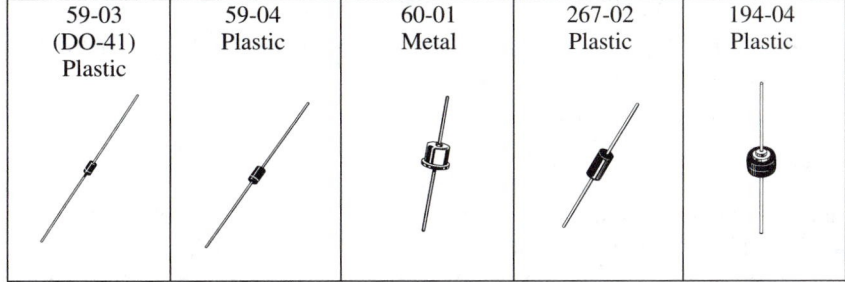

| 59-03 (DO-41) Plastic | 59-04 Plastic | 60-01 Metal | 267-02 Plastic | 194-04 Plastic |

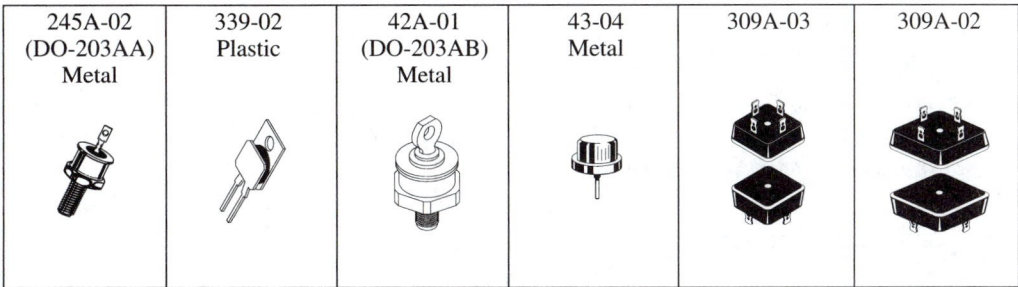

| 245A-02 (DO-203AA) Metal | 339-02 Plastic | 42A-01 (DO-203AB) Metal | 43-04 Metal | 309A-03 | 309A-02 |

▲ **FIGURE A–6**

Diode packages (*Copyright of Semiconductor Component Industries, LLC. Used by permission*)

Shottky Diodes

These diodes feature a very high switching speed and are consequently used in high frequency and fast-switching applications. The key parameter in their selection is the speed at which the diode goes from the forward to reverse-biased operation.

Light-emitting Diodes

Light-emitting diodes are used as indicators or displays or to transmit information optically. As indicators, the LEDs are usually used in individual packages. As displays, 7 segment or 5×7 dot matrix LEDs are common. LEDs are used to transmit optical information down glass and plastic fiber in fiber-optic applications. The key selection parameters are:

1. The wavelength or color of the output light

2. The intensity of the output light

3. The switching speed

4. Efficiency (the amount of output light intensity per the input current)

Photodiodes

The photodiode is operated reverse-biased. When light is applied to the reverse-biased photodiode the leakage current increases. The key operational parameters for selecting a photodiode are:

1. The wavelength of maximum sensitivity

2. The sensitivity—this is the amount of reverse current per the input optical power

A–5 ▶ Transistors

Transistor selection involves first the choosing of either bipolar (BJTs) or unipolar (FETs) devices. BJTs are characterized by faster switching speeds and poorer power efficiency. FETs are generally slower but draw very little current and are therefore very efficient. The available transistor packages are shown in Figure A–7.

Bipolar Junction Transistor (BJT)

BJTs are generally used in small- to medium-power applications. The key parameters for selection are the maximum collector to emitter voltage, the maximum collector current, and the DC current gain, β.

Field Effect Transistor (FET)

The FET is also used in small- to medium-power applications where power efficiency is more important than speed. High-power FETs are called MOSFETs and are discussed next. The key FET parameters are the drain-to-source and the gate-

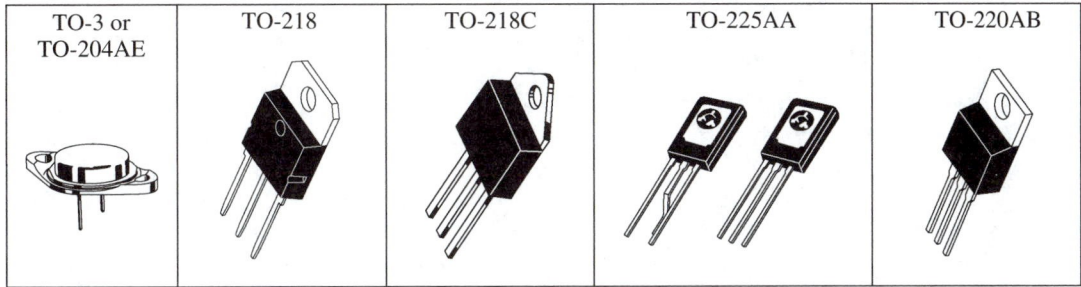

▲ **FIGURE A–7**

Transistor packages (*Copyright of Semiconductor Component Industries, LLC. Used by permission*)

to-source voltages, the drain to source current and the forward transconductance. The forward transconductance is the change in drain-to-source current per the change in gate-to-source voltage. This is similar to the current gain, β, in BJTs.

Metal Oxide Semiconductor FET (MOSFET)

The primary application for MOSFETs are as power transistors called *Power MOSFETs*. The Power MOSFET is capable of high currents because of the very small voltage drop across the drain to source. The key MOSFET parameters are the drain-to-source and the gate-to-source voltages, the drain-to-source current, and the forward transconductance.

A–6 ▶ Integrated Circuits

There are a wide variety of analog, digital, and hybrid (analog/digital) integrated circuits available. Their selection will involve all of the usual parameters—input and output voltage and current, power supply voltage, temperature coefficients, and frequency/speed capabilities. The different integrated circuit packages available are shown in Figure A–8 and A–9.

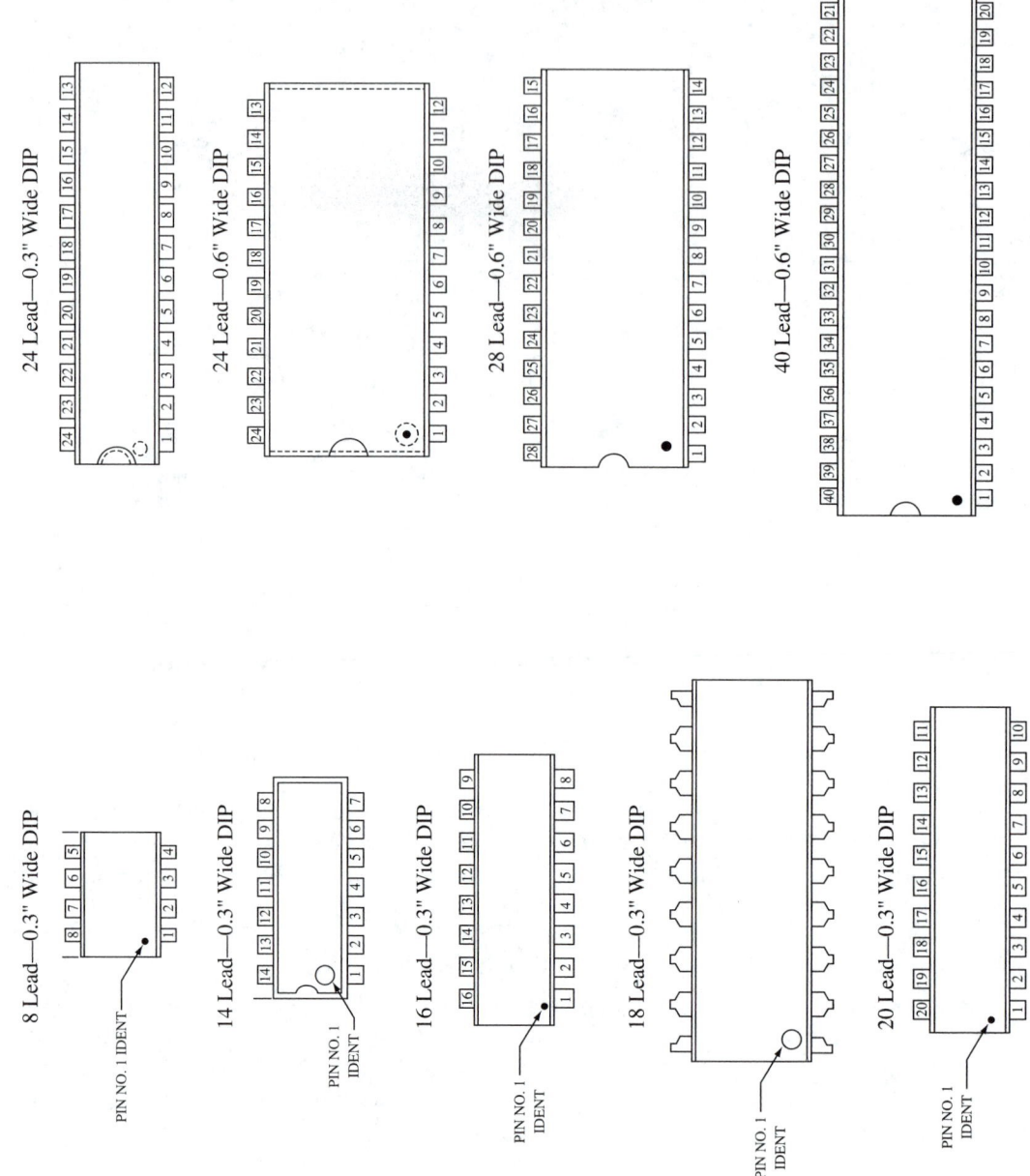

▲ **FIGURE A-8**
Integrated circuit packages

428

20-lead PLCC Package

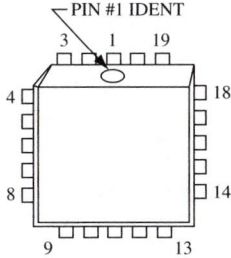

28-lead PLCC Package

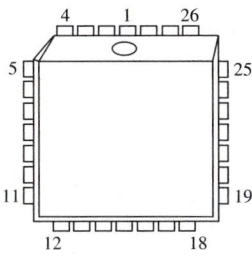

44-lead PLCC Package

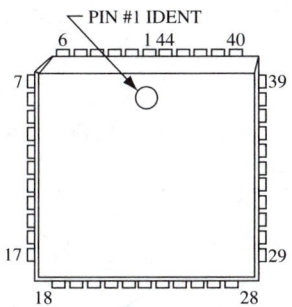

44-lead Quad Flat Package

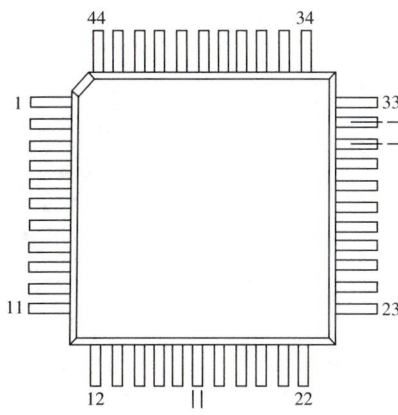

44-lead Cerquad Package

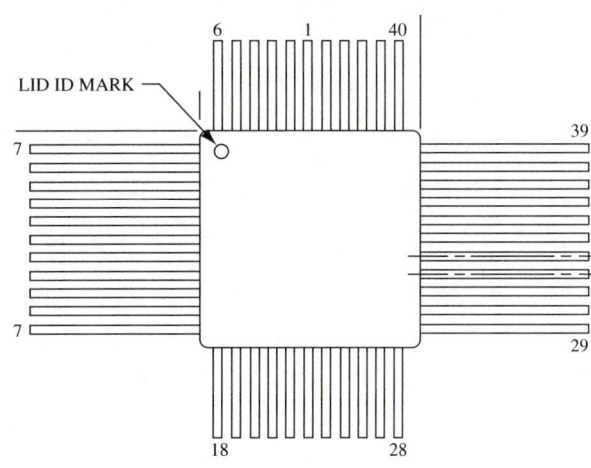

▲ **FIGURE A–9**
Integrated circuit packages

Index

TK   Stadtmiller, D. Joseph
7836   Applied electronic
.S728   design

2003

Date Due